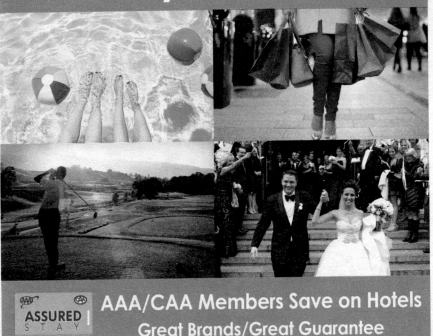

ASSURED STAY
Total Satisfaction Guarantee

AAA/CAA Members Save on Hotels
Great Brands/Great Guarantee

VISIT over 1,100 AAA/CAA Offices
CLICK AAA.com/greatrates | CALL 1-866-222-7283

AAA Mobile
CAA Mobile

free to rock the boat

TripAssist travel insurance allows you to go with the flow. It can free you up to make the most of your vacation. Nothing will hold you back knowing that you and your travel plans are safe.

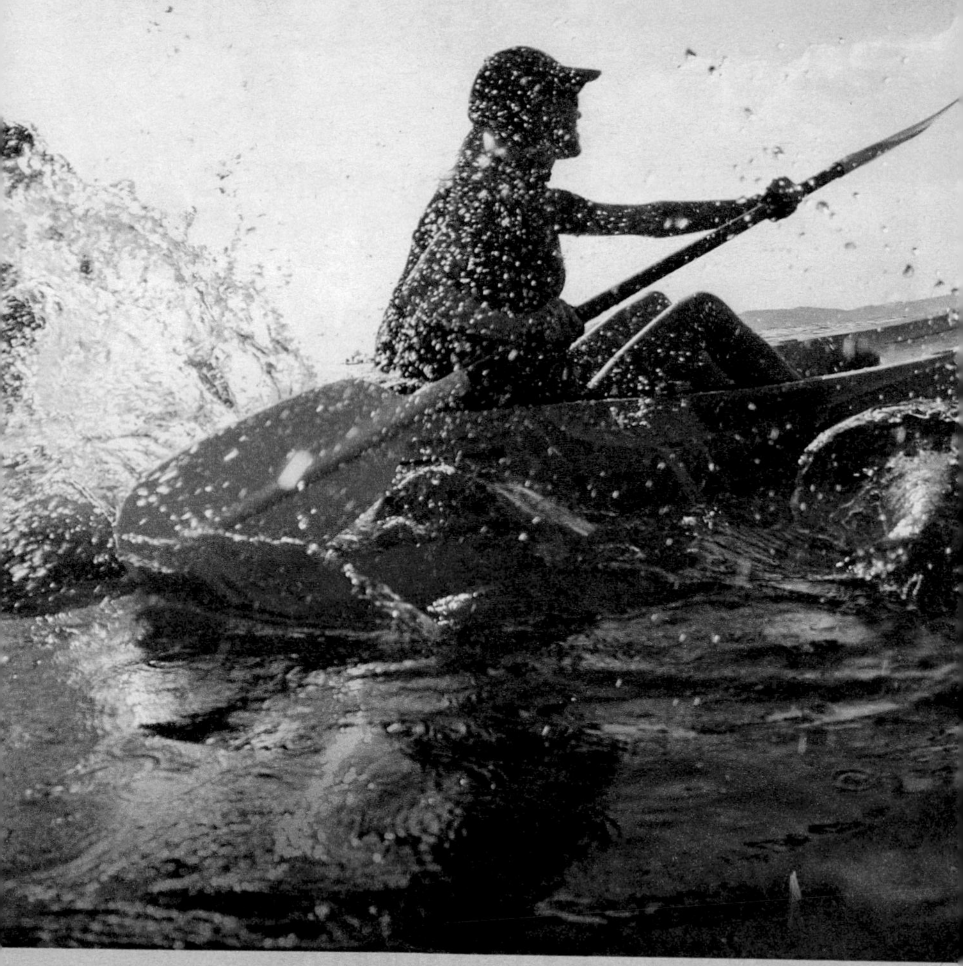

Talk to your AAA Travel Agent today for more information.

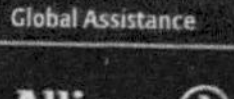

Terms, conditions and exclusions apply. Insurance products are underwritten by BCS Insurance Company or Jefferson Insurance Company. AGA Service Company is the licensed producer and administrator of these plans.

400003588_053018

Red Roof®

Sleep Easy. Spend Less.™

Discover why Red Roof is **#1 in online guest reviews** — for 9 years running — with **FREE Wi-Fi, flat-screen TVs** in every room and, for even faster FREE Wi-Fi, we have **Verified Wi-Fi™** coming to more locations every day. It's all the conveniences you'll need for a clean, comfortable and affordable stay.

VERIFIED **WI-FI™**

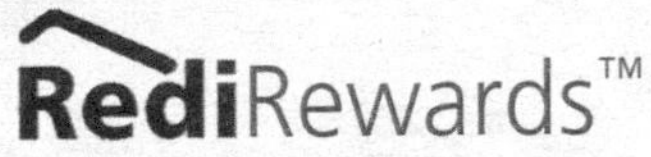

Earn FREE nights and more.
Choose from FREE nights, discounts, gift cards and merchandise.

10% OFF our already low rates for our AAA guests

Use VP+®/Promo Code 526810 to receive 10% off at any of our locations.
Simply visit redroof.com or call 800.RED.ROOF (800.733.7663) Español 877.733.7244

Restrictions may apply based on availability. Offer cannot be combined with any other discount or offer. Not valid during special events.

THE Red COLLECTION®

HOMETOWNE STUDIOS by Red Roof

For reservations visit redroof.com or call 800.RED.ROOF (800.733.7663)

*Pet accommodations policy may vary at some HomeTowne Studios by Red Roof® locations.

Make the Connection

For trip planning and local activities, AAA guidebooks are just the beginning.

Open the door to a whole lot more on **AAA.com**. Get extra travel insight, more information and online booking.

Find this symbol for places to look, book and save on AAA.com.

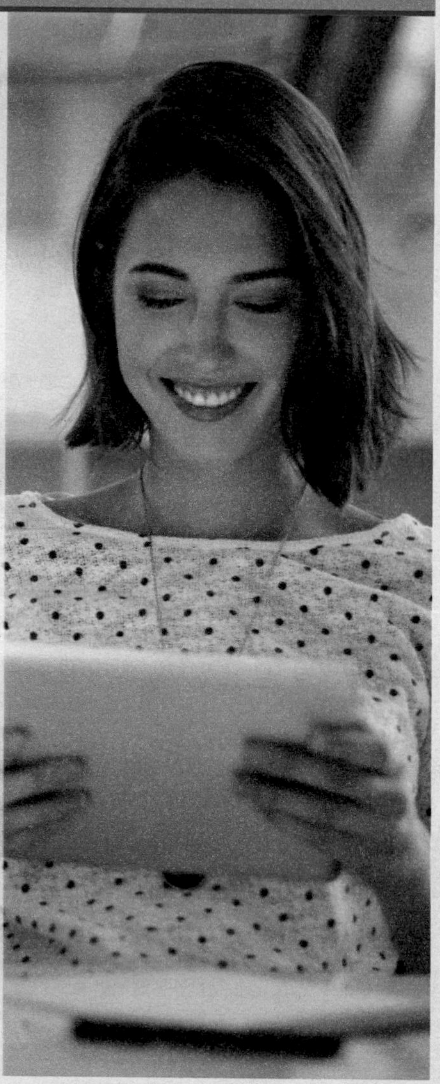

iStockphoto.com_shapecharge

Central Florida

Published by AAA Publishing
1000 AAA Drive, Heathrow, FL 32746-5063
Copyright AAA 2019, All rights reserved

The publisher has made every effort to provide accurate, up-to-date information but accepts no responsibility for loss or injury sustained by any person using this book. TourBook® guides are published for the exclusive use of AAA members. Not for sale.

Advertising Rate and Circulation Information: (407) 444-8280

Printed in the USA by Quad/Graphics

This book is printed on paper certified by third-party standards for sustainably managed forestry and production.

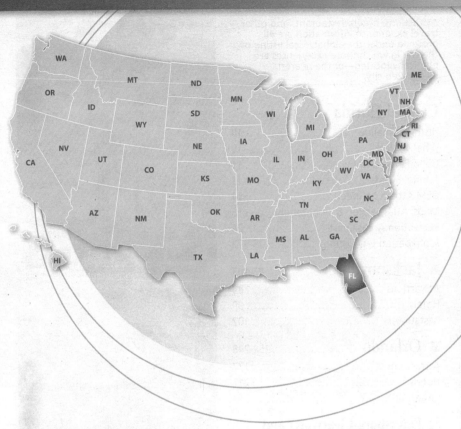

Printed on recyclable paper.
Please recycle whenever possible.

Stock #4664

CONTENTS

Get more travel information at AAA.com/travelguides and AAA.com/traveltips

Attractions, hotels, restaurants and other travel experience information are all grouped under the alphabetical listing of the city in which those experiences are physically located—or the nearest recognized city.

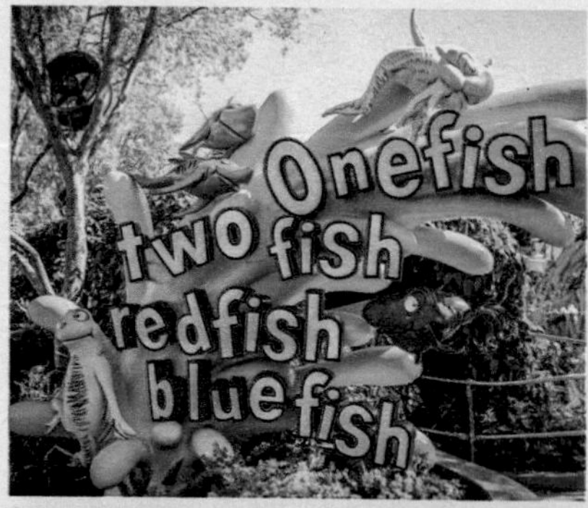

Central Florida

Featured Information

Using Your Guide

AAA TourBook guides are packed with travel insights, maps and listings of places to stay, play, eat and save. For more listings, more details and online booking, visit **AAA.com/travelguides**.

Helping You Make the Connection

Look for this symbol throughout the guides for direct links to related content.

A to Z City Listings

Cities and places are listed alphabetically within each state or province. Attractions, hotels and restaurants are listed once — under the city in which they are physically located.

Cities that are considered part of a larger destination city or area have an expanded city header. The header identifies the larger region and cross-references pages that contain shared trip-planning resources:

- Destination map – outline map of the cities that comprise a destination city or area
- Attraction spotting map – regional street map marked with attraction locations
- Hotel/restaurant spotting map and index – regional street map numbered with hotel and restaurant locations identified in an accompanying index

Cities that are not considered part of a larger destination city or area but have a significant number of listings may have these resources within the individual city section:

- Attraction spotting map
- Hotel/restaurant spotting map and index

Location Abbreviations

Directions are from the center of town unless otherwise specified, using these highway abbreviations:

Bus. Rte.=business route

CR=county road

FM=farm to market

FR=forest road

Hwy.=Canadian highway

I=interstate highway

LR=legislative route

R.R.=rural route

SR/PR=state or provincial route

US=federal highway

About Listed Establishments

AAA/CAA Inspected & Approved hotels and restaurants are listed on the basis of merit alone after careful evaluation and approval by full-time, professionally trained AAA inspectors. An establishment's decision to advertise in the TourBook guide has no bearing on its evaluation or rating; nor does inclusion of advertising imply AAA endorsement of products and services.

Information in this guide was believed accurate at the time of publication. However, since changes inevitably occur between annual editions, please contact your AAA travel professional, visit **AAA.com/travelguides** or download the free AAA Mobile app to confirm prices and schedules.

Attraction Listing Icons

SAVE AAA Discounts & Rewards® member discount

Electric vehicle charging station on premises. Domestic station information provided by the U.S. Department of Energy. Canadian station information provided by Plug'n Drive Ontario.

GT Guided Tours available

Camping facilities

Food on premises

Recreational activities

Pet friendly (Call for restrictions/fees.)

Picnicking allowed

In select cities only:

Mass transit station within 1 mile. Icon is followed by station name and AAA/CAA designated station number within listing.

GEM AAA/CAA travel experts may designate an attraction of exceptional interest and quality as a AAA GEM — a *Great Experience for Members®*. See GEM Attraction Index (listed on CONTENTS page) for a complete list of locations.

Consult the online travel guides at **AAA.com/travelguides** or visit AAA Mobile for additional things to do if you have time.

Hotel Listing Icons

May be preceded by CALL and/or SOME UNITS.

Member Information:

SAVE Member rates: discounted standard room rate or lowest public rate available at time of booking for dates of stay.

- Eco-certified by government or private organization.
- Electric vehicle charging station on premises. Domestic station information provided by the U.S. Department of Energy. Canadian station information provided by Plug'n Drive Ontario.
- Smoke-free premises

In select cities only:

- Mass transit station within 1 mile. Icon is followed by station name and AAA/CAA designated station number within listing.

Services:

- Airport transportation
- Pet friendly (Call for restrictions/fees.)
- Restaurant on premises
- Restaurant off premises
- Room service for 2 or more meals
- Full bar
- Child care
- Business center
- Accessible features (Call property for available services and amenities.)

Activities:

- Full-service casino
- Pool
- Health club or exercise room on premises

In-Room Amenities:

- High-speed Internet service
- High-speed Internet service (Call property for fees.)
- Wireless Internet service
- Wireless Internet service (Call property for fees.)
- No wireless Internet service
- Pay movies
- Refrigerator
- Microwave
- Coffeemaker
- No air conditioning
- No TV
- No telephones

Restaurant Listing Icons

- AAA Discounts & Rewards® member discount
- Eco-certified by government or private organization.
- Electric vehicle charging station on premises. Domestic station information provided by the U.S. Department of Energy. Canadian station information provided by Plug'n Drive Ontario.
- No air conditioning
- Accessible features (Call property for available services and amenities.)
- Designated smoking section
- Breakfast
- Lunch
- Dinner
- Open 24 hours
- Open after 11 p.m.
- Pet friendly (Call for restrictions/fees.)

In select cities only:

- Mass transit station within 1 mile. Icon is followed by station name and AAA/CAA designated station number within listing.

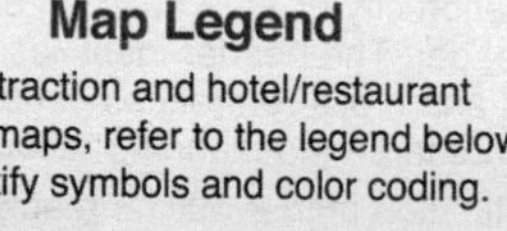

Map Legend

For attraction and hotel/restaurant spotting maps, refer to the legend below to identify symbols and color coding.

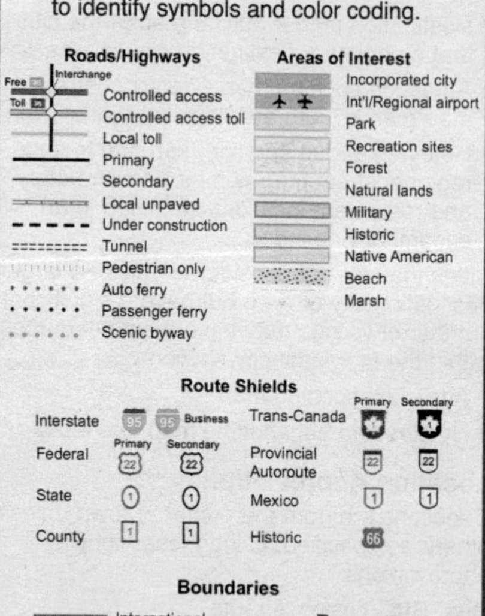

Boundaries

- International
- State
- Time zone
- Continental Divide

Points of Interest

- National capital
- State/Prov capital
- AAA/CAA club location
- Feature of interest
- GEM attraction
- Hotel listing
- Restaurant listing
- College/University
- Town
- Campground
- Winery
- Customs station
- Historic
- Mountain peak
- Rapid transit
- Stations
- Metromover

Understanding the Diamond Ratings

Hotel and restaurant inspections are unscheduled to ensure our trained professionals encounter the same unbiased experience members do.

Inspected & Approved

- The first step for every hotel and restaurant is to demonstrate they meet expected standards of cleanliness, comfort and hospitality.
- Only hotels and restaurants that pass AAA's rigorous on-site inspection are designated **AAA Inspected & Approved.**

But all AAA Inspected & Approved properties aren't the same: The difference is in the **Diamonds.** Each additional Diamond means greater comfort, amenities and service. Learn more at **AAA.com/Diamonds**.

Hotels

Budget-oriented, offering basic comfort and hospitality.

Affordable, with modestly enhanced facilities, décor and amenities.

Distinguished, multifaceted with enhanced physical attributes, amenities and guest comforts.

Refined, stylish with upscale physical attributes, extensive amenities and high degree of hospitality, service and attention to detail.

Ultimate luxury, sophistication and comfort with extraordinary physical attributes, meticulous personalized service, extensive amenities and impeccable standards of excellence.

Restaurants

Simple, economical food, often quick-serve, in a functional environment.

Familiar food, often cooked to order, served in casual surroundings.

Trendy cuisine, skillfully prepared and served, with expanded beverage options, in an enhanced setting.

Distinctive fine-dining. Creative preparations, skillfully served, often with wine steward, amid upscale ambience.

Leading-edge cuisine of the finest ingredients, uniquely prepared by an acclaimed chef, served by expert service staff led by maître d' in extraordinary surroundings.

Guest Safety

Inspectors view a sampling of rooms during hotel evaluations and, therefore, AAA/CAA cannot guarantee working locks and operational fire safety equipment in every guest unit.

Contacting AAA/CAA About the TourBook Guide

Tell us what you think about the TourBook guides or your experience at a listed hotel, restaurant or attraction. If your visit doesn't meet your expectations, please contact us **during your visit or within 30 days**. Be sure to save your receipts. We also welcome your recommendations on places to inspect.

Use the easy online form at **AAA.com/MemberFeedback**, email memberrelations@national.aaa.com or mail your feedback to: AAA Member Comments, 1000 AAA Dr., Box 61, Heathrow, FL 32746.

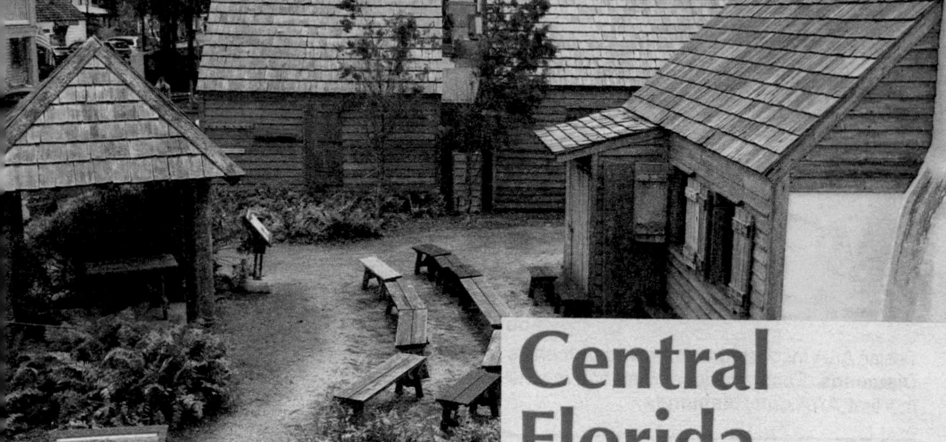
Colonial Quarter, St. Augustine

Central Florida

What comes to mind when you hear the words "Central Florida"? It's a good question that has no easy answer. This swath of the Sunshine State conjures up so many different images that you'd be challenged to sum it all up in 25 words or less.

From a historical perspective there's St. Augustine, earning a place in school history books due to the fact that it's the oldest European settlement in the United States. The site was claimed by Spanish explorers in 1565 for its strategic advantage—encircled by waterways on three sides, it was a prime spot to establish Spain's military headquarters in North America.

Jacksonville could be considered the working son in a family of Florida playboys. It's the largest deepwater port in the South, a financial center, a corporate headquarters and is home to multiple military facilities. Tampa is an equally hard-working sibling; today this former pirate stronghold and cigar-rolling center is a major player in everything from heavy industry to major league sports.

Tampa

For many, Central Florida is synonymous with a mouse who answers to Mickey and a man by the name of Walt. Prior to Magic Kingdom® Park's 1971 opening Orlando was a sedate little city situated amid orange groves and sparkling blue lakes. But in the mid-1960s "Uncle Walt" paid a series of hush-hush visits to survey undeveloped swamplands in southwestern Orange County. The opening of Mr. Disney's park was an unprecedented success, transforming "O-Town" into one of the most popular tourist destinations in the world.

There are plenty of nice beaches in this part of the state. Sarasota has the breezy look of a quintessential resort community—the Gulf of Mexico's turquoise waters, brilliant white sand and gracefully arching palms, not to mention gleaming condo towers and that Spanish-inspired, distinctively Floridian architectural motif of stucco and red tile. Beach getaways like Anna Maria, Pass-a-Grille and Caladesi Island State Park are the perfect solution to the delightful dilemma of how to spend that hard-earned

3-day weekend.

Days at the Beach

Over on the Atlantic side you've got Vero Beach, Melbourne Beach and Cocoa Beach, just to name a few. The Intracoastal Waterway, a network of interconnected inlets, bays, estuaries and saltwater rivers that runs along the entire east coast of Florida, provides an exceptionally scenic backdrop. It's the setting for a laid-back lifestyle where fishing, boating, sunning and kicking back at casual beachside restaurants are all high on the list of life's priorities.

At Daytona Beach sand not only gets between your toes; it gets between your tire treads. Although the speed limit for beach driving is a mere 10 miles per hour, land speed records were set here during the early days of the automobile. At nearby Canaveral National Seashore the sand is reserved for marine life like barnacles, mollusks and ghost crabs as well as people; 24 miles of uninterrupted shoreline constitute the longest stretch of undeveloped public beach on Florida's east coast.

Central Florida rules when it comes to family vacations. Every website and glossy travel brochure worth its promotional salt touts this region's many lures, chief among them benevolent winter weather and a plethora of sightseeing attractions.

Theme Park Nirvana

In the 4 decades following the Magic Kingdom® Park's opening, theme parks have sprouted in Orlando like mushrooms after a heavy rain. In addition to the Walt Disney World® Resort, which encompasses four theme parks, the area is home to SeaWorld Orlando and the Universal Orlando Resort. And that's just the tip of the entertainment iceberg; water parks, dinner shows, championship golf and heavy-duty shopping are a few other ways to spend your time. From Space Mountain to Shamu to The Wizarding World of Harry Potter's Hogsmeade and Diagon Alley (ride the Hogwarts Express train from one to the other), Orlando's got it covered when it comes to family fun.

But it's certainly not the only option. Nearby Kennedy Space Center appeals not only to budding astronauts but to anyone who's ever gazed up at the night sky and pondered the mysteries it holds. Throw on your orange sweatshirt and cheer on the Florida Gators at the University of Florida in Gainesville. Wander among the miniature versions of New York City and Washington, D.C. at LEGOLAND Florida Resort in Winter Haven. Head to Busch Gardens Tampa and scream to your heart's content on coasters like the floorless SheiKra. Or gaze at works by a master Spanish surrealist at St. Petersburg's The Dalí Museum.

Then there are the old standbys that have been welcoming visitors for generations. Silver Springs State Park (formerly Florida's Silver Springs), near Ocala, offers such simple pleasures as a ride in a glass-bottomed boat, cruising past riverbanks lined with bald cypresses and inhabited by alligators, turtles and herons—a more primeval Florida that existed long before the arrival of mouse ears and space shuttles. In St. Augustine, where Juan Ponce de León first set foot more than 500 years ago, hang out at Castillo de San Marcos National Monument, a massive fort built 1672-95. In Tarpon Springs, you can learn all about sponge diving, explore the local Greek culture and sample delicacies like flaming cheese. Opa!

Watch fish-tailed mermaids do their underwater thing in Weeki Wachee Springs' cool, crystal-clear spring waters. Gasp in astonishment as 8-foot-long reptiles jump clear out of the water to snatch raw chicken from an outstretched hand at Gatorland. Purchase bottled water from the Fountain of Youth, a dried puffer fish or a pink plastic yard flamingo to take back home. Central Florida is truly a place that has its kitsch in sync.

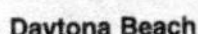

Daytona Beach

Historic Timeline

1513	Juan Ponce de León, searching for the Fountain of Youth, sails around Florida and lands near the future site of St. Augustine.
1565	Spanish explorer Pedro Menéndez de Aviles destroys a French Huguenot colony and establishes St. Augustine.
1763	The First Treaty of Paris cedes Florida to England; in 1783 the Second Treaty of Paris returns Florida to Spain.
1817	Gen. Andrew Jackson comes to punish the Native Americans for attacking the settlers, thus instigating the First Seminole War.
1819	Spain sells Florida to the United States.
1845	Florida achieves statehood.
1958	The first U.S. satellite launches from Cape Canaveral; the National Aeronautics and Space Administration is created.
1971	Walt Disney World® Resort opens, leading the way for new attractions and drawing millions of tourists to central Florida.
1986	The space shuttle *Challenger* explodes seconds after liftoff, killing all seven aboard.
2011	The space shuttle *Atlantis* launches from Kennedy Space Center, ending the space shuttle program.
2018	SpaceX launches the *Falcon Heavy* rocket from Kennedy Space Center sending Elon Musk's Tesla Roadster toward Mars.

What To Pack

Temperature Averages Maximum/Minimum	JANUARY	FEBRUARY	MARCH	APRIL	MAY	JUNE	JULY	AUGUST	SEPTEMBER	OCTOBER	NOVEMBER	DECEMBER
Daytona Beach	70/47	71/49	76/54	80/58	85/65	89/71	91/72	90/73	88/72	83/65	77/57	71/50
Jacksonville	64/42	67/44	73/50	79/55	84/62	89/60	91/72	89/72	86/69	79/60	73/51	66/44
Ocala	70/46	73/47	78/52	83/56	88/63	91/69	92/71	92/71	90/69	84/61	77/53	72/47
Orlando	72/50	74/51	79/56	83/60	88/66	91/71	92/73	92/73	90/72	85/65	79/59	73/53
Tampa	70/52	72/54	76/58	81/62	86/69	89/74	90/75	90/75	89/74	84/68	78/61	72/65
Vero Beach	73/53	74/54	78/58	81/62	85/67	89/72	90/73	90/73	89/73	84/69	79/62	75/55

From the records of The Weather Channel Interactive, Inc.

Good Facts To Know

ABOUT THE STATE

POPULATION: 18,801,310.

AREA: 65,758 square miles; ranks 22nd.

CAPITAL: Tallahassee.

HIGHEST POINT: 345 ft., Walton County.

LOWEST POINT: Sea level, Atlantic Ocean.

TIME ZONE(S): Eastern/Central. DST.

GAMBLING

MINIMUM AGE FOR GAMBLING: 18 for pari-mutuel betting; 21 for casino gambling.

REGULATIONS

TEEN DRIVING LAWS: There are no passenger restrictions. Driving is not permitted 11 p.m.-6 a.m. for age 16 and 1 a.m.-5 a.m. for age 17, unless accompanied by a licensed driver who is at least 21 years old in the front seat. The minimum age for an unrestricted driver's license is 18. For more information about Florida driver's license regulations phone (850) 617-2000.

SEAT BELT/CHILD RESTRAINT LAWS: Seat belts are required for driver and front-seat passengers. Seat belt is required for children ages 6-17. Appropriate child restraints are required for children under age 6. AAA recommends seat belts/child restraints for driver and all passengers.

CELLPHONE RESTRICTIONS: Text messaging is prohibited for all drivers. Handheld cell phone use is prohibited in school and construction zones where workers are present.

HELMETS FOR MOTORCYCLISTS: Required for riders under 21. Persons 21 and over may ride without helmets only if they can show proof they are covered by a medical insurance policy.

RADAR DETECTORS: Permitted. Prohibited for commercial vehicles.

MOVE OVER LAW: Driver is required to slow down and vacate the lane nearest stopped police, fire and rescue vehicles using audible or flashing signals. Law also requires drivers to move over for tow truck drivers assisting motorists, municipal vehicles and utility vehicles.

FIREARMS LAWS: Vary by state and/or county. Contact the Florida Department of Agriculture and Consumer Services, Division of Licensing, P.O. Box 6687, Tallahassee, FL 32314-6687; phone (850) 245-5691.

SPECIAL REGULATIONS: All motorists who drive trucks or pull trailers must stop at road guard agricultural inspection stations. Recreational vehicles and private passenger vehicles without trailers are not required to stop at these stations.

Permanently disabled persons with "handicapped" license plates from any state receive special parking privileges in Florida.

HOLIDAYS

HOLIDAYS: Jan. 1 ▪ Martin Luther King Jr. Day, Jan. (3rd Mon.) ▪ Memorial Day, May (4th Mon.) ▪ July 4 ▪ Labor Day, Sept. (1st Mon.) ▪ Veterans Day, Nov. 11 ▪ Thanksgiving, Nov. (4th Thurs.), and following Fri. ▪ Christmas, Dec. 25.

MONEY

TAXES: Florida's statewide sales tax is 6 percent, with counties allowed to impose additional levies. There is a tax on accommodations and meals, and counties have the option to add a tourist impact tax and a tourist development tax of varying levels.

VISITOR INFORMATION

INFORMATION CENTERS: State welcome centers can be found just south of the Florida/Alabama border on US 231 at Campbellton ▪ south of the Florida/Georgia border off I-75 near Jennings ▪ near the Florida/Alabama border off I-10, 16 miles west of Pensacola ▪ south of the Florida/Georgia border off I-95 near Yulee ▪ and in Tallahassee at the Florida State Capitol.

SPECIAL NOTE: Lovebugs are very sticky insects that swarm during the day in April, May, September and October, clogging car radiators, smearing windshields and corroding a car's finish.

FURTHER INFORMATION FOR VISITORS:
Visit Florida Inc.
2540 W. Executive Center Cir., Suite 200
Tallahassee, FL 32301
(850) 488-5607 (Main Office)
(850) 488-6167 (Florida Capitol Welcome Center)
(888) 735-2872 (Information specialist)

NATIONAL FOREST INFORMATION:
National Forests in Florida
325 John Knox Rd., Suite F-100
Tallahassee, FL 32303-4160
(850) 523-8500
(877) 444-6777 (Reservations)

FISHING AND HUNTING REGULATIONS:
Florida Fish and Wildlife Conservation Commission
620 S. Meridian St.
Tallahassee, FL 32399-1600
(850) 488-4676 (Main Office)
(888) 347-4356 (fishing licenses)

RECREATION INFORMATION:
Florida Department of Environmental Protection
3900 Commonwealth Blvd., Mail Station 49
Tallahassee, FL 32399-3000
(850) 245-2118

Central Florida Annual Events

Please call ahead to confirm event details.

Visit AAA.com/travelguides/events to find AAA-listed events for every day of the year

WINTER

Dec. - Historic Inns Bed & Breakfast Holiday Tour / St. Augustine / 904-824-2229
- Victorian Christmas Stroll / Tampa 813-258-7302

Jan. - Epiphany Celebration / Tarpon Springs / 727-937-3540
- Gasparilla Pirate Fest / Tampa 813-353-8070
- Zora Neale Hurston Festival of the Arts and Humanities / Eatonville 407-647-3307

Feb. - Florida State Fair / Tampa 813-621-7821
- Daytona 500 / Daytona Beach / 904-253-7223
- Mount Dora Arts Festival / Mount Dora / 352-383-0880

SPRING

Mar. - Bike Week / Daytona Beach / 904-255-0981
- Florida Strawberry Festival / Plant City / 813-752-9194
- Winter Park Sidewalk Art Festival Winter Park / 407-644-7207

Apr. - Wanee Music Festival / Live Oak / 800-594-8499
- Ormond Beach Celtic Festival Ormond Beach / 386-492-2938
- Shark's Tooth Festival / Venice 941-412-0402

May - Jacksonville Jazz Festival Jacksonville / 904-630-3690
- Isle of Eight Flags Shrimp Festival Fernandina Beach / 800-226-3542
- Orlando International Fringe Theatre Festival / Orlando / 407-648-0077

SUMMER

June - Harvest Festival / Clermont 352-394-8627
- Tampa Bay Boat Show / Tampa 727-893-8523
- KIAFest Main Street Blast / New Port Richey / 727-842-8066

July - Bayfront Fireworks Spectacular Sarasota / 941-371-8820, ext. 1800
- Caladium Festival / Lake Placid / 863-465-4331
- Greater Jacksonville Kingfish Tournament / Jacksonville 904-745-3223

Aug. - Harvest Grape Stomp / Clermont 352-394-8627
- Antiques Fair (August) / Mount Dora / 352-383-8393

FALL

Sept. - Sponge Docks Labor Day Festival Tarpon Springs / 352-344-0657
- NKF Rich Salick Pro-Am Surfing Festival / Cocoa Beach / 321-784-5661
- QuiltFest of Jacksonville Jacksonville / 904-396-0078

Oct. - Epcot International Food & Wine Festival / Lake Buena Vista / 407-939-3378
- Biketoberfest / Daytona Beach / 866-296-8970
- Clearwater Jazz Holiday / Clearwater 727-461-5200

Nov. - Daytona Turkey Run Car Show and Swap Meet / Daytona Beach / 386-255-7355
- Halifax Art Festival / Daytona Beach / 800-544-0415
- Crystal Classic International Sandsculpting Festival / Sarasota 941-349-3800

Love the great outdoors? Find places to camp at AAA.com/campgrounds

World Golf Hall of Fame & Museum at World Golf Village, St. Augustine

Universal's Volcano Bay™, Orlando

Cocoa Beach

Epicurean Hotel, Autograph Collection, Tampa

Kennedy Space Center Visitor Center Complex

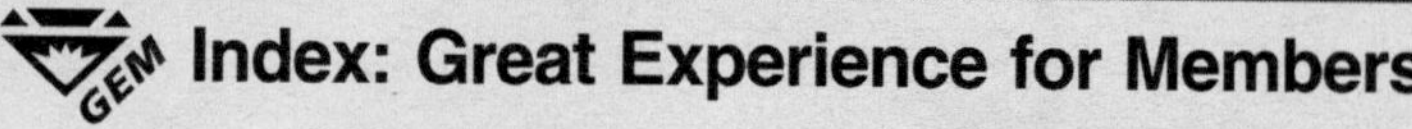

Index: Great Experience for Members

AAA editor's picks of exceptional note

Castillo de San Marcos National Monument

Highlands Hammock State Park

Bok Tower Gardens

Kennedy Space Center Visitor Complex

See Orientation map on p. 22 for corresponding grid coordinates, if applicable.
*Indicates the GEM is temporarily closed.

STAY CONNECTED

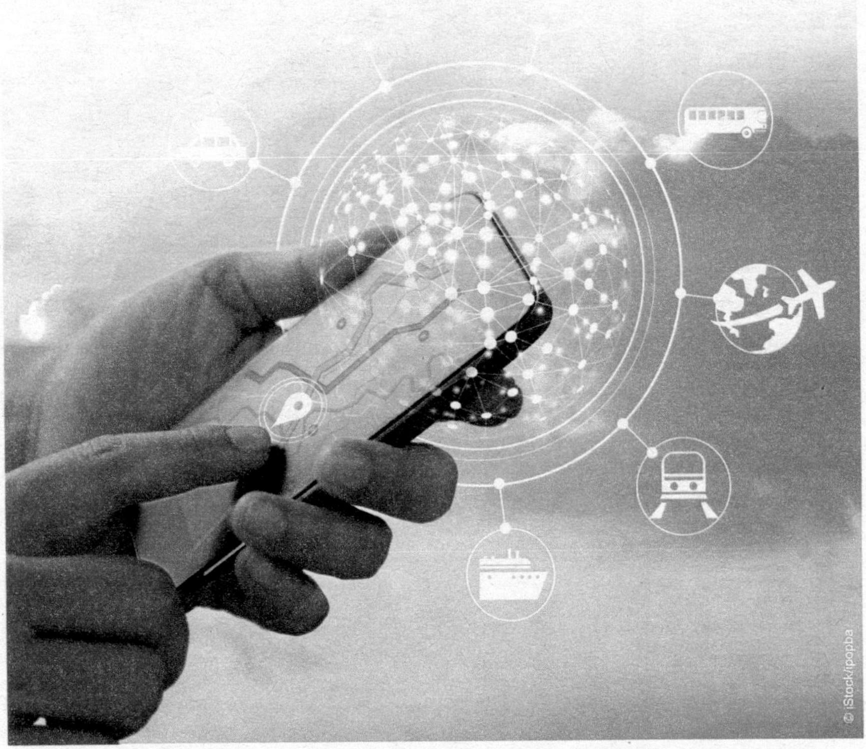

© iStock/ipopba

to all the things membership can do for you

- Member discounts around you
- Cheapest gas nearby
- Diamond Rated hotels and restaurants
- Travel information and reservations
- Roadside assistance

Download today.
Connect every day.
AAA.com/mobile | CAA.ca/mobile

Central Florida Atlas Section

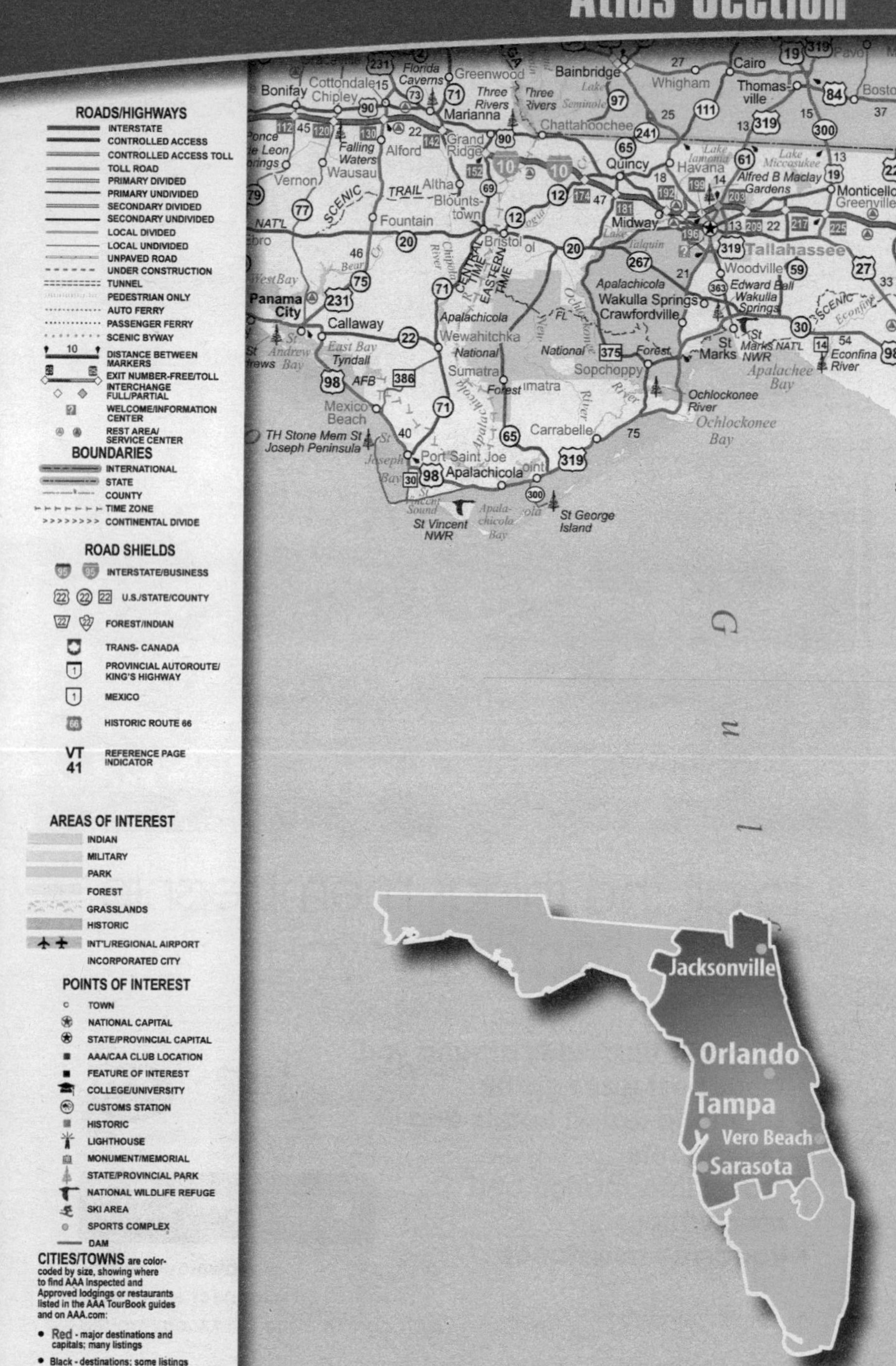

ROADS/HIGHWAYS
INTERSTATE
CONTROLLED ACCESS
CONTROLLED ACCESS TOLL
TOLL ROAD
PRIMARY DIVIDED
PRIMARY UNDIVIDED
SECONDARY DIVIDED
SECONDARY UNDIVIDED
LOCAL DIVIDED
LOCAL UNDIVIDED
UNPAVED ROAD
UNDER CONSTRUCTION
TUNNEL
PEDESTRIAN ONLY
AUTO FERRY
PASSENGER FERRY
SCENIC BYWAY
DISTANCE BETWEEN MARKERS
EXIT NUMBER-FREE/TOLL
INTERCHANGE FULL/PARTIAL
WELCOME/INFORMATION CENTER
REST AREA/ SERVICE CENTER
BOUNDARIES
INTERNATIONAL
STATE
COUNTY
TIME ZONE
CONTINENTAL DIVIDE
ROAD SHIELDS
INTERSTATE/BUSINESS
U.S./STATE/COUNTY
FOREST/INDIAN
TRANS- CANADA
PROVINCIAL AUTOROUTE/ KING'S HIGHWAY
MEXICO
HISTORIC ROUTE 66
VT 41
REFERENCE PAGE INDICATOR
AREAS OF INTEREST
INDIAN
MILITARY
PARK
FOREST
GRASSLANDS
HISTORIC
INT'L/REGIONAL AIRPORT
INCORPORATED CITY
POINTS OF INTEREST
TOWN
NATIONAL CAPITAL
STATE/PROVINCIAL CAPITAL
AAA/CAA CLUB LOCATION
FEATURE OF INTEREST
COLLEGE/UNIVERSITY
CUSTOMS STATION
HISTORIC
LIGHTHOUSE
MONUMENT/MEMORIAL
STATE/PROVINCIAL PARK
NATIONAL WILDLIFE REFUGE
SKI AREA
SPORTS COMPLEX
DAM
CITIES/TOWNS are color-coded by size, showing where to find AAA inspected and Approved lodgings or restaurants listed in the AAA TourBook guides and on AAA.com:
Red - major destinations and capitals; many listings
Black - destinations; some listings
Grey - no listings
Bonifay
Cottondale
Chipley
Florida Caverns
Greenwood
Marianna
Three Rivers
Bainbridge
Whigham
Cairo
Thomasville
Boston
Chattahoochee
Alford
Falling Waters
Grand Ridge
Wausau
Vernon
Quincy
Havana
Lake Miccosukee
Alfred B Maclay Gardens
Monticello
Greenville
Altha
Blountstown
Fountain
Bristol
Midway
Tallahassee
Woodville
Panama City
Callaway
Apalachicola
Wakulla Springs
Crawfordville
Edward Ball Wakulla Springs
Wewahitchka
East Bay
Tyndall AFB
Sumatra
Sopchoppy
St Marks
St Marks NWR
Apalachee Bay
Econfina River
Mexico Beach
Carrabelle
Ochlockonee River
Ochlockonee Bay
TH Stone Mem St Joseph Peninsula
Port Saint Joe
Apalachicola
St Vincent NWR
St George Island
CENTRAL TIME
EASTERN TIME
Jacksonville
Orlando
Tampa
Vero Beach
Sarasota

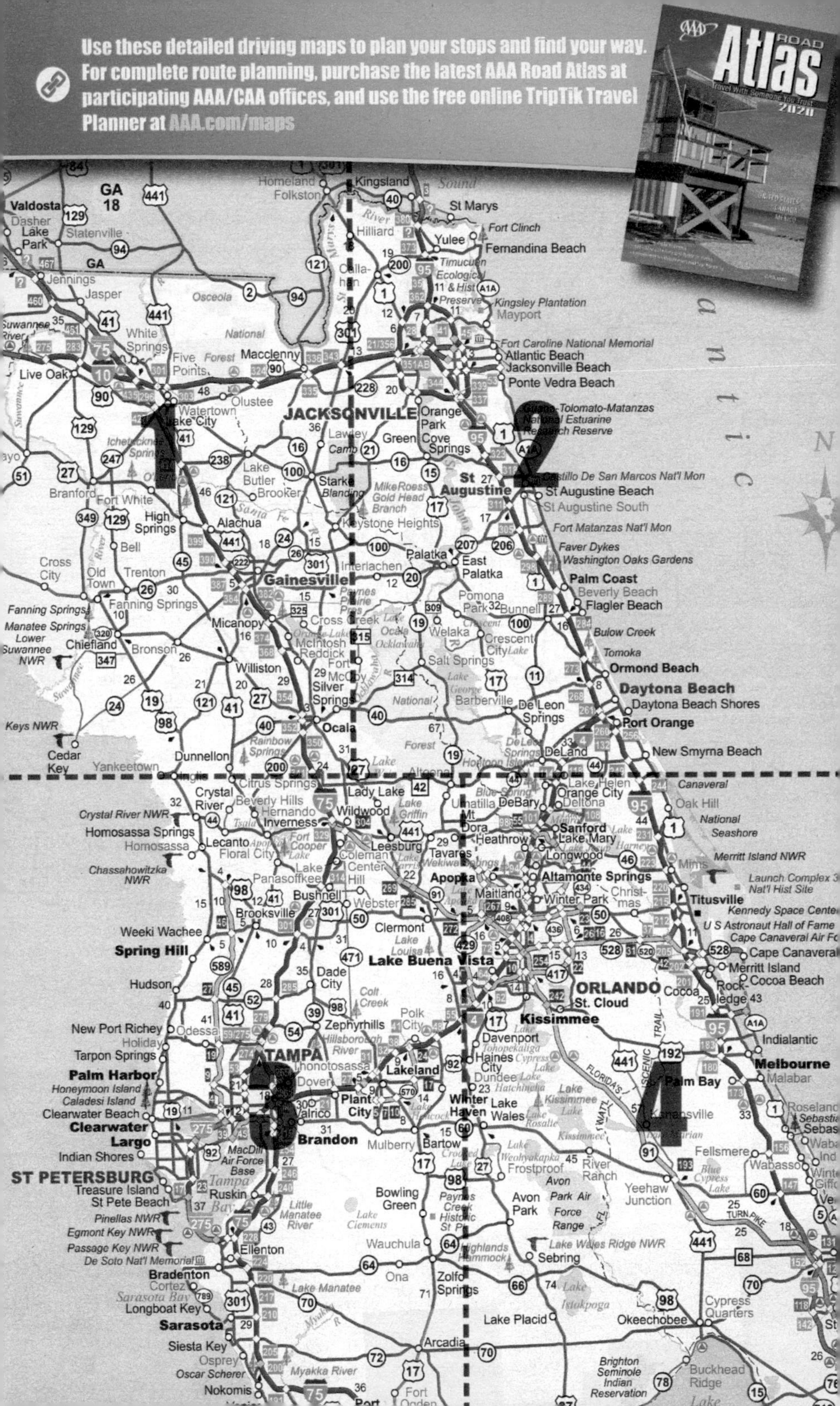
Use these detailed driving maps to plan your stops and find your way.
For complete route planning, purchase the latest AAA Road Atlas at participating AAA/CAA offices, and use the free online TripTik Travel Planner at AAA.com/maps
AAA
Road Atlas
2020
Valdosta
GA 18
Jennings
Jasper
White Springs
Live Oak
Lake City
Macclenny
Kingsland
St Marys
Fernandina Beach
Yulee
Hilliard
Callahan
JACKSONVILLE
Atlantic Beach
Jacksonville Beach
Ponte Vedra Beach
Orange Park
Green Cove Springs
Starke
Lake Butler
Alachua
High Springs
Gainesville
St Augustine
St Augustine South
Palatka
East Palatka
Palm Coast
Flagler Beach
Ormond Beach
Daytona Beach
Daytona Beach Shores
Port Orange
New Smyrna Beach
DeLand
Ocala
Silver Springs
Williston
Micanopy
Chiefland
Cedar Key
Dunnellon
Crystal River
Inverness
Wildwood
Lady Lake
Leesburg
Sanford
Lake Mary
Longwood
Altamonte Springs
Apopka
Winter Park
Titusville
Kennedy Space Center
Cape Canaveral
Cocoa Beach
Merritt Island
ORLANDO
St. Cloud
Kissimmee
Lake Buena Vista
Clermont
Brooksville
Spring Hill
Hudson
New Port Richey
Tarpon Springs
Palm Harbor
Clearwater
Largo
ST PETERSBURG
St Pete Beach
TAMPA
Brandon
Plant City
Lakeland
Winter Haven
Bartow
Lake Wales
Haines City
Davenport
Melbourne
Palm Bay
Indialantic
Bradenton
Sarasota
Siesta Key
Osprey
Nokomis
Wauchula
Zolfo Springs
Arcadia
Avon Park
Sebring
Lake Placid
Okeechobee
Frostproof
Bowling Green
Ellenton
Ruskin
Yeehaw Junction
Cypress Quarters
Fellsmere
Roseland
Sebastian
Atlantic

GA
28
Valdosta
Lake Park
Jennings
Pinetta
Hanson
Fargo
Folkston
Sargent
Eddy
GA
HAMILTON
Jasper
COLUMBIA
Osceola
Big Gum Swamp Wilderness Area
Taylor
BAKER
Nat'l Forest
Olustee Battlefield Historic SP
Suwannee River
Suwannee Springs
Stephen Foster Folk Culture Center
Genoa
White Springs
Lee
Newburn
Live Oak
Five Points
Glen St Mary
Macclenny
Sanderson
Olustee
Wellborn
Watertown
Lake City
Dowling Park
Day
Pine Mount
SUWANNEE
Luraville
UNION
Ellerbee
Sapp
Lawtey
Raiford
Lake Butler
Columbia
Mayo
O'Brien
Ichetucknee Springs
Providence
New River
Starke
Branford
Hildreth
Fort White
Worthington Springs
BRADFORD
Brooker
Graham
LAFAYETTE
Hatchbend
O'Leno
Alachua
ALACHUA
Waldo
High Springs
San Felasco Hammock Preserve
Gainesville
Earleton
Tennille
Hines
DIXIE
Bell
GILCHRIST
Wannee
(GNV)
Newnans Lake
Newberry
Jena
Shamrock
Cross City
Trenton
Hawthorne
Old Town
Fanning Springs
Archer
Micanopy
Lochloosa Lake
Lochloosa
Cross Creek
Manatee Springs
Paynes Prairie Preserve
Chiefland
Bronson
McIntosh
Citra
Horseshoe Beach
Shired Island
Lower Suwannee
LEVY
Williston
Reddick
Sparr
Suwannee
Ellzey
Otter Creek
Goethe State Forest
Morriston
Silver Springs
National Wildlife Refuge
Gulf Hammock
Rosewood
Rainbow Lakes Estates
Cotton Plant
Ocala
Cedar Key
Lebanon
Rainbow Springs
Dunnellon
Belleview
Cedar Keys NWR
Yankeetown
Citrus Springs
The Villages
Inglis
Citronelle
Holder
SUMTER
Crystal River Archaeological St Pk
Beverly Hills
Hernando
Wildwood
Crystal River
Lecanto
Inverness
Rutland

2
Atlantic
Kingsland
St Marys
Fort Clinch
Fernandina Plaza Historic SP
Hilliard
NASSAU
Yulee
Fernandina Beach
Callahan
Amelia City
(JAX)
Timucuan Ecological & Hist Preserve
Bryceville
DUVAL
Baldwin
Jacksonville
Atlantic Beach
Jacksonville Beach
Ponte Vedra Beach
Jennings State Forest
Orange Park
Guana-Tolomato-Matanzas National Estuarine Research Reserve
Fruit Cove
Fleming Island
Middleburg
Hilden
CLAY
Castillo de San Marcos National Monument
Anastasia
Penney Farms
Green Cove Springs
St Augustine
St Augustine Beach
St Augustine Shores
Mike Roess Gold Head Branch
McRae
PUTNAM
Elkton
Crescent Beach
Keystone Heights
Bostwick
Putnam Hall
Fort Matanzas National Monument
Carraway
Hastings
Faver Dykes
Grandin
Melrose
Springside
East Palatka
ST JOHNS
Washington Oaks Gardens
Interlachen
Hollister
Palatka
San Mateo
Palm Coast
Rodman Res
Satsuma
FLAGLER
Beverly Beach
Pomona Park
Flagler Beach
Welaka
Lake Como
Orange Springs
FLORIDA NAT'L
Crescent Lake
Bunnell
Gamble Rogers Memorial State Recreation Area
Georgetown
Crescent City
Ormond-by-the-Sea
Ocala
Tomoka
Drayton Island
Ormond Beach
Fort McCoy
Salt Springs
Seville
Lake George
Juniper Prairie Wilderness Area
Pierson
(DAB)
Daytona Beach
Barberville
De Leon Springs
Silver Springs
Astor
National Pine Castle Bombing Range
Alexander Springs Wilderness
Ponce Inlet
Silver Springs Shores
De Leon Springs
Halifax River
MARION
Lake Woodruff NWR
Glencoe
New Smyrna Beach
DeLand
Edgewater
Ocklawaha
Forest
Lake Weir
Altoona
SCENIC
Hontoon Island
Lake Helen
Canaveral National Seashore
Weirsdale
Paisley
Orange City
VOLUSIA
Lady Lake
Grand Island
Umatilla
Deltona
Fruitland Park
Lake Griffin
Lake Eustis
LAKE
DeBary
Osteen
Oak Hill
Silver Lake
Eustis
Sanford
Indian River

3
Key
Lebanon
Forest
Rainbow Springs
Dunnellon
Belleview
Shores
MARION
Bombing Range
Ocklawaha
Forest
Altoona
Yankeetown
Inglis
Citrus Springs
Citronelle
The Villages
Lake Weir
Weirsdale
Lady Lake
Grand Island
Holder
Beverly Hills
Hernando
SUMTER
Crystal River Archaeological St Pk
Crystal River
Lecanto
Inverness
Rutland
Wildwood
Fruitland Park
Lake Griffin
Silver Lake
Eustis
Preserve State Park
Ozello
Homosassa Springs
CITRUS
Lake Panasoffkee
Sumterville
Leesburg
Tavares
Ellie Schiller Homosassa Springs Wildlife
Homosassa
Withlacoochee State Forest
Fort Cooper
Yalaha
Howey-in-the-Hills
Chassahowitzka National Wildlife Refuge
State Forest (Citrus Res)
Floral City
Bushnell
Center Hill
HERNANDO
Dade Battlefield Hist St Pk
Minneola
Brooksville
Webster
Mascotte
Groveland
Clermont
Weeki Wachee
Linden
Withlacoochee St Forest (Croom Res)
Ridge Manor
Withlacoochee State Forest (Richloam Reservation)
Lake Louisa
Spring Hill
Aripeka
Lacoochee
Dade City
Walt Disney World Resort
Hudson
PASCO
Bayonet Point
Richland
Colt Creek
Champions-Gate
Port Richey
Land O'Lakes
Wesley Chapel
New Port Richey
Odessa
Trinity
Elfers
Zephyrhills
Polk City
Holiday
Lakeland
Lake Alfred
Hillsborough River
Tarpon Springs
PINELLAS
ALT
Lutz
Winter
(TPA)
Dover
Plant City
Seffner
Highland City
West Lake Wales
Clearwater
(PIE)
Valrico
Brandon
Mulberry
Bartow
TAMPA
ST PETERSBURG
Lithia
Bradley
Homeland
Crooked Lake
Balm
HILLSBOROUGH
Fort Meade
Tampa Bay
Sun City Center
Bowling Green
Paynes Creek Historic State Park
Fort Green Springs
Wauchula
De Soto Nat'l Mem
Manatee River
Vandolah
Bradenton
Oneco
Ona
Zolfo Springs
26
MANATEE
Horse Cr.
(SRQ)
Lakewood Ranch
Myakka City
Limestone
Sweetwater
Gardner
Longboat Key
Myakka River
Peace River
Brownville
Sarasota
Siesta Key
Arcadia
Osprey
DESOTO
Oscar Scherer
SARASOTA
Hull
Nocatee
Nokomis
Lake Suzy
Fort Ogden
Venice
North Port
South Venice

4
DeLand
New Smyrna Beach
Edgewater
Lake Helen
Canaveral National Seashore
Orange City
DeBary
Deltona
Osteen
VOLUSIA
Oak Hill
Sanford
Heathrow
Geneva
Lake Harney
Scottsmoor
Indian River Lagoon
INTRACOASTAL
Apopka
Altamonte Springs
Mims
SEMINOLE
Chuluota
Titusville
Kennedy Space Ctr
INSET
Winter Park
Bithlo
Christmas
Cape Canaveral Air Force Station
ORLANDO
BEACH LINE EXPY
Cape Canaveral
Cocoa Beach
Lake Buena Vista
ORANGE
Kissimmee
St Cloud
Reunion
Lake Tohopekaliga
Davenport
OSCEOLA
Haines City
Indialantic
Melbourne
Malabar
Palm Bay
Grant-Valk
Dundee
Lake Hatchineha
Cypress Gardens
Lake Wales
Lake Kissimmee
Kenansville
BREVARD
Micco
Sebastian Inlet
Roseland
Sebastian
St Sebastian River Preserve
Babson Park
River Ranch
POLK
Fellsmere
Wabasso
Blue Cypress Lake
Winter Beach
Gifford
Frostproof
Yeehaw Junction
Vero Beach
Avon Park
Ridge State Forest
Air Force Range
Kissimmee Prairie Preserve State Park
INDIAN RIVER
Oslo
Lakewood Park
Avalon
Lake Wales Ridge NWR
OKEECHOBEE
Fort Drum
Sebring
Highlands Hammock
DeSoto City
Lorida
Crewsville
Lake Istokpoga
Basinger
ST LUCIE
Cypress Quarters
HIGHLANDS
Okeechobee
Port Saint Lucie
Lake Placid
Brighton
MARTIN
Hicoria
Buckhead Ridge
Indiantown
Venus
Brighton Seminole Indian Reservation
Lake
Lake Baldwin
Lakeport
DuPuis
Ocean

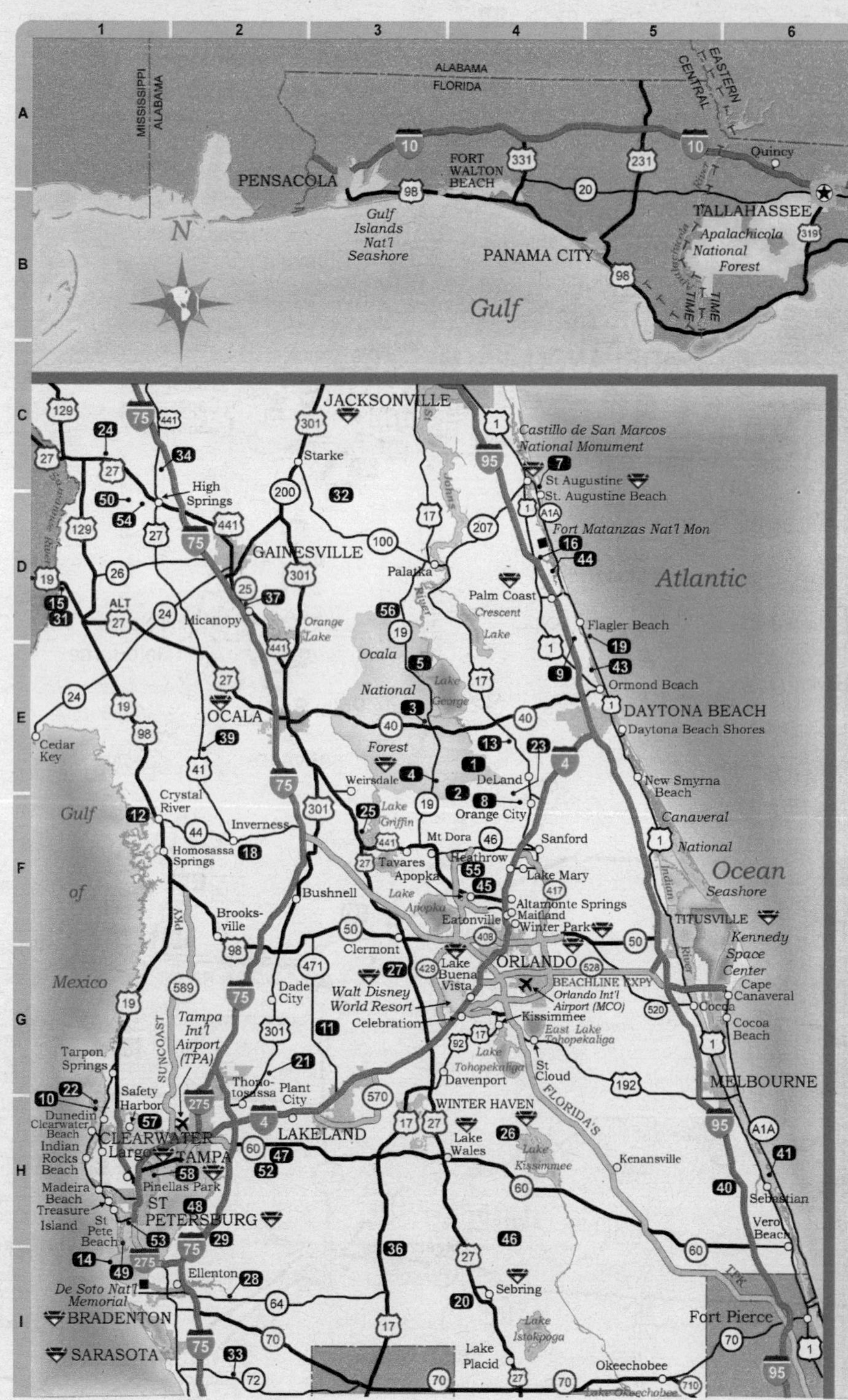

ALABAMA
FLORIDA
MISSISSIPPI
ALABAMA
CENTRAL
EASTERN
PENSACOLA
FORT WALTON BEACH
Quincy
TALLAHASSEE
Gulf Islands Nat'l Seashore
PANAMA CITY
Apalachicola National Forest
Gulf
JACKSONVILLE
Castillo de San Marcos National Monument
St Augustine
St. Augustine Beach
Fort Matanzas Nat'l Mon
Starke
High Springs
GAINESVILLE
Palatka
Palm Coast
Crescent Lake
Atlantic
Flagler Beach
Ormond Beach
DAYTONA BEACH
Daytona Beach Shores
Micanopy
Orange Lake
Ocala National Forest
Lake George
OCALA
Cedar Key
Weirsdale
DeLand
New Smyrna Beach
Crystal River
Lake Griffin
Orange City
Canaveral National Seashore
Gulf of Mexico
Inverness
Mt Dora
Sanford
Homosassa Springs
Tavares
Heathrow
Lake Mary
Ocean
Apopka
Lake Apopka
Altamonte Springs
Maitland
Winter Park
Eatonville
Bushnell
Brooksville
TITUSVILLE
Kennedy Space Center
Clermont
Lake Buena Vista
ORLANDO
BEACHLINE EXPY
Orlando Int'l Airport (MCO)
Cape Canaveral
Cocoa
Cocoa Beach
Dade City
Walt Disney World Resort
Celebration
Kissimmee
East Lake Tohopekaliga
Tampa Int'l Airport (TPA)
SUNCOAST
PKY
Tarpon Springs
Lake Tohopekaliga
Davenport
St Cloud
MELBOURNE
Safety Harbor
Thonotosassa
Plant City
WINTER HAVEN
FLORIDA'S
Dunedin
Clearwater Beach
CLEARWATER
Largo
TAMPA
LAKELAND
Lake Wales
Indian Rocks Beach
Lake Kissimmee
Kenansville
Pinellas Park
Madeira Beach
Treasure Island
ST PETERSBURG
St Pete Beach
Sebastian
Vero Beach
Ellenton
Sebring
De Soto Nat'l Memorial
BRADENTON
Lake Istokpoga
Fort Pierce
SARASOTA
Lake Placid
Okeechobee
Lake Okeechobee
TPK
Indian River
St Johns River
Suwannee River

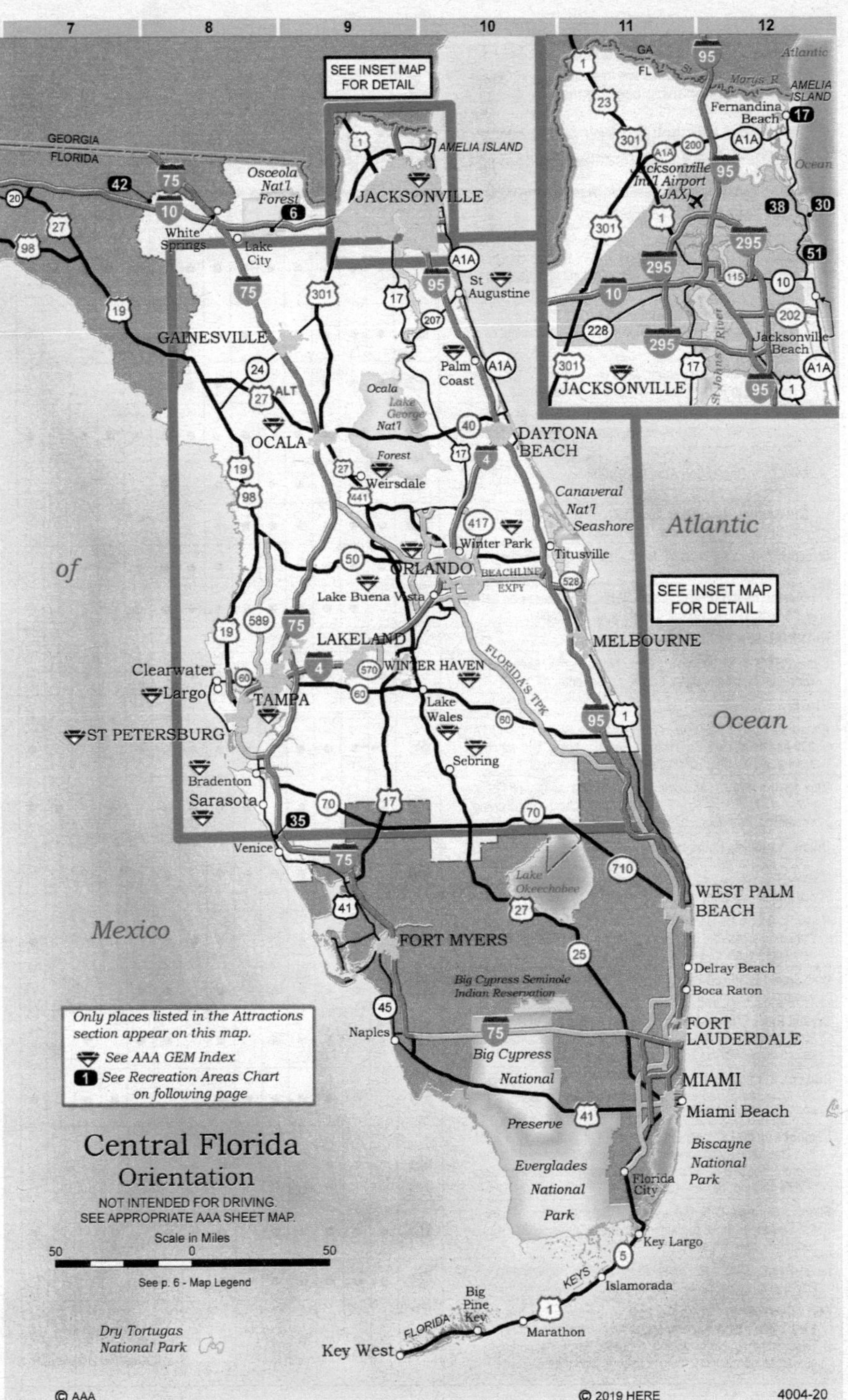

SEE INSET MAP FOR DETAIL
GEORGIA
FLORIDA
Osceola Nat'l Forest
White Springs
Lake City
JACKSONVILLE
AMELIA ISLAND
St Augustine
GAINESVILLE
Palm Coast
Ocala
Lake George
Nat'l
Forest
OCALA
DAYTONA BEACH
Weirsdale
Canaveral Nat'l Seashore
Atlantic
Winter Park
Titusville
of
ORLANDO
BEACHLINE EXPY
Lake Buena Vista
SEE INSET MAP FOR DETAIL
LAKELAND
MELBOURNE
Clearwater
Largo
WINTER HAVEN
FLORIDA'S TPK
TAMPA
Lake Wales
ST PETERSBURG
Ocean
Sebring
Bradenton
Sarasota
Venice
Lake Okeechobee
WEST PALM BEACH
Mexico
FORT MYERS
Big Cypress Seminole Indian Reservation
Delray Beach
Boca Raton
Naples
FORT LAUDERDALE
Big Cypress National Preserve
MIAMI
Miami Beach
Biscayne National Park
Everglades National Park
Florida City
Key Largo
Islamorada
KEYS
Big Pine Key
FLORIDA
Marathon
Key West
Dry Tortugas National Park
GA
FL
Atlantic
Ocean
AMELIA ISLAND
Fernandina Beach
Jacksonville Int'l Airport (JAX)
Jacksonville Beach
St Johns River
JACKSONVILLE
Only places listed in the Attractions section appear on this map.
See AAA GEM Index
See Recreation Areas Chart on following page
Central Florida
Orientation
NOT INTENDED FOR DRIVING.
SEE APPROPRIATE AAA SHEET MAP.
Scale in Miles
50 0 50
See p. 6 - Map Legend
© AAA
© 2019 HERE
4004-20

Recreation Areas Chart

The map location numerals in column 2 show an area's location on the preceding map.

Find thousands of places to camp at AAA.com/campgrounds

	MAP LOCATION	CAMPING	PICNICKING	HIKING TRAILS	BOATING	BOAT RAMP	BOAT RENTAL	FISHING	SWIMMING	PET FRIENDLY	BICYCLE TRAILS	SKIN/SCUBA	VISITOR CENTER	LODGE/CABINS	FOOD SERVICE
NATIONAL FORESTS *(See place listings.)*															
Ocala (E-3) 383,573 acres. North-central Florida. Scenic. Hunting, scuba diving, snorkeling, water skiing; ATV and dirt bike trails, canoe and kayak rental, horse rental, natural springs, scenic drive.		•	•	•	•	•	•	•	•	•	•	•	•	•	•
Alexander Springs Recreation Area (E-4) 30 acres 13 mi. n.e. of Umatilla via SR 19 and CR 445. Scuba diving; canoe and kayak rentals.	1	•	•	•	•		•	•	•	•	•	•			•
Clearwater Lake Recreation Area (E-4) 15 acres .9 mi. s.w. on SR 42 in Paisley. Mountain biking; canoe rentals.	2	•	•	•	•			•	•		•				
Juniper Springs Recreation Area (E-3) 47 acres 28 mi. e. of Ocala on SR 40. Bird-watching, canoeing, kayaking, paddling, snorkeling; canoe rental, pool.	3	•	•	•	•		•		•	•	•	•	•		•
Lake Dorr Recreation Area (E-3) 10 acres 5 mi. n. of Umatilla on SR 19.	4	•	•		•	•	•	•		•			•		
Salt Springs Recreation Area (E-3) 93 acres off SR 19 just n. of CR 314 in Salt Springs. Canoe rentals.	5	•	•	•	•	•	•	•	•						
Osceola (A-8) 198,484 acres. Northeastern Florida. Hunting; horse rentals and trails.		•	•	•	•	•		•	•	•	•				
Olustee Beach (B-9) 15 acres .25 mi. n. of Olustee on CR 231 (Pine Street). Kayaking, water skiing; fishing pier.	6		•	•	•	•	•	•	•	•	•				
NATIONAL SEASHORES *(See place listings.)*															
Canaveral (F-5) 57,000 acres. East-central Florida. Scenic. Bird-watching, hunting, surfing; beach, canoe rental.		•	•	•	•	•	•	•	•				•		
STATE															
Anastasia (C-4) 1,643 acres at St. Augustine Beach off SR A1A at 300 Anastasia Park Rd. Historic. Beachcombing, bird-watching, surfing, windsurfing; amphitheater, beach, playground.	7	•	•	•	•		•	•	•	•	•				•
Blue Spring (F-4) 2,643 acres 2 mi. w. of Orange City off US 17/92 on W. French Ave. Historic. Bird-watching, scuba diving, snorkeling; boat tours, canoe and kayak rental, river cruises.	8	•	•	•	•		•	•	•	•		•		•	•
Bulow Plantation Ruins Historic (E-4) 152 acres 3 mi. w. on CR 100, 3 mi. s.e. on CR 2001 (Old Kings Rd.) to 3501 S. Old Kings Rd. Historic. Canoeing, kayaking; canoe rental, interpretive center, museum, ruins.	9		•	•	•	•	•	•		•	•				
Caladesi Island (H-1) 2,470 acres in the Gulf of Mexico w. of Dunedin. Accessible only by boat or ferry. Bird-watching, boat camping, kayaking; beach, marina, playground.	10		•	•	•			•	•	•					•
Colt Creek (G-3) 5,067 acres 4 mi. n. of US 98 on CR 471. Bird-watching, camping (primitive), canoeing, kayaking; horse trails.	11	•	•	•	•	•		•		•	•				
Crystal River Preserve (F-1) 30,000 acres 2 mi. n. of Crystal River on US 19. Educational programs. Exhibits. Canoeing and kayaking, wildlife viewing; boat tour, interpretive trails.	12			•	•	•		•		•	•		•		
De Leon Springs (E-4) 625 acres 1 mi. w. of De Leon Springs off US 17. Historic. Bird-watching, boat tours, scuba diving, snorkeling; canoe, kayak and paddleboat rentals.	13		•	•	•	•	•	•	•			•	•		•
Egmont Key (I-1) 400 acres at the mouth of Tampa Bay, s.w. of Fort DeSoto Beach. Accessible only by boat or ferry. Historic. Interpretive exhibits. Beachcombing, bird-watching, snorkeling, wildlife viewing; beach, lighthouse.	14		•	•	•			•	•						
Fanning Springs (D-1) 198 acres on US 19/98 on the e. bank of the Suwannee River in Fanning Springs. Canoeing, kayaking, scuba diving, snorkeling; primitive camping.	15	•	•	•	•	•		•	•	•		•		•	•
Faver-Dykes (D-4) 1,465 acres 15 mi. s. of St. Augustine off US 1. Bird-watching, canoeing, kayaking, wildlife viewing; playground.	16	•	•	•	•	•	•	•			•				
Fort Clinch (A-12) 1,361 acres 2 mi. e. of Fernandina Beach on SR A1A/Atlantic Ave. on n. end of Amelia Island. Historic. Beachcombing, bird-watching, canoeing, kayaking, surfing; beach, garden, guided tours, museum, playground.	17	•	•	•	•			•	•	•	•		•		

Recreation Areas Chart

The map location numerals in column 2 show an area's location on the preceding map.

Find thousands of places to camp at AAA.com/campgrounds

	MAP LOCATION	CAMPING	PICNICKING	HIKING TRAILS	BOATING	BOAT RAMP	BOAT RENTAL	FISHING	SWIMMING	PET FRIENDLY	BICYCLE TRAILS	SKIN/SCUBA	VISITOR CENTER	LODGE/CABINS	FOOD SERVICE
Fort Cooper (F-2) 753 acres 2 mi. s. of Inverness off US 41. Historic. Bird-watching, boating (rental canoes; water level permitting), camping (primitive), wildlife viewing; recreation hall. Call ahead to confirm boating and swimming conditions; phone (352) 726-0315.	18	●	●	●	●		●	●	●	●	●				
Gamble Rogers Memorial State Recreation Area (E-5) 133 acres .5 mi. s. of Flagler Beach at SR A1A/S. Ocean Shore Blvd. Beachcombing, bird-watching, canoeing, kayaking, surfing; beach, bicycle, canoe and kayak rentals.	19	●	●	●	●	●	●	●	●	●	●				
Highlands Hammock (I-4) 9,251 acres 3.5 mi. w. of US 27 on CR 634. Scenic. Bird-watching; amphitheater, boardwalk, equestrian camping, guided tours, horse trails, museum, playground, rental bicycles and kayaks.	20	●	●	●						●	●		●		
Hillsborough River (G-2) 3,383 acres 6 mi. s. of Zephyrhills off US 301. Canoeing, kayaking; bicycle and canoe rentals, guided tours, living-history program, playground, swimming pool (seasonal).	21	●	●	●	●		●	●	●	●	●		●		●
Honeymoon Island (G-1) 2,810 acres 3 mi. n. of Dunedin on SR 586, w. of US 19A. Beachcombing, bird-watching, canoeing, kayaking, snorkeling, surfing; beach, playground.	22		●	●	●			●	●	●	●				●
Hontoon Island (E-4) 1,654 acres 6 mi. w. of DeLand off SR 44. Camping (primitive, tent and boat); boat slip and canoe rentals, cabins (rustic); museum, playground.	23	●	●	●	●			●		●	●		●	●	
Ichetucknee Springs (C-1) 2,356 acres off US 27 .5 mi. e. of Hildreth. Scenic. Bird-watching, canoeing, kayaking, scuba diving (seasonal), snorkeling, tubing, wildlife viewing; boardwalk, playground.	24		●	●	●				●	●		●	●		●
Lake Griffin (F-3) 620 acres 1 mi. e. of Fruitland Park off US 27. Amphitheater, boat tours, canoe and kayak rental, playground.	25	●	●	●	●	●	●	●		●					
Lake Kissimmee (H-4) 5,933 acres 8 mi. e. of Lake Wales via SR 60, 5 mi. n. on Boy Scout Rd., then 5 mi. e. on Camp Mack Rd. following signs. Bird-watching, canoeing, kayaking; equestrian camping, horse trails, living-history program, observation tower, playground, guided Segway tours.	26	●	●	●	●	●		●		●					●
Lake Louisa (G-3) 4,407 acres 7 mi. s.e. of Clermont on Lake Nellie Rd. Canoeing, kayaking; cabins, equestrian camping, horse trails, playground.	27	●	●	●	●			●	●	●	●			●	
Lake Manatee (I-2) 548 acres 15 mi. e. of Bradenton on SR 64. Bird-watching, canoeing, kayaking; playground.	28	●	●	●	●	●	●	●	●	●	●				
Little Manatee River (H-2) 2,417 acres 5 mi. s. of Sun City off US 301. Camping (primitive and equestrian), canoeing, kayaking; amphitheater, horse trails, playground.	29	●	●	●	●		●	●		●	●				
Little Talbot Island (B-12) 1,766 acres 17 mi. n.e. of Jacksonville on SR A1A. Beachcombing, bird-watching, canoeing, kayaking, surfing; beach, guided paddle tours, pier, playground.	30	●	●	●	●			●	●	●	●		●		
Manatee Springs (D-1) 2,200 acres 6 mi. w. of Chiefland on SR 320. Bird-watching, canoeing, kayaking, scuba diving, snorkeling; canoe and kayak rental (seasonal), guided tours.	31	●	●	●	●		●	●	●	●	●	●			●
Mike Roess Gold Head Branch (D-3) 2,174 acres 6 mi. n.e. of Keystone Heights on SR 21. Bird-watching, boating (canoes and kayaks only; water level permitting), camping (primitive); bicycle and canoe rental, horse trails, playground. Note: The availability of recreational water activities varies with water levels.	32	●	●	●	●			●	●	●	●			●	
Myakka River (I-2) 37,000 acres 17 mi. e. of Sarasota on SR 72. Bird-watching, canoeing, kayaking; airboat and tram tours, bicycle rentals, boardwalk, horse trails.	33	●	●	●	●	●	●	●		●	●		●	●	●
O'Leno (C-2) 6,700 acres 6 mi. n. of High Springs off US 41. Historic. Bird-watching, canoeing, kayaking; bicycle and canoe rentals, playground.	34	●	●	●	●	●	●	●	●	●	●			●	
Oscar Scherer (F-9) 1,383 acres 2 mi. s. of Osprey on US 41. Bird-watching, canoeing, kayaking, inline skating, kayaking, snorkeling; beach, guided tours, playground.	35	●	●	●	●	●	●	●	●	●	●	●	●		

Recreation Areas Chart

The map location numerals in column 2 show an area's location on the preceding map.

Find thousands of places to camp at AAA.com/campgrounds

	MAP LOCATION	CAMPING	PICNICKING	HIKING TRAILS	BOATING	BOAT RAMP	BOAT RENTAL	FISHING	SWIMMING	PET FRIENDLY	BICYCLE TRAILS	SKIN/SCUBA	VISITOR CENTER	LODGE/CABINS	FOOD SERVICE
Paynes Creek Historic (I-3) 400 acres .5 mi. e. of Bowling Green at 888 Lake Branch Rd. Historic. Bird-watching, canoeing, kayaking; guided walks, interpretive center, playground.	36	●	●	●	●	●		●		●	●		●		
Paynes Prairie Preserve (D-2) 21,000 acres 1 mi. n. of Micanopy on US 441. Bird-watching, boating (electric motors only), canoeing, kayaking; equestrian camping, horse trail, wildlife observation tower.	37	●	●	●	●	●		●		●	●		●		
Pumpkin Hill Creek (B-12) 4,000 acres 4 mi. n. on New Berlin to Cedar Point Rd. via I-95 in Jacksonville, then 10 mi. e. to Pumpkin Hill Rd., and 1 mi. n. to parking area. Bird-watching, canoeing, horseback riding, kayaking, wildlife viewing; canoe launch, horse trails, interpretive exhibits, threatened and endangered wildlife.	38		●	●	●	●		●		●	●				
Rainbow Springs (E-2) 1,083 acres 3 mi. n. of Dunnellon on US 41. Bird-watching, canoeing, kayaking, snorkeling, tubing; amphitheater, canoe and kayak rentals, garden, waterfalls.	39	●	●	●	●				●	●		●			
St. Sebastian River Preserve (H-6) 22,705 acres 1.8 mi. e. of I-95 off SR 512 in Fellsmere. Bird-watching, canoeing, kayaking, wildlife viewing; equestrian and primitive camping, guided tours, horse trails.	40	●	●	●	●			●			●		●		
Sebastian Inlet (H-6) 917 acres 15 mi. n. of Vero Beach on SR A1A. Beachcombing, bird-watching, canoeing, kayaking, scuba diving, snorkeling, stargazing, surfing; beach, marina, museum, playground.	41	●	●	●	●	●	●	●	●	●	●	●	●		●
Suwannee River (A-7) 1,928 acres 13 mi. w. of Live Oak on US 90. Historic. Bird-watching, canoeing, kayaking; playground.	42	●	●	●	●	●		●		●	●			●	
Tomoka (E-5) 1,610 acres 3 mi. n. of Ormond Beach. Museum. Bird-watching, canoeing, kayaking; canoe rentals, playground.	43	●	●	●	●	●	●	●		●					
Washington Oaks Gardens (D-5) 425 acres at 6400 Oceanshore Blvd. Interpretive center. Bird-watching; beach, garden, playground.	44		●	●				●		●	●		●		
Wekiwa Springs (F-4) 7,725 acres off Wekiwa Springs Road at 1800 Wekiwa Cir. in Apopka. Bird-watching, equestrian camping, snorkeling; canoe and kayak rentals, horse trails, playground.	45	●	●	●	●		●	●	●	●	●	●	●		●
OTHER															
Avon Park Air Force Range (H-4) 106,000 acres off CR 64 at 29 S. Boulevard in Avon Park. Open Thurs.-Mon. Note: Photo ID is required. Bird-watching, hunting.	46	●	●	●	●	●		●		●			●		
Edward Medard Regional (H-2) 1,284 acres off Turkey Creed Rd. at 6140 Edward Medard Pkwy. in Plant City. Bird-watching, disc golf, inline skating, volleyball; beach, boardwalk, canoe and kayak rental, fishing pier, horse trails, observation tower, playground.	47	●	●	●	●	●		●	●	●	●				
E.G. Simmons Regional (H-2) 258 acres on Tampa Bay, 1 mi. w. of US 41 at 2401 19th Ave. N.W. in Ruskin. Bird-watching, canoeing, kayaking, volleyball; canoe and kayak rentals, fishing pier.	48	●	●		●	●		●	●	●	●		●		
Fort De Soto (I-1) 1,136 acres off I-275 exit 17 to 3500 S. Pinellas Bayway. Historic. Beach, dog park, fishing piers; guided tours, museum, playground.	49	●	●	●	●	●		●	●	●	●		●		●
Ginnie Springs (D-1) 200 acres 7 mi. w. of High Springs off CR 340 at N.E. 60th Ave. Canoeing, kayaking, river tubing, scuba diving, snorkeling, volleyball; canoes and kayak rentals, playground.	50	●	●	●	●	●	●	●	●		●	●		●	●
Kathryn Abbey Hanna (B-12) 446 acres next to Mayport Naval Station off SR A1A in Jacksonville Beach. Canoeing, horseback riding, kayaking, shelling, surfing; beach, horse rentals, shuffleboard, splash park.	51	●	●	●	●		●	●	●	●	●			●	●
Lithia Springs Regional (H-2) 160 acres 7.2 mi. s. of Brandon off Lithia Pinecrest Rd. at 3932 Lithia Springs Rd. Volleyball; canoe and kayak rental; playground.	52	●	●	●	●	●		●	●	●					

Recreation Areas Chart

The map location numerals in column 2 show an area's location on the preceding map.

Find thousands of places to camp at AAA.com/campgrounds

	MAP LOCATION	CAMPING	PICNICKING	HIKING TRAILS	BOATING	BOAT RAMP	BOAT RENTAL	FISHING	SWIMMING	PET FRIENDLY	BICYCLE TRAILS	SKIN/SCUBA	VISITOR CENTER	LODGE/CABINS	FOOD SERVICE
Maximo (H-1) 70 acres in St. Petersburg at 34th St. and Pinellas Point Dr. S. Disc golf; beach, observation tower, playground.	53		•		•	•		•	•	•	•				
Poe Springs (D-1) 202 acres 3 mi. w. of High Springs on CR 340 at 28800 N.W. 182nd Ave. Canoeing, kayaking, snorkeling; playground, soccer and softball fields, volleyball court.	54		•	•	•	•	•	•	•			•			•
Kelly Park and Rock Springs (F-4) 245 acres 6 mi. n. of Apopka on SR 435. Canoeing, kayaking, snorkeling, tubing; playground, volleyball court.	55	•	•	•					•		•				
Rodman Reservoir (D-3) 9,000 acres 10 mi. s.w. of Palatka off SR 19 access roads on the Ocklawaha River. Bird-watching; horse trails.	56	•	•	•	•	•		•	•						
Upper Tampa Bay Regional (H-1) 596 acres off SR 580 at 8001 Double Branch Rd. in Tampa. Boardwalk, canoe and kayak rental, fishing pier, nature center, playground.	57		•	•	•	•	•	•		•			•		
Weedon Island Preserve (H-2) 3,190 acres 1 mi. e. of St. Petersburg on 83rd Ave. (Patica Rd.) off 4th St. N., then 1 mi. n.e. on San Martin Blvd., following signs to entrance on Weedon Dr. NE. Education center. Exhibits. Bird-watching, canoeing, kayaking; boardwalk, canoe and kayak rental and launches, guided tours, observation tower, paddling trails.	58		•	•	•			•					•		

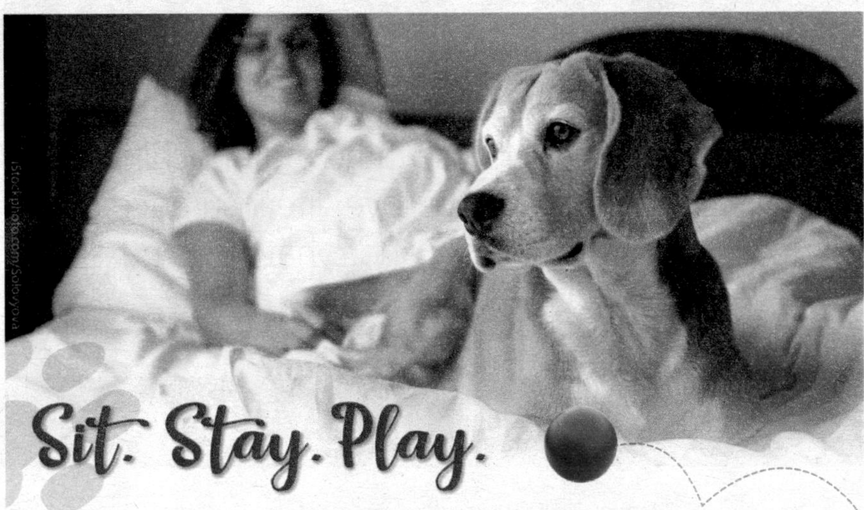

Discover thousands of pet-friendly places to stay, play and dine. Get insight to guide your decisions. And enter your favorite photo in the next AAA Pet Travel Photo Contest*.

Visit AAA.com/PetTravel

*Contest entry open to U.S. residents only.

Have you ever stopped to think about the countless reasons why you need life insurance?

Your why isn't just about who you're protecting, it's about what you're doing to protect them.

Whether it's a new house, a new grandchild or a new life with the one we love, life insurance can cover you for the now and whatever's next.

What's your why?

Get a free quote at AAALife.com

Products and their features may not be available in all states. Life insurance underwritten by AAA Life Insurance Company, Livonia, MI. AAA Life (CA Certificate of Authority #07861) is licensed in all states except NY. Automobile Club of Southern California CA License #0003259. CSAA Life Insurance Agency of California, Inc. CA License #0D12130. Insurance products in Northern California offered through AAA Northern California Insurance Agency, License #0175868,in Nevada by AAA Nevada and in Utah by AAA Utah. Your local AAA club and/or its affiliates act as agents for AAA Life.

ALAN-25514-519-XX

ALTAMONTE SPRINGS (F-4) pop. 41,496, elev. 85'

• **Hotels & Restaurants map & index p. 188**
• **Part of Orlando area — see map p. 2**

This lively Orlando suburb abounds with opportunities for shopping and outdoor recreation. Altamonte Mall (451 E. Altamonte Dr.) has been a mainstay for some 40 years and features Barnes & Noble, Dillard's, JCPenney, Macy's, Sears and more than 100 specialty stores. Adjectives Market (1200 E. Altamonte Dr.) holds a treasure trove of antique curiosities for every taste from Victorian to midcentury modern.

For outdoor fun, try Sanlando Park (401 W. Highland St.). With 25 lighted tennis courts, racquetball courts, basketball courts, a beach volleyball court, four wallyball courts, and a link to Seminole Wekiva Trail's 60 miles of trails, it's a sports lover's paradise; phone (407) 665-2100.

Red, Hot & Boom, a huge Independence Day celebration, is held every July 3 at Cranes Roost Park (274 Cranes Roost Blvd.). More than 100,000 revelers pack the park for music by live bands topped off with a spectacular fireworks display. The beautifully landscaped park includes a 1-mile path around a lake populated with ducks and turtles, as well as an amphitheater with stadium seating.

EMBASSY SUITES BY HILTON ORLANDO NORTH
407/834-2400 41

Hotel

AAA Benefit: Members save 5% or more!

Address: 225 Shorecrest Dr 32701 **Location:** I-4 exit 92 (SR 436), just e to Cranes Roost Blvd, then just n. **Facility:** 277 units. 4-7 stories, interior corridors. **Amenities:** safes. **Dining:** Omaha Steakhouse, see separate listing. **Pool:** heated indoor. **Activities:** hot tub, exercise room. **Guest Services:** valet and coin laundry, boarding pass kiosk, rental car service, area transportation. **Featured Amenity: full hot breakfast.**

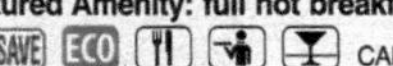   

HAMPTON INN & SUITES ORLANDO-NORTH/ALTAMONTE SPRINGS
407/331-0220 40

Hotel

AAA Benefit: Members save 5% or more!

Address: 161 N Douglas Ave 32714 **Location:** I-4 exit 92 (SR 436), just w to Douglas Ave, then just n. **Facility:** 128 units. 6 stories, interior corridors. **Pool:** outdoor. **Activities:** exercise room. **Guest Services:** valet and coin laundry. **Featured Amenity: breakfast buffet.**

/ SOME UNITS

HAWTHORN SUITES BY WYNDHAM-ALTAMONTE SPRINGS
407/767-5757 39

Extended Stay Hotel. **Address:** 644 Raymond Ave 32701

HILTON ORLANDO/ALTAMONTE SPRINGS
407/830-1985 43

Hotel

AAA Benefit: Members save 5% or more!

Address: 350 S Northlake Blvd 32701 **Location:** I-4 exit 92 (SR 436), just e to Northlake Blvd, then 0.4 mi s. **Facility:** 309 units. 8 stories, interior corridors. **Terms:** check-in 4 pm. **Dining:** 2 restaurants. **Pool:** heated outdoor. **Activities:** sauna, hot tub, exercise room. **Guest Services:** valet laundry, rental car service, area transportation.

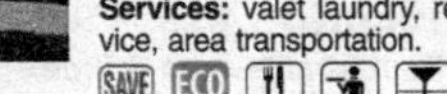

TOWNEPLACE SUITES BY MARRIOTT ORLANDO ALTAMONTE SPRINGS/MAITLAND
321/316-3111 42

Extended Stay Hotel

TOWNEPLACE SUITES MARRIOTT

AAA Benefit: Members save 5% or more!

Address: 151 Douglas Ave 32714 **Location:** I-4 exit 92 (SR 436), just w to Douglas Ave, then just n. **Facility:** 117 kitchen units. 5 stories, interior corridors. **Pool:** outdoor. **Activities:** exercise room. **Guest Services:** valet and coin laundry. **Featured Amenity: continental breakfast.**

SAVE CALL BIZ

/ SOME UNITS

WHERE TO EAT

AMIGOS RESTAURANT & CANTINA 407/774-4334
Tex-Mex. Casual Dining. **Address:** 120 N Westmonte Dr 32714

BAHAMA BREEZE ISLAND GRILLE 407/831-2929 123
Caribbean. Casual Dining. **Address:** 499 E Altamonte Dr 32701

BUBBALOU'S BODACIOUS BAR-B-QUE 407/478-1212
Barbecue. Casual Dining. **Address:** 1049 E Altamonte Dr 32701

CAFE MURANO 407/834-5880 122
Italian. Fine Dining. **Address:** 309 Cranes Roost Blvd 32701

DUFFY'S SPORTS GRILL 407/636-9980
American. Sports Bar. **Address:** 525 E Altamonte Dr 32701

KOHINOOR INDIAN RESTAURANT 407/788-6004 126
Indian. Casual Dining. **Address:** 249 W SR 436 32714

MR. MARGARITA MEXICAN KITCHEN & TEQUILA BAR 407/636-8634 121
Mexican. Casual Dining. **Address:** 995 N SR 434 32714

OMAHA STEAKHOUSE 407/571-3457 125
Steak. Casual Dining. **Address:** 225 Shorecrest Dr 32701

SANTIAGO'S BODEGA 407/960-2605 120
International Small Plates. Fine Dining. **Address:** 1185 Spring Center South Blvd 32714

(See map & index p. 188.)

SEASONS 52 FRESH GRILL 407/767-1252 124

New American. Fine Dining. **Address:** 463 E Altamonte Dr 32701

TERRAMIA WINE BAR & TRATTORIA 407/774-8466 119

Italian Pizza. Fine Dining. **Address:** 1150 Douglas Ave 32714

TOOJAY'S GOURMET DELI 407/830-1770

American. Casual Dining. **Address:** 515 E Altamonte Dr 32701

AMELIA ISLAND (A-12)

• **Hotels & Restaurants map & index p. 92**
• **Part of Jacksonville area — see map p. 84**

Thirteen miles of Appalachian quartz beaches and towering sand dunes distinguish Amelia Island, a picturesque island off the northeast tip of Florida's Atlantic coast. Formerly a haven for smugglers in the mid-19th century, the island became the site of Florida's first cross-state railroad and, consequently, the state's first resort. The many Victorian buildings in Fernandina Beach, the island's only city *(see place listing p. 72)*, remain a testament to the era.

Henry Flagler's Florida East Coast Railway soon lured tourists farther south in search of new playgrounds, locking the island in its Victorian atmosphere. With its bed and breakfast inns, quaint shops and galleries within walking distance of the Atlantic Ocean, Amelia Island encapsulates the charm of a Victorian seaport village. Visitors find relief from the modern world in the island's relaxed pace and such recreational pursuits as golf, swimming and horseback riding.

At the southern end of the island is American Beach, one of the country's last predominately African-American beaches. The town of American Beach was founded in the 1930s, an era during which many beaches were closed to African-Americans.

Amelia Island/Fernandina Beach/Yulee Chamber of Commerce: 961687 Gateway Blvd., Suite 101-G, Amelia Island, FL 32034. **Phone:** (904) 261-3248.

AMELIA RIVER CRUISES & CHARTERS departs from Fernandina Harbor Marina, 1 N. Front St. Historical narrative and sightings of wildlife are highlights of cruises along the Amelia River and Cumberland Sound. The 2-hour Cumberland Island Tour features views of Cumberland Island National Seashore. The 90-minute Beach Creek Tour offers views of saltwater marshes and the ruins of Carnegie's Dungeness Mansion. An Adult Twilight BYOB Cruise, a Shrimping Eco Tour and a Family-Friendly Sunset Tour also are available seasonally.

Food and beverages are allowed on all cruises. **Time:** Allow 2 hours minimum. **Hours:** Office open daily 9-last cruise departure. Cumberland Island Tours depart daily at 10. Beach Creek Tours depart daily at 2:30. Adult Twilight BYOB Cruise, Shrimping Eco Tour and Family-Friendly Sunset Tour times vary seasonally. Closed some holidays. Phone ahead to confirm schedule. **Cost:** Cumberland Island Tour $30; $28 (ages 65+); $24 (ages 4-12). Adult Twilight BYOB Cruise $30. Shrimping Eco Tour $27; $17 (ages 4-12). Beach Creek Tour $25; $23 (ages 65+); $19 (ages 4-12). Family-Friendly Sunset Tour $22; $16 (ages 4-12). **Phone:** (904) 261-9972. GT

AMELIA HOTEL AT THE BEACH 904/206-5200 50

Hotel. **Address:** 1997 S Fletcher Ave 32034

AMELIA ISLAND WILLIAMS HOUSE 904/277-2328 48

Classic Historic Bed & Breakfast. **Address:** 103 S 9th St 32034

ELIZABETH POINTE LODGE 904/277-4851 46

Boutique Bed & Breakfast

Address: 98 S Fletcher Ave 32034 **Location:** Oceanfront. In Fernandina Beach; jct Atlantic Ave, just s on S Fletcher Ave (SR A1A). **Facility:** The Nantucket-style home features a wrap-around porch, a cozy fireplace and nautical-themed décor. Each room features a unique style. The evening wine reception and beachfront location are highlights. 25 units, some cottages. 2-4 stories, interior/exterior corridors. **Amenities:** safes. **Activities:** bicycles. **Guest Services:** valet laundry. **Featured Amenity: breakfast buffet.**

SAVE

/ SOME UNITS

THE FAIRBANKS HOUSE 904/277-0500 49

Historic Bed & Breakfast. **Address:** 227 S 7th St 32034

HAMPTON INN AMELIA ISLAND AT FERNANDINA BEACH 904/321-1111 51

SAVE Hotel. **Address:** 2549 Sadler Rd 32034

AAA Benefit: Members save 5% or more!

HAMPTON INN & SUITES-AMELIA ISLAND 904/491-4911 47

SAVE Hotel. **Address:** 19 S 2nd St 32034

AAA Benefit: Members save 5% or more!

THE HOYT HOUSE 904/277-4300 45

Historic Bed & Breakfast. **Address:** 804 Atlantic Ave 32034

OMNI AMELIA ISLAND PLANTATION RESORT 904/261-6161 54

Resort Hotel

Address: 39 Beach Lagoon Rd 32034 **Location:** Oceanfront. In Fernandina Beach; SR A1A (Atlantic Ave), 6.5 mi s of the bridge. **Facility:** Secluded, wooded grounds envelop the expansive waterfront property with restaurants, shops and a spa. Every room has an ocean view and private balcony. The resort amenities are seemingly endless. 404 units, some kitchens. 8 stories, exterior corridors. **Parking:** on-site (fee) and valet. **Terms:** check-in 4 pm. **Amenities:** safes. **Dining:** 9 restaurants, also, Bob's Steak & Chop House, see separate listing, entertainment. **Pool:** outdoor, heated outdoor, heated indoor. **Activities:** sauna, hot tub, steamroom, boat dock, fishing, regulation golf, miniature golf, tennis, recreation programs, bicycles, playground, game room, health club, spa. **Guest Services:** valet laundry, area transportation.

SAVE ECO CALL BIZ

HS / SOME UNITS

(See map & index p. 92.)

RESIDENCE INN BY MARRIOTT-AMELIA ISLAND 904/277-2440 52

Extended Stay Contemporary Hotel. **Address:** 2301 Sadler Rd 32034

AAA Benefit: Members save 5% or more!

THE RITZ-CARLTON, AMELIA ISLAND 904/277-1100 53

Resort Hotel

AAA Benefit: Unequaled service at special member savings!

Address: 4750 Amelia Island Pkwy 32034 **Location:** Oceanfront. In Fernandina Beach; on SR A1A (Atlantic Ave). **Facility:** Wispy oaks, tropical surroundings and Southern elegance define the setting at this island gem. Your private balcony overlooks a pristine coast of white sand and manicured gardens. 446 units. 8 stories, interior corridors. **Parking:** valet only. **Terms:** check-in 4 pm. **Amenities:** video games, safes. **Dining:** 4 restaurants, also, Salt, see separate listing, entertainment. **Pool:** heated outdoor, heated indoor. **Activities:** sauna, hot tub, steamroom, cabanas, regulation golf, tennis, recreation programs, kids club, bicycles, playground, game room, health club, spa. **Guest Services:** valet laundry, boarding pass kiosk.

 CALL BIZ SHS

SEASIDE AMELIA INN 904/206-5300 44

Boutique Hotel. **Address:** 2900 Atlantic Ave 32034

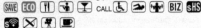

WHERE TO EAT

29 SOUTH 904/277-7919 57

New American. Fine Dining. **Address:** 29 S 3rd St 32034

AMELIA TAVERN 904/310-6088 53

Small Plates. Brewpub. **Address:** 318 Centre St 32034

BOB'S STEAK & CHOP HOUSE 904/432-2201 66

Steak Seafood. Fine Dining. **Address:** 80 Amelia Village Cir 32034

BRETT'S WATERWAY CAFE 904/261-2660 54

Regional American. Casual Dining. **Address:** 1 S Front St 32034

CEDAR RIVER SEAFOOD 904/491-0445 63

Seafood. Casual Dining. **Address:** 2728 Sadler Rd 32034

CIAO ITALIAN BISTRO 904/206-4311 52

Italian. Casual Dining. **Address:** 614 Centre St 32034

THE CRAB TRAP 904/261-4749 49

Seafood. Casual Dining. **Address:** 31 N 2nd St 32034

DAVID'S RESTAURANT & LOUNGE 904/310-6049 58

Seafood Steak. Fine Dining. **Address:** 802 Ash St 32034

ESPANA RESTAURANT & TAPAS 904/261-7700 56

Spanish Small Plates. Fine Dining. **Address:** 22 S 4th St 32034

FANCY SUSHI 904/261-9855 64

Japanese Sushi. Casual Dining. **Address:** 1478 Sadler Rd 32034

HANA SUSHI 904/277-8838 60

Japanese Sushi. Casual Dining. **Address:** 1930 S 14th St 32034

JOE'S 2ND STREET BISTRO 904/321-2558 55

American. Fine Dining. **Address:** 14 S 2nd St 32034

MARINA SEAFOOD RESTAURANT 904/261-5310 50

Seafood Comfort Food. Casual Dining. **Address:** 101 Center St 32034

PEPPER'S MEXICAN GRILL & CANTINA 904/277-2011 51

Mexican. Casual Dining. **Address:** 530 Centre St 32034

SALT 904/277-1100 65

American Fine Dining $33-$150

AAA Inspector Notes: Beautiful ocean views are easily captured through the many windows in the stylish restaurant that offers a relaxed ambience with elegant appeal. The culinary team focuses on creative, savory cuisine which includes artfully presented dishes such as beef tenderloin served with lobster, Nebraskan free range chicken and a variety of Prime meats. The "chef's adventure" adds a bit of intrigue for the adventurous diner. The beverage selection is extensive and reasonably priced with over 300 wines. **Features:** full bar. **Reservations:** required. Semiformal attire. **Address:** 4750 Amelia Island Pkwy 32034 **Location:** In Fernandina Beach; on SR A1A (Atlantic Ave); in The Ritz-Carlton, Amelia Island. **Parking:** valet only. D CALL

SLIDERS SEASIDE GRILL 904/277-6652 61

Seafood. Casual Dining. **Address:** 1998 S Fletcher Ave 32034

TONY'S NEW YORK STYLE BRICK OVEN PIZZA & RESTAURANT 904/277-7661 62

Italian Pizza. Casual Dining. **Address:** 1425 Sadler Rd 32034

T-RAYS BURGER STATION 904/261-6310 59

American. Quick Serve. **Address:** 202 S 8th St 32034

APOPKA (F-4) pop. 41,542, elev. 131'

- **Hotels p. 32 • Restaurants p. 32**
- **Hotels & Restaurants map & index p. 188**
- **Part of Orlando area — see map p. 2**

Like many settlements in central Florida, Apopka's growth can be traced to the emergence of the citrus industry; development stalled, however, after citrus groves were all but destroyed by a series of devastating freezes in the late 1800s. The Museum of the Apopkans, 122 E. 5th St., chronicles historical events and the lives of early settlers through a variety of exhibit topics; phone (407) 703-1707.

KELLY PARK AND ROCK SPRINGS are 6 mi. n. on SR 435 to 400 E. Kelly Park Rd. Rock Springs, a half-mile east of the park entrance, discharges 26,000 gallons of clear, 68-degree Fahrenheit water per minute into a spring that is popular for tubing and swimming; farther down the run, the temperature warms up to approximately 72 degrees Fahrenheit. Shelters, bathhouses, tube rentals (outside park), and hiking trails are available. *See Recreation Areas Chart.*

Note: Due to high-volume visitation in summer months, the park may fill to capacity early in the day. Visitors are not admitted after capacity is reached. **Hours:** Daily 8-8, during DST; 8-6, rest of year. Waterfront area closes 1 hour before park. **Cost:** $5 (per private vehicle with three to eight people); $3 (per private vehicle with one to two people); $1 (per additional passenger or person arriving by bicycle,

(See map & index p. 188.)

motorcycle or on foot); free (ages 0-5). **Phone:** (407) 254-1902 or (407) 836-6200.

HAMPTON INN & SUITES ORLANDO-APOPKA 407/880-7861 36

Contemporary Hotel. **Address:** 321 Lake Cortez 32703

AAA Benefit: Members save 5% or more!

HOLIDAY INN EXPRESS & SUITES ORLANDO-APOPKA 407/880-7868 35

Hotel. **Address:** 238 S Line Dr 32703

WHERE TO EAT

1-6-8 CHINESE RESTAURANT 407/862-1688 102

Chinese. Casual Dining. **Address:** 3030 E Semoran Blvd 32703

CAFFÉ POSITANO 407/774-8080 103

Italian. Casual Dining. **Address:** 3030 E Semoran Blvd 32703

CATFISH PLACE OF APOPKA 407/889-7980 104

Seafood. Casual Dining. **Address:** 311 S Forest Ave 32703

GATOR'S DOCKSIDE 407/869-4222

American. Casual Dining. **Address:** 3030 E Semoran Blvd 32703

SONNY'S REAL PIT BAR-B-Q 407/814-8888

Barbecue. Casual Dining. **Address:** 2210 E Semoran Blvd 32703

ATLANTIC BEACH pop. 12,655

• Hotels & Restaurants map & index p. 92
• Part of Jacksonville area — see map p. 84

BEST WESTERN MAYPORT INN & SUITES 904/435-3500 57

Hotel

AAA Benefit: Members save up to 15% and earn bonus points!

Address: 2389 Mayport Rd 32233 **Location:** 2 mi n on SR A1A; 1.4 mi s of naval base. **Facility:** 60 units. 2 stories, interior corridors. **Pool:** outdoor. **Activities:** exercise room. **Guest Services:** coin laundry. **Featured Amenity: breakfast buffet.**

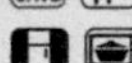    / SOME UNITS

ONE OCEAN RESORT & SPA 904/249-7402 58

Boutique Resort Hotel

Address: One Ocean Blvd 32233 **Location:** Jct SR A1A, just e on Atlantic Blvd. **Facility:** Elegant rooms offer a pleasant stay and luxuries such robes and refreshments. The docent staff offers an enhanced level of personalized services. For relaxation, take time to enjoy the pool area. 193 units. 8 stories, interior corridors. **Parking:** valet only. **Terms:** check-in 4 pm. **Amenities:** safes. **Dining:** Azurea, see separate listing. **Pool:** heated outdoor. **Activities:** hot tub, steamroom, recreation programs, bicycles, health club, spa. **Guest Services:** valet laundry.

  CALL 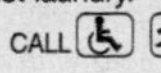   / SOME UNITS

WHERE TO EAT

AL'S PIZZA 904/249-0002

Italian Pizza. Casual Dining. **Address:** 303 Atlantic Blvd 32233

AZUREA 904/249-7402 70

International Fine Dining
$26-$48

AAA Inspector Notes: Prepare for a culinary adventure as you relax and dine on delicious, distinctive items like jumbo lump crab cakes, a fresh fish sampling that is grilled, bronzed or beignet battered, or "The Adventurous Palate," which is a five-course chef's tasting menu with the option of wine paring. Desserts are creative and as memorable as the cuisine. Service is excellent. The seasonal menu is subject to change. **Features:** full bar, patio dining, Sunday brunch. **Reservations:** suggested. **Address:** One Ocean Blvd 32233 **Location:** Jct SR A1A, just e on Atlantic Blvd; in One Ocean Resort & Spa. **Parking:** valet only.

B L D CALL

CULHANE'S IRISH PUB 904/249-9595 73

Irish. Casual Dining. **Address:** 967 Atlantic Blvd 32233

JOSEPH'S PIZZA & ITALIAN RESTAURANT 904/270-1122 69

Italian Pizza. Casual Dining. **Address:** 30 Ocean Blvd 32233

M SHACK 904/241-2599 71

Burgers. Quick Serve. **Address:** 299 Atlantic Blvd 32233

SEAFOOD KITCHEN 904/241-8470 72

Seafood. Casual Dining. **Address:** 31 Royal Palms Dr 32233

AUBURNDALE pop. 13,507

BEST WESTERN AUBURNDALE INN & SUITES 863/551-3400

Hotel

AAA Benefit: Members save up to 15% and earn bonus points!

Address: 1008 US Hwy 92 W 33823 **Location:** Polk Pkwy (SR 570) exit 17, 0.9 mi ne on US 92 (Auburndale Hwy). **Facility:** 57 units. 3 stories, interior corridors. **Pool:** heated outdoor. **Activities:** exercise room. **Guest Services:** valet and coin laundry. **Featured Amenity: full hot breakfast.**

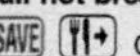 CALL 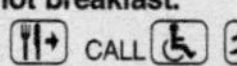 

   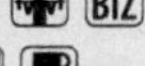

WHERE TO EAT

SWEET MAGNOLIAS TEA & BISTRO 863/965-1684

Coffee/Tea Sandwiches. Casual Dining. **Address:** 212 Howard St 33823

BARTOW pop. 17,298

ABC PIZZA 863/533-1177

Italian. Casual Dining. **Address:** 890 W Main St 33830

HACIENDA MEXICAN RESTAURANT 863/533-7600

Mexican. Casual Dining. **Address:** 195 E Main St 33830

HAVANA DELIGHTS CAFE 863/533-6947

Cuban. Casual Dining. **Address:** 155 E Main St 33830

SONNY'S REAL PIT BAR-B-Q 863/534-1429

Barbecue. Casual Dining. **Address:** 595 N Broadway Ave 33830

TROPICAL SMOOTHIE CAFE 863/519-9111

Sandwiches Natural/Organic. Quick Serve. **Address:** 1490 N Broadway Ave 33830

BELLEAIR BLUFFS pop. 2,031

- **Hotels & Restaurants map & index p. 286**
- **Part of St. Petersburg-Clearwater and Beaches area — see map p. 275**

E & E STAKEOUT GRILL 727/585-6399 (72)

Continental. Casual Dining. **Address:** 100 N Indian Rocks Rd 33770

BOWLING GREEN pop. 2,930

BEST WESTERN HERITAGE INN & SUITES 863/773-2378

Hotel

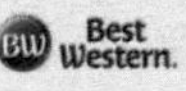

AAA Benefit: Members save up to 15% and earn bonus points!

Address: 2727 US 17 N 33834 **Location:** On US 17, 3 mi s; 0.3 mi n of SR 62. **Facility:** 48 units, some kitchens. 3 stories, interior corridors. **Pool:** outdoor. **Activities:** hot tub, exercise room. **Guest Services:** coin laundry. **Featured Amenity: breakfast buffet.**

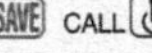    

BRADENTON (E-8) pop. 49,546, elev. 21'

- **Restaurants p. 34**
- **Hotels & Restaurants map & index p. 300**

Nearby Gulf beaches attract visitors to Bradenton (BRAY-den-ton), on Florida's west coast. The ArtCenter Manatee, 209 Ninth St. W., displays works of local artists. Classes, demonstrations and workshops are offered year-round; phone (941) 746-2862.

Pirate City, 1701 27th St. E., is the Pittsburgh Pirates' minor league and spring training facility. The major league team trains here in February, while the Pirates' minor-leaguers play here March through May. The Gulf Coast League plays here June through August, and the Florida Instructional League plays September through October. Visitors can watch the Pirates prepare for the regular season as they battle other major league teams in March at McKechnie Field, 1611 9th St. W. Phone (941) 747-3031.

From mid-December to early May the world-renowned Herrmann's Royal Lipizzan Stallions from Austria are trained at Colonel Herrmanns' Ranch, 32755 Singletary Rd., in nearby Myakka City. Visitors are welcome Thursday through Saturday at the training sessions; phone (941) 322-1501.

Bradenton Area Convention & Visitors Bureau: One Haben Blvd., Palmetto, FL 34221. **Phone:** (941) 729-9177.

Shopping: DeSoto Square Mall, 303 301 Blvd. W. at US 41 and Cortez Road, features JCPenney and Sears among more than 100 stores.

DE SOTO NATIONAL MEMORIAL—see place listing p. 68.

THE BISHOP MUSEUM OF SCIENCE AND NATURE, 201 10th St. W., is said to be the largest natural and cultural history museum on Florida's Gulf Coast. The museum interprets the region from the Pleistocene to the present.

The first floor features the Montague Tallant collection, fossil evidence of Florida's earliest animal inhabitants and archaeological material representing Paleo-Indian, archaic and pre-contact cultures. Exhibitions on the second floor feature local maritime history and regional biodiversity.

The Planetarium at The Bishop uses advanced digital projection systems to present astronomy programs in a dome theater. The Parker Manatee Rehabilitation Habitat, part of Florida's manatee rehabilitation network, is home to manatees under rehabilitation. **Time:** Allow 1 hour, 30 minutes minimum. **Hours:** Tues.-Sat. 10-5, Sun. noon-5. Closed Jan. 1, first Sat. in Nov., Thanksgiving and Christmas. **Cost:** Museum/planetarium/aquarium $19; $17 (ages 65+); $14 (ages 12-17 and college students with ID); $10 (ages 5-11); free (ages 0-5 with paying adult). Phone ahead to confirm schedule and admission. **Phone:** (941) 746-4131.

FAMILY HERITAGE HOUSE MUSEUM, 5840 26th St. W. on the State College of Florida Bradenton campus, features exhibits tracing the African-American experience and has a large collection of reference material, including photographs, books, articles, artifacts and memorabilia. Topics of interest include the Underground Railroad and Florida communities. **Time:** Allow 1 hour minimum. **Hours:** Tues.-Thurs. 11-6, or by appointment. Closed major holidays. **Cost:** Free. **Phone:** (941) 752-5319.

BEST WESTERN PLUS BRADENTON GATEWAY HOTEL 941/238-0800 (34)

Hotel

AAA Benefit: Members save up to 15% and earn bonus points!

Address: 2215 Cortez Rd W 34207 **Location:** On SR 684 (Cortez Rd), 0.5 mi w of jct US 41 (Tamiami Tr). **Facility:** 51 units, some kitchens. 3 stories, interior corridors. **Pool:** heated outdoor. **Activities:** exercise room. **Guest Services:** valet and coin laundry. **Featured Amenity: full hot breakfast.**

(See map & index p. 300.)

BEST WESTERN PLUS BRADENTON HOTEL & SUITES 941/757-5555 (30)

Hotel

AAA Benefit: Members save up to 15% and earn bonus points!

Address: 648 67th St Cir E 34208 **Location:** I-75 exit 220 southbound; exit 220B northbound, 0.3 mi w on SR 64, just n on 66th St Ct E. **Facility:** 60 units. 3 stories, interior corridors. **Pool:** heated outdoor. **Activities:** exercise room. **Guest Services:** valet and coin laundry, boarding pass kiosk. **Featured Amenity: breakfast buffet.**

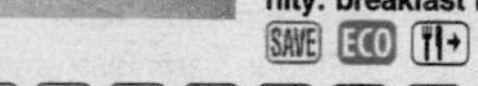

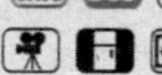

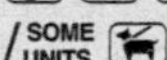

COUNTRY INN & SUITES BY RADISSON-BRADENTON 941/363-4000 (37)

Hotel

Address: 5610 Manor Hill Ln 34203 **Location:** I-75 exit 217 southbound; exit 217B northbound, just w on SR 70, then just s. **Facility:** 79 units. 3 stories, interior corridors. **Pool:** heated outdoor. **Activities:** exercise room. **Guest Services:** coin laundry. **Featured Amenity: breakfast buffet.**

COURTYARD BY MARRIOTT BRADENTON/SARASOTA RIVERFRONT 941/747-3727 (31)

Hotel

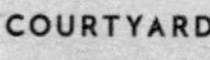

AAA Benefit: Members save 5% or more!

Address: 100 Riverfront Dr W 34205 **Location:** Waterfront. Just w of US 41 and 301; south side of Hernando Desoto Bridge; just n of jct SR 64 (Manatee Ave W) on 3rd St W. **Facility:** 153 units. 5 stories, interior corridors. **Pool:** heated outdoor. **Activities:** hot tub, exercise room. **Guest Services:** valet and coin laundry, boarding pass kiosk.

COURTYARD BY MARRIOTT SARASOTA UNIVERSITY PARK 941/360-2626 (39)

Hotel. **Address:** 8305 Tourist Center Dr 34201

AAA Benefit: Members save 5% or more!

HAMPTON INN & SUITES BRADENTON-DOWNTOWN HISTORIC DISTRICT 941/746-9400 (33)

Historic Boutique Hotel. **Address:** 309 10th St W 34205

AAA Benefit: Members save 5% or more!

HAMPTON INN & SUITES SARASOTA-UNIVERSITY PARK 941/355-8619 (40)

Hotel. **Address:** 8565 Cooper Creek Blvd 34201

AAA Benefit: Members save 5% or more!

HOLIDAY INN EXPRESS HOTEL & SUITES BRADENTON WEST 941/795-4633 (36)

Hotel. **Address:** 4450 47th St W 34210

HOLIDAY INN EXPRESS INN & SUITES BRADENTON EAST-LAKEWOOD RANCH 941/755-0055 (35)

Hotel. **Address:** 5464 Lena Rd 34211

HYATT PLACE SARASOTA/LAKEWOOD RANCH 941/748-3100 (38)

Hotel

HYATT PLACE **AAA Benefit:** Members save up to 10%!

Address: 6021 Exchange Way 34202 **Location:** I-75 exit 213, just e on University Pkwy, then just n on Market St. **Facility:** 112 units. 5 stories, interior corridors. **Pool:** heated outdoor. **Activities:** cabanas, exercise room. **Guest Services:** coin laundry, area transportation.

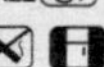

SPRINGHILL SUITES BY MARRIOTT BRADENTON DOWNTOWN/RIVERFRONT 941/226-2200 (32)

Hotel. **Address:** 102 12th St W 34205

AAA Benefit: Members save 5% or more!

WHERE TO EAT

ANNA MARIA OYSTER BAR

Seafood. Casual Dining.

LOCATIONS:

Address: 6906 14th St W 34207 **Phone:** 941/758-7880

Address: 6696 Cortez Rd W 34210 **Phone:** 941/792-0077

ANNA'S DELI 941/893-5908 (49)

Sandwiches. Quick Serve. **Address:** 8207 Tourist Center Dr 34201

ANOTHER BROKEN EGG CAFE 941/388-6898 (48)

Breakfast Sandwiches. Casual Dining. **Address:** 6115 Exchange Way 34202

CADDY'S AT THE POINTE 941/708-3777 (41)

Seafood. Casual Dining. **Address:** 801 Riverside Dr E 34208

CODY'S ORIGINAL ROADHOUSE 941/727-6700

American. Casual Dining. **Address:** 895 Cortez Rd W 34207

D. AMERICO'S PIZZERIA 941/747-7888 (40)

Italian. Quick Serve. **Address:** 812 62nd St Cir E 34208

THE GRILL AT O'BRICK'S 941/896-8860 (42)

American. Casual Dining. **Address:** 427 W 12th St 34205

MACALLISTERS GRILL & TAVERN 941/359-2424 (47)

Irish. Casual Dining. **Address:** 8110 Lakewood Main St 34202

MIXON'S GROVESIDE CAFE 941/746-6127 (46)

Sandwiches Pizza. Quick Serve. **Address:** 2525 27th St E 34208

PEACH'S RESTAURANT 941/747-2894 (43)

Breakfast Sandwiches. Casual Dining. **Address:** 3201 Manatee Ave W 34205

(See map & index p. 300.)

SHAKE PIT 941/748-4016 (44)

Sandwiches Desserts. Quick Serve. **Address:** 3801 Manatee Ave W 34205

SONNY'S REAL PIT BAR-B-Q 941/746-6166

Barbecue. Casual Dining. **Address:** 631 67th St Cir E 34208

SWEET BERRIES FROZEN CUSTARD & EATERY 941/750-6771 (45)

Sandwiches Desserts. Quick Serve. **Address:** 4500 Manatee Ave W 34208

BRANDON pop. 103,483

• Hotels & Restaurants map & index p. 347
• Part of Tampa area — see map p. 313

HOLIDAY INN EXPRESS TAMPA BRANDON 813/643-3800 (12)

Hotel

Address: 510 Grand Regency Blvd 33510 **Location:** I-75 exit 257, just e on SR 60, then 0.6 mi n; in Regency Corporate Office Park. **Facility:** 119 units. 4 stories, interior corridors. **Pool:** heated outdoor. **Activities:** exercise room. **Guest Services:** valet and coin laundry. **Featured Amenity: breakfast buffet.**

WOODSPRING SUITES TAMPA BRANDON 813/255-2566 (13)

Extended Stay Hotel. **Address:** 2450 S Falkenburg Rd 33619

WHERE TO EAT

ANTHONY'S COAL FIRED PIZZA 813/409-3830

Pizza. Casual Dining. **Address:** 1912 W Brandon Blvd 33511

BABE'S PIZZA 813/689-2282 (14)

Pizza. Casual Dining. **Address:** 107 N Kings Ave 33510

BONEFISH GRILL 813/571-5553 (35)

Seafood. Fine Dining. **Address:** 1015 Providence Rd 33511

BRANDON BAGELS 813/654-9672 (16)

Breakfast. Quick Serve. **Address:** 942 W Brandon Blvd 33511

THE BRUNCHERY RESTAURANT 813/654-9036

Breakfast Sandwiches. Casual Dining. **Address:** 4389 Lynx Paw Tr 33596

BUBBAQUE'S BBQ 813/685-1800 (10)

Barbecue. Quick Serve. **Address:** 957 E Brandon Blvd 33511

CALI VIEJO RESTAURANT ROTISSERIE & BAKERY 813/685-3715 (13)

Colombian. Casual Dining. **Address:** 436 E Brandon Blvd 33511

CAMPBELL'S DAIRYLAND 813/685-1189 (19)

Sandwiches Desserts. Quick Serve. **Address:** 200 S Parsons Ave 33511

CHICAGO'S BEST BURGERS 813/654-3232 (24)

Burgers. Quick Serve. **Address:** 1925A W Brandon Blvd 33511

CHICK-N-BONES CAFE & CATERING COMPANY 813/689-9531 (38)

Chicken Sandwiches. Quick Serve. **Address:** 1953 W Lumsden Rd 33511

CHINA 1 813/849-9994 (44)

Chinese. Quick Serve. **Address:** 125 E Bloomingdale Ave 33511

CHOPSTICKS CHINESE RESTAURANT 813/653-0258 (12)

Chinese. Quick Serve. **Address:** 801 E Brandon Blvd 33511

CRISPERS 813/654-9940

Sandwiches Soup. Quick Serve. **Address:** 11019 Causeway Blvd 33511

DELLA'S DELECTABLES 813/684-3354 (22)

Sandwiches Deli. Quick Serve. **Address:** 608 Oakfield Dr 33511

DOWN TO THE BONE BAR-B-Q & CATERING 813/653-9903 (20)

Barbecue. Quick Serve. **Address:** 110 S Kings Ave 33511

FIRST WATCH 813/684-3447 (34)

Breakfast Sandwiches. Casual Dining. **Address:** 11305 Causeway Blvd 33511

FORDS GARAGE 813/661-3673 (36)

American. Casual Dining. **Address:** 11105 Causeway Blvd 33511

GENGHIS GRILL 813/662-2695 (32)

Chinese. Casual Dining. **Address:** 910 Providence Rd 33511

JASMINE THAI RESTAURANT 813/662-3635 (37)

Thai. Fine Dining. **Address:** 1947 W Lumsden Rd 33511

JO-TO JAPANESE STEAK HOUSE & SUSHI BAR 813/684-0221 (27)

Japanese. Casual Dining. **Address:** 905 Lithia Pinecrest Rd 33511

KOIZI ENDLESS HIBACHI & SUSHI EATERY 813/653-2999 (41)

Japanese Sushi. Casual Dining. **Address:** 11245 Causeway Blvd 33511

LA CUBANITA CAFE 813/661-2253 (31)

Cuban. Quick Serve. **Address:** 723A W Lumsden Rd 33511

LA SEPTIMA CAFE 813/685-0502 (28)

Spanish. Casual Dining. **Address:** 702 W Lumsden Rd 33511

LATIN GRILL 813/654-8000 (43)

Cuban. Casual Dining. **Address:** 3318 John Moore Rd 33511

LIN'S GARDEN CHINESE RESTAURANT 813/689-6868 (40)

Chinese. Quick Serve. **Address:** 11237 Causeway Blvd 33511

MELLOW MUSHROOM 813/685-1122 (39)

Pizza Sandwiches. Casual Dining. **Address:** 10959 Causeway Blvd 33511

O'BRIEN'S IRISH PUB & RESTAURANT 813/661-9688 (33)

Irish. Casual Dining. **Address:** 701 W Lumsden Rd 33511

OLDE TOWN PIZZERIA BLOOMINGDALE 813/684-4200 (46)

Pizza Sandwiches. Casual Dining. **Address:** 115 W Bloomingdale Ave 33511

O'TOOLE'S IRISH PUB & RESTAURANT 813/684-2600 (21)

Irish. Casual Dining. **Address:** 1215 W Brandon Blvd 33511

(See map & index p. 347.)

PLOY THAI RESTAURANT 813/684-5007 (25)

💎💎💎 Thai Sushi. Fine Dining. **Address:** 1941 W Brandon Blvd 33511

RECIPE BOX DINER 813/655-2686 (47)

💎💎 Comfort Food Breakfast. Casual Dining. **Address:** 147 E Bloomingdale Ave 33511

ROMANO'S GREEK ITALIAN RESTAURANT 813/653-9477 (18)

💎💎 Greek. Casual Dining. **Address:** 901 W Brandon Blvd 33510

SABOR A MEXICO RESTAURANT 813/654-4900 (9)

💎💎 Mexican. Casual Dining. **Address:** 706 E Brandon Blvd 33511

SHELLS 813/689-4691 (15)

💎💎 Seafood. Casual Dining. **Address:** 115 E Brandon Blvd 33511

SILVER SPOON PAKISTANI & INDIAN RESTAURANT 813/681-3626 (11)

💎💎 Indian. Casual Dining. **Address:** 955 E Brandon Blvd 33511

SQUARE 1 BURGERS & BAR 813/689-1611 (30)

💎💎 Burgers. Casual Dining. **Address:** 2042 Badlands Dr 33511

STONEWOOD GRILL & TAVERN 813/655-9561 (42)

💎💎💎 American. Fine Dining. **Address:** 612 E Bloomingdale Ave 33511

TASTE OF BERLIN GERMAN RESTAURANT 813/685-9392 (23)

💎💎 German. Casual Dining. **Address:** 526 Oakfield Dr 33511

TASTE OF INDIA 813/689-4040 (8)

💎💎 Indian. Casual Dining. **Address:** 902 E Brandon Blvd 33511

TIJUANA FLATS 813/643-3020

💎 Tex-Mex. Quick Serve. **Address:** 11007 Causeway Blvd 33511

TIMES SQUARE PIZZA 813/651-0122 (45)

💎 Pizza Sandwiches. Quick Serve. **Address:** 927 E Bloomingdale Ave 33511

TOP'S CHINA SUPER BUFFET 813/655-6888 (17)

💎 Chinese. Quick Serve. **Address:** 1528 W Brandon Blvd 33511

TRES AMIGOS CANTINA 813/689-6476 (26)

💎💎 Mexican. Casual Dining. **Address:** 2025 W Brandon Blvd 33511

WESTSHORE PIZZA 813/661-2424

💎 Pizza. Casual Dining. **Address:** 1279 Kingsway Rd 33510

YOKOHAMA JAPANESE RESTAURANT AND SUSHI BAR 813/684-3485 (29)

💎💎 Japanese Sushi. Casual Dining. **Address:** 760 W Lumsden Rd 33511

BROOKSVILLE (F-2) pop. 7,719, elev. 126'

Scenic riverbanks, brackish creeks, cypress ponds, hardwood hammocks and shallow bays accent the rolling terrain surrounding Brooksville. The founding of Brooksville predates the Civil War, and many of its residential streets are lined with Victorian antebellum homes. Murals on downtown buildings depict historic events.

Winding through Lake Townsen Regional Park, 28011 Lake Lindsey Rd., and the nearby countryside are miles of hiking, biking and horseback riding trails, including those of nearby Withlacoochee State Forest; phone (352) 754-4031.

Florida's Adventure Coast Visitor & Information Center: 31085 Cortez Blvd., Brooksville, FL 34602. **Phone:** (352) 754-4405 or (800) 601-4580.

Self-guiding tours: Brochures for a self-guiding walking or driving tour of the historic district are available from the visitor & information center.

HOLIDAY INN EXPRESS HOTEL & SUITES 352/597-4540

💎💎 Hotel. **Address:** 14112 Cortez Blvd 34613

WHERE TO EAT

CONEY ISLAND DRIVE INN 352/796-9141

💎 Hot Dogs Burgers. Quick Serve. **Address:** 1112 E Jefferson St 34601

DEEP SOUTH BBQ 352/799-5060

💎 Barbecue. Quick Serve. **Address:** 7247 Cedar Ln 34601

MAIN STREET EATERY 352/799-2789

💎💎 Sandwiches. Casual Dining. **Address:** 101 N Main St 34601

MONTICELLO'S PIZZERIA 352/799-3787

💎 Italian. Casual Dining. **Address:** 31150 Cortez Blvd 34602

BUSHNELL (F-2) pop. 2,418, elev. 75'

Rural Bushnell, where the Withlacoochee River flows through a cypress swamp as a small stream, features small lakes once fished by Native Americans and Spanish explorers. Most are still popular with anglers today, as is Lake Panasoffkee, to the north. Withlacoochee State Forest, which covers 113,000 acres in three units, is west of town; phone (352) 754-6896.

Florida National Veterans Cemetery, off I-75 exit 309 off SR 476B at 6502 S.W. 102nd Ave., is among America's largest; phone (352) 793-7740. On SR 471 in nearby Webster shoppers enjoy Monday events at the Sumter County Farmers Market, one of the largest flea markets in the country and oldest in Florida; phone (352) 793-2021.

DADE BATTLEFIELD HISTORIC STATE PARK, off I-75 exit 314, e. on CR 48, 1.5 mi. s. on US 301, then 1 mi. w. to 7200 CR 603, commemorates the massacre of Maj. Francis L. Dade and his troops, who were ambushed by Seminole Indians the morning of Dec. 28, 1835; the incident helped spark the Second Seminole War. Highlights include reproductions of the log barricade used in the battle and monuments honoring Dade and his men. A visitor center has exhibits and artifacts, and an interpretive trail marks the military road and battlefield. Some of the site has been returned to the natural habitat that would have existed in the 19th century.

Events and children's activities are available; phone for schedule. **Time:** Allow 1 hour minimum. **Hours:** Grounds daily 8-dusk. Visitor center daily

9-5. **Cost:** $3 (per private vehicle with maximum eight people); $2 (per additional passenger or person arriving by bicycle or on foot). Exact change is required. There may be additional fees for admission and parking during programs and events; phone ahead. Cash only. **Phone:** (352) 793-4781 or (850) 245-2157.

SONNY'S REAL PIT BAR-B-Q 352/569-0200

Barbecue. Casual Dining. **Address:** 2684 W CR 48 33513

CANAVERAL NATIONAL SEASHORE (F-5)

Canaveral National Seashore lies north of the Kennedy Space Center *(see place listing p. 105)*. This 57,000-acre unit of the National Park Service encompasses 24 miles of unspoiled barrier beaches, shallow lagoons and dunes. Alligators, turtles, manatees and a variety of birds are among the abundant wildlife.

Swimming, boating, surf fishing and ranger-led activities can be enjoyed at Playalinda Beach at the southern tip of the seashore and at Apollo Beach at the area's northern end. The Merritt Island National Wildlife Refuge adjoins the national seashore. The Apollo Visitor Center at 7611 S. Atlantic Ave. in New Smyrna Beach is open daily 9-5; phone (386) 428-3384.

The seashore is open daily 6 a.m.-8 p.m., late Apr.-late Oct.; 6-6, rest of year. Admission $10 (per private vehicle or motorcycle); $1 (per person arriving on foot or by bicycle). An annual pass is $35. For further information, phone (321) 267-1110. For a recorded rocket launch schedule, phone (321) 867-4636. *See Recreation Areas Chart.*

CAPE CANAVERAL (G-6) pop. 9,912, elev. 10'

- **Restaurants p. 38**
- **Hotels & Restaurants map & index p. 50**

EXPLORATION TOWER AT PORT CANAVERAL is at 670 Dave Nisbet Dr. The modern, white Exploration Tower at Port Canaveral towers over the port and features interactive maritime and historical exhibits, displays about the space program and an observation tower on the seventh floor with a grand view of the port and surrounding area; you can watch cruise ships go out to sea. **Hours:** Daily 10-5. Closed Thanksgiving and Christmas. **Cost:** $6.50; $4 (ages 65+ and military with ID); $3.75 (ages 3-10). **Phone:** (321) 394-3408 or (321) 394-3405.

Make the Connection

Find this symbol for places to look, book and save on AAA.com.

COUNTRY INN & SUITES BY RADISSON-PORT CANAVERAL 321/784-8500 27

Hotel

Address: 9009 Astronaut Blvd 32920 **Location:** On SR A1A, 0.3 mi s of jct SR 528. **Facility:** 150 units. 4 stories, interior corridors. **Pool:** heated outdoor. **Activities:** hot tub, exercise room. **Guest Services:** valet and coin laundry, area transportation. **Featured Amenity: breakfast buffet.**

SAVE ECO CALL BIZ HS

HOLIDAY INN CLUB VACATIONS CAPE CANAVERAL BEACH RESORT 321/799-4900 26

Resort Hotel

Address: 1000 Shorewood Dr 32920 **Location:** Oceanfront. SR 528 (Beachline Expwy) exit George King Blvd, 1.4 mi e to Shorewood Dr, then just s. **Facility:** Near Port Canaveral and the Kennedy Space Center, the resort offers plenty of fun activities for the family. Condo-style units are spacious ranging from moderate to luxurious and some have balconies. 248 units, some two bedrooms, efficiencies and kitchens. 1-5 stories, interior/exterior corridors. **Terms:** check-in 4 pm. **Amenities:** safes. **Pool:** heated outdoor. **Activities:** sauna, hot tub, miniature golf, tennis, recreation programs, kids club, bicycles, playground, game room, picnic facilities, exercise room, massage. **Guest Services:** complimentary laundry.

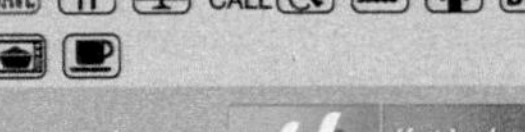

SAVE CALL BIZ

1 and 2-bedroom villas, 4-story waterslide, lazy river, kids pool, Grill & Bar + Free Wi-Fi/parking.

HOMEWOOD SUITES BY HILTON CAPE CANAVERAL-COCOA BEACH 321/868-1841 28

Extended Stay Contemporary Hotel

HOMEWOOD SUITES BY HILTON

AAA Benefit: Members save 5% or more!

Address: 9000 Astronaut Blvd 32920 **Location:** On SR A1A, 0.3 mi s of jct SR 528. Adjacent to Port Canaveral. **Facility:** 153 kitchen units. 6 stories, interior corridors. **Parking:** on-site (fee). **Pool:** outdoor. **Activities:** exercise room. **Guest Services:** valet and coin laundry. **Featured Amenity: full hot breakfast.**

SAVE CALL BIZ HS / SOME UNITS

RESIDENCE INN BY MARRIOTT CAPE CANAVERAL/COCOA BEACH 321/323-1100 29

SAVE Extended Stay Contemporary Hotel. **Address:** 8959 Astronaut Blvd 32920

AAA Benefit: Members save 5% or more!

ROYAL MANSIONS OCEANFRONT CONDOMINIUM RESORT 321/784-8484 30

Vacation Rental Hotel. **Address:** 8600 Ridgewood Ave 32920

(See map & index p. 50.)

WHERE TO EAT

FISHLIPS 321/784-4533 (19)

Seafood. Casual Dining. **Address:** 610 Glen Cheek Dr 32920

GRILLS WATERFRONT SEAFOOD DECK & TIKI BAR 321/868-2226 (18)

Seafood. Casual Dining. **Address:** 505 Glen Cheek Dr 32920

KELSEY'S RESTAURANT & PIZZERIA 321/783-9191 (21)

Italian Pizza. Casual Dining. **Address:** 8699 Astronaut Blvd 32920

SAGE BISTRO 321/783-4548 (22)

Continental. Fine Dining. **Address:** 6615 N Atlantic Ave 32920

ZACHARY'S RESTAURANT 321/784-9007 (20)

Greek. Casual Dining. **Address:** 8799 Astronaut Blvd 32920

CEDAR KEY (E-1) pop. 702, elev. 8'

Due to its location among a group of small barrier islands off the Gulf Coast of Florida, Cedar Key was a strategic point from which blockade runners exported cotton and lumber and imported food and supplies for the Confederacy during the Civil War. Following the war, lumbering and then fishing and shipbuilding formed the town's economic base. An 1896 hurricane leveled the original town.

Now sustained by tourism and the seafood industry, which includes clam farming, oystering, fishing and crabbing, Cedar Key is home to many artists. Its surrounding area is popular with bird-watchers.

Cedar Key Area Chamber of Commerce: 450 Second St., Cedar Key, FL 32625. **Phone:** (352) 543-5600.

Self-guiding tours: The Cedar Key Historical Society Museum offers brochures with tours of the historic district.

NATURE'S LANDING CONDOMINIUMS 352/543-9161

Vacation Rental Condominium. **Address:** 7050 C St 32625

WHERE TO EAT

ISLAND HOTEL RESTAURANT 352/543-5111

Seafood. Casual Dining. **Address:** 373 2nd St 32625

THE ISLAND ROOM RESTAURANT AT CEDAR COVE 352/543-6520

fyi

Seafood Casual Dining $10-$35

Under major renovation, call for details. **Last rated:** **AAA Inspector Notes:** Adjacent to the public beach and overlooking the bay to the south, this dining room is on the ground floor of a condominium complex. Menu offerings include steamed clams, linguine scampi, crab cakes, grouper Savannah, shrimp cocktail and crab bisque. For landlubbers, they offer rib-eye steak and herbed chicken. The restaurant is open for breakfast and lunch on the weekends. **Features:** full bar, Sunday brunch. **Reservations:** suggested. **Address:** 192 2nd St 32625 **Location:** Jct Depot Rd.

D

STEAMERS CLAM BAR & GRILL 352/543-5142

Seafood. Casual Dining. **Address:** 420 Dock St 32625

Exciting Itineraries | Engaging Experiences | Exclusive Values

AAA Vacations

DESIGNED FOR AAA MEMBERS

AAA Vacations® offers vacation options and experiences all over the world. In addition to our 24/7 Member Care and Best Price Guarantee*, we deliver value with every itinerary.

Call your AAA Travel Agent or visit AAA.com/AAAVacations

* Must be a qualifying *AAA Vacations*® cruise or tour vacation. Certain Restrictions apply. Visit AAA.com/AAAVacations for full details.

CELEBRATION (G-4) pop. 7,427, elev. 82'

• Hotels & Restaurants map & index p. 202
• Part of Orlando area — see map p. 2

Celebration is an upscale master-planned community conceptualized and built by the Disney Company, which began construction on the development in 1996. Reminiscent of New England, this small, well-manicured town is about 10 miles from the Walt Disney World® Resort and comes complete with parks, a community pool, a golf course and playgrounds. Within a 5-minute walk of most residents, downtown's Town Center is home to delightful mom-and-pop shops and restaurants. The palm-tree lined Celebration Boulevard features a movie theater, a high school and businesses housed inside Art Deco-style buildings, many designed by famous architects, including a post office designed by Michael Graves.

In keeping with its family-oriented atmosphere, Celebration goes all out when it comes to celebrating annual events, which include car shows throughout the year, late April's Great American Pie Festival and Art & Wine Stroll, A Sci-Fi 4th of July, Oktoberfest in mid-October, the World Food Championships in early November and, from late November though late December, Now Snowing, a Christmas event where simulated snow drifts from the sky.

For getaways off the beaten path, visit AAA.com/campgrounds

iStockphoto.com_pixelfit

BOHEMIAN HOTEL CELEBRATION, AUTOGRAPH COLLECTION 407/566-6000 (123)

SAVE Boutique Hotel. **Address:** 700 Bloom St 34747

AAA Benefit: Members save 5% or more!

MELIA ORLANDO SUITE HOTEL AT CELEBRATION 407/964-7000 (122)

Extended Stay Contemporary Hotel

Address: 225 Celebration Pl 34747 **Location:** I-4 exit 64 (US 192), just e. **Facility:** 289 units, some two bedrooms and kitchens. 5 stories, interior corridors. **Parking:** on-site (fee). **Terms:** check-in 4 pm. **Amenities:** safes. **Pool:** heated outdoor. **Activities:** hot tub. **Guest Services:** valet and coin laundry, boarding pass kiosk, area transportation. *(See ad this page, p. 120.)*

SAVE ECO BIZ sHS

/ SOME UNITS

WHERE TO EAT

CAFE D'ANTONIO 407/566-2233 (68)
Italian. Fine Dining. **Address:** 691 Front St 34747

COLUMBIA RESTAURANT 407/566-1505 (69)
Spanish. Casual Dining. **Address:** 649 Front St 34747

JOE'S CRAB SHACK 321/939-6880 (64)
SAVE Seafood. Casual Dining. **Address:** 10 Blake Blvd 34747

LE CHINA CHINESE RESTAURANT 321/939-2462 (65)
Chinese. Casual Dining. **Address:** 37 Blake Blvd 34747

MARKET STREET CAFE 407/566-1144 (70)
American. Casual Dining. **Address:** 701 Front St 34747

SWEET ESCAPE 407/566-0603 (66)
Sandwiches Desserts. Quick Serve. **Address:** 603 Market St 34747

THAI THANI 407/566-9444 (67)
Thai. Casual Dining. **Address:** 600 Market St, Suite 110 34747

▼ See AAA listing this page ▼

MELIÁ ORLANDO SUITE HOTEL AT CELEBRATION
TAKING IT TO THE NEXT LEVEL

MELIÃ ORLANDO HOTEL AT CELEBRATION www.melia.com

An oasis of chic comfort designed around a 360 Degree Infinity Edge Pool and Jacuzzi. Lounge, relax, or prep for fun at the surrounding theme parks, it's all a stone's throw away.

Free WiFi | Outdoor Pool | 360 American Bistro and Bar

225 Celebration Place | Celebration, FL 34747 | 888.956.3542

CHAMPIONSGATE

• Hotels & Restaurants map & index p. 197
• Part of Orlando area — see map p. 2

OMNI ORLANDO RESORT AT CHAMPIONSGATE

407/390-6664 (24)

Resort Hotel

Address: 1500 Masters Blvd 33896 **Location:** I-4 exit 58, 0.5 mi w on ChampionsGate Blvd (CR 532) to Masters Blvd, then just n. **Facility:** The traditional guest rooms have an elegant appeal and feature comfortable easy chairs. Many rooms have great views of the scenic grounds. The luxurious villas create a perfect, full-amenity getaway. 720 units. 16 stories, interior corridors. **Parking:** on-site (fee) and valet. **Terms:** check-in 4 pm. **Amenities:** safes. **Dining:** 8 restaurants, also, Zen, see separate listing. **Pool:** heated outdoor. **Activities:** sauna, hot tub, steamroom, cabanas, regulation golf, tennis, recreation programs, playground, game room, exercise room, spa. **Guest Services:** valet laundry, rental car service, area transportation.

 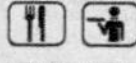  

TROPICAL ESCAPE AT CHAMPIONS GATE

863/588-3777 (23)

Vacation Rental House

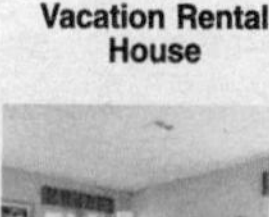

Location: I-4 exit 55, 4.1 mi n. **Facility:** Located near attractions, eateries and shops, each of the upscale vacation homes features a private, screened-in pool. The homes vary in size; some can accommodate up to 10 guests. 50 kitchen house units. 1-2 stories (no elevator), interior corridors. **Terms:** check-in 4 pm. **Pool:** heated outdoor. **Activities:** hot tub, cabanas, regulation golf, par 3 golf, tennis, recreation programs in season, game room, exercise room, massage. **Guest Services:** complimentary laundry.

WHERE TO EAT

ZEN 407/390-6664 (19)

Asian. Casual Dining. **Address:** 1500 Masters Blvd 33896

CHIEFLAND pop. 2,245, elev. 40'

QUALITY INN NEAR MANATEE SPRINGS STATE PARK

352/493-0663

Motel

Address: 1125 N Young Blvd 32626 **Location:** On Alternate Rt US 27/19/98, just n of jct US 129. **Facility:** 60 units. 2 stories (no elevator), exterior corridors. **Pool:** outdoor. **Guest Services:** coin laundry. **Featured Amenity: full hot breakfast.**

WHERE TO EAT

ABC PIZZA 352/493-1432

Italian. Casual Dining. **Address:** 1285 NW Hwy 19 32626

BAR-B-Q BILL'S 352/493-4444

Barbecue. Casual Dining. **Address:** 1901 N Young Blvd 32626

CLEARWATER (E-8) pop. 107,685, elev. 29'

• Restaurants p. 43
• Hotels & Restaurants map & index p. 286
• Part of St. Petersburg-Clearwater and Beaches area — see map p. 275

A resort city and popular retirement community on the Pinellas Peninsula, Clearwater overlooks the Gulf of Mexico.

Broadway and comedy shows, orchestral and jazz pop performances, ballet, opera and children's theater are staged throughout the year at Ruth Eckerd Hall in Richard B. Baumgardner Center for the Performing Arts, 1111 McMullen Booth Rd.; phone (727) 791-7400.

Aficionados of performing arts won't want to miss the Clearwater Jazz Holiday. The 4-day festival, held the third weekend in October at downtown Coachman Park, features performers of national and international acclaim; phone (727) 461-5200.

The Philadelphia Phillies hold spring training and play exhibition games from late February to late March at Bright House Field; their Class A affiliates, the Clearwater Threshers, train at Bright House Field and play April through August; phone (727) 467-4457.

Clearwater and the beach communities have two trolley systems for visitors. Operated by PSTA, Suncoast Beach Trolley travels Gulf Boulevard north to Clearwater's Sand Key and south to St. Pete Beach Mon.-Thurs. and Sun.; phone (727) 540-1900. The Jolley Trolley covers Clearwater and Clearwater Beach, and includes Dunedin, Palm Harbor and Tarpon Springs on weekends; phone (727) 445-1900.

Clearwater Regional Chamber of Commerce: 600 Cleveland St., Suite 200, Clearwater, FL 33755. **Phone:** (727) 461-0011.

Visit St. Petersburg/Clearwater: 8200 Bryan Dairy Rd. #200, Seminole, FL 33777. **Phone:** (727) 464-7200 or (877) 352-3224.

Shopping: The Westfield Countryside Mall, 27001 US 19 N., lures adolescent mall rats with an ice-skating rink and such stores as American Eagle Outfitters, Buckle, Forever 21 and Hot Topic, while anchors Dillard's, JCPenney, Macy's and Sears accommodate visiting fashionistas.

Serious bargain hunters navigate a trinkets-, crafts- and furniture-crammed maze at the 49er Flea Market, 10525 49th St. N. This collector's paradise features indoor vendors on weekends, but it's best to shop 'til you drop on Sundays, when outdoor booths augment the usual stockpile of secondhand treasures.

SAVE **CLEARWATER MARINE AQUARIUM,** 249 Windward Passage, is a rescue, rehabilitation and release facility specializing in dolphins, otters and sea turtles. Marine exhibits, a theater, underwater viewing tanks, daily ecocruises and animal care presentations are offered. The facility is home to Winter, a tailless dolphin able to swim freely with

(See map & index p. 286.)

the help of a prosthetic tail. Winter's Dolphin Tale Adventure, 300 Cleveland St., features scenes and props used in "Dolphin Tale," a movie starring Winter. A behind-the-scenes tour focuses on efforts to rescue, rehabilitate and release marine animals. A complimentary shuttle provides transportation between the two facilities in spring and summer; phone ahead to confirm schedule.

Time: Allow 1 hour, 30 minutes minimum. **Hours:** Daily 10-6. Winter's Dolphin Tale Adventure daily 10-6, in spring and summer. Closed Thanksgiving and Christmas. Phone ahead to confirm schedule. **Cost:** (includes Winter's Dolphin Tale Adventure) $21.95; $19.95 (ages 60+); $16.95 (ages 3-12). Combination ticket with Sea Life Safari $40.90; $37.90 (ages 60+); $29.90 (ages 3-12). Combination ticket with a behind-the-scenes tour $34.90; $31.90 (ages 60+); $26.90 (ages 7-12). **Phone:** (727) 441-1790. GT

COURTYARD BY MARRIOTT ST. PETERSBURG CLEARWATER 727/572-8484 24

Hotel

COURTYARD® **AAA Benefit:** Members save 5% or more!

Address: 3131 Executive Dr 33762 **Location:** I-275 exit 31 southbound, just w on SR 688 (Ulmerton Rd); exit 30 northbound, 1.4 mi w on SR 686, just w SR 688 (Ulmerton Rd); in The Centres Office Park. **Facility:** 149 units. 3 stories, interior corridors. **Pool:** heated outdoor. **Activities:** exercise room. **Guest Services:** valet and coin laundry, area transportation.

SAVE ECO CALL BIZ HS

FAIRFIELD INN & SUITES BY MARRIOTT CLEARWATER BAYSIDE 727/724-6223 21

SAVE Hotel. **Address:** 3070 Gulf-to-Bay Blvd 33759

AAA Benefit: Members save 5% or more!

FAIRFIELD INN & SUITES BY MARRIOTT ST. PETERSBURG/CLEARWATER 727/572-4400 25

SAVE Hotel. **Address:** 3211 Executive Dr 33762

AAA Benefit: Members save 5% or more!

HAMPTON INN & SUITES CLEARWATER/ST. PETERSBURG 727/572-7456 27

Hotel

AAA Benefit: Members save 5% or more!

Address: 4050 Ulmerton Rd 33762 **Location:** I-275 exit 31 southbound, 1.8 mi w on SR 688; exit 30 northbound, 1.4 mi w on SR 686, then 0.8 mi w. **Facility:** 128 units. 6 stories, interior corridors. **Pool:** heated outdoor. **Activities:** exercise room. **Guest Services:** valet and coin laundry, area transportation. **Featured Amenity: full hot breakfast.**

SAVE CALL BIZ

 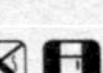  

HOLIDAY INN EXPRESS CLEARWATER EAST-ICOT CENTER 727/536-7275 28

Hotel. **Address:** 13625 Icot Blvd 33760

HOMEWOOD SUITES BY HILTON CLEARWATER 727/573-1500 23

Extended Stay Hotel

AAA Benefit: Members save 5% or more!

Address: 2233 Ulmerton Rd 33762 **Location:** I-275 exit 31, 1.3 mi w on SR 688; exit 30 northbound, 1.4 mi w on SR 686, then 0.6 mi e on SR 688. **Facility:** 112 kitchen units, some two bedrooms. 2 stories, interior corridors. **Pool:** heated outdoor. **Activities:** exercise room. **Guest Services:** valet and coin laundry, boarding pass kiosk, area transportation. **Featured Amenity: breakfast buffet.**

RESIDENCE INN BY MARRIOTT CLEARWATER DOWNTOWN 727/562-5400 22

SAVE Extended Stay Hotel. **Address:** 940 Court St 33756

AAA Benefit: Members save 5% or more!

RESIDENCE INN BY MARRIOTT ST. PETERSBURG/CLEARWATER 727/573-4444 29

SAVE Extended Stay Hotel. **Address:** 5050 Ulmerton Rd 33760

AAA Benefit: Members save 5% or more!

Save on travel, shopping and more:

AAA.com/discounts

(See map & index p. 286.)

SPRINGHILL SUITES BY MARRIOTT ST. PETERSBURG-CLEARWATER 727/571-1600 26

SAVE Hotel. **Address:** 3485 Ulmerton Rd 33762

AAA Benefit: Members save 5% or more!

TOWNEPLACE SUITES BY MARRIOTT ST. PETERSBURG/ CLEARWATER 727/299-9229 30

SAVE Extended Stay Hotel. **Address:** 13200 49th St N 33762

AAA Benefit: Members save 5% or more!

▼ *See AAA listing p. 255* ▼

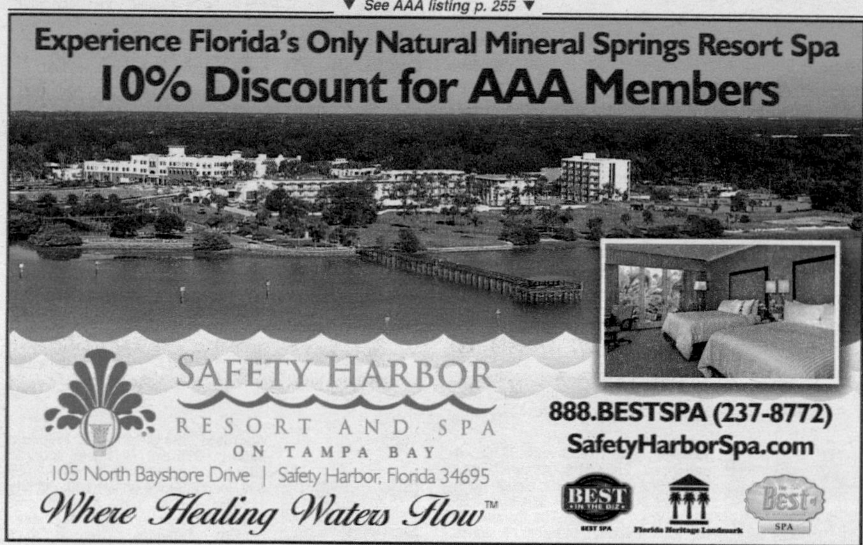
Experience Florida's Only Natural Mineral Springs Resort Spa
10% Discount for AAA Members
SAFETY HARBOR
RESORT AND SPA
ON TAMPA BAY
105 North Bayshore Drive | Safety Harbor, Florida 34695
Where Healing Waters Flow™
888.BESTSPA (237-8772)
SafetyHarborSpa.com
BEST IN THE BIZ

Hit the Road with Foreign Currency

A treasure trove of artisan masterpieces awaits.

Visit your local AAA office or online at
AAA.com/ForeignCurrency

All products not available at all locations.

AAA

(See map & index p. 286.)

WHERE TO EAT

ALFANO'S RESTAURANT 727/584-2125 (40)

💎💎💎 Italian. Fine Dining. **Address:** 1702 Clearwater-Largo Rd 33756

ANTHONY'S COAL FIRED PIZZA 727/797-0929

💎💎 Pizza. Casual Dining. **Address:** 2532 McMullen Booth Rd 33761

BASCOM'S CHOP HOUSE STEAKS & FRESH SEAFOOD 727/573-3363 (41)

💎💎💎 Steak Seafood. Fine Dining. **Address:** 3665 Ulmerton Rd 33762

CAFE PONTE 727/538-5768 (42)

💎💎💎 Fusion. Fine Dining. **Address:** 13505 Icot Blvd, Suite 214 33760

CAPOGNA'S DUGOUT 727/441-4791 (37)

💎 Sandwiches Pizza. Casual Dining. **Address:** 1653 Gulf-to-Bay Blvd 33755

CODY'S ORIGINAL ROADHOUSE 727/726-6800

💎💎 American. Casual Dining. **Address:** 26200 US 19 N 33763

FLORIDA SUBS & GYROS 727/447-5850 (35)

💎 Sandwiches Burgers. Quick Serve. **Address:** 2017 Gulf-To-Bay Blvd 33765

GREEN MARKET CAFE 727/725-2819 (32)

💎 Natural/Organic Sandwiches. Quick Serve. **Address:** 2570 Gulf-To-Bay Blvd N 33765

LENNY'S RESTAURANT 727/799-0402 (30)

💎💎 Breakfast Sandwiches. Casual Dining. **Address:** 21220 US 19 N 33765

O'KEEFE'S TAVERN & RESTAURANT 727/442-9034 (39)

💎💎 American. Casual Dining. **Address:** 1219 S Fort Harrison Ave 33756

ORIENTAL SUPER BUFFET 727/725-2083 (33)

💎

Chinese Quick Serve

$9-$14

AAA Inspector Notes: This popular restaurant's extensive Chinese buffet features more than 130 items each day, including sushi, snow crab legs and mussels. Enhanced by lots of bamboo and neon lighting, the main buffet dining area has a modern vibe. Enjoy watching the koi fish in the attractive water feature in the foyer. The staff is quite friendly and helpful. **Features:** beer & wine. **Address:** 2456 Gulf-To-Bay Blvd 33765 **Location:** On SR 60, just w of jct US 19. (L) (D)

PAPA'S NEW YORK DINER 727/446-8283 (36)

💎💎 Comfort Food. Casual Dining. **Address:** 1764 Gulf to Bay Blvd 33755

PETE & SHORTY'S TAVERN 727/799-0580 (31)

💎💎 American. Casual Dining. **Address:** 2820 Gulf-To-Bay Blvd 33759

PICKLES PLUS DELI 727/725-3325 (28)

💎💎 Sandwiches Breakfast. Casual Dining. **Address:** 2530 N McMullen Booth Rd 33761

QUEEN'S PIZZA & RESTAURANT 727/446-6016 (29)

💎💎 Italian. Casual Dining. **Address:** 1834 N Belcher Rd 33765

RUMBA ISLAND BAR & GRILL 727/446-7027 (34)

💎💎 Caribbean. Casual Dining. **Address:** 1800 Gulf-to-Bay Blvd 33755

THAI COCONUT RESTAURANT 727/441-1650 (38)

💎💎 Thai. Casual Dining. **Address:** 1280 S Missouri Ave 33756

WESTSHORE PIZZA

💎 Pizza. Casual Dining.

LOCATIONS:

Address: 1969 Drew St 33755 **Phone:** 727/446-4444

Address: 2481 McMullen Booth Rd 33763 **Phone:** 727/725-0300

CLEARWATER BEACH (H-1) elev. 5'

• Hotels p. 44 • Restaurants p. 47
• Hotels & Restaurants map & index p. 286
• Part of St. Petersburg-Clearwater and Beaches area — see map p. 275

Clearwater Beach is connected with the mainland by the Clearwater Memorial Causeway, a landscaped, 2-mile drive. The broad, white-sand beach attracts both residents and visitors. Beach Walk, a winding, half-mile-long brick pedestrian promenade paralleling South Gulfview Boulevard in the area of Pier 60, provides beachgoers with unobstructed views and plenty of covered seating.

The Clearwater Marina harbors a large sport-fishing fleet of deep-sea charter boats and a variety of sightseeing cruise boats. The Tropics Boat Tours' Dolphin Exploration Tour offers an opportunity to view dolphins and feed seabirds on a 2-hour excursion (dolphin sighting is guaranteed or next trip is free); for schedule and fare information, phone (727) 442-7433.

Nightlife: While enjoying an early evening stroll on the Beach Walk, you're apt to find yourself immersed in the goings-on of Sunsets at Pier 60. Snap a few shots of the resplendent coast at sundown while conversing with local artisans along the beach umbrella-festooned walkway. You'll also encounter bold street entertainers posing for photos with gaggles of giggling teenyboppers, red-hot local bands, break-dancers and a juggling fire-breather. Two playgrounds and a variety of carnival-style amusements edge the crowded dock, with young children sliding, bouncing and swinging into the night. The daily event begins 2 hours before dusk and ends 2 hours after dusk (weather permitting).

For dinner and drinks, head to Frenchy's Rockaway Grill, about .5 miles north of Pier 60 at 7 Rockaway St. This beachfront oasis is popular with locals and visitors, so arrive early to snag a table overlooking the Gulf of Mexico; phone (727) 446-4844. Next door at the Palm Pavilion Beachside Grill & Bar, spirited sports fans high-five over televised touchdowns and home runs as more subdued patrons relish tropical drinks on the wraparound deck; phone (727) 446-2642.

Shephard's Beach Resort, 601-619 S. Gulfview Blvd., (727) 442-5107, offers two bass-thumping party spots for sand and surf lovers. Although uninhibited spring breakers certainly stir up the scene, live reggae and rock bands harmonizing with the stunning surroundings make this seaside retreat appealing year-round. Wade through a sea of bikinis and boardshorts at the Tiki Beach Bar & Grill, which stays packed with piña colada-sipping locals and visiting undergrads from mid-afternoon to after dark. Well-groomed twentysomethings let loose Friday

(See map & index p. 286.)

through Sunday evenings at The Wave, a two-story nightclub swathed in chrome and metallic hues.

***CALYPSO QUEEN* CRUISES** departs from Clearwater Marina at 25 Causeway Blvd. The captain gives a historical narration during 1.5-hour afternoon and 2.5-hour evening sightseeing cruises along Clearwater Harbor and the Intracoastal Waterway. The open top deck provides opportunities for viewing seabirds and marine life. A buffet meal is available.

Note: Passengers must get a parking permit at the cruises' kiosk to get the $6 parking rate, which allows passengers to park 11-6 or 5 p.m.-1 a.m. **Hours:** Sightseeing cruises depart daily at 12:30 and 7, mid-Mar. through Sept. 30; at 12:30 and 6, rest of year. Boarding begins 30 minutes before departure. Phone ahead to confirm schedule and fare. **Cost:** Afternoon cruise $14.95; $9.95 (ages 3-10). Afternoon cruise with buffet $29.90; $17.70 (ages 3-10). Evening cruise $19.95; $12.95 (ages 3-10). Evening cruise with buffet $39.90; $22.90 (ages 3-10). Reservations are recommended. **Parking:** $6 at metered parking lot. **Phone:** (727) 461-3113. GT

SAVE ***SEA SCREAMER*** departs from slip 15 at Clearwater Marina. Narrated, 1-hour speedboat rides begin with a slow cruise out of Clearwater Harbor. The boat accelerates as it enters the Gulf of Mexico, providing an exhilarating trip accompanied by dolphins. **Time:** Allow 1 hour, 30 minutes minimum. **Hours:** Cruises daily at noon, 2 and 4 (also at dusk, June 1-Sept. 15). Tickets are sold 30 minutes before departure. **Cost:** $24; $18 (ages 5-12). Reservations are recommended. **Phone:** (727) 447-7200, or (888) 238-9020 for reservations. GT

FAIRFIELD INN & SUITES BY MARRIOTT CLEARWATER BEACH 727/298-2600 36

SAVE Hotel. **Address:** 650 Bay Esplanade 33767

AAA Benefit: Members save 5% or more!

HAMPTON INN & SUITES CLEARWATER BEACH 727/451-1111 47

SAVE Hotel. **Address:** 635 S Gulfview Blvd 33767

AAA Benefit: Members save 5% or more!

HILTON CLEARWATER BEACH RESORT & SPA 727/461-3222 39

Resort Hotel

AAA Benefit: Members save 5% or more!

Address: 400 Mandalay Ave 33767 **Location:** Oceanfront. Just n of jct SR 60 (roundabout). **Facility:** Nestled along the shores of the Gulf of Mexico; the hotel's public areas boast a South Beach-like décor. Most rooms have a private balcony with either Gulf or city views. 418 units. 9 stories, interior corridors. **Parking:** valet only. **Terms:** check-in 4 pm. **Amenities:** safes. **Dining:** 6 restaurants, entertainment. **Pool:** heated outdoor. **Activities:** steamroom, cabanas, recreation programs, exercise room, spa. **Guest Services:** valet and coin laundry, boarding pass kiosk.

SAVE ECO CALL BIZ SHS / SOME UNITS

HOLIDAY INN & SUITES 727/447-6461 45

Hotel. **Address:** 521 S Gulfview Blvd 33767

(See map & index p. 286.)

HYATT REGENCY CLEARWATER BEACH RESORT & SPA

727/373-1234 41

Resort Hotel

AAA Benefit: Members save up to 10%!

Address: 301 S Gulfview Blvd 33767 **Location:** Oceanfront. Just s of jct SR 60 (roundabout), enter via Coronado Dr. **Facility:** Located across from the Gulf of Mexico, this property is very upscale in nature. A popular area of the property is the rooftop pool deck, which offers great views of the beach and gorgeous sunsets. 287 units, some efficiencies and kitchens. 17 stories, interior corridors. **Parking:** on-site (fee) and valet. **Terms:** check-in 4 pm. **Amenities:** safes. **Dining:** SHOR American Seafood Grill, see separate listing. **Pool:** heated outdoor. **Activities:** hot tub, beach access, cabanas, kids club, health club, spa. **Guest Services:** valet and coin laundry, boarding pass kiosk.

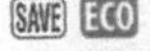  CALL  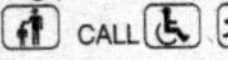

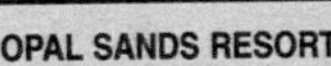

RESIDENCE INN BY MARRIOTT CLEARWATER BEACH

727/218-1088 42

Extended Stay Hotel

Residence INN. **AAA Benefit:** Members save 5% or more!

Address: 309-1 Coronado Dr 33767 **Location:** Just s of jct SR 60 (roundabout). **Facility:** 140 kitchen units, some two bedrooms. 7 stories, interior corridors. **Parking:** valet only. **Pool:** heated outdoor. **Activities:** beach access, exercise room. **Guest Services:** valet and coin laundry. **Featured Amenity: breakfast buffet.**

CALL / SOME UNITS 

OPAL SANDS RESORT

727/450-0380 44

Contemporary Resort Hotel

Address: 430 S Gulfview Blvd 33767 **Location:** Oceanfront. 0.5 mi s of SR 60 (roundabout). **Facility:** This impressive hotel on the Gulf is a work of art. Gorgeous blue hues of the nearby water are pulled into the color palette of this establishment where spacious and luxurious guest rooms await. 230 units, some two bedrooms and kitchens. 15 stories, interior corridors. **Parking:** valet only. **Terms:** check-in 4 pm. **Amenities:** safes. **Dining:** 2 restaurants, entertainment. **Pool:** heated outdoor. **Activities:** bicycles, health club, spa. **Guest Services:** valet laundry, area transportation.

CALL 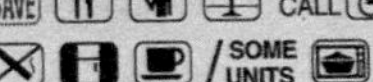

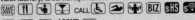

/ SOME UNITS

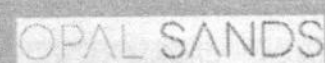

A luxurious resort on Clearwater Beach. Featuring panoramic Gulf views from every room.

SANDPEARL RESORT

727/441-2425 38

Resort Hotel

Address: 500 Mandalay Ave 33767 **Location:** Oceanfront. 0.4 mi n of jct SR 60 (roundabout). **Facility:** This beautiful high-rise resort is located directly on the Gulf of Mexico. Luxurious appointments can be found throughout the property. Guest rooms have panoramic city or gorgeous beach views. 249 units, some two bedrooms and kitchens. 8 stories, interior corridors. **Parking:** valet only. **Terms:** check-in 4 pm. **Amenities:** safes. **Dining:** 3 restaurants, also, Caretta On The Gulf, see separate listing, entertainment. **Pool:** heated outdoor. **Activities:** sauna, hot tub, steamroom, cabanas, self-propelled boats, marina, recreation programs, kids club, bicycles, lawn sports, health club, spa. **Guest Services:** valet laundry, boarding pass kiosk, area transportation. Affiliated with Preferred Hotels & Resorts.

CALL / SOME UNITS

Sandpearl RESORT CLEARWATER BEACH

An award-winning Clearwater Beach resort that reflects the casual elegance of Florida's Gulf Coast.

PALM PAVILION INN

727/446-6777 37

Hotel. **Address:** 18 Bay Esplanade 33767

SHEPHARD'S BEACH RESORT

727/442-5107 46

Hotel

Address: 619 S Gulfview Blvd 33767 **Location:** Oceanfront. 1 mi s of jct SR 60 (roundabout). **Facility:** 140 units, some two bedrooms, efficiencies and kitchens. 2-6 stories, interior corridors. **Parking:** on-site (fee) and valet. **Amenities:** video games, safes. **Dining:** nightclub, entertainment. **Pool:** heated outdoor. **Activities:** hot tub, cabanas, exercise room. **Guest Services:** valet and coin laundry.

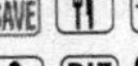 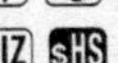 CALL  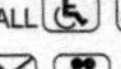 

QUALITY BEACH RESORT

727/442-7171 48

Hotel

Address: 655 S Gulfview Blvd 33767 **Location:** Oceanfront. 0.9 mi s of jct SR 60 (roundabout). **Facility:** 93 units. 5 stories, interior/exterior corridors. **Parking:** valet only. **Amenities:** safes. **Pool:** heated outdoor. **Guest Services:** valet and coin laundry.

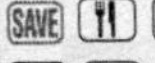  

▼ See AAA listing p. 47 ▼

WYNDHAM GRAND®
Clearwater Beach

Offering 343 guestrooms, come experience America's best beach, with views of the Gulf of Mexico and Intracoastal Waterway.

Indulge in the tranquil Pallavi Luxury Spa and waterfront dining at our signature restaurant, Ocean Hai, the only Asian-fusion cuisine on Clearwater Beach.

LIFE IS GRAND
WYNDHAMGRANDCLEARWATER.COM
727-281-9500
100 CORONADO DRIVE
CLEARWATER, FL 33767

(See map & index p. 286.)

Be Vacation Ready

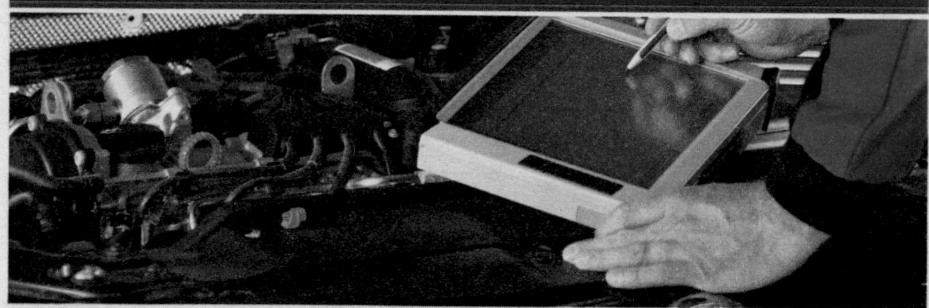

Have your car checked out by a dependable AAA/CAA Approved Auto Repair facility.

AAA.com/autorepair

(See map & index p. 286.)

SHERATON SAND KEY RESORT 727/595-1611 49

Resort Hotel

AAA Benefit: Members save 5% or more!

Address: 1160 Gulf Blvd 33767 **Location:** Oceanfront. 2 mi s on SR 699; at south end of Clearwater Pass Bridge. **Facility:** Located on the Gulf of Mexico, this resort offers rooms with private patios or balconies, some of which have an excellent view of the beach. Rooms are spacious and decorated in dark wood tones. 390 units. 9 stories, interior corridors. **Amenities:** safes. **Dining:** 4 restaurants, entertainment. **Pool:** heated outdoor. **Activities:** hot tub, fishing, tennis, lawn sports, health club, massage. **Guest Services:** valet and coin laundry.

 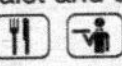  CALL  BIZ

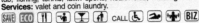

SPRINGHILL SUITES BY MARRIOTT CLEARWATER BEACH 727/218-1090 43

Hotel

AAA Benefit: Members save 5% or more!

Address: 309-2 Coronado Dr 33767 **Location:** Just s of SR 60 (roundabout). **Facility:** 115 units. 7 stories, interior corridors. **Parking:** valet only. **Pool:** heated outdoor. **Activities:** beach access, exercise room. **Guest Services:** valet and coin laundry. **Featured Amenity: full hot breakfast.**

 CALL 

 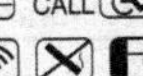 

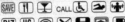

/SOME UNITS

WYNDHAM GRAND CLEARWATER BEACH 727/281-9500 40

Contemporary Resort Hotel

Address: 100 Coronado Dr 33767 **Location:** Oceanfront. Just s of jct SR 60 (roundabout). **Facility:** An ultra-modern exterior and pool with a cascading water feature and fantastic views of the Gulf of Mexico are just the beginning of your experience. The lobby is relaxing with an upscale beachy vibe. 343 units, some three bedrooms and kitchens. 15 stories, interior corridors. **Parking:** valet only. **Terms:** check-in 4 pm. **Amenities:** safes. **Dining:** 4 restaurants, also, Ocean Hai, see separate listing. **Pool:** heated outdoor. **Activities:** hot tub, steamroom, recreation programs, health club, spa. **Guest Services:** valet laundry, boarding pass kiosk. *(See ad p. 46.)*

 CALL  BIZ SHS

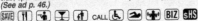

 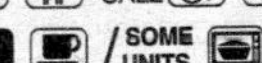 /SOME UNITS

WHERE TO EAT

BACKWATER'S ON SAND KEY 727/517-7383 65

Steak Seafood. Casual Dining. **Address:** 1261 Gulf Blvd 33767

BOBBY'S BISTRO & WINE BAR 727/446-9463 55

Continental. Casual Dining. **Address:** 447 Mandalay Ave 33767

BOB HEILMAN'S BEACHCOMBER 727/442-4144 56

Steak Seafood. Fine Dining. **Address:** 447 Mandalay Ave 33767

CARETTA ON THE GULF 727/441-2425 53

Continental Fine Dining $12-$54

AAA Inspector Notes: The restaurant offers a wonderful retreat after a day of beachside activities. The dining room is quite inviting with an upscale flair, and the view, ranging from the beach and nightly sunset, is outstanding. The seasonal menu highlights selections like Durham Ranch Buffalo, line-caught salmon, poached lobster, Colorado rack of lamb, pan-seared halibut, Dutch Harbor King crab legs, and Blue Point oysters. A professional service staff awaits to treat you to a well-deserved dinner. **Features:** full bar, Sunday brunch. **Reservations:** suggested. **Address:** 500 Mandalay Ave 33767 **Location:** 0.4 mi n of jct SR 60 (roundabout); in Sandpearl Resort. **Parking:** valet only.

B L D CALL

COLUMBIA RESTAURANT 727/596-8400

Spanish. Casual Dining. **Address:** 1241 Gulf Blvd 33767

COOTERS RESTAURANT & BAR 727/462-2668 57

Seafood. Casual Dining. **Address:** 423 Poinsettia Ave 33767

FRENCHY'S CAFE 727/446-3607 54

Seafood. Casual Dining. **Address:** 41 Baymont St 33767

FRENCHY'S ROCKAWAY GRILL 727/446-4844 52

Caribbean. Casual Dining. **Address:** 7 Rockaway St 33767

FRENCHY'S SALTWATER CAFE 727/461-6295 58

Seafood. Casual Dining. **Address:** 419 Poinsettia Ave 33767

FRENCHY'S SOUTH BEACH CAFE 727/441-9991 61

Seafood. Casual Dining. **Address:** 351 S Gulfview Blvd 33767

GONDOLIER ITALIAN RESTAURANT AND PIZZA 727/441-3353

Italian Pizza. Casual Dining. **Address:** 674 S Gulfview Blvd 33767

OCEAN HAI 727/281-9500 59

Asian Fusion Fine Dining $14-$42

AAA Inspector Notes: Located just off the lobby of an ultra-modern hotel, this upscale restaurant serves sushi and sashimi dishes prepared with local and farm-raised ingredients. Popular dishes include Mongolian lamb chops, Korean short ribs, Kurobuta pork chops, Peking duck breast, Asian sea bass, Wild Isles organic salmon and Hokkaido scallops. **Features:** full bar, patio dining. **Address:** 100 Coronado Dr 33767 **Location:** Just s of jct SR 60 (roundabout); in Wyndham Grand Clearwater Beach. **Parking:** valet only. *(See ad p. 46.)*

B L D CALL

PALM PAVILION BEACHSIDE GRILL & BAR 727/446-2642 51

American. Casual Dining. **Address:** 10 Bay Esplanade 33767

POST CORNER PIZZA 727/461-7795 62

American. Casual Dining. **Address:** 431 S Gulfview Blvd 33767

SEA-GUINI 727/450-6236 63

Italian. Casual Dining. **Address:** 430 S Gulfview Blvd 33767

(See map & index p. 286.)

SHOR AMERICAN SEAFOOD GRILL 727/373-4780 (60)

Seafood
Steak
Casual Dining
$10-$46

AAA Inspector Notes: This upscale restaurant is set on the second floor and offers fabulous views of the Gulf. The earth tone decor features a touch of fine dining appeal. The dinner menu features black grouper, salmon, red snapper and mahi mahi, along with New York strip, filet mignon, Angus ribeye, braised lamb shank, and Adobo glazed chicken breast. Their lobster ravioli and wild mushroom risotto are popular choices. The staff is professional and knowledgeable. **Features:** full bar, Sunday brunch. **Reservations:** suggested. **Address:** 301 S Gulfview Blvd 33767 **Location:** Just s of jct SR 60 (roundabout), enter via Coronado Dr; in Hyatt Regency Clearwater Beach Resort & Spa. **Parking:** on-site (fee) and valet. B L D CALL

TACO BUS 727/754-5304 (64)

Mexican. Quick Serve. **Address:** 505A S Gulfview Blvd 33767

CLERMONT (F-3) pop. 28,742, elev. 190'

- **Hotels & Restaurants map & index p. 202**
- **Part of Orlando area — see map p. 2**

Clermont founder A.F. Wrotnoski named this town of wide, shady streets and rolling hills after his French birthplace. Lake Louisa State Park *(see Recreation Areas Chart)*, 7 miles southeast of Clermont on Lake Nellie Road, is one of 13 in a chain of lakes connected by the Palatlakaha River.

South Lake Chamber of Commerce: 620 W. Montrose St., Clermont, FL 34711. **Phone:** (352) 394-4191.

PRESIDENTS HALL OF FAME, just n. of SR 50 at 123 US 27N, features changing exhibits of memorabilia related to U.S. presidents and their first ladies. Among displays are campaign and inaugural artifacts, first ladies' evening gowns, replicas of china place settings and miniature re-creations of White House rooms. Video presentations include a tour of the White House and presidential biographies.

Time: Allow 2 hours minimum. **Hours:** Mon.-Sat. 10-4, Sun. noon-4. Closed Jan. 1, Easter, Thanksgiving and Christmas. **Cost:** (good for 1 year; includes tour) $15 (ages 13+, ages 65+ and military with ID); $8 (ages 6-12). **Phone:** (352) 394-2836. GT

EXPLORIA EXPRESS BY EXPLORIA RESORTS 407/239-8315 (79)

Hotel. **Address:** 105 Summer Bay Blvd 34714

FAIRFIELD INN & SUITES BY MARRIOTT CLERMONT 352/394-6585

Hotel

Fairfield **AAA Benefit:** Members save 5% or more!

Address: 1750 Hunt Trace Blvd 34711 **Location:** 0.5 mi e of jct US 27 on SR 50, just n on Citrus Tower Blvd. **Facility:** 85 units, some two bedrooms. 3 stories, interior corridors. **Terms:** check-in 4 pm. **Pool:** outdoor. **Activities:** hot tub, exercise room. **Guest Services:** coin laundry. **Featured Amenity: breakfast buffet.**

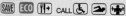

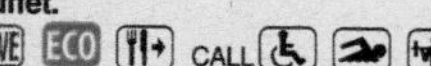

BIZ HS / SOME UNITS

HAMPTON INN & SUITES CLERMONT 352/536-6600

SAVE Hotel. **Address:** 2200 E SR 50 34711

AAA Benefit: Members save 5% or more!

HOME2 SUITES BY HILTON, CLERMONT, FL 352/227-2900

SAVE Extended Stay Hotel. **Address:** 1450 Champions Way 34711

AAA Benefit: Members save 5% or more!

SUMMER BAY ORLANDO BY EXPLORIA RESORTS 352/242-1100 (78)

Vacation Rental Condominium. **Address:** 17805 US Hwy 192 34714

WHERE TO EAT

CRISPERS 352/243-5111

Sandwiches Soup. Quick Serve. **Address:** 1754 E Hwy 50 34711

LEGENDS GRILLE & TAVERN 352/243-1118

Sandwiches. Casual Dining. **Address:** 1700 Legendary Blvd 34711

SAN JOSE'S ORIGINAL MEXICAN RESTAURANT 352/536-2006

Mexican. Casual Dining. **Address:** 4315 S Hwy 27, Suite A-1 34711

SONNY'S REAL PIT BAR-B-Q 352/243-6422

Barbecue. Casual Dining. **Address:** 1500 E Hwy 50 34711

COCOA (G-5) pop. 17,140, elev. 25'

- **Hotels & Restaurants map & index p. 50**

Cocoa's first families arrived at this site along the Indian River in 1860, and the town was platted beginning in 1882. Although there are differing accounts of the name's origin, records show that Cocoa was selected in the 1880s when the town's original name, Indian River City, was deemed by postal authorities to be too long for a postmark.

Throughout its early history, Cocoa experienced periodic growth spurts interrupted by such reversals as a catastrophic fire, a freeze that damaged the area's citrus crops and the Great Depression. The town's prospects improved considerably in the latter half of the 20th century thanks to its proximity to the Kennedy Space Center *(see place listing p. 105)*.

The Brevard Museum of History and Natural Science, 2201 Michigan Ave., offers local history exhibits as well as a hands-on display of Ice Age mammals and fossils; phone (321) 632-1830. The museum's grounds include a 22-acre nature preserve with trails.

Cocoa Beach Regional Chamber of Commerce—Cocoa: 400 Fortenberry Rd., Merritt Island, FL 32952. **Phone:** (321) 459-2200.

EASTERN FLORIDA STATE COLLEGE PLANETARIUM & OBSERVATORY is 2.5 mi. e. of I-95 exit 201 on SR 520, then 1.75 mi. n. on SR 501 to 1519 Clearlake Rd. The planetarium is in Building 19 at the back of the Eastern Florida State College

(See map & index p. 50.)

campus. Visitors can look through a 24-inch telescope at the observatory to see objects in the solar system. The Science Quest Demonstration Hall features hands-on space science exhibits. The planetarium gallery displays changing art exhibits. Other options include planetarium shows, large-format films in the Iwerks Discovery Theatre and laser shows.

Hours: Planetarium shows Wed. at 2, Fri.-Sat. at 7. Large-format films Wed. at 3:15, Fri.-Sat. at 8:15 p.m. Laser show Fri.-Sat. at 9 p.m. Exhibit hall Wed. 1:30-4:30, Fri.-Sat. 6:30-10:30 p.m. Observatory telescope Fri.-Sat. dusk-10 p.m. (weather permitting). Phone ahead to confirm schedule. **Cost:** Film, planetarium or laser show $8; $7 (ages 55+ and students and military with ID); $5 (ages 0-12). Rooftop observatory and exhibit halls free. **Phone:** (321) 433-7373 for recorded show information or (321) 433-7372.

BEST WESTERN COCOA INN 321/632-1065 (22)

Hotel

AAA Benefit: Members save up to 15% and earn bonus points!

Address: 4225 W King St 32926 **Location:** I-95 exit 201 (SR 520), just e. **Facility:** 120 units. 2 stories (no elevator), exterior corridors. **Amenities:** safes. **Pool:** outdoor. **Activities:** exercise room. **Guest Services:** valet and coin laundry. **Featured Amenity: full hot breakfast.**

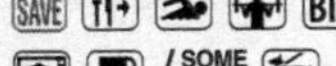

/ SOME UNITS

HOLIDAY INN EXPRESS HOTEL & SUITES COCOA 321/635-9975 (23)

Hotel. **Address:** 301 Tucker Ln 32926

WHERE TO EAT

CAFE MARGAUX 321/639-8343 (15)

European. Fine Dining. **Address:** 220 Brevard Ave 32922

THE TULIP RESTAURANT & LOUNGE 321/631-1133 (14)

Continental. Fine Dining. **Address:** 207 Brevard Ave 32922

COCOA BEACH (G-6) pop. 11,231, elev. 12'

• Hotels p. 52 • Restaurants p. 53
• Hotels & Restaurants map & index p. 50

Long a popular spot with locals, Cocoa Beach also is known for its location at the heart of the Space Coast. Cocoa Beach Pier extends 800 feet into the Atlantic, affording opportunities for fishing, surfing, dining and dancing.

Florida's Space Coast Office of Tourism—Cocoa Beach: 430 Brevard Ave., Suite 150, Cocoa, FL 32922. **Phone:** (321) 433-4470 or (877) 572-3224.

Shopping: When in Cocoa Beach, a stop at Ron Jon Surf Shop, 4151 N. Atlantic Ave., is definitely a requirement. From bikinis, beach toys and boards to sandals, sunscreen and tiki décor, this multilevel megastore of surf holds everything you need for the beach and the beach lifestyle. Even non-surfers won't feel out of place here, and no one should leave without picking up the ultimate Cocoa Beach souvenir: a Ron Jon T-shirt. Phone (321) 799-8888.

How about a saber cat fossil or a dinosaur egg as a souvenir? While a shop that specializes in dinosaur paraphernalia isn't the first thing you'd expect to find by the beach, The Dinosaur Store, 250 W. Cocoa Beach Cswy., is a happy surprise (unless you have ornithoscelidaphobia, i.e., a fear of dinosaurs). Dig into the assortment of dinosaur-related merchandise, which includes everything from fossils and shark-tooth necklaces to toy triceratops and museum-quality pieces; phone (321) 783-7300.

Nightlife: After a long, hot day in the sun, nothing quenches a thirst like an ice-cold mug of suds. There's plenty of beer to be had in Cocoa Beach, and what better place to get one than an air-conditioned Irish pub? Paddy Cassidy's Irish Pub, 2009 N. Atlantic Ave., and Nolan's Irish Pub, 204 W. Cocoa Beach Cswy., are both laid-back establishments with inviting Irish interiors and welcoming bartenders; phone (321) 783-0810 or (321) 783-8499, respectively.

Local favorite Cocoa Beach Brewing Company, 150 N. Atlantic Ave., is a nanobrewery that sits inside what could be your neighbor's house, except for the glowing neon sign in the window that says "OPEN." Join the off-duty rocket scientists who frequent the place and sip one of the pub's homemade brews in the living room, kitchen or backyard patio; phone (321) 613-2941.

If a dark jazz club featuring talented local performers is what you have in mind, Heidi's Jazz Club, 7 N. Orlando Ave., fits the bill perfectly; phone (321) 783-4559. Get set for guffaws, chuckles and belly laughs at Gregory's Upstairs Comedy Club, 900 N. Atlantic Ave. Nationally known comics take the stage every Thursday through Saturday at 9 p.m. and patrons can indulge in a full or bar menu; phone (321) 799-2557.

Step out of the hot sand and amble along the Cocoa Beach Pier until you reach the Rikki Tiki Tavern at the very end. Order a hurricane (not the real kind) or just name your poison, then kick back and enjoy the salty air, ocean breezes and tiki bar ambience; phone (321) 783-7549.

Rest assured: AAA.com/travelguides/hotels

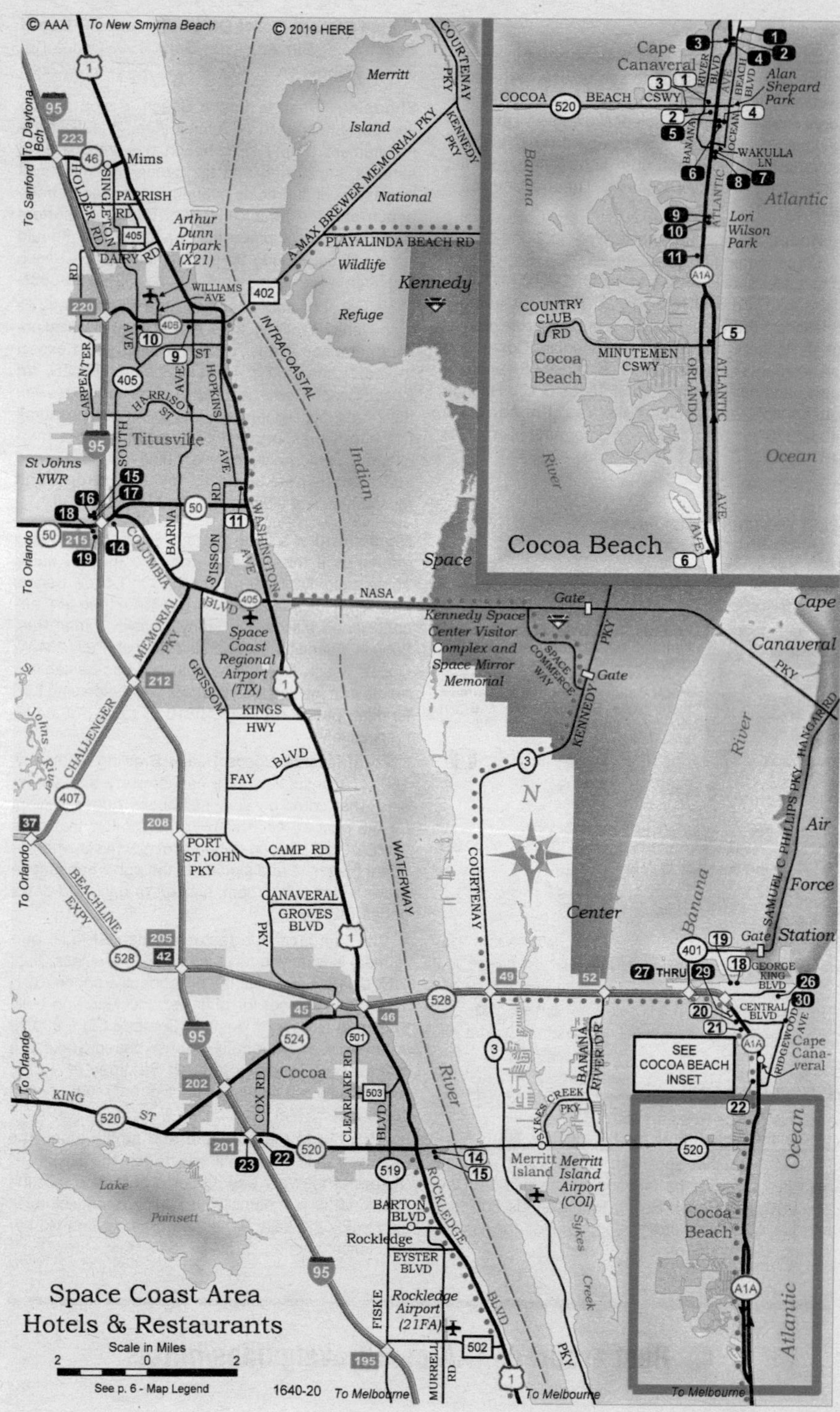
© AAA
© 2019 HERE
To New Smyrna Beach
Merritt Island National Wildlife Refuge
Kennedy Space Center
Cocoa Beach
Cape Canaveral
Alan Shepard Park
Lori Wilson Park
Atlantic Ocean
Banana River
Indian River
Titusville
Mims
Cocoa
Rockledge
Merritt Island
St Johns NWR
Arthur Dunn Airpark (X21)
Space Coast Regional Airport (TIX)
Kennedy Space Center Visitor Complex and Space Mirror Memorial
Merritt Island Airport (COI)
Rockledge Airport (21FA)
Cape Canaveral Air Force Station
SEE COCOA BEACH INSET
Space Coast Area
Hotels & Restaurants
Scale in Miles
See p. 6 - Map Legend
1640-20
To Melbourne
To Orlando
To Sanford
To Daytona Bch
Lake Poinsett

Space Coast

This index helps you "spot" where approved hotels and restaurants are located on the corresponding detailed maps. Restaurant price range is a combination of lunch and/or dinner. Turn to the listing page for more information and consult display ads for special promotions.

For more details, rates and reservations: AAA.com/travelguides/hotels

COCOA BEACH

Map Page	Hotels	Diamond Rated	Member Savings	Page
1 p. 50	Discovery Beach Resort	◆◆◆		52
2 p. 50	**Best Western Cocoa Beach Hotel & Suites**	◆◆	✔	52
3 p. 50	Holiday Inn Express Hotel & Suites-Cocoa Beach	◆◆◆		53
4 p. 50	Days Inn Cocoa Beach-Port Canaveral	◆◆		52
5 p. 50	Four Points by Sheraton-Cocoa Beach	◆◆◆	✔	52
6 p. 50	**Quality Inn & Suites Port Canaveral Area**	◆◆	✔	53
7 p. 50	**Courtyard by Marriott Cocoa Beach-Port Canaveral**	◆◆◆	✔	52
8 p. 50	**Hampton Inn Cocoa Beach/Cape Canaveral**	◆◆◆	✔	52
9 p. 50	The Resort On Cocoa Beach	◆◆◆		53
10 p. 50	**Hilton Cocoa Beach Oceanfront**	◆◆◆	✔	52
11 p. 50	**La Quinta Inn Cocoa Beach-Port Canaveral**	◆◆	✔	53

Map Page	Restaurants	Diamond Rated	Cuisine	Price Range	Page
1 p. 50	Old Fish House Restaurant	◆◆	Seafood	$8-$36	53
2 p. 50	Nolan's Irish Pub	◆◆	Irish	$7-$11	53
3 p. 50	Sunset Waterfront Bar and Grill	◆◆	Seafood	$10-$30	53
4 p. 50	Shark Pit Bar & Grill	◆◆	American	$8-$30	53
5 p. 50	Yen Yen Chinese Restaurant	◆◆	Chinese	$8-$27	53
6 p. 50	Squid Lips Overwater Grill	◆◆	Seafood	$8-$27	53

TITUSVILLE

Map Page	Hotels	Diamond Rated	Member Savings	Page
14 p. 50	**Best Western Space Shuttle Inn**	◆◆	✔	364
15 p. 50	**Fairfield Inn & Suites by Marriott-Titusville/ Kennedy Space Center**	◆◆◆	✔	364
16 p. 50	Hampton Inn Titusville/I-95 Kennedy Space Center	◆◆◆	✔	364
17 p. 50	Holiday Inn Titusville-Kennedy Space Center	◆◆◆		364
18 p. 50	Days Inn Titusville Kennedy Space Center	◆◆		364
19 p. 50	TownePlace Suites by Marriott Kennedy Space Center	◆◆◆	✔	364

Map Page	Restaurants	Diamond Rated	Cuisine	Price Range	Page
9 p. 50	Dixie Crossroads Seafood Restaurant	◆◆	American	$9-$46	364
10 p. 50	Kelsey's Pizzeria Eatery	◆◆	Italian Pizza	$4-$22	364
11 p. 50	el Leoncito Mexican & Cuban Restaurant	◆◆	Mexican	$6-$15	364

COCOA

Map Page	Hotels	Diamond Rated	Member Savings	Page
22 p. 50	**Best Western Cocoa Inn**	◆◆	✔	49
23 p. 50	Holiday Inn Express Hotel & Suites Cocoa	◆◆◆		49

Map Page	Restaurants	Diamond Rated	Cuisine	Price Range	Page
14 p. 50	The Tulip Restaurant & Lounge	◆◆◆	Continental	$15-$29	49

Map Page	Restaurants (cont'd)	Diamond Rated	Cuisine	Price Range	Page
15 p. 50	Cafe Margaux	◆◆◆	European	$24-$185	49

CAPE CANAVERAL

Map Page	Hotels	Diamond Rated	Member Savings	Page
26 p. 50	**Holiday Inn Club Vacations Cape Canaveral Beach Resort**	◆◆◆	✔	37
27 p. 50	**Country Inn & Suites by Radisson-Port Canaveral**	◆◆◆	✔	37
28 p. 50	**Homewood Suites by Hilton Cape Canaveral-Cocoa Beach**	◆◆◆	✔	37
29 p. 50	Residence Inn by Marriott Cape Canaveral/Cocoa Beach	◆◆◆	✔	37
30 p. 50	Royal Mansions Oceanfront Condominium Resort	◆◆		37

Map Page	Restaurants	Diamond Rated	Cuisine	Price Range	Page
18 p. 50	Grills Waterfront Seafood Deck & Tiki Bar	◆◆	Seafood	$11-$34	38
19 p. 50	Fishlips	◆◆	Seafood	$10-$24	38
20 p. 50	Zachary's Restaurant	◆◆	Greek	$6-$20	38
21 p. 50	Kelsey's Restaurant & Pizzeria	◆◆	Italian Pizza	$10-$22	38
22 p. 50	Sage Bistro	◆◆◆	Continental	$18-$32	38

BEST WESTERN COCOA BEACH HOTEL & SUITES
321/783-7621 **2**

AAA Benefit: Members save up to 15% and earn bonus points!

Address: 5600 N Atlantic Ave 32931 **Location:** SR A1A (Atlantic Ave), 0.8 mi n of jct SR 520. **Facility:** 229 units, some efficiencies and kitchens. 2-7 stories, interior/exterior corridors. **Terms:** check-in 4 pm. **Pool:** heated outdoor. **Activities:** beach access, picnic facilities, exercise room. **Guest Services:** coin laundry. **Featured Amenity: breakfast buffet.**

/ SOME UNITS

COURTYARD BY MARRIOTT COCOA BEACH-PORT CANAVERAL
321/784-4800 **7**

COURTYARD **AAA Benefit:** Members save 5% or more!

Address: 3435 N Atlantic Ave 32931 **Location:** SR A1A (Atlantic Ave), 0.5 mi s of jct SR 520. **Facility:** 156 units. 4-7 stories, interior corridors. **Parking:** on-site (fee). **Terms:** check-in 4 pm. **Pool:** heated outdoor. **Activities:** hot tub, exercise room. **Guest Services:** valet and coin laundry, boarding pass kiosk.

DAYS INN COCOA BEACH-PORT CANAVERAL
321/784-2550 **4**

◆◆ Motel. **Address:** 5500 N Atlantic Ave 32931

DISCOVERY BEACH RESORT 321/868-7777 **1**

◆◆◆ Resort Hotel. **Address:** 300 Barlow Ave 32931

FOUR POINTS BY SHERATON-COCOA BEACH
321/783-8717 **5**

◆◆◆ SAVE Hotel. **Address:** 4001 N Atlantic Ave 32931

AAA Benefit: Members save 5% or more!

HAMPTON INN COCOA BEACH/CAPE CANAVERAL
321/799-4099 **8**

AAA Benefit: Members save 5% or more!

Address: 3425 N Atlantic Ave 32931 **Location:** SR A1A (Atlantic Ave), 0.5 mi s of jct SR 520. **Facility:** 150 units. 8 stories, interior/exterior corridors. **Terms:** check-in 4 pm. **Pool:** heated outdoor. **Activities:** beach access, exercise room. **Guest Services:** valet and coin laundry. **Featured Amenity: breakfast buffet.**

HILTON COCOA BEACH OCEANFRONT
321/799-0003 **10**

◆◆◆ Resort Hotel

AAA Benefit: Members save 5% or more!

Address: 1550 N Atlantic Ave 32931 **Location:** Oceanfront. SR A1A (Atlantic Ave), 1.5 mi s of jct SR 520. **Facility:** Welcoming rooms are comfortably designed with dark wood tones, marble accents, upscale bedding and plenty of space to move around. Many of the rooms feature ocean views, but none have a balcony. 295 units. 7 stories, interior corridors. **Parking:** on-site (fee) and valet. **Terms:** check-in 4 pm. **Amenities:** safes. **Dining:** 3 restaurants. **Pool:** heated outdoor. **Activities:** recreation programs, bicycles, exercise room. **Guest Services:** valet and coin laundry.

HOLIDAY INN EXPRESS HOTEL & SUITES-COCOA BEACH 321/868-2525 3

Hotel. **Address:** 5575 N Atlantic Ave 32931

LA QUINTA INN COCOA BEACH-PORT CANAVERAL 321/783-2252 11

Hotel

Address: 1275 N Atlantic Ave 32931 **Location:** SR A1A (Atlantic Ave), 1.7 mi s of SR 520. **Facility:** 127 units. 2 stories (no elevator), exterior corridors. **Terms:** check-in 4 pm. **Dining:** 2 restaurants. **Pool:** heated outdoor. **Activities:** beach access. **Guest Services:** coin laundry. **Featured Amenity: breakfast buffet.**

SAVE CALL / SOME UNITS

QUALITY INN & SUITES PORT CANAVERAL AREA 321/783-2221 6

Hotel

Address: 3901 N Atlantic Ave 32931 **Location:** On SR A1A (Atlantic Ave), 0.3 mi s of jct SR 520. **Facility:** 170 units, some efficiencies. 1-6 stories, exterior corridors. **Terms:** check-in 4 pm. **Amenities:** safes. **Pool:** heated outdoor. **Activities:** hot tub, beach access, playground, game room, lawn sports, exercise room. **Guest Services:** coin laundry. **Featured Amenity: continental breakfast.**

SAVE BIZ HS / SOME UNITS

THE RESORT ON COCOA BEACH 321/783-4000 9

Resort Condominium. **Address:** 1600 N Atlantic Ave 32931

WHERE TO EAT

NOLAN'S IRISH PUB 321/783-8499 2

Irish. Casual Dining. **Address:** 204 Cocoa Beach Cswy 32931

OLD FISH HOUSE RESTAURANT 321/799-9190 1

Seafood. Casual Dining. **Address:** 249 W Cocoa Beach Cswy 32931

SHARK PIT BAR & GRILL 321/868-8952 4

American. Casual Dining. **Address:** 4001 N Atlantic Ave 32931

SQUID LIPS OVERWATER GRILL 321/783-1350 6

Seafood. Casual Dining. **Address:** 2200 S Orlando Ave 32931

SUNSET WATERFRONT BAR AND GRILL 321/783-8485 3

Seafood. Casual Dining. **Address:** 500 W Cocoa Beach Cswy 32931

YEN YEN CHINESE RESTAURANT 321/783-9512 5

Chinese. Casual Dining. **Address:** 2 N Atlantic Ave 32931

CRESCENT BEACH pop. 931

• **Hotels & Restaurants map & index p. 266**

SOUTH BEACH GRILL 904/471-8700 17

International. Casual Dining. **Address:** 45 Cubbedge Rd 32080

CRYSTAL RIVER (F-1) pop. 3,108, elev. 4'

Crystal River denotes both a town and the river that runs through it into Kings Bay. The waters accommodate anglers and scuba divers.

The Citrus County Visitors & Convention Bureau: 915 N. Suncoast Blvd., Crystal River, FL 34429. **Phone:** (352) 794-5506 or (800) 587-6667.

BEST WESTERN CRYSTAL RIVER RESORT 352/795-3171

Motel

AAA Benefit: Members save up to 15% and earn bonus points!

Address: 614 NW Hwy 19 34428 **Location:** Waterfront. On US 19/98, 0.8 mi n of jct SR 44. **Facility:** 114 units, some efficiencies. 2 stories (no elevator), exterior corridors. **Terms:** check-in 4 pm. **Amenities:** safes. **Pool:** heated outdoor. **Activities:** hot tub, boat dock, fishing, scuba diving, snorkeling, picnic facilities. **Guest Services:** coin laundry. **Featured Amenity: breakfast buffet.**

SAVE BIZ HS / SOME UNITS

HAMPTON INN BY HILTON CRYSTAL RIVER 352/564-6464

Hotel

AAA Benefit: Members save 5% or more!

Address: 1103 N Suncoast Blvd 34429 **Location:** On US 19/98, just s of jct Fort Island Tr/SE 8th Ave. **Facility:** 68 units. 3 stories, interior corridors. **Pool:** heated outdoor. **Activities:** exercise room. **Guest Services:** valet and coin laundry. **Featured Amenity: breakfast buffet.**

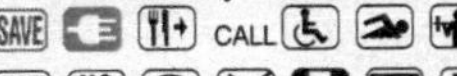

SAVE CALL

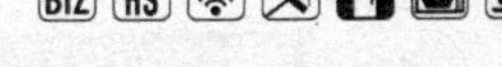

BIZ HS

HOLIDAY INN EXPRESS CRYSTAL RIVER 352/563-1111

Hotel

Address: 1203 NE 5th St 34429 **Location:** On SR 44, 0.9 mi ne of jct US 19. **Facility:** 75 units, some two bedrooms. 4 stories, interior corridors. **Pool:** heated outdoor. **Activities:** exercise room. **Guest Services:** valet and coin laundry. **Featured Amenity: full hot breakfast.**

SAVE CALL BIZ HS

WHERE TO EAT

CHARLIE'S FISH HOUSE 352/795-3949

Seafood. Casual Dining. **Address:** 224 US 19 NW 34228

CLAWDADDY'S RAW BAR & GRILL 352/564-2529

Seafood. Casual Dining. **Address:** 1601 SE N Suncoast Blvd 34428

CODY'S ORIGINAL ROADHOUSE 352/795-7223

American. Casual Dining. **Address:** 305 SE US 19 N 34429

THE CRAB PLANT 352/795-4700

Seafood. Casual Dining. **Address:** 201 NW 5th St 34428

VINTAGE ON 5TH 352/794-0004

Southern. Casual Dining. **Address:** 114 NE 5th St 34429

DADE CITY (G-2) pop. 6,437, elev. 89'

• Part of Tampa area — see map p. 313

Originally settled as Fort Dade in the 1840s, the settlement's name was changed to Dade City in 1884. Historic Church Avenue, the restored Old Courthouse, antiques shops, and a lively calendar of events add to the community's quaint atmosphere.

Greater Dade City Chamber of Commerce: 14112 8th St., Dade City, FL 33525. **Phone:** (352) 567-3769.

PIONEER FLORIDA MUSEUM AND VILLAGE is 1.5 mi. n. via US 301, then e. to 15602 Pioneer Museum Rd. Highlights include a one-room pioneer schoolhouse, the 1860s John Overstreet House, Enterprise Methodist Church, an 1896 depot with a 1913 Porter steam engine, sawmill buildings, a general store, and a moonshine still. The museum also displays early farm machinery, vintage carriages, Roseville pottery, textiles, and antique toys and dolls. **Time:** Allow 2 hours minimum. **Hours:** Tues.-Sat. 10-5. Closed major holidays. **Cost:** $8; $6 (ages 55+); $4 (ages 6-18 and students with ID); free (ages 0-5 and active military with ID). **Phone:** (352) 567-0262.

HAMPTON INN DADE CITY/ZEPHYRHILLS 352/567-5277

Hotel. **Address:** 13215 US Hwy 301 33525

AAA Benefit: Members save 5% or more!

WHERE TO EAT

ABC PIZZA 352/567-1414

Italian. Casual Dining. **Address:** 37941 Heather Pl 33525

A MATTER OF TASTE CAFE 352/567-5100

American. Casual Dining. **Address:** 14121 7th St 33525

ANGEL TEA ROOM & HEAVENLY TREASURES GIFT SHOP 352/518-5683

Sandwiches Coffee/Tea. Casual Dining. **Address:** 37847 Meridian Ave 33525

KAFE KOKOPELLI 352/523-0055

Steak Seafood. Casual Dining. **Address:** 37940 Live Oak Ave 33523

LITTLE MEXICO RESTAURANT 352/521-5675

Mexican. Casual Dining. **Address:** 14314 7th Ave 33523

LUNCH ON LIMOGES 352/567-5685

Sandwiches. Casual Dining. **Address:** 14139 7th St 33525

DAVENPORT (G-4) pop. 2,888, elev. 138'

• Hotels & Restaurants map & index p. 197, 202
• Part of Orlando area — see map p. 2

Off I-4, the community serves as a convenient gateway to Lake Buena Vista and Walt Disney World® Resort. The mixed-use Posner Park, 1300 Posner Blvd., contains Cinépolis Polk Co. IMAX theater and a handful of chain retailers like JC Penney, Kay Jewelers and Target.

Central Florida's Visitor Information Center: 101 Adventure Ct., Davenport, FL 33837. **Phone:** (863) 420-2586 or (800) 828-7655.

BAHAMA BAY RESORT & SPA 863/547-1200 127

Vacation Rental Condominium

Address: 400 Gran Bahama Blvd 33897 **Location:** Jct US 27, just n on Florence Villa Grove Rd. **Facility:** Located in a gated community on 70 tropical acres with a lake, the resort's spacious two and three-bedroom units feel like home. Each has a living room, dining room and a washer and dryer. 498 condominiums. 1-3 stories (no elevator), exterior corridors. **Terms:** check-in 4 pm. **Amenities:** safes. **Dining:** 2 restaurants. **Pool:** heated outdoor. **Activities:** sauna, hot tub, fishing, tennis, playground, game room, picnic facilities, exercise room, spa. **Guest Services:** complimentary laundry. *(See ad p. 108.)*

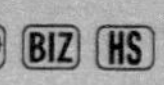

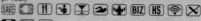

HAMPTON INN DAVENPORT MAINGATE SOUTH 863/420-9898

Hotel. **Address:** 44117 US 27 33897

AAA Benefit: Members save 5% or more!

HOLIDAY INN CLUB VACATIONS ORLANDO BREEZE RESORT 863/420-3838 126

Hotel

Address: 100 Orlando Breeze Cir 33897 **Location:** 0.5 mi s of US 192. **Facility:** 64 kitchen units, some two and three bedrooms. 2 stories, exterior corridors. **Terms:** check-in 4 pm. **Amenities:** video games. **Pool:** heated outdoor. **Activities:** hot tub, miniature golf, recreation programs, game room, exercise room.

HOLIDAY INN EXPRESS & SUITES ORLANDO SOUTH DAVENPORT 863/420-6611

Hotel. **Address:** 4050 Hotel Dr 33897

WHERE TO EAT

DIROMIO'S PIZZA & GRILL 863/420-2001 73

Italian. Casual Dining. **Address:** 101 Divine Dr 33897

GRAND CHINA BUFFET 863/420-2064

Chinese. Quick Serve. **Address:** 43554 N US 27 33837

MIA PIZZA PASTA KITCHEN 863/420-3336 16

Pizza. Quick Serve. **Address:** 2440 Sand Mine Rd 33897

OVATION BISTRO & BAR 863/354-6967

American. Casual Dining. **Address:** 42605 Hwy 27 33837

ZEN ASIAN GRILL 863/420-9958

Asian. Casual Dining. **Address:** 4812 Grandview Pkwy 33837

DAYTONA BEACH (C-10) pop. 61,005, elev. 10'

• Hotels p. 61 • Restaurants p. 65
• Hotels & Restaurants map & index p. 58

Daytona Beach has been a popular family vacation destination for more than a century. But it was

(See map & index p. 58.)

more speedway than beach in the early days of the automobile. Between 1903 and 1935 some 15 speed records were set on the beach racecourse by Barney Oldfield, Sir Henry Segrave and Sir Malcolm Campbell. The racing tradition continues at Daytona International Speedway *(see attraction listing p. 57)*.

During the day cars may be driven on designated sections of the 23 miles of the hard-packed sand. For safety, beach driving should be done during a low or outgoing tide and never in the water, however shallow. The speed limit on the beach is 10 miles per hour. Drivers should heed all signs, including those indicating conservation areas, where vehicles are prohibited. Overnight parking or camping on the beach is not permitted. Pets are not permitted; this law is strictly enforced.

The beach is not open to motor vehicles between Seabreeze and International Speedway boulevards; south of Emelia Avenue in Daytona Beach Shores to Beach Street in Ponce Inlet; at Lighthouse Point Park in Ponce Inlet; between Millsap Avenue and Andy Romano Park; or north of Granada Boulevard in Ormond Beach. A daily beach access toll of $10 per vehicle; tollbooths are at each approach. For beach information phone (386) 239-7873.

A wide promenade along the ocean is the center of an amusement area anchored on the south by the Daytona Beach Pier. The Daytona Beach Bandshell at the north end of the promenade is the setting for concerts and events, and an entertainment complex provides dining and shopping options.

A scenic portion of SR A1A extends along the ocean from Ormond Beach north to Fernandina Beach, a distance of 110 miles.

Ocean lovers enjoy sailing, surfing and riding personal watercraft; the Halifax River is a favorite for scenic boat tours as well as boating, fishing, kayaking and sailboarding.

Mary McLeod Bethune founded Bethune-Cookman University for the training of African-American women in 1904; it later became an accredited coed college. The campus, off International Speedway Boulevard, includes Bethune's home and gravesite, early buildings and the Dr. Mary McLeod Bethune Performing Arts Center.

Daytona Beach Area Convention and Visitors Bureau: 126 E. Orange Ave., Daytona Beach, FL 32114. **Phone:** (386) 255-0415 or (800) 854-1234.

Shopping: T-shirts, swimsuits, surfboards and...leather jackets? Yes, the amount and variety of shopping options impress in Daytona Beach, which welcomes beachgoers, bikers, deal seekers and window shoppers alike. Most of the well-known retailers are located by International Speedway Boulevard and LPGA Boulevard, while you'll find the most boutiques, souvenirs and biker gear around Beach Street, Main Street and beachside along Atlantic Avenue (SR A1A). Flea markets, an outlet mall and bargain shops are scattered between I-95 and Beach Street.

If you're here for NASCAR, you can't miss The Pit Shop, 1801 W. International Speedway Blvd., at Daytona International Speedway *(see attraction listing)*, one of the city's most well-known destinations. Stock car fans can buy merchandise featuring their favorite drivers on apparel, mugs and towels. Don't have room in your suitcase for all the die-cast miniature cars? They also ship.

Facing the grandstands on the track is One Daytona, at 1 Daytona Blvd., which attracts visitors not only for convenience but also for its range of shops, local restaurants and entertainment. Things to see include Victory Circle and stores featuring popular brands such as Bass Pro Shops, Guitar Center, IT'SUGAR and Sunglass World.

A number of other large shopping centers present apparel, décor and gifts from national brands. Tomoka Town Center, 1401 Cornerstone Blvd., is the city's latest retail complex with Burlington Stores, Ross Dress for Less, Hobby Lobby and a 15,000-square-foot Barnes & Noble, which includes a book theater, kids section and seating areas; phone (386) 281-4960. Volusia Mall, 1700 W. International Speedway Blvd., offers anchors such as Dillard's, JCPenney and Macy's as well as 120 other services and stores, including American Eagle Outfitters, PacSun and Victoria's Secret; phone (386) 253-6783.

Tanger Outlets Daytona Beach, 1100 Cornerstone Blvd., offers deals on designer brands. Among the 60 outlet stores are Carter's Babies and Kids, J. Crew, Nike Factory Store and Under Armour. Phone (386) 843-7459.

The Daytona Beach Downtown Farmers Market, off Magnolia Avenue and adjacent to Jackie Robinson Ballpark at City Island, runs 7 to 1 each Saturday morning. Bring your pet—it's pet-friendly—to keep you company as you shop for fresh produce, desserts and artisanal goods. Phone (386) 671-3272.

Riverfront Shops of Daytona Beach, a collection of retailers between Bay Street and Orange Avenue, is the place to admire antiques and objets d'art. Ask the proprietors of Arlequin Antiques, 122 S. Beach St., about their collection of Art Deco jewelry and European antiques; phone (386) 252-6531. Browse the stacks (and greet the resident feline) at Abraxas Books, 256 S. Beach St., where there is everything from secondhand paperbacks to rare books; phone (386) 307-6478. For a fun thing for couples to do, visit Angell & Phelps Chocolate Factory *(see attraction listing p. 57)* to go on a free tour and shop for sweets (the chocolate is made on-site) at 154 S. Beach St. The fudge and chocolate-covered potato chips are what to buy; phone (386) 252-6531.

Across town—and open Friday through Sunday—is the well-known Daytona Flea & Farmers Market, adjacent to I-95 and US 92 at 1425 Tomoka Farms Rd. With a majority of the registered 650 vendors inside or under a roof, the market's a great

(See map & index p. 58.)

place to go if it's raining or you're looking for indoor things to do this weekend. There's everything from collectibles to souvenirs. If you didn't already pack something to nibble on at the beach, check out the available produce, snacks and refreshments. Phone (386) 253-3330.

Beachwear and souvenir shops line North Atlantic Avenue (SR A1A). Open since 1989, Maui Nix Surf Shop might be Daytona's most quintessential place to go for swimsuits, hats and surfing accessories. If you're missing anything for your day at the beach, you'll find it at one of the retailer's three locations: in the Ocean Walk Shoppes, at 250 N. Atlantic Ave.; inside Volusia Mall, at 1700 W. International Speedway Blvd.; or the original site at 635 N. Atlantic Ave.; phone (386) 253-1234. Sand Box Beachwear, another longtime beach shop at 1340 S. Atlantic Ave., also provides bathing suits and beach gear; phone (386) 252-6676.

Nestled among the bars and nightclubs along Seabreeze Boulevard is the legendary Sussman's (303 Seabeeze Blvd.), which has been offering fashion expertise since 1929. This is where to buy cocktail dresses, sportswear and high-end accessories; phone (386) 212-9614.

Be sure to check out a large collection of the latest albums as well as classic vinyl records at Atlantic Sounds, 138 W. International Blvd. In business since 1982, the independent record store is part shop and part community gathering space. Phone (386) 258-1420.

If you're a motorcyclist looking for where to go in Daytona Beach, you'll want to head toward Main Street at the junction of Halifax and Ocean avenues. In addition to the legendary biker bars in Daytona Beach, there is a mix of shops ranging from leather goods to motorcycle parts. One of the best known might be Hot Leathers, 801 Main St., which sells leather belts, jackets and tank tops year-round; phone (386) 238-1048. During Bike Week and Biketoberfest, score some Daytona Beach souvenirs at pop-up stores along Main Street and North Atlantic Avenue.

Nightlife: Ready to turn your day at the beach into a night on the town? Daytona Beach has a lot to offer, and you might be surprised to learn that there are more than just beachside bars where you can walk in wearing little more than flip-flops and cutoffs. There are beachside bars aplenty, but you'll also find pubs, clubs, discos and other venues offering a selection of music from rock to reggae, blues to jazz, and country to classical. No matter what your musical taste is, you're sure to find a spot in Daytona Beach to satisfy it and keep the beach party spirit going well into the night.

If your idea of beach music is the Beach Boys, pay no attention to this paragraph. However, if Led Zeppelin and AC/DC cover bands are more your style, then join the party at one of the many biker bars that call Main Street home. Daytona is world-renowned for its annual celebration of motorcycles; bikers gather in March for Bike Week and in October for Biketoberfest. Main Street is where they rally for raucous partying both night and day. Sandwiched between the Halifax River and the Atlantic Ocean, the area could be considered biker heaven; bars are tucked in among shops selling leather attire, motorcycles and bike parts. The Bank & Blues Club, 701 Main St., hosts live blues and rock bands in a 1920s bank and has the original brick walls and stained glass; the vault now keeps the beer and wine safe. Across the street from a cemetery, Boot Hill Saloon, 310 Main St., is quasi-legendary among the biker set; its slogan is "You're better off here than across the street." Be careful, though; the live rock music is loud enough to wake the dead. Memorabilia covers every surface, and bras hang from the ceiling; it's a tradition for women to leave one behind. For more ice-cold brews, deafening rock music and good times, check out Dirty Harry's, 705 Main St.; Froggy's Saloon, 800 Main St.; and Full Moon Saloon, 700 Main St.

For those who like to dance more than they like to rock, there's plenty of room on the huge dance floor at Razzle's, 611 Seabreeze Blvd., along with 11 bars, pool tables, an upscale dress code and décor, and the Ultra Lounge, featuring VIP booths and bottle service. DJs spin techno, house, trance and hip-hop.

You'll pick up more mellow vibes at oceanfront watering holes. A favorite of locals and out-of-towners alike, The Ocean Deck Restaurant and Beach Club, 127 S. Ocean Ave., faces the Atlantic and is decked out in sea shanty décor with colorful marlins hanging from the ceiling and restrooms marked Gulls and Buoys. Sip a margarita and sway to live reggae music on the outdoor deck on sultry summer evenings.

Every town has at least one Irish pub, and Daytona Beach is no different. Tir Na Nog Irish Pub, 612 E. International Speedway Blvd., draws local artists, whose works hang on the wall, and local musicians, whom you can listen to nightly. Jovial bartenders will happily draw you a pint from the extensive beer list, as befits any Irish pub worth its shamrocks.

The restored Daytona Beach Bandshell, built in the 1930s by the Works Progress Administration, presents live music ranging from country, classical, blues and big band to rock, jazz and even military bands. Concerts are offered Friday and Saturday at 7 p.m., May through September. Friday concerts are $3; Saturday concerts are free and conclude with fireworks. Bring the kids, a picnic basket (no alcohol is allowed) and some folding chairs (chair rentals are available on site) for an old-fashioned, hand-clapping good time. The band shell is on the beach near Ocean Walk Shoppes, 250 N. Atlantic Ave., between Ora and Earl streets.

Daytona Beach is the last place you might expect to find live classical music, but orchestras from all over the world perform in this beachside town,

(See map & index p. 58.)

thanks to the Daytona Beach Symphony Society. Its chief venue is the Peabody Auditorium, 600 Auditorium Blvd., which has played host to the Boston Pops, the Czech Philharmonic and Itzhak Perlman; the season runs November through February.

ANGELL & PHELPS CHOCOLATE FACTORY TOUR, just s. of US 92 (International Speedway Blvd.) at 154 S. Beach St., offers tours of a working factory where visitors can watch handmade chocolates being created. Samples are given at the end of the tour. **Time:** Allow 30 minutes minimum. **Hours:** Tours depart on the hour Mon.-Sat. 10-11 and 1-4. **Cost:** Free. **Phone:** (386) 252-6531 or (800) 969-2634. GT

DAYTONA INTERNATIONAL SPEEDWAY is 1 mi. e. of I-95 exit 261 at 1801 W. International Speedway Blvd. NASCAR founder Bill France opened the tri-oval racetrack in 1959 with the inaugural Daytona 500 race. Every February the Daytona 500 thrills racing fans and is the culmination of Speedweeks, a series of sports- and stock-car races and test runs held throughout January and February. With at least eight major race weekends each year, the speedway's busy calendar includes the Rolex 24 At Daytona in late January, motorcycle events during Bike Week in March, Coke Zero 400 Powered By Coca-Cola in July, Fall Cycle Scene in October, and the Ferrari World Finals and karting events in December.

Daytona International Speedway features a 2.5-mile superspeedway and a 3.56-mile infield road course. When races are not scheduled, the 500-acre complex is used for vehicle testing and development, automobile-related shows and events, and the Richard Petty Driving Experience. The 30-minute Speedway Tour includes the infield, Gatorade Victory Lane, the start/finish line and Pit Road.

The 90-minute All-Access Tour includes everything from the 30-minute tour and adds entrance into the driver's meeting room and garages as well as an inside look at the renovated stadium. The 3-hour VIP Tour includes everything from the All-Access Tour plus a visit to the Archives and Research Center where guests can view photographs, trophies, memorabilia, a re-creation of Bill France Sr.'s office from the 1960s and Marvin Panch's 1961 DAYTONA 500 champion car. Entrance for grandstand viewing is through the ticket office lobby.

Hours: Guided All-Access Tours are given daily on the hour 10-3 (weather and track schedule permitting). Guided Speedway Tours are given daily at 11:30, 1:30, 3:30 and 4. All-Access Tours and Speedway Tours are available on a first-come, first-served basis. Ticket sales begin at 9. VIP Tours are given on some Tues., Thurs. and Sat. 1-4; reservations are recommended. Tours are not available on race days or during car shows. Closed Christmas. Phone ahead to confirm schedule. **Cost:** All-Access Tour $25; $19 (ages 6-12). Speedway Tour $18; $12 (ages 6-12). VIP Tour $52. Grandstand viewing free. **Phone:** (800) 748-7467 for race information and tickets or TTY (386) 681-6700. GT

HALIFAX HISTORICAL SOCIETY MUSEUM is 2 blks. s. of US 92 at 252 S. Beach St. Housed in the restored 1910 Merchants Bank building, the museum's displays of artifacts detail local history. Of special interest are Native American artifacts, a scale model of the 1938 boardwalk, a racing exhibit and the War Room. Grandma's Attic is an exhibit of vintage toys, children's clothing and memorabilia dating to the early 1900s. A 20-minute film covers 130,000 years of area history, from prehistoric times to the present.

Guided tours are available by appointment. **Time:** Allow 1 hour minimum. **Hours:** Tues.-Fri. 10:30-4:30, Sat. 10-4. **Cost:** Tues.-Wed. and Fri.-Sat. $7; $1 (ages 0-12); Thurs. by donation. **Phone:** (386) 255-6976. GT

MUSEUM OF ARTS & SCIENCES (MOAS) is at 352 S. Nova Rd. On a 90-acre nature preserve, this Smithsonian Institution affiliate museum features a wide range of permanent and changing exhibits. Included are African, early American, European, Chinese and Cuban fine art and furniture; and a 13-foot-tall skeleton of a giant ground sloth. The museum also includes a planetarium, environmental complex, nature trails, sculpture garden and children's science museum. Pieces once in storage, including European and American furniture, are showcased in the glass-fronted Helen B. Roberson Visible Storage Building.

The Root Family Museum pays homage to Americana with original railroad artifacts, two midcentury railcars, race cars, teddy bears, quilts and a large collection of Coca-Cola memorabilia. The Cici and Hyatt Brown Museum of Art displays 400 pieces from its permanent collection of more than 2,600 oil and watercolor paintings depicting historic Florida and has six galleries with changing exhibits.

Time: Allow 1 hour minimum. **Hours:** MOAS (including Cici and Hyatt Brown Museum) Mon.-Sat. 10-5, Sun. 11-5. Planetarium shows daily on the hour 1-4 (also Sun. at noon, Fri. at 5, and Sat. at 11, noon and 5). Closed Jan. 1, Thanksgiving, Christmas Eve and Christmas. **Cost:** MOAS (includes planetarium show) $12.95; $10.95 (ages 65+ and students with ID); $6.95 (ages 6-17). Cici and Hyatt Brown Museum of Art $10.95; $8.95 (ages 65+ and students with ID); $4.95 (ages 6-17). Planetarium show only $5; $3 (ages 0-17). Combination Ticket (MOAS, Cici and Hyatt Brown Museum and planetarium show): $18.95; $16.95 (ages 65+ and students with ID); $9.95 (ages 6-17). **Phone:** (386) 255-0285 or (866) 439-4769.

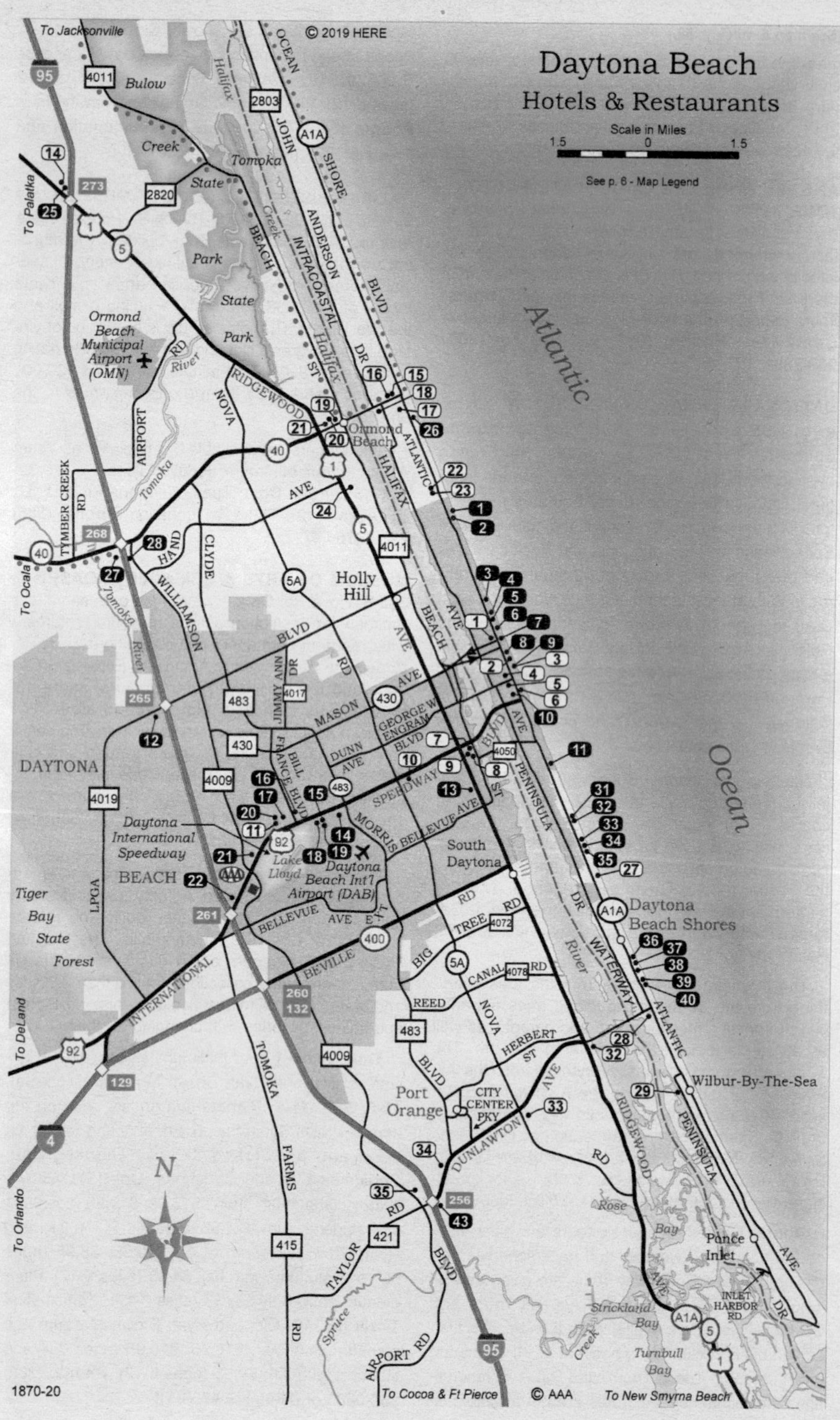
Daytona Beach
Hotels & Restaurants
Scale in Miles
1.5 0 1.5
See p. 6 - Map Legend
© 2019 HERE
Atlantic
Ocean
To Jacksonville
To Palatka
To Ocala
To DeLand
To Orlando
To Cocoa & Ft Pierce
To New Smyrna Beach
Bulow Creek State Park
Tomoka State Park
Ormond Beach Municipal Airport (OMN)
Ormond Beach
Holly Hill
DAYTONA BEACH
Daytona International Speedway
Daytona Beach Int'l Airport (DAB)
Lake Lloyd
South Daytona
Daytona Beach Shores
Wilbur-By-The-Sea
Port Orange
Ponce Inlet
Tiger Bay State Forest
Rose Bay
Strickland Bay
Turnbull Bay
N
© AAA

Airport Hotels

Map Page	**DAYTONA BEACH INTERNATIONAL** (Maximum driving distance from airport: 2.2 mi)	Diamond Rated	Member Savings	Page
14 p. 58	**Courtyard by Marriott-Daytona Beach Speedway/Airport, 1.5 mi**	◆◆◆	✔	62
20 p. 58	**The Daytona, Autograph Collection, 2.0 mi**	◆◆◆◆	✔	62
17 p. 58	**Fairfield Inn & Suites by Marriott Daytona Beach Speedway/Airport, 1.7 mi**	◆◆◆	✔	62
15 p. 58	**Hampton Inn Daytona Beach Speedway-Airport, 1.2 mi**	◆◆◆	✔	62
18 p. 58	**Hilton Garden Inn Daytona Beach-Airport, 1.0 mi**	◆◆◆	✔	63
16 p. 58	Homewood Suites by Hilton Daytona Beach Speedway-Airport, 1.4 mi	◆◆◆	✔	65
21 p. 58	**Quality Inn Daytona Speedway, 2.2 mi**	◆◆	✔	65
19 p. 58	**Residence Inn by Marriott-Daytona Beach Speedway/Airport, 1.1 mi**	◆◆◆	✔	65

Daytona Beach

This index helps you "spot" where approved hotels and restaurants are located on the corresponding detailed maps. Restaurant price range is a combination of lunch and/or dinner. Turn to the listing page for more information and consult display ads for special promotions.

For more details, rates and reservations: **AAA.com/travelguides/hotels**

DAYTONA BEACH

Map Page	Hotels	Diamond Rated	Member Savings	Page
1 p. 58	**Daytona Beach Resort & Conference Center**	fyi	✔	62
2 p. 58	Hilton Garden Inn Daytona Beach Oceanfront	◆◆◆	✔	63
3 p. 58	Hampton Inn by Hilton Daytona Beach/Beachfront	◆◆◆	✔	62
4 p. 58	Holiday Inn Hotel & Suites Daytona Beach On The Ocean	◆◆◆		63
5 p. 58	**Hard Rock Hotel Daytona Beach**	◆◆◆◆	✔	62
6 p. 58	**Best Western Plus Daytona Inn Seabreeze Oceanfront**	◆◆	✔	61
7 p. 58	**The Plaza Resort & Spa** *(See ad p. 64.)*	◆◆◆	✔	65
8 p. 58	Wyndham Ocean Walk	◆◆◆		65
9 p. 58	**Hilton Daytona Beach Oceanfront Resort** *(See ad p. 63.)*	◆◆◆	✔	63
10 p. 58	Streamline Hotel	◆◆◆		65
11 p. 58	**Holiday Inn Resort Daytona Beach Oceanfront** *(See ad p. 64.)*	◆◆◆	✔	65
12 p. 58	Holiday Inn LPGA	◆◆◆		63
13 p. 58	Days Inn Daytona Downtown	◆◆		62
14 p. 58	**Courtyard by Marriott-Daytona Beach Speedway/Airport**	◆◆◆	✔	62
15 p. 58	**Hampton Inn Daytona Beach Speedway-Airport**	◆◆◆	✔	62
16 p. 58	Homewood Suites by Hilton Daytona Beach Speedway-Airport	◆◆◆	✔	65
17 p. 58	**Fairfield Inn & Suites by Marriott Daytona Beach Speedway/Airport**	◆◆◆	✔	62
18 p. 58	**Hilton Garden Inn Daytona Beach-Airport**	◆◆◆	✔	63
19 p. 58	**Residence Inn by Marriott-Daytona Beach Speedway/Airport**	◆◆◆	✔	65
20 p. 58	**The Daytona, Autograph Collection**	◆◆◆◆	✔	62
21 p. 58	**Quality Inn Daytona Speedway**	◆◆	✔	65

DAYTONA BEACH (cont'd)

Map Page	Hotels (cont'd)	Diamond Rated	Member Savings	Page
22 p. 58	**Best Western International Speedway Hotel**	◆◆◆	✔	61

Map Page	Restaurants	Diamond Rated	Cuisine	Price Range	Page
1 p. 58	The Oyster Pub	◆◆	American	$6-$24	66
2 p. 58	Sloppy Joe's	◆◆	American	$11-$24	66
3 p. 58	Hyde Park Prime Steakhouse	◆◆◆	Steak	$14-$89	65
4 p. 58	Hog Heaven Real Pit Bar-B-Q	◆◆	Barbecue	$7-$24	65
5 p. 58	**Cruisin' Cafe Bar & Grill**	◆◆	American	$10-$28	65
6 p. 58	Ocean Deck Restaurant & Beach Club	◆◆	American	$11-$23	65
7 p. 58	The Dancing Avocado Kitchen	◆◆	American	$10-$16	65
8 p. 58	McK's Tavern	◆◆	Irish	$7-$19	65
9 p. 58	The Cellar Restaurant	◆◆◆	Italian	$23-$46	65
10 p. 58	Crab Stop II	◆◆	Seafood	$8-$38	65
11 p. 58	Oklahoma Joe's	◆◆	Barbecue	$11-$26	65

ORMOND BEACH

Map Page	Hotels	Diamond Rated	Member Savings	Page
25 p. 58	**Clarion Inn Ormond Beach**	◆◆	✔	248
26 p. 58	**Best Western Castillo Del Sol**	◆◆	✔	248
27 p. 58	**Hampton Inn Daytona-Ormond Beach**	◆◆	✔	248
28 p. 58	Sleep Inn Ormond Beach	◆◆		248

Map Page	Restaurants	Diamond Rated	Cuisine	Price Range	Page
14 p. 58	Colt's Pig Stand	◆	Barbecue	$9-$20	248
15 p. 58	Peach Valley Cafe	◆◆	Breakfast Sandwiches	$6-$13	248
16 p. 58	Genovese's Italian Cafe	◆◆	Italian Pizza	$8-$25	248
17 p. 58	Stonewood Grill & Tavern	◆◆◆	American	$11-$36	248
18 p. 58	Wild Rabbit Cafe & Bistro	◆◆	American	$9-$15	248
19 p. 58	Grind GastroPub and Kona Tiki Bar	◆◆	American	$11-$32	248
20 p. 58	63 Sovereign	◆◆	International	$8-$28	248
21 p. 58	Hull's Seafood Restaurant & Market	◆◆	Seafood	$7-$30	248
22 p. 58	Charlie Horse Restaurant	◆◆	American	$9-$65	248
23 p. 58	Bonefish Grill	◆◆◆	Seafood	$15-$34	248
24 p. 58	Mario's Italian Restaurant & Lounge	◆◆	Italian	$15-$25	248

DAYTONA BEACH SHORES

Map Page	Hotels	Diamond Rated	Member Savings	Page
31 p. 58	**Best Western Aku Tiki Inn**	◆◆	✔	66
32 p. 58	**Tropical Manor**	◆◆	✔	67
33 p. 58	**Sun Viking Lodge**	◆◆	✔	66
34 p. 58	Shoreline All Suites Inn	◆◆		66

DAYTONA BEACH SHORES (cont'd)

Map Page	Hotels (cont'd)	Diamond Rated	Member Savings	Page
35 p. 58	Delta Hotels by Marriott Daytona Beach Oceanfront	♦♦♦	✔	66
36 p. 58	Hampton Inn Daytona Shores-Oceanfront	♦♦♦	✔	66
37 p. 58	**Hyatt Place Daytona Beach Oceanfront**	♦♦♦	✔	66
38 p. 58	Residence Inn by Marriott-Daytona Beach Oceanfront	♦♦♦	✔	66
39 p. 58	**Atlantic Ocean Palm Inn**	♦♦	✔	66
40 p. 58	Holiday Inn Express & Suites Oceanfront Daytona Beach Shores	♦♦♦		66

Map Page	Restaurants	Diamond Rated	Cuisine	Price Range	Page
27 p. 58	Azure	♦♦♦	Continental	$14-$40	67
28 p. 58	Genovese's Italian Cafe	♦♦	Italian	$8-$25	67
29 p. 58	Boondocks Restaurant	♦♦	Seafood	$4-$19	67

PORT ORANGE

Map Page	Hotel	Diamond Rated	Member Savings	Page
43 p. 58	Country Inn & Suites by Radisson, Port Orange-Daytona	♦♦♦		254

Map Page	Restaurants	Diamond Rated	Cuisine	Price Range	Page
32 p. 58	Aunt Catfish's On The River	♦♦	Southern Seafood	$9-$40	254
33 p. 58	Port Orange Steakhouse	♦♦	Steak Seafood	$8-$28	254
34 p. 58	Monterey Grill	♦♦	American	$10-$20	254
35 p. 58	Malibu Beach Grill	♦♦♦	New American	$11-$28	254

BEST WESTERN INTERNATIONAL SPEEDWAY HOTEL
386/258-6333 22

♦♦♦ Hotel

AAA Benefit: Members save up to 15% and earn bonus points!

Address: 2620 W International Speedway Blvd 32114 **Location:** I-95 exit 261 (US 92), just e. **Facility:** 151 units. 2 stories, interior corridors. **Pool:** outdoor. **Activities:** tennis, exercise room. **Guest Services:** valet and coin laundry. **Featured Amenity: breakfast buffet.**

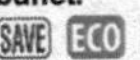

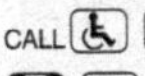

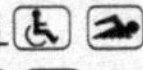
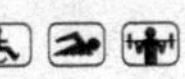

BEST WESTERN PLUS DAYTONA INN SEABREEZE OCEANFRONT
386/255-5491 6

♦♦ Hotel

AAA Benefit: Members save up to 15% and earn bonus points!

Address: 730 N Atlantic Ave 32118 **Location:** Oceanfront. On SR A1A (Atlantic Ave), 1.1 mi n of jct US 92 (International Speedway Blvd). **Facility:** 97 units, some efficiencies. 5 stories, interior/exterior corridors. **Terms:** check-in 4 pm. **Amenities:** safes. **Pool:** outdoor. **Activities:** exercise room. **Featured Amenity: breakfast buffet.**

Let Your Voice Be Heard

If your visit to a listed property doesn't meet your expectations, tell us about it.

AAA.com/MemberFeedback

(See map & index p. 58.)

COURTYARD BY MARRIOTT-DAYTONA BEACH SPEEDWAY/AIRPORT

386/255-3388 **14**

Hotel

COURTYARD **AAA Benefit:** Members save 5% or more!

Address: 1605 Richard Petty Blvd 32114 **Location:** I-95 exit 261 (US 92), 2.8 mi e to Corsair Dr, just s to Richard Petty Blvd, then just e. **Facility:** 122 units. 3 stories, interior corridors. **Pool:** heated outdoor. **Activities:** hot tub, exercise room. **Guest Services:** valet and coin laundry, boarding pass kiosk, area transportation.

SAVE ECO CALL BIZ / SOME UNITS

DAYS INN DAYTONA DOWNTOWN

386/255-4500 **13**

Hotel. **Address:** 544 S Ridgewood Ave 32114

THE DAYTONA, AUTOGRAPH COLLECTION

386/323-9777 **20**

Boutique Hotel

AUTOGRAPH COLLECTION HOTELS **AAA Benefit:** Members save 5% or more!

Address: 1870 Victory Cir 32114 **Location:** I-95 exit 261 (US 92), 2.1 mi e to Bill France Blvd, then just n; in ONE DAYTONA complex. **Facility:** In ONE DAYTONA and across from the Daytona International Speedway, the hotel features a captivating racing theme. Oversize rooms are upscale with a streamlined design. The fitness center is expansive. 144 units. 6 stories, interior corridors. *Bath:* shower only. **Terms:** check-in 4 pm. **Amenities:** safes. **Dining:** 2 restaurants. **Pool:** heated outdoor. **Activities:** hot tub, bicycles, exercise room. **Guest Services:** valet and coin laundry, area transportation.

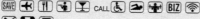

SAVE CALL BIZ

DAYTONA BEACH RESORT & CONFERENCE CENTER

386/672-3770 **1**

fyi

Resort Hotel

Under major renovation, call for details. **Last Rated:** **Address:** 2700 N Atlantic Ave 32118 **Location:** Oceanfront. I-95 exit 261 (US 92), 6 mi e to SR A1A (Atlantic Ave), then 3.2 mi n. **Facility:** Nestled along the beach, this resort features indoor and outdoor pools, hot tubs and a sauna. Beach-themed rooms vary in size; all include a fully stocked kitchen. 193 efficiencies. 5-14 stories, interior/exterior corridors. **Parking:** on-site (fee). **Terms:** check-in 4 pm. **Dining:** 2 restaurants. **Pool:** heated outdoor, heated indoor. **Activities:** sauna, hot tub, exercise room. **Guest Services:** valet and coin laundry.

SAVE ECO BIZ SHS

FAIRFIELD INN & SUITES BY MARRIOTT DAYTONA BEACH SPEEDWAY/AIRPORT

386/254-4700 **17**

Hotel

Fairfield **AAA Benefit:** Members save 5% or more!

Address: 1820 Checkered Flag Blvd 32114 **Location:** I-95 exit 261 (US 92), 2.1 mi e to Bill France Blvd, then just n; in One Daytona complex. 1.7 mi from airport. **Facility:** 105 units. 4 stories, interior corridors. **Pool:** outdoor. **Activities:** exercise room. **Guest Services:** valet and coin laundry, area transportation.

SAVE CALL BIZ

HAMPTON INN BY HILTON DAYTONA BEACH/BEACHFRONT

386/944-2570 **3**

SAVE Contemporary Hotel. **Address:** 1024 N Atlantic Ave 32118

AAA Benefit: Members save 5% or more!

HAMPTON INN DAYTONA BEACH SPEEDWAY-AIRPORT

386/257-4030 **15**

Contemporary Hotel

AAA Benefit: Members save 5% or more!

Address: 1715 W International Speedway Blvd 32114 **Location:** I-95 exit 261 (US 92), 2.5 mi e. **Facility:** 122 units. 4 stories, interior corridors. **Pool:** outdoor. **Activities:** hot tub, exercise room. **Guest Services:** valet laundry. **Featured Amenity: full hot breakfast.**

SAVE ECO

HARD ROCK HOTEL DAYTONA BEACH

386/947-7300 **5**

Hotel

Address: 918 N Atlantic Ave 32118 **Location:** Oceanfront. On SR A1A (Atlantic Ave), 1.2 mi n of US 92 (International Speedway Blvd). **Facility:** This music lover's paradise has unique, themed décor. The well-designed rooms are inviting and spacious. Spoil yourself with a luxurious spa treatment or enjoy a work out in the large fitness center. 200 units, some two bedrooms. 7 stories, interior corridors. **Parking:** on-site (fee). **Terms:** check-in 4 pm. **Amenities:** safes. **Dining:** 3 restaurants, entertainment. **Pool:** heated outdoor. **Activities:** sauna, hot tub, steamroom, recreation programs, game room, lawn sports, exercise room, in-room exercise equipment, spa. **Guest Services:** valet laundry. **Featured Amenity: continental breakfast.**

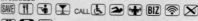

SAVE CALL BIZ

For complete hotel, dining and attraction listings: AAA.com/travelguides

(See map & index p. 58.)

HILTON DAYTONA BEACH OCEANFRONT RESORT
386/254-8200 9

Resort Hotel

AAA Benefit:
Members save 5% or more!

Address: 100 N Atlantic Ave 32118 **Location:** Oceanfront. I-95 exit 261A, 6.1 mi e to SR A1A (Atlantic Ave), then 0.5 mi n. Across from the Convention Center. **Facility:** The warm aura and light décor in rooms lend way to a tropical vibe. Cozy, comfortable bedding and scenic views are what to expect when retiring at the end of the day. 744 units. 11-16 stories, interior corridors. **Parking:** on-site (fee) and valet. **Terms:** check-in 4 pm. **Amenities:** safes. **Dining:** 7 restaurants, also, Hyde Park Prime Steakhouse, see separate listing. **Pool:** heated outdoor. **Activities:** hot tub, recreation programs, bicycles, exercise room, spa. **Guest Services:** valet and coin laundry. *(See ad this page.)*

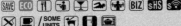

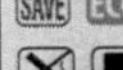 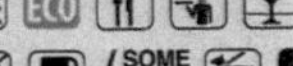  

SOME UNITS

Hilton Daytona Beach Oceanfront Resort

Oceanfront Resort, 7 Restaurants/Lounges, 2 Heated Outdoor Pools, Spa, 24-Hr Fitness, Shops & More.

HILTON GARDEN INN DAYTONA BEACH-AIRPORT
386/944-4000 18

Hotel

Hilton Garden Inn

AAA Benefit:
Members save 5% or more!

Address: 189 Midway Ave 32114 **Location:** I-95 exit 261 (US 92), 2.4 mi e, then just s; adjacent to Daytona International Speedway. **Facility:** 115 units. 5 stories, interior corridors. **Pool:** outdoor. **Activities:** hot tub, exercise room. **Guest Services:** valet and coin laundry. **Featured Amenity: breakfast buffet.**

SAVE ECO CALL BIZ

SOME UNITS HS

HILTON GARDEN INN DAYTONA BEACH OCEANFRONT
386/265-0511 2

SAVE Hotel. **Address:** 2560 N Atlantic Ave 32118

AAA Benefit:
Members save 5% or more!

HOLIDAY INN HOTEL & SUITES DAYTONA BEACH ON THE OCEAN
386/255-5494 4

Hotel. **Address:** 930 N Atlantic Ave 32118

HOLIDAY INN LPGA 386/236-0200 12

Hotel. **Address:** 137 Automall Cir 32124

▼ See AAA listing this page ▼

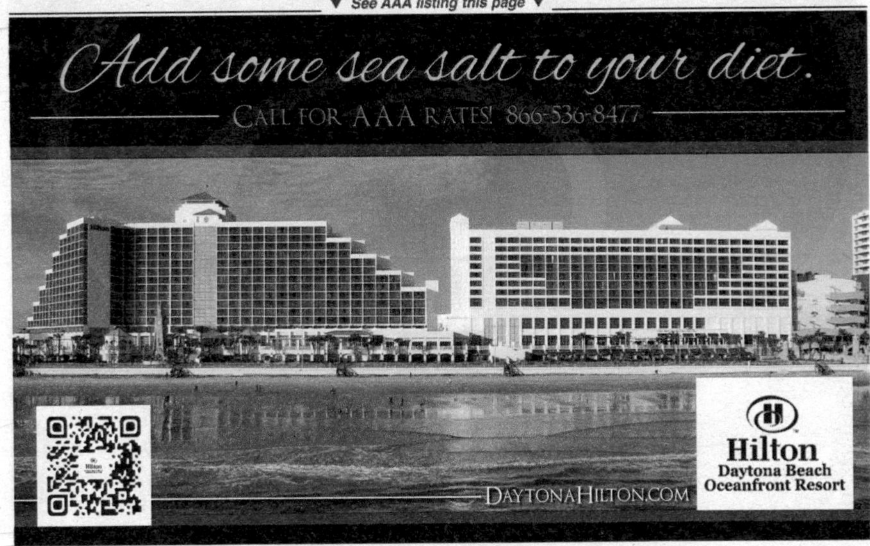

Save on travel, shopping, dining and more:
AAA.com/discounts

▼ See AAA listing p. 65 ▼

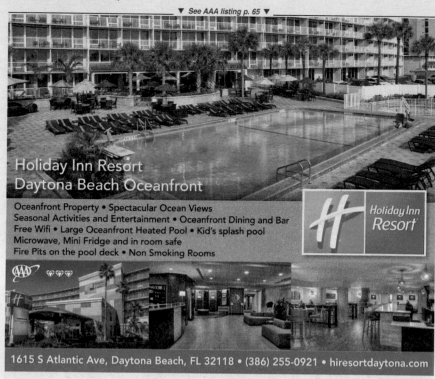

Holiday Inn Resort
Daytona Beach Oceanfront

Oceanfront Property • Spectacular Ocean Views
Seasonal Activities and Entertainment • Oceanfront Dining and Bar
Free Wifi • Large Oceanfront Heated Pool • Kid's splash pool
Microwave, Mini Fridge and in room safe
Fire Pits on the pool deck • Non Smoking Rooms

Holiday Inn Resort

AAA

1615 S Atlantic Ave, Daytona Beach, FL 32118 • (386) 255-0921 • hiresortdaytona.com

▼ See AAA listing p. 65 ▼

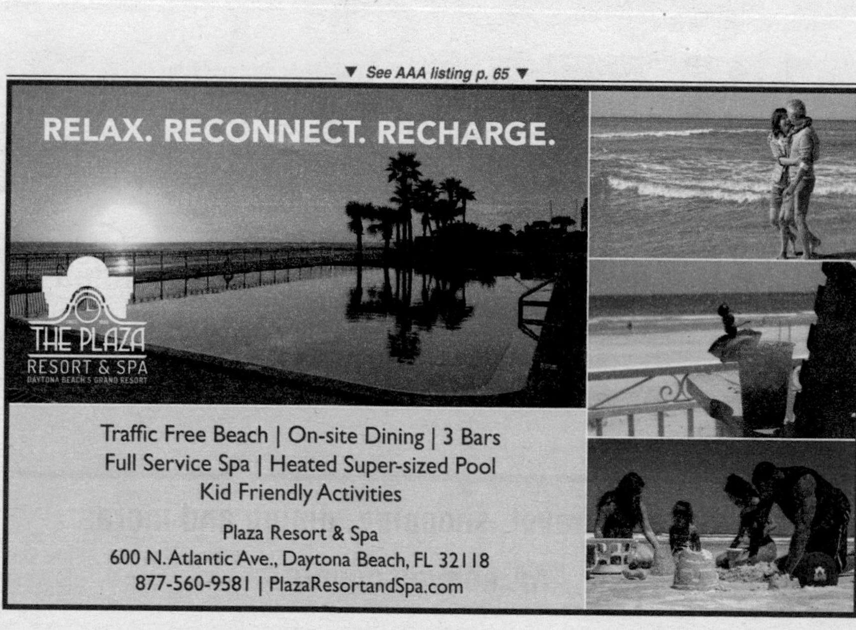

(See map & index p. 58.)

HOLIDAY INN RESORT DAYTONA BEACH OCEANFRONT 386/255-0921 11

Contemporary Resort Hotel

Address: 1615 S Atlantic Ave 32118 **Location:** Oceanfront. On SR A1A (Atlantic Ave), 1.3 mi s of jct US 92 (International Speedway Blvd). **Facility:** Spacious rooms with deep wood tones and vibrant décor provide guests with a bit of serenity. The attractive outdoor pool area and inviting on-site restaurant are standout amenities. 188 units, some efficiencies. 8 stories, exterior corridors. **Parking:** on-site (fee). **Amenities:** safes. **Pool:** heated outdoor. **Activities:** hot tub, recreation programs, game room, exercise room. **Guest Services:** valet and coin laundry. *(See ad p. 64.)*

SAVE CALL BIZ SHS

HOMEWOOD SUITES BY HILTON DAYTONA BEACH SPEEDWAY-AIRPORT 386/258-2828 16

SAVE Extended Stay Hotel. **Address:** 165 Bill France Blvd 32114

AAA Benefit: Members save 5% or more!

THE PLAZA RESORT & SPA 386/255-4471 7

Classic Historic Resort Hotel

Address: 600 N Atlantic Ave 32118 **Location:** Oceanfront. I-95 exit 261 (US 92), 6 mi e to SR A1A (Atlantic Ave), 1 mi n. **Facility:** You'll enjoy the space allotted in the traditional-style rooms which feature comfortable beds and a wet bar. Some rooms have either a patio or a balcony. Get revived and pampered in the on-site spa. 323 units, some efficiencies. 14 stories, interior corridors. **Parking:** on-site (fee) and valet. **Terms:** check-in 4 pm. **Amenities:** safes. **Dining:** 3 restaurants. **Pool:** heated outdoor. **Activities:** steamroom, recreation programs in season, bicycles, lawn sports, exercise room, spa. **Guest Services:** valet and coin laundry. *(See ad p. 64.)*

SAVE ECO BIZ HS

QUALITY INN DAYTONA SPEEDWAY 386/255-3661 21

Motel

Address: 2250 W International Speedway Blvd 32114 **Location:** I-95 exit 261 (US 92), 1.3 mi e. Opposite Daytona International Speedway. **Facility:** 64 units. 2 stories (no elevator), exterior corridors. **Activities:** limited exercise equipment. **Guest Services:** coin laundry.

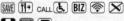

SAVE CALL BIZ

Where Diamonds make the difference:

AAA.com/travelguides/hotels

RESIDENCE INN BY MARRIOTT-DAYTONA BEACH SPEEDWAY/AIRPORT 386/252-3949 19

Extended Stay Hotel

Residence INN **AAA Benefit:** Members save 5% or more!

Address: 1725 Richard Petty Blvd 32114 **Location:** I-95 exit 261 (US 92), 2.4 mi e to Midway Ave, just s to Richard Petty Blvd, then just e. **Facility:** 122 units, some two bedrooms, efficiencies and kitchens. 5 stories, interior corridors. **Pool:** heated outdoor. **Activities:** hot tub, picnic facilities, exercise room. **Guest Services:** valet and coin laundry, area transportation. **Featured Amenity:** breakfast buffet.

SAVE ECO CALL BIZ HS / SOME UNITS

STREAMLINE HOTEL 386/947-7470 10

Historic Vintage Hotel. **Address:** 140 S Atlantic Ave 32118

WYNDHAM OCEAN WALK 386/323-4800 8

Condominium. **Address:** 300 N Atlantic Ave 32118

WHERE TO EAT

THE CELLAR RESTAURANT 386/258-0011 9

Italian. Fine Dining. **Address:** 220 Magnolia Ave 32114

CRAB STOP II 386/253-4616 10

Seafood. Casual Dining. **Address:** 933 W International Speedway Blvd 32114

CRUISIN' CAFE BAR & GRILL 386/253-5522 5

American Casual Dining $10-$28

AAA Inspector Notes: This is a race lover's dream restaurant. The interior is decked out in full NASCAR regalia and memorabilia, which includes tributes to the sport's most popular drivers. You even can sit in replica race car while enjoying your meal. The tables are dedicated to the Daytona 500 winners over the past 50 plus years. Menu options include salads, sandwiches, burgers, pizza, wings and steaks. Ask your server about the Crusin Cup Burger Challenge - see if you can finish it. **Features:** full bar, patio dining, happy hour. **Address:** 2 S Atlantic Ave 32118 **Location:** Corner of SR A1A (Atlantic Ave) and Main St; just n of jct US 92 (International Speedway Blvd) on SR A1A (Atlantic Ave). **Parking:** on-site and street. L D LATE

THE DANCING AVOCADO KITCHEN 386/947-2022 7

American. Casual Dining. **Address:** 110 S Beach St 32114

HOG HEAVEN REAL PIT BAR-B-Q 386/257-1212 4

Barbecue. Casual Dining. **Address:** 37 N Atlantic Ave 32118

HYDE PARK PRIME STEAKHOUSE 386/226-9844 3

Steak. Fine Dining. **Address:** 100 N Atlantic Ave 32118

MCK'S TAVERN 386/238-3321 8

Irish. Casual Dining. **Address:** 218 S Beach St 32114

OCEAN DECK RESTAURANT & BEACH CLUB 386/253-5224 6

American. Casual Dining. **Address:** 127 S Ocean Ave 32118

OKLAHOMA JOE'S 386/366-2669 11

Barbecue. Casual Dining. **Address:** 1866 Victory Cir 32114

(See map & index p. 58.)

THE OYSTER PUB 386/255-6348 (1)

American. Casual Dining. **Address:** 555 Seabreeze Blvd 32118

SLOPPY JOE'S 386/239-0014 (2)

American. Casual Dining. **Address:** 250 N Atlantic Blvd 32118

DAYTONA BEACH SHORES (E-5)

pop. 4,247, elev. 13'

• **Hotels & Restaurants map & index p. 58**

Four miles south of Daytona Beach and 60 miles northeast of Orlando, this beach town is on a barrier island that lies between the Atlantic Ocean and part of the Intracoastal Waterway. Family entertainment reigns supreme here, with putt-putt golf courses, plenty of parks and, of course, the beach and the Atlantic Ocean, perfect for fishing, sailing and other water sports. Music fans, take note: Gregg and Duane Allman spent their teenage years in Daytona Beach Shores.

ATLANTIC OCEAN PALM INN 386/761-8450 (39)

Motel

Address: 3247 S Atlantic Ave 32118 **Location:** Oceanfront. On SR A1A (Atlantic Ave), 5 mi s of jct US 92 (International Speedway Blvd). **Facility:** 50 units, some efficiencies. 3 stories, exterior corridors. **Pool:** heated outdoor. **Guest Services:** coin laundry.

/ SOME UNITS

AAA members save 10%
Located on ocean w/ all partial Oceanview Rms. Kitchen Rms avail.
Newly Renov Rms.

BEST WESTERN AKU TIKI INN 386/252-9631 (31)

Hotel

Best Western. **AAA Benefit:** Members save up to 15% and earn bonus points!

Address: 2225 S Atlantic Ave 32118 **Location:** Oceanfront. On SR A1A (Atlantic Ave), 2.2 mi s of jct US 92 (International Speedway Blvd). **Facility:** 132 units, some efficiencies. 5 stories, interior corridors. **Amenities:** safes. **Pool:** heated outdoor. **Activities:** exercise room. **Guest Services:** valet and coin laundry. **Featured Amenity: breakfast buffet.**

SAVE CALL

DELTA HOTELS BY MARRIOTT DAYTONA BEACH OCEANFRONT 386/366-8515 (35)

SAVE Hotel. **Address:** 2505 S Atlantic Ave 32118

AAA Benefit: Members save 5% or more!

HAMPTON INN DAYTONA SHORES-OCEANFRONT 386/767-8533 (36)

SAVE Hotel. **Address:** 3135 Atlantic 32118

AAA Benefit: Members save 5% or more!

HOLIDAY INN EXPRESS & SUITES OCEANFRONT DAYTONA BEACH SHORES 386/767-1711 (40)

Hotel. **Address:** 3301 S Atlantic Ave 32118

HYATT PLACE DAYTONA BEACH OCEANFRONT 386/944-2010 (37)

Hotel

HYATT PLACE **AAA Benefit:** Members save up to 10%!

Address: 3161 S Atlantic Ave 32118 **Location:** Oceanfront. I-95 exit 256 (SR 421), 5 mi e to SR A1A (Atlantic Ave), then 0.8 mi n. **Facility:** 143 units. 10 stories, interior corridors. **Terms:** check-in 4 pm. **Amenities:** safes. **Pool:** heated outdoor. **Activities:** hot tub, exercise room. **Guest Services:** valet and coin laundry. **Featured Amenity: breakfast buffet.**

SAVE CALL BIZ

/ SOME UNITS HS

RESIDENCE INN BY MARRIOTT-DAYTONA BEACH OCEANFRONT 386/944-2000 (38)

SAVE Extended Stay Contemporary Hotel. **Address:** 3209 S Atlantic Ave 32118

AAA Benefit: Members save 5% or more!

SHORELINE ALL SUITES INN 386/252-1692 (34)

Motel. **Address:** 2435 S Atlantic Ave 32118

SUN VIKING LODGE 386/252-6252 (33)

Resort Hotel

Address: 2411 S Atlantic Ave 32118 **Location:** Oceanfront. Jct US 92 (International Speedway Blvd), 2.5 mi s on SR A1A (Atlantic Ave). **Facility:** Rooms vary in size and design, each has a beach vibe. The 60 ft. slide makes a splash with kids and an attractive, enclosed pool area resembles a greenhouse. The on-site café opens seasonally. 91 units, some efficiencies and kitchens. 2-8 stories, exterior corridors. **Amenities:** safes. **Pool:** heated outdoor, heated indoor. **Activities:** sauna, hot tub, recreation programs, playground, game room, lawn sports, picnic facilities, exercise room. **Guest Services:** coin laundry.

SAVE BIZ / SOME UNITS

20% OFF-Promo: AAA
Oceanfront Hotel
60-Foot Waterslide
FREE Activity Program
Rooms, Kitchens & Suites

(See map & index p. 58.)

TROPICAL MANOR 386/252-4920 32

Boutique Motel

Address: 2237 S Atlantic Ave 32118 **Location:** Oceanfront. On SR A1A (Atlantic Ave), 2.2 mi s of jct US 92 (International Speedway Blvd). **Facility:** Lush landscaping, hand-painted murals and the Atlantic Ocean as a backdrop make this one of the more novel properties around. Room types vary, including a few value rooms, which offer a pleasant stay. 38 units, some two bedrooms, three bedrooms, efficiencies and kitchens. 1-2 stories, exterior corridors. **Amenities:** *Some:* safes. **Pool:** heated outdoor. **Activities:** picnic facilities. **Guest Services:** coin laundry.

SAVE

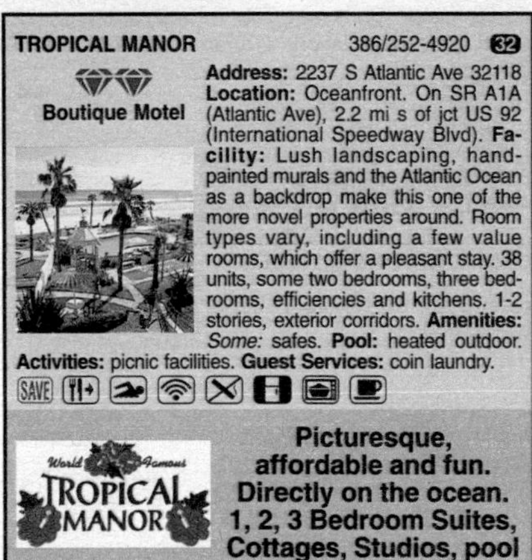

World Famous TROPICAL MANOR

Picturesque, affordable and fun. Directly on the ocean. 1, 2, 3 Bedroom Suites, Cottages, Studios, pool

WHERE TO EAT

AZURE 386/322-7231 27

Continental. Casual Dining. **Address:** 2637 S Atlantic Ave 32118

BOONDOCKS RESTAURANT 386/760-9001 29

Seafood. Casual Dining. **Address:** 3948 S Peninsula Dr 32127

GENOVESE'S ITALIAN CAFE 386/767-4151 28

Italian. Casual Dining. **Address:** 116 Dunlawton Ave 32118

DEBARY pop. 19,320

HAMPTON INN DEBARY/DELTONA/ORANGE CITY 386/668-5758

SAVE Hotel. **Address:** 308 Sunrise Blvd 32713

AAA Benefit: Members save 5% or more!

WHERE TO EAT

GENUINE BISTRO & LOUNGE 386/320-0217

American. Gastropub. **Address:** 2 S Charles Richard Beall Blvd 32713

THE ORIGINAL ANTHONY'S PIZZA & ITALIAN RESTAURANT 386/668-9477

Italian Pizza. Casual Dining. **Address:** 155 S Charles Richard Beall Blvd 32713

SWAMP HOUSE RIVERFRONT GRILL 386/668-8891

American. Casual Dining. **Address:** 488 W Highbanks Rd 32713

DELAND (E-4) pop. 27,031, elev. 27'

• Hotels p. 68 • Restaurants p. 68

With its rolling hills and towering pine trees, the area so allured New York baking-soda tycoon Henry A. DeLand that he purchased 159.1 acres upon first glimpse in 1876. DeLand refined his newly established community by donating land for a road; seeding lovely magnolia, oak and orange trees; and founding a college, which he christened DeLand Academy.

DeLand's involvement in the lucrative orange-growing industry backfired when a bitter mid-1880s freeze left him financially unable to support the university. He sought help from renowned hat maker John Stetson, for whom the school was eventually renamed. Boasting a number of early 20th-century buildings on its 175-acre campus, Stetson University, 421 N. Woodland Blvd., is a must-see for architecture and history buffs; phone (386) 822-7000.

Add some science and art to the equation by exploring the college's Gillespie Museum of Minerals, 234 E. Michigan Ave., and Homer and Dolly Hand Art Center, 139 E. Michigan Ave. The former exhibits some 15,000 rocks, gems and minerals; the latter showcases modern paintings by Oscar Bluemner as well as pieces by students, faculty and professional artists. Phone (386) 822-7330 or (386) 822-7270, respectively.

Picturing a typical early to mid-20th-century day in "the Athens of Florida" isn't all that difficult. Scattered throughout downtown are polychromatic murals unveiling scenes from DeLand's past. These elaborate works of local artists have made the town a favorite stop along the Florida Mural Trail. Mix in a little culture with the DeLand Sculpture Walk, made up of 12 annually changing outdoor sculptures placed throughout downtown. Swing by MainStreet DeLand Association, 100 N. Woodland Blvd., for a mural- and sculpture-walk brochure; phone (386) 734-4371.

While browsing specialty shops, scoping out the perfect café or watering hole, or enjoying a simple stroll along Woodland Boulevard and its neighboring streets, notice how history is preserved in the Greek Revival and masonry vernacular-style buildings. If you *really* want to explore the past, embark on an antiquing adventure. This has the potential to be an all-day expedition on any day but Sunday, when many mom-and-pops are closed.

Catch a concert, classic flick or theatrical performance at the restored Athens Theatre, 124 N. Florida Ave.; phone (386) 736-1500 for tickets. A fine example of Italian Renaissance architecture, the Athens opened as a vaudeville house in 1922 and over the years served as a movie cinema, dinner theater, video-game room and prom-party venue.

Stimulate your brain in a different way at tree-shaded Chess Park, on the north side of W. New York Avenue. Here you can challenge your travel buddy to a game of chess on one of the built-in checkerboard tables surrounded by benches and a waterfall-backed platform.

Grab some grub and head over to Bill Dreggors Park and Freedom Playground, 230 N. Stone St., for a picnic; phone (386) 626-7280. Immerse yourself in the sights, scents and textures of the Sensory Butterfly Garden, which was designed for physically and visually impaired visitors. Also on the grounds is the DeLand Memorial Hospital Museum, with a re-created 1920s surgery room and apothecary exhibit, and the Burgess Building, with exhibits featuring vintage toys, elephant-themed collectibles, military memorabilia, vintage electrical appliances and items highlighting the area's African-American heritage. The Veterans Memorial Wall honors veterans of the World Wars and Korean War. Phone (904) 740-5800 for the DeLand Memorial Hospital Museum.

During World War II, Navy combat bomber pilots completed 3-month training assignments in DeLand. Aircraft, practice bombs and vintage photographs are among the treasures you'll find in DeLand Naval Air Station Museum and Historical Hangar, 910 Biscayne Blvd.; phone (386) 738-4149.

Rent a pontoon or fishing boat from a local outfitter and unwind in Florida's longest river, the St. Johns. If 120 miles per hour is more your pace and the sky is your limit, try free falling from a whopping 14,000 feet at Skydive DeLand, 1600 Flightline Blvd.; phone (386) 738-3539. The town, believed to have been the site of the first tandem jump in history, has experienced a huge economic boost as a result of the sport's popularity.

For more of the great outdoors, hop on the free ferry to Hontoon Island State Park *(see Recreation Areas Chart)*, 2309 River Ridge Rd., where fishing, canoeing, kayaking, camping, hiking and biking opportunities abound; phone (386) 736-5309. The Timucuan Indians, who once called the 1,650-acre island home, feasted on snails from the St. Johns' shoals. Over time the discarded shells fused together into sizable mounds like the one you'll encounter along the park's nature trail.

West Volusia Tourism Bureau: 116 W. New York Ave., Deland, FL 32720. **Phone:** (386) 734-0162 or (800) 749-4350.

THE STETSON MANSION is at 1031 Camphor Ln. You'll be awed by the extraordinary mix of Tudor, Gothic, Polynesian and Moorish architectural styles exhibited in hat manufacturer John Stetson's former winter home; the ornate 1886 residence is one of just a few in Florida that remain from the Gilded Age.

Among the kings, presidents and other prominent individuals to cross the three-story house's threshold was Thomas Edison, who supervised the electrical installation; you can see the original circuit box and some of his original fixtures. Highlights include 16 intricately patterned parquet floors and 10,000 original leaded-glass window panes. From Nov. 15-Jan. 15, the mansion is resplendent in Christmas finery.

Note: Photography, video cameras, high-heeled shoes, large handbags and camera bags are not permitted inside the mansion. Tours require guests to climb two flights of stairs. **Time:** Allow 1 hour, 30 minutes minimum. **Hours:** Guided tours are given Thurs.-Sat. at 10:30 and 1:30, early Feb. through mid-Sept. Christmas tours are given Mon.-Sat. at 10:30, 1:30 and 5 (also Sun. at 1:30 and 5), Nov. 15-Jan. 15. Phone ahead to confirm schedule. **Cost:** 75-minute Standard Tour (first and second floor and guest cottage) $20; $15 (ages 6-22). 100-minute Grand Tour (first, second and third floors, Stetson memorabilia room, boardroom, four bathrooms, three bedrooms and balcony) $30; $15 (ages 6-22). 75-90 minute Christmas Tour $25; $15 (ages 6-22). Cash only. Reservations are required. **Phone:** (386) 873-0167. GT

COMFORT INN DELAND 386/736-3100

Hotel. **Address:** 400 E International Speedway Blvd 32724

COURTYARD BY MARRIOTT DELAND HISTORIC DOWNTOWN 386/943-9500

SAVE Hotel. **Address:** 308 N Woodland Blvd 32720

AAA Benefit: Members save 5% or more!

HAMPTON INN & SUITES DELAND 386/279-7808

SAVE Contemporary Hotel. **Address:** 20 Summit Oak Pl 32720

AAA Benefit: Members save 5% or more!

WHERE TO EAT

BELLINI'S DELICATESSEN 386/736-1747

Italian. Casual Dining. **Address:** 111 E Rich Ave 32724

CONNIE'S CAFÉ 386/738-5030

Deli. Quick Serve. **Address:** 101 N Woodland Blvd 32720

COOK'S BUFFET, CAFE, BAKERY 386/734-4339

American. Buffet Style. **Address:** 704 N Woodland Blvd 32720

GRAM'S KITCHEN 386/736-9340

Comfort Food. Casual Dining. **Address:** 844 E New York Ave 32724

GRAM'S KITCHEN 386/734-9460

Comfort Food. Casual Dining. **Address:** 915 N Spring Garden Ave 32724

DE SOTO NATIONAL MEMORIAL (I-1)

On the south shore of the Manatee River, 5 miles west of Bradenton on SR 64, then 2 miles north on 75th Street N.W., De Soto National Memorial commemorates the first major European exploration of what is now the southeastern United States.

The expedition began in 1539 when Hernando de Soto and about 600 Spanish soldiers landed somewhere in the Tampa Bay area. Marked by many Native American battles, the expedition covered 4,000 miles to the north and west. De Soto crossed the Mississippi River in 1541 and was buried in it when he died a year later. About half the group survived the 4-year ordeal.

The visitor center contains artifacts and exhibits explaining the expedition's effect on Native Americans. A 21-minute film depicting the expedition is shown hourly. Talks and weapons demonstrations by costumed rangers are given daily mid-December to late April based on staff availability; phone ahead to confirm schedule. There also is a nature trail; guided tours are available based on staff availability and weather permitting. Popular activities include fishing, bird-watching, picnicking and boating. Allow 1 hour minimum. Grounds open daily dawn-dusk;

parking lot gate closes at 5. Visitor Center open daily 9-5; closed Jan. 1, Thanksgiving and Christmas. Free. Phone (941) 792-0458.

DUNEDIN (H-1) pop. 35,321, elev. 13'

- **Hotels p. 70 • Restaurants p. 70**
- **Hotels & Restaurants map & index p. 286**
- **Part of St. Petersburg-Clearwater and Beaches area — see map p. 275**

Dunedin's rejuvenated downtown—a historic district complete with a red-, white- and blue-striped barber pole and an array of charming white picket fences—recalls a simpler way of life, while quirky boutiques and hip eateries bolster the town's far-from-dullsville rep. By day, antique shops, a weekly farmers market and artist-owned galleries lure vacationing shopaholics; by night, happy hour-seeking natives pack laid-back establishments that run the gamut from chic martini lounge to cozy Irish pub.

In addition, you'll find something special going on in this edgy small town every month—from arts and crafts exhibitions to ethnic fairs. Dunedin, a name closely resembling the Gaelic word from which Edinburgh is derived, celebrates its Scottish heritage with the Dunedin Highland Games and Festival in late March or early April, the Military Tattoo in early April, and the Celtic Music and Craft Beer Festival in mid-November. Other calendar highlights include the Art Harvest, a juried art show held the first weekend in November at Highlander Park, and Mardi Gras Celebration, featuring an outrageous Main Street parade in mid-February.

Along with window shoppers, twilight partyers and spirited festivalgoers, bicyclists, joggers and inline skaters wind through the downtown area on a portion of the Pinellas Trail, a 34-mile-long corridor spanning from Tarpon Springs to St. Petersburg. North of downtown at 1050 Palm Blvd., golfers work on lowering their handicap at the Dunedin Golf Club, home of the PGA 1945-62; phone (727) 733-2134. Meanwhile, from early March to early April droves of sports fanatics assemble just south of downtown at Florida Auto Exchange Stadium, 373 Douglas Ave., (727) 733-9302, to watch the Toronto Blue Jays baseball club during spring training. Throughout the summer, the Class A Florida State League Dunedin Blue Jays dazzle spectators.

Subtropical surroundings and miles of striking shoreline also bring day trippers to Dunedin, which originated as a seaport and trading center in the 1800s. Between the mainland and the islands outdoor enthusiasts can windsurf, sail catamarans and ride personal watercraft on the protected St. Joseph Sound. If you're a boater, cruise into the city marina, on the Intracoastal Waterway between the Dunedin and Clearwater causeways, then disembark for a stroll along the palm tree- and bench-studded linear park curving beside the water's edge on Edgewater Drive (US 19A).

Or, navigate your vessel to the 108-slip marina at Dunedin's most revered coastal attraction: Caladesi Island State Park *(see Recreation Areas Chart)*. Pint-size shell collectors happily lug burgeoning collections of delicate sand dollars, freckled conchs and porcelain cowries along Caladesi's secluded 3-mile beach—often regarded as one of the nation's best—as playful couples splash about the turquoise-tinted surf. Traverse a 3-mile kayak trail shaded by sinuous mangrove trees during your visit, or look for signs of gopher tortoises, armadillos and raccoons on a hike through pine forests and coastal strand and maritime hammock communities.

Passenger ferries to the barrier island also are available and depart daily beginning at 10 a.m. from Honeymoon Island State Park *(see Recreation Areas Chart)*, at the west end of the Dunedin Causeway (SR 586); phone (727) 734-5263 for ferry information. Both state parks offer opportunities for bird-watching (observe such endangered species as egrets, herons, ospreys and storks), swimming (plunge into warm waters averaging 75 F) and fishing (cast your line for everything from redfish to sheepshead).

Shopping: Before hitting the antique shops and chic boutiques lining the streets of downtown Dunedin—a compact historic district radiating old Florida charm—fuel up with a wholesome breakfast shake from the Dunedin Downtown Market, held Friday and Saturday mornings from early November through May at Pioneer Park (420 Main St.). Scan the veggie- and fruit-laden tables at the farmers market, then join the packs of pedestrians pausing before well-designed storefront windows and tempting sidewalk cafés on Main Street. After lunch, sift through vintage treasures and coastal home accents on Broadway, or model crocheted silk shawls and handmade jewelry in the bungalows-turned-showrooms on Douglas Avenue. Throughout the year, bazaars and special events highlighting everything from arts and crafts to cherished collectibles boost Dunedin's retail appeal.

Nightlife: You'll have a tough time deciding where to wet your whistle in Dunedin—home to trendsetting establishments and watering holes evoking old country traditions—so keep things simple and opt for a pub crawl. Play a quick game of darts at Mike & Lisa's Cricketers British Pub & Restaurant at 2634 Bayshore Blvd. before savoring their homemade steak and kidney pie. From Cricketers, it's just a short cab ride to downtown Dunedin. Make fast friends over sudsy beverages at Flanagan's Irish Pub, 465 Main St., where draft beers—including Guinness, Smithwick's, Newcastle and Killian's—are served, and where the St. Patrick's Day street festival is launched every year. Phone (727) 736-1322 for Mike & Lisa's Cricketers British Pub & Restaurant or (727) 401-3477 for Flanagan's Irish Pub.

Booth or table?

AAA.com/travelguides/restaurants

(See map & index p. 286.)

Just a few doors down from Flanagan's, Casa Tina, 365 Main St., emulates the aromas and vibrancy of Mexico with a delightfully unorthodox approach. Weekend-night patrons sip mojitos while watching performers from Dance & Circus Arts of Tampa Bay contort and twirl inside this colorful, folk art-adorned space; phone (727) 734-9226.

For some unadulterated local flavor, walk to Dunedin Brewery, about 2 blocks north of Main Street at 937 Douglas Ave. Ask the barkeep about the unconventional people who inspired Razz-BEERy Wheat Ale, or knock back a frosty mug of Apricot Peach Ale while planning your own fantastic shoreline-inspired saga; phone (727) 736-0606.

Whether you're in the mood for gorgonzola-stuffed pork chops, a caramel appletini, or a few rounds of drag queen-hosted bingo, the Kelly's suite of dining and entertainment establishments have you covered. Natives looking to see and be seen adore this artsy Main Street strip comprising a kitschy restaurant (Kelly's, for Just About Anything!), a fabulously retro martini lounge (The Chic-a-Boom Room), and a dynamic nightclub and show bar (Blur). Kick back on the spacious patio—purring with a jumbled soundtrack of clinking glasses, candid chortles, and jazz and hip-hop beats—or wave your hands in the air like you just don't care on the mirror-fronted dance floor. Show your face the next day (unless things got a bit *too* wild the night before), and Kelly's friendly staff will nurse your hangover with fresh-squeezed OJ, mouthwatering flapjacks, and lots and lots of eye-opening coffee; phone (727) 736-0206 for The Chic-a-Boom Room and Blur or (727) 736-5284 for Kelly's.

Greater Dunedin Chamber of Commerce: 301 Main St., Dunedin, FL 34698. **Phone:** (727) 733-3197.

DUNEDIN FINE ART CENTER is at 1143 Michigan Blvd. Five galleries feature changing exhibits of local, regional and national artists. The David L. Mason Children's Art Museum provides interactive and hands-on experiences that make art fun for both children and their parents. **Time:** Allow 1 hour minimum. **Hours:** Fine Art Center Mon.-Fri. 10-5, Sat. 10-2, Sun. 1-4. Children's Art Museum Mon.-Fri. 10-5, Sat. 10-2, Sun. 1-4, mid-Sept. through June 30; Mon.-Fri. 3:30-5, Sat. 10-2, Sun. 1-4, rest of year. Closed major holidays. Phone ahead to confirm schedule. **Cost:** Donations. Children's art museum $4; $3 (ages 65+); free (ages 0-2). **Phone:** (727) 298-3322.

DUNEDIN HISTORICAL MUSEUM is at 349 Main St. The area's history from 1870s to the present is depicted through various exhibits including vintage clothing, household implements and railroad artifacts. Special programs such as 1890s baseball games and living-history re-enactments also are offered. **Time:** Allow 1 hour, 30 minutes minimum. **Hours:** Tues.-Sat. 10-4. Closed major holidays. **Cost:** $3; free (ages 0-12). **Phone:** (727) 736-1176.

BEST WESTERN PLUS YACHT HARBOR INN
727/733-4121 **17**

Motel

AAA Benefit: Members save up to 15% and earn bonus points!

Address: 150 Marina Plaza 34698 **Location:** Waterfront. Jct Alternate Rt US 19 (Bayshore Blvd) and gulf end of Main St, 0.5 mi s of SR 580. **Facility:** 54 units, some two bedrooms. 2 stories, exterior corridors. **Dining:** Bon Appetit Restaurant & Marina Cafe, see separate listing. **Pool:** heated outdoor. **Activities:** hot tub, bicycles, exercise room. **Guest Services:** valet and coin laundry. **Featured Amenity: breakfast buffet.**

SAVE CALL 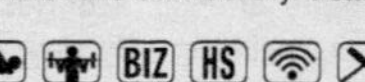

FENWAY HOTEL, AUTOGRAPH COLLECTION
727/683-5999 **18**

Historic Hotel

AUTOGRAPH COLLECTION HOTELS **AAA Benefit:** Members save 5% or more!

Address: 453 Edgewater Dr 34698 **Location:** Waterfront. 0.5 mi n of Main St. **Facility:** Built in 1925, the property has an interesting history with having been a hotel with a speakeasy, the site of the first local radio station and it served as a local college. It has now been reborn. 83 units. 2-3 stories, interior corridors. *Bath:* shower only. **Parking:** valet only. **Amenities:** safes. **Dining:** 2 restaurants, entertainment. **Pool:** heated outdoor. **Activities:** recreation programs, bicycles, lawn sports, health club. **Guest Services:** valet laundry.

SAVE CALL HS

HOLIDAY INN EXPRESS HOTEL & SUITES CLEARWATER NORTH/DUNEDIN 727/450-1200 **16**

Hotel. **Address:** 975 Broadway St 34698

WHERE TO EAT

BON APPETIT RESTAURANT & MARINA CAFE
727/733-2151 **18**

Continental. Fine Dining. **Address:** 148 Marina Plaza 34698

CAFE ALFRESCO 727/736-4299 **20**

Italian. Casual Dining. **Address:** 344 Main St 34698

CAFE HONEYMOON 727/736-2132

Sandwiches. Quick Serve. **Address:** 1 Causeway Blvd 34698

CASA TINA 727/734-9226 **23**

Mexican. Casual Dining. **Address:** 365 Main St 34698

FLANAGAN'S IRISH PUB & RESTAURANT
727/736-4994 **19**

Irish. Casual Dining. **Address:** 465 Main St 34698

HONEYMOON SOUTH BEACH PAVILION 727/260-5503

American. Quick Serve. **Address:** 1 Causeway Blvd 34698

JULIAN'S LITTLE ITALY 727/734-8989 **17**

Italian. Casual Dining. **Address:** 916-A Patricia Ave 34698

KELLY'S CHIC-A-BOOM-ROOM 727/736-5284 **22**

Continental. Casual Dining. **Address:** 319 Main St 34698

(See map & index p. 286.)

LONNI'S SANDWICHES, ETC. 727/734-0121

Sandwiches. Quick Serve. **Address:** 1153 Main St 34698

MARGUERITE'S CAFE AND CATERING 727/734-7040 (25)

Breakfast Sandwiches. Casual Dining. **Address:** 405 Plaza Dr 34698

THE RESTORATIVE (24)

American. Casual Dining. **Address:** 420 Patricia Ave 34698

SEA SEA RIDERS RESTAURANT 727/734-1445 (21)

Seafood. Casual Dining. **Address:** 221 Main St 34698

EAST PALATKA pop. 1,654

BEST WESTERN INN OF PALATKA 386/325-7800

Motel

AAA Benefit: Members save up to 15% and earn bonus points!

Address: 119 S Hwy 17 32131 **Location:** On US 17, just s of St. Johns River Bridge. **Facility:** 54 units, some efficiencies. 2 stories (no elevator), exterior corridors. **Terms:** check-in 4 pm. **Pool:** outdoor. **Activities:** exercise room. **Guest Services:** coin laundry. **Featured Amenity: breakfast buffet.**

WHERE TO EAT

MUSSELWHITE'S SEAFOOD & GRILL 386/326-9111

Seafood. Casual Dining. **Address:** 125 Hwy 17 S 32131

EATONVILLE (F-4) pop. 2,159, elev. 95'

• Part of Orlando area — see map p. 2

In 1887, the town of Eatonville was the first African-American community in the United States to become incorporated. Growing up in this small bedroom community just minutes from Orlando inspired author Zora Neale Hurston in much of her work. Eatonville's beloved native daughter is best known for her novel "Their Eyes Were Watching God."

The town celebrates its most well-known resident annually with the Zora Neale Hurston Festival of the Arts and Humanities, also known as the ZORA! Festival, held in late January. The festival features entertainment by well-known gospel, R & B, Latin, spoken word and jazz artists such as Ashford & Simpson and the Ramsey Lewis Trio. African-American culture also is explored through visual art exhibitions and vendors, public forums and panel discussions.

ZORA NEALE HURSTON NATIONAL MUSEUM OF FINE ART is at 227 E. Kennedy Blvd. The museum serves as a platform for the arts and heritage experience as depicted in the literary works of writer, folklorist and anthropologist Zora Neale Hurston. Temporary exhibits showcase the work of African-American artists. **Time:** Allow 1 hour minimum. **Hours:** Mon.-Fri. 9-4, Sat. 11-1. Closed major holidays. **Cost:** Donations. **Phone:** (407) 647-3307.

EDGEWATER pop. 20,750

BEST WESTERN EDGEWATER INN 386/427-7101

Hotel

AAA Benefit: Members save up to 15% and earn bonus points!

Address: 1730 S Ridgewood Ave 32132 **Location:** I-95 exit 244 (SR 442), 3.7 mi e to US 1 (Ridgewood Ave), then just n. **Facility:** 45 units. 2 stories, interior corridors. **Pool:** outdoor. **Guest Services:** coin laundry. **Featured Amenity: continental breakfast.**

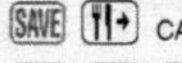 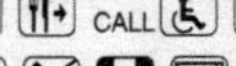 

WHERE TO EAT

ATHENS FAMILY RESTAURANT 386/423-8159

Greek. Casual Dining. **Address:** 1401 S Ridgewood Ave 32132

DUSTIN'S BAR-B-Q 386/423-5299

Barbecue. Quick Serve. **Address:** 1208 S Ridgewood Ave 32132

ELLENTON (I-2) pop. 4,275, elev. 11'

• Hotels & Restaurants map & index p. 300

Ellenton, a small community on the northern bank of the Manatee River, offers fine fishing opportunities, nearby white sandy beaches and a climate favorable to agricultural endeavors.

Shopping: Ellenton Prime Outlets, off I-75 exit 224 at 5461 Factory Shops Blvd., features more than 135 factory outlet stores, including Kate Spade New York, Nike Factory Store, Saks Fifth Avenue OFF 5th and Van Heusen.

HAMPTON INN ELLENTON-BRADENTON 941/721-4000 (27)

SAVE Hotel. **Address:** 5810 20th Ct E 34222

AAA Benefit: Members save 5% or more!

WHERE TO EAT

ANNA MARIA OYSTER BAR 941/721-7773

Seafood. Casual Dining. **Address:** 1525 51st Ave E 34222

HICKORY HOLLOW RESTAURANT 941/722-3932 (36)

Comfort Food. Casual Dining. **Address:** 4705 US Hwy 301 N 34222

PEACH'S RESTAURANT 941/721-7838 (34)

Breakfast Sandwiches. Casual Dining. **Address:** 2207 60th Ave E 34222

RIPPERS ROADSTAND 941/479-7999 (33)

Burgers Hot Dogs. Quick Serve. **Address:** 5967 Factory Shops Blvd 34222

SHAKE STATION 941/722-7866 (37)

Burgers Sandwiches. Casual Dining. **Address:** 4219 US 301 N 34222

WOODY'S RIVER ROO PUB & GRILL 941/722-2391 (35)

American. Casual Dining. **Address:** 5717 18th St E 34222

EUSTIS pop. 18,558

• Hotels & Restaurants map & index p. 188
• Part of Orlando area — see map p. 2

GATOR'S DOCKSIDE 352/357-1255

American. Casual Dining. **Address:** 15241 US Hwy 441 32726

HAYSTAX RESTAURANT 352/589-0510 (66)

Comfort Food. Casual Dining. **Address:** 15939 US Hwy 441 32726

SONNY'S REAL PIT BAR-B-Q 352/589-6888

Barbecue. Casual Dining. **Address:** 15800 Hwy 441 32726

FERNANDINA BEACH (A-12) pop. 11,487, elev. 10'

• Part of Jacksonville area — see map p. 84

This centuries-old town on Amelia Island *(see place listing p. 30)* features a variety of architectural styles. The Victorian district is scattered across 50 blocks, including residential and commercial buildings and a popular shopping area. The heart of downtown is Centre Street, an eight-block pedestrian-friendly corridor leading to the Intracoastal Waterway and a marina, where shrimp boats unload the catch of the day and charter boats depart for sightseeing and fishing. On Centre Street at Second Avenue is the Palace Saloon, built in 1878 and reputedly the oldest in the state. A hand-carved, 40-foot mahogany bar and hand-painted murals decorate the interior; phone (844) 441-2444.

Fernandina Beach is the northern terminus for a portion of scenic highway extending 105 miles south via SR A1A to Daytona Beach.

The first week in May the town celebrates the local shrimping industry and its early days under the flags of eight nations with the Isle of Eight Flags Shrimp Festival.

Self-guiding tours: A brochure outlining a tour of the historic district is available from the Amelia Island/Fernandina Beach/Yulee Chamber of Commerce *(see Amelia Island).*

FLAGLER BEACH pop. 4,484, elev. 7'

Self-guiding tours: A brochure outlining a tour of historic downtown is available from the Flagler Beach Historical Museum.

THE WHITE ORCHID OCEANFRONT INN & SPA 386/439-4944

Bed & Breakfast. **Address:** 1104 S Oceanshore Blvd 32136

WHERE TO EAT

DAHLIA MEXICAN KITCHEN 386/338-3514

Mexican. Casual Dining. **Address:** 422 Beach Village Dr 32136

THE FLAGLER FISH COMPANY 386/439-0000

Seafood. Casual Dining. **Address:** 180 S Daytona Ave 32136

FUNKY PELICAN 386/439-0011

American Seafood. Casual Dining. **Address:** 215 S Oceanshore Blvd 32136

THE GOLDEN LION CAFE 386/439-3004

American Casual Dining
$10-$38

AAA Inspector Notes: Across the street from the beach, this casual spot has scenic views from just about every table. The upstairs deck is perched high above everything and is a great place to enjoy a refreshing drink and a tasty meal. Menu items include delicious burgers, peel and eat shrimp, and the famous fish and chips, which are super crispy, fresh and delicious. Live music is featured on select days. Check out the specialty drinks. **Features:** full bar, patio dining, happy hour. **Address:** 501 N Oceanshore Blvd 32136 **Location:** I-95 exit 284 (SR 100/Moody Blvd), 3.4 mi e to SR A1A (Oceanshore Blvd), then just n. **Parking:** on-site and street.

L D

FORT MATANZAS NATIONAL MONUMENT (D-4)

Off SR A1A 14 miles south of St. Augustine, Fort Matanzas National Monument includes the southern tip of Anastasia Island and the northern third of Rattlesnake Island. There is ferry service to the fort from which the monument took its name every hour on the half hour daily 9:30-4:30; to determine if the ferry is operating, phone (904) 471-0116. Ferry tickets are issued on a first-come, first-served basis and are required for boarding; visitors can pick one up at the visitor center. The fort can be seen from the dock on Anastasia Island.

Built of coquina 1740-42 by the Spanish, Fort Matanzas replaced temporary watch stations that had guarded the southern approach to St. Augustine since 1569. In 1564 French Huguenots established a settlement in the area, threatening the Spaniards with territorial encroachment and what the latter considered to be religious heresy.

Pedro Menéndez de Avilés was sent to remove the French and establish a colony in 1565. Following a hurricane that scattered the attacking French ships, he captured Fort Caroline, about 35 miles north of St. Augustine. Upon returning to St. Augustine, Menéndez located the shipwrecked survivors of the French fleet some 14 miles south of town, where most of them surrendered and were killed.

By the time the Castillo de San Marcos in St. Augustine and Fort Matanzas were built, it was the English that threatened Spanish Florida. After surviving two attacks at the castillo, the Spanish constructed Fort Matanzas watchtower, at the southern approach to the city. Used briefly by the British during the American Revolution, the forts became the property of the United States in 1821. Fort Matanzas and nearly 300 acres of natural barrier island became a national monument in 1924.

A small visitor center on Anastasia Island contains exhibits pertaining to the fort's history. Swimming east of SR A1A at Matanzas Inlet is dangerous because of the currents. Grounds open daily 9-5:30. Visitor center open daily 9-5. Closed Christmas. Free. Phone (904) 471-0116.

GAINESVILLE (C-9) pop. 124,354, elev. 170'

• Hotels p. 77 • Restaurants p. 79
• Hotels & Restaurants map & index p. 75

Gainesville was founded in 1853 and named for Edmund Pendleton Gaines, a U.S. Army officer who served in the War of 1812 and as a commander during the Seminole and Mexican-American Wars. Gaines' surname also provided the inspiration for the naming of the cities of Gainesville in Georgia and Texas as well as Gainesboro, Tenn.

The community has strong roots in both agriculture and education, as it is home to the headquarters of several federal and state agricultural agencies, populous Santa Fe College and the University of Florida, one of the country's largest collegiate institutions. Set on a 2,000-acre campus just off I-75, the university is renowned for its research in such fields as medicine. The campus' historic district comprises more than two dozen buildings and properties, some dating to the early 20th century. On the main campus, Century Tower, a 157-foot-tall carillon, pays homage to alumni and students who died in the World Wars. The university's athletic program also is strong; the men's basketball team earned consecutive NCAA titles in 2006-07, while its football team has claimed three national championships since 1996.

Student-guided walking tours of the campus are offered Monday through Friday at 11 a.m. and 1 or 2 p.m.; phone (352) 392-2959. A map of the campus is available at the AAA office at 1201 N.W. 13th St., or at the university's Welcome Center in the J. Wayne Reitz Union building on Museum Road.

Regional history exhibits at Matheson History Museum, 513 E. University Ave., cover such topics as the Timucuan Indians, Spanish occupation and travels of William Bartram. The museum complex also includes one of Gainesville's oldest residences (built in 1867), a botanical garden and a tool museum; phone (352) 378-2280.

The Hippodrome Theatre, 25 S.E. 2nd Pl., presents professional theater performances in a renovated 1911 federal building that once housed courtrooms, government offices and a post office. Additional offerings include a cinema series, playwright festivals and an art gallery featuring pieces crafted by local artisans. Performance schedules and ticketing information are available from the theater's box office; phone (352) 375-4477.

The Gainesville to Hawthorne State Trail, a 16-mile trail designed for bicycling, horseback riding and walking, extends from Boulware Springs, on S.E. 15th Street in Paynes Prairie Preserve State Park *(see attraction listing p. 152 and Recreation Areas Chart)*, through Lochloosa Wildlife Management Area to the town of Hawthorne. For trail information, phone the Florida Park Service Information Center at (850) 245-2157 or (352) 466-3397.

Held rain or shine each Wednesday from 4-7 p.m., the Union Street Farmers' Market, 111 E. University Ave. at the Bo Diddley Community Plaza, provides local vendors with the opportunity to offer such goods as produce and dairy as well as baked and organic items. Art and such accessories as handmade jewelry also may be purchased.

The city caters to an abundance of its diverse community's persuasions and tastes, offering a wide range of dining experiences and nightlife options. Themed and specialized restaurants, the latter of which entail a variety of ethnic and vegetarian eateries, are located throughout the city and its outskirts. The downtown neighborhoods are abuzz on a nightly basis, as a number of live music venues showcase local and traveling talent and an array of bars and college hangouts attract college students and citizens alike.

Visit Gainesville: 30 E. University Ave., Gainesville, FL 32601. **Phone:** (352) 374-5260 or (866) 778-5002.

Shopping: Among the more than 140 stores at The Oaks Mall, off I-75 exit 387 at 6419 W. Newberry Rd., are Belk, Dillard's, JCPenney and Sears.

Road Trip? We'll be there for you.
AAA/CAA Mobile Battery Service.
Delivered & Installed on the Spot!
Download our apps today
Power You Can Trust!™

(See map & index p. 75.)

UNIVERSITY OF FLORIDA campus is accessed by I-75 exits 382-384; tours depart from the J. Wayne Reitz Union, just w. of jct. Museum Rd. and US 441/SR 24/S.W. Thirteenth St. The university, with an approximate enrollment of some 51,000 students, was founded in 1853. In the 2012-13 season, UF claimed eight conference crowns in such sports as men's basketball, gymnastics, women's tennis and soccer. The campus features Century Tower, one of only four carillons in the state, 10 libraries and a multipurpose arena.

Time: Allow 2 hours minimum. **Hours:** 1.5-hour student-guided walking tours of the central campus are offered, weather permitting, following information sessions Mon.-Fri. at 11 and 1 or 3 (also at 2 or 4 on select days). Guided tours are not offered on university holidays and home football game weekends. Closed major holidays. Phone ahead to confirm schedule. **Cost:** Tours free. Reservations are required. **Parking:** $5. **Phone:** (352) 392-2959. ***(See ad p. 78.)*** GT

Florida Museum of Natural History is at 3215 Hull Rd. in Powell Hall at the University of Florida Cultural Plaza. The Butterfly Rainforest features waterfalls, lush tropical foliage and hundreds of free-flying butterflies. Museum exhibits include a full-scale North Florida limestone cave replica and mammoth and mastodon skeletons standing more than 12 feet tall. The Florida Fossils exhibit traces 65 million years of state history. Visitors may experience a Calusa Indian welcoming ceremony. The museum also has temporary exhibits.

Note: Butterfly release Mon.-Fri. at 2; Sat.-Sun. at 2 and 3. **Time:** Allow 1 hour minimum. **Hours:** Mon.-Sat. 10-5, Sun. 1-5. Last admission to Butterfly Rainforest and temporary exhibits is 30 minutes before closing. Closed Thanksgiving, Christmas Eve and Christmas. **Cost:** Permanent museum exhibits by donation. Butterfly Rainforest $14; $12 (FL residents and FL students with ID); $7 (ages 3-17). Free (University of Florida students with ID and ages 0-2); Admission may be charged during temporary exhibits. **Parking:** Mon.-Fri. $4 (cash only); Sat.-Sun. and state holidays free. **Phone:** (352) 846-2000. ***(See ad p. 78.)***

Samuel P. Harn Museum of Art, 3259 Hull Rd. in the University of Florida Cultural Plaza, houses more than 9,000 works focusing on African and Asian art, modern and contemporary art and photography. On view are examples from the permanent collections as well as temporary exhibitions of loaned artwork. Five themed gardens surround the building.

Time: Allow 1 hour minimum. **Hours:** Tues.-Fri. 11-5, Sat. 10-5, Sun. 1-5 (also second Thurs. of the month 6-9 p.m.). Guided tours Sat.-Sun. at 2. Last admission 15 minutes before closing. Closed state holidays. **Cost:** Donations. **Parking:** $4; free on weekends and state holidays. **Phone:** (352) 392-9826. GT

University Gallery is at jct. S.W. 13th St. and S.W. 4th Ave. in the College of Fine Arts (Building B) at the University of Florida. The gallery showcases contemporary art with an emphasis on interdisciplinary content. Faculty and student work also is exhibited. **Time:** Allow 1 hour minimum. **Hours:** Tues.-Fri. 10-5 (also Thurs. 5-7), Sat. noon-4. Closed academic holidays. **Cost:** Free. **Phone:** (352) 273-3000.

Visit with us on your favorite social media sites for the latest updates on hot discounts, cool destinations and handy automotive know-how. *Talk with us!*

AAA.com/Facebook
AAA.com/Twitter
Instagram.com/aaa_national
YouTube.com/AAA

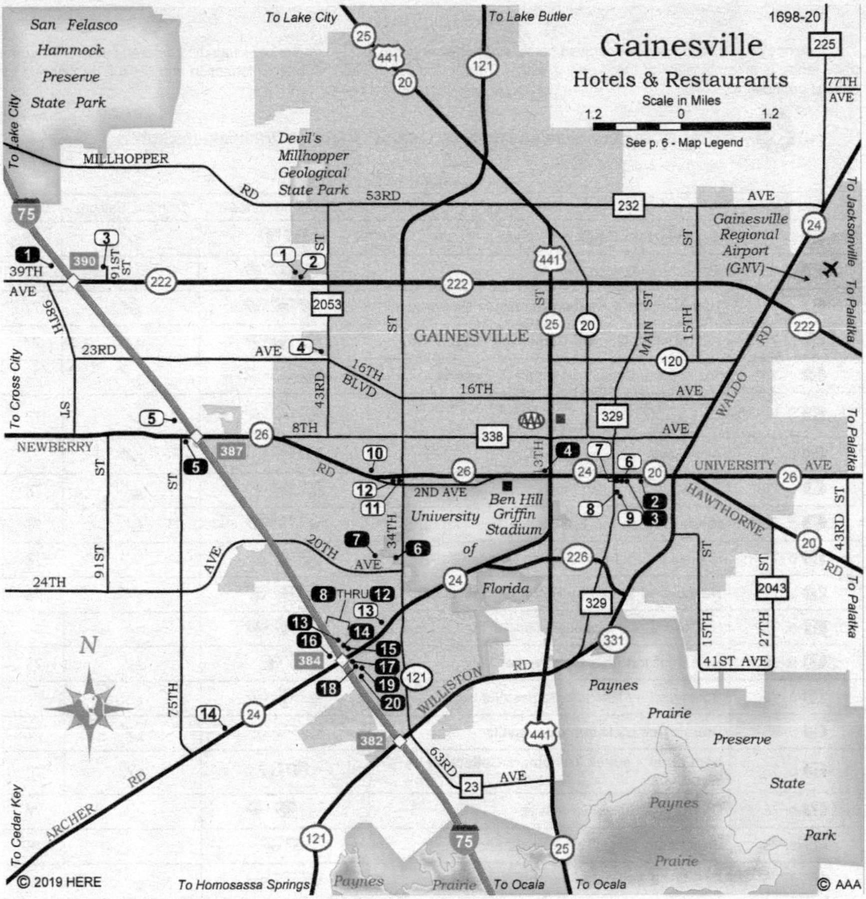

Gainesville

Hotels & Restaurants

Scale in Miles
1.2 0 1.2

See p. 6 - Map Legend

1698-20

San Felasco Hammock Preserve State Park

Devil's Millhopper Geological State Park

Gainesville Regional Airport (GNV)

GAINESVILLE

University of Florida

Ben Hill Griffin Stadium

Paynes Prairie Preserve State Park

To Lake City
To Lake Butler
To Jacksonville
To Palatka
To Cross City
To Cedar Key
To Homosassa Springs
To Ocala

MILLHOPPER RD
53RD AVE
39TH AVE
23RD AVE
16TH AVE
8TH AVE
NEWBERRY RD
UNIVERSITY AVE
2ND AVE
20TH AVE
24TH AVE
ARCHER RD
WILLISTON RD
HAWTHORNE RD
WALDO RD
41ST AVE
63RD
23 AVE
16TH BLVD
MAIN ST
13TH ST
15TH ST
34TH ST
43RD ST
75TH ST
91ST ST
27TH ST
98TH ST
77TH AVE

© 2019 HERE
© AAA

Share the security and savings with those you love

Add drivers in your household as Associate members and give them the same great benefits you trust and enjoy.

Add an Associate membership today:

- Online at AAA.com/membership
- Visit your local club office
- Call 800-Join-AAA (564-6222)

AAA

Gainesville

This index helps you "spot" where approved hotels and restaurants are located on the corresponding detailed maps. Restaurant price range is a combination of lunch and/or dinner. Turn to the listing page for more information and consult display ads for special promotions.

For more details, rates and reservations: AAA.com/travelguides/hotels

GAINESVILLE

Map Page	Hotels	Diamond Rated	Member Savings	Page
1 p. 75	**Best Western Gateway Grand**	◆◆	✔	77
2 p. 75	Sweetwater Branch Inn	◆◆◆		78
3 p. 75	**Hampton Inn & Suites Gainesville Downtown**	◆◆◆	✔	77
4 p. 75	**AC Hotel by Marriott Gainesville Downtown**	◆◆◆	✔	77
5 p. 75	TownePlace Suites by Marriott Gainesville	◆◆◆	✔	78
6 p. 75	Hilton University of Florida Conference Center Gainesville	◆◆◆	✔	78
7 p. 75	Aloft Gainesville University Area	◆◆◆	✔	77
8 p. 75	Residence Inn by Marriott Gainesville I-75	◆◆◆	✔	78
9 p. 75	**Hilton Garden Inn Gainesville**	◆◆◆	✔	77
10 p. 75	Holiday Inn Express & Suites Gainesville I-75	◆◆◆		78
11 p. 75	**Homewood Suites by Hilton Gainesville FL**	◆◆◆	✔	78
12 p. 75	Staybridge Suites Gainesville I-75	◆◆◆		78
13 p. 75	**Red Roof Inn Plus Gainesville**	◆◆	✔	78
14 p. 75	**Courtyard by Marriott Gainesville**	◆◆◆	✔	77
15 p. 75	**DoubleTree by Hilton Gainesville**	◆◆◆	✔	77
16 p. 75	**hom hotel + suites Trademark Collection by Wyndham**	◆◆	✔	78
17 p. 75	Drury Inn & Suites Gainesville	◆◆◆		77
18 p. 75	Sleep Inn & Suites University/Shands	◆◆		78
19 p. 75	**SpringHill Suites by Marriott Gainesville**	◆◆◆	✔	78
20 p. 75	Hampton Inn	◆◆◆	✔	77

Map Page	Restaurants	Diamond Rated	Cuisine	Price Range	Page
1 p. 75	One Love Cafe	◆◆	American	$7-$13	79
2 p. 75	Taste Sushi Bar & Asian Cuisine	◆◆	Asian Sushi	$10-$20	79
3 p. 75	**Pomodoro Cafe**	◆◆	Italian	$13-$18	79
4 p. 75	43rd Street Deli & Breakfast House	◆◆	Breakfast Comfort Food	$7-$12	79
5 p. 75	The Bakery Mill & Deli	◆	Deli Breads/ Pastries	$4-$12	79
6 p. 75	Emiliano's Cafe	◆◆	Latin American	$8-$28	79
7 p. 75	The Gelato Company and Eatery	◆	Sandwiches	$8-$11	79
8 p. 75	Amelia's Italian Cuisine	◆◆◆	Italian	$18-$28	79
9 p. 75	Liquid Ginger	◆◆	Asian Sushi	$7-$22	79
10 p. 75	Ballyhoo Grill	◆◆	Seafood Steak	$8-$26	79
11 p. 75	Mi Apa Latin Cafe	◆	Cuban	$6-$8	79
12 p. 75	**Mildred's Big City Food**	◆◆◆	American	$8-$32	79
13 p. 75	Bonefish Grill	◆◆◆	Seafood	$15-$34	79
14 p. 75	Backstreet Blues Chophouse and Oyster Bar	◆◆◆	Steak	$15-$100	79

(See map & index p. 75.)

AC HOTEL BY MARRIOTT GAINESVILLE DOWNTOWN 352/792-1151 4

Hotel

AAA Benefit: Members save 5% or more!

Address: 151 NW 14th St 32603 **Location:** Jct W University Ave and SR 26, just n. **Facility:** 144 units. 10 stories, interior corridors. **Parking:** valet only. **Pool:** heated outdoor. **Activities:** exercise room. **Guest Services:** valet laundry.

 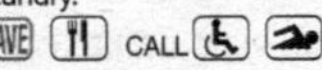   

ALOFT GAINESVILLE UNIVERSITY AREA 352/378-1100 7

Hotel. **Address:** 3743 Hull Rd 32607

AAA Benefit: Members save 5% or more!

BEST WESTERN GATEWAY GRAND 352/331-3336 1

Hotel

AAA Benefit: Members save up to 15% and earn bonus points!

Address: 4200 NW 97th Blvd 32606 **Location:** I-75 exit 390, just w on SR 222, then just n. **Facility:** 152 units. 3 stories, interior corridors. **Terms:** check-in 4 pm. **Pool:** outdoor. **Activities:** hot tub, lawn sports, picnic facilities, exercise room, massage. **Guest Services:** valet and coin laundry, area transportation. **Featured Amenity: continental breakfast.**

 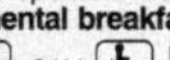  SOME UNITS

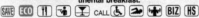

COURTYARD BY MARRIOTT GAINESVILLE 352/335-9100 14

Hotel

COURTYARD **AAA Benefit:** Members save 5% or more!

Address: 3700 SW 42nd St 32608 **Location:** I-75 exit 384, just e on SR 24 (Archer Rd), then just n. **Facility:** 81 units. 3 stories, interior corridors. **Pool:** heated outdoor. **Activities:** exercise room. **Guest Services:** valet and coin laundry, boarding pass kiosk.

 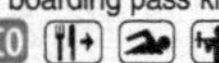   SOME UNITS

DOUBLETREE BY HILTON GAINESVILLE 352/375-2400 15

Hotel

AAA Benefit: Members save 5% or more!

Address: 3726 SW 40th Blvd 32608 **Location:** I-75 exit 384, just e on SR 24 (Archer Rd), then just n. **Facility:** 205 units. 3 stories, interior corridors. **Pool:** outdoor. **Activities:** lawn sports, exercise room. **Guest Services:** valet laundry, area transportation.

 SOME UNITS

DRURY INN & SUITES GAINESVILLE 352/372-5600 17

Hotel. **Address:** 4000 SW 40th Blvd 32608

HAMPTON INN 352/371-4171 20

Hotel. **Address:** 4225 SW 40th Blvd 32608

AAA Benefit: Members save 5% or more!

HAMPTON INN & SUITES GAINESVILLE DOWNTOWN 352/240-9300 3

Hotel

AAA Benefit: Members save 5% or more!

Address: 101 SE 1st Ave 32601 **Location:** Jct SE 1st St (Main St); downtown. **Facility:** 124 units. 6 stories, interior corridors. **Parking:** on-site (fee) and valet. **Terms:** check-in 4 pm. **Pool:** heated outdoor. **Activities:** exercise room, massage. **Guest Services:** valet laundry. **Featured Amenity: full hot breakfast.**

SOME UNITS

HILTON GARDEN INN GAINESVILLE 352/338-1466 9

Hotel

AAA Benefit: Members save 5% or more!

Address: 4075 SW 33rd Pl 32608 **Location:** I-75 exit 384, just e on SR 24 (Archer Rd), just ne on Clark Butler Blvd, then just w. **Facility:** 104 units. 4 stories, interior corridors. **Pool:** outdoor. **Activities:** exercise room. **Guest Services:** valet and coin laundry.

Get an expert view from AAA inspectors:

AAA.com/travelguides/hotels

(See map & index p. 75.)

HILTON UNIVERSITY OF FLORIDA CONFERENCE CENTER GAINESVILLE 352/371-3600 **6**

SAVE Hotel. **Address:** 1714 SW 34th St 32607

AAA Benefit: Members save 5% or more!

HOLIDAY INN EXPRESS & SUITES GAINESVILLE I-75 352/378-1300 **10**

Hotel. **Address:** 3370 SW 42nd St 32608

HOMEWOOD SUITES BY HILTON GAINESVILLE FL 352/335-3133 **11**

Extended Stay Hotel

HOMEWOOD SUITES BY HILTON **AAA Benefit:** Members save 5% or more!

Address: 3333 SW 42nd St 32608 **Location:** I-75 exit 384, just e on SR 24 (Archer Rd). **Facility:** 103 efficiencies, some two bedrooms. 4 stories, interior corridors. **Terms:** check-in 4 pm. **Pool:** outdoor. **Activities:** exercise room. **Guest Services:** valet and coin laundry. **Featured Amenity: breakfast buffet.**

SAVE ECO CALL  

BIZ HS

/ SOME UNITS

Florida Museum
Butterfly Rainforest
Experience hundreds of living butterflies from around the world!
FLORIDA MUSEUM
UF UNIVERSITY of FLORIDA
3215 Hull Road, Gainesville, FL 32611
floridamuseum.ufl.edu/butterflies

HOM HOTEL + SUITES TRADEMARK COLLECTION BY WYNDHAM 352/376-0004 **16**

Hotel

Address: 3905 SW 43rd St 32608 **Location:** I-75 exit 384, just w on SR 24 (Archer Rd), then just n. **Facility:** 114 units. 4 stories, interior corridors. **Pool:** heated outdoor. **Activities:** exercise room. **Guest Services:** valet and coin laundry. **Featured Amenity: breakfast buffet.**

SAVE CALL BIZ

HS

/ SOME UNITS

RED ROOF INN PLUS GAINESVILLE 352/336-3311 **13**

Hotel

Address: 3500 SW 42nd St 32608 **Location:** I-75 exit 384, Just e on SR 24 (Archer Rd), then just n. **Facility:** 129 units. 4 stories, interior corridors. **Terms:** check-in 4 pm. **Amenities:** safes. **Pool:** outdoor.

SAVE

/ SOME UNITS

RESIDENCE INN BY MARRIOTT GAINESVILLE I-75 352/264-0000 **8**

SAVE Extended Stay Hotel. **Address:** 3275 SW 40th Blvd 32608

AAA Benefit: Members save 5% or more!

SLEEP INN & SUITES UNIVERSITY/SHANDS 352/376-4145 **18**

Hotel. **Address:** 4110 SW 40th Blvd 32608

SPRINGHILL SUITES BY MARRIOTT GAINESVILLE 352/376-8873 **19**

Hotel

SPRINGHILL SUITES MARRIOTT **AAA Benefit:** Members save 5% or more!

Address: 4155 SW 40th Blvd 32608 **Location:** I-75 exit 384, just e, then just s. Located at the end of a quiet street. **Facility:** 126 units. 4 stories, interior corridors. **Pool:** heated outdoor. **Activities:** exercise room. **Guest Services:** valet and coin laundry. **Featured Amenity: breakfast buffet.**

SAVE ECO CALL

BIZ HS

STAYBRIDGE SUITES GAINESVILLE I-75 352/378-1900 **12**

Extended Stay Hotel. **Address:** 3401 SW 40th Blvd 32608

SWEETWATER BRANCH INN 352/373-6760 **2**

Historic Bed & Breakfast. **Address:** 625 E University Ave 32601

TOWNEPLACE SUITES BY MARRIOTT GAINESVILLE 352/415-1111 **5**

SAVE Extended Stay Hotel. **Address:** 7451 W Newberry Rd 32605

AAA Benefit: Members save 5% or more!

(See map & index p. 75.)

WHERE TO EAT

43RD STREET DELI & BREAKFAST HOUSE 352/373-5656

Breakfast Sandwiches. Casual Dining. **Address:** 3483 SW Williston Rd 32608

43RD STREET DELI & BREAKFAST HOUSE 352/373-2927 (4)

Breakfast Comfort Food. Casual Dining. **Address:** 4401 NW 25th Pl 32606

ADAMS RIB CO. 352/373-8882

Barbecue. Casual Dining. **Address:** 2109 NW 13th St 32609

ADAMS RIB CO. 352/727-4005

Barbecue. Casual Dining. **Address:** 1515 SW 13th St 32608

AMELIA'S ITALIAN CUISINE 352/373-1919 (8)

Italian. Fine Dining. **Address:** 235 S Main St 32601

BACKSTREET BLUES CHOPHOUSE AND OYSTER BAR 352/363-6792 (14)

Steak. Casual Dining. **Address:** 6500 SW Archer Rd 32608

THE BAKERY MILL & DELI 352/331-3354 (5)

Deli Breads/Pastries. Quick Serve. **Address:** 1143 NW 76th Blvd 32606

BALLYHOO GRILL 352/373-0059 (10)

Seafood Steak. Casual Dining. **Address:** 3700 W University Ave 32607

BENTO ASIAN KITCHEN + SUSHI 352/377-8686

Japanese. Quick Serve. **Address:** 3832 W Newberry Rd 32607

BENTO ASIAN KITCHEN + SUSHI 352/224-5123

Japanese. Quick Serve. **Address:** 3841 SW Archer Rd 32608

BONEFISH GRILL 352/377-8383 (13)

Seafood. Fine Dining. **Address:** 3237 SW 35th Blvd 32608

EMILIANO'S CAFE 352/375-7381 (6)

Latin American. Casual Dining. **Address:** 7 SE 1st Ave 32601

GATOR'S DOCKSIDE 352/338-4445

American. Casual Dining. **Address:** 3842 Newberry Rd 32607

THE GELATO COMPANY AND EATERY 352/373-3153 (7)

Sandwiches. Quick Serve. **Address:** 11 SE 1st Ave 32601

LIQUID GINGER 352/371-2323 (9)

Asian Sushi. Casual Dining. **Address:** 101 SE 2nd Pl 32601

MI APA LATIN CAFE 352/376-7020 (11)

Cuban. Quick Serve. **Address:** 114 SW 34th St 32607

MILDRED'S BIG CITY FOOD 352/371-1711 (12)

American Casual Dining
$8-$32

AAA Inspector Notes: By day, this is a casual coffee shop which serves tempting lunch items such as interesting sandwiches that include the hot ham and brie, Mildred's club and seared tuna club. By night, service and fare is elevated as the spot is transformed into a trendy bistro with a sophisticated vibe. Evening menu temptations include roasted hen, scallops and lamb trio. To ensure freshness, the menu changes almost daily. A featured wine is listed on the evening menu. Rating reflects evening dinner service. **Features:** full bar, patio dining, Sunday brunch, happy hour. **Reservations:** suggested, for dinner. **Address:** 3445 W University Ave 32607 **Location:** I-75 exit 387, 3 mi e on SR 26 (Newberry Rd); at west end of Westgate Regency Shopping Center. L D

ONE LOVE CAFE 352/509-3131 (1)

American. Casual Dining. **Address:** 4989 NW 40th Pl 32606

POMODORO CAFE 352/380-9886 (3)

Italian Casual Dining
$13-$18

AAA Inspector Notes: Colorful murals adorn the walls here and help to create a lively, festive feeling. The menu is steeped in Italian traditions with offerings of bruschetta, capellini Francesco and tiramisu. During lunch hours, specially priced pasta dishes are featured. Indoor and covered patio seating is available. The staff is friendly and welcoming. **Features:** beer & wine, patio dining, happy hour. **Address:** 9200 NW 39th Ave, Suite 100 32606 **Location:** I-75 exit 390, just e. L D CALL

SONNY'S REAL PIT BAR-B-Q

Barbecue. Casual Dining.

LOCATIONS:

Address: 3635 SW Archer Rd 32608 **Phone:** 352/375-6667
Address: 2700 NE Waldo Rd 32609 **Phone:** 352/378-7881
Address: 9213 NW 39th Ave 32606 **Phone:** 352/381-7333

TASTE SUSHI BAR & ASIAN CUISINE 352/372-8686 (2)

Asian Sushi. Casual Dining. **Address:** 4860 NW 39th Ave, Suite C 32606

TIJUANA FLATS 352/692-3093

Tex-Mex. Quick Serve. **Address:** 1720 W University Ave 32602

GULFPORT pop. 12,029

• **Hotels & Restaurants map & index p. 286**
• **Part of St. Petersburg-Clearwater and Beaches area — see map p. 275**

HABANA CAFE 727/321-8855 (120)

Cuban. Casual Dining. **Address:** 5402 Gulfport Blvd S 33707

HEATHROW (F-4) pop. 5,896, elev. 50'

• **Restaurants p. 81**
• **Hotels & Restaurants map & index p. 188**
• **Part of Orlando area — see map p. 2**

Heathrow is the site of the AAA National Office. North of Orlando at I-4 and Lake Mary Boulevard, the Heathrow community includes recreational, commercial and residential areas.

COURTYARD BY MARRIOTT-ORLANDO LAKE MARY/NORTH 407/444-1000 (32)

SAVE Hotel. **Address:** 135 International Pkwy 32746

AAA Benefit: Members save 5% or more!

iStockphoto.com_LeoPatrizi

For travel and everyday activities, insight from those you trust can make a good experience great!

AAA inspectors and travel writers spend their days evaluating hotels, sampling menus and exploring new sights so you don't have to. Use their recommended picks and itineraries to find the best places to go, stay, dine and play.

Photo source iStockphoto.com

Get AAA travel information at club offices and on AAA.com for experiences you'll remember for a lifetime.

(See map & index p. 188.)

WHERE TO EAT

PEACH VALLEY CAFE 407/833-9440 (98)

Breakfast Sandwiches. Casual Dining. **Address:** 1210 S International Pkwy, Suite 108 32746

SAMURAI SUSHI JAPANESE CUISINE & SUSHI BAR 407/829-3299 (97)

Japanese Sushi. Casual Dining. **Address:** 100 International Pkwy, Suite 118-122 32746

STONEWOOD GRILL & TAVERN 407/333-3292 (99)

American. Fine Dining. **Address:** 1210 S International Pkwy 32746

HIGH SPRINGS (D-1) pop. 5,350, elev. 69'

High Springs, once a mining and railroad town, now offers antiquing and recreational opportunities in a small-town atmosphere. The downtown business section, representative of old Florida, features antique shops and several historic buildings.

O'Leno State Park *(see Recreation Areas Chart)*, one of the first state parks developed in Florida, is 6 miles north and offers camping, swimming, boating, fishing, nature trails, horseback riding trails, bicycle trails and a playground; phone (386) 454-1853.

Other state and privately owned parks with natural springs surround High Springs. Blue Springs Park, west off CR 340 at 7450 N.E. 60th St., features a boardwalk and offers swimming; phone (386) 454-1369. Ginnie Springs and Poe Springs Park, west off CR 340 at 28800 N.W. 182nd Ave., and Ichetucknee Springs State Park, 14 mi. n.w. to 12087 S.W. US 27, offer swimming, tubing, canoeing and underwater cave exploration *(see Recreation Areas Chart)*.

High Springs Chamber of Commerce: 23517 N.W. 185th Rd., High Springs, FL 32643. **Phone:** (386) 454-3120.

THE RUSTIC INN 386/454-1223

Bed & Breakfast. **Address:** 15529 NW SR 45 32643

WHERE TO EAT

BEV'S BETTER BURGERS 386/454-3131

American. Quick Serve. **Address:** 315 NE Santa Fe Blvd 32643

BEV'S BURGER CAFE AND BBQ 386/454-9434

Comfort Food Burgers. Casual Dining. **Address:** 18732 N US Highway 441 32643

GREAT OUTDOORS RESTAURANT 386/454-1288

American. Casual Dining. **Address:** 65 N Main St 32643

HOLMES BEACH pop. 3,836

• Hotels & Restaurants map & index p. 300

WATERLINE MARINA RESORT & BEACH CLUB, AUTOGRAPH COLLECTION 941/238-6262 (43)

Hotel

AUTOGRAPH COLLECTION HOTELS **AAA Benefit:** Members save 5% or more!

Address: 5325 Marina Dr 34217 **Location:** Waterfront. Jct Gulf Dr, just n. **Facility:** 37 units, some two bedrooms and kitchens. 3 stories, interior/exterior corridors. **Amenities:** safes. **Pool:** heated outdoor. **Activities:** self-propelled boats, bicycles, exercise room. **Guest Services:** complimentary laundry, area transportation.

SAVE CALL BIZ HS

WHERE TO EAT

BEACH BISTRO 941/778-6444 (52)

Continental. Fine Dining. **Address:** 6600 Gulf Dr 34217

HOMOSASSA SPRINGS (F-1) pop. 13,791, elev. 6'

• Restaurants p. 82

ELLIE SCHILLER HOMOSASSA SPRINGS WILDLIFE STATE PARK is on US 19 at 4150 S. Suncoast Blvd., 6 mi. n. of jct. US 19/98, following signs. Source of the Homosassa River, the freshwater spring emits millions of gallons each hour at a constant temperature of 72 F. Manatees and fresh- and saltwater fish can be seen through the windows of a floating observatory. The Wildlife Walk provides views of native wildlife, including two Florida panthers, whooping cranes and Key deer. Manatee, wildlife encounters and alligator and hippo programs are presented daily. Pontoon boats and trams shuttle visitors to and from the park.

Time: Allow 3 hours minimum. **Hours:** Daily 9-5:30. Last admission 45 minutes before closing; last boat departs 2.5 hours before closing. Wildlife Encounters programs are at 10:30 and 2:30, manatee programs at 11:30, 1:30 and 3:30, and an alligator and hippo program at 12:30. **Cost:** $13; $5 (ages 6-12). **Phone:** (352) 628-5343, or (352) 628-2311 for recorded information.

RIVER SAFARIS & GULF CHARTERS departs from 10823 W. Yulee Dr. Offered is a variety of pontoon boat tours and airboat rides on the Homosassa River and to the Gulf of Mexico. Seasonal manatee and scalloping trips also are available. Rental pontoons and jon boats are available. A live alligator exhibit is also on site.

Time: Allow 1 hour minimum. **Hours:** Trips depart daily at 9, 11, 1, 3 and 5. Closed Thanksgiving and Christmas. **Cost:** Pontoon boat tour $25-$45. Airboat rides $39-$59. Manatee snorkel tour (includes equipment) $59-$69. Rates vary according to type and length of tour. Reservations are recommended. **Phone:** (352) 628-5222 or (800) 758-3474. GT

THE FREEZER - CEDAR KEY FISH & OYSTER CO. 352/628-2452

Seafood. Quick Serve. **Address:** 5590 S Boulevard Dr 34447

HOWEY-IN-THE-HILLS pop. 1,098

• Part of Orlando area — see map p. 2

MISSION INN RESORT & CLUB 352/324-3101

Resort Hotel

Address: 10400 CR 48 34737 **Location:** Jct SR 19. **Facility:** Set on several lush acres, the inn features traditional-style rooms, many with great views of the grounds. The patio is a popular spot to gather and enjoy the beautiful scenery. 182 units, some two and three bedrooms. 1-4 stories (no elevator), interior/exterior corridors. **Parking:** on-site and valet. **Terms:** check-in 4 pm. **Amenities:** safes. **Dining:** 4 restaurants. **Pool:** heated outdoor. **Activities:** hot tub, marina, fishing, regulation golf, tennis, bicycles, playground, exercise room, spa. **Guest Services:** valet and coin laundry. *(See ad p. 219.)*

SAVE ECO CALL BIZ HS / SOME UNITS

HUDSON pop. 12,158

• Part of St. Petersburg-Clearwater and Beaches area — see map p. 275

SAM'S HUDSON BEACH RESTAURANT 727/868-1971

Seafood. Casual Dining. **Address:** 6325 Clark St 34667

INDIALANTIC pop. 2,720

• Hotels & Restaurants map & index p. 148

TUCKAWAY SHORES RESORT 321/723-3355 12

Extended Stay Hotel. **Address:** 1441 S Miramar Av 32903

WHERE TO EAT

THE BLUEBERRY MUFFIN RESTAURANT 321/725-7117 11

Breakfast Sandwiches. Casual Dining. **Address:** 1130 N Hwy A1A 32903

LONG DOGGERS 321/725-1115 13

American. Casual Dining. **Address:** 890 N A1A 32903

MOO'S SOFT SERVE 321/723-4990 12

Hot Dogs Desserts. Quick Serve. **Address:** 930 N A1A Hwy 32903

SKEWERS A MEDITERRANEAN GRILLE 321/727-8944 15

Mediterranean Vegetarian. Casual Dining. **Address:** 144 5th Ave 32903

VILLA PALMA RISTORANTE 321/951-0051 14

Italian. Casual Dining. **Address:** 874 N Hwy A1A 32903

INDIAN ROCKS BEACH (H-1) pop. 4,113, elev. 10'

• Hotels & Restaurants map & index p. 286
• Part of St. Petersburg-Clearwater and Beaches area — see map p. 275

Indian Rocks Beach is a resort community near the midpoint of Sand Key, a long, narrow island in the Gulf off the Pinellas County coast. It is accessible by SR 688 north of St. Petersburg.

Beach Welcome Center: 105 Fifth Ave., Indian Rocks Beach, FL 33785. **Phone:** (727) 595-4575 or (800) 926-9303.

CRABBY BILL'S 727/595-4825

Seafood. Casual Dining. **Address:** 401 Gulf Blvd 33785

GUPPY'S ON THE BEACH SEAFOOD GRILL & BAR 727/593-2032 69

Seafood. Casual Dining. **Address:** 1701 Gulf Blvd 33785

THAI-PAN ALLEY & BAMBOO BEACH BAR 727/593-3663 68

Thai. Casual Dining. **Address:** 2300 Gulf Blvd 33785

INDIAN SHORES pop. 1,420, elev. 5'

• Hotels & Restaurants map & index p. 286
• Part of St. Petersburg-Clearwater and Beaches area — see map p. 275

BAREFOOT BEACH RESORT 727/593-5303 61

Vacation Rental Condominium. **Address:** 19417 Gulf Blvd 33785

WHERE TO EAT

CADDY'S PUB WATERFRONT RESTAURANT 727/595-3172 90

Seafood. Casual Dining. **Address:** 20025 Gulf Blvd 33785

SALT ROCK GRILL 727/593-7625 91

Seafood. Casual Dining. **Address:** 19325 Gulf Blvd 33785

INVERNESS (F-2) pop. 7,210, elev. 38'

WILD BILL'S AIRBOAT TOURS is on SR 44, 6.3 mi. e. of US 41 or 9 mi. w. of I-75. Narrated 45-minute airboat rides on the Withlacoochee River provide sightings of native wildlife, including wading birds, ospreys, eagles, deer and alligators. **Time:** Allow 1 hour minimum. **Hours:** Tours depart daily on the hour 10-4. **Cost:** $45; $35 (ages 3-10). Reservations are required. **Phone:** (352) 726-6060. GT

COACH'S PUB & EATERY 352/344-3333

American. Casual Dining. **Address:** 114 W Old Main St 34450

HEIDI'S ITALIAN RESTAURANT 352/637-1355

Italian. Casual Dining. **Address:** 901 Hwy 41 N 34450

JMJ PHILIPPINE CUISINE & ORIENTAL MARKET 352/344-5212

Philippine. Casual Dining. **Address:** 3788 E Gulf to Lake Hwy 34450

STUMPKNOCKERS ON THE SQUARE 352/726-2212

Seafood. Casual Dining. **Address:** 110 W Main St 34450

GET THE APP
Download today.
Connect every day.
AAA.com/mobile
CAA.ca/mobile

Jacksonville

Then & Now

Jacksonville embraces more than 500 neighborhoods within more than 800 square miles, an impressive expanse that makes this busy seaport the biggest city in the contiguous United States. Its size inflated by a consolidation of city and county governments in 1968, the mammoth destination also boasts the largest population in Florida.

The vicinity was home to the Mocama Indians when French Protestants known as Huguenots arrived in 1562 and founded Fort Caroline. Spanish troops from nearby St. Augustine destroyed the ill-fated Huguenot village just three years later.

Spanish control of the area ended in 1763, when Spain traded Florida to Britain. Under British rule, The King's Road between Savannah, Georgia and St. Augustine was completed. A settlement developed where the road crossed the St. Johns River, roughly where downtown Jacksonville is today.

AAA.com/travelguides—
more ways to look, book and save

As a result of the 1783 Treaty of Paris, Britain returned Florida to Spain. Despite Spanish ownership, citizens of the new United States of America began settling in northern Florida. In 1819, Spain struck a deal with the U. S., trading its interests in the Oregon Country and Florida in exchange for recognition of Spanish sovereignty over Texas. Soon after the U.S. took formal possession of the Florida Territory, Jacksonville—named after the region's first military governor, Gen. Andrew Jackson—was founded.

Jacksonville skyline

The town prospered as a port of entry until the Civil War, during which it was burned and abandoned several times. Though the city was resurrected as a winter resort for wealthy tourists in the 1880s, by the end of the 19th century, Jacksonville's status as a popular vacation destination had declined, partly due to yellow fever outbreaks. In 1901 tragedy visited the city again when a fire destroyed nearly the entire downtown area.

But the resilient city rebounded. During the early 20th century, more than 300 silent movies were shot in the area. Naval bases built during World War II contributed to the city's further growth. Today, three Fortune 500 companies—CSX Corp., Fidelity National Financial and Fidelity National Information Service Inc.—are headquartered in this distribution hub set in the double loop of the St. Johns River. And the armed forces' presence is still strong, with military bases, including Naval Station Mayport and the Marine

(Continued on p. 85.)

Destination Jacksonville

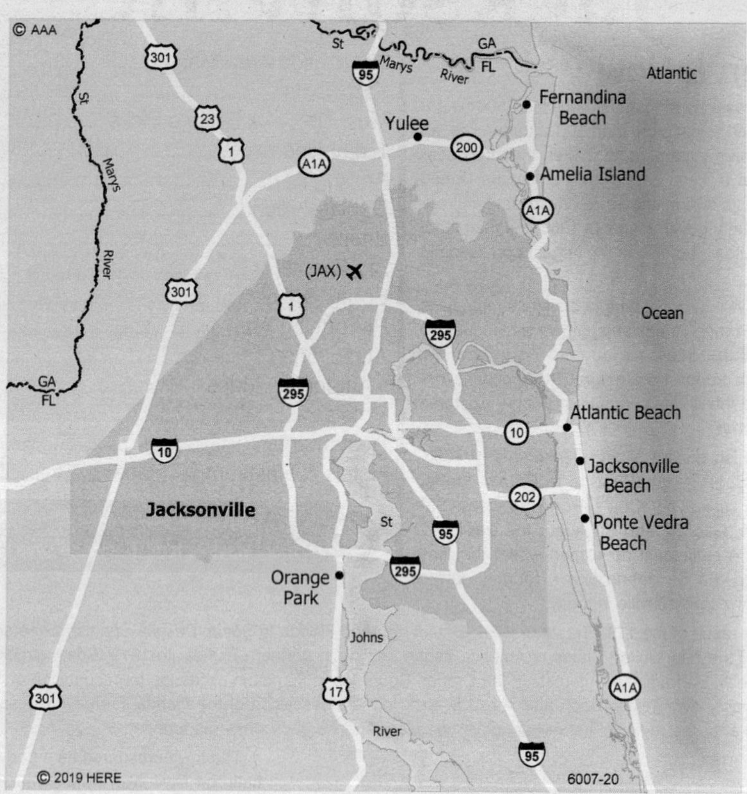

This map shows cities in the Jacksonville vicinity where you will find attractions, hotels and restaurants. Cities are listed alphabetically in this book on the following pages.

Fast Facts

ABOUT THE CITY

POP: 842,583 ■ **ELEV:** 20 ft.

MONEY

SALES TAX: The sales tax is 7 percent in Clay, Duval and Nassau counties and 6.5 percent in St. Johns County. The bed tax is 4 to 6 percent in St. Johns County and 6 percent in Duval County; the tourist development tax is 3 percent in Clay County and 4 percent in Nassau and St. Johns counties.

WHOM TO CALL

EMERGENCY: 911

POLICE (non-emergency): (904) 630-0500

FIRE (non-emergency): (904) 630-0434

TEMPERATURE: (904) 741-4311

HOSPITALS: Baptist Medical Center, (904) 202-2000 ■ Mayo Clinic, (904) 953-2000 ■ Memorial Hospital of Jacksonville, (904) 399-6111 ■ St. Vincent's Medical Center Southside, (904) 296-3700 ■ UF Health Jacksonville, (904) 244-0411.

VISITOR INFORMATION

Visit Jacksonville: 208 N. Laura St., Suite 102, Jacksonville, FL 32202. **Phone:** (904) 798-9111 or (800) 733-2668.

TRANSPORTATION

AIR TRAVEL: More than a dozen major and regional carriers serve Jacksonville International Airport (JAX), which is about 13 miles north of downtown near the northern junction of I-95 and I-295.

Several taxi and limousine companies serve the airport, although the baggage claim area is served exclusively by Gator City Taxi, (904) 999-9999 or (904) 741-0008. Taxi fares to downtown average $35.

RENTAL CARS: Hertz, at the airport, offers discounts to AAA members; phone (904) 741-2151.

Book and save at AAA.com/hertz

RAIL SERVICE: The Amtrak station is at 3570 Clifford Ln., 5 miles northwest of downtown. For arrival information phone (904) 766-5110; for reservations and information phone (800) 872-7245.

BUSES: The main Greyhound Lines Inc. bus terminal is at 10 N. Pearl St.; phone (904) 356-9976.

TAXIS: Major cab companies are Checker Yellow Cab Co., (904) 345-3333 or (904) 765-9999 ■ Coastal Cab, (904) 246-9999 ■ and Gator City Taxi, (904) 999-9999. Base fare is $2 with a rate of $2 per mile.

PUBLIC TRANSPORTATION: Jacksonville Transportation Authority operates a system of buses, trolleys and shuttles that serves Jacksonville and the beaches. A Baldwin Wildcat Commuter Shuttle offers weekday service to Baldwin and Macclenny. The Skyway, an automated monorail system, provides downtown transportation between the Prime Osborn Convention Center, Hemming Plaza and Rosa L. Parks Transit Station on the Northbank and San Marco and Kings Avenue Station across the river.

The fare for buses, trolleys and shuttles is $1.50, free (ages 65+); express buses are $2, $1.50 (ages 60+). Unlimited one-day fare is $4, $1.50 (ages 60+). The Skyway is free. Discounted fares are available through the purchase of a multiday STAR card. For information phone (904) 630-3100.

BOATS: River taxi service between points along the St. Johns River is available from Jacksonville Water Taxi, departing every half-hour Tues.-Thurs. and Sun. 11 a.m. to 9 p.m. and Fri.-Sat. (also holidays) 11 a.m. to 11 p.m.; phone (904) 630-2489. A daily pass is $10; $8 (ages 3-12 and 65+). Fare to the stadium or Downtown Loop during football games and special events is $10 (round-trip); $20 (unlimited all day); cash only.

(Continued from p. 83.)

Corps' Blount Island Command, contributing about $6.1 billion annually to the local economy.

While the Jacksonville Jaguars have yet to bring home the Lombardi Trophy, the city's first professional football franchise has won two division championships and made several trips to the playoffs since joining the NFL in 1995. Gridiron fans in this rivalry-loving destination cheer on the Jaguars at TIAA Bank Field, Super Bowl XXXIX venue and continuing host to such annual college games as the Florida vs. Georgia Football Classic and the Gator Bowl Classic. Nearby Ponte Vedra Beach, home to the PGA Tour, also attracts golfers with THE PLAYERS Championship in March.

But while touchdowns and eagles electrify the city, the St. Johns River remains at the heart of modern-day Jacksonville, with downtown's opposing Riverwalks attracting sightseers and natives year-round with fun things to do. The Museum of Science & History is the highlight of the 1.2-mile Southbank Riverwalk, which also shelters Friendship Fountain. Across the river, the downtown Sports and Entertainment Complex is home to TIAA Bank Field, the VyStar Veterans Memorial Arena, the Baseball Grounds of Jacksonville, Daily's Place Amphitheater and Intuition Ale Works, the first brewery in the state of Florida to can its beer.

Must Do: AAA Editor's Picks

- Discover the magic of the lazily looping St. Johns River, which made Jacksonville an important port. The rare, north-flowing river is best enjoyed by boat. Take a ride on the St. Johns River Taxi to explore all the sights.
- Visit the **Riverside Arts Market** (715 Riverside Ave.), tucked under the Fuller Warren Bridge, where you can buy food and handmade gifts each Saturday—rain or shine—from 10 a.m. to 3 p.m. Or just walk around and observe the singers and other performers entertaining the locals. More than 100 vendors come to the weekly market, so it's a great way to see what Jacksonville has to offer.
- Learn more about Florida's founding at the Timucuan Ecological and Historic Preserve. The oldest site, **Fort Caroline National Memorial** (12713 Fort Caroline Rd.), marks the ill-fated spot where French Huguenots settled in 1564. A more "recent" settlement is **Kingsley Plantation** (11676 Palmetto Ave.) which a former slave operated for her slave trader husband. Built in the late 18th century, it is Florida's oldest remaining plantation.
- Dip your toes into the Atlantic Ocean. Or just dive in! Jax has more than 22 miles of alabaster-sand **beaches** not far from downtown. Jax is the birthplace of the Salt Life movement and it is best enjoyed at the **Beaches Town Center** (0 Atlantic Blvd., Neptune Beach, FL 32266). Better yet, stay in a beachside resort and wake up to the sound of the surf lapping at the shore.
- Continue your lesson in state history—from prehistoric times onward—at **The Museum of Science & History** (1025 Museum Cir.). Walk through the Florida Naturalist's Center, learn about science from one of many hands-on exhibits or stay for a show at the Bryan-Gooding Planetarium.
- See the world—or at least many animals in it—at the **Jacksonville Zoo and Gardens** (370 Zoo Pkwy.). The Zoo Train meanders through themed areas such as South America and Africa featuring animals such as endangered jaguars and elephants. Garden lovers will want to reserve time to see its lush gardens before they hop back on the train to get to a Keeper Talk.
- Hang out at **Tree Hill Nature Center** (7152 Lone Star Rd.) for a fun learning experience. The 50-acre environmental education site includes a nature center, three ecosystems and an amphitheater. Kids especially enjoy the butterfly garden and exhibits with native animals.
- Get back to the city at pedestrian-friendly **San Marco Square** (Hendricks Ave. and Atlantic Blvd.) Named after St. Mark's Square in Venice, the neighborhood intersection is home to boutiques and chic **Matthew's Restaurant** (2107 Hendricks Ave.).
- Step through 8,000 years of art history at the **Cummer Museum of Art & Gardens** (829 Riverside Ave.). A former private residence, the museum opened its doors with 60 pieces of art in 1961 and now contains nearly 5,000 objects. Cast your eyes upon works by Winslow Homer, Auguste Rodin, Peter Paul Rubens and John Singer Sargent. The surrounding gardens, ornamented with reflecting pools, fountains, arbors and sculptures, draw visitors from throughout the Southeast. Don't miss the Italian Garden.
- Satisfy your appetite for contemporary art at the **Museum of Contemporary Art Jacksonville** (333 N. Laura St.). Owned by the University of North Florida, the collection includes more than 800 pieces of art created after 1960. Visitors lucky enough to come on the first Wednesday of the month should take part in the **Art Walk**, a free event showcasing art in the museum and in various locations downtown.
-

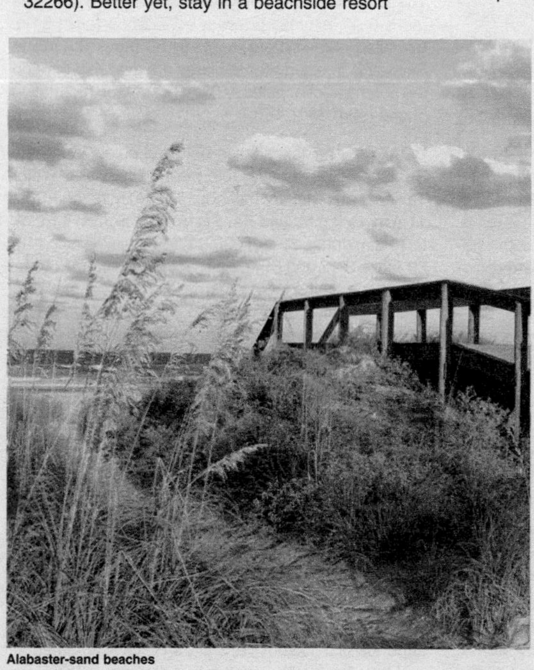

Alabaster-sand beaches

Jacksonville 1-day Itinerary

AAA editors suggest these activities for a great short vacation experience.

Morning

- Start the day with an adventure at the 46,000-acre Timucuan Ecological and Historic Preserve. Spend some time hiking, biking and canoeing, or head to **Fort Caroline National Memorial** (12713 Fort Caroline Rd.) to experience the historical side of the preserve. A French Huguenot settlement here in 1564 led to a bloody conflict with Spain. **Kingsley Plantation** (11676 Palmetto Ave.) is where a former enslaved African—married to a slave trader—ran a large, profitable plantation before the racial laws of the United States took effect in the former Spanish territory.
- You might see an alligator or bear at the Timucuan Ecological and Historic Preserve, but for guaranteed wildlife sightings, visit the **Jacksonville Zoo and Gardens** (370 Zoo Pkwy.). With a Wild Florida exhibit and exhibits of other animals from around the world, the Wildlife Carousel and a train, the park offers plenty of exhibits and activities to keep the whole family entertained.

Afternoon

- Hungry yet? Head toward downtown and dine at **Juliette's Bistro** (245 Water St.). You can get everything from syrupy sweet tea and a burger to the catch of the day.
- Explore the Riverwalk by the St. Johns River, especially on a Saturday. The **Riverside Arts Market,** southwest of downtown, fills the space under Fuller Warren Bridge from 10-3, and offers live music and local artisans.
- Investigate how your body—as well as the universe—can function and change at **The Museum of Science & History** (1025 Museum Cir.) and its Bryan-Gooding Planetarium. You can also take a walk on the aquatic side and see the permanent aquarium exhibit in addition to MOSH's resident animals at the Florida Naturalist's Center.
- The neighborhood of **San Marco** features some of the best restaurants in Jacksonville, so you might want to eat early if you haven't made reservations. Try **bb's restaurant + bar,** which features the utterly delicious pan Asian chop chop salad among other creative salads and sandwiches. Don't miss the specialty cake. Options may change hourly!

Evening

- **Matthew's Restaurant** (2107 Hendricks Ave.) is one to book ahead. Chef Matthew Medure, who established the city's premiere dining destination, offers international cuisine and award-winning wines in an intimate setting.
- The **Museum of Contemporary Art Jacksonville** (333 N Laura St.) has a collection of work from the '60s to today and hosts visiting exhibits. It extends its hours for Art Walk on the first Wednesday of the month and on Thursday evenings. During Art Walk, galleries, businesses and artists join the museum to showcase art and live music within a 15-block area.

Cummer Museum of Art & Gardens

- On Tuesday, the GEM **Cummer Museum of Art & Gardens** (829 Riverside Ave.) extends its hours. Created as a gift from an avid art collector and gardener, the facility showcases historic gardens, including a formal English Garden designed in 1910, and an art collection of 5,000 pieces.
- To mix it up a little, head toward the eclectic **Mossfire Grill** (1537 Margaret St.) which features New American and Southwest cuisine. The local "hot spot" is named after the source of the devastating 1901 fire that burned Jacksonville: Spanish moss. On that unfortunate day, a wood stove cooking dinner sparked a fire on the platform where moss—used inside of mattresses—was drying. An estimated 2,368 buildings were burned, and most of the city had to be rebuilt.
- For those wanting to make an entire night of it, head to **Five Points District** (1001 Park St.) in Riverside and enjoy more than a dozen bars, restaurants and local hangouts. You'll find happy hours and a burgeoning nightlife scene.
- If you prefer a more relaxing evening, settle into a seat inside the European-style **Jacoby Symphony Hall** at the **Times-Union Center for the Performing Arts** (300 Water St.) on the St. Johns River and listen to the dulcet sounds of the **Jacksonville Symphony Orchestra**.

Arriving

By Car

Two important interstate highways, I-95 and I-10, intersect in the Jacksonville downtown area. I-95 traverses the United States from north to south beginning in Maine and ending in Miami. It is frequently congested as it approaches downtown.

I-10 connects Jacksonville on the East Coast with Los Angeles by way of New Orleans, Houston, San Antonio, Tucson and Phoenix.

I-295 loops around the city, connecting with I-95 both south and north of downtown. I-295 also intersects with I-10 directly west of the city.

A more scenic approach is SR A1A, which follows the coastline through Jacksonville. Northeast of the city, SR A1A travels through historic Fernandina Beach.

US 1 is another important route. This highway runs the length of America's east coast, from Lubec, Maine, to Key West, Fla. US 17 approaches from the west and provides yet another route into Jacksonville.

Getting Around

Street System

Like most newer cities, the street system of downtown Jacksonville is a simple grid. Bay Street divides the city north-south, while Main Street is the east-west divider. The destination does not adhere to a street naming convention, and thus a road's name (that is, whether it is called a street, avenue or boulevard) does not indicate its compass orientation.

Downtown Jacksonville

The downtown speed limit is 30 mph. Traffic is most congested 7 to 9 a.m. and 4 to 6 p.m.

Parking

Both on-street parking and several parking garages are available downtown. Parking meters require 25c per half hour ($6 maximum per day).

Shopping

In addition to major shopping malls, the city boasts a multitude of small shopping centers and an array of antique stores and flea markets.

St. Johns Town Center, 4663 River City Dr., has 150 stores in its 1 million square feet of shopping and dining space in an open-air configuration anchored by Dillard's and Nordstrom.

The Avenues, 10300 Southside Blvd., has more than 150 stores including Belk, Dillard's, JCPenney and Sears. **Orange Park Mall,** 1910 Wells Rd., counts Belk, Dillard's and JCPenney among its 120 stores. **Regency Square Mall,** 9501 Arlington Expwy., has 170 stores including Dillard's Clearance, JCPenney and Sears.

San Marco, 5 miles south of downtown, and **The Shoppes of Avondale,** 3567 St. Johns Ave., entice with specialty boutiques, antique shops and galleries. The shops around Riverside's Five Points and on Main Street in the Springfield neighborhood have a funkier feel and offer plenty of things to see and buy.

Big Events

Jacksonville is host to exciting events throughout the year. College football fans celebrate the new year with the **TaxSlayer Gator Bowl,** which is played late December or early January and is one of the city's top sports events.

The **World of Nations Celebration** that focuses on Jacksonville's cultural mix; the event is held in late February at **Metropolitan Park.**

In March the **Gate River Run** attracts more than 23,000 runners for a 15-kilometer race along the city's roads and bridges. Also in March, in nearby **Ponte Vedra Beach**, is **THE PLAYERS Championship** golf tournament, the PGA Tour's premier spring event.

Early April brings the **Springing the Blues Music Festival,** 3 days of blues music held at **SeaWalk Pavilion.** The **Jacksonville Jazz Festival,** which features concerts at various indoor and outdoor venues, is held Memorial Day weekend.

The **Greater Jacksonville Kingfish Tournament** features prizes, a fish fry, seafood festival and entertainment in July.

The **Greater Jacksonville Agricultural Fair** in November offers livestock, a petting zoo, horticultural exhibits, arts and crafts, carnival rides and country entertainment.

Ring in the new year during the **New Year's Eve Celebration** on the riverfront in downtown Jacksonville.

Sports & Rec

Swimming is fantastic at the more than 22 miles of white sandy beaches on the intricate chain of barrier islands off the coast adjacent to Jacksonville. Just 20 miles northeast of the destination are the pristine beaches and wild natural beauty of **Little Talbot Island State Park** and **Fort George Island Cultural State Park.** The beach communities of the area—**Atlantic Beach**, **Neptune Beach**, **Jacksonville Beach** and, to the south, **Ponte Vedra Beach**—combine surf and sand with the amenities of hotels and local restaurants.

Boating is a popular pastime in the area due to Jacksonville's access to water and things to see. The city operates more than 50 public docks, the most popular ones are at the following locations: Huguenot Memorial Park, Kathryn Abbey Hanna Park, Metropolitan Park, NorthBank and SouthBank Riverwalk.

Kayaking services offer trips through the coastal salt marshes and on quiet waterways; contact **Kayak Amelia/Long Island Outfitters,** (904) 251-0016, or **Black Creek Guides,** (904) 645-7003.

Fishing can be enjoyed along the **St. Johns River** and **Intracoastal Waterway** and in the **Atlantic Ocean.** Speckled trout, striped bass, bluefish, redfish, flounder and whiting are a few of the fish frequently caught at **Little Talbot Island State Park.** Saltwater fishing and more than 60 acres of freshwater fishing lakes are available at **Kathryn Abbey Hanna Park** *(see Recreation Areas Chart).*

Golf and Florida's balmy climate go together perfectly, and Jacksonville offers more than 50 area golf courses. Courses include **Bent Creek Golf Course** at 10440 Tournament Ln., (904) 779-0800; **Deerfield Lakes Golf Club** at 54002 Deerfield Country Club Rd. in Callahan, (904) 879-1210; **Fernandina Beach Golf Club** at 2800 Bill Melton Rd., (904) 310-3175; **Jacksonville Beach Golf Club** at 605 S. Penman Rd., (904) 247-6184; and **Windsor Parke Golf Club** at 13823 Sutton Park Dr. N., phone (904) 223-4653.

Tennis courts can be found throughout the Jacksonville area.

Hiking Numerous hiking trails and one **biking** path through several distinct ecological communities are at the **Timucuan Ecological & Historic Preserve,** 12713 Fort Caroline Rd.; phone (904) 641-7155. Three self-guiding nature trails are at the **University of North Florida Wildlife Sanctuary**; phone (904) 620-2998. **Bird-watching** is a popular pastime along the hiking trails of both Big and Little Talbot islands.

Football The **Jacksonville Jaguars** began their first National Football League season in 1995 and came within one game of going to the Super Bowl in their second season. The team's **TIAA Bank Field** is at 1 Everbank Field Dr.; phone (904) 633-2000 for ticket information.

Baseball The **Jacksonville Jumbo Shrimp,** play AA Southern League baseball at the **Baseball Grounds of Jacksonville,** 301 A Philip Randolph Blvd., in the sports complex; phone (904) 358-2846.

Fort George Island Cultural State Park

Performing Arts

The **Jacksonville Symphony Orchestra** presents performances throughout the year including a guest artist series, an outdoor concert series and smaller group concerts. **Times-Union Center for the Performing Arts,** 300 Water St., is a state-of-the-art performance venue overlooking the St. Johns River downtown. Its three halls include **Jacoby Symphony Hall,** home of the Jacksonville Symphony Orchestra; **Moran Theater,** which can accommodate large-scale concerts and Broadway touring shows; and **Terry Theater,** which is used for smaller performances. For more information phone (904) 354-5547 or (904) 633-6110.

The Florida State College at Jacksonville's **Artist Series** brings Broadway productions along with national and international ballet, opera and contemporary dance companies; phone (904) 442-2929 or (888) 860-2929.

Located downtown at 128 E. Forsyth St., the lavish **Florida Theatre** was built in 1927 and serves as a performing arts center; phone (904) 355-5661 for information or (904) 355-2787 for tickets.

ATTRACTIONS

For a complete list of attractions, visit AAA.com/travelguides/attractions

CUMMER MUSEUM OF ART & GARDENS, 829 Riverside Ave., offers more than 5,000 objects in its permanent collection and three historic

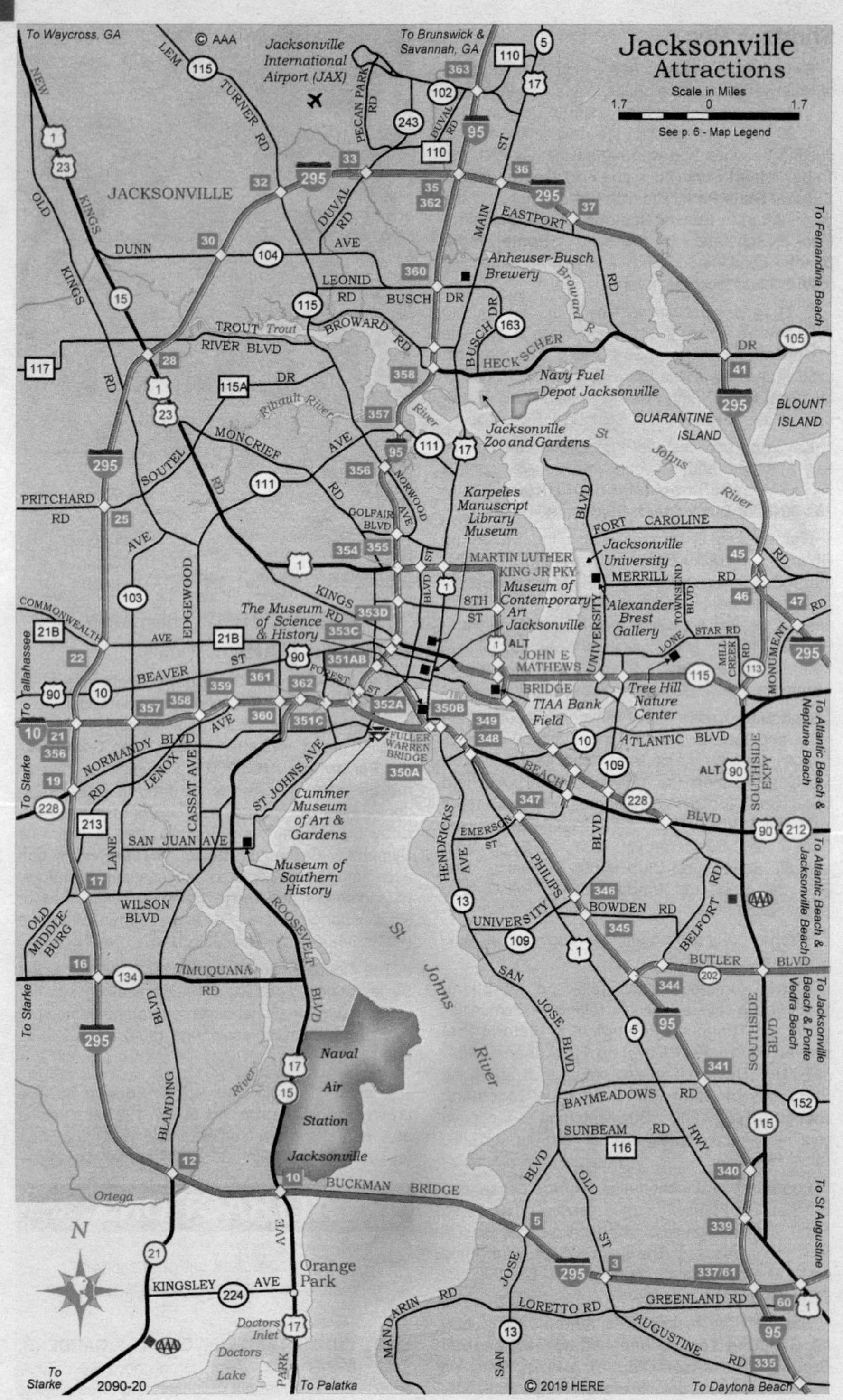

Jacksonville Attractions
Scale in Miles
1.7 0 1.7
See p. 6 - Map Legend
© AAA
Jacksonville International Airport (JAX)
Anheuser-Busch Brewery
Navy Fuel Depot Jacksonville
Jacksonville Zoo and Gardens
Karpeles Manuscript Library Museum
Jacksonville University
Museum of Contemporary Art Jacksonville
Alexander Brest Gallery
The Museum of Science & History
Tree Hill Nature Center
TIAA Bank Field
Cummer Museum of Art & Gardens
Museum of Southern History
Naval Air Station Jacksonville
JACKSONVILLE
BLOUNT ISLAND
QUARANTINE ISLAND
St Johns River
Orange Park
Doctors Inlet
Doctors Lake
Ortega
To Waycross, GA
To Brunswick & Savannah, GA
To Fernandina Beach
To Tallahassee
To Starke
To Atlantic Beach & Neptune Beach
To Atlantic Beach & Jacksonville Beach
To Jacksonville Beach & Ponte Vedra Beach
To St Augustine
To Daytona Beach
To Palatka
N
2090-20
© 2019 HERE

gardens along the St. Johns River built by pioneering landscape architects of the early 20th century. World-class art spanning from 2100 B.C. through the 21st century includes such masterworks as paintings by Thomas Moran, Norman Rockwell, Winslow Homer, Agnolo Gaddi and Lucas Cranach the Elder. Also of interest is a significant collection of 18th-century Meissen porcelain.

Art Connections, the museum's interactive education gallery, provides multi-sensory opportunities for visitors to look more closely at art, explore the museum's collection more deeply, and apply their own creativity by creating artwork of their own. Traveling exhibitions complement the permanent collection.

Time: Allow 2 hours minimum. **Hours:** Tues. 10-9, Wed.-Sat. 10-4, Sun. noon-4. Guided tours depart Tues. at 7 p.m. and the first Sat. of the month at 2. Closed Jan. 1, July 4, Thanksgiving, Christmas Eve, Christmas and Dec. 31. **Cost:** $10; $6 (ages 65+, military and students); free (ages 0-5, college students with ID Tues.-Fri. and to all Tues. 4-9 and first Sat. of the month). Guided tour free with admission. **Phone:** (904) 356-6857. GT 🍴

FORT CAROLINE NATIONAL MEMORIAL, 13 mi. e. near jct. Monument and Fort Caroline rds., is within the Timucuan Ecological and Historic Preserve and marks the site near which French colonials established a settlement in 1564. A year later Spaniards massacred many of them at Matanzas Inlet. The memorial contains a model of the fort, interpretive trails and Ribault Monument, an obelisk commemorating the first landing at St. Johns in 1562. The visitor center has displays. **Time:** Allow 1 hour minimum. **Hours:** Visitor center daily 9-5. Closed Jan. 1, Thanksgiving and Christmas. **Cost:** Free. **Phone:** (904) 641-7155.

JACKSONVILLE ZOO AND GARDENS, 370 Zoo Pkwy., features more than 2,000 animals and 1,000 plant species from around the world on 92 acres. In addition to Great Apes of the World, Plains of East Africa and Range of the Jaguar, the park has Giraffe Overlook, an exhibit that allows visitors to feed giraffes, the Komodo Dragon exhibit, and the Tuxedo Coast Penguin exhibit. At Stingray Bay, guests can touch and feed stingrays. Savanna Blooms, the Gardens of Trout River Plaza and the Monsoon Asia provide respite. Lorikeet birds feed from visitors' hands at Australian Adventure. Train, carousel and 4-D rides also are available. A 2.5-acre Play Park, which includes the seasonal Splash Ground, affords children the opportunity to discover, experience and explore additional exhibits and play areas.

Picnicking is permitted in designated areas outside the zoo. **Time:** Allow 2 hours minimum. **Hours:** Mon.-Fri. 9-5, Sat.-Sun. 9-6. Last admission 1 hour before closing. Closed Christmas. **Cost:** $17.95; $15.95 (ages 65+); $12.95 (ages 3-12). Train ride or 4-D theater $4; $2 (ages 3-12). Carousel ride, giraffe feeding or Stingray Bay $2. Stingray or lorikeet bird feed $1. Combination tickets available. **Phone:** (904) 757-4463.

KINGSLEY PLANTATION, 11676 Palmetto Ave., is part of the Timucuan Ecological and Historic Preserve. This 19th-century cotton plantation was operated 1813-39 by Zephaniah Kingsley. It is one of the last remaining examples of the plantation system of territorial Florida. The main house and the remains of 23 slave cabins are visible. Interpretive displays reflect 19th-century plantation life. An audio tour is available.

Hours: Grounds daily 9-5. House tours Sat.-Sun. at 11 and 3; reservations are required. Closed Jan. 1, Thanksgiving and Christmas. **Cost:** Free. **Phone:** (904) 251-3537 or (904) 251-3626. GT

MUSEUM OF SOUTHERN HISTORY, 4304 Herschel St., houses an extensive collection of artifacts, clothing and memorabilia from the Civil War era, in addition to a 5,000-volume research library and genealogical records. **Time:** Allow 1 hour minimum. **Hours:** Tues.-Sat. 10-4. Closed major holidays. Phone ahead to confirm schedule. **Cost:** $3; free (ages 0-15). **Phone:** (904) 388-3574.

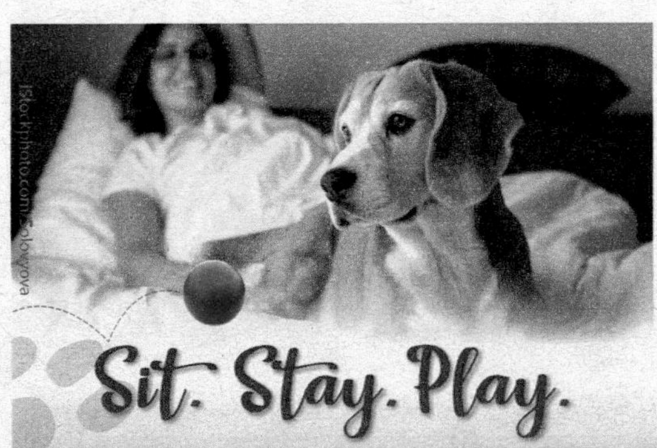

Discover thousands of pet-friendly places to stay, play and dine. Get insight to guide your decisions. And enter your favorite photo in the next AAA Pet Travel Photo Contest*.

Visit AAA.com/PetTravel

*Contest entry open to U.S. residents only.

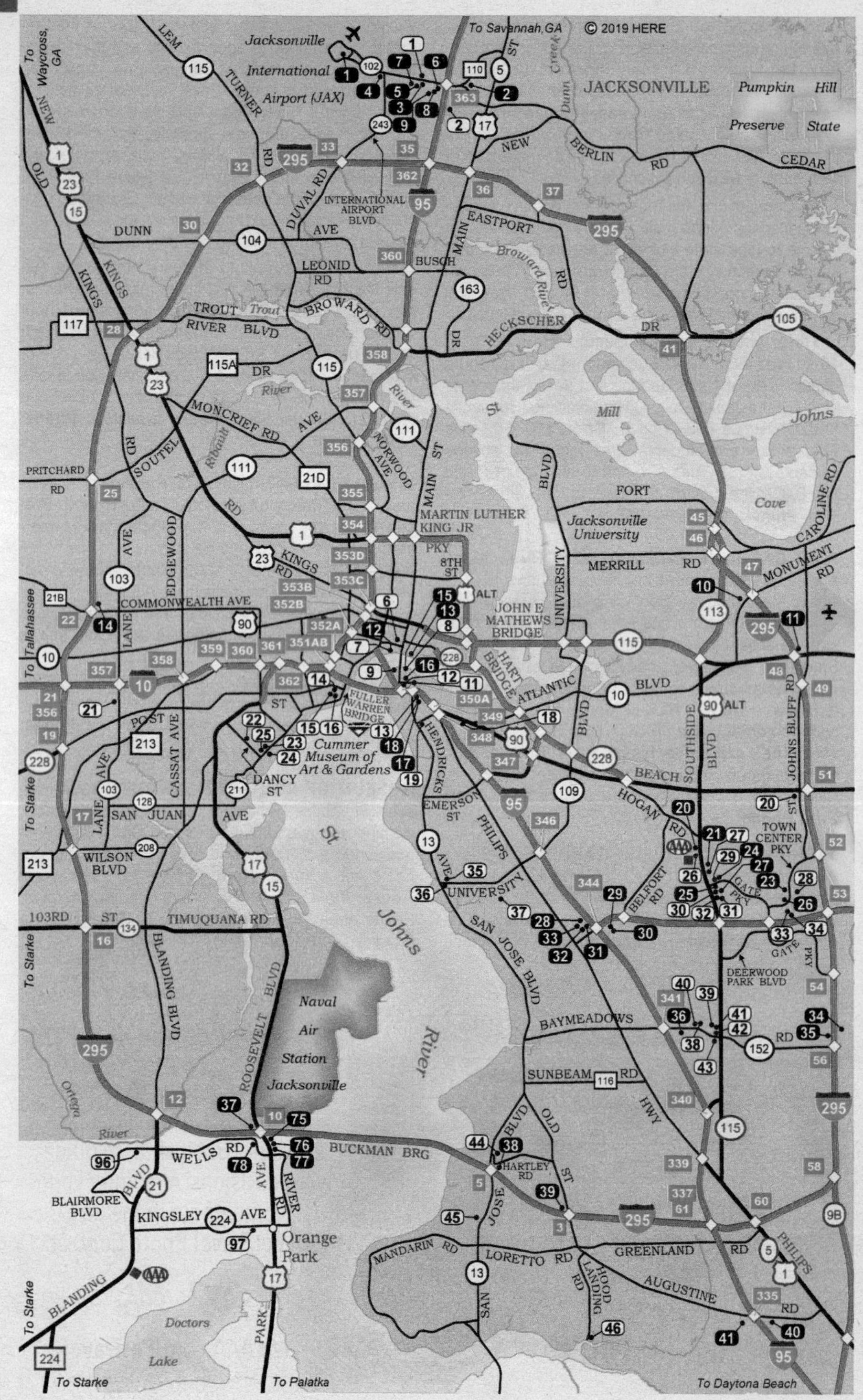
To Savannah,GA
© 2019 HERE
Jacksonville International Airport (JAX)
JACKSONVILLE
Pumpkin Hill Preserve State
To Waycross, GA
NEW KINGS
OLD KINGS
LEM TURNER RD
DUVAL RD
INTERNATIONAL AIRPORT BLVD
NEW BERLIN RD
CEDAR
DUNN AVE
EASTPORT RD
MAIN ST
LEONID RD
BUSCH
Broward River
TROUT RIVER BLVD
BROWARD RD
HECKSCHER DR
Trout River
115A DR
Ribault River
MONCRIEF RD
AVE
NORWOOD AVE
Mill
Johns
St
PRITCHARD RD
SOUTEL RD
FORT
Cove
CAROLINE RD
MARTIN LUTHER KING JR PKY
Jacksonville University
UNIVERSITY BLVD
EDGEWOOD AVE
KINGS RD
8TH ST
MERRILL RD
MONUMENT RD
COMMONWEALTH AVE
JOHN E MATHEWS BRIDGE
LANE AVE
ALT
To Tallahassee
HART BRIDGE
ATLANTIC BLVD
POST ST
FULLER WARREN BRIDGE
Cummer Museum of Art & Gardens
HENDRICKS
BEACH BLVD
SOUTHSIDE BLVD
JOHNS BLUFF RD
DANCY ST
CASSAT AVE
SAN JUAN AVE
EMERSON ST
PHILIPS
HOGAN RD
To Starke
WILSON BLVD
TOWN CENTER PKY
UNIVERSITY
BELFORT RD
GATE PKY
103RD ST
TIMUQUANA RD
SAN JOSE BLVD
DEERWOOD PARK BLVD
BLANDING BLVD
ROOSEVELT BLVD
Naval Air Station Jacksonville
Johns River
BAYMEADOWS RD
SUNBEAM RD
HWY
Ortega River
BUCKMAN BRG
WELLS RD
HARTLEY RD
OLD ST
BLAIRMORE BLVD
KINGSLEY AVE
RIVER RD
Orange Park
MANDARIN RD
LORETTO RD
GREENLAND RD
HOOD LANDING RD
AUGUSTINE RD
BLANDING
Doctors Lake
PARK
SAN JOSE
To Starke
To Palatka
To Daytona Beach

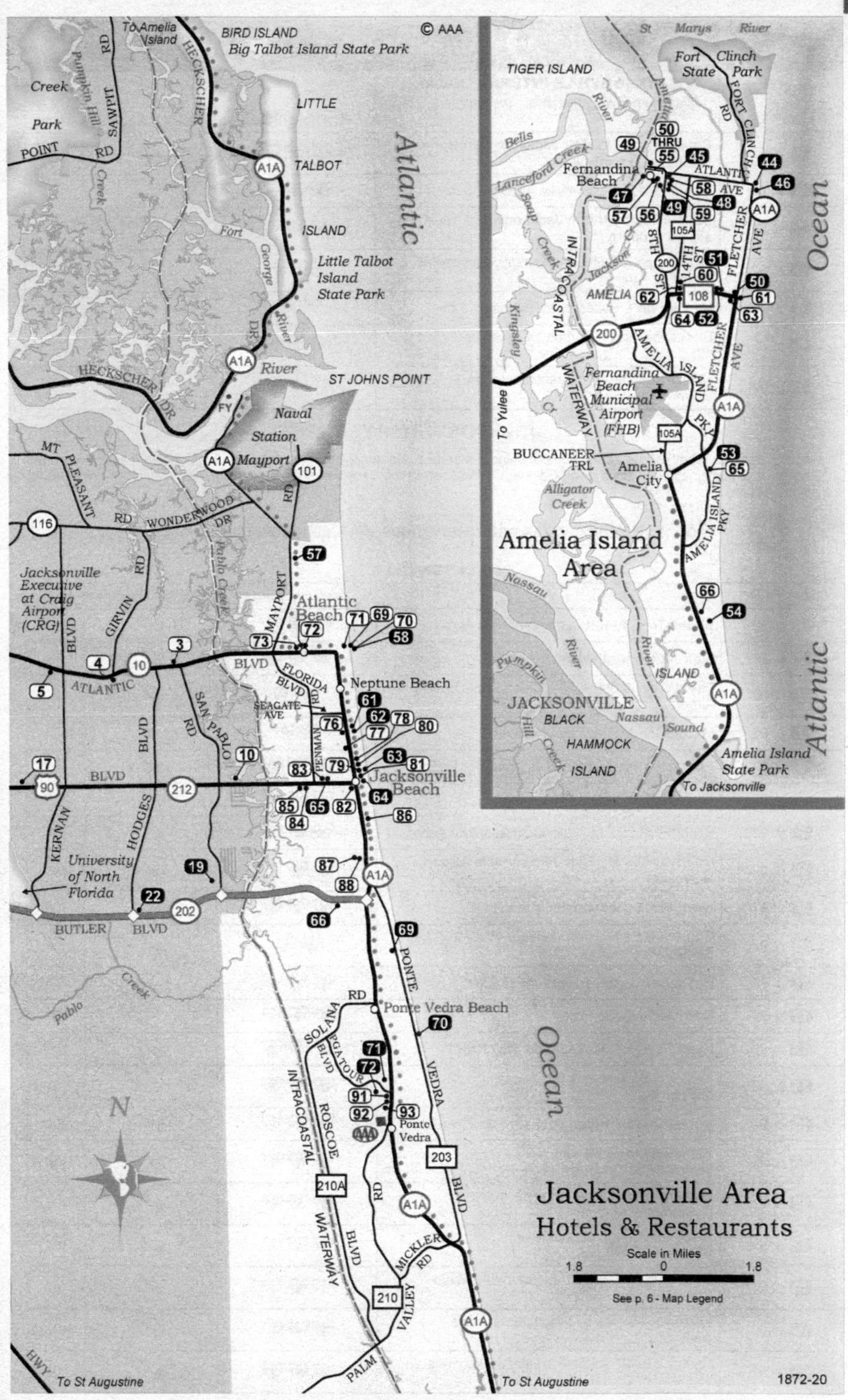

Jacksonville Area
Hotels & Restaurants
Scale in Miles
1.8 0 1.8
See p. 6 - Map Legend
Amelia Island Area
© AAA
1872-20
To St Augustine
To Jacksonville
To Yulee
Atlantic Ocean
Jacksonville Beach
Neptune Beach
Atlantic Beach
Ponte Vedra Beach
Fernandina Beach
Amelia City

Airport Hotels

Map Page	JACKSONVILLE INTERNATIONAL (Maximum driving distance from airport: 2.6 mi)	Diamond Rated	Member Savings	Page
8 p. 92	**Courtyard by Marriott Jacksonville Airport Northeast, 2.6 mi**	♦♦♦	✔	99
6 p. 92	Crowne Plaza Jacksonville Airport, 2.5 mi	♦♦♦		100
1 p. 92	**DoubleTree by Hilton Jacksonville Airport, on airport property**	♦♦♦	✔	100
3 p. 92	Fairfield Inn & Suites by Marriott Jacksonville Airport, 2.1 mi	♦♦	✔	100
4 p. 92	Microtel Inn & Suites by Wyndham, 1.8 mi	♦♦		101
5 p. 92	Residence Inn by Marriott Jacksonville Airport, 2.5 mi	♦♦♦	✔	101
7 p. 92	SpringHill Suites by Marriott Jacksonville Airport, 2.0 mi	♦♦♦	✔	101

Jacksonville Area

This index helps you "spot" where approved hotels and restaurants are located on the corresponding detailed maps. Restaurant price range is a combination of lunch and/or dinner. Turn to the listing page for more information and consult display ads for special promotions.

For more details, rates and reservations: AAA.com/travelguides/hotels

JACKSONVILLE

Map Page	Hotels	Diamond Rated	Member Savings	Page
1 p. 92	**DoubleTree by Hilton Jacksonville Airport**	♦♦♦	✔	100
2 p. 92	Aloft Jacksonville Airport	♦♦♦	✔	99
3 p. 92	Fairfield Inn & Suites by Marriott Jacksonville Airport	♦♦	✔	100
4 p. 92	Microtel Inn & Suites by Wyndham	♦♦		101
5 p. 92	Residence Inn by Marriott Jacksonville Airport	♦♦♦	✔	101
6 p. 92	Crowne Plaza Jacksonville Airport	♦♦♦		100
7 p. 92	SpringHill Suites by Marriott Jacksonville Airport	♦♦♦	✔	101
8 p. 92	**Courtyard by Marriott Jacksonville Airport Northeast**	♦♦♦	✔	99
9 p. 92	**Hyatt Place Jacksonville Airport**	♦♦♦	✔	101
10 p. 92	**Courtyard by Marriott Jacksonville I-295 East Beltway**	♦♦	✔	99
11 p. 92	Holiday Inn Express Jacksonville East	♦♦♦		101
12 p. 92	Omni Jacksonville Hotel	♦♦♦		101
13 p. 92	**Hyatt Regency Jacksonville Riverfront**	♦♦♦	✔	101
14 p. 92	Holiday Inn Express & Suites Jacksonville W - I295 & I10	♦♦♦		101
15 p. 92	**DoubleTree by Hilton Jacksonville Riverfront**	♦♦♦	✔	100
16 p. 92	**Hampton Inn by Hilton Jacksonville-Downtown-I-95**	♦♦♦	✔	100
17 p. 92	Homewood Suites by Hilton Jacksonville Downtown/Southbank	♦♦♦	✔	101
18 p. 92	Hilton Garden Inn Jacksonville Downtown/Southbank	♦♦♦	✔	101
19 p. 92	**Courtyard by Marriott Jacksonville Mayo Clinic/Beaches**	♦♦♦	✔	99
20 p. 92	Homewood Suites by Hilton Jacksonville Deerwood Park	♦♦♦	✔	101
21 p. 92	Hampton Inn & Suites by Hilton Jacksonville-St Johns Town Center Area	♦♦♦	✔	100

JACKSONVILLE (cont'd)

Map Page	Hotels (cont'd)	Diamond Rated	Member Savings	Page
22 p. 92	Holiday Inn Express & Suites Jacksonville SE Med Ctr Area	◆◆◆		101
23 p. 92	Tru by Hilton Jacksonville St. Johns Town Center	◆◆	✔	102
24 p. 92	Hilton Garden Inn Deerwood Park	◆◆◆	✔	100
25 p. 92	**Aloft Jacksonville Tapestry Park**	◆◆◆	✔	99
26 p. 92	**Hyatt Place Jacksonville St. Johns Town Center**	◆◆◆	✔	101
27 p. 92	Hotel Indigo Jacksonville Deerwood Park	◆◆◆		101
28 p. 92	TownePlace Suites by Marriott Jacksonville Butler Boulevard	◆◆	✔	101
29 p. 92	Jacksonville Marriott Hotel	◆◆◆	✔	101
30 p. 92	Holiday Inn Express Hotel & Suites-South	◆◆◆		101
31 p. 92	**Courtyard by Marriott Jacksonville Butler Boulevard**	◆◆	✔	99
32 p. 92	**Hampton Inn Jacksonville South/I-95 at JTB**	◆◆◆	✔	100
33 p. 92	Fairfield Inn & Suites by Marriott Jacksonville Butler Boulevard	◆◆◆	✔	100
34 p. 92	**Holiday Inn Jacksonville E 295 Baymeadows**	◆◆◆	✔	101
35 p. 92	Hampton Inn by Hilton Jacksonville I-295 E & Baymeadows	◆◆	✔	100
36 p. 92	**Embassy Suites by Hilton Jacksonville Baymeadows**	◆◆◆	✔	100
37 p. 92	**Best Western Southside Hotel & Suites**	◆◆	✔	99
38 p. 92	Ramada by Wyndham Conference Center Jacksonville	◆◆		101
39 p. 92	Holiday Inn Express Hotel & Suites Jacksonville/ I-295 South	◆◆◆		101
40 p. 92	Courtyard by Marriott Jacksonville Flagler Center	◆◆◆	✔	99
41 p. 92	Hampton Inn & Suites by Hilton Jacksonville South-Bartram Park	◆◆◆	✔	100

Map Page	Restaurants	Diamond Rated	Cuisine	Price Range	Page
1 p. 92	Millhouse	◆◆	American	$13-$34	103
2 p. 92	Green Papaya	◆◆	Thai	$8-$20	102
3 p. 92	German Schnitzel Haus	◆◆	German	$10-$25	102
4 p. 92	Epik Burger	◆	Burgers	$5-$10	102
5 p. 92	Soul Food Bistro	◆	Soul Food	$9-$15	103
6 p. 92	Zodiac Bar & Grill	◆◆	Mediterranean	$6-$24	103
7 p. 92	Juliette's Bistro	◆◆	American	$21-$38	102
8 p. 92	Ruth's Chris Steak House	◆◆◆	Steak	$32-$124	103
9 p. 92	River City Brewing Company Galley & Tavern	◆◆	American	$9-$36	103
10 p. 92	Marker 32	◆◆◆	Continental	$20-$30	102
11 p. 92	bb's restaurant + bar	◆◆	International	$11-$36	102
12 p. 92	The Wine Cellar	◆◆◆	International	$10-$39	103
13 p. 92	The Bearded Pig	◆	Barbecue	$8-$25	102
14 p. 92	Hawkers Asian Street Fare	◆◆	Asian Small Plates	$6-$15	102
15 p. 92	Mossfire Grill	◆◆	Southwestern	$4-$16	103
16 p. 92	Black Sheep Restaurant	◆◆◆	New American	$12-$32	102

Map Page	Restaurants (cont'd)	Diamond Rated	Cuisine	Price Range	Page
17 p. 92	PK Noodles	◆◆	Vietnamese	$7-$12	103
18 p. 92	Havana Jax	◆◆	Cuban	$10-$22	102
19 p. 92	**Matthew's Restaurant**	◆◆◆◆	International	$25-$47	102
20 p. 92	Q-Cup Boba Tea	◆◆	Vietnamese	$4-$12	103
21 p. 92	Cross Creek Steakhouse & Ribs	◆◆	American	$8-$30	102
22 p. 92	**Restaurant Orsay**	◆◆◆◆	French	$9-$40	103
23 p. 92	Blue Fish Restaurant & Oyster Bar	◆◆	Seafood	$8-$34	102
24 p. 92	Biscottis	◆◆	International	$11-$37	102
25 p. 92	Brick Restaurant	◆◆	New American	$10-$31	102
26 p. 92	PizzaPaddle	◆	Italian Pizza	$7-$23	103
27 p. 92	Pho Today	◆◆	Vietnamese	$9-$14	103
28 p. 92	M Shack Town Center	◆	Burgers	$6-$12	103
29 p. 92	Seven Bridges Grille & Brewery	◆◆	International	$10-$30	103
30 p. 92	Yashi Sushi	◆◆	Japanese Sushi	$8-$28	103
31 p. 92	Lime Leaf Thai Restaurant	◆◆	Thai	$14-$27	102
32 p. 92	III Forks Steakhouse	◆◆◆	Steak Seafood	$16-$95	102
33 p. 92	Brio Tuscan Grille	◆◆◆	Italian	$12-$30	102
34 p. 92	Moxie Kitchen + Cocktails	◆◆◆	New American	$12-$34	103
35 p. 92	Mojo Bar-B-Que "A Southern Blues Kitchen"	◆◆	Barbecue	$10-$22	103
36 p. 92	Fusion Sushi	◆◆	Japanese Sushi	$8-$29	102
37 p. 92	Athens Cafe	◆◆	Greek	$9-$36	102
38 p. 92	Athenian Owl	◆◆	Greek	$7-$22	102
39 p. 92	Bowl of Pho	◆◆	Vietnamese	$8-$14	102
40 p. 92	5th Element Taste of India	◆◆	Indian	$10-$17	102
41 p. 92	Mandaloun Mediterranean Cuisine	◆◆	Mediterranean	$15-$30	102
42 p. 92	Deerwood Deli & Diner	◆	American	$6-$11	102
43 p. 92	India's Restaurant	◆◆	Indian	$10-$17	102
44 p. 92	Enza's Italian Restaurant	◆◆	Italian	$12-$28	102
45 p. 92	The Tree Steak House	◆◆◆	Steak Seafood	$26-$55	103
46 p. 92	Clark's Fish Camp Seafood Restaurant	◆◆	Seafood Wild Game	$5-$32	102

AMELIA ISLAND

Map Page	Hotels	Diamond Rated	Member Savings	Page
44 p. 92	Seaside Amelia Inn	◆◆		31
45 p. 92	The Hoyt House	◆◆◆		30
46 p. 92	**Elizabeth Pointe Lodge**	◆◆◆	✔	30
47 p. 92	Hampton Inn & Suites-Amelia Island	◆◆◆	✔	30
48 p. 92	Amelia Island Williams House	◆◆◆		30
49 p. 92	The Fairbanks House	◆◆◆		30
50 p. 92	Amelia Hotel at the Beach	◆◆		30
51 p. 92	Hampton Inn Amelia Island at Fernandina Beach	◆◆◆	✔	30

AMELIA ISLAND (cont'd)

Map Page	Hotels (cont'd)	Diamond Rated	Member Savings	Page
52 p. 92	Residence Inn by Marriott-Amelia Island	◆◆◆	✔	31
53 p. 92	**The Ritz-Carlton, Amelia Island**	◆◆◆◆◆	✔	31
54 p. 92	**Omni Amelia Island Plantation Resort**	◆◆◆◆	✔	30

Map Page	Restaurants	Diamond Rated	Cuisine	Price Range	Page
49 p. 92	The Crab Trap	◆◆	Seafood	$11-$40	31
50 p. 92	Marina Seafood Restaurant	◆◆	Seafood Comfort Food	$8-$30	31
51 p. 92	Pepper's Mexican Grill & Cantina	◆◆	Mexican	$8-$19	31
52 p. 92	Ciao Italian Bistro	◆◆	Italian	$14-$30	31
53 p. 92	Amelia Tavern	◆◆	Small Plates	$9-$23	31
54 p. 92	Brett's Waterway Cafe	◆◆	Regional American	$11-$35	31
55 p. 92	Joe's 2nd Street Bistro	◆◆◆	American	$19-$34	31
56 p. 92	Espana Restaurant & Tapas	◆◆◆	Spanish Small Plates	$19-$32	31
57 p. 92	29 South	◆◆◆	New American	$8-$28	31
58 p. 92	David's Restaurant & Lounge	◆◆◆	Seafood Steak	$26-$60	31
59 p. 92	T-Rays Burger Station	◆	American	$3-$9	31
60 p. 92	Hana Sushi	◆◆	Japanese Sushi	$5-$25	31
61 p. 92	Sliders Seaside Grill	◆◆	Seafood	$11-$29	31
62 p. 92	Tony's New York Style Brick Oven Pizza & Restaurant	◆	Italian Pizza	$7-$15	31
63 p. 92	Cedar River Seafood	◆◆	Seafood	$8-$45	31
64 p. 92	Fancy Sushi	◆◆	Japanese Sushi	$8-$30	31
65 p. 92	**Salt**	◆◆◆◆◆	American	$33-$150	31
66 p. 92	Bob's Steak & Chop House	◆◆◆	Steak Seafood	$30-$79	31

ATLANTIC BEACH

Map Page	Hotels	Diamond Rated	Member Savings	Page
57 p. 92	**Best Western Mayport Inn & Suites**	◆◆	✔	32
58 p. 92	**One Ocean Resort & Spa**	◆◆◆◆	✔	32

Map Page	Restaurants	Diamond Rated	Cuisine	Price Range	Page
69 p. 92	Joseph's Pizza & Italian Restaurant	◆◆	Italian Pizza	$7-$24	32
70 p. 92	**Azurea**	◆◆◆◆	International	$26-$48	32
71 p. 92	M Shack	◆	Burgers	$6-$19	32
72 p. 92	Seafood Kitchen	◆	Seafood	$7-$17	32
73 p. 92	Culhane's Irish Pub	◆◆	Irish	$9-$19	32

JACKSONVILLE BEACH

Map Page	Hotels	Diamond Rated	Member Savings	Page
61 p. 92	**Courtyard by Marriott Jacksonville Beach Oceanfront**	◆◆◆	✔	104
62 p. 92	**Hampton Inn Jacksonville Beach-Oceanfront**	◆◆◆	✔	104
63 p. 92	**Best Western Oceanfront**	◆◆	✔	104
64 p. 92	**Four Points by Sheraton Jacksonville Beachfront**	◆◆◆	✔	104
65 p. 92	**Holiday Inn Express Jacksonville Beach**	◆◆◆	✔	105

JACKSONVILLE BEACH (cont'd)

Map Page	Hotels (cont'd)	Diamond Rated	Member Savings	Page
66 p. 92	Hampton Inn by Hilton Jacksonville/Mayo Clinic Area/Ponte Vedra	◆◆	✔	104

Map Page	Restaurants	Diamond Rated	Cuisine	Price Range	Page
76 p. 92	Metro Diner	◆◆	American	$8-$17	105
77 p. 92	Salt Life Food Shack	◆◆	International	$8-$20	105
78 p. 92	Graffiti Junktion	◆	Burgers	$5-$15	105
79 p. 92	Hoptinger Bier Garden & Sausage House	◆◆	Burgers Hot Dogs	$8-$17	105
80 p. 92	The Blind Rabbit	◆◆	Burgers	$10-$26	105
81 p. 92	Campeche Bay Cantina	◆◆	Mexican	$9-$17	105
82 p. 92	Burrito Gallery	◆	Mexican	$7-$12	105
83 p. 92	Jaxon Social Restaurant & Bar	◆◆◆	New American	$14-$22	105
84 p. 92	Mojo Kitchen, BBQ Pit and Blues Bar	◆◆	Barbecue	$11-$37	105
85 p. 92	TacoLu Baja Mexicana	◆◆	Mexican	$5-$10	105
86 p. 92	Eleven South	◆◆◆	New American	$11-$39	105
87 p. 92	Roy's	◆◆◆	Pacific Rim Fusion	$26-$55	105
88 p. 92	Bonefish Grill	◆◆◆	Seafood	$15-$34	105

PONTE VEDRA BEACH

Map Page	Hotels	Diamond Rated	Member Savings	Page
69 p. 92	**Ponte Vedra Inn & Club** *(See ad p. 253.)*	◆◆◆◆◆	✔	252
70 p. 92	**The Lodge & Club at Ponte Vedra Beach**	◆◆◆◆	✔	252
71 p. 92	Hilton Garden Inn Jacksonville/Ponte Vedra	◆◆◆	✔	252
72 p. 92	**Sawgrass Marriott Golf Resort & Spa**	◆◆◆	✔	252

Map Page	Restaurants	Diamond Rated	Cuisine	Price Range	Page
91 p. 92	Pusser's Bar and Grille	◆◆	Caribbean	$10-$28	252
92 p. 92	Ruth's Chris Steak House	◆◆◆	Steak	$32-$124	252
93 p. 92	**Restaurant Medure**	◆◆◆◆	Fusion	$21-$58	252

ORANGE PARK

Map Page	Hotels	Diamond Rated	Member Savings	Page
75 p. 92	Days Inn Orange Park	◆		158
76 p. 92	Hampton Inn & Suites Jacksonville - Orange Park	◆◆◆	✔	158
77 p. 92	Hilton Garden Inn	◆◆◆	✔	158
78 p. 92	**Holiday Inn & Suites Orange Park**	◆◆◆	✔	158

Map Page	Restaurants	Diamond Rated	Cuisine	Price Range	Page
96 p. 92	The Hilltop	◆◆	American	$14-$29	158
97 p. 92	OP Fish House and Oyster Bar	◆◆	Seafood	$10-$24	158

For complete hotel, dining and attraction listings: AAA.com/travelguides

JACKSONVILLE

- **Restaurants p. 102**
- **Hotels & Restaurants map & index p. 92**

ALOFT JACKSONVILLE AIRPORT 904/714-3800 **2**

SAVE Hotel. **Address:** 751 Skymarks Dr 32218

AAA Benefit: Members save 5% or more!

ALOFT JACKSONVILLE TAPESTRY PARK 904/998-4448 **25**

AAA Benefit: Members save 5% or more!

Address: 4812 Deer Lake Dr W 32246 **Location:** I-95 exit 340, 4.5 mi n to Southside Blvd, then e. **Facility:** 137 units. 5 stories, interior corridors. *Bath:* shower only. **Amenities:** safes. **Pool:** heated outdoor. **Activities:** exercise room. **Guest Services:** valet and coin laundry, area transportation.

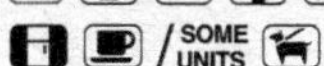

BEST WESTERN SOUTHSIDE HOTEL & SUITES 904/264-4466 **37**

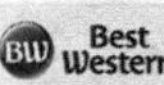

AAA Benefit: Members save up to 15% and earn bonus points!

Address: 4580 Collins Rd 32244 **Location:** I-295 exit 10 (US 17), just nw. **Facility:** 99 units. 5 stories, interior corridors. **Pool:** outdoor. **Activities:** exercise room. **Guest Services:** coin laundry. **Featured Amenity: breakfast buffet.**

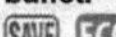

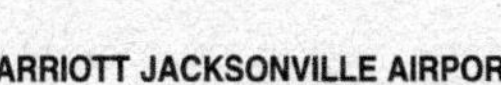

COURTYARD BY MARRIOTT JACKSONVILLE AIRPORT NORTHEAST 904/741-1122 **8**

COURTYARD **AAA Benefit:** Members save 5% or more!

Address: 14668 Duval Rd 32218 **Location:** I-95 exit 363B, just w on Airport Rd, then just s. **Facility:** 81 units. 3 stories, interior corridors. **Pool:** outdoor. **Activities:** hot tub, exercise room. **Guest Services:** valet and coin laundry, boarding pass kiosk, area transportation.

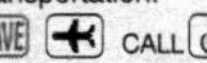

COURTYARD BY MARRIOTT JACKSONVILLE BUTLER BOULEVARD 904/296-2828 **31**

COURTYARD **AAA Benefit:** Members save 5% or more!

Address: 4670 Lenoir Ave S 32216 **Location:** I-95 exit 344 (Butler Blvd/SR 202), just sw, then just nw. **Facility:** 137 units. 5 stories, interior corridors. **Pool:** outdoor. **Activities:** exercise room. **Guest Services:** valet and coin laundry, boarding pass kiosk.

SOME UNITS HS

COURTYARD BY MARRIOTT JACKSONVILLE FLAGLER CENTER 904/260-2027 **40**

SAVE Hotel. **Address:** 14402 Old St Augustine Rd 32258

AAA Benefit: Members save 5% or more!

COURTYARD BY MARRIOTT JACKSONVILLE I-295 EAST BELTWAY 904/247-6782 **10**

Hotel

COURTYARD **AAA Benefit:** Members save 5% or more!

Address: 9815 Lantern St 32225 **Location:** I-295 exit 47, Monument Rd, just w, then just n. **Facility:** 97 units. 4 stories, interior corridors. **Pool:** heated outdoor. **Activities:** hot tub, exercise room. **Guest Services:** valet and coin laundry, boarding pass kiosk.

SAVE ECO CALL BIZ

COURTYARD BY MARRIOTT JACKSONVILLE MAYO CLINIC/BEACHES 904/223-1700 **19**

COURTYARD **AAA Benefit:** Members save 5% or more!

Address: 14390 Mayo Blvd 32224 **Location:** SR 202 (Butler Blvd) exit San Pablo Rd, 0.4 mi n, then just w; adjacent to Mayo Clinic. **Facility:** 146 units. 3 stories, interior corridors. **Pool:** heated outdoor. **Activities:** exercise room. **Guest Services:** valet and coin laundry, boarding pass kiosk, area transportation.

AAA.com/maps—Dream, plan, go with AAA travel planning tools

(See map & index p. 92.)

CROWNE PLAZA JACKSONVILLE AIRPORT
904/741-4404 6

Hotel. **Address:** 14670 Duval Rd 32218

DOUBLETREE BY HILTON JACKSONVILLE AIRPORT
904/741-1997 1

Hotel

AAA Benefit: Members save 5% or more!

Address: 2101 Dixie Clipper 32218 **Location:** I-95 exit 363B, Jct Pecan Park rd, just w. **Facility:** 201 units. 2-6 stories, interior corridors. **Parking:** on-site (fee). **Amenities:** safes. **Pool:** outdoor. **Activities:** exercise room. **Guest Services:** valet and coin laundry, area transportation.

SAVE BIZ

DOUBLETREE BY HILTON JACKSONVILLE RIVERFRONT
904/398-8800 15

Hotel

AAA Benefit: Members save 5% or more!

Address: 1201 Riverplace 32207 **Location:** On south bank of river; just e of Main St Bridge; center. **Facility:** 293 units. 10 stories, interior corridors. **Parking:** on-site (fee) and valet. **Terms:** check-in 4 pm. **Amenities:** safes. **Dining:** Ruth's Chris Steak House, see separate listing. **Pool:** outdoor. **Activities:** exercise room. **Guest Services:** valet laundry.

SAVE ECO BIZ / SOME UNITS

EMBASSY SUITES BY HILTON JACKSONVILLE BAYMEADOWS
904/731-3555 36

Hotel

AAA Benefit: Members save 5% or more!

Address: 9300 Baymeadows Rd 32256 **Location:** I-95 exit 341 (Baymeadows Rd/SR 152), 0.5 mi e. **Facility:** 277 units. 4-7 stories, interior corridors. **Amenities:** safes. **Pool:** heated indoor. **Activities:** hot tub, exercise room. **Guest Services:** valet and coin laundry, area transportation. **Featured Amenity: breakfast buffet.**

SAVE ECO BIZ / SOME UNITS

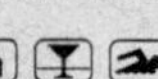

FAIRFIELD INN & SUITES BY MARRIOTT JACKSONVILLE AIRPORT
904/741-3500 3

SAVE Hotel. **Address:** 1300 Airport Rd 32218

AAA Benefit: Members save 5% or more!

FAIRFIELD INN & SUITES BY MARRIOTT JACKSONVILLE BUTLER BOULEVARD
904/854-6200 33

SAVE Hotel. **Address:** 4888 Lenoir Ave S 32216

AAA Benefit: Members save 5% or more!

FAIRFIELD INN & SUITES BY MARRIOTT JACKSONVILLE WEST/CHAFFEE POINT
904/693-4400

SAVE Hotel. **Address:** 561 Chaffee Point 32221

AAA Benefit: Members save 5% or more!

HAMPTON INN & SUITES BY HILTON JACKSONVILLE SOUTH-BARTRAM PARK
904/268-6264 41

SAVE Hotel. **Address:** 13950 Village Lake Cir 32258

AAA Benefit: Members save 5% or more!

HAMPTON INN & SUITES BY HILTON JACKSONVILLE-ST JOHNS TOWN CENTER AREA
904/997-9100 21

SAVE Hotel. **Address:** 4415 Southside Blvd 32216

AAA Benefit: Members save 5% or more!

HAMPTON INN BY HILTON I-10/WEST
904/783-8277

SAVE Hotel. **Address:** 548 Chaffee Point Blvd 32221

AAA Benefit: Members save 5% or more!

HAMPTON INN BY HILTON JACKSONVILLE-DOWNTOWN-I-95
904/396-7770 16

Hotel

AAA Benefit: Members save 5% or more!

Address: 1331 Prudential Dr 32207 **Location:** South side of Main St Bridge. **Facility:** 118 units. 5 stories, interior corridors. **Pool:** outdoor. **Activities:** limited exercise equipment. **Guest Services:** valet laundry. **Featured Amenity: breakfast buffet.**

SAVE CALL BIZ HS

HAMPTON INN BY HILTON JACKSONVILLE I-295 E & BAYMEADOWS
904/363-7150 35

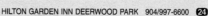

SAVE Hotel. **Address:** 8127 Point Meadows Dr 32256

AAA Benefit: Members save 5% or more!

HAMPTON INN JACKSONVILLE SOUTH/I-95 AT JTB
904/281-2600 32

Hotel

AAA Benefit: Members save 5% or more!

Address: 4681 Lenoir Ave 32216 **Location:** I-95 exit 344 (Butler Blvd/SR 202), just w, then just n. **Facility:** 100 units. 4 stories, interior corridors. **Pool:** outdoor. **Activities:** exercise room. **Guest Services:** valet laundry, area transportation. **Featured Amenity: breakfast buffet.**

SAVE ECO CALL BIZ

HILTON GARDEN INN DEERWOOD PARK 904/997-6600 24

SAVE Hotel. **Address:** 9745 Gate Pkwy N 32246

AAA Benefit: Members save 5% or more!

(See map & index p. 92.)

HILTON GARDEN INN JACKSONVILLE DOWNTOWN/SOUTHBANK 904/396-6111 **18**

SAVE Hotel. **Address:** 1201 Kings Ave 32207

AAA Benefit: Members save 5% or more!

HOLIDAY INN EXPRESS & SUITES JACKSONVILLE SE MED CTR AREA 904/421-7000 **22**

Hotel. **Address:** 4791 Windsor Commons Ct 32224

HOLIDAY INN EXPRESS & SUITES JACKSONVILLE W - I295 & I10 904/693-5100 **14**

Hotel. **Address:** 1120 Suemac Rd 32254

HOLIDAY INN EXPRESS HOTEL & SUITES JACKSONVILLE/ I-295 SOUTH 904/899-9000 **39**

Hotel. **Address:** 11262 Old St. Augustine Rd 32257

HOLIDAY INN EXPRESS HOTEL & SUITES-SOUTH 904/332-9500 **30**

Hotel. **Address:** 4675 Salisbury Rd 32256

HOLIDAY INN EXPRESS JACKSONVILLE EAST 904/997-9190 **11**

Hotel. **Address:** 53 Jefferson Rd 32225

HOLIDAY INN JACKSONVILLE E 295 BAYMEADOWS 904/854-8000 **34**

Hotel

Address: 11083 Nurseryfields Dr 32256 **Location:** SR 9A and Baymeadows Rd, just ne. **Facility:** 98 units. 5 stories, interior corridors. **Pool:** outdoor. **Activities:** hot tub, exercise room. **Guest Services:** valet and coin laundry.

SAVE CALL BIZ HS

HOMEWOOD SUITES BY HILTON JACKSONVILLE DEERWOOD PARK 904/253-7120 **20**

SAVE Extended Stay Hotel. **Address:** 8511 Touchton Rd 32216

AAA Benefit: Members save 5% or more!

HOMEWOOD SUITES BY HILTON JACKSONVILLE DOWNTOWN/SOUTHBANK 904/396-6888 **17**

SAVE Extended Stay Hotel. **Address:** 1201 Kings Ave 32207

AAA Benefit: Members save 5% or more!

HOTEL INDIGO JACKSONVILLE DEERWOOD PARK 904/996-7199 **27**

Hotel. **Address:** 9840 Tapestry Park Cir 32246

HYATT PLACE JACKSONVILLE AIRPORT 904/741-4184 **9**

Hotel

HYATT PLACE **AAA Benefit:** Members save up to 10%!

Address: 14565 Duval Rd 32218 **Location:** I-95 exit 363B, just w, then just s. **Facility:** 127 units. 6 stories, interior corridors. **Pool:** outdoor. **Activities:** exercise room. **Guest Services:** valet and coin laundry, area transportation.

SAVE BIZ HS

/ SOME UNITS

HYATT PLACE JACKSONVILLE ST. JOHNS TOWN CENTER 904/641-7200 **26**

Hotel

HYATT PLACE **AAA Benefit:** Members save up to 10%!

Address: 4742 Town Center Pkwy 32246 **Location:** Waterfront. Jct Town Center Pkwy. and Gate Pkwy., just ne. **Facility:** 160 units. 5 stories, interior corridors. **Pool:** heated outdoor. **Activities:** exercise room. **Guest Services:** valet and coin laundry. **Featured Amenity:** **breakfast buffet.**

SAVE CALL BIZ

/ SOME UNITS

HYATT REGENCY JACKSONVILLE RIVERFRONT 904/588-1234 **13**

Hotel

HYATT REGENCY **AAA Benefit:** Members save up to 10%!

Address: 225 E Coast Line Dr 32202 **Location:** Downtown; just e of The Landing. **Facility:** 951 units. 4-19 stories, interior corridors. **Parking:** on-site (fee) and valet. **Amenities:** safes. **Dining:** 3 restaurants. **Pool:** heated outdoor. **Activities:** exercise room. **Guest Services:** valet and coin laundry, boarding pass kiosk, area transportation.

SAVE ECO BIZ HS / SOME UNITS

JACKSONVILLE MARRIOTT HOTEL 904/296-2222 **29**

SAVE Hotel. **Address:** 4670 Salisbury Rd 32256

AAA Benefit: Members save 5% or more!

MICROTEL INN & SUITES BY WYNDHAM 904/741-4911 **4**

Hotel. **Address:** 13200 International Airport Blvd 32218

OMNI JACKSONVILLE HOTEL 904/355-6664 **12**

Hotel. **Address:** 245 Water St 32202

RAMADA BY WYNDHAM CONFERENCE CENTER JACKSONVILLE 904/268-8080 **38**

Hotel. **Address:** 3130 Hartley Rd 32257

RESIDENCE INN BY MARRIOTT JACKSONVILLE AIRPORT 904/741-6550 **5**

SAVE Extended Stay Hotel. **Address:** 1310 Airport Rd 32218

AAA Benefit: Members save 5% or more!

SPRINGHILL SUITES BY MARRIOTT JACKSONVILLE AIRPORT 904/741-8002 **7**

SAVE Hotel. **Address:** 13550 Airport Ct 32218

AAA Benefit: Members save 5% or more!

TOWNEPLACE SUITES BY MARRIOTT JACKSONVILLE BUTLER BOULEVARD 904/296-1661 **28**

SAVE Extended Stay Hotel. **Address:** 4801 Lenoir Ave 32216

AAA Benefit: Members save 5% or more!

(See map & index p. 92.)

TRU BY HILTON JACKSONVILLE ST. JOHNS TOWN CENTER 904/420-4200 (23)

Hotel. **Address:** 4640 Tropea Way 32246

Members save 5% or more!

WHERE TO EAT

III FORKS STEAKHOUSE 904/928-9277 (32)

Steak Seafood. Fine Dining. **Address:** 9822 Tapestry Park Cir, Suite 111 32246

4 RIVERS SMOKEHOUSE 855/368-7748

Barbecue. Quick Serve. **Address:** 9220 Baymeadows Rd 32256

5TH ELEMENT TASTE OF INDIA 904/448-8265 (40)

Indian. Casual Dining. **Address:** 9485 Baymeadows Rd 32256

ATHENIAN OWL 904/503-3008 (38)

Greek. Casual Dining. **Address:** 9551 Baymeadows Rd 32256

ATHENS CAFE 904/733-1199 (37)

Greek. Casual Dining. **Address:** 6271 St. Augustine Rd 32217

BB'S RESTAURANT + BAR 904/306-0100 (11)

International. Casual Dining. **Address:** 1019 Hendricks Ave 32207

THE BEARDED PIG 904/619-2247 (13)

Barbecue. Quick Serve. **Address:** 1224 Kings Ave 32207

BISCOTTIS 904/387-2060 (24)

International. Casual Dining. **Address:** 3556 St. Johns Ave 32204

BLACK SHEEP RESTAURANT 904/380-3091 (16)

New American. Casual Dining. **Address:** 1534 Oak St 32204

BLUE FISH RESTAURANT & OYSTER BAR 904/387-0700 (23)

Seafood. Casual Dining. **Address:** 3551 St. Johns Ave 32205

BONO'S PIT BAR-B-Q

Barbecue. Casual Dining.

LOCATIONS:

Address: 10065 Skinner Lake Dr 32246 **Phone:** 904/998-1997

Address: 10645 Philips Hwy 32256 **Phone:** 904/886-2801

Address: 8011 Merrill Rd, Suite 23 32277 **Phone:** 904/743-3727

Address: 5711 Bowden Rd 32216 **Phone:** 904/448-5395

Address: 705 Lane Ave S 32205 **Phone:** 904/783-1404

Address: 9820 San Jose Blvd 32257 **Phone:** 904/268-2666

Address: 3303 S San Pablo Rd 32224 **Phone:** 904/223-1391

Address: 12620 Bartram Park Blvd 32258 **Phone:** 904/652-2989

Address: 100 Bartram Oaks Walk 32259 **Phone:** 904/287-7710

BOWL OF PHO 904/646-4455 (39)

Vietnamese. Casual Dining. **Address:** 9902 Old Baymeadows Rd 32256

BRICK RESTAURANT 904/387-0606 (25)

New American. Casual Dining. **Address:** 3585 St. Johns Ave 32205

BRIO TUSCAN GRILLE 904/807-9960 (33)

Italian. Casual Dining. **Address:** 4910 Big Island Dr 32246

CANTINA LAREDO 904/997-6110

Mexican. Casual Dining. **Address:** 10282 Bistro Dr 32246

CLARK'S FISH CAMP SEAFOOD RESTAURANT 904/268-3474 (46)

Seafood Wild Game. Casual Dining. **Address:** 12903 Hood Landing Rd 32258

CROSS CREEK STEAKHOUSE & RIBS 904/783-9579 (21)

American. Casual Dining. **Address:** 850 Lane Ave S 32205

DEERWOOD DELI & DINER 904/641-4877 (42)

American. Casual Dining. **Address:** 9934 Old Baymeadows Rd 32256

ENZA'S ITALIAN RESTAURANT 904/268-4458 (44)

Italian. Casual Dining. **Address:** 10601 San Jose Blvd, Suite 109 32257

EPIK BURGER 904/374-7326 (4)

Burgers. Quick Serve. **Address:** 12740 Atlantic Blvd 32250

FUSION SUSHI 904/636-8688 (36)

Japanese Sushi. Casual Dining. **Address:** 1550 University Blvd W 32217

GATOR'S DOCKSIDE 904/448-0500

American. Casual Dining. **Address:** 8650 Baymeadows Rd 32256

GERMAN SCHNITZEL HAUS 904/221-9700 (3)

German. Casual Dining. **Address:** 13475 Atlantic Blvd 32225

GREEN PAPAYA 904/696-8886 (2)

Thai. Casual Dining. **Address:** 13141 City Station Dr, Suite 149 32218

HAVANA JAX 904/399-0609 (18)

Cuban. Casual Dining. **Address:** 2578 Atlantic Blvd 32207

HAWKERS ASIAN STREET FARE 904/508-0342 (14)

Asian Small Plates. Casual Dining. **Address:** 1001 Park St 32204

INDIA'S RESTAURANT 904/620-0777 (43)

Indian. Casual Dining. **Address:** 9802-8 Baymeadows Rd 32256

JULIETTE'S BISTRO 904/355-7118 (7)

American. Casual Dining. **Address:** 245 Water St 32202

LIME LEAF THAI RESTAURANT 904/645-8568 (31)

Thai. Casual Dining. **Address:** 9822 Tapestry Park Cir, Suite 109 32246

MANDALOUN MEDITERRANEAN CUISINE 904/646-1881 (41)

Mediterranean. Casual Dining. **Address:** 9862 Old Baymeadows Rd 32256

MARKER 32 904/223-1534 (10)

Continental. Fine Dining. **Address:** 14549 Beach Blvd 32250

MATTHEW'S RESTAURANT 904/396-9922 (19)

International Fine Dining
$25-$47

AAA Inspector Notes: Recognized as one of the area's premiere dining rooms, the elegant restaurant features an intriguing menu in which renowned chef Matthew Medure tantalizes diners with innovative cuisine and award-winning wines. The diverse menu showcase includes caviar, a salumi and cheese tasting, Australian lamb and Wagyu beef. Soufflé for dessert is highly recommended. Reservations typically fill up in advance. Valet parking is available Thursday through Saturday. **Features:** full bar, happy hour. **Reservations:** suggested. **Address:** 2107 Hendricks Ave 32207 **Location:** Jct Atlantic Blvd, just s on SR 13 (Hendricks Ave); s of downtown; in historic San Marco. **Parking:** valet and street only.

(D)

(See map & index p. 92.)

MILLHOUSE 904/741-8722 (1)

American. Casual Dining. **Address:** 1341 Airport Rd 32218

MOJO BAR-B-QUE "A SOUTHERN BLUES KITCHEN" 904/732-7200 (35)

Barbecue. Casual Dining. **Address:** 1607 University Blvd 32217

MOSSFIRE GRILL 904/355-4434 (15)

Southwestern. Casual Dining. **Address:** 1537 Margaret St 32204

MOXIE KITCHEN + COCKTAILS 904/998-9744 (34)

New American. Casual Dining. **Address:** 4972 Big Island Dr 32246

M SHACK TOWN CENTER 904/642-5000 (28)

Burgers. Quick Serve. **Address:** 10281 MidTown Pkwy 32246

PHO TODAY 904/551-7367 (27)

Vietnamese. Casual Dining. **Address:** 9700 Deer Lake Ct, #5A 32246

PIZZAPADDLE 904/440-0000 (26)

Italian Pizza. Casual Dining. **Address:** 4320 Deerwood Lake Pkwy, Unit 204 32216

PK NOODLES 904/646-0707 (17)

Vietnamese. Casual Dining. **Address:** 11925 Beach Blvd 32246

Q-CUP BOBA TEA 904/329-2623 (20)

Vietnamese. Casual Dining. **Address:** 11380 Beach Blvd, Suite 20 32246

RESTAURANT ORSAY 904/381-0909 (22)

French Casual Dining $9-$40

AAA Inspector Notes: The cozy, upscale restaurant features attentive staff and a menu deeply focused on fine-quality ingredients sourced from local farms, ranches and waters. Enjoy the house-made charcuterie and the in-house cured and smoked Maple Leaf bacon. Entrées include P.E.I. mussels, lobster pot pie and braised beef short ribs with truffle fries. Hints of various ethnic influences are infused throughout the menu. **Features:** full bar, patio dining, Sunday brunch, happy hour. **Reservations:** suggested. **Address:** 3630 Park St 32205 **Location:** Just e of Roosevelt Blvd; s of downtown; in historic Avondale. [D]

RIVER CITY BREWING COMPANY GALLEY & TAVERN 904/398-2299 (9)

American. Casual Dining. **Address:** 835 Museum Cir 32207

RUTH'S CHRIS STEAK HOUSE 904/396-6200 (8)

Steak. Fine Dining. **Address:** 1201 Riverplace Blvd 32207

SEVEN BRIDGES GRILLE & BREWERY 904/997-1999 (29)

International. Casual Dining. **Address:** 9735 Gate Pkwy N 32246

SONNY'S REAL PIT BAR-B-Q

Barbecue. Casual Dining.

LOCATIONS:

Address: 4434 Blanding Blvd 32210 **Phone:** 904/777-0730

Address: 1923 S Lane Ave 32210 **Phone:** 904/786-0081

Address: 5097 University Blvd 32216 **Phone:** 904/737-4906

Address: 12485 San Jose Blvd 32223 **Phone:** 904/288-7928

SOUL FOOD BISTRO 904/394-2801 (5)

Soul Food. Buffet Style. **Address:** 11876 Atlantic Blvd 32225

STICKY FINGERS RIB HOUSE 904/309-7427

Barbecue. Casual Dining. **Address:** 13150 City Station Dr 32218

TIJUANA FLATS

Tex-Mex. Quick Serve.

LOCATIONS:

Address: 9942 Old Baymeadows Rd 32256 **Phone:** 904/641-1090

Address: 13529 Beach Blvd 32224 **Phone:** 904/223-0041

Address: 5907 Roosevelt Blvd 32244 **Phone:** 904/908-4343

Address: 651 Nautica Dr 32218 **Phone:** 904/738-7642

Address: 5635 San Jose Blvd 32207 **Phone:** 904/737-9938

Address: 13820 Old St Augustine Rd, Suite 125 32258 **Phone:** 904/262-0484

Address: 2025 Riverside Ave, Suite 205 32204 **Phone:** 904/389-5630

THE TREE STEAK HOUSE 904/262-0006 (45)

Steak Seafood. Casual Dining. **Address:** 11362 San Jose Blvd, Suite 1 32223

THE WINE CELLAR 904/398-8989 (12)

International. Fine Dining. **Address:** 1314 Prudential Dr 32207

YASHI SUSHI 904/997-9887 (30)

Japanese Sushi. Casual Dining. **Address:** 4820 W Deer Lake Dr 32246

ZODIAC BAR & GRILL 904/354-8283 (6)

Mediterranean. Casual Dining. **Address:** 120 W Adams St 32202

JACKSONVILLE BEACH (B-12) pop. 21,362, elev. 14'

- **Hotels p. 104 • Restaurants p. 105**
- **Hotels & Restaurants map & index p. 92**
- **Part of Jacksonville area — see map p. 84**

It's all about the beach in Jacksonville Beach, where salty Atlantic Ocean waters are said to offer the best surfing in the area. If folks aren't riding the waves, they're strolling on the boardwalk (aka the Sea Walk), spiking volleyballs, or just leaning back in a beach chair on the fine white sand and taking it easy. Dining, shopping and barhopping on the beachfront's 1-mile-long boardwalk (on the oceanfront between 1st Avenue North and 6th Avenue North) also attract beachgoers. Swimming, snorkeling and sailing are popular outdoor sports, as is saltwater fishing off the pier, 503 N. 1st St. A license is not required, and bait and tackle can be purchased at a concession stand; phone (904) 241-1515. The pier is open daily 6 a.m.-10 p.m., Apr.-Nov. (6 a.m.-7 p.m., rest of year); entry fee $4, $1 (spectators), free (ages 0-5).

The beach also is popular with much smaller visitors: Endangered loggerhead turtles wade out of the ocean at night to lay their eggs during sea turtle nesting season May-Oct. Take care not to disturb the turtles; do not touch them, light campfires or use flashlights, cell phones or cameras with flash. It's illegal to do so and could cause the female to abandon her nest.

Break away from the sand and ocean and attempt a hole-in-one at the 18-hole Jacksonville Beach Golf Course, 605 Penman Rd. S.; phone (904) 247-6184. Or head for South Beach Park and Sunshine Playground, 2514 S. Beach Pkwy., and shoot some hoops, swing a tennis racquet, work out on the fitness trail, and let the kids go wild on the large playground; it features sections for different age groups

(See map & index p. 92.)

and includes a lighthouse, a splash pad and a wooden ship complete with swinging bridge and covered slides.

Spring and summer months bring music and movies to the beach. At the SeaWalk Pavilion, 75 N. 1st St., you can attend blues, jazz, pops and classical music concerts or catch a classic flick. Phone the events hotline at (904) 247-6157, for information. Indoor productions including dramas, comedies and musicals at Players-By-The-Sea Theatre, 106 6th St. N., will capture the attention of theater devotees; phone (904) 249-0289 for reservations.

SAVE **ADVENTURE LANDING,** 1944 Beach Blvd., features Shipwreck Island Water Park, with four extreme waterslides, a wave pool and a pirate play village with 12 slides. Among other amusements are go-carts, laser tag, miniature golf and batting cages. Rental lockers and cabanas are available.

Hours: Amusements open Sun.-Thurs. 10-10, Fri.-Sat. 10 a.m.-midnight. Water park open daily at 10, mid-May to late Aug.; Sat.-Sun. at 10, mid-Mar. to mid-May and late Aug.-Sept. 30. Closing times vary; phone ahead. **Cost:** Water park $28.99; $23.99 (under 42 inches tall); $19.99 (after 3 p.m.); free (ages 0-3 when accompanied by an adult). Amusement prices vary. **Phone:** (904) 246-4386.

BEST WESTERN OCEANFRONT 904/249-4949 63

Motel

AAA Benefit: Members save up to 15% and earn bonus points!

Address: 305 1st St N 32250 **Location:** Oceanfront. 0.4 mi n of Beach Blvd (US 90). **Facility:** 51 units. 3 stories, interior corridors. **Amenities:** safes. **Pool:** heated outdoor. **Guest Services:** valet and coin laundry, area transportation. **Featured Amenity: breakfast buffet.**

Love the
Great Outdoors?

For getaways off the beaten path, visit AAA.com/campgrounds

iStockphoto.com_pixelfit

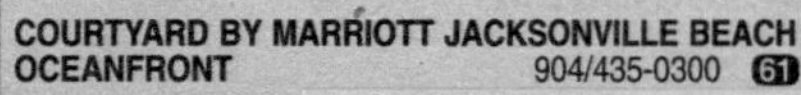
COURTYARD BY MARRIOTT JACKSONVILLE BEACH OCEANFRONT 904/435-0300 61

Hotel

AAA Benefit: Members save 5% or more!

Address: 1617 N 1st St 32250 **Location:** Oceanfront. Just e of SR A1A; at 16th Ave N. **Facility:** 150 units. 4-7 stories, interior/exterior corridors. **Terms:** check-in 4 pm. **Pool:** heated outdoor. **Activities:** hot tub, exercise room. **Guest Services:** valet and coin laundry, boarding pass kiosk.

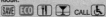

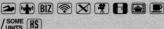

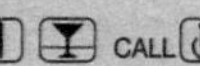
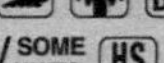

SOME UNITS HS

COURTYARD

Amazing Oceanfront Views, Beachfront Patio with Pool, Whirlpool & Bar, Dining & Cocktails at The Bistro

FOUR POINTS BY SHERATON JACKSONVILLE BEACHFRONT 904/435-3535 64

Hotel

FOUR POINTS BY SHERATON **AAA Benefit:** Members save 5% or more!

Address: 11 1st St N 32250 **Location:** Oceanfront. Just n of Beach Blvd (US 90). **Facility:** 80 units. 6 stories, interior corridors. **Terms:** check-in 4 pm. **Amenities:** safes. **Pool:** heated outdoor. **Activities:** hot tub, exercise room. **Guest Services:** valet and coin laundry, area transportation.

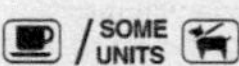

HAMPTON INN BY HILTON JACKSONVILLE/MAYO CLINIC AREA/PONTE VEDRA 904/280-9101 66

SAVE Hotel. **Address:** 1220 Marsh Landing Pkwy 32250

AAA Benefit: Members save 5% or more!

HAMPTON INN JACKSONVILLE BEACH-OCEANFRONT 904/241-2311 62

Hotel

AAA Benefit: Members save 5% or more!

Address: 1515 1st St N 32250 **Location:** Oceanfront. Just e of SR A1A; at 14th Ave N. **Facility:** 177 units. 7 stories, interior corridors. **Terms:** check-in 4 pm. **Dining:** 2 restaurants. **Pool:** heated outdoor. **Activities:** hot tub, exercise room. **Guest Services:** valet and coin laundry. **Featured Amenity: breakfast buffet.**

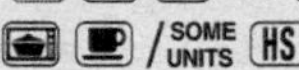

SOME UNITS HS

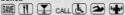

(See map & index p. 92.)

HOLIDAY INN EXPRESS JACKSONVILLE BEACH

904/435-3000 (65)

Hotel

Address: 1101 Beach Blvd 32250 **Location:** 0.7 mi w of 3rd St/SR A1A. **Facility:** 82 units. 3 stories, interior corridors. **Amenities:** safes. **Pool:** heated outdoor. **Activities:** hot tub, exercise room. **Guest Services:** valet and coin laundry, area transportation. **Featured Amenity: breakfast buffet.**

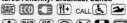

SAVE ECO CALL BIZ HS / SOME UNITS

WHERE TO EAT

THE BLIND RABBIT 904/595-5915 (80)
Burgers. Gastropub. **Address:** 311 3rd St N 32250

BONEFISH GRILL 904/247-4234 (88)
Seafood. Casual Dining. **Address:** 2400 S 3rd St 32250

BONO'S PIT BAR-B-Q 904/249-8704
Barbecue. Casual Dining. **Address:** 1266 3rd St S 32250

BURRITO GALLERY 904/246-6521 (82)
Mexican. Casual Dining. **Address:** 300 Beach Blvd 32250

CAMPECHE BAY CANTINA 904/249-3322 (81)
Mexican. Casual Dining. **Address:** 127 1st Ave N 32250

ELEVEN SOUTH 904/241-1112 (86)
New American. Fine Dining. **Address:** 216 11th Ave S 32250

GRAFFITI JUNKTION 904/372-9985 (78)
Burgers. Casual Dining. **Address:** 265 5th Ave N 32250

HOPTINGER BIER GARDEN & SAUSAGE HOUSE 904/222-0796 (79)
Burgers Hot Dogs. Casual Dining. **Address:** 331 1st Ave N 32250

JAXON SOCIAL RESTAURANT & BAR 904/595-5660 (83)
New American. Casual Dining. **Address:** 1161 Beach Blvd 32250

METRO DINER 904/853-6817 (76)
American. Casual Dining. **Address:** 1534 3rd St N 32250

MOJO KITCHEN, BBQ PIT AND BLUES BAR 904/247-6636 (84)
Barbecue. Casual Dining. **Address:** 1500 Beach Blvd 32250

ROY'S 904/241-7697 (87)
Pacific Rim Fusion. Fine Dining. **Address:** 2400 S 3rd St 32250

SALT LIFE FOOD SHACK 904/372-4456 (77)
International. Casual Dining. **Address:** 1018 3rd St N 32250

TACOLU BAJA MEXICANA 904/249-8226 (85)
Mexican. Casual Dining. **Address:** 1712 Beach Blvd 32250

KENNEDY SPACE CENTER (F-6)

Forty-seven miles east of Orlando via the Beachline Expressway (toll) or SR 50, the John F. Kennedy Space Center (KSC) is accessible from the mainland off US 1, 6 miles across the SR 405 causeway over the Indian River, or from the beaches across the SR 520 or 528 causeways to Merritt Island, then north on SR 3 and Space Commerce Way. The center is located within the 140,000-acre Merritt Island National Wildlife Refuge and extends some 34 miles along the coast.

Since 1981, when *Columbia* flew into Earth's orbit, through July 2011, when the last shuttle was launched, Kennedy Space Center has been the launch and landing site for the space shuttle, NASA's reusable space transportation system. It is home to two launch pads, one of the world's longest runways and the nation's third-largest building, the Vehicle Assembly Building. KSC also is the only place in the world where man has launched from Earth and traveled to the moon.

Cape Canaveral Air Force Station, east of the space center, was the site of the historic Mercury and Gemini flights, including America's first suborbital space flight taken by Navy Cmdr. Alan B. Shepard Jr. on May 5, 1961, and the country's first manned orbital flight by Marine Lt. Col. John H. Glenn Jr. on Feb. 20, 1962. Cape Canaveral is now the site for unmanned rocket launches. For additional information about Kennedy Space Center, phone (866) 737-5235.

KENNEDY SPACE CENTER VISITOR COMPLEX is 10 mi. e. of I-95 on Space Commerce Way. Built in 1967, the modern facility explores the past, present and future of the U.S. space program. The orbiter *Atlantis*, which flew the last space shuttle mission in July 2011, is at the heart of the center's Space Shuttle *Atlantis* exhibit. *Atlantis* bears the scars of its 33 missions and sits at a 43-degree angle with its cargo bay doors open, allowing spectators to walk around the massive spacecraft and gaze at almost every square inch.

Space Shuttle *Atlantis* also features more than 60 interactive exhibits, including simulators and cinematic presentations, that explore the 30-year history of the space shuttle program; replicas of the Hubble space telescope and International Space Station modules are highlights. Guests can also become "crew members" on the Shuttle Launch Experience, vertically launching into space and orbiting earth aboard NASA's space shuttle.

The complex also features more multimedia displays and hands-on exhibits, 3-D theater, spacecraft and artifacts, face-to-face encounters with astronauts and behind-the-scenes tours. In the Rocket Garden, space equipment traces the program's development. Admission to the complex includes a behind-the-scenes bus tour of NASA's launch facilities, offering views of rocket launch pads. At the Apollo/Saturn V Center, visitors can walk beneath the 363-foot *Saturn V* rocket and watch footage of Neil Armstrong's history-making walk on the moon. The Firing Room Theater simulates an earth-shaking *Apollo 8* rocket launch.

Question-and-answer sessions and personal stories are part of Astronaut Encounter, which brings guests face-to-face with men and women who have launched into space. The exhibit Forever Remembered showcases a section of fuselage from the shuttle *Challenger* and *Columbia's* cockpit windows,as well as personal memorabilia of the astronauts who lost their lives in these tragedies.

Special-interest programs also are available for an additional fee: Dine with an Astronaut enables visitors to share a meal with a space explorer, and Cape Canaveral Early Space Tour chronicles the space program in the early days. Heroes and Legends, featuring the U.S. Astronaut Hall of Fame offers simulated holograms, high-tech elements and special effects to tell the story of pioneering astronauts and the dangers of earlier missions.

Note: The Cape Canaveral Early Space Tour is available Wed.-Sun. only. Due to restricted access, each visitor must register with Visitor Complex security officers between 9 a.m. and 11 a.m. on the day of the tour. Register at the information center located at the main entrance. Food and free pet kennels are available. Allow 6 hours minimum to see the visitor complex and take the KSC bus tour. Arrive early to avoid crowds. **Hours:** Complex open daily at 9-6. Bus tours depart daily every 15 minutes beginning at 10; last tour departs at 3:30. Phone ahead to confirm schedule.

Cost: (includes all shows, exhibits, 3-D films, KSC bus tour, Shuttle Launch Experience and Heroes and Legends featuring the U.S. Astronaut Hall of Fame) $57; $50 (ages 55+ and active military with ID); $47 (ages 3-11); $41 (children ages 3-11 of active military with ID). Phone ahead to verify prices. **Parking:** $10; $5 (motorcycle); $15 (RV). **Phone:** (855) 433-4210 for ticket information. GT

Space Films is 11 mi. e. of I-95 on SR 405 within the Kennedy Space Center Visitor Complex. An IMAX theater equipped with five-and-a-half-story-tall screens presents the 3-D films "Journey to Space," narrated by Sir Patrick Stewart, and "Hubble 3-D," narrated by Leonardo DiCaprio.

Hours: 3-D shows are presented daily. Phone ahead to confirm schedule. **Cost:** (includes Kennedy Space Center Visitor Complex shows, exhibits, KSC bus tour, Shuttle Launch Experience and Heroes and Legends Featuring the U.S. Astronaut Hall of Fame) $50; $46 (ages 55+ and active military with ID); $40 (ages 3-11); $37 (children ages 3-11 of active military with ID). Phone ahead to verify prices. **Parking:** $10; $5 (motorcycle); $15 (RV). **Phone:** (855) 433-4210 for ticket information.

GEM **Space Mirror Memorial** is accessible through the entrance to Kennedy Space Center Visitor Complex. Dedicated in 1991 to American astronauts who died in the line of duty, this 60-ton black granite monument is carved with the names of 24 men and women, including the *Challenger* and *Columbia* crews. The mirrored surface reflects each name against the sky.

Time: Allow 30 minutes minimum. **Hours:** Daily 9-dusk. **Cost:** (includes Kennedy Space Center Visitor Complex shows, exhibits, IMAX films, KSC bus tour, Shuttle Launch Experience and Heroes and Legends Featuring the U.S. Astronaut Hall of Fame) $50; $46 (ages 55+ and active military with ID); $40 (ages 3-11); $37 (children ages 3-11 of active military with ID). Phone ahead to verify prices. **Parking:** $10; $5 (motorcycle); $15 (RV). **Phone:** (877) 313-2610.

KISSIMMEE (G-4) pop. 59,682, elev. 62'

- **Restaurants p. 114**
- **Hotels & Restaurants map & index p. 197, 202, 215**
- **Part of Orlando area — see map p. 2**

Kissimmee (Kiss-SEM-mee), is near the southern terminus of a scenic portion of Florida's Turnpike, which extends 65 miles southeast from Wildwood. It is more widely known to visitors to the central Florida region as being a near neighbor of Walt Disney World® Resort (located farther northeast in Orlando are Universal Orlando Resort and SeaWorld Orlando). Many downtown businesses occupy structures dating from the late 1800s; landscaping and renovations preserve the town's old-time aura.

While tourism and agriculture have long dominated the business climate, recent economic development initiatives encourage advancements in plastics, engineering and electronics. The Florida Cattlemen's Association has its headquarters in town.

Kissimmee also attracts the sports-minded to Osceola County Stadium, in Osceola Heritage Park at 631 Heritage Park Way; phone (321) 697-3220 for ticket information.

AAA DISCOUNTS»REWARDS
DISCOUNTS
WITHOUT LIMITS
AAA.com/discounts

(See maps & indexes p. 197, 202, 215.)

Silver Spurs Arena, 1875 Silver Spur Ln. in Osceola Heritage Park, hosts the popular Silver Spurs Rodeo, concerts and major sports events. Picnic tables and boat ramps are available at Lakefront Park, .25 mile southeast of US 17/92 at 201 Lakeview Dr.; phone (407) 518-2501. Near the park at 300 E. Monument Ave. is the Monument of States, a 40-foot-high pyramid consisting of stones from every state and 20 countries; phone (407) 847-2821.

Experience Kissimmee: 215 Celebration Pl., Suite 200, Kissimmee, FL 34747. **Phone:** (407) 742-8200 or (800) 333-5477.

Shopping: The Loop and Loop West, 3208 N. John Young Pkwy., offer 800,000 square feet of open-air shopping as well as multiple dining and entertainment options. Old Town, just east of I-4 on US 192 at 5770 W. Irlo Bronson Memorial Hwy., features 75 specialty shops as well as restaurants and amusement rides in a re-created turn-of-the-20th-century setting. Hundreds of classic cars cruise the streets of Old Town every Friday and Saturday night.

CAPONE'S DINNER AND SHOW, 4740 W. Irlo Bronson Memorial Hwy. (US 192), 1 mi. e. of jct. SR 535, presents an action-packed musical comedy stage show set in the 1930s prohibition era featuring a cast of zany mobsters and dames. Guests can win prizes during a gangster shootout. A buffet meal, dessert and beverages are included. **Time:** Allow 2 hours, 30 minutes minimum. **Hours:** Performances are given at 8 p.m., mid-June through mid-Aug.; at 7:30 p.m., rest of year. Matinee dates vary; phone ahead for schedule. **Cost:** $65.99; $41.99 (ages 4-12). Reservations are recommended. **Phone:** (407) 397-2378 or (800) 220-8428.

GREEN MEADOWS PETTING FARM, 1368 S. Poinciana Blvd., offers guided tours of a 50-acre farm with more than 300 farm animals. The hands-on philosophy encourages learning as visitors milk a cow, ride a pony or hold a chicken. Petting pens with various farm animals are a highlight of the tour. Tractor-drawn hayrides and a train ride are included. **Time:** Allow 2 hours minimum. **Hours:** Tours are given daily 9:30-4 (weather permitting). Last tour departs 90 minutes before closing. **Cost:** $23; $20 (ages 3-12); $19 (ages 62+ and military with ID); $5 (age 2). **Phone:** (407) 846-0770. GT Poinciana, 1

MEDIEVAL TIMES DINNER AND TOURNAMENT, 4510 W. Irlo Bronson Memorial Hwy. (US 192/W. Vine St.), is in a replica of an 11th-century European castle. Pageantry, romance and excitement unfold at a medieval, hands-on feast served by staff members costumed in period attire. Spectators sit a few feet from tournament action in the Great Ceremonial Arena, where knights on Andalusian stallions compete in jousting matches and medieval games of skill.

Time: Allow 2 hours minimum. **Hours:** Performances nightly. Phone ahead to confirm schedule. **Cost:** (includes four-course meal) $62.95; $36.95 (ages 3-12). Reservations are required. **Phone:** (407) 396-1518 or (866) 543-9637.

Medieval Life, 4510 W. Irlo Bronson Memorial Hwy. (US 192/W. Vine St.), is a permanent re-creation of a medieval village. This 8-cottage hamlet showcases medieval artifacts and costumed artisans working their trades. **Time:** Allow 1 hour minimum. **Hours:** Open daily 2 hours before Medieval Times Dinner and Tournament show time. Phone ahead to confirm schedule. **Cost:** Free. **Phone:** (407) 396-1518.

MUSEUM OF MILITARY HISTORY, 5210 W. Irlo Bronson Memorial Hwy., offers insight into World Wars I and II as well as the Korean, Vietnam, Gulf and Civil Wars with its interactive exhibits and displays of vehicles, uniforms, historic photos, weapons and gear. An extensive library is on site. **Time:** Allow 1 hour minimum. **Hours:** Tues.-Sun. 10-6. Closed major holidays. **Cost:** $7; $6 (ages 65+); $5 (ages 5-17). **Phone:** (407) 507-3894.

OSCEOLA COUNTY WELCOME CENTER AND HISTORY MUSEUM, 4155 W. Vine St., offers a detailed history of Osceola County with interactive displays about its discovery by the Spanish, the lives of pioneers and cracker cowboys, early industry and early tourism. Illustrating the county's history are historic photos, tools, clothing and a hand-dug 1750 canoe. Exhibits also provide details about such area habitats as swamplands, pine flatwoods, oak hammocks and lakefront. A trailhead to the Shingle Creek Regional Trail is located on the grounds.

Time: Allow 1 hour minimum. **Hours:** Daily 9-5. Closed major holidays. **Cost:** Free. **Phone:** (407) 396-8644.

BAREFOOT SUITES 407/507-2750 111

Condominium. **Address:** 2750 Florida Plaza Blvd 34746

BEST WESTERN PLUS KISSIMMEE LAKE BUENA VISTA SOUTH INN AND SUITES 407/997-1700 95

Hotel

AAA Benefit: Members save up to 15% and earn bonus points!

Address: 3484 Polynesian Isle Blvd 34746 **Location:** I-4 exit 67, 0.9 mi e on SR 536, 1 mi se on SR 535 (Vineland Rd), just se. **Facility:** 148 units. 4 stories, interior corridors. **Amenities:** safes. **Pool:** heated outdoor. **Activities:** hot tub, game room, exercise room. **Guest Services:** valet and coin laundry, area transportation.

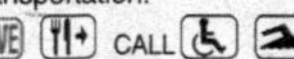

SAVE CALL BIZ

HS

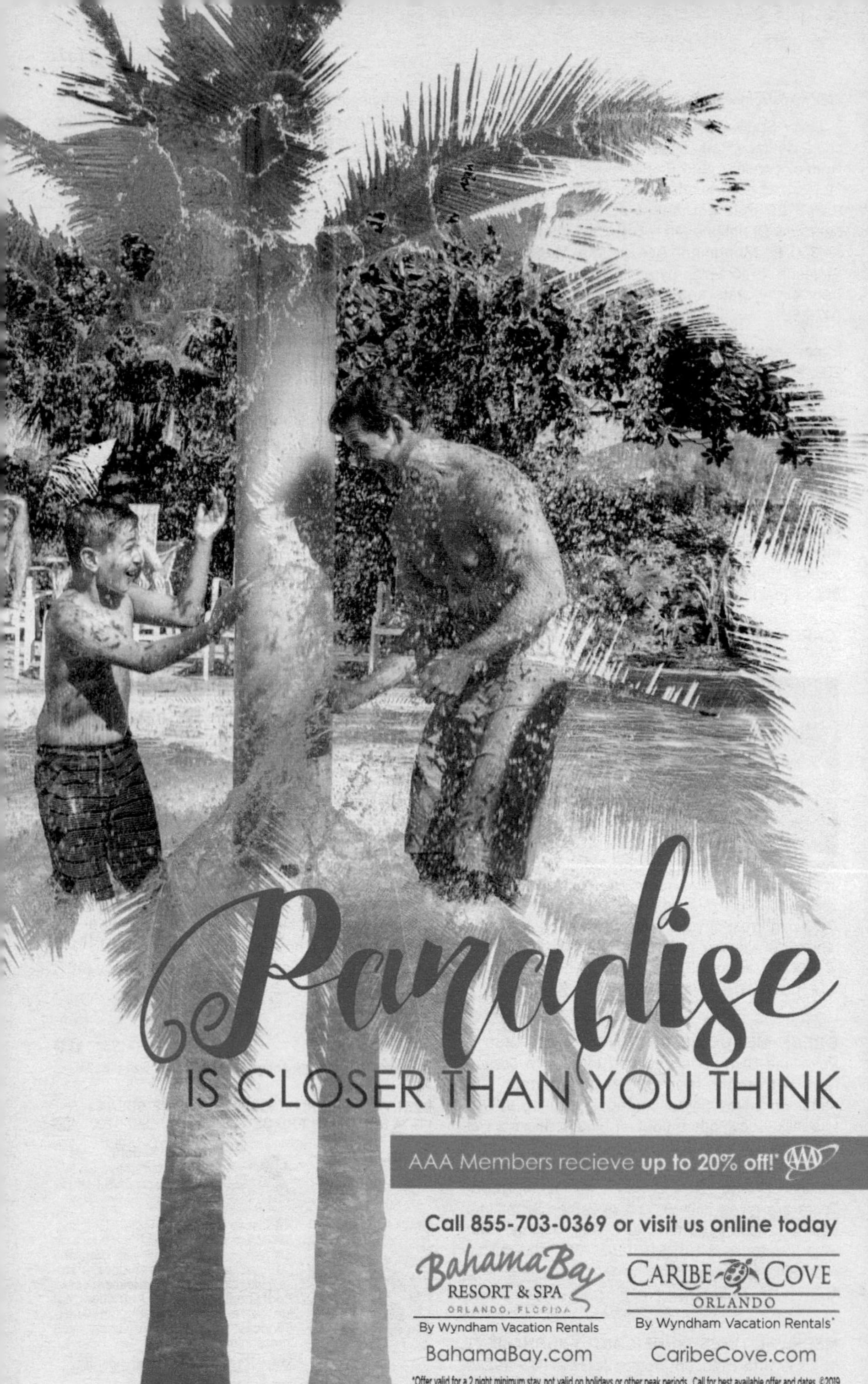
Paradise
IS CLOSER THAN YOU THINK
AAA Members recieve up to 20% off!*
AAA
Call 855-703-0369 or visit us online today
Bahama Bay
RESORT & SPA
ORLANDO, FLORIDA
By Wyndham Vacation Rentals
CARIBE COVE
ORLANDO
By Wyndham Vacation Rentals
BahamaBay.com
CaribeCove.com
*Offer valid for a 2 night minimum stay, not valid on holidays or other peak periods. Call for best available offer and dates. ©2019 Wyndham Vacation Rentals North America, LLC. 14 Sylvan Way, Parsippany, NJ 07054. Wyndham Vacation Rentals and related marks are registered trademarks and/or service marks in the United States and internationally. All rights reserved. Printed in the USA.

▼ See AAA listing p. 110 ▼

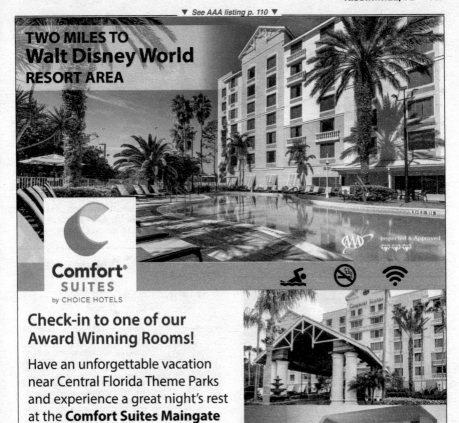

Check-in to one of our Award Winning Rooms!

Have an unforgettable vacation near Central Florida Theme Parks and experience a great night's rest at the **Comfort Suites Maingate East at Old Town.**

- Free breakfast buffet served daily
- Walk to Old Town, shops & restaurants
- Seasonally heated pool open 24 hours
- **No Resort, parking or WiFi fees**

2775 Florida Plaza Blvd. Kissimmee, FL 34746
407.397.7848 | Toll Free 888.784.8379 | ComfortSuitesFL.com

(See maps & indexes p. 197, 202, 215.)

For complete hotel, dining and attraction listings: AAA.com/travelguides

(See maps & indexes p. 197, 202, 215.)

CARIBE COVE RESORT BY WYNDHAM VACATION RENTALS 407/997-4444 119

Vacation Rental Condominium

Address: 9000 Treasure Trove Ln 34747 **Location:** Waterfront. I-4 exit 64, 6.7 mi w on US 192, then 0.6 mi s on Westside Blvd. **Facility:** This property is bordered by two small ponds and a nature preserve. Enjoy relaxing in units with an abundance of space, homelike comforts and peaceful surroundings. 187 condominiums. 4-5 stories, exterior corridors. **Terms:** check-in 4 pm. **Amenities:** safes. **Pool:** heated outdoor. **Activities:** hot tub, picnic facilities, exercise room. **Guest Services:** complimentary laundry. *(See ad p. 108.)*

SAVE CALL BIZ HS

WYNDHAM VACATION RENTALS

Luxury spa services available. Minutes from attractions, restaurants and shopping.

CLARION SUITES MAINGATE 407/390-9888 108

Motel

Address: 7888 W Irlo Bronson Memorial Hwy 34747 **Location:** I-4 exit 64, 4.7 mi w on US 192. **Facility:** 150 units. 3 stories, exterior corridors. **Terms:** check-in 4 pm. **Amenities:** safes. **Pool:** heated outdoor. **Activities:** hot tub, game room. **Guest Services:** valet and coin laundry, area transportation. **Featured Amenity: breakfast buffet.** *(See ad p. 111.)*

SAVE CALL BIZ

COMFORT INN MAINGATE 407/396-4000 112

Hotel

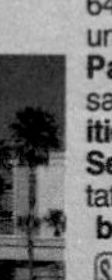

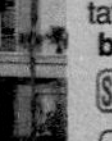

Address: 7675 W Irlo Bronson Memorial Hwy 34747 **Location:** I-4 exit 64, 4.2 mi w on US 192. **Facility:** 197 units. 5 stories, interior corridors. **Parking:** on-site (fee). **Amenities:** safes. **Pool:** heated outdoor. **Activities:** hot tub, exercise room. **Guest Services:** coin laundry, area transportation. **Featured Amenity: full hot breakfast.**

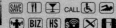

SAVE CALL BIZ HS

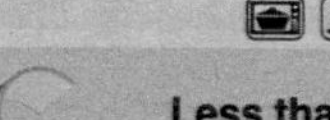

Less than 1 mile to Disney. Timed shuttle to the parks. Hot buffet breakfast. Family rooms sleep 6.

COMFORT SUITES MAINGATE EAST AT OLD TOWN 407/397-7848 109

Hotel

Address: 2775 Florida Plaza Blvd 34746 **Location:** I-4 exit 64, 2.2 mi e on W Irlo Bronson Memorial Hwy (US 192), then just s. **Facility:** 198 units. 7 stories, interior corridors. **Amenities:** safes. **Pool:** heated outdoor. **Activities:** hot tub, game room, exercise room. **Guest Services:** valet and coin laundry, area transportation. **Featured Amenity: breakfast buffet.** *(See ad p. 109.)*

SAVE CALL BIZ HS

Suite property includes free hot breakfast and great prices for AAA Members. 2 miles to Disney.

EMBASSY SUITES BY HILTON ORLANDO LAKE BUENA VISTA SOUTH 407/597-4000 3

Hotel

AAA Benefit: Members save 5% or more!

Address: 4955 Kyngs Heath Rd 34746 **Location:** I-4 exit 67, 0.9 mi e on SR 536, 1.8 mi se on SR 535 (Vineland Rd). **Facility:** 300 units. 10 stories, interior corridors. **Parking:** on-site (fee) and valet. **Terms:** check-in 4 pm. **Amenities:** safes. **Pool:** heated outdoor. **Activities:** hot tub, game room, exercise room. **Guest Services:** valet and coin laundry, boarding pass kiosk, rental car service, area transportation. **Featured Amenity: full hot breakfast.** *(See ad p. 228.)*

SAVE CALL BIZ SHS

ENCANTADA RESORT 407/997-3231 118

Vacation Rental Condominium

Address: 3070 Secret Lake Dr 34747 **Location:** Waterfront. I-4 exit 64, 6 mi w on US 192 (W Irlo Bronson Hwy), then just s. **Facility:** Set away from the bustle of traffic, this resort offers a slew of amenities and recreational facilities. Each spacious unit has a private screened lanai with a hot tub; four units have a plunge pool. 135 condominiums. 2 stories (no elevator), exterior corridors. **Terms:** check-in 4 pm. **Amenities:** safes. **Pool:** heated outdoor. **Activities:** hot tub, fishing, recreation programs, playground, game room, exercise room. **Guest Services:** complimentary laundry.

SAVE HS

(See maps & indexes p. 197, 202, 215.)

FAIRFIELD INN & SUITES BY MARRIOTT ORLANDO KISSIMMEE/CELEBRATION 407/390-1532 105

Hotel

Fairfield **AAA Benefit:** Members save 5% or more!

Address: 6073 W Irlo Bronson Memorial Hwy 34747 **Location:** I-4 exit 64, 1.5 mi e on US 192. **Facility:** 150 units. 4 stories, interior corridors. **Pool:** heated outdoor. **Activities:** exercise room. **Guest Services:** valet and coin laundry. **Featured Amenity: continental breakfast.** *(See ad this page.)*

SAVE CALL BIZ HS

FANTASY WORLD RESORT 407/396-8530 99

Vacation Rental Condominium

Address: 5005 Kyngs Heath Rd 34746 **Location:** I-4 exit 64, 4.1 mi e on W Irlo Bronson Memorial Hwy (US 192), then just n on Hart Ave. **Facility:** The popular resort offers spacious condos with a home-away-from-home feel. The units feature private, screened patios and kitchens with stainless-steel appliances. Recreational amenities are vast. 302 condominiums. 2 stories (no elevator), exterior corridors. **Terms:** check-in 4 pm. **Amenities:** safes. **Pool:** heated outdoor. **Activities:** sauna, hot tub, steamroom, cabanas, tennis, recreation programs, playground, game room, exercise room. **Guest Services:** complimentary laundry, area transportation.

SAVE BIZ SHS

▼ See AAA listing p. 110 ▼

Clarion Suites Maingate.

- Fun & Excitement right outside your door
- Heated Pool, Children's Pool area, Cabana Bar, Hot Tub
- Gift Shop, Game Room, Business Center, Guest Laundry
- Transportation to Walt Disney World, Universal Resort, Sea World Parks
- Full Hot Breakfast Buffet Daily
- Host hotel to Osceola County's only winery, Island Grove Wine Company at Formosa Gardens

7888 West Irlo Bronson Memorial Hwy., Kissimmee, Fl 34747 | clarionsuiteskissimmee.com | 888-390-9888

▼ See AAA listing this page ▼

Fairfield®
BY MARRIOTT

6073 W Irlo Bronson Memorial Hwy
Kissimmee, FL 34747

407-390-1532

(See maps & indexes p. 197, 202, 215.)

GALLERIA PALMS HOTEL 407/396-6300 114

Hotel

Address: 3000 Maingate Ln 34747 **Location:** I-4 exit 64, 3.8 mi w, just n on US 192. **Facility:** 118 units. 5 stories, interior corridors. **Amenities:** safes. **Pool:** heated outdoor. **Guest Services:** valet and coin laundry, area transportation. **Featured Amenity: full hot breakfast.**

SAVE CALL BIZ HS

GAYLORD PALMS RESORT & CONVENTION CENTER 407/586-0000 97

Resort Hotel

AAA Benefit: Members save 5% or more!

Address: 6000 W Osceola Pkwy 34746 **Location:** I-4 exit 65, just e; SR 417 exit 3 (Osceola Pkwy), just w. **Facility:** Striking architecture greets guests at the eco-friendly hotel that offers top-notch service paired with impressive décor. Thematic rooms offer upscale décor and a balcony, many overlook the atrium. 1416 units. 9 stories, interior corridors. **Parking:** on-site (fee) and valet. **Terms:** check-in 4 pm. **Amenities:** safes. **Dining:** 6 restaurants, also, Villa De Flora, see separate listing. **Pool:** heated outdoor. **Activities:** hot tub, cabanas, recreation programs, playground, game room, exercise room, spa. **Guest Services:** valet and coin laundry, area transportation.

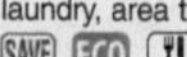  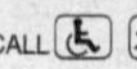  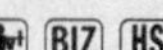

GRAND ORLANDO RESORT AT CELEBRATION 407/396-7000 106

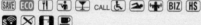

Resort Hotel

Address: 2900 Parkway Blvd 34747 **Location:** I-4 exit 64 (US 192), 0.3 mi e, then just n. **Facility:** Rooms are traditional in style and offer ample move about space. Some units sleep up to six people. The pool area provides a nice spot to relax. The on-site coffee shop and restaurant add convenience. 718 units. 3-8 stories, interior corridors. **Parking:** on-site (fee). **Terms:** check-in 4 pm. **Amenities:** safes. **Dining:** 2 restaurants. **Pool:** outdoor, heated outdoor. **Activities:** hot tub, tennis, recreation programs, exercise room, massage. **Guest Services:** valet and coin laundry, rental car service, area transportation.

  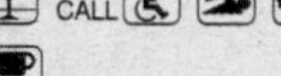

SAVE ECO CALL BIZ HS

HAMPTON INN & SUITES ORLANDO - SOUTH LAKE BUENA VISTA 407/396-8700 1

SAVE Hotel. **Address:** 4971 Calypso Cay Way 34746

AAA Benefit: Members save 5% or more!

HAPIMAG LAKE BERKLEY 407/390-9083 6

Vacation Rental Condominium

Address: 1010 Park Ridge Cir 34746 **Location:** Jct US 192 (Irlo Bronson Hwy), 0.4 mi w on Oren Brown Rd, then 0.4 mi s on Roma Way. **Facility:** Off the beaten path in a guard-gated community, the spacious, simply decorated townhouses offer kitchens, living rooms and private patios. The residential-style neighborhood is inviting. 100 condominiums. 2 stories (no elevator), exterior corridors. **Terms:** check-in 4 pm. **Amenities:** safes. **Pool:** heated outdoor. **Activities:** hot tub, fishing, tennis, playground, exercise room. **Guest Services:** complimentary laundry.

SAVE BIZ HS

Spacious fully equipped 1, 2 or 3 bedroom 2-story townhomes in gated community. Free Wi-Fi & 2 pools.

HAWTHORN SUITES BY WYNDHAM MAINGATE KISSIMMEE 407/507-0060 113

Motel. **Address:** 3020 Reedy Creek Rd 34747

HOLIDAY INN CLUB VACATIONS AT ORANGE LAKE RESORT 407/239-0000 103

Resort Condominium

Address: 8505 W Irlo Bronson Memorial Hwy 34747 **Location:** Waterfront. I-4 exit 64 (US 192), 5.7 mi w, just n on W Orange Lake Dr. **Facility:** Found among 1,450 acres of beautifully landscaped grounds and a large lake, units include traditional hotel rooms, villas and condos. Various pool areas, water sports and golf courses are highlights. 2478 condominiums. 1-8 stories, interior/exterior corridors. **Terms:** check-in 4 pm. **Amenities:** safes. **Dining:** 8 restaurants, entertainment. **Pool:** heated outdoor. **Activities:** hot tub, limited beach access, fishing, regulation golf, par 3 golf, miniature golf, tennis, recreation programs, playground, game room, picnic facilities, exercise room, massage. **Guest Services:** complimentary laundry, boarding pass kiosk, rental car service, area transportation. *(See ad p. 233.)*

SAVE BIZ HS

1-, 2- and 3-bedroom villas, near Disney, 7 pools, lazy river, water sports, Free Wi-Fi and parking.

HOLIDAY INN EXPRESS & SUITES ORLANDO-SOUTH LAKE BUENA VISTA 407/997-1400 96

Hotel

Address: 5001 Calypso Cay Way 34746 **Location:** I-4 exit 67 (SR 536), 0.9 mi e, 1.6 mi se on SR 535 (Vineland Rd). **Facility:** 162 units. 7 stories, interior corridors. **Amenities:** safes. **Pool:** heated outdoor. **Activities:** hot tub, miniature golf, playground, exercise room. **Guest Services:** valet and coin laundry, area transportation. **Featured Amenity: full hot breakfast.**

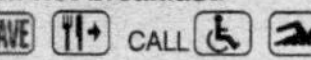 

(See maps & indexes p. 197, 202, 215.)

HOLIDAY INN ORLANDO SW-CELEBRATION AREA 407/396-4222 **101**

Two Diamond **Hotel**

Address: 5711 W Irlo Bronson Memorial Hwy 34746 **Location:** I-4 exit 64, 2.5 mi e on US 192. **Facility:** 444 units. 8 stories, interior corridors. **Amenities:** safes. **Pool:** heated outdoor. **Activities:** hot tub, playground, game room, exercise room. **Guest Services:** valet and coin laundry, boarding pass kiosk, rental car service, area transportation.

SAVE CALL BIZ HS / SOME UNITS

MARGARITAVILLE RESORT ORLANDO 407/479-0950 **110**

Four Diamond **Resort Hotel**

Address: 8000 Fins Up Cir 34747 **Location:** Jct US 192 and SR 429, just sw. **Facility:** Of course there are obvious nods to the Jimmy Buffet theme, but this resort offers something more with upscale accents, relaxed dining, plush furnishings and well designed rooms and bathrooms. 184 units. 5 stories, interior/exterior corridors. **Parking:** valet only. **Terms:** check-in 4 pm. **Amenities:** safes. **Dining:** 4 restaurants, entertainment. **Pool:** heated outdoor. **Activities:** sauna, hot tub, steamroom, cabanas, recreation programs, kids club, playground, lawn sports, trails, exercise room, spa. **Guest Services:** valet laundry, rental car service, area transportation. *(See ad this page.)*

SAVE CALL BIZ / SOME UNITS

QUALITY INN HERITAGE PARK 407/449-4777 **5**

Two Diamond Hotel. **Address:** 2039 E Irlo Bronson Memorial Hwy 34744

RED LION HOTEL LAKE BUENA VISTA SOUTH 407/997-2800 **100**

Three Diamond Hotel. **Address:** 5150 W Irlo Bronson Memorial Hwy 34746

RED LION HOTEL ORLANDO/KISSIMMEE MAINGATE 407/396-7300 **117**

Two Diamond **Motel**

Address: 7300 W Irlo Bronson Memorial Hwy 34747 **Location:** I-4 exit 64 (US 192), 2.4 mi w; jct Reedy Creek Blvd. **Facility:** 516 units. 2 stories, exterior corridors. **Terms:** check-in 4 pm. **Amenities:** safes. **Pool:** heated outdoor. **Activities:** tennis, bicycles, playground, game room, picnic facilities, exercise room. **Guest Services:** valet and coin laundry, boarding pass kiosk, area transportation.

SAVE BIZ

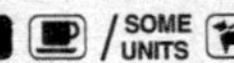

/ SOME UNITS

AAA.com/campgrounds—

For overnights under the stars

▼ See AAA listing this page ▼

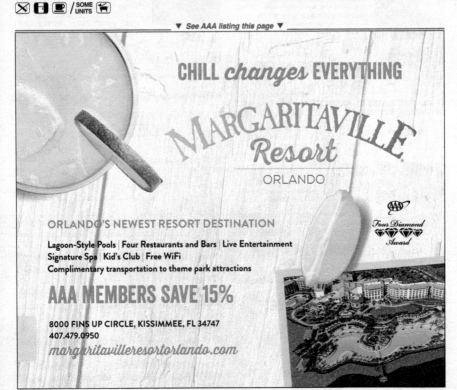

CHILL *changes* EVERYTHING

MARGARITAVILLE Resort ORLANDO

AAA Four Diamond Award

ORLANDO'S NEWEST RESORT DESTINATION

Lagoon-Style Pools | Four Restaurants and Bars | Live Entertainment
Signature Spa | Kid's Club | Free WiFi
Complimentary transportation to theme park attractions

AAA MEMBERS SAVE 15%

8000 FINS UP CIRCLE, KISSIMMEE, FL 34747
407.479.0950
margaritavilleresortorlando.com

(See maps & indexes p. 197, 202, 215.)

REUNION RESORT & GOLF CLUB 407/662-1000 **20**

Resort Condominium

Address: 7593 Gathering Dr 34747 **Location:** I-4 exit 58, 1.1 mi e on CR 532; 1 mi n on Reunion Blvd. **Facility:** Guest rooms are luxurious with custom furnishings, abundant space, walk-in showers and garden tubs. For a bit of fun and games, check out the pool area in the cove or visit the water park. 42 condominiums. 11 stories, interior corridors. **Parking:** on-site and valet. **Terms:** check-in 4 pm. **Amenities:** safes. **Dining:** 6 restaurants. **Pool:** outdoor, heated outdoor. **Activities:** hot tub, regulation golf, tennis, recreation programs, kids club, bicycles, playground, game room, lawn sports, health club, spa.

SAVE ECO CALL BIZ HS

Luxury villas & vacation homes. 3 golf courses, dining & water park. Free Wi-Fi & self-parking.

SARATOGA RESORT VILLAS 407/997-3300 **4**

Hotel

Address: 4787 W Irlo Bronson Memorial Hwy 34746 **Location:** I-4 exit 64, 4.9 mi e on US 192. **Facility:** 150 kitchen units, some two and three bedrooms. 2 stories, exterior corridors. **Terms:** check-in 4 pm. **Amenities:** safes. **Pool:** heated outdoor. **Activities:** hot tub, playground, game room, exercise room. **Guest Services:** valet and coin laundry, area transportation. *(See ad p. 121.)*

SAVE CALL BIZ sHS

/ SOME UNITS

SPRINGHILL SUITES BY MARRIOTT ORLANDO/KISSIMMEE 407/997-1300 **2**

Hotel

SPRINGHILL SUITES MARRIOTT **AAA Benefit:** Members save 5% or more!

Address: 4991 Calypso Cay Way 34746 **Location:** I-4 exit 67, 0.9 mi se on SR 536, 1.6 mi se on SR 535 (Vineland Rd). **Facility:** 150 units. 6 stories, interior corridors. **Amenities:** safes. **Activities:** miniature golf, playground, picnic facilities, exercise room. **Guest Services:** valet and coin laundry, area transportation. **Featured Amenity: breakfast buffet.**

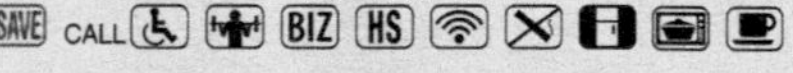

SAVE CALL BIZ HS

Use the free travel planning tools at AAA.com/maps

STAR ISLAND RESORT & CLUB 407/997-8000 **104**

Resort Condominium. **Address:** 5000 Avenue of the Stars 34746

STAYBRIDGE SUITES ROYALE PARC 407/396-8040 **107**

Extended Stay Hotel

Address: 5876 W Irlo Bronson Memorial Hwy 34746 **Location:** I-4 exit 64, 1.9 mi e on US 192. **Facility:** 224 kitchen units, some two bedrooms. 5 stories, interior corridors. **Parking:** on-site (fee). **Terms:** check-in 4 pm. **Amenities:** safes. **Pool:** heated outdoor. **Activities:** hot tub, playground, game room, exercise room. **Guest Services:** valet and coin laundry, area transportation. **Featured Amenity: breakfast buffet.**

SAVE CALL BIZ sHS / SOME UNITS

SUPER 8 MAINGATE 407/396-8883 **102**

Motel. **Address:** 5875 W Irlo Bronson Memorial Hwy 34746

WESTGATE TOWERS RESORT 407/396-2500 **115**

Resort Condominium

Address: 7600 W Irlo Bronson Memorial Hwy 34747 **Location:** I-4 exit 64, 3 mi w on US 192 at jct Morgan-Williams Rd. **Facility:** The hotel is located just minutes from popular attractions. All rooms have either a balcony or a patio, many with a pool view. Some have a living room, a washer and dryer, and a jetted tub. 267 condominiums. 3-6 stories, interior corridors. **Terms:** check-in 4 pm. **Amenities:** safes. **Pool:** heated outdoor. **Activities:** hot tub, playground, game room, exercise room. **Guest Services:** complimentary laundry, area transportation.

SAVE CALL BIZ sHS / SOME UNITS

WINGATE BY WYNDHAM KISSIMMEE AT CELEBRATION 407/997-9999 **98**

Hotel. **Address:** 3104 Parkway Blvd 34747

WHERE TO EAT

FLIPPERS PIZZERIA 407/397-9509 **59**

Pizza Sandwiches. Casual Dining. **Address:** 5770 W US 192 34746

FORD'S GARAGE 407/815-3673 **60**

American. Casual Dining. **Address:** 3210 Margarita Blvd 34747

GIORDANO'S FAMOUS STUFFED PIZZA 407/397-0044

Pizza. Casual Dining. **Address:** 7866 W Irlo Bronson Memorial Hwy 34747

ICHIBAN CHINESE & JAPANESE BUFFET 407/396-6668 **57**

Chinese. Quick Serve. **Address:** 5269 W Irlo Bronson Memorial Hwy 34746

MOOR 407/586-1101 **56**

Caribbean. Casual Dining. **Address:** 6000 W Osceola Pkwy 34746

ON VACATION 407/479-0950 **61**

Regional American. Casual Dining. **Address:** 8000 Fins Up Cir 34747

PACINO'S ITALIAN RISTORANTE 407/396-8022 **58**

Italian. Casual Dining. **Address:** 5795 W Hwy 192 34746

(See maps & indexes p. 197, 202, 215.)

PAUL'S ITALIAN DELI & RESTAURANT 407/933-0766 (1)

Sandwiches. Quick Serve. **Address:** 812 E Vine St 34744

VILLA DE FLORA 407/586-1114 (55)

Continental. Casual Dining. **Address:** 6000 W Osceola Pkwy 34746

LADY LAKE pop. 13,926

• Part of Orlando area — see map p. 2

COMFORT SUITES THE VILLAGES 352/259-6578

Hotel

Address: 1202 Avenida Central N 32159 **Location:** Just w of jct US 441/27. **Facility:** 80 units. 3 stories, interior corridors. **Pool:** heated outdoor. **Activities:** exercise room. **Guest Services:** valet and coin laundry.

MICROTEL INN & SUITES BY WYNDHAM LADY LAKE/THE VILLAGES 352/259-0184

Hotel. **Address:** 850 S US 27/441 32159

TOWNEPLACE SUITES BY MARRIOTT THE VILLAGES 352/753-8686

Extended Stay Hotel

TOWNEPLACE SUITES MARRIOTT **AAA Benefit:** Members save 5% or more!

Address: 1141 Alonzo Ave 32159 **Location:** Just w of jct US 27/441 on Main St, just n. **Facility:** 119 units, some two bedrooms, efficiencies and kitchens. 4 stories, interior corridors. **Pool:** heated outdoor. **Activities:** hot tub, exercise room. **Guest Services:** coin laundry. **Featured Amenity: breakfast buffet.**

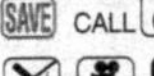

/ SOME UNITS

WHERE TO EAT

MARGARITA REPUBLIC CARIBBEAN GRILL & BAR 352/753-4660

American. Casual Dining. **Address:** 1102 Main St 32159

OAKWOOD SMOKEHOUSE & GRILL 352/751-5640

Barbecue. Casual Dining. **Address:** 860 S Hwy 27/441 32159

TOOJAY'S GOURMET DELI 352/753-3510

American. Casual Dining. **Address:** 990 Del Mar Dr 32162

LAKE BUENA VISTA (D-10) pop. 10, elev. 100'

• Hotels p. 120 • Restaurants p. 135
• Hotels & Restaurants map & index p. 202
• Part of Orlando area — see map p. 2

Although claiming only a handful of fulltime residents, Lake Buena Vista is home to tens of thousands of temporary citizens—also known as tourists—on any day of the year thanks to its status as host community to the Walt Disney World® Resort. With its sprawling, meticulously planned theme parks and family-friendly hotels, Lake Buena Vista definitely lives up to its Spanish name, offering visitors "good views" that have been preserved in countless vacation photos. The name comes from the street in Burbank, Calif., where Walt Disney's animation studios have been since the early 1940s.

Celebration Welcome Center: 851 Celebration Ave., Celebration, FL 34747. **Phone:** (407) 566-1200.

GEM SAVE **WALT DISNEY WORLD® RESORT,** accessible from Florida's Tpke., US 192, Osceola Pkwy. and several exits off I-4 s. of Orlando, covers 40 square miles. The resort includes four theme parks: Magic Kingdom® Park, Epcot®, Disney's Hollywood Studios® and Disney's Animal Kingdom® Theme Park; two water parks; more than 25 resort hotels; ESPN Wide World of Sports Complex; and Disney Springs®, a shopping, dining and entertainment district.

Drawn to the area by its climate, highway access and inexpensive land, Walt Disney and his "Imagineers" began transforming acres of swamps and orange groves into a magical vacationland that opened in 1971. Magic Kingdom® Park was an instant success. Other theme parks were soon on the drawing board. Epcot®, a celebration of technology and world cultures, opened in 1982. Disney-MGM Studios (later Disney's Hollywood Studios®), a natural addition considering Disney's background in animation and TV and film production, followed in 1989. Disney's Animal Kingdom® Theme Park completed the quartet in 1998.

Navigating the resort property is simple thanks to concise road signs as well as monorail, boat and bus transportation. At the theme parks, parking lot tram service helps save time, too.

Large crowds and long lines are to be expected, especially during holiday periods. Options such as Magic Your Way allow you to customize your theme park tickets. All guest tickets come with the FastPass+ option. This reservation system allows guests to select up to three FastPass+ experiences for each day of their ticket up to 30 days before their visit, with the option to add more experiences once at the parks. Walt Disney World Resort hotel guests can reserve their FastPass+ experiences 60 days prior to their hotel check-in; access the FastPass+ line using your theme park ticket or MagicBand any time during the 1-hour arrival window.

Hours: Theme parks open daily generally at 9; closing times vary. **Cost:** One-Day Base Magic Kingdom® Park $109-$129; $103-$123 (ages 3-9). 1-Day Base Epcot® or Disney's Hollywood Studios® or Disney's Animal Kingdom® Theme Park $102-$122; $93-$113 (ages 3-9). Prices vary by season. Two-day ticket $199; $187 (ages 3-9). Three-day ticket $289; $271 (ages 3-9). Four-day ticket $350; $330 (ages 3-9). Five-day ticket $370; $350 (ages 3-9). Six-day ticket $390; $370 (ages 3-9).

(See map & index p. 202.)

Seven-day ticket $410; $390 (ages 3-9). Eight-day ticket $420; $400 (ages 3-9). Nine-day ticket $430; $410 (ages 3-9). Ten-day ticket $440; $420 (ages 3-9). *Park Hopper®* Option $60 more with the purchase of a 2- or 3-day base ticket. *Park Hopper®* PlusOption $75 more with the purchase of a 2-or-3-day base ticket; $90 more with a 4- to 10-day base ticket. Ticket options for additional fees include admission to other entertainment areas and "hopping" between theme parks. Prices do not include tax. Tickets and options are non-transferable, non-refundable and expire 14 days from first use. Tickets valid for one theme park per day unless the *Park Hopper®* and *Park Hopper®* Plus Options are purchased. All parks, attractions and entertainment may be changed, canceled or discontinued without notice and without liability. Select theme park tickets are available at participating AAA/CAA Travel offices. **Parking:** $22; $27 (bus, camper or tractor-trailer); free (Disney resort guests with valid resort ID). The fee allows parking for that entire day. **Phone:** (407) 824-4321.

GEM **Disney's Animal Kingdom® Theme Park,** on Osceola Pkwy., celebrates nature and promotes conservation. At the island's center stands the 145-foot Tree of Life® with more than 300 intricate carvings of animals. Shown in a theater inside the tree, "It's Tough to be a Bug!®" is a comical 3-D, special-effects adventure inspired by the Disney•Pixar movie "A Bug's Life." In the attraction queue and on the Discovery Island® Trails there are many opportunities for up close viewing of the Tree of Life. Bridges branch off from the island into themed lands.

The newest is Pandora—The World of Avatar, which celebrates the magic of nature. Be sure to take an expedition through the Valley of Mo'ara, where one can walk amid floating mountains as well as encounter two attractions. On Avatar Flight of Passage, riders can fly on the back of a "mountain banshee" during a 3-D ride above a vast moon. For a more peaceful excursion, journey deep into a bioluminescent rainforest in search of the Na'vi Shaman of Songs on Na'vi River Journey.

Cross into Africa to explore Harambe, a village designed to look like a modern-day African town. Kilimanjaro Safaris® Expedition takes passengers on a bumpy ride in an open-air vehicle through a 100-acre savanna where antelopes, cheetahs, crocodiles, elephants, giraffes, lions, ostriches, rhinos and other animals roam freely.

Safari guides drop riders off at the Gorilla Falls Exploration Trail where animal viewing includes gorillas, hippos and exotic birds. The Wildlife Express Train transports visitors to Rafiki's Planet Watch®, an interactive, educational experience that includes Conservation Station®, Habitat Habit! and Affection Section.

Festival of the Lion King, an extravagant theatrical show based on the film, is performed in Harambe Theatre.

The land of Asia features Expedition Everest®, a high-speed train ride through the Himalayas, where the legendary yeti, also known as the abominable snowman, lurks. Then cool off during a white-water rafting adventure at Kali River Rapids®.

Beautiful Asian tigers can be seen from multiple vantage points on the Maharajah Jungle Trek®, where the pathway provides glimpses of other animals, including a Komodo dragon. Try to time your excursion to Asia to coincide with UP!—A Great Bird Adventure, where you can discover some of the world's most exotic birds during an all-new show starring those fun-loving pals from Disney•Pixar's Up!

DinoLand U.S.A.® is the home of the thrill ride DINOSAUR, which blasts back 65 million years to rescue a dinosaur from a deadly asteroid speeding toward Earth. Young kids and adults can hop on TriceraTop Spin to ride a flying dinosaur. The Boneyard® Dig Site is an open-air playground where children can maneuver through a maze of dinosaur skeletons and look for giant mammoth "bones." DinoLand USA also features Primeval whirl, a time-machine coaster where one can spin and slide back to the dinosaur age through a madcap maze of curves and drops. DinoLand USA is teeming with colorful new décor and festively dressed characters at Donald's Dino-Bash! You'll find more old friends

▼ *See AAA listing p. 233* ▼

HILTON ORLANDO

Central to Everything, **UNLIKE ANYTHING**

Centrally located near all Orlando theme parks. Enjoy two pools, a lazy river, NEW Splash Zone & poolside cabanas, seven unique dining options, a full service spa and more!

SAVE EXTRA WITH YOUR AAA MEMBERSHIP*

6001 Destination Parkway
Orlando, FL 32819
407.313.4300
thehiltonorlando.com

**Based on availability. Proof of AAA membership required. Offer cannot be combined with any other discount and is not applicable to group rates. © 2019 Hilton*

(See map & index p. 202.)

than Disney's Animal Kingdom park has ever seen before—including Donald himself, Daisy, Goofy, Pluto and Launchpad McQuack. You'll even catch Chip 'n Dale in their all-new dino-inspired costumes.

Dive into the sea with the characters of "Finding Nemo—The Musical." Inspired by the Disney•Pixar film, the show features puppetry, dancers, acrobats, special effects and animated backdrops. **Hours:** Park opens daily generally at 9; closing time varies. **Cost:** One-day Disney Magic Your Way® Base Ticket $109-$159; $104-$154 (ages 3-9). Prices vary by season; phone ahead. **Parking:** $22; $27 (bus, camper or tractor-trailer); free (Disney resort guests with valid resort ID). The fee allows parking for that entire day. **Phone:** (407) 824-4321. [fork-and-knife symbol]

Disney's Blizzard Beach Water Park, 1500 W. Buena Vista Dr., is the polar opposite of other water parks; it's themed as a "melted ski resort" in the middle of Florida. Those who dare can plunge down a 120-foot drop with Summit Plummet waterslide, tackle a fast-paced tube run, take on the Teamboat Springs family raft ride or float leisurely along a creek.

For little ones, there's Tike's Peak—a special play area full of scaled-down, kid-size slides, rides and water jets. Inquire about how weather policies. **Hours:** Hours may vary due to refurbishment as well as seasonal and weather closures. Phone ahead to confirm schedule. **Cost:** $65; $59 (ages 3-9). Admission may vary, depending on season; phone ahead. **Phone:** (407) 560-9283. [fork-and-knife symbol]

GEM **Disney's Hollywood Studios®,** 50 Animation Dr., has been inspired by popular films, television, music and animation. Art Deco architecture and design elements throughout the park recall old Hollywood. Guests begin their immersion in entertainment via Hollywood Boulevard.

Catch the pulsating beat of Rock 'n' Roller Coaster® Starring Aerosmith in a twistin', turnin', loopin', high-speed limo ride that is sure to get the adrenaline jammin'. And never experience the same fear twice as you hurtle up and down on The Twilight Zone Tower of Terror™ haunted "elevator" attraction.

Take aim and ride on the interactive 4D Toy Story Mania!® attraction inspired by Disney•Pixar's "Toy Story" films, where you'll grab some 3D glasses, board a ride vehicle and zip off into a world of immersive, midway-style games hosted by popular Toy Story characters. In the all-new Toy Story Land, the Alien Swirling Saucers and the Slinky-Dog Dash coaster add to the fun.

Have younger kids? Then head to an all-new Disney Junior show "Disney Junior Dance Party!" where little ones can sing, clap and dance along with some favorite friends from Mickey Mouse Clubhouse, Doc McStuffins and more!

Of course, people of all ages can enjoy watching the Broadway-style extravaganza "Beauty and the Beast—Live on Stage" and taking a dive under the sea with Ariel, Sebastian and Flounder on "Voyage of The Little Mermaid."

Star Wars: Galaxy's Edge boasts thrilling adventures like Millennium Falcon: Smugglers Run and in Dec. 2019, Star Wars: Rise of the Resistance. Build your own lightsaber in Savi's Workshop and design a customized droid at the Droid Depot. For an out-of-this-world 3-D thrill, nothing beats Star Tours®—The Adventures Continue! Featuring a constellation of interplanetary destinations and encounters with characters, such as C-3PO, R2-D2 and Darth Vader, you'll never know where the Force might take you.

Then head to the Hyperion Theater and enjoy "For the First Time in Forever: A Frozen Sing-Along Celebration" featuring Elsa and Anna, immersive storytelling, a mountain of songs from the movie and more. And finally, be dazzled by "Fantasmic!" where Sorcerer Mickey defeats some Disney Villains amid an extravaganza of lasers, lights, dancing waters and special effects.

Note: Mickey and Minnie's Runaway Railway attraction is under construction and anticipated to open in Spring 2020; the park remains open. **Hours:** Park opens daily generally at 9; closing times vary. **Cost:** One-day Magic Your Way® Base Ticket $109-$159; $104-$154 (ages 3-9). Prices vary by season; phone ahead. **Parking:** $22; $27 (bus, camper or tractor-trailer); free (Disney resort guests with valid resort ID). The fee allows parking for that entire day. **Phone:** (407) 824-4321. [fork-and-knife symbol]

Disney's Typhoon Lagoon Water Park, 1195 E. Buena Vista Dr., re-creates a tropical paradise as imagined after "the storm of storms" blew through and left twisting slides, sandy beaches and one of the world's largest inland wave pool. Thrill-seekers can conquer Miss Adventure Falls, the family raft attraction, or Crush 'n' Gusher water coaster. Then there's the opportunity to chill out either on the beach or while one floats down a creek.

Ketchakiddee Creek offers slides, rides and bubbling jets for the little ones. **Hours:** Hours may vary due to refurbishment as well as seasonal and weather closures. Phone ahead to confirm schedule. **Cost:** $65; $59 (ages 3-9). Admission may vary, depending on season; phone ahead. **Phone:** (407) 560-9283. [fork-and-knife symbol]

GEM **Epcot®,** 1580 Avenue of the Stars, stands for Experimental Prototype Community of Tomorrow. At Epcot®, high-tech fun and Disney imagination are combined with the wonder of diverse cultures in two distinct themed worlds bursting with thrills and excitement: Future World and World Showcase.

Design It. Floor It. On Test Track® Presented by Chevrolet®, you can design a virtual concept vehicle before boarding a special "SIM Car" and put your design through its paces. Discover how your custom concept vehicle performs on the hills, hairpin turns

(See map & index p. 202.)

and straightaways of the Test Track circuit, at peak speeds of 65 mph. Afterward there are even more interactive experience to enjoy with your vehicle design. Steer over changing terrain and extreme conditions on a digital driving table, produce a TV commercial starring your "dream ride," and immerse yourself in a Chevrolet showroom among other highlights.

Hoist the sails in Arendelle aboard an ancient Norwegian vessel as you set out into the wintry world of "Frozen!" On Frozen Ever After, you'll be whisked away to a frozen willow forest. Soon you will be rubbing shoulders with some "boulders"—aka Kristoff's family from Troll Valley—before bracing for the cold of the icy North Mountain, where Queen Elsa's enchanting palace awaits. (You might spot other "Frozen" characters as well.) When you're done, head to Royal Sommerhus where "for the first time in forever," you're invited to meet with Anna and Elsa inside a cozy summer cabin.

Strap yourselves in for Soarin' Around the World, an epic re-imagining of a beloved Future World attraction. On the airborne adventure, you'll go hang gliding above some of the breathtaking wonders of the world. Whether you're soaring above man-made marvels like the Great Wall of China, cruising over natural sights like Iguazu Falls in South America or swooping past sailboats in Australia's spectacular Sydney Harbour, this is your chance to experience the joy of hang gliding as you never have before.

On The Seas with Nemo & Friends®, you don't need gills to dive into undersea adventure—just a "clam-mobile." So climb aboard and journey alongside Marlin and Dory on an exciting quest to find Nemo. Along the way, you'll meet up with Bruce the shark, ride the EAC and come face-to-fin with some real-life fish in a gigantic aquarium. It's an ocean of adventure inspired by Disney•Pixar's "Finding Nemo."

And while we're on the subject of our underwater friends, gather 'round a window to the ocean for a real-time Q-and-A session with a totally tubular turtle at the Turtle Talk with Crush experience also inspired by the film. Using his high-tech "hydrophone," Crush can communicate directly with little dudes and dudettes about literally anything that's on their minds. Righteous!

Then come have a ball inside the incredible icon of Epcot—Spaceship Earth! Narrated by actress Dame Judi Dench, this classic attraction will take you from living in the past to picturing yourself in the future. Afterward, you'll get to experience an interactive playground area where you can build, play, create, compete and explore.

Then there's the cartoon clubhouse of the future at Epcot® Character Spot. The future is here ... along with Mickey Mouse, Minnie Mouse and Pluto.

Over in World Showcase, you can travel around the world without needing a passport. Here, 11 great nations offer the best of their food, music, products and culture. Journey through the poetic mountains of China, soar in a balloon over France and sail down a river in Mexico. Plus, you can shop 'til you drop, indulging in tempting Guerlain fragrances, Goebel Hummel figurines, glass etchings, antiques, trinkets, jewelry, gifts, toys and more.

And while you're in World Showcase, you can become a secret agent and go undercover during Disney Phineas and Ferb: Agent P's World Showcase Adventure. Join Agent P (better known as Perry the Platypus) on this interactive quest and help solve clues to thwart some of Dr. Doofenshmirtz's most daringly evil plots.

The grand finale to your day? IllumiNations: Reflections of Earth, an inspiration of music, fireworks, lasers and special effects celebrating the planet we call home and the spirit of humanity.

Of course, during special times of the year, there's even more magic to discover, and it's included with your admission—like the fantastically fresh Epcot® International Festival of the Arts, where you can kick off your year with world-class cuisine, visual art and amazing live entertainment; and Epcot® International Flower & Garden Festival (early March-late May), where you can celebrate all things spring. At this incredible event, you can enjoy locally grown gardens and Disney Character topiaries, freshly picked music, garden-inspired recipes at a variety of outdoor kitchens and more.

Then come taste your way around the world in the fall during the Epcot® International Food & Wine Festival (late August to mid-November), where you'll discover more than 30 international food and beverage marketplaces, signature dining experiences with celebrated chefs, culinary demonstrations and wine seminars. There's also the live Eat to the Beat Concert Series, featuring nightly performances from popular artists.

Note: Attractions based on films "Guardians of the Galaxy" and "Ratatouille" are scheduled for the former Universe of Energy pavilion on the Future World side and the France pavilion in World Showcase, respectively; the park remains open. Lunch and dinner reservations at full-service restaurants should be made in advance of your visit. **Hours:** Future World opens daily generally at 9. World Showcase opens daily generally at 11. Closing times vary. **Cost:** One-day Magic Your Way® Base Ticket $109-$159; $104-$154 (ages 3-9). Prices vary by season; phone ahead. **Parking:** $22; $27 bus, camper or tractor-trailer); free (Disney resort guests with valid resort ID). The fee allows parking for that entire day. **Phone:** (407) 824-4321, or (407) 939-3463 for dining reservations.

ESPN Wide World of Sports Complex, 700 S. Victory Way (in Kissimmee), is a 230-acre, state-of-the-art sports venue, which hosts more than 60 sports and thousands of events for athletes of all ages and abilities. Train and compete with your team—or cheer as a spectator—in this grand sports setting where classic athletic ideals meet contemporary innovation. **Hours:** Hours vary. Phone ahead to

(See map & index p. 202.)

confirm schedule. **Cost:** $18; $13 (ages 3-9). Some special events may require an additional admission fee. **Phone:** (407) 828-3267.

GEM **Magic Kingdom® Park** is at 3111 World Dr.; guests can choose to take a brief ferry or monorail ride to the main entrance from the Transportation and Ticket Center.

Delight in classic attractions (more than 40 of them), enchanting fireworks, musical parades and Disney characters across six themed lands. Fantasy becomes reality while experiencing Adventureland®, Frontierland®, Liberty Square®, Fantasyland®, Tomorrowland® and Main Street, U.S.A®, areas. Visits to the park begin on Main Street, U.S.A., representative of a typical late 19th-century boulevard complete with restaurants, shops and horse-drawn streetcars. The Victorian boulevard leads to Cinderella Castle, a 189-foot icon. Walk through the archway to see the beautiful mosaic images depicting Cinderella's fairy tale.

For some big-time enchantment, take a rollicking ride into the mine "where a million diamonds shine" aboard Seven Dwarfs Mine Train. Set sail on a swashbuckling voyage to a long-forgotten time and place when pirates and privateers ruled the seas on Pirates of the Caribbean®. And discover haunting surprises as you board a Doom Buggy and journey through Haunted Mansion® with your Ghost Host.

Looking for a thrill? Blast off on an indoor rocket-shaped coaster ride through the inky black of space on Space Mountain®, glide along a colorful bayou in a log flume and zip down 5 stories into the Laughing Place on Splash Mountain®, or streak through a haunted gold-mining town aboard a runaway train on the Big Thunder Mountain Railroad® coaster.

And that's just for starters. Venture into Prince Eric's Castle and join Ariel and friends for the musical Under the Sea~Journey of the Little Mermaid attraction and become part of the "tale as old as time" during the interactive Enchanted Tales with Belle storytelling experience. Soar aboard Dumbo the Flying Elephant® before cooling off at Casey Jr. Splash 'n' Soak Station. Fly high on The Barnstormer featuring the Great Goofini. Then join your "Monster of Ceremonies" Mike Wazowski for Monsters, Inc. Laugh Floor®—a zany comedy showcase inspired by Disney•Pixar's "Monsters, Inc."

And since everyone loves a parade, during the Disney Festival of Fantasy Parade, you can celebrate the Disney stories you know and love in a whole new way with a mix of innovative floats, vibrant costumes and original music.

Finally, experience the grandest of finales with the newest fireworks show in the park: Happily Ever After. Happily Ever After starts with a dream and showcases the heart, humor and heroism of many favorite Disney characters. So gather around Cinderella Castle for a show with more lasers, lights and fireworks than ever before.

For an extra fee, guests can attend Mickey's Not-So-Scary Halloween Party and Mickey's Very Merry Christmas Party select evenings during the Halloween and Christmas seasons. **Hours:** Park opens daily generally at 9, with earlier openings for guests staying at a Disney resort hotel; closing times vary. **Cost:** One-day Magic Your Way® Base Ticket $109-$129; $103-$123 (ages 3-9). Prices vary by season; phone ahead. **Parking:** $22; $27 (bus, camper or tractor-trailer); free (Disney resort guests with valid resort ID). The fee allows parking for that entire day. **Phone:** (407) 824-4321.

INSIDER INFO:

Disney Tickets

Parking and Pets

The entrance road leads to parking. The $25 ($30 for camper) fee allows standard parking at any of the four theme parks for that entire day; parking is free for Disney resort guests with valid resort ID. Free tram service connects the parking area with the Ticket and Transportation Center, Epcot®, Disney's Hollywood Studios® and Disney's Animal Kingdom® Theme Park. Transportation also is available to all guest areas. Best Friends Pet Care Inc. full-service pet facility on Bonnett Creek Parkway provides dog and cat boarding and offers such amenities as grooming and opportunities for exercise.

Admissions

Customize your Disney vacation by selecting the ticket options that best match your budget, needs and preferences. Magic Your Way®, the Walt Disney World® Resort ticket pricing structure, allows you to customize your theme park tickets to fit your needs. Plus, tickets include Disney FastPass+ service, which lets you reserve access to select attractions and entertainment experiences in advance at no extra cost. It's as easy as "1,2,3."

1. Choose up to 10 days.

• A ***Magic Your Way*** **Base Ticket** is valid for one theme park per day. For each day of your ticket, you'll gain admission to one of the four Walt Disney World® Theme Parks. Essentially, the longer you visit, the less you will pay per day.

2. Add Options.

• The ***Park Hopper®*** **Option** allows guests to come and go as you please through multiple Theme Parks on the same day for each of your ticket.

• The Park Hopper® Plus Option adds Disney fun beyond just the parks. Visit more than one theme park per day, plus get a certain number of visits—based on the length of the ticket purchased—to one of the following: Disney's Blizzard Beach Water Park, Disney's Typhoon Lagoon Water Park, Disney's Oak Trail Golf Course, Disney's Fantasia Gardens Miniature Golf Course, Disney's Winter Summerland Miniature Golf Course or ESPN Wide World of Sports Complex. Phone ahead to confirm

(See map & index p. 202.)

schedules, additional fees, reservations, and weather or seasonal closures.

3. Save even more when you bundle.

Ticket prices do not include tax. All tickets must be used by Dec. 31, 2020. All tickets and options are nontransferable and exclude activities or events separately priced. Ticket prices may change without notice. Visiting multiple Theme Parks on the same day requires The Park Hopper® or Park Hopper® Plus Options.

One-Day Magic Your Way® Theme Park Tickets and Options: One-Day Magic Kingdom® Park $109-$159 (ages 10+); $104-$154 (ages 3-9). One-Day ticket to your choice of Epcot® or Disney's Hollywood Studios® or Disney's Animal Kingdom® Theme Park $107-$155 (ages 10+); $102-$150 (ages 3-9). You can also add the Park Hopper® or Park Hopper® Plus Option for an additional charge. One-Day ticket with Park Hopper® Option $169-$219 (ages 10+); $164-$214 (ages 3-9). One-Day ticket with Park Hopper® Plus Option $189-$239 (ages 10+); $184-$234 (ages 3-9).

Multi-Day Magic Your Way® Tickets and Options: Two-day base ticket $212-$310 (ages 10+); $203-$300 (ages 3-9). Three-day base ticket $311-$447 (ages 10+); $297-$433 (ages 3-9). Four-day base ticket $400-$560 (ages 10+); $383-$543 (ages 3-9). Five-day base ticket $410-$568 (ages 10+); $392-$550 (ages 3-9). Six-day base ticket $418-$574 (ages 10+); $399-$555 (ages 3-9). Seven-day base ticket $425-$579 (ages 10+); $406-$560 (ages 3-9). Eight-day base ticket $440-$591 (ages 10+); $421-$571 (ages 3-9). Nine-day base ticket $453-$594 (ages 10+); $433-$574 (ages 3-9). Ten-day base ticket $463-$604 (ages 10+); $443-$583 (ages 3-9). Park Hopper® Option: $70 more with the purchase of a 2- or 3-day base ticket; $80 more with a 4-to-10-day base ticket. Park Hopper® Plus Option $90 more with the purchase of a 2- or 3-day base ticket; $100 more with a 4-to-10-day base ticket.

Prices do not include tax. Tickets and Options are non-transferable, non-refundable and exclude activities or events separately priced. One-day tickets must be used by Dec. 31, 2020. Multi-day tickets and any options added to a ticket expire 14 days from date of first use. First use must be by Dec. 31, 2020.

Florida Residents: Florida Residents can enjoy the excitement and fun at the four Walt Disney World® Resort Theme Parks with discounted Florida Resident 3-Day and 4-Day Disney Select Tickets. With a Florida Resident Disney Select Ticket, you can enjoy admission to one theme park per day. Choose from Magic Kingdom® Park, Epcot®, Disney's Hollywood Studios®, and Disney's Animal Kingdom® Theme Park. Florida Residents are also eligible for discounts on Annual Passes as well as the Park Hopper® and Park Hopper® Plus Options.

Prices do not include tax. Tickets and Options are non-transferable, non-refundable and expire 14 days from first use. Passes are non-transferable, non-refundable and expire one year from date of issue. All Parks, attractions, and entertainment may be changed, canceled or discontinued without notice and without liability.

Select Theme Park tickets are available at participating AAA/CAA Travel offices.

BAY LAKE TOWER AT DISNEY'S CONTEMPORARY RESORT
407/934-7639 **1**

Contemporary Resort Hotel. **Address:** 4600 N World Dr 32830

BEST WESTERN LAKE BUENA VISTA RESORT HOTEL
407/828-2424 **38**

Hotel

Best Western. **AAA Benefit:** Members save up to 15% and earn bonus points!

Address: 2000 Hotel Plaza Blvd 32830 **Location:** Waterfront. I-4 exit 68, 0.5 mi n on SR 535, then just w. **Facility:** 308 units. 19 stories, interior corridors. **Parking:** on-site (fee) and valet. **Amenities:** *Some:* safes. **Dining:** 2 restaurants. **Pool:** heated outdoor. **Activities:** exercise room. **Guest Services:** valet and coin laundry, area transportation. **Featured Amenity: continental breakfast.**

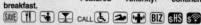

 CALL  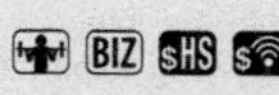

/ SOME UNITS

▼ See AAA listing p. 39 ▼

www.melia.com

An oasis of chic comfort designed around a 360 Degree Infinity Edge Pool and Jacuzzi. Lounge, relax, or prep for fun at the surrounding theme parks, it's all a stone's throw away.

Free WiFi | Outdoor Pool | 360 American Bistro and Bar

225 Celebration Place | Celebration, FL 34747 | 888.956.3542

(See map & index p. 202.)

BLUE TREE RESORT AT LAKE BUENA VISTA-SPM RESORTS 407/238-6000 20

Vacation Rental Condominium

Address: 12007 Cypress Run Rd 32836 **Location:** I-4 exit 68, 1 mi n on SR 535, then 0.4 mi e on Vinings Way Blvd. **Facility:** Located near major attractions, the property features spacious rooms that cater well to families. Each has a living room, a sofa sleeper and a patio. Not all buildings have elevator service. 275 condominiums. 3 stories, exterior corridors. **Terms:** check-in 4 pm. **Amenities:** safes. **Pool:** outdoor, heated outdoor. **Activities:** hot tub, miniature golf, tennis, recreation programs, playground, game room, picnic facilities, exercise room. **Guest Services:** coin laundry, area transportation.

  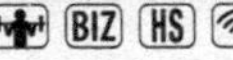   

BOULDER RIDGE VILLAS AT DISNEY'S WILDERNESS LODGE 407/934-7639 3

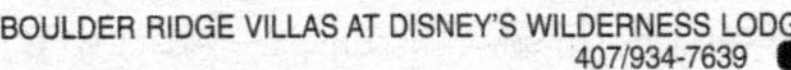

Vacation Rental Condominium. **Address:** 901 W Timberline Dr 32830

B RESORT & SPA LAKE BUENA VISTA 407/828-2828 37

Hotel. **Address:** 1905 Hotel Plaza Blvd 32830

For complete hotel, dining and attraction listings: AAA.com/travelguides

BUENA VISTA SUITES 407/239-8588  58

Hotel

Address: 8203 World Center Dr 32821 **Location:** I-4 exit 68, 1.1 mi s on SR 535, then just e. **Facility:** 279 units. 7 stories, interior corridors. **Amenities:** safes. **Dining:** 2 restaurants. **Pool:** heated outdoor. **Activities:** hot tub, tennis, exercise room. **Guest Services:** valet and coin laundry, rental car service, area transportation. **Featured Amenity:** full hot breakfast.

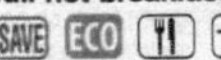     

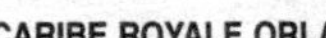

CARIBE ROYALE ORLANDO 407/238-8000 55

Hotel

Address: 8101 World Center Dr 32821 **Location:** I-4 exit 68, 1.6 mi s on SR 535, then 0.3 mi e. **Facility:** 1335 units, some two bedrooms and kitchens. 4-10 stories, interior/exterior corridors. **Parking:** on-site (fee) and valet. **Amenities:** safes. **Dining:** 5 restaurants, also, The Venetian Chop House, see separate listing, entertainment. **Pool:** heated outdoor. **Activities:** hot tub, cabanas, tennis, recreation programs, bicycles, playground, game room, trails, health club, spa. **Guest Services:** valet and coin laundry, rental car service, area transportation.

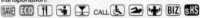

  CALL    

 /SOME UNITS

▼ See AAA listing p. 114 ▼

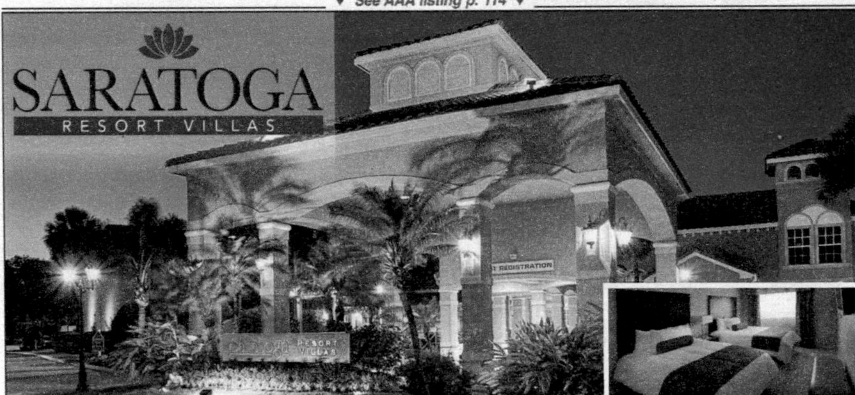

- In the heart of Kissimmee!
- All Villa Resort, 2 & 3 bedrooms, fully equipped kitchens
- FREE Shuttle to Disney & LBV Outlet Mall
- Free WI-FI, Business Center, Fitness Center
- Full Service Restaurant & Bar
- Pool • Gated Entrance
- Disney Good Neighbor® Hotel

Disneyland GOOD NEIGHBOR HOTEL

Saratogaresortvillas.com • 877-767-0147

4787 W Irlo Bronson Memorial Hwy. Kissimmee, FL 34746

(See map & index p. 202.)

CLARION INN LAKE BUENA VISTA, A ROSEN HOTEL 407/996-7300 **22**

Hotel

Address: 8442 Palm Pkwy 32836 **Location:** I-4 exit 68, 0.6 mi n on SR 535, then 0.5 mi e. **Facility:** 640 units. 5 stories, exterior corridors. **Terms:** check-in 4 pm. **Amenities:** safes. **Dining:** 2 restaurants. **Pool:** heated outdoor. **Activities:** recreation programs in season, playground, game room. **Guest Services:** valet and coin laundry, area transportation. *(See ad p. 224.)*

SAVE CALL BIZ HS / SOME UNITS

COPPER CREEK VILLAS AND CABINS 407/934-7639 **5**
Resort Hotel. **Address:** 901 W Timberline Dr 32830

COURTYARD BY MARRIOTT LAKE BUENA VISTA @ VISTA CENTRE 407/239-6900 **25**
SAVE Hotel. **Address:** 8501 Palm Pkwy 32836

AAA Benefit: Members save 5% or more!

COURTYARD BY MARRIOTT ORLANDO LAKE BUENA VISTA IN THE MARRIOTT VILLAGE 407/938-9001 **35**

COURTYARD **AAA Benefit:** Members save 5% or more!

Address: 8623 Vineland Ave 32821 **Location:** I-4 exit 68, just s on SR 535, 0.3 mi e. **Facility:** 312 units. 5 stories, interior corridors. **Parking:** on-site (fee). **Terms:** check-in 4 pm. **Pool:** heated outdoor, heated indoor. **Activities:** hot tub, recreation programs, exercise room. **Guest Services:** valet and coin laundry, boarding pass kiosk, area transportation.

CROWNE PLAZA LAKE BUENA VISTA 407/239-8400 **27**

Address: 8686 Palm Pkwy 32836 **Location:** I-4 exit 68, 0.6 mi n on SR 535, then 0.3 mi e. **Facility:** 200 units. 7 stories, interior corridors. **Parking:** on-site (fee). **Pool:** outdoor. **Activities:** exercise room. **Guest Services:** valet and coin laundry, area transportation.

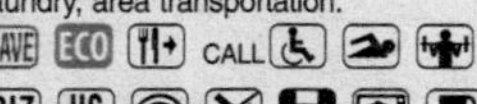

Save on travel, shopping, dining and more:

AAA.com/discounts

DELTA HOTELS BY MARRIOTT ORLANDO LAKE BUENA VISTA 407/387-9999 **29**

DELTA HOTELS **AAA Benefit:** Members save 5% or more!

Address: 12490 Apopka-Vineland Rd 32836 **Location:** I-4 exit 68, 0.7 mi n on SR 535. **Facility:** 241 units. 7 stories, interior corridors. **Parking:** on-site (fee). **Terms:** check-in 4 pm. **Amenities:** safes. **Pool:** heated outdoor. **Activities:** hot tub, cabanas, game room, exercise room. **Guest Services:** valet laundry, area transportation. **Featured Amenity: breakfast buffet.**

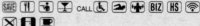

DISNEY'S ALL-STAR MOVIES RESORT 407/934-7639 **75**
Resort Hotel. **Address:** 1901 W Buena Vista Dr 32830

DISNEY'S ALL-STAR MUSIC RESORT 407/934-7639 **74**
Resort Hotel. **Address:** 1801 W Buena Vista Dr 32830

DISNEY'S ALL-STAR SPORTS RESORT 407/934-7639 **73**
Resort Hotel. **Address:** 1701 W Buena Vista Dr 32830

DISNEY'S ANIMAL KINGDOM VILLAS-JAMBO HOUSE 407/934-7639 **72**
Resort Hotel. **Address:** 2901 Osceola Pkwy 32830

DISNEY'S ANIMAL KINGDOM VILLAS-KIDANI VILLAGE 407/934-7639 **71**
Vacation Rental Condominium. **Address:** 2901 Osceola Pkwy 32830

DISNEY'S ART OF ANIMATION RESORT 407/938-7000 **70**
Hotel. **Address:** 1850 Century Dr 32830

DISNEY'S BEACH CLUB RESORT 407/934-7639 **49**
Resort Hotel. **Address:** 1800 Epcot Resorts Blvd 32830

DISNEY'S BEACH CLUB VILLAS 407/934-7639 **50**
Vacation Rental Condominium. **Address:** 1800 Epcot Resorts Blvd 32830

DISNEY'S BOARDWALK INN 407/934-7639 **57**
Resort Hotel. **Address:** 2101 N Epcot Resorts Blvd 32830

DISNEY'S BOARDWALK VILLAS 407/934-7639 **56**
Vacation Rental Condominium. **Address:** 2101 N Epcot Resorts Blvd 32830

DISNEY'S CARIBBEAN BEACH RESORT 407/934-7639 **60**
Resort Hotel. **Address:** 900 Cayman Way 32830

DISNEY'S CONTEMPORARY RESORT 407/934-7639 **2**
Resort Hotel. **Address:** 4600 N World Dr 32830

DISNEY'S CORONADO SPRINGS RESORT 407/934-7639 **65**
Resort Hotel. **Address:** 1001 W Buena Vista Blvd 32830

DISNEY'S FORT WILDERNESS RESORT & CAMPGROUND 407/934-7639 **19**
Vacation Rental Cabin. **Address:** 4510 N Fort Wilderness Tr 32830

DISNEY'S GRAND FLORIDIAN RESORT & SPA 407/934-7639 **6**
Resort Hotel. **Address:** 4401 Grand Floridian Way 32830

DISNEY'S OLD KEY WEST RESORT 407/934-7639 **47**
Vacation Rental Condominium. **Address:** 1510 N Cove Rd 32830

(See map & index p. 202.)

DISNEY'S POLYNESIAN VILLAGE RESORT 407/934-7639 10

Resort Hotel. **Address:** 1600 Seven Seas Dr 32830

DISNEY'S POP CENTURY RESORT 407/934-7639 69

Resort Hotel. **Address:** 1050 Century Dr 32830

DISNEY'S PORT ORLEANS RESORT-FRENCH QUARTER 407/934-7639 39

Resort Hotel. **Address:** 2201 Orleans Dr 32830

DISNEY'S PORT ORLEANS RESORT-RIVERSIDE 407/934-7639 30

Resort Hotel. **Address:** 1251 Riverside Dr 32830

DISNEY'S SARATOGA SPRINGS RESORT & SPA 407/934-7639 41

Vacation Rental Condominium. **Address:** 1960 Broadway 32830

DISNEY'S WILDERNESS LODGE 407/934-7639 4

Resort Hotel. **Address:** 901 W Timberline Dr 32830

DISNEY'S YACHT CLUB RESORT 407/934-7639 51

Resort Hotel. **Address:** 1700 Epcot Resorts Blvd 32830

DOUBLETREE SUITES BY HILTON HOTEL ORLANDO IN THE WALT DISNEY WORLD RESORT 407/934-1000 34

Hotel

DOUBLETREE BY HILTON **AAA Benefit:** Members save 5% or more!

Address: 2305 Hotel Plaza Blvd 32830 **Location:** I-4 exit 68, 0.5 mi n on SR 535, just w. **Facility:** 229 units, some two bedrooms. 7 stories, interior corridors. **Parking:** on-site (fee) and valet. **Terms:** check-in 4 pm. **Amenities:** safes. *Some:* video games. **Pool:** heated outdoor. **Activities:** hot tub, tennis, playground, exercise room. **Guest Services:** valet and coin laundry, rental car service, area transportation.

SAVE ECO CALL BIZ HS

EMBASSY SUITES BY HILTON ORLANDO-LAKE BUENA VISTA RESORT 407/239-1144 15

Hotel

EMBASSY SUITES by HILTON **AAA Benefit:** Members save 5% or more!

Address: 8100 Lake St 32836 **Location:** I-4 exit 68, 0.6 mi n on SR 535, 1 mi e on Palm Pkwy, then just se. **Facility:** 334 units. 5-6 stories, interior/exterior corridors. **Parking:** on-site (fee) and valet. **Terms:** check-in 4 pm. **Amenities:** safes. **Pool:** heated outdoor, heated indoor. **Activities:** sauna, hot tub, cabanas, tennis, playground, game room, exercise room. **Guest Services:** valet and coin laundry, area transportation. **Featured Amenity: full hot breakfast.**

SAVE ECO CALL BIZ HS

FAIRFIELD INN & SUITES BY MARRIOTT ORLANDO-LAKE BUENA VISTA 407/239-1115 23

 Hotel. **Address:** 12191 S Apopka-Vineland Rd 32836

AAA Benefit: Members save 5% or more!

FAIRFIELD INN & SUITES BY MARRIOTT ORLANDO LAKE BUENA VISTA IN THE MARRIOTT VILLAGE 407/938-9001 36

Hotel

Fairfield **AAA Benefit:** Members save 5% or more!

Address: 8615 Vineland Ave 32821 **Location:** I-4 exit 68, just s on SR 535, 0.3 mi e. **Facility:** 388 units. 5 stories, interior corridors. **Parking:** on-site (fee). **Terms:** check-in 4 pm. **Pool:** heated outdoor. **Activities:** hot tub, recreation programs, exercise room. **Guest Services:** valet and coin laundry, boarding pass kiosk, area transportation. **Featured Amenity: breakfast buffet.**

SAVE ECO CALL BIZ HS

FOUR SEASONS RESORT ORLANDO AT WALT DISNEY WORLD RESORT 407/313-7777 7

Resort Hotel

Address: 10100 Dream Tree Blvd 32836 **Location:** Waterfront. I-4 exit 67, 1.1 mi nw, 1.5 mi n on Bonnet Creek Pkwy, 0.9 mi n; in Golden Oak. **Facility:** Fall into the lap of luxury at this impressive resort. Rooms are designed with comfort and technology in mind. Exciting restaurants, a luxurious spa and spectacular pool complex complete the scene. 443 units. 17 stories, interior corridors. **Parking:** valet only. **Terms:** check-in 4 pm. **Amenities:** safes. **Dining:** 4 restaurants, also, Capa, PB & G, Ravello, see separate listings, entertainment. **Pool:** heated outdoor. **Activities:** sauna, hot tub, steamroom, cabanas, regulation golf, tennis, recreation programs, kids club, playground, game room, health club, spa. **Guest Services:** valet laundry, rental car service, area transportation.

SAVE CALL BIZ HS

/ SOME UNITS

GRAND BEACH RESORT 407/238-2500 52

Vacation Rental Condominium. **Address:** 8317 Lake Bryan Beach Blvd 32821

HAMPTON INN ORLANDO-LAKE BUENA VISTA 407/465-8150 16

 Hotel. **Address:** 8150 Palm Pkwy 32836

AAA Benefit: Members save 5% or more!

HAWTHORN SUITES BY WYNDHAM LAKE BUENA VISTA 407/597-5000 18

Hotel

Address: 8303 Palm Pkwy 32836 **Location:** I-4 exit 68, 0.6 mi n on SR 535, then 0.4 mi e. **Facility:** 120 efficiencies. 5 stories, interior corridors. **Amenities:** safes. **Pool:** heated outdoor. **Activities:** hot tub, game room, exercise room. **Guest Services:** valet and coin laundry, area transportation. **Featured Amenity: full hot breakfast.**

(See map & index p. 202.)

HILTON GARDEN INN LAKE BUENA VISTA/ORLANDO

407/239-9550 9

Hotel

AAA Benefit: Members save 5% or more!

Address: 11400 Marbella Palm Ct 32836 **Location:** I-4 exit 68, 0.6 mi n on SR 535, 1 mi e on Palm Pkwy. **Facility:** 137 units. 6 stories, interior corridors. **Amenities:** safes. **Pool:** heated outdoor. **Activities:** hot tub, game room, exercise room. **Guest Services:** valet and coin laundry, area transportation. *(See ad this page.)*

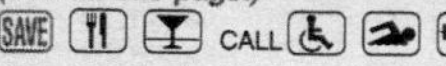

HILTON ORLANDO BONNET CREEK

407/597-3600 66

Resort Hotel

AAA Benefit: Members save 5% or more!

Address: 14100 Bonnet Creek Resort Ln 32821 **Location:** I-4 exit 65, 1.3 mi w on W Osceola Pkwy, 1.2 mi n on Victory Way, 0.5 mi e on Buena Vista Dr, then 1.2 mi s on Chelonia Pkwy. **Facility:** Just minutes from Disney Springs, the hotel has ultra-modern public areas decorated in light wood tones and huge ceiling murals of fun swimming scenes. The spacious rooms have a modern vibe. 1009 units. 17 stories, interior corridors. **Parking:** on-site (fee) and valet. **Terms:** check-in 4 pm. **Amenities:** safes. **Dining:** 5 restaurants. **Pool:** heated outdoor. **Activities:** hot tub, cabanas, regulation golf, recreation programs, bicycles, game room, trails, exercise room. **Guest Services:** valet laundry, boarding pass kiosk, rental car service, area transportation. *(See ad p. 125.)*

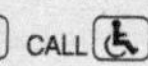

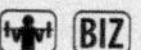

Free Parking, Free WiFi and
No Resort Service Fee!
Our complex is located just outside of Disney Springs and
Centrally Located to EVERYTHING Orlando has to offer!
• Choose a Room or upgrade to a Suite!
• Fitness Center, Game Room, Heated Pool & Hot Tub
• Mini Fridge, Microwave & Keurig Coffee Maker in every room
• Garden Grille Restaurant serving Breakfast and Dinner
• Suite Shop and Pavilion Pantry on-site!
• Complimentary Disney Transportation!
Hilton Garden Inn
Hilton Garden Inn
Lake Buena Vista/Orlando
11400 Marbella Palm Ct
Lake Buena Vista, FL 32836 • 407-239-9550
HOMEWOOD SUITES BY HILTON
Homewood Suites
by Hilton Lake Buena Vista
11428 Marella Palm Ct
Lake Buena Vista, FL 32836 • 407-239-4540
Daily Breakfast Included!

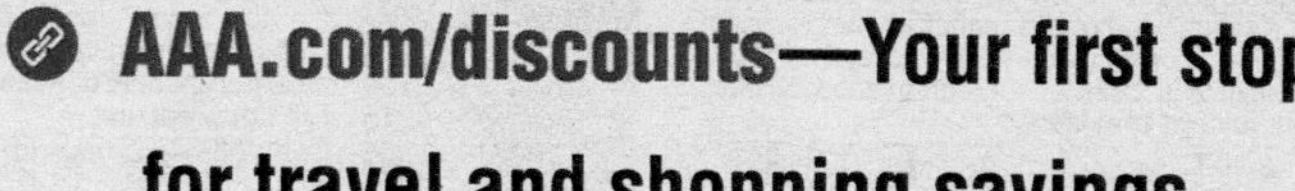

AAA.com/discounts—Your first stop
for travel and shopping savings

▼ See AAA listing p. 124 ▼

DISCOVER THE PERKS OF EXTRA MAGIC

Enjoy access to Disney's *FastPass+* Service up to 60 days in advance and Disney's *Extra Magic Hours* benefit when you stay at Hilton Orlando Bonnet Creek, an Official *Walt Disney World®* Hotel. Complete with Disney shuttle, 3-acre lazy river pool, and 12 onsite dining options, your family's stay will be filled with non-stop magic and memories!

ORLANDO BONNET CREEK

Special rates available to AAA Members.
Call 1-888-353-2013 or visit hiltonbonnetcreek.com

Official *Walt Disney World®* Hotel benefits available through Dec 31, 2020 with valid theme park ticket.

(See map & index p. 202.)

▼ See AAA listing p. 126 ▼

ORLANDO BUENA VISTA PALACE

1900 East Buena Vista Drive
Lake Buena Vista, FL 32830
407-827-2727

Where Diamonds make the difference:

AAA.com/travelguides/hotels

(See map & index p. 202.)

HILTON ORLANDO BUENA VISTA PALACE, DISNEY SPRINGS RESORT 407/827-2727 43

Hotel

AAA Benefit: Members save 5% or more!

Address: 1900 E Buena Vista Dr 32830 **Location:** I-4 exit 68, just n on SR 535 to Hotel Plaza Blvd (Walt Disney World Resort), 0.7 mi sw, then just nw. **Facility:** 1011 units. 6-27 stories, interior corridors. **Parking:** on-site (fee) and valet. **Terms:** check-in 4 pm. **Amenities:** safes. **Dining:** 5 restaurants. **Pool:** heated outdoor. **Activities:** sauna, hot tub, playground, game room, lawn sports, health club, massage. **Guest Services:** valet and coin laundry, boarding pass kiosk, area transportation. *(See ad p. 125, p. 127.)*

SAVE ECO   CALL   BIZ sHS

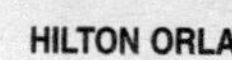   / SOME UNITS 

HILTON ORLANDO LAKE BUENA VISTA 407/827-4000 45

Hotel

AAA Benefit: Members save 5% or more!

Address: 1751 Hotel Plaza Blvd 32830 **Location:** I-4 exit 68, 0.5 mi n on SR 535, then 0.9 mi w. **Facility:** 814 units. 10 stories, interior corridors. **Parking:** on-site (fee) and valet. **Terms:** check-in 4 pm. **Amenities:** video games, safes. **Dining:** 6 restaurants. **Pool:** heated outdoor. **Activities:** hot tub, game room, exercise room, massage. **Guest Services:** valet and coin laundry, rental car service, area transportation. *(See ad p. 127.)*

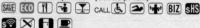

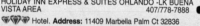

SAVE ECO CALL BIZ sHS 

HOLIDAY INN EXPRESS & SUITES ORLANDO -LK BUENA VISTA AREA 407/778-7888 8

Hotel. **Address:** 11409 Marbella Palm Ct 32836

Mobile Battery Service

1-800-AAA-HELP • 1-800-CAA-HELP

AAA.com/mobile • CAA.ca/mobile

Power You Can Trust!™

HOLIDAY INN ORLANDO-DISNEY SPRINGS AREA 407/828-8888 40

Hotel

Address: 1805 Hotel Plaza Blvd 32830 **Location:** I-4 exit 68, 0.5 mi n on SR 535, 0.4 mi w. **Facility:** 323 units. 6-14 stories, interior corridors. **Parking:** on-site (fee) and valet. **Terms:** check-in 4 pm. **Amenities:** safes. **Pool:** heated outdoor. **Activities:** hot tub, game room, exercise room. **Guest Services:** valet and coin laundry, area transportation.

SAVE CALL BIZ HS

HOLIDAY INN RESORT ORLANDO-LAKE BUENA VISTA 407/239-4500 46

Hotel

Address: 13351 SR 535 32821 **Location:** I-4 exit 68, 0.3 mi se. **Facility:** 496 units. 6 stories, interior corridors. **Parking:** on-site (fee). **Amenities:** safes. **Pool:** heated outdoor. **Activities:** hot tub, recreation programs, playground, game room, exercise room, massage. **Guest Services:** valet and coin laundry, rental car service, area transportation. *(See ad p. 224.)*

SAVE CALL BIZ / SOME UNITS

HOLIDAY INN RESORT ORLANDO SUITES-WATERPARK 407/387-5437 61

Resort Hotel

Address: 14500 Continental Gateway 32821 **Location:** I-4 exit 67, 1 mi e on SR 536. **Facility:** All guest rooms come equipped with plenty of sleeping accommodations which includes a kids room featuring bunk beds, the bottom bunk is queen size. The marketplace features food outlets and a bar. 777 units, some two bedrooms, three bedrooms and kitchens. 6 stories, exterior corridors. **Parking:** on-site (fee). **Terms:** check-in 4 pm. **Amenities:** safes. **Dining:** 5 restaurants, entertainment. **Pool:** heated outdoor. **Activities:** hot tub, cabanas, miniature golf, recreation programs, playground, game room, exercise room. **Guest Services:** valet and coin laundry, area transportation. *(See ad p. 128.)*

SAVE ECO CALL BIZ HS  

HOMEWOOD SUITES BY HILTON LAKE BUENA VISTA/ ORLANDO 407/239-4540 11

Extended Stay Hotel

AAA Benefit: Members save 5% or more!

Address: 11428 Marbella Palm Ct 32836 **Location:** I-4 exit 68, 0.6 mi n on SR 535, 1 mi e on Palm Pkwy. **Facility:** 130 units, some two bedrooms and efficiencies. 7 stories, interior corridors. **Amenities:** safes. **Pool:** heated outdoor. **Activities:** hot tub, exercise room. **Guest Services:** valet and coin laundry, area transportation. *(See ad p. 124.)*

SAVE  BIZ HS  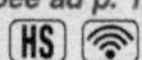 

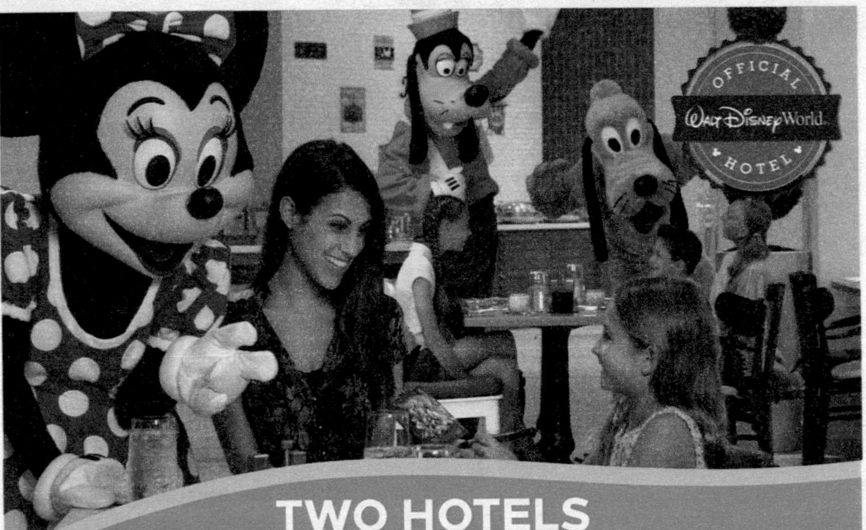

TWO HOTELS
One Amazing Location

STEPS FROM DISNEY SPRINGS®

Hilton Lake Buena Vista and Hilton Buena Vista Palace are walking distance from world-class shopping, dining and entertainment at Disney Springs®

As official *Walt Disney World®* hotels, guests enjoy these Disney benefits:

- ***Extra Magic Hours****
- **FastPass+ Service with extended 60-day booking window***
- Shuttle transportation to Disney Theme Parks
- Sunday Disney Character Breakfast

*Benefits available through 2020. Valid theme park ticket required.

SPECIAL DISCOUNTS FOR AAA MEMBERS

ORLANDO BUENA VISTA PALACE

407.827.2727 | buenavistapalace.com

1900 E Buena Vista Dr. Lake Buena Vista, FL 32830

Hilton

ORLANDO LAKE BUENA VISTA

407.827.4000 | hiltonlakebuenavista.com

1751 Hotel Plaza Blvd. Lake Buena Vista, FL 32830

▼ See AAA listing p. 126 ▼

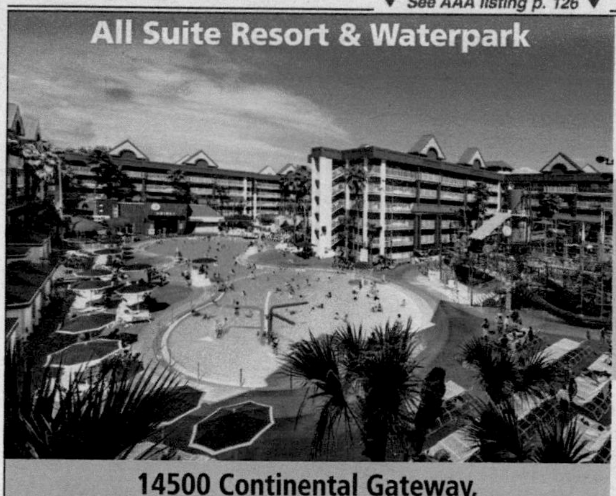

Holiday Inn Resort
ORLANDO SUITES - WATERPARK

Orlando's family-inspired all-suite destination offering Fun, Sun and Entertainment with immediate access to Orlando's greatest theme parks and attractions. One mile from Disney World.

- **AAA Members Save Up to 25%**
- All Suite Accommodations
- Lagoon Waterpark and Family Pool Areas
- Multiple Dining Options
- Live Entertainment, 4-D Theater, Bank Heist Laser Challenge
- Earn IHG Rewards Club Points

14500 Continental Gateway,
Orlando, FL United States 32821
For reservations call 800.465.4329
or visit HIsuitesorlando.com

(See map & index p. 202.)

Connect with AAA for the latest updates.

 AAA.com/Facebook

 AAA.com/Twitter

 Instagram.com/aaa_national

 YouTube.com/AAA

(See map & index p. 202.)

HYATT PLACE ORLANDO/LAKE BUENA VISTA
407/778-5500 **28**

Hotel

HYATT PLACE **AAA Benefit:** Members save up to 10%!

Address: 8688 Palm Pkwy 32836 **Location:** I-4 exit 68, 0.6 mi n on SR 535, then just e. **Facility:** 169 units. 6 stories, interior corridors. **Amenities:** safes. **Pool:** heated outdoor. **Activities:** hot tub, exercise room. **Guest Services:** valet and coin laundry, area transportation. **Featured Amenity:** **breakfast buffet.**

HYATT REGENCY GRAND CYPRESS
407/239-1234 **31**

Resort Hotel

AAA Benefit: Members save up to 10%!

Address: 1 Grand Cypress Blvd 32836 **Location:** Waterfront. I-4 exit 68, 0.8 mi nw on SR 535, just s. **Facility:** Set on a small lake, the hotel has great views of a protected preserve and rooms with inviting design elements. Guests enjoy leisure time in pool areas enhanced with bronze statues and waterfalls. 779 units. 18 stories, interior corridors. **Parking:** on-site (fee) and valet. **Terms:** check-in 4 pm. **Amenities:** safes. **Dining:** 3 restaurants, also, Hemingway's, see separate listing. **Pool:** outdoor, heated outdoor. **Activities:** hot tub, self-propelled boats, fishing, regulation golf, tennis, recreation programs, kids club, bicycles, playground, game room, lawn sports, picnic facilities, trails, health club, spa. **Guest Services:** valet and coin laundry, rental car service, area transportation. *(See ad p. 130.)*

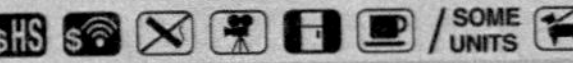

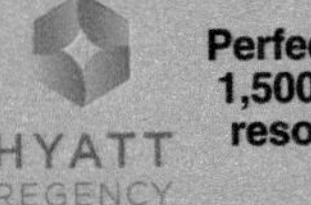

Perfection near the Parks on 1,500 acres with an array of resort amenities everyone will enjoy.

LAKE BUENA VISTA RESORT VILLAGE & SPA
407/597-0214 **63**

Vacation Rental Condominium

Address: 8113 Resort Village Dr 32821 **Location:** I-4 exit 68, 1.8 mi se on SR 535. **Facility:** Located near the attractions, this condominium-style hotel is within walking distance of restaurants and shops. The luxurious, spacious units feature a kitchen, a living area and a private balcony. 496 condominiums. 8-15 stories, exterior corridors. **Terms:** check-in 4 pm. **Amenities:** safes. **Dining:** 3 restaurants, also, Frankie Farrell's Irish Pub & Grille, see separate listing. **Pool:** heated outdoor. **Activities:** hot tub, game room, exercise room, spa. **Guest Services:** complimentary laundry, area transportation.

    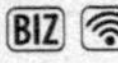   

LEGACY VACATION CLUB RESORTS- LAKE BUENA VISTA
407/238-1700 **24**

Vacation Rental Condominium. **Address:** 8451 Palm Pkwy 32836

ORLANDO WORLD CENTER MARRIOTT
407/239-4200 **54**

Resort Hotel

AAA Benefit: Members save 5% or more!

Address: 8701 World Center Dr 32821 **Location:** I-4 exit 67, 1.5 mi s on SR 536. **Facility:** At the end of a long, winding road, the impressive resort features cozy, inviting rooms with upscale décor. The sprawling pool area is not to be missed, especially during the nightly laser show. 2009 units. 5-28 stories, interior corridors. **Parking:** on-site (fee) and valet. **Terms:** check-in 4 pm. **Amenities:** video games, safes. **Dining:** 8 restaurants, also, Latitude and Longitude, see separate listing. **Pool:** heated outdoor, heated indoor. **Activities:** sauna, hot tub, steamroom, regulation golf, tennis, recreation programs, kids club, playground, game room, lawn sports, health club, spa. **Guest Services:** valet and coin laundry, boarding pass kiosk, rental car service, luggage security pick-up, area transportation.

RADISSON HOTEL ORLANDO-LAKE BUENA VISTA
407/597-3400 **32**

Hotel. **Address:** 12799 Apopka-Vineland Rd 32836

RESIDENCE INN BY MARRIOTT ORLANDO LAKE BUENA VISTA
407/465-0075 **12**

Extended Stay Hotel. **Address:** 11450 Marbella Palms Ct 32836

AAA Benefit: Members save 5% or more!

SHERATON LAKE BUENA VISTA RESORT
407/239-0444 **26**

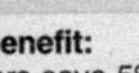

Hotel

AAA Benefit: Members save 5% or more!

Address: 12205 Apopka-Vineland Rd 32836 **Location:** I-4 exit 68, 0.6 mi n on SR 535. **Facility:** 486 units. 6 stories, interior/exterior corridors. **Parking:** on-site (fee) and valet. **Amenities:** safes. **Dining:** 2 restaurants. **Pool:** heated outdoor. **Activities:** hot tub, cabanas, recreation programs, game room, exercise room, spa. **Guest Services:** valet and coin laundry, boarding pass kiosk, rental car service. *(See ad p. 131.)*

 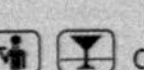 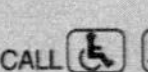  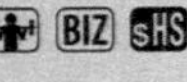

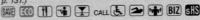

SHERATON'S VISTANA RESORT VILLAS, LAKE BUENA VISTA/ORLANDO
407/239-3100 **48**

Resort Condominium. **Address:** 8800 Vistana Centre Dr 32821

AAA Benefit: Members save 5% or more!

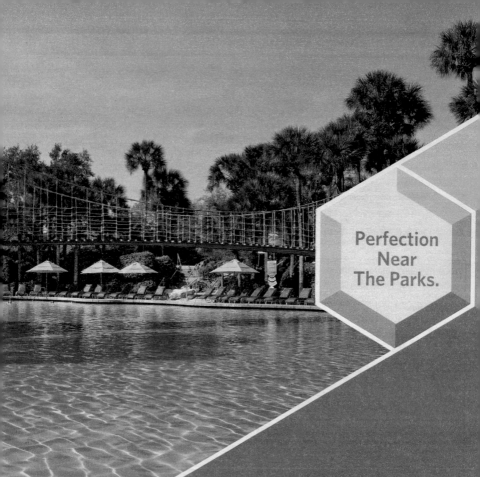

Perfection
Near
The Parks.

MAKE MEMORIES at the award-winning, 1,500 acre Hyatt Regency Grand Cypress, located minutes from Orlando's famous theme parks. Enjoy a host of amenities and activities, ranging from a full-service spa, championship golf and lagoon pool with waterfalls to whirlpools, water slide, rock climbing, and splash zone.

For reservations or more information, call 407-239-1234 or visit **grandcypress.regency.hyatt.com**

HYATT REGENCY GRAND CYPRESS
One Grand Cypress Boulevard
Orlando, Florida 32836

(See map & index p. 202.)

SPRINGHILL SUITES BY MARRIOTT AT THE MARRIOTT VILLAGE LAKE BUENA VISTA 407/938-9001 33

Hotel

SPRINGHILL SUITES MARRIOTT **AAA Benefit:** Members save 5% or more!

Address: 8601 Vineland Ave 32821 **Location:** I-4 exit 68, just s on SR 535, 0.3 mi e. **Facility:** 400 units. 5 stories, interior corridors. **Parking:** on-site (fee). **Terms:** check-in 4 pm. **Pool:** heated outdoor. **Activities:** hot tub, recreation programs, exercise room. **Guest Services:** valet and coin laundry, area transportation. **Featured Amenity:** breakfast buffet.

SPRINGHILL SUITES BY MARRIOTT ORLANDO THEME PARKS/LAKE BUENA VISTA 407/635-8500 14

Hotel

SPRINGHILL SUITES MARRIOTT **AAA Benefit:** Members save 5% or more!

Address: 8040 Palm Pkwy 32836 **Location:** I-4 exit 68, 0.6 mi n on SR 535, then 1.4 mi e. **Facility:** 180 units, some kitchens. 6 stories, interior corridors. **Pool:** heated outdoor. **Activities:** game room, exercise room. **Guest Services:** valet and coin laundry, area transportation.

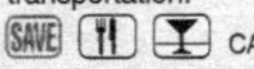
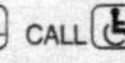

STAYBRIDGE SUITES-ORLANDO/LAKE BUENA VISTA 407/238-0777 17

Extended Stay Contemporary Hotel. **Address:** 8751 Suiteside Dr 32836

TOWNEPLACE SUITES BY MARRIOTT ORLANDO THEME PARKS/LAKE BUENA VISTA 407/239-4005 13

Extended Stay Hotel

TOWNEPLACE SUITES MARRIOTT **AAA Benefit:** Members save 5% or more!

Address: 8040 Palm Pkwy 32836 **Location:** I-4 exit 68, 0.6 mi n on SR 535, then 1.4 mi e. **Facility:** 155 units, some two bedrooms and kitchens. 6 stories, interior corridors. **Pool:** heated outdoor. **Activities:** game room, exercise room. **Guest Services:** valet and coin laundry, area transportation. **Featured Amenity:** continental breakfast.

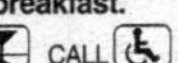

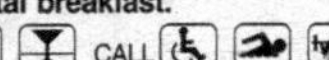

▼ See AAA listing p. 129 ▼

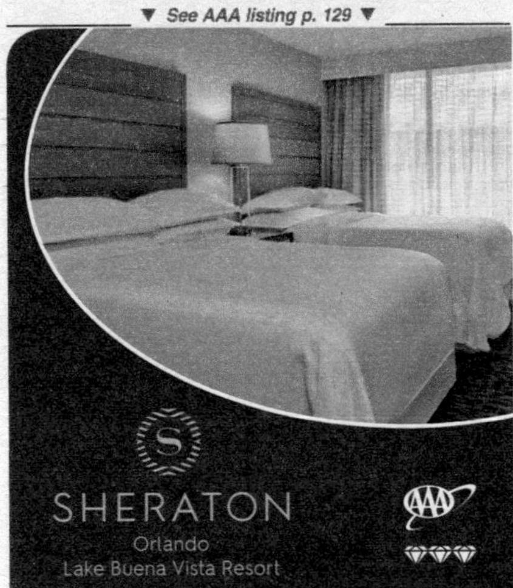

Whether traveling as a family, in a group or for a getaway, **Sheraton Lake Buena Vista** offers spacious resort accommodations right in the center of Orlando's great attractions and just a few blocks from Disney Springs™.

Featuring Sheraton Signature Bed®, flat panel HD TVs, high-speed Wi-Fi access and Free Disney Theme Park Shuttle.

12205 Apopka-Vineland Road
Lake Buena Vista FL 32836
407-239-0444
sheratonlbv.com

Walt Disney World GOOD NEIGHBOR HOTEL

Discover member savings around the world: AAA.com/discounts

(See map & index p. 202.)

WALDORF ASTORIA ORLANDO 407/597-5500 68

Resort Hotel

AAA Benefit: Members save 5% or more!

Address: 14200 Bonnet Creek Resort Ln 32821 **Location:** I-4 exit 65, 1.3 mi w on W Osceola Pkwy, 1.2 mi n on Victory Way, 0.5 mi e on Buena Vista Dr, then 1.2 mi s on Chelonia Pkwy. **Facility:** The spa, golf course and gorgeous pool area with cabanas and a lazy river offer plenty of opportunities for fun and relaxation. After a full day, retreat to your inviting room for a good night's rest. 502 units, some two bedrooms. 11 stories, interior corridors. **Parking:** on-site (fee) and valet. **Amenities:** safes. **Dining:** 8 restaurants, also, Bull & Bear Restaurant, see separate listing, entertainment. **Pool:** heated outdoor. **Activities:** hot tub, steamroom, cabanas, regulation golf, recreation programs, bicycles, health club, spa. **Guest Services:** valet laundry, boarding pass kiosk, area transportation. *(See ad this page.)*

SAVE CALL BIZ $HS

WALT DISNEY WORLD DOLPHIN 407/934-4000 53

Resort Hotel

SHERATON

AAA Benefit: Members save 5% or more!

Address: 1500 Epcot Resorts Blvd 32830 **Location:** Waterfront. I-4 exit 67, follow Epcot Resort area signs; 0.3 mi e of Walt Disney World Resort; 2 mi n of US 192. **Facility:** The expansive hotel's iconic, rooftop dolphin statue is hard to miss. After a full day of activities, the modern rooms and comfortable bedding makes it a breeze to rest easy. 1514 units. 20 stories, interior corridors. **Parking:** on-site (fee) and valet. **Terms:** check-in 4 pm. **Amenities:** safes. **Dining:** 5 restaurants, also, Shula's America's Steak House, Todd English's bluezoo, see separate listings, entertainment. **Pool:** heated outdoor. **Activities:** hot tub, recreation programs, playground, game room, health club, spa. **Guest Services:** valet and coin laundry, area transportation. Affiliated with Sheraton Hotels.

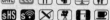

SAVE ECO CALL BIZ $HS

▼ *See AAA listing this page* ▼

Discover the luxury of extra magic during your Orlando getaway.

Experience an unforgettable family getaway at Waldorf Astoria Orlando, an Official *Walt Disney World*® Hotel. Enjoy luxurious accommodations, tranquil resort pools with private cabanas, championship golf, and award-winning spa. Plus, guests receive access to Disney's *FastPass+* Service up to 60 days in advance and Disney's *Extra Magic Hours* benefit, with transportation to and from all Disney parks.

OFFICIAL Walt Disney World HOTEL

Special rates available to AAA Members.
Call 1-888-353-2009 or visit waldorfastoriaorlando.com

WALDORF ASTORIA ORLANDO

Official *Walt Disney World*® Hotel benefits available through Dec 31, 2020 with valid theme park ticket.

Get an expert view from AAA inspectors:

AAA.com/travelguides/hotels

(See map & index p. 202.)

WALT DISNEY WORLD SWAN RESORT
407/934-3000 59

Resort Hotel

WESTIN HOTELS & RESORTS **AAA Benefit:** Members save 5% or more!

Address: 1200 Epcot Resorts Blvd 32830 **Location:** Waterfront. I-4 exit 67, follow Epcot Resort area signs; 0.3 mi e of Walt Disney World Resort main gate access road; 2 mi n of US 192. **Facility:** The elegant, iconic swan proudly rests atop the hotel which creates a warm welcome for guests. The comfortably designed, modern rooms are a joy to retire to at the end of a busy day. 756 units. 12 stories, interior corridors. **Parking:** on-site (fee) and valet. **Terms:** check-in 4 pm. **Amenities:** safes. **Dining:** 3 restaurants, also, Il Mulino, see separate listing. **Pool:** heated outdoor. **Activities:** hot tub, playground, health club, massage. **Guest Services:** valet laundry, area transportation. Affiliated with Westin Hotels.

   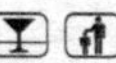 CALL  

WESTGATE BLUE TREE RESORT AT LAKE BUENA VISTA
407/597-2200 21

Vacation Rental Condominium

Address: 12007 Cypress Run Rd 32836 **Location:** I-4 exit 68, 1 mi n on SR 535, 0.4 mi e on to Vinings Way Blvd. **Facility:** Located near major attractions and many restaurants, the property is well designed for families and large groups. The spacious one and two-bedroom units have a living room, a kitchen and a patio. 119 condominiums. 3 stories (no elevator), exterior corridors. **Terms:** check-in 4 pm. **Amenities:** safes. **Pool:** outdoor, heated outdoor. **Activities:** hot tub, miniature golf, tennis, recreation programs, kids club, playground, game room, picnic facilities, exercise room. **Guest Services:** coin laundry.

CALL 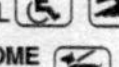 / SOME UNITS

WORLDQUEST RESORT 407/387-3800 67

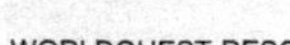 Vacation Rental Condominium. **Address:** 8849 World Quest Blvd 32821

WYNDHAM BONNET CREEK RESORT
407/238-3500 62

Vacation Rental Condominium

Address: 9560 Via Encinas 32830 **Location:** Waterfront. I-4 exit 65, 1.3 mi w on W Osceola Pkwy, 1.2 mi n on Victory Way, 0.4 mi ne on Buena Vista Dr, then 0.6 mi s on Chelonia Pkwy. **Facility:** The sprawling resort with condo-style suites offers many recreational amenities that appeal to families. Enjoy the popular lazy river, which meanders around the pool. 1149 condominiums. 4-15 stories, interior corridors. **Terms:** check-in 4 pm. **Amenities:** safes. **Dining:** 3 restaurants, entertainment. **Pool:** heated outdoor. **Activities:** hot tub, cabanas, miniature golf, recreation programs, kids club, playground, game room, lawn sports, picnic facilities, trails, exercise room, massage. **Guest Services:** complimentary laundry.

 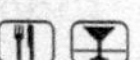 CALL 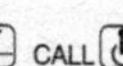    

WYNDHAM GARDEN LAKE BUENA VISTA DISNEY SPRINGS RESORT AREA 407/842-6644 42

Hotel

Address: 1850B Hotel Plaza Blvd 32830 **Location:** I-4 exit 68, 0.5 mi n on SR 535, then 0.6 mi sw. **Facility:** 394 units. 5 stories, exterior corridors. **Parking:** on-site and valet. **Terms:** check-in 4 pm. **Amenities:** safes. **Dining:** 4 restaurants. **Pool:** outdoor, heated outdoor. **Activities:** hot tub, cabanas, tennis, recreation programs, kids club, game room, exercise room, massage. **Guest Services:** valet and coin laundry, rental car service, area transportation. *(See ad on inside front cover, p. 134.)*

CALL

WYNDHAM GARDEN
Lake Buena Vista
Disney Springs™ Resort area

Featuring Disney's 60 Day FastPass+, Extra Magic Hours, & Disney Character Breakfast 3 Days A Week.

WYNDHAM GRAND ORLANDO RESORT BONNET CREEK
407/390-2300 64

Contemporary Resort Hotel

Address: 14651 Chelonia Pkwy 32821 **Location:** I-4 exit 65, 1.3 mi w on W Osceola Pkwy, 1.2 mi n on Victory Way, 0.4 mi ne on Buena Vista Dr, then 0.9 mi s. **Facility:** Guest rooms vary in layout with many offering great views of the beautifully landscaped grounds. Some deluxe suites have an area with bunk beds and a separate TV for the kids to enjoy. 400 units, some two bedrooms. 14 stories, interior corridors. **Parking:** on-site (fee) and valet. **Terms:** check-in 4 pm. **Amenities:** safes. **Dining:** 3 restaurants, also, deep blu Seafood Grille, see separate listing. **Pool:** heated outdoor. **Activities:** hot tub, steamroom, recreation programs, game room, picnic facilities, trails, health club, spa. **Guest Services:** valet laundry, boarding pass kiosk, rental car service, area transportation. *(See ad p. 134.)*

CALL / SOME UNITS

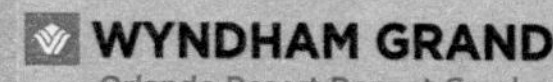

Four Diamond, Walt Disney World® Gateway Hotel with 5 pools and lazy rivers. AAA Members SAVE 20%!

GET THE APP
Download today.
Connect every day.
AAA.com/mobile
CAA.ca/mobile

▼ See AAA listing p. 133 ▼

MEMBERSHIP PAYS,
SAVE 20%!

Splash around in five sparkling pools, two lazy rivers, two kid's splash parks, or challenge your family to miniature golf — all within Bonnet Creek Resort. Then, relax in our luxurious Blue Harmony Spa or catch the complimentary shuttle to Walt Disney World® Resort.

407-390-2300
WyndhamGrandOrlando.com
infoWyndhamGrandOrlando@wyndham.com

WYNDHAM GRAND®
Orlando Resort Bonnet Creek

MEMBER OF
WYNDHAM REWARDS®

All Wyndham® hotels are either franchised by the company or managed by Wyndham Hotel Management, Inc., one of its affiliates or through a joint-venture partner. ©2018 Wyndham Hotels and Resorts, LLC. All rights reserved.

Exclusive Disney Benefits

- Disney's 60 Day FastPass+ and Extra Magic Hours Access
- Across the street from Disney Springs™
- Shuttle To Disney® Parks
- Disney Character Breakfast

as to the Disney artwork, logos and property: ©Disney

WYNDHAM GARDEN
Lake Buena Vista
Disney Springs® Resort Area

WYNDHAM
Lake Buena Vista
Disney Springs® Resort Area

For Wyndham Reservations Call **1-800-624-4109**
For Wyndham Garden Reservations Call **1-844-482-8444**
www.wyndhamlakebuenavista.com
1850 Hotel Plaza Boulevard, Lake Buena Vista, FL 32830

Hit the Road with Foreign Currency

A treasure trove of artisan masterpieces awaits.

Visit your local AAA office or online at
AAA.com/ForeignCurrency

All products not available at all locations.

(See map & index p. 202.)

WYNDHAM LAKE BUENA VISTA DISNEY SPRINGS RESORT AREA 407/828-4444 (44)

Resort Hotel

Address: 1850 Hotel Plaza Blvd 32830 **Location:** Waterfront. I-4 exit 68, 0.5 mi n on SR 535, then 0.6 mi sw. **Facility:** Enjoy the convenience of staying near Disney Springs and the theme parks. The rooms are chic, inviting and comfortable. Some have views of the Disney parks. 232 units. 19 stories, interior corridors. **Parking:** on-site (fee) and valet. **Terms:** check-in 4 pm. **Amenities:** safes. **Dining:** 4 restaurants. **Pool:** outdoor, heated outdoor. **Activities:** hot tub, cabanas, tennis, recreation programs, kids club, game room, exercise room, massage. **Guest Services:** valet and coin laundry, rental car service, area transportation. *(See ad on inside front cover, p. 134.)*

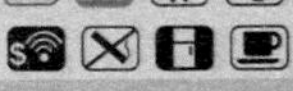

SAVE ECO CALL BIZ SHS

Featuring Disney's 60 Day FastPass+, Extra Magic Hours, & Disney Character Breakfast 3 Days A Week.

WHERE TO EAT

50'S PRIME TIME CAFE 407/939-3463

American. Casual Dining.

ARTIST POINT 407/939-3463 (2)

Regional American. Casual Dining. **Address:** 901 W Timberline Dr 32830

BAHAMA BREEZE ISLAND GRILLE 407/938-9010 (12)

Caribbean. Casual Dining. **Address:** 8735 Vineland Ave 32821

THE BOATHOUSE WATERFRONT DINING 407/939-2628 (20)

Seafood Steak. Fine Dining. **Address:** 1620 E Buena Vista Dr 32830

BOATWRIGHT'S DINING HALL 407/934-3463

Cajun. Casual Dining. **Address:** 1251 Riverside Dr 32830

BONGOS CUBAN CAFE ORLANDO 407/828-0999 (25)

Cuban. Casual Dining. **Address:** 1498 E Buena Vista Dr 32830

BULL & BEAR RESTAURANT 407/597-5500 (40)

New Steak Seafood. Fine Dining. **Address:** 14200 Bonnet Creek Resort Ln 32821

CALIFORNIA GRILL 407/934-3463 (1)

Regional American. Fine Dining. **Address:** 4660 World Dr 32830

CAPA 407/313-7777 (6)

Basque. Fine Dining. **Address:** 10100 Dream Tree Blvd, Suite C 32836

CINDERELLA'S ROYAL TABLE 407/939-3463

American. Casual Dining. **Address:** 3111 World Dr 32830

CITRICOS 407/939-3463 (3)

Southern Mediterranean. Fine Dining. **Address:** 4401 Grand Floridian Way 32830

THE CRYSTAL PALACE 407/939-3463

American. Casual Dining.

DEEP BLU SEAFOOD GRILLE 407/390-2420 (37)

Seafood Fine Dining $28-$78

AAA Inspector Notes: The open kitchen offers an opportunity to observe the chefs at work in the trendy, upscale spot where focus is placed on sustainable items procured from local farms. Menu selections include a variety of oysters, various seafood options and steak. For starters, the excellent crab cake is a big win. For your entree, try the loaded lobster which is full flavored and satisfying. Presentation is skilled with attention to detail. Tables near the windows overlook the expansive pool area. **Features:** full bar, happy hour. **Reservations:** suggested. **Address:** 14651 Chelonia Pkwy 32821 **Location:** I-4 exit 65, 1.3 mi w on W Osceola Pkwy, 1.2 mi n on Victory Way, 0.4 mi ne on Buena Vista Dr, then 0.9 mi s; in Wyndham Grand Orlando Resort Bonnet Creek. **Parking:** on-site and valet. D CALL

THE EDISON 407/560-9288 (21)

American. Casual Dining. **Address:** 1570 E Buena Vista Dr 32830

EL PATRON MEXICAN RESTAURANT & CANTINA 407/238-5300 (9)

Mexican. Casual Dining. **Address:** 12167 S Apopka-Vineland Rd 32836

ENZO'S HIDEAWAY TUNNEL BAR 407/560-3696 (24)

Italian. Casual Dining. **Address:** 1560 E Buena Vista Dr 32830

ESPN® CLUB 407/939-3463

Sandwiches. Casual Dining. **Address:** 2101 N Epcot Resorts Blvd 32830

FLYING FISH CAFE 407/939-3463 (29)

Seafood. Fine Dining. **Address:** 2101 N Epcot Resort Blvd 32830

FRANKIE FARRELL'S IRISH PUB & GRILLE 407/238-1003 (36)

Irish. Casual Dining. **Address:** 8112 Poinciana Blvd 32821

GOURMETO'S NY PIZZA & CLASSIC ITALIAN CUISINE 407/465-1818 (35)

Italian. Quick Serve. **Address:** 8216 World Center Dr 32836

HAVANA'S CAFE 407/238-5333 (10)

Cuban. Casual Dining. **Address:** 8544 Palm Pkwy 32836

HEMINGWAY'S 407/239-1234 (11)

Seafood. Fine Dining. **Address:** 1 Grand Cypress Blvd 32836

THE HOLLYWOOD BROWN DERBY 407/939-3463 (39)

American. Fine Dining. **Address:** Hollywood Blvd 32830

HOMECOMIN' KITCHEN 407/560-0100 (22)

Southern Comfort Food. Casual Dining. **Address:** 1602 E Buena Vista Dr 32830

IL MULINO 407/934-1609 (34)

Italian. Fine Dining. **Address:** 1200 Epcot Resorts Blvd 32830

JIKO-THE COOKING PLACE 407/939-3463 (41)

African. Fine Dining. **Address:** 2901 Osceola Pkwy 32820

KONA CAFÉ 407/939-3463

American. Casual Dining. **Address:** 1600 Seven Seas Dr 32830

LATITUDE AND LONGITUDE 407/238-8829 (32)

American. Casual Dining. **Address:** 8701 World Center Dr 32821

LIBERTY TREE TAVERN 407/939-3463

American. Casual Dining. **Address:** 4600 World Dr 32836

(See map & index p. 202.)

MAMA MELROSE'S RISTORANTE ITALIANO 407/939-3463

Italian. Casual Dining.

MORIMOTO ASIA 407/939-6686 (15)

Asian Dim Sum Sushi. Casual Dining. **Address:** 1600 E Buena Vista Dr 32830

NARCOOSSEE'S 407/939-3463 (5)

Seafood. Fine Dining. **Address:** 4401 Floridian Way 32830

'OHANA 407/939-3463

Polynesian. Casual Dining. **Address:** 1600 Seven Seas Dr 32830

PADDLEFISH 407/934-2628 (14)

Seafood. Casual Dining. **Address:** 1670 Buena Vista Dr 32830

PARADISO 37 TASTE OF THE AMERICAS 407/934-3700 (27)

Continental. Casual Dining. **Address:** 1590 E Buena Vista Dr 32830

PB & G 407/313-7777 (8)

Comfort Food. Casual Dining. **Address:** 10100 Dream Tree Blvd 32836

THE POLITE PIG 407/938-7444 (19)

Barbecue. Casual Dining. **Address:** 1536 Buena Vista Dr 32821

RAGLAN ROAD IRISH PUB AND RESTAURANT 407/938-0300 (18)

Irish. Casual Dining. **Address:** 1640 E Buena Vista Dr 32830

RAINFOREST CAFE 407/827-8500 (13)

SAVE American. Casual Dining. **Address:** 1800 E Buena Vista Dr 32830

RAVELLO 407/313-7777 (7)

Italian. Casual Dining. **Address:** 10100 Dream Tree Blvd B 32836

SCI-FI DINE-IN THEATRE RESTAURANT 407/939-3463

American. Casual Dining. **Address:** Backlot 32830

SHULA'S AMERICA'S STEAK HOUSE 407/934-1362 (31)

Steak. Fine Dining. **Address:** 1500 Epcot Resorts Blvd 32830

SPLITSVILLE LUXURY LANES 407/938-7467 (26)

American. Casual Dining. **Address:** 1494 E Buena Vista Dr 32830

STK ORLANDO 407/917-7440 (23)

Steak. Fine Dining. **Address:** 1580 E Buena Vista Dr 32830

TODD ENGLISH'S BLUEZOO 407/934-4644 (30)

Seafood. Fine Dining. **Address:** 1500 Epcot Resorts Blvd 32830

TOLEDO 407/934-7639 (38)

Steak Seafood. Casual Dining. **Address:** 1001 W Buena Vista Blvd 32830

TONY'S TOWN SQUARE RESTAURANT 407/939-3463

Italian. Casual Dining.

T-REX CAFE 407/828-8739 (17)

American. Casual Dining. **Address:** 1676 E Buena Vista Dr 32830

THE VENETIAN CHOP HOUSE 407/238-8060 (33)

Continental Fine Dining $36-$43

AAA Inspector Notes: Rich woods, carved frosted glass, impressive chandeliers and classic red accents create an atmosphere of warmth and sophistication in the intimate dining room. Menu selections include a savory lump crab cake with pommery mustard butter sauce, lobster bisque baked with puff pastry and several cuts of premium, aged Black Angus beef. The decadent and artfully presented desserts will make you glad you ended on a sweet note. **Features:** full bar, patio dining. **Reservations:** suggested. **Address:** 8101 World Center Dr 32821 **Location:** I-4 exit 68, 1.6 mi s on SR 535, then 0.3 mi e; in Caribe Royale Orlando. **Parking:** on-site and valet. D CALL

VICTORIA & ALBERT'S 407/939-3862 (4)

New American Fine Dining $185-$250

AAA Inspector Notes: This is Disney's finest restaurant with luxurious, intimate surroundings that complement the personalized service and extensive wine list. The dinner menu offers an ever-changing culinary adventure through 10 exquisite courses. Chef Scott Hunnel creates meticulous and incredibly delicious contemporary cuisine which reflects both American and International influences and uses the finest ingredients available. The coffee and tea presentations are extraordinary. **Features:** full bar. **Reservations:** required. **Address:** 4401 Grand Floridian Way 32830 **Location:** I-4 exit 67, 3.4 mi nw following signs to the Magic Kingdom; in Disney's Grand Floridian Resort & Spa. **Parking:** on-site and valet. D CALL

WINE BAR GEORGE 407/490-1800 (16)

American. Casual Dining. **Address:** 1610 E Buena Vista Dr 32820

YACHTSMAN STEAKHOUSE 407/934-3818 (28)

Steak. Casual Dining. **Address:** 1700 Epcot Resorts Blvd 32830

LAKE CITY (B-8) pop. 12,046, elev. 197'

Prior to 1830, Lake City was called Alpata Telophka, or Alligator Village, by its original residents, the Seminole Tribe of Florida. Sixty miles west of Jacksonville, today Lake City also is known as "The Gateway to Florida," since many tourists drive through the town via I-75 and I-10 on their way to destinations further south.

Stop here for some outdoor fun: Ride a bike or hike on trails along the Suwanee River or hit the links at several local country clubs. Be inspired by football player and sportscaster Pat Summerall, who hailed from Lake City and played baseball, basketball, football and tennis at Columbia High School.

BEST WESTERN PLUS LAKE CITY 386/754-5944

Hotel

AAA Benefit: Members save up to 15% and earn bonus points!

Address: 350 SW Florida Gateway Dr 32024 **Location:** I-75 exit 427, just w on US 90. **Facility:** 60 units. 3 stories, interior corridors. **Pool:** heated indoor. **Activities:** exercise room. **Guest Services:** valet and coin laundry.

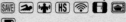

FAIRFIELD INN & SUITES BY MARRIOTT LAKE CITY 386/466-1014

Hotel

Fairfield **AAA Benefit:** Members save 5% or more!

Address: 538 SW Corporate Dr 32055 **Location:** I-75 exit 427, just w to Florida Gateway Blvd, 0.5 mi s, then w. **Facility:** 89 units. 4 stories, interior corridors. **Pool:** heated indoor. **Activities:** hot tub, exercise room. **Guest Services:** valet and coin laundry. **Featured Amenity:** breakfast buffet.

SAVE ECO CALL BIZ HS

HAMPTON INN & SUITES LAKE CITY 386/487-0580

SAVE Hotel. **Address:** 450 SW Florida Gateway Dr 32024

AAA Benefit: Members save 5% or more!

HOLIDAY INN HOTEL & SUITES 386/754-1411

Hotel. **Address:** 213 SW Commerce Dr 32025

HOME2 SUITES BY HILTON 386/487-9890

SAVE Extended Stay Hotel. **Address:** 414 SW Florida Gateway Dr 32024

AAA Benefit: Members save 5% or more!

WHERE TO EAT

KEN'S BAR-B-QUE 386/752-5919

Barbecue. Casual Dining. **Address:** 1659 W US 90 32056

MARION STREET BISTRO & BREW HOUSE 386/487-6194

American. Casual Dining. **Address:** 281 N Marion Ave 32055

SONNY'S REAL PIT BAR-B-Q 386/752-1117

Barbecue. Casual Dining. **Address:** 3177 W US Hwy 90 32055

LAKELAND (E-9) pop. 97,422, elev. 227'

• Hotels p. 138 • Restaurants p. 140

Lakeland encompasses 13 lakes that provide many opportunities for fishing, boating and water skiing. The area also offers pleasant surroundings for such sports as golf and tennis. Long known for its citrus growing and phosphate mining industries, Lakeland also boasts an infusion of high-tech and service industries into the commercial mix.

The world's largest group of buildings designed by Frank Lloyd Wright is on the Florida Southern College campus at 750 Frank Lloyd Wright Way. The 1938 Annie Pfeiffer Chapel was the first structure here; others were patterned after its "Child of the Sun" theme. The Sharp Family Tourism and Education Center has exhibits about Wright's work. Maps for a self-guiding tour are available at the center or outside the administration building; phone (863) 680-4597 for information on guided tours.

Hollis Garden, 702 E. Orange St., is a formal botanical garden that includes water features, a koi pond, a butterfly garden, ornamental shrubs, flowering plants and herbs; phone (863) 834-2280. Barnett Family Park, adjacent to Hollis Garden, has several play areas for children, including a water park, a labyrinth, swings and large sculptures.

During March the city is the spring-training camp for baseball's Detroit Tigers, and from April through August it is the home of the Lakeland Flying Tigers. Exhibition games are played at Publix Field at Joker Marchant Stadium; phone (863) 686-8075 or (866) 668-4437. Ice hockey games, concerts, ballet performances and trade shows are among the entertainment presented at The Lakeland Center, 701 W. Lime St.; phone (863) 834-8111 for ticket information.

In mid-April, Lakeland is the site of the 5-day Sun 'n Fun International Fly-In & Expo, which attracts visitors and vendors from around the world. In addition to 500 commercial exhibitors, there are workshops, forums and daily air shows, and the exhibits and aircraft of the Aerospace Discovery at the Florida Air Museum *(see attraction listing this page)*. For information, phone (863) 644-2431.

Lakeland Area Chamber of Commerce: 35 Lake Morton Dr., Lakeland, FL 33801. **Phone:** (863) 688-8551.

Self-guiding tours: Information about tours of the downtown historic district is available from the chamber of commerce.

Shopping: Lakeland Square Mall, off I-4 exit 32 at 3800 US 98N, contains Dillard's, JCPenney and Sears. Art and antique lovers can find an eclectic choice of shops and dealers in the city's antiques district, 2 blocks north of Main Street along Kentucky Avenue and Pine Street.

AEROSPACE DISCOVERY AT THE FLORIDA AIR MUSEUM is at 4175 Medulla Rd. at the Lakeland Linder Regional Airport. The museum houses collectible aircraft including many unusual experimental and homebuilt models. Amphibious aircraft, biplanes, sailplanes, sports planes, ultralights, simulators and a collection of aircraft engines are among the items on display. Visitors can see aeronautical memorabilia from the collection of tycoon Howard Hughes. An interactive activity area features S.T.E.M. learning stations and immersive aerospace activities. Interactive smartphone tours are available.

Time: Allow 1 hour minimum. **Hours:** Tues.-Sat. 10-4 (also Mon. 10-4, Nov.-Apr.), Sun. noon-4. Closed Easter, Thanksgiving and Christmas. **Cost:** $12; $10 (ages 55+ and active military with ID); $8 (ages 6-17); free (ages 0-5 and active military with ID). **Phone:** (863) 644-6833. GT

COURTYARD BY MARRIOTT LAKELAND 863/802-9000

Hotel

COURTYARD **AAA Benefit:** Members save 5% or more!

Address: 3725 Harden Blvd 33803 **Location:** SR 570 (Polk Pkwy) exit 5, just n on SR 563. **Facility:** 78 units. 3 stories, interior corridors. **Pool:** outdoor. **Activities:** exercise room. **Guest Services:** valet and coin laundry, boarding pass kiosk.

SAVE CALL   BIZ HS

DAYS INN & SUITES 863/683-5095

Hotel

Address: 4502 N Socrum Loop Rd 33809 **Location:** I-4 exit 33, 0.6 mi sw via access road, just nw on CR 582. **Facility:** 72 units, some two bedrooms. 3 stories, interior corridors. **Amenities:** safes. **Pool:** outdoor. **Guest Services:** valet and coin laundry. **Featured Amenity: full hot breakfast.**

SAVE CALL  BIZ HS

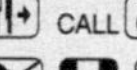 

ECCO SUITES LAKELAND 863/904-2050

Extended Stay Hotel. **Address:** 4360 Lakeland Park Dr 33809

For exclusive AAA member savings and benefits:

AAA.com/hertz

HAMPTON INN & SUITES LAKELAND-SOUTH/POLK PARKWAY 863/603-7600

Hotel

AAA Benefit: Members save 5% or more!

Address: 3630 Lakeside Village Blvd 33803 **Location:** SR 570 (Polk Pkwy) exit 5, 0.4 mi n on Harden Blvd (SR 563), then just w on Town Center Dr. **Facility:** 117 units. 6 stories, interior corridors. **Amenities:** video games. **Pool:** heated outdoor. **Activities:** exercise room. **Guest Services:** valet and coin laundry. **Featured Amenity: full hot breakfast.** *(See ad this page.)*

SAVE  CALL  BIZ HS  

/SOME UNITS

HAMPTON INN LAKELAND 863/816-2525

Hotel

AAA Benefit: Members save 5% or more!

Address: 4420 N Socrum Loop Rd 33809 **Location:** I-4 exit 33, 0.6 mi s on SR 33, then just nw. **Facility:** 73 units. 3 stories, interior corridors. **Pool:** heated outdoor. **Activities:** limited exercise equipment. **Guest Services:** valet and coin laundry. **Featured Amenity: breakfast buffet.**

SAVE CALL  BIZ HS

HILTON GARDEN INN LAKELAND 863/647-0066

SAVE Hotel. **Address:** 3839 Don Emerson Dr 33811

AAA Benefit: Members save 5% or more!

HOLIDAY INN EXPRESS & SUITES LAKELAND NORTH 863/595-4500

Hotel. **Address:** 4500 Lakeland Park Dr 33809

LAKESIDE VILLAGE HOTELS IN LAKELAND

Both hotels are next to each other in Lakeside Village which features many dining and shopping options.

Hampton Inn & Suites Lakeland-South/Polk Parkway
3630 Lakeside Village Blvd
Lakeland, FL 33803
863-603-7600

- Guest Rooms and Suites
- Free Hot Breakfast and WiFi
- Outdoor Pool & Fitness Room

Home2 Suites Lakeland-South
3610 Lakeside Village Blvd
Lakeland, FL 33803
863-500-6869

- All Suites Hotel
- Pet Friendly*
- Free Breakfast and WiFi

*Fees Apply

HOME2 SUITES LAKELAND-SOUTH 863/500-6869

Extended Stay Hotel

AAA Benefit: Members save 5% or more!

Address: 3610 Lakeside Village Blvd 33803 **Location:** SR 570 (Polk Pkwy) exit 5, 0.4 mi n on Harden Blvd (SR 563), then just w on Town Center Dr. **Facility:** 110 units, some efficiencies and kitchens. 4 stories, interior corridors. **Pool:** heated outdoor. **Activities:** exercise room. **Guest Services:** valet and coin laundry. **Featured Amenity: breakfast buffet.** *(See ad p. 138.)*

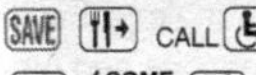 CALL 

/ SOME UNITS

RESIDENCE INN BY MARRIOTT LAKELAND 863/680-2323

Extended Stay Hotel

AAA Benefit: Members save 5% or more!

Address: 3701 Harden Blvd 33803 **Location:** SR 570 (Polk Pkwy) exit 5, just n on SR 563. **Facility:** 78 kitchen units, some two bedrooms. 3 stories, interior corridors. **Pool:** outdoor. **Activities:** hot tub, exercise room. **Guest Services:** valet and coin laundry. **Featured Amenity: continental breakfast.**

 CALL 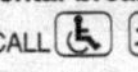  

/ SOME UNITS

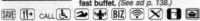

HYATT PLACE LAKELAND 863/413-1122

Hotel

AAA Benefit: Members save up to 10%!

Address: 525 SW Orange St 33815 **Location:** I-4 exit 31, 2.6 mi se on Kathleen Rd, then just w; adjacent to The Lakeland Center. **Facility:** 127 units. 6 stories, interior corridors. **Pool:** heated outdoor. **Activities:** exercise room. **Guest Services:** valet laundry. **Featured Amenity: breakfast buffet.** *(See ad this page.)*

 CALL  

/ SOME UNITS

STAYBRIDGE SUITES-LAKELAND WEST 863/225-2886

Extended Stay Hotel. **Address:** 3855 Don Emerson Dr 33811

TOWNEPLACE SUITES BY MARRIOTT LAKELAND 863/680-1115

Extended Stay Hotel

AAA Benefit: Members save 5% or more!

Address: 3370 N US Hwy 98 33805 **Location:** I-4 exit 32, just n; in Lakeland Crossing. **Facility:** 112 units, some efficiencies and kitchens. 4 stories, interior corridors. **Pool:** heated outdoor. **Activities:** exercise room. **Guest Services:** valet and coin laundry. **Featured Amenity: breakfast buffet.**

 CALL   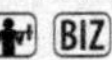

/ SOME UNITS

▼ *See AAA listing this page* ▼

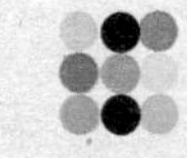

Enjoy a relaxing and easy stay with amenities that help you live life your way.

- Spacious guest rooms
- Plush Hyatt Grand Bed®
- 24/7 Gallery Menu and Coffee to Cocktails Bar
- 24-hour StayFit™ Gym
- State-of-the-art media and work centers
- 42″ HDTV
- Free Wi-Fi and remote printing

HYATT PLACE LAKELAND
525 W. Orange Street
Lakeland, FL 33815
863-413-1122
hyattplacelakelandcenter.com

TRAVELODGE LAKELAND 863/858-4481

Motel. **Address:** 3425 Hwy 98 N 33809

WHERE TO EAT

THE CHOP SHOP BAR & GRILL HOT ROD CAFE 863/603-4040

Burgers Sandwiches. Casual Dining. **Address:** 118 S Kentucky Ave 33801

COUNTRY CHICKEN 'N FISH 863/686-2564

Chicken Seafood. Quick Serve. **Address:** 1263 Kathleen Rd 33805

CRISPERS 863/682-7708

Sandwiches Soup. Quick Serve. **Address:** 217 N Kentucky Ave 33801

DIVICIOUS DELI & COFFEE SHOP 863/940-9779

Sandwiches Coffee/Tea. Quick Serve. **Address:** 128 E Main 33801

FORD'S GARAGE 863/337-3673

American. Casual Dining. **Address:** 879 Lakeland Park Center Dr 33809

FRED'S MARKET RESTAURANT 863/603-7080

Southern Comfort Food. Buffet Style. **Address:** 2120 Harden Blvd 33803

HARRY'S SEAFOOD BAR GRILLE 863/686-2228

Cajun. Casual Dining. **Address:** 101 N Kentucky Ave 33801

KING'S WOK 863/816-8187

Chinese. Quick Serve. **Address:** 5383 N Socrum Loop Rd 33809

LOUIS PAPPAS MARKET CAFE 863/284-1010

Greek. Quick Serve. **Address:** 1318 Town Center Dr 33803

MANNYS ORIGINAL CHOPHOUSE 863/940-9924

American. Casual Dining. **Address:** 5125 S Florida Ave 33813

PALACE PIZZA DOWNTOWN 863/688-0045

Italian. Casual Dining. **Address:** 114 S Kentucky Ave 33801

PIZZERIA VALDIANO 863/686-3730

Italian. Quick Serve. **Address:** 1610 NW Town Center Dr 33803

SONNY'S REAL PIT BAR-B-Q

Barbecue. Casual Dining.

LOCATIONS:

Address: 3611 US Hwy 98 N 33809 **Phone:** 863/853-8283

Address: 5910 Florida Ave S 33813 **Phone:** 863/646-2990

TACO BUS 863/333-4139

Mexican. Quick Serve. **Address:** 126 S Kentucky Ave 33801

TAPATIO'S RESTAURANTE MEXICANO 863/646-2199

Mexican. Casual Dining. **Address:** 6645 S Florida Ave 33813

TAPATIO'S RESTAURANTE MEXICANO 863/686-6958

Mexican Casual Dining $7-$26

AAA Inspector Notes: Lunch and dinner are busy times at this eatery, where vibrant and colorful murals decorate the walls and set the festive tone. Sizzling plates of fajitas and enormous burritos are the norm. Those who are not in a hurry might try the Cajun plate, which offers seven jumbo shrimp stuffed with cheese and rolled in bacon. Fresh homemade chips and salsa are brought to your table as you wait for your meal to be prepared. **Features:** full bar, patio dining, happy hour. **Address:** 734 E Memorial Blvd 33801 **Location:** 0.3 mi e of jct US 98 and 92.

L D CALL

THAI OISHI AUTHENTIC THAI SUSHI AND SEAFOOD 863/333-0657

Thai Sushi. Casual Dining. **Address:** 1535 Town Center Dr 33803

LAKE MARY (F-4) pop. 13,822, elev. 62'

• **Hotels & Restaurants map & index p. 188**
• **Part of Orlando area — see map p. 2**

The "City of Lakes" bustles with weekday commuters employed at thriving businesses representing high-tech, telemarketing and other concerns. This Orlando bedroom community also accommodates travelers who want to make a base within an hour's drive of east coast beaches and the theme parks. Restaurants and boutiques border Central Park (100 N. Country Club Rd.), where visitors can relish the small-town vibe at the Saturday morning farmers market and at WineART Wednesday evenings (first week of the month).

CANDLEWOOD SUITES LAKE MARY 407/585-3000 29

Extended Stay Hotel. **Address:** 1130 Greenwood Blvd 32746

HAMPTON INN & SUITES LAKE MARY AT COLONIAL TOWNPARK 407/995-9000 23

SAVE Hotel. **Address:** 850 Village Oak Ln 32746

AAA Benefit: Members save 5% or more!

HILTON GARDEN INN ORLANDO NORTH/LAKE MARY 407/531-9900 27

Hotel

Hilton Garden Inn **AAA Benefit:** Members save 5% or more!

Address: 705 Currency Cir 32746 **Location:** I-4 exit 98, just ne via Lake Mary and Primera blvds. **Facility:** 123 units. 3 stories, interior corridors. **Pool:** heated outdoor. **Activities:** hot tub, exercise room. **Guest Services:** valet and coin laundry, area transportation.

SAVE CALL

HYATT PLACE LAKE MARY/ORLANDO-NORTH 407/995-5555 28

Hotel

HYATT PLACE **AAA Benefit:** Members save up to 10%!

Address: 1255 S International Pkwy 32746 **Location:** I-4 exit 98, just w. **Facility:** 128 units. 4 stories, interior corridors. **Amenities:** safes. **Pool:** heated outdoor. **Activities:** hot tub, exercise room. **Guest Services:** valet and coin laundry, area transportation. **Featured Amenity: breakfast buffet.**

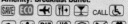

SAVE ECO CALL BIZ HS / SOME UNITS

(See map & index p. 188.)

ORLANDO MARRIOTT LAKE MARY

407/995-1100 25

Hotel

AAA Benefit: Members save 5% or more!

Address: 1501 International Pkwy 32746 **Location:** I-4 exit 101A, just w. **Facility:** 304 units. 10 stories, interior corridors. **Dining:** Bistro 1501, see separate listing. **Pool:** heated outdoor. **Activities:** hot tub, exercise room. **Guest Services:** valet and coin laundry, area transportation. *(See ad this page.)*

SAVE ECO CALL BIZ HS / SOME UNITS

RESIDENCE INN BY MARRIOTT-ORLANDO LAKE MARY

407/995-3400 26

SAVE Extended Stay Contemporary Hotel. **Address:** 825 Heathrow Park Ln 32746

AAA Benefit: Members save 5% or more!

Make the Connection

Find this symbol for places to look, book and save on AAA.com.

THE WESTIN LAKE MARY, ORLANDO NORTH

407/531-3555 24

Hotel

AAA Benefit: Members save 5% or more!

Address: 2974 International Pkwy 32746 **Location:** I-4 exit 101A, 0.5 mi w. **Facility:** 253 units. 7 stories, interior corridors. **Amenities:** safes. **Dining:** Shula's 347, see separate listing. **Pool:** heated outdoor. **Activities:** hot tub, exercise room. **Guest Services:** valet laundry, rental car service, area transportation.

SAVE BIZ / SOME UNITS

WHERE TO EAT

4TH STREET GRILL 407/732-6979 83

American. Casual Dining. **Address:** 132 N 4th St, Suite 1200 32746

AMURA 407/936-6001 72

Japanese Sushi. Casual Dining. **Address:** 950 Market Promenade Ave 32746

APPLETON'S CAFE 407/323-7663 85

Comfort Food. Casual Dining. **Address:** 3575 W Lake Mary Blvd 32746

BISTRO 1501 407/995-7053 79

New American. Fine Dining. **Address:** 1501 International Pkwy 32746

CHENG'S CHINESE RESTAURANT 407/333-0099 92

Chinese. Casual Dining. **Address:** 3705 Lake Emma Rd 32746

DALLI'S RESTAURANT & PIZZERIA 407/302-2707 82

Italian Pizza. Casual Dining. **Address:** 101 N Country Club Rd, #111 32746

DEXTER'S 407/805-3090

New American. Casual Dining. **Address:** 950 Market Promenade Ave, Suite 1201 32746

▼ See AAA listing this page ▼

1501 INTERNATIONAL PARKWAY
LAKE MARY, FLORIDA 32746
407.995.1100

MARRIOTT
ORLANDO LAKE MARY

LET YOUR MIND TRAVEL IN REDESIGNED GUEST ROOMS

Experience newly renovated accommodations, on-site dining, Bistro 1501 open for breakfast, lunch and dinner. Cobalt's Martini Bar serving light fare and Expresso Lounge, proudly serving Starbucks Coffee. Complimentary self-parking and complimentary Wi-Fi.

Call your travel agent or 1-800-380-7724 or visit Marriott.com/MCOML.

(See map & index p. 188.)

DIGINO'S PIZZA 407/333-2733 (89)

Pizza Sandwiches. Casual Dining. **Address:** 3895 Lake Emma Rd, Suite 151 32746

DON JULIO 321/363-0025 (90)

Mexican. Casual Dining. **Address:** 4275 W Lake Mary Blvd 32746

F&D KITCHEN & BAR 407/915-5687 (78)

New American. Gastropub. **Address:** 1541 International Pkwy 32746

FISHBONES 407/581-2399 (76)

Seafood Steak. Fine Dining. **Address:** 7005 CR 46A 32746

FRED'S MARKET RESTAURANT 407/915-6808

Southern Comfort Food. Buffet Style. **Address:** 835 Currency Cir 32746

GATOR'S DOCKSIDE 407/330-2557

American. Casual Dining. **Address:** 4349 W Lake Mary Blvd 32746

GIOVANNI'S ITALIAN RESTAURANT & PIZZERIA 407/330-4350 (80)

Italian. Casual Dining. **Address:** 875 Rinehart Rd 32746

GRATO ITALIAN GRILL & PIZZERIA 407/268-3715 (86)

Italian Pizza. Casual Dining. **Address:** 3801 W Lake Mary Blvd 32746

THE GREEK VILLAGE RESTAURANT 407/333-3776 (94)

Greek. Casual Dining. **Address:** 3577 Lake Emma Rd, Suite 111 32746

KELLER'S REAL SMOKED BAR-B-Q 407/333-1444 (88)

Barbecue. Casual Dining. **Address:** 3893 Lake Emma Rd 32746

KRAZY GREEK KITCHEN 407/330-7482 (81)

Greek. Casual Dining. **Address:** 142 W Lakeview Ave, Suite 1000 32746

LA ANTIOQUENA RESTAURANT 407/829-2532 (91)

Colombian. Casual Dining. **Address:** 3861 Lake Emma Rd 32746

LIAM FITZPATRICK'S IRISH RESTAURANT & PUB 407/936-3782 (73)

Irish. Sports Bar. **Address:** 951 Market Promenade Ave 32746

LONNIES FUSION CUISINE 407/878-5804 (84)

Regional American. Casual Dining. **Address:** 124 N Fourth St 32746

PAPA JOE'S PIZZA 407/323-9222 (87)

Italian Pizza. Casual Dining. **Address:** 4205 Lake Mary Blvd 32746

PAPA JOE'S PIZZA - COLONIAL TOWNPARK 407/936-3300 (69)

Italian Pizza. Casual Dining. **Address:** 960 Colonial Grand Ln 32746

RUTH'S CHRIS STEAK HOUSE 407/804-8220 (75)

Steak. Fine Dining. **Address:** 80 Colonial Center Pkwy 32746

SHULA'S 347 407/531-3567 (74)

Steak. Casual Dining. **Address:** 2974 International Pkwy 32746

TERRAMIA BRICK OVEN PIZZA 407/333-1233 (77)

Italian Pizza. Casual Dining. **Address:** 7025 CR 46A, Suite 1051 32746

THAI CORNER RESTAURANT 407/833-8066 (93)

Thai
Casual Dining
$9-$19

AAA Inspector Notes: Tucked in a plaza with chain restaurants and markets, the unobtrusive eatery has been serving up flavorful Thai dishes for years. Dark woods, rust color accents and soft background music create a calming aura for patrons. The menu features traditional favorites such as tom yum soup, fried rice and pad thai. Appetizers include crispy thai spring rolls and the ever-popular crab rangoons. Several vegetarian options are offered. Staff is friendly and take out is available. **Features:** beer & wine. **Address:** 3589 Lake Emma Rd 32746 **Location:** I-4 exit 98, just e to Lake Emma Rd, then 0.3 mi s; in Lake Mary Centre.

(L) (D)

TIJUANA FLATS 407/328-0907

Tex-Mex. Quick Serve. **Address:** 3005 W Lake Mary Blvd 32746

TOOJAY'S GOURMET DELI 407/833-0848

American. Casual Dining. **Address:** 3577 Lake Emma Rd 32746

THE VINEYARD WINE COMPANY 407/833-9463 (71)

New American. Casual Dining. **Address:** 1140 TownPark Ave, Suite 1260 32746

LAKE PLACID (I-4) pop. 2,223, elev. 136'

Lake Stearns was renamed Lake Placid in the late 1920s by Melvil Dewey, creator of the Dewey Decimal Classification, a system for cataloging library books. A resident of Lake Placid, N.Y., Dewey wintered in Florida and was instrumental in the town's development as a resort. The town boasts dozens of murals that depict the area's history and ecology. It is also the Caladium Capital of the World.

Lake Placid is surrounded by 29 freshwater lakes that provide innumerable opportunities for fishing and boating. Lake June-in-Winter Scrub State Park is approximately 7 miles west off US 27; phone (863) 386-6099.

Greater Lake Placid Chamber of Commerce and Welcome Center: 18 N. Oak Ave., Lake Placid, FL 33852. **Phone:** (863) 465-4331.

THE MURALS OF LAKE PLACID are downtown. Forty-six colorful murals (some with sound) depict the history and ecology of the town and surrounding area. The artwork adorns town buildings and other structures, including fences and trash cans. Booklets for self-guiding tours can be purchased at shops and from the chamber of commerce, 18 N. Oak Ave. **Time:** Allow 1 hour minimum. **Hours:** A 10-minute orientation video plays at the chamber office Mon.-Fri. 9-4, Apr.-Dec.; 9-1, rest of year. **Cost:** Free. **Phone:** (863) 465-4331.

HOLIDAY INN EXPRESS & SUITES LAKE PLACID 863/465-9916

Hotel. **Address:** 608 S Lakeview Rd 33852

WHERE TO EAT

CHEF BUDDY'S ITALIAN AMERICAN DELI 863/465-6800

Sandwiches Pizza. Quick Serve. **Address:** 381 E Interlake Blvd 33852

LAKE WALES (E-10) pop. 14,225, elev. 252'

On North Wales Drive at Dr. J.A. Whiltshire Drive in Lake Wales a bizarre phenomenon occurs: Through optical illusion, cars appear to roll uphill. To experience this mystery, park your car at the bottom of the incline known as Spook Hill and release the brake.

It is said that the Spook Hill mystery stems from a Seminole legend in which Chief Cufcowellax and his tribe settled on Lake Wailes. Soon a huge bull alligator moved into the lake and regularly attacked the Native Americans. Aided by the Great Spirit, the chief stalked the beast and engaged him in a monthlong battle, after which the chief rose from the water in victory.

During the battle a small lake, now Crystal Lake, appeared next to the big one. The chief was later buried on the shores of the new lake. Some attribute the Spook Hill enigma to the alligator seeking revenge, while others speculate that Cufcowellax has returned to defend his homeland from encroachment.

Housed in a 1927 mission-style structure that served as a Catholic church for 60 years, Polk State College's Lake Wales Arts Center at 1099 SR 60 E. provides gallery and performance space for actors and artists; phone (863) 298-6883 or (863) 676-8426. Florida's Natural Grove House Visitor Center at 20160 US 27 offers displays and video presentations about the citrus industry and information about local attractions, as well as a free glass of juice; phone (863) 679-4110.

Lake Wales Area Chamber of Commerce: 340 W. Central Ave., Lake Wales, FL 33859. **Phone:** (863) 676-3445.

Shopping: Dillard's and JCPenney are the anchor stores at Eagle Ridge Mall, 5 miles north on US 27 to 451 Eagle Ridge Dr. Art galleries, antique shops and specialty stores can be found in the downtown Lake Wales Historic District, 2 blocks east of US 27.

BOK TOWER GARDENS, 3 mi. n. off CR 17A (Burns Ave.) at 1151 Tower Blvd., consists of 250 acres with Olmsted-designed gardens, a 205-foot marble and coquina bell tower and Pinewood Estate, a Mediterranean-style mansion. One of Florida's oldest attractions, the tower and gardens were dedicated to the American people in 1929 by President Calvin Coolidge on behalf of founder Edward Bok, a Dutch immigrant. New gardens include a children's garden and a Florida wild garden and bog.

Other features include daily concerts from the 60-bell carillon, a nature observatory and Pine Ridge Nature Preserve Trail. The visitor center presents art exhibits, an orientation film and exhibits about the Bok legacy, the carillon, and endangered plants and animals found on the property.

Hours: Gardens daily 8-6. Last admission 1 hour before closing. Visitor center daily 9-5. Pinewood Estate tours daily 11-3, in summer; otherwise varies. Carillon concerts are given at 1 and 3. Phone ahead to confirm schedule. **Cost:** $14; $5 (ages 5-12); free (active military with ID and to veterans on Veteran's Day, Memorial Day, July 4 and Armed Forces Day). Gardens and Pinewood Estate $20; $10 (ages 5-12). **Phone:** (863) 676-1408 or (863) 734-1222. GT 🍴 ⛱

HAMPTON INN & SUITES LAKE WALES 863/734-3000

◆◆◆ SAVE Contemporary Hotel. **Address:** 22900 Hwy 27 33859

AAA Benefit: Members save 5% or more!

WHERE TO EAT

BLUE PALMETTO CAFE 863/676-1355

◆ American. Quick Serve. **Address:** 1151 Tower Blvd 33853

CRAZY FISH BAR & GRILL 863/676-6361

◆◆ Seafood. Casual Dining. **Address:** 802 Henry St 33853

LAND O' LAKES pop. 31,996

• Part of Tampa area — see map p. 313

SPRINGHILL SUITES BY MARRIOTT TAMPA NORTH, LAND O'LAKES 813/536-1900

◆◆◆ SAVE Hotel. **Address:** 16615 Crosspointe Run 34638

AAA Benefit: Members save 5% or more!

LARGO (E-8) pop. 77,648, elev. 50'

• Hotels p. 144 • Restaurants p. 144
• Hotels & Restaurants map & index p. 286
• Part of St. Petersburg-Clearwater and Beaches area — see map p. 275

Largo is bordered on three sides by water—the Gulf of Mexico circles around the west and south sides, and Tampa Bay is on the eastern border. In 1905 when it became a city, it had 291 residents and covered 1 square mile.

Tee off at Bardmoor Golf and Tennis Club, 8001 Cumberland Rd., or at East Bay Golf Club, 702 Country Club Dr.; phone (727) 392-1234 or (727) 581-3333, respectively. City-run Largo Golf Course, 12500 N. Vonn Rd., offers nine holes; phone (727) 518-3024.

Central Pinellas Chamber of Commerce: 801 W. Bay Center, Suite 602, Largo, FL 33770. **Phone:** (727) 584-2321.

Shopping: Catch some rays while browsing clothing, jewelry and books at the Largo Mall. The open-air shopping center on the corner of Ulmerton Road (SR 688) and Seminole Boulevard is home to a cinema and more than 70 other businesses, including eateries, local boutiques, and such chain retailers as Bealls and Marshalls.

HERITAGE VILLAGE is at 11909 125th St. N. Thirty-three restored structures on the grounds of this 21-acre living-history museum depict life during the early days of Pinellas County. **Hours:** Wed.-Sat.

(See map & index p. 286.)

10-4, Sun. 1-4. Closed major holidays. **Cost:** Donations. **Phone:** (727) 582-2123.

HOLIDAY INN EXPRESS & SUITES LARGO CENTRAL PARK 727/581-3900 52

Hotel. **Address:** 210 Seminole Blvd 33770

WHERE TO EAT

CAFÉ CLASSICO EXPRESS 727/538-5240 77

Italian. Quick Serve. **Address:** 3200 E Bay Dr N 33771

CARMELITA'S MEXICAN RESTAURANT 727/533-8555

Mexican. Casual Dining. **Address:** 7705 Ulmerton Rd 33771

THE HAUS COFFEE SHOP 727/333-7999 75

Coffee/Tea Sandwiches. Quick Serve. **Address:** 3690 E Bay Dr, Suite Y 33771

ROOSTERFISH GRILL 727/584-5888 76

Seafood. Casual Dining. **Address:** 776 Missouri Ave N 33770

SAGES WEST BAY BISTRO 727/585-6600 79

Italian. Casual Dining. **Address:** 883 W Bay Dr 33770

SONNY'S REAL PIT BAR-B-Q 727/501-9000

Barbecue. Casual Dining. **Address:** 2250 Seminole Blvd 33778

TIJUANA FLATS 727/210-1190

Tex-Mex. Quick Serve. **Address:** 180 S Belcher Rd 33771

ZIO'S ITALIAN MARKET DELI & BAKERY 727/536-2119 78

Italian. Quick Serve. **Address:** 2575 E Bay Dr 33771

LEESBURG pop. 20,117

• Part of Orlando area — see map p. 2

BEST WESTERN PLUS CHAIN OF LAKES INN & SUITES 352/460-0118

Hotel

AAA Benefit: Members save up to 15% and earn bonus points!

Address: 1321 N 14th St 34748 **Location:** Jct US 27 and 441. **Facility:** 70 units. 3 stories, interior corridors. **Amenities:** safes. **Pool:** outdoor. **Activities:** hot tub, exercise room. **Guest Services:** valet and coin laundry. **Featured Amenity: full hot breakfast.**

SAVE CALL BIZ HS

/ SOME UNITS

HAMPTON INN LEESBURG/TAVARES 352/315-1053

SAVE Hotel. **Address:** 9630 US Hwy 441 34788

AAA Benefit: Members save 5% or more!

MICROTEL INN & SUITES BY WYNDHAM LEESBURG/MT. DORA 352/315-1234

Hotel. **Address:** 9700 US Hwy 441 34788

WHERE TO EAT

NAPLES ITALIAN RESTAURANT 352/323-1616

Italian. Casual Dining. **Address:** 1107 W North Blvd 34748

OAKWOOD SMOKEHOUSE & GRILL 352/435-4633

Barbecue. Casual Dining. **Address:** 27745 S Hwy 27 34748

LIVE OAK pop. 6,850

HOLIDAY INN EXPRESS HOTEL & SUITES 386/362-2600

Hotel

Address: 6694 US 129 N 32060 **Location:** I-10 exit 283, just s. **Facility:** 69 units. 3 stories, interior corridors. **Pool:** outdoor. **Activities:** exercise room. **Guest Services:** coin laundry. **Featured Amenity: breakfast buffet.**

SAVE CALL BIZ HS

LONGBOAT KEY pop. 6,888

• Hotels & Restaurants map & index p. 300

THE RESORT AT LONGBOAT KEY CLUB 941/383-8821 47

Resort Condominium

Address: 220 Sands Point Rd 34228 **Location:** Oceanfront. On SR 789, just n of New Pass Bridge. **Facility:** Situated along a wide strip of scenic beach, this sprawling resort offers extensive recreational amenities. Each guest unit has a private balcony with a view of the beach or surrounding countryside. 226 condominiums. 4-10 stories, exterior corridors. **Parking:** on-site and valet. **Terms:** check-in 4 pm. **Amenities:** safes. **Dining:** 6 restaurants, entertainment. **Pool:** heated outdoor. **Activities:** hot tub, steamroom, cabanas, self-propelled boats, marina, snorkeling, regulation golf, tennis, recreation programs, kids club, bicycles, playground, lawn sports, trails, health club, spa. **Guest Services:** valet and coin laundry, area transportation.

SAVE ECO CALL BIZ HS

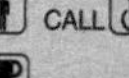

Newly renovated suites, all with private balconies. Golf, tennis, dining, spa, and fitness center.

For getaways off the beaten path, visit AAA.com/campgrounds

iStockphoto.com_pixelfit

(See map & index p. 300.)

ZOTA BEACH RESORT 941/383-2451 (46)

Boutique Contemporary Hotel

Address: 4711 Gulf of Mexico Dr 34228 **Location:** Oceanfront. On SR 789, 5.7 mi se of jct SR 684 (Cortez Rd). **Facility:** This hotel has a fantastic location right on the Gulf of Mexico. It is quite upscale in design and offers a fantastic pool area that overlooks the beach. There is poolside food service and cabanas. 187 units, some two bedrooms. 5-6 stories, interior corridors. **Parking:** valet only. **Terms:** check-in 4 pm. **Amenities:** safes. **Dining:** 2 restaurants. **Pool:** heated outdoor. **Activities:** hot tub, cabanas, health club. **Guest Services:** valet laundry.

SAVE ECO CALL BIZ / SOME UNITS

Located on a breathtaking stretch of white sand beach on Longboat Key. Close to St. Armands Circle.

WHERE TO EAT

CHART HOUSE 941/383-5593 (59)
SAVE Seafood Steak. Fine Dining. **Address:** 201 Gulf of Mexico Dr 34228

DRY DOCK WATERFRONT GRILL 941/383-0102 (58)
Seafood. Casual Dining. **Address:** 412 Gulf of Mexico Dr 34228

EUPHEMIA HAYE RESTAURANT 941/383-3633 (57)
Continental. Fine Dining. **Address:** 5540 Gulf of Mexico Dr 34228

HARRY'S CONTINENTAL KITCHENS 941/383-0777 (56)
Continental. Fine Dining. **Address:** 525 St. Judes Dr 34228

MAR VISTA DOCKSIDE RESTAURANT & PUB 941/383-2391 (55)
Seafood. Casual Dining. **Address:** 760 Broadway St 34228

LONGWOOD pop. 13,657, elev. 75'

- **Hotels & Restaurants map & index p. 188**
- **Part of Orlando area — see map p. 2**

4 RIVERS SMOKEHOUSE 407/474-8377
Barbecue. Quick Serve. **Address:** 1869 W SR 434 32750

BAYRIDGE SUSHI 407/331-0000 (111)
Japanese Sushi. Casual Dining. **Address:** 1000 W SR 434 32750

BONEFISH GRILL 407/331-0131 (113)
Seafood. Fine Dining. **Address:** 1761 W SR 434 32750

CAFE PAISANO 407/767-0011 (108)
Italian. Casual Dining. **Address:** 182 W SR 434, Suite 1000 32750

ENZO'S ON THE LAKE 407/834-9872 (112)
Regional Italian. Fine Dining. **Address:** 1130 S Hwy 17-92 32750

GATEWAY TO INDIA 407/339-9996 (107)
Northern Indian. Casual Dining. **Address:** 790 E SR 434 32750

HURRICANE GRILL & WINGS 407/772-5504 (116)
American. Casual Dining. **Address:** 2401 W SR 434, Suite 141 32779

KOREA HOUSE 407/767-5918 (110)
Korean. Casual Dining. **Address:** 1155 W SR 434 32750

PICKLES AUTHENTIC NEW YORK DELICATESSEN 407/951-8662 (114)
Deli Sandwiches. Casual Dining. **Address:** 1891 W SR 434 32750

THAILICIOUS 321/316-4882 (109)
Thai. Casual Dining. **Address:** 470 W SR 434 32750

VICTORIO'S OYSTER BAR & GRILLE 407/834-9800 (115)
American. Casual Dining. **Address:** 300 Dog Track Rd 32750

LUTZ pop. 19,344

- **Restaurants p. 146**
- **Part of Tampa area — see map p. 313**

HILTON GARDEN INN-TAMPA-SUNCOAST PKWY 813/491-4900
SAVE Hotel. **Address:** 2155 Northpointe Pkwy 33558

AAA Benefit: Members save 5% or more!

HYATT PLACE TAMPA WESLEY CHAPEL IN LUTZ 813/803-5600

Hotel

AAA Benefit: Members save up to 10%!

Address: 26000 Sierra Center Blvd 33559 **Location:** I-75 exit 265, Just w on SR 56. **Facility:** 132 units. 6 stories, interior corridors. **Amenities:** safes. **Pool:** heated outdoor. **Activities:** exercise room. **Guest Services:** valet and coin laundry. **Featured Amenity: breakfast buffet.**

SAVE CALL BIZ HS / SOME UNITS

RESIDENCE INN BY MARRIOTT TAMPA SUNCOAST PARKWAY AT NORTHPOINTE VILLAGE 813/792-8400

Extended Stay Hotel

AAA Benefit: Members save 5% or more!

Address: 2101 NorthPointe Pkwy 33558 **Location:** Suncoast Pkwy exit 19, just e on SR 54, then just ne; in Northpointe at Suncoast Crossings. **Facility:** 100 kitchen units, some two bedrooms. 5 stories, interior corridors. **Terms:** check-in 4 pm. **Pool:** heated outdoor. **Activities:** exercise room. **Guest Services:** valet and coin laundry, boarding pass kiosk. **Featured Amenity: full hot breakfast.**

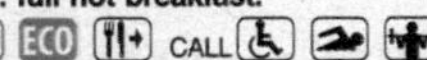

WHERE TO EAT

BANGKOK SUSHI AUTHENTIC THAI CUISINE & SUSHI BAR 813/920-9777

Thai. Casual Dining. **Address:** 16541 Pointe Village Dr 33558

FORD'S GARAGE 813/540-3673

American. Casual Dining. **Address:** 25526 Sierra Center Blvd 33559

MR. EMPANADA 813/908-6232

Cuban. Quick Serve. **Address:** 17693 N Dale Mabry Hwy 33558

SAN JOSE MEXICAN RESTAURANT 813/920-8833

Mexican. Casual Dining. **Address:** 16450 Pointe Village Dr 33558

MADEIRA BEACH (H-1) pop. 4,263, elev. 6'

• Hotels & Restaurants map & index p. 286
• Part of St. Petersburg-Clearwater and Beaches area — see map p. 275

Joined to the mainland near St. Petersburg by a free causeway, Madeira Beach offers good swimming and parasailing as well as personal watercraft rentals. Boats can be chartered from several marinas for fishing in the Gulf of Mexico. Water sports of all kinds, including parasailing, are the focal point at John's Pass Village & Boardwalk, 1.3 mi. s. on Gulf Boulevard at 150 John's Pass Boardwalk.

Shopping: Tourists on the lookout for kitschy gifts and beach essentials lollygag beneath swaying palms and a deluge of rainbow-lettered banners at John's Pass Village & Boardwalk. Slurp a frozen treat while negotiating the nautically themed marketplace offering more than 100 souvenir shops, restaurants, and apparel and accessories stores. After stocking up on sarongs, surf gear and airbrushed T-shirts, lunch at one of the boardwalk's tropical dockside eateries and snap a few photos of the boaters and water sports enthusiasts jetting across the inlet.

BAREFOOT BEACH CLUB 727/393-6133 69

Hotel

Address: 13238 Gulf Blvd 33708 **Location:** Oceanfront. On SR 699, 1.3 mi s of jct SR 666 (Tom Stuart Cswy). **Facility:** 42 units, some two bedrooms and kitchens. 4 stories, exterior corridors. **Pool:** heated outdoor. **Activities:** hot tub. **Guest Services:** coin laundry.

Save on travel, shopping and more: AAA.com/discounts

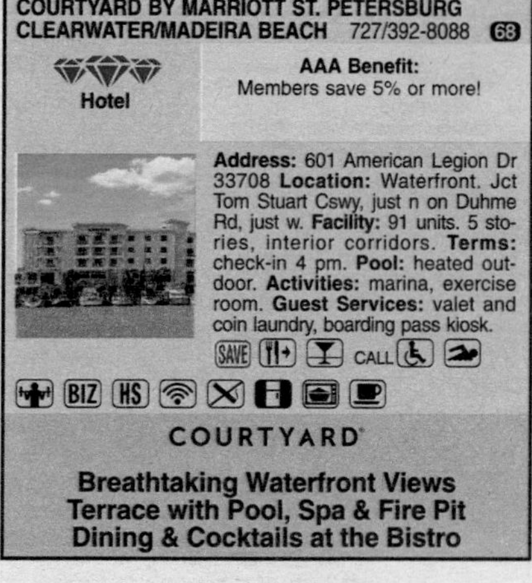

COURTYARD BY MARRIOTT ST. PETERSBURG CLEARWATER/MADEIRA BEACH 727/392-8088 68
Hotel
AAA Benefit:
Members save 5% or more!
Address: 601 American Legion Dr 33708 Location: Waterfront. Jct Tom Stuart Cswy, just n on Duhme Rd, just w. Facility: 91 units. 5 stories, interior corridors. Terms: check-in 4 pm. Pool: heated outdoor. Activities: marina, exercise room. Guest Services: valet and coin laundry, boarding pass kiosk.
SAVE
CALL
BIZ
HS
COURTYARD
Breathtaking Waterfront Views
Terrace with Pool, Spa & Fire Pit
Dining & Cocktails at the Bistro

WHERE TO EAT

DE LOSA'S PIZZA & ITALIAN RESTAURANT 727/398-4657 102

Italian. Quick Serve. **Address:** 12800 Village Blvd 33708

FRIENDLY FISHERMAN WATERFRONT SEAFOOD RESTAURANT 727/391-6025 103

Seafood. Casual Dining. **Address:** 150 John's Pass Boardwalk Pl 33708

THE HUT BAR & GRILL 727/233-3311 101

Sandwiches Burgers. Casual Dining. **Address:** 190 128th Ave E 33708

MAITLAND (F-4) pop. 15,751, elev. 91'

• Hotels & Restaurants map & index p. 188
• Part of Orlando area — see map p. 2

Maitland's 19th-century growth followed a pattern familiar to many central Florida towns. A pioneer fort in the Second Seminole War, the settlement prospered during the citrus-producing era and later swelled as the railroad brought an influx of climate-conscious tourists and entrepreneurs.

The Maitland Historical Museum, 221 W. Packwood Ave., highlights area history in a timeline format and features changing exhibits. The nearby Telephone Museum houses an extensive collection of antique telephones and equipment and traces the growth of the family-owned Winter Park Telephone Co. through photographs, equipment and related memorabilia. For additional information phone Art & History Museums–Maitland at (407) 644-1364.

Audubon Center for Birds of Prey, 1101 Audubon Way, is an urban environmental nature center specializing in the rescue, rehabilitation and release of sick, injured and orphaned birds of prey. The center also is a permanent home to approximately 20 species of raptors that cannot be returned to the wild due to past injuries; phone (407) 644-0190.

Maitland Area Chamber of Commerce: 110 N. Maitland Ave., Maitland, FL 32751. **Phone:** (407) 644-0741.

(See map & index p. 188.)

THE HOLOCAUST MEMORIAL RESOURCE AND EDUCATION CENTER OF FLORIDA is 1.25 mi. e. of I-4 exit 90A at 851 N. Maitland Ave. (jct. Maitland Blvd./SR 414). The center illustrates key events of the Holocaust through chronological displays, photographs and audiovisual presentations. Six lamps and a memorial wall built of Jerusalem stone remember the 6 million Jews who died at the hands of the Nazis. **Time:** Allow 1 hour minimum. **Hours:** Mon.-Thurs. 9-4, Fri. 9-1, Sun. 1-4. Closed major national and Jewish holidays. **Cost:** Free. **Phone:** (407) 628-0555. Maitland, 11

COURTYARD BY MARRIOTT ORLANDO-ALTAMONTE SPRINGS/MAITLAND 407/659-9100 47

Hotel

COURTYARD **AAA Benefit:** Members save 5% or more!

Address: 1750 Pembrook Dr 32810 **Location:** I-4 exit 90B, 0.5 mi w to Keller Rd, just s Pembrook Dr, then just w. **Facility:** 112 units. 4 stories, interior corridors. **Terms:** check-in 4 pm. **Pool:** heated outdoor. **Activities:** exercise room. **Guest Services:** complimentary and valet laundry, boarding pass kiosk, area transportation.

SAVE ECO BIZ / SOME UNITS

HOMEWOOD SUITES BY HILTON-ORLANDO NORTH/MAITLAND 407/875-8777 48

SAVE Extended Stay Hotel. **Address:** 290 Southhall Ln 32751

AAA Benefit: Members save 5% or more!

SHERATON ORLANDO NORTH 407/660-9000 46

Hotel

SHERATON **AAA Benefit:** Members save 5% or more!

Address: 600 N Lake Destiny Dr 32751 **Location:** I-4 exit 90B, just w. **Facility:** 389 units, some two bedrooms. 6 stories, interior corridors. **Parking:** on-site (fee). **Amenities:** safes. **Dining:** 4 restaurants. **Pool:** heated outdoor. **Activities:** hot tub, exercise room. **Guest Services:** valet laundry, rental car service, area transportation.

SAVE ECO CALL

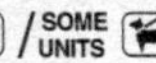

BIZ / SOME UNITS

WHERE TO EAT

ANTONIO'S MARKET & CAFE DOWNSTAIRS 407/645-1039 131

Italian. Casual Dining. **Address:** 611 S Orlando Ave 32751

ANTONIO'S UPSTAIRS 407/645-5523 132

Italian. Fine Dining. **Address:** 611 S Orlando Ave 32751

FRANCESCO'S RISTORANTE & PIZZERIA 407/960-5533 130

Italian. Fine Dining. **Address:** 400 S Orlando Ave, Suite 104 32751

KAPPY'S 407/647-9099 129

American. Quick Serve. **Address:** 501 N Orlando Ave 32751

SAM SNEAD'S OAK GRILL & TAVERN 407/622 - 8800

American. Casual Dining. **Address:** 1801 Maitland Blvd 32810

MELBOURNE (D-11) pop. 76,068, elev. 21'

• **Hotels p. 150 • Restaurants p. 151**
• **Hotels & Restaurants map & index p. 148**

The town was named after the postmaster's Australian hometown in 1879. Economic growth came in the late 1890s with the arrival of the Florida East Coast Railway. The introduction of another innovative form of travel—space flight—led to the development of high-tech and electronics industries, an additional benefit of the city's proximity to the Kennedy Space Center *(see place listing p. 105).*

Shopping: Melbourne Square Mall, 2 miles east of I-95 on US 192 at 1700 W. New Haven Ave., contains Dillard's, JCPenney and Macy's. The downtown Historic District has specialty and antique shops.

BREVARD ZOO, .5 mi. e. of I-95 exit 191 to 8225 N. Wickham Rd., features more than 800 animals representing some 182 species in regional habitats that include Florida, South and Central America, Asia, Australia and Africa. Visitors can feed giraffes and lorikeets; a Rhino Encounter also is available. Kayak tours allow visitors to get a unique perspective of selected habitats. Treetop Trek Aerial Adventures features zip lines and obstacle challenges. Paddle boat rentals, train rides and behind-the-scenes tours are available.

Time: Allow 2 hours minimum. **Hours:** Daily 9:30-5. Last zoo admission 45 minutes before closing; last Treetop Trek admission 2 hours before closing. Kayak tours and paddle boat rental daily 10-4. Closed Thanksgiving and Christmas. **Cost:** $19.95; $18.95 (ages 65+); $14.95 (ages 3-11). Treetop Trek $29.95-$64.95; $14.95 (ages 5-12). Rhino Encounter $19.95. Kayak tours $9.95; ages 5-12 must be with an adult, and ages 0-4 are not permitted. Train $3 (ages 2+). Paddle boats $14.95; ages 0-12 must be with an adult. **Phone:** (321) 254-9453. GT

FOOSANER ART MUSEUM, 2 blks. e. of US 1 at 1463 Highland Ave., presents changing exhibits of works by artists of regional, national and international acclaim. Lectures, workshops and classes are given on a regular basis. Rotating exhibits highlight international modern and contemporary art. The Museum Studio at the Renee Foosaner Education Center offers more than 200 art-instruction classes and workshops. **Time:** Allow 1 hour minimum. **Hours:** Wed.-Sat. 10-4 (also first Fri. of the month 4-7:30). Jazz concert first Fri. of the month at 5:30. Closed major holidays. **Cost:** Free. **Phone:** (321) 674-8916.

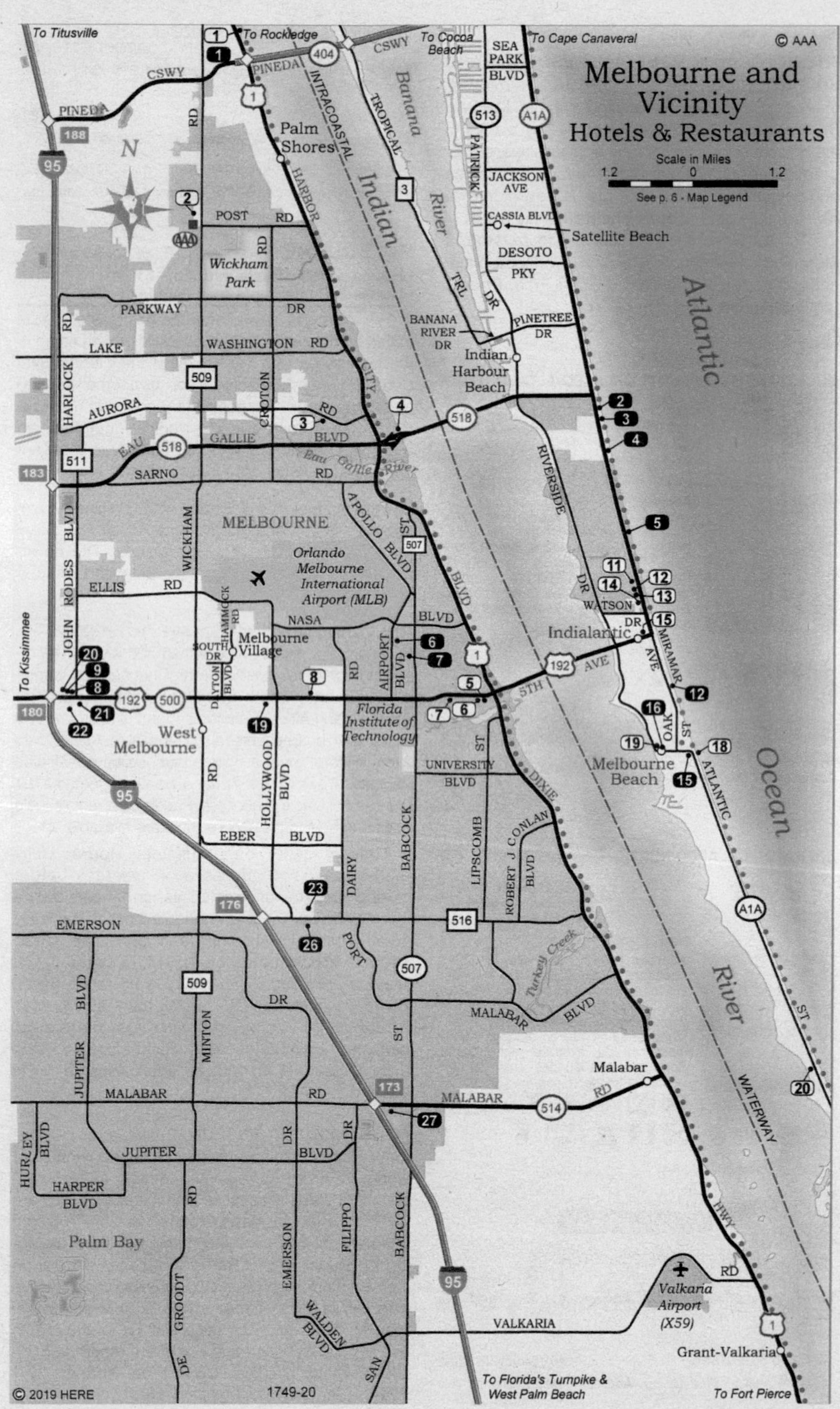
Melbourne and Vicinity
Hotels & Restaurants
Scale in Miles
1.2 0 1.2
See p. 6 - Map Legend
© AAA
To Titusville
To Rockledge
To Cocoa Beach
To Cape Canaveral
Palm Shores
Wickham Park
Satellite Beach
Indian Harbour Beach
MELBOURNE
Orlando Melbourne International Airport (MLB)
Melbourne Village
West Melbourne
Florida Institute of Technology
Indialantic
Melbourne Beach
Malabar
Palm Bay
Valkaria Airport (X59)
Grant-Valkaria
Indian River
Banana River
Atlantic Ocean
To Kissimmee
To Florida's Turnpike & West Palm Beach
To Fort Pierce
© 2019 HERE
1749-20

Airport Hotels

Map Page	MELBOURNE INTERNATIONAL (Maximum driving distance from airport: 1.5 mi)	Diamond Rated	Member Savings	Page
6 p. 148	**Hilton Melbourne Rialto Place, 1.0 mi**	◆◆◆	✔	150
7 p. 148	**Residence Inn by Marriott Melbourne, 1.5 mi**	◆◆◆	✔	151

Melbourne and Vicinity

This index helps you "spot" where approved hotels and restaurants are located on the corresponding detailed maps. Restaurant price range is a combination of lunch and/or dinner. Turn to the listing page for more information and consult display ads for special promotions.

For more details, rates and reservations: AAA.com/travelguides/hotels

MELBOURNE

Map Page	Hotels	Diamond Rated	Member Savings	Page
1 p. 148	Candlewood Suites Melbourne/Viera	◆◆		150
2 p. 148	Radisson Suite Hotel Oceanfront	◆◆◆		151
3 p. 148	**Hilton Melbourne Beach Oceanfront**	◆◆◆	✔	150
4 p. 148	Crowne Plaza Melbourne Oceanfront	◆◆◆		150
5 p. 148	**DoubleTree Suites by Hilton Melbourne Beach Oceanfront**	◆◆◆	✔	150
6 p. 148	**Hilton Melbourne Rialto Place**	◆◆◆	✔	150
7 p. 148	**Residence Inn by Marriott Melbourne**	◆◆◆	✔	151
8 p. 148	**Days Inn Melbourne**	◆◆	✔	150
9 p. 148	**La Quinta Inn & Suites Melbourne**	◆◆◆	✔	151

Map Page	Restaurants	Diamond Rated	Cuisine	Price Range	Page
1 p. 148	Grills Riverside Seafood Deck & Tiki Bar	◆◆	Seafood	$5-$30	151
2 p. 148	The Soup Shop	◆	Soup	$6-$16	151
3 p. 148	Shep's Diner	◆◆	Comfort Food Breakfast	$3-$12	151
4 p. 148	**Squid Lips Overwater Grill**	◆◆	Seafood	$8-$27	151
5 p. 148	Jacqueline's Bakery & Cafe	◆	French Breads/ Pastries Sandwiches	$3-$15	151
6 p. 148	Meg O'Malley's Restaurant & Irish Pub	◆◆	Irish	$9-$27	151
7 p. 148	Mustard's Last Stand	◆	Hot Dogs	$3-$7	151
8 p. 148	Shells of Melbourne	◆◆	Seafood	$8-$20	151

INDIALANTIC

Map Page	Hotel	Diamond Rated	Member Savings	Page
12 p. 148	Tuckaway Shores Resort	◆◆		82

Map Page	Restaurants	Diamond Rated	Cuisine	Price Range	Page
11 p. 148	The Blueberry Muffin Restaurant	◆◆	Breakfast Sandwiches	$6-$14	82
12 p. 148	Moo's Soft Serve	◆	Hot Dogs Desserts	$2-$3	82
13 p. 148	Long Doggers	◆◆	American	$4-$14	82
14 p. 148	Villa Palma Ristorante	◆◆◆	Italian	$13-$25	82
15 p. 148	Skewers A Mediterranean Grille	◆◆	Mediterranean Vegetarian	$8-$29	82

MELBOURNE BEACH

Map Page	Hotels	Diamond Rated	Member Savings	Page
15 p. 148	**Port d'Hiver Bed & Breakfast Inn**	◆◆◆◆	✔	151

MELBOURNE BEACH (cont'd)

Map Page	Hotels (cont'd)	Diamond Rated	Member Savings	Page
16 p. 148	**SeaGlass Inn Bed & Breakfast**	◆◆◆◆	✔	151

Map Page	Restaurants	Diamond Rated	Cuisine	Price Range	Page
18 p. 148	Sand on the Beach	◆◆	Seafood	$8-$26	151
19 p. 148	Djon's Steak & Lobster House	◆◆◆	Steak Seafood	$16-$64	151
20 p. 148	Cafe Coconut Cove	◆◆	German	$17-$36	151

WEST MELBOURNE

Map Page	Hotels	Diamond Rated	Member Savings	Page
19 p. 148	**Courtyard by Marriott Melbourne West**	◆◆◆	✔	368
20 p. 148	Hampton Inn Melbourne	◆◆◆	✔	368
21 p. 148	**Fairfield Inn & Suites by Marriott Melbourne Palm Bay/Viera**	◆◆◆	✔	368
22 p. 148	Holiday Inn Express & Suites	◆◆◆		368
23 p. 148	Hampton Inn & Suites by Hilton West Melbourne-Palm Bay Road	◆◆◆	✔	368

PALM BAY

Map Page	Hotels	Diamond Rated	Member Savings	Page
26 p. 148	Quality Inn Palm Bay	◆◆		249
27 p. 148	Holiday Inn Express Hotel & Suites Palm Bay	◆◆◆		249

CANDLEWOOD SUITES MELBOURNE/VIERA
321/821-9009 1

◆◆ Extended Stay Hotel. **Address:** 2930 Pineda Plaza Way 32940

CROWNE PLAZA MELBOURNE OCEANFRONT
321/777-4100 4

◆◆◆ Hotel. **Address:** 2605 N SR A1A 32903

DAYS INN MELBOURNE

321/724-2051 8

◆◆ **Motel**

Address: 4500 W New Haven Ave 32904 **Location:** I-95 exit 180, just e on US 192. **Facility:** 97 units. 2 stories (no elevator), exterior corridors. **Guest Services:** valet and coin laundry.

/ SOME UNITS

DOUBLETREE SUITES BY HILTON MELBOURNE BEACH OCEANFRONT

321/723-4222 5

◆◆◆ **Hotel**

AAA Benefit: Members save 5% or more!

Address: 1665 N SR A1A 32903 **Location:** Oceanfront. 1.5 mi n of jct US 192. **Facility:** 207 units. 9 stories, exterior corridors. **Parking:** on-site (fee). **Terms:** check-in 4 pm. **Amenities:** safes. **Dining:** 2 restaurants. **Pool:** heated outdoor. **Activities:** hot tub, self-propelled boats, exercise room, massage. **Guest Services:** valet and coin laundry, area transportation.

HAMPTON INN MELBOURNE-VIERA
321/255-6868

◆◆◆ SAVE Hotel. **Address:** 130 Sheriff Dr 32940

AAA Benefit: Members save 5% or more!

HILTON MELBOURNE BEACH OCEANFRONT

321/777-5000 3

◆◆◆ **Hotel**

Hilton

AAA Benefit: Members save 5% or more!

Address: 3003 N SR A1A 32903 **Location:** Oceanfront. 3 mi n of jct US 192. **Facility:** 199 units. 11 stories, interior corridors. **Parking:** on-site (fee). **Terms:** check-in 4 pm. **Amenities:** safes. **Dining:** 2 restaurants. **Pool:** heated outdoor. **Activities:** hot tub, self-propelled boats, fishing, exercise room, massage. **Guest Services:** valet laundry, area transportation.

SAVE ECO CALL BIZ / SOME UNITS HS

HILTON MELBOURNE RIALTO PLACE

321/768-0200 6

◆◆◆ **Hotel**

AAA Benefit: Members save 5% or more!

Address: 200 Rialto Pl 32901 **Location:** I-95 exit 180 (US 192/New Haven Ave), 4.8 mi e to Airport Blvd, then 0.8 mi n to Rialto Pl. **Facility:** 238 units. 8 stories, interior corridors. **Amenities:** safes. **Pool:** heated outdoor. **Activities:** hot tub, tennis, exercise room, massage. **Guest Services:** valet and coin laundry, area transportation.

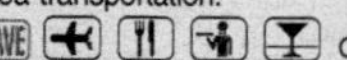

(See map & index p. 148.)

HOLIDAY INN MELBOURNE-VIERA HOTEL & CONFERENCE CENTER 321/255-0077

Hotel. **Address:** 8298 N Wickham Rd 32940

LA QUINTA INN & SUITES MELBOURNE
321/724-2050 9

Hotel

Address: 4510 W New Haven Ave 32904 **Location:** I-95 exit 180 (US 192/New Haven Ave), just e. **Facility:** 68 units. 5 stories, interior corridors. **Amenities:** *Some:* safes. **Pool:** outdoor. **Activities:** limited exercise equipment. **Guest Services:** valet laundry. **Featured Amenity: breakfast buffet.**

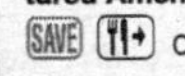
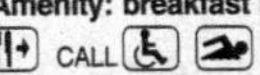

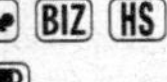

RADISSON SUITE HOTEL OCEANFRONT 321/773-9260 2

Hotel. **Address:** 3101 N Hwy A1A 32903

RESIDENCE INN BY MARRIOTT MELBOURNE
321/723-5740 7

Extended Stay Hotel

Residence INN. **AAA Benefit:** Members save 5% or more!

Address: 1430 S Babcock St 32901 **Location:** I-95 exit 180, 5.1 mi e on US 192(New Haven Ave), then 0.5 mi n. **Facility:** 133 units, some two bedrooms, efficiencies and kitchens. 6 stories, interior corridors. **Terms:** check-in 4 pm. **Pool:** heated outdoor. **Activities:** picnic facilities, exercise room. **Guest Services:** valet and coin laundry. **Featured Amenity: full hot breakfast.**

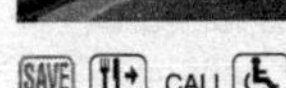

/ SOME UNITS

WHERE TO EAT

CHARLIE & JAKE'S BREWERY GRILLE 321/752-7675

Barbecue. Casual Dining. **Address:** 6300 N Wickham Rd, Suite 137 32940

DUSTIN'S BAR-B-Q 321/242-7871

Barbecue. Casual Dining. **Address:** 411 N Wickham Rd 32935

EL CHICO 321/722-4622

Tex-Mex. Casual Dining. **Address:** 1751 Evans Rd 32904

GRILLS RIVERSIDE SEAFOOD DECK & TIKI BAR
321/242-8999 (1)

Seafood. Casual Dining. **Address:** 6075 N US 1 32940

JACQUELINE'S BAKERY & CAFE 321/312-6594 (5)

French Breads/Pastries Sandwiches. Quick Serve. **Address:** 906 E New Haven Ave 32901

MEG O'MALLEY'S RESTAURANT & IRISH PUB
321/952-5510 (6)

Irish. Casual Dining. **Address:** 812 E New Haven Ave 32901

MUSTARD'S LAST STAND 321/951-3469 (7)

Hot Dogs. Quick Serve. **Address:** 415 E New Haven Ave 32901

SHELLS OF MELBOURNE 321/722-1122 (8)

Seafood. Casual Dining. **Address:** 1490 W New Haven Ave 32904

SHEP'S DINER 321/255-2999 (3)

Comfort Food Breakfast. Casual Dining. **Address:** 1409 Aurora Rd 32935

SONNY'S REAL PIT BAR-B-Q 321/242-4600

Barbecue. Casual Dining. **Address:** 150 Sheriff Dr 32940

THE SOUP SHOP 321/622-6914 (2)

Soup. Quick Serve. **Address:** 4100 N Wickham Rd 32935

SQUID LIPS OVERWATER GRILL 321/259-3101 (4)

Seafood Casual Dining $8-$27

AAA Inspector Notes: *Classic Historic.* Situated along the Intracoastal Waterway and housed in a historic landmark, this casual eatery's history began in 2004 and quickly made a name for itself as one of the most popular restaurants in the area. Patrons should expect waits at peak dining times and always on the weekends. The menu offers something for everyone with a wide variety of choices. **Features:** full bar, patio dining, happy hour. **Address:** 1477 W Pineapple Ave 32935 **Location:** I-95 exit 183, 5.1 mi e on SR 518(Eau Gallic Blvd), then just n. L D

MELBOURNE BEACH pop. 3,101

• **Hotels & Restaurants map & index p. 148**

PORT D'HIVER BED & BREAKFAST INN
321/722-2727 15

Bed & Breakfast

Address: 201 Ocean Ave 32951 **Location:** Jct US 192 and SR A1A/Miramar Ave, 1.7 mi s to Ocean Ave, then just e. **Facility:** Just steps from the salty waters of the Atlantic Ocean, this beautiful bed and breakfast offers guests a perfect retreat. A tropically landscaped pool area is highlighted by a gorgeous water feature. 10 units. 2 stories (no elevator), interior/exterior corridors. **Amenities:** safes. **Pool:** heated outdoor. **Activities:** beach access, bicycles, massage. **Featured Amenity: full hot breakfast.**

SAVE BIZ

/ SOME UNITS

SEAGLASS INN BED & BREAKFAST
321/725-7558 16

Bed & Breakfast

Address: 514 Ocean Ave 32951 **Location:** Jct US 192 and SR A1A/Miramar Ave, 1.7 mi s to Ocean Ave, just w. **Facility:** Nestled serenely between the beach and Intracoastal Waterway, this boutique lodging boasts an upscale décor with hints of Key West and the West Indies. 7 units. 2 stories (no elevator), interior/exterior corridors. **Pool:** heated outdoor. **Activities:** bicycles. **Guest Services:** boarding pass kiosk. **Featured Amenity: full hot breakfast.**

SAVE

WHERE TO EAT

CAFE COCONUT COVE 321/727-3133 (20)

German. Casual Dining. **Address:** 4210 SR A1A S 32951

DJON'S STEAK & LOBSTER HOUSE 321/722-2737 (19)

Steak Seafood. Fine Dining. **Address:** 522 Ocean Blvd 32951

SAND ON THE BEACH 321/327-8951 (18)

Seafood. Casual Dining. **Address:** 1005 Atlantic St 32951

MERRITT ISLAND pop. 34,743

SONNY'S REAL PIT BAR-B-Q 321/449-9102

Barbecue. Casual Dining. **Address:** 310 N Courtenay Pkwy 32953

TIJUANA FLATS 321/453-1881

Tex-Mex. Quick Serve. **Address:** 76 E Merritt Island Cswy 32952

MICANOPY (D-2) pop. 600, elev. 100'

The former site of a Timucuan Indian village, Micanopy (MIK-uh-no-pee) is the state's oldest inland town not on a waterway. Many antique, art and curio shops help to create an atmosphere of a small Florida village during the 19th century.

Micanopy Area Chamber of Commerce: P.O. Box 331, Micanopy, FL 32667. **Phone:** (352) 466-3327 or (352) 466-9229.

PAYNES PRAIRIE PRESERVE STATE PARK, 1 mi. n. on US 441, encompasses 21,000 acres of freshwater marsh, hammocks, pine flatwoods, swamps and ponds. More than 30 miles of trails are available, including the 16-mile Gainesville to Hawthorne State Trail *(see Gainesville p. 73)*. Visitor center exhibits interpret the natural and cultural history of this important ecological area. A 50-foot observation tower stands near the center of the preserve and a recreation area is at Lake Wauberg. Pets on leash are allowed only in designated areas. *See Recreation Areas Chart.*

Time: Allow 1 hour minimum. **Hours:** Park open daily 8-dusk. Visitor center open daily 9-4. Ranger-led activities are available November through March by reservation. **Cost:** $6 (per private vehicle with two to eight people), $4 (motorcyclists or single-occupant private vehicle); $2 (per person arriving by bicycle or on foot). LaChua Trail $4. Bolen Bluff Trail $2. **Phone:** (352) 466-3397 or (352) 466-4100.

ANTONIO'S 352/591-4141

Italian. Fine Dining. **Address:** 22050 N US Hwy 441 32667

BLUE HIGHWAY A PIZZERIA 352/466-0062

Pizza Sandwiches. Casual Dining. **Address:** 204 NE US Hwy 441 32667

COFFEE N CREAM 352/466-1101

Sandwiches. Quick Serve. **Address:** 201 NE Cholokka Blvd 32667

OLD FLORIDA CAFE 352/466-3663

Sandwiches. Quick Serve. **Address:** 203A Cholokka Blvd 32667

MOUNT DORA (F-3) pop. 12,370, elev. 174'

- **Hotels & Restaurants map & index p. 188**
- **Part of Orlando area — see map p. 2**

As you stroll the downtown streets, you may see a passerby or a shop with a T-shirt sporting the phrase "I climbed Mount Dora"—an inside joke among locals and in-the-know tourists. Mount Dora, named for its location on a plateau with a 174-foot elevation, is certainly no mountain, but it's considered pretty high in the relatively flat state of Florida.

Boutiques, antique malls and restaurants sometimes draw throngs of people to the old-fashioned downtown. On Donnelly Street between 5th and 6th avenues stands the 1893 Queen Anne-style Donnelly House, former home of the town's first mayor and now a Masonic lodge. This grand yellow and white house features colorful stained-glass windows and a large wraparound porch. Across the street is Donnelly Park, a focal point of downtown with benches and shuffleboard and tennis courts. The park is particularly lovely during the holiday season when nearly 2 million Christmas lights adorn the trees. The lights are lit at Light Up Mount Dora in late November and continue each evening through the season.

Lake Dora, one of seven lakes comprising the Harris Chain of Lakes, draws boaters and fishers. Several parks line the waterfront. Elizabeth Evans Park at the end of Donnelly Street offers benches, picnic tables and a small covered gazebo right above the lake—a great place for viewing the water and local wildlife in the shade. It's also home to the Mount Dora Lawn Bowling Club. Spectators are permitted; phone (352) 383-2294. A boat ramp is available at nearby Grantham Point, where the highlight is a red-and-white-striped inland lighthouse.

Adjacent Palm Island Park offers grills, a small covered pavilion with tables, and a nature trail that includes a boardwalk jutting out into Lake Dora. As you stroll along you're likely to see a variety of birds and if you keep your eyes peeled on the water, you might even see a turtle or alligator. Across the street is Gilbert Park, which has a large children's playground area. Contact the parks and recreation department for more information; phone (352) 735-7183.

Mount Dora History Museum, 450 Royellou Ln., is filled with photos, memorabilia, period clothing and other items of interest to local history buffs. It is operated by the Mount Dora Historical Society; phone (352) 383-0006 for hours of operation.

The city hosts a major festival nearly each month, including the Mount Dora Arts Festival in February, the Mount Dora Regatta in March or April and the Craft Fair in October. There are special events held throughout the year, too, like outdoor movies in Donnelly Park on the second Friday of each month.

The IceHouse Theatre Company performs at the 270-seat Sonnentag Theatre at the IceHouse at 1100 N. Unser St.; phone (352) 383-4616 or (352) 383-3133.

Mount Dora Chamber of Commerce: 341 N. Alexander St., Mount Dora, FL 32757. **Phone:** (352) 383-2165.

Shopping: Downtown Mount Dora is a delightful shopping destination offering many types of items, including antiques, books, clothing, collectibles, dolls, gift items, homemade dog treats, jewelry, kitchen and bath items, scrapbook supplies, shoes and toys. The chamber of commerce, housed in the former railroad depot, offers shopping directories and maps.

(See map & index p. 188.)

Two more options for antique shopping are not far from downtown. Village Antique Mall, 405 N. Highland St., features more than 60 dealers; phone (352) 385-0257. The biggest draw to the region, though, is Renninger's Florida Twin Markets at 20651 US 441, which is open Friday through Sunday. It caters to antique and flea market fans alike. On one side is the Farmers & Flea Market, and the Antiques Center with about 200 dealers is on the other. A guitar, antique car and motorcycle swap is held the second Sunday of the month. Three-day antique fairs (Friday through Sunday) are held the third weekend of the month March through October and in December and bring additional dealers—sometimes up to 200—who set up on the grounds and in covered outdoor pavilions. The January, February and November third-weekend shows are extravaganzas, and with more than 1500 dealers on the site these 3-day shows are the ultimate destination for antique collectors. Throughout the year a variety of special events are held on the grounds, too. For more information about Renninger's phone (352) 383-8393.

ADORA INN 352/735-3110 (20)

Historic Bed & Breakfast. **Address:** 610 N Tremain St 32757

WHERE TO EAT

1921 352/385-1921 (59)

New American. Casual Dining. **Address:** 142 E 4th Ave 32757

FIESTA GRANDE MEXICAN GRILL 352/385-3540 (58)

Mexican. Casual Dining. **Address:** 421 N Baker St 32757

FROGGERS GRILL & BAR 352/385-3555 (54)

American. Casual Dining. **Address:** 4931 Lake Park Ct 32757

THE GOBLIN MARKET 352/735-0059 (62)

American. Casual Dining. **Address:** 330 Dora Drawdy Ln 32757

THE HIGHLAND ST CAFE 352/383-1446 (63)

Comfort Food. Casual Dining. **Address:** 185 S Highland St 32757

JEREMIAH'S 352/383-7444 (55)

American. Casual Dining. **Address:** 500 N Highlands St 32757

LAKE HOUSE BAR & GRILL 352/735-7433 (56)

American. Casual Dining. **Address:** 315 N Highlands St 32757

ONE FLIGHT UP CAFÉ 352/735-1446 (57)

Sandwiches. Quick Serve. **Address:** 440 N Donnelly St 32757

PISCES RISING 352/385-2669 (60)

Seafood Steak. Casual Dining. **Address:** 239 W 4th Ave 32757

THE WINDSOR ROSE RESTAURANT & ENGLISH TEA ROOM 352/735-2551 (61)

English. Casual Dining. **Address:** 142 W 4th Ave 32757

NEW PORT RICHEY pop. 14,911

• Part of St. Petersburg-Clearwater and Beaches area — see map p. 275

CARMELITA'S MEXICAN RESTAURANT 727/376-4800

Mexican. Casual Dining. **Address:** 8526 Old CR 54 34653

CENTRAL PARK FAMILY RESTAURANT 727/376-7402

Comfort Food. Casual Dining. **Address:** 7657 State Rd. 54 34653

PIT BOSS BAR-B-Q 727/376-2677

Barbecue. Casual Dining. **Address:** 4221 Little Rd 34655

SONNY'S REAL PIT BAR-B-Q 727/375-9555

Barbecue. Casual Dining. **Address:** 5130 Little Rd 34655

TASO ITALIANO 727/807-7900

Italian. Casual Dining. **Address:** 4016 Little Rd 34653

THAI BISTRO 727/815-8600

Thai. Casual Dining. **Address:** 5414 Main St 34652

NEW SMYRNA BEACH (E-5) pop. 22,464, elev. 10'

• Hotels p. 154 • Restaurants p. 154

On this beach north of Cape Canaveral, automobiles may be driven along the stretch of firm white sand from the inlet south to 27th Avenue. Drivers should heed signs noting unsafe areas. Overnight parking or camping are not permitted on the beach. A daily driving toll of $10 per car is charged; annual passes are available for both residents ($25) and nonresidents ($100). Tollbooths are at each approach.

The foundations of the Turnbull Ruins/Old Fort, built of coquina, are on N. Riverside Drive between Washington and Julia streets. These ruins, made of walls 3 feet thick, represent a local mystery—it has never been established if the foundation is the unfinished remains of a pre-colonial fort or the incomplete beginnings of a mansion for the Turnbull family. The remains of a large plantation's sugar mill can be seen at Sugar Mill Ruins, 600 Old Mission Rd. Built in the early 1800s, the mill was destroyed during the Second Seminole War.

The Atlantic Center for the Arts, 1414 Art Center Ave., provides studio space and facilities for resident artists and offers exhibitions and events throughout the year; phone (386) 427-6975.

New Smyrna Beach Visitors Bureau: 2238 SR 44, New Smyrna Beach, FL 32168. **Phone:** (386) 428-1600 or (800) 541-9621.

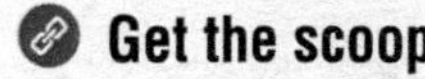

from AAA inspectors:

AAA.com/travelguides/restaurants

BEST WESTERN NEW SMYRNA BEACH HOTEL & SUITES 386/426-0020

Hotel

Best Western. **AAA Benefit:** Members save up to 15% and earn bonus points!

Address: 1401 S Atlantic Ave 32169 **Location:** Oceanfront. Jct SR 44, just s on SR A1A (Atlantic Ave). **Facility:** 101 units, some two bedrooms. 8 stories, interior corridors. **Terms:** check-in 4 pm. **Pool:** outdoor. **Activities:** exercise room. **Guest Services:** valet and coin laundry. *(See ad this page.)*

SAVE BIZ

BLACK DOLPHIN INN 386/410-4868

Boutique Bed & Breakfast

Address: 916 S Riverside Dr 32168 **Location:** I-95 exit 249 (SR 44), 4.1 mi e to Riverside Dr, then 0.4 mi s. **Facility:** Enjoy quiet seclusion in rooms that feature stylish décor, luxurious bed linens, jetted tubs and cozy bathrobes. The property is serenely located near the Indian River in a quaint residential area. 14 units. 3 stories (no elevator), interior/exterior corridors. **Amenities:** safes. **Activities:** boat dock, fishing, bicycles, lawn sports, massage. **Featured Amenity: full hot breakfast.**

SAVE CALL BIZ HS / SOME UNITS

HAMPTON INN NEW SMYRNA BEACH 386/898-9444

Hotel

AAA Benefit: Members save 5% or more!

Address: 214 Flagler Ave 32169 **Location:** I-95 exit 249 (SR 44), 5.3 mi e to Peninsula Ave, 0.6 mi n to Flagler Ave, then just e; downtown. **Facility:** 112 units. 3 stories, interior corridors. **Pool:** heated outdoor. **Activities:** exercise room. **Guest Services:** coin laundry. **Featured Amenity: full hot breakfast.**

SAVE CALL BIZ

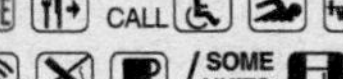

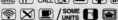

/ SOME UNITS

SPRINGHILL SUITES NEW SMYRNA BEACH 386/427-0512
Hotel. **Address:** 512 Flagler Ave 32169

WHERE TO EAT

CAFE HEAVENLY 386/427-7475
American. Quick Serve. **Address:** 115 Flagler Ave 32169

FLAGLER TAVERN 386/402-8861
Seafood. Casual Dining. **Address:** 414 Flagler Ave 32169

THE GARLIC 386/424-6660
Italian. Casual Dining. **Address:** 556 E 3rd Ave 32169

GNARLY BRIDGE HOUSE GRILL 386/957-3844
Fusion. Casual Dining. **Address:** 114 Flagler Ave 32169

THE GRILLE AT RIVERVIEW 386/428-1865
American. Fine Dining. **Address:** 101 Flagler Ave 32169

JB'S FISH CAMP & RESTAURANT 386/427-5747
Seafood. Casual Dining. **Address:** 859 Pompano Ave 32169

NEW SMYRNA STEAKHOUSE 386/424-9696
Steak Seafood. Casual Dining. **Address:** 723 E 3rd Ave 32169

NORWOOD'S RESTAURANT AND WINE SHOP 386/428-4621
Seafood Steak. Fine Dining. **Address:** 400 2nd Ave 32169

THE SEASHACK 386/428-8850
American. Casual Dining. **Address:** 491 E 3rd Ave 32169

THIRD WAVE CAFE 386/402-7864
American. Casual Dining. **Address:** 204 Flagler Ave 32169

YELLOW DOG EATS KITCHEN & BAR 386/410-4824
Barbecue Sandwiches. Casual Dining. **Address:** 147 Canal St 32168

NORTH REDINGTON BEACH pop. 1,417

- **Hotels & Restaurants map & index p. 286**
- **Part of St. Petersburg-Clearwater and Beaches area — see map p. 275**

DOUBLETREE BEACH RESORT BY HILTON HOTEL TAMPA BAY-NORTH REDINGTON BEACH 727/391-4000 64
SAVE Hotel. **Address:** 17120 Gulf Blvd 33708

AAA Benefit: Members save 5% or more!

SAILS RESORT MOTEL 727/391-6000 65
Motel. **Address:** 17004 Gulf Blvd 33708

▼ *See AAA listing this page* ▼

Best Western.

1401 South Atlantic Avenue
New Smyrna Beach, FL 32169
386-426-0020

(See map & index p. 286.)

WHERE TO EAT

THE CONCH REPUBLIC GRILL & RAW BAR 727/320-0536 (98)

Seafood. Casual Dining. **Address:** 16699 Gulf Blvd 33708

THE FROG POND RESTAURANT 727/392-4117 (97)

Breakfast Sandwiches. Casual Dining. **Address:** 16909 Gulf Blvd 33708

OCALA (C-9) pop. 56,315, elev. 104'

• **Restaurants p. 156**

Ocala (oh-KAL-a) has moss-draped oaks and stately old Southern homes along many of its streets. The 1888 Ocala Bible Chapel (729 N.E. 2nd St.), formerly United Hebrews of Ocala, is said to be the second oldest standing synagogue in Florida and among the oldest in the United States, though it is no longer used as a synagogue.

The surrounding area is considered the heartland of Florida's Thoroughbred industry. It is possible to visit some of the horse farms. Particularly scenic segments of two highways approach Ocala: US 301 from Waldo and US 27 from Williston.

Ocala-Marion County Visitors & Convention Bureau: 112 N. Magnolia Ave., Ocala, FL 34475. **Phone:** (352) 438-2800 or (888) 356-2252.

Shopping: Paddock Mall, a half-mile east of I-75 on SR 200 to 3100 S.W. College Rd., features JCPenney, Macy's and Sears. Dillard's and Dick's Sporting Goods anchor Market Street at Heath Brook, west of I-75 on SR 200 to 4414 S.W. College Rd.

GEM **APPLETON MUSEUM OF ART,** 4333 E. Silver Springs Blvd., houses European paintings, sculpture and decorative arts; contemporary art; pre-Columbian artworks; West African, Islamic and Asian artworks; as well as antiquities. The Edith-Marie Appleton wing features the ARTSpace, where you can create various types of art, as well as classrooms and additional galleries. Special exhibits, lectures, live musical entertainment and films also are offered.

Time: Allow 1 hour minimum. **Hours:** Tues.-Sat. 10-5, Sun. noon-5. Closed Jan. 1, Thanksgiving and Christmas. **Cost:** $10; $8 (ages 55+, educators and students ages 18+ with ID); $5 (ages 10-18); free (ages 0-5 and active military with ID). **Phone:** (352) 291-4455.

DON GARLITS' MUSEUM OF DRAG RACING is e. of I-75 exit 341 on CR 484, then s. on CR 475A. The museum traces the evolution of drag racing through a collection of more than 200 race cars and varied memorabilia. Also on the premises is the Museum of Classic Automobiles featuring many antique and classic cars. **Time:** Allow 1 hour minimum. **Hours:** Daily 9-5. Closed Thanksgiving and Christmas. **Cost:** $20; $15 (ages 13-18, ages 60+ and students and military veterans with ID); $10 (ages 5-12). Ages 0-5 must be with an adult. **Phone:** (352) 245-8661 or (877) 271-3278.

BEST WESTERN OCALA PARK CENTRE 352/237-4848

Hotel

Best Western **AAA Benefit:** Members save up to 15% and earn bonus points!

Address: 3701 SW 38th Ave 34474 **Location:** I-75 exit 350, just s on SR 200; in Park Centre. **Facility:** 138 units. 4 stories, interior corridors. **Pool:** heated outdoor. **Guest Services:** coin laundry. **Featured Amenity: full hot breakfast.**

SAVE CALL BIZ

/ SOME UNITS HS

COMFORT INN 352/629-7300

Hotel. **Address:** 1212 S Pine Ave 34474

COURTYARD BY MARRIOTT OCALA 352/237-8000

SAVE Hotel. **Address:** 3712 SW 38th Ave 34474

AAA Benefit: Members save 5% or more!

FAIRFIELD INN & SUITES BY MARRIOTT OCALA 352/861-8400

Fairfield **AAA Benefit:** Members save 5% or more!

Address: 4101 SW 38th Ct 34474 **Location:** I-75 exit 350, just sw on SR 200 (SW College Rd). **Facility:** 96 units. 3 stories, interior corridors. **Terms:** check-in 4 pm. **Pool:** heated outdoor. **Activities:** hot tub, exercise room. **Guest Services:** valet and coin laundry. **Featured Amenity: breakfast buffet.**

CALL

BIZ HS

/ SOME UNITS

HAMPTON INN & SUITES OCALA 352/867-0300

AAA Benefit: Members save 5% or more!

Address: 3601 SW 38th Ave 34474 **Location:** I-75 exit 350, just w on SR 200 (SW College Rd), then just nw. **Facility:** 101 units. 4 stories, interior corridors. **Terms:** check-in 4 pm. **Pool:** heated outdoor. **Activities:** exercise room. **Guest Services:** valet and coin laundry. **Featured Amenity: breakfast buffet.**

SAVE CALL

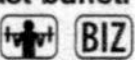

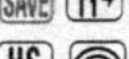

HS

/ SOME UNITS

For complete hotel, dining and attraction listings:

AAA.com/travelguides

HAMPTON INN & SUITES OCALA SOUTH 352/347-1600

Hotel

AAA Benefit: Members save 5% or more!

Address: 2075 SW Hwy 484 34473 **Location:** I-75 exit 341, just w. **Facility:** 109 units. 4 stories, interior corridors. **Pool:** heated outdoor. **Activities:** exercise room. **Guest Services:** valet and coin laundry. **Featured Amenity: breakfast buffet.**

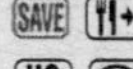 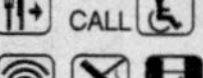 CALL  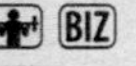 BIZ HS

HOLIDAY INN & SUITES OCALA CONFERENCE CENTER 352/629-9500

Hotel

Address: 3600 SW 38th Ave 34474 **Location:** I-75 exit 350, just s on SR 200 (SW College Rd), then just nw. **Facility:** 133 units. 6 stories, interior corridors. **Dining:** 2 restaurants. **Pool:** heated outdoor. **Activities:** exercise room. **Guest Services:** valet and coin laundry.

   CALL  BIZ HS

HOMEWOOD SUITES BY HILTON OCALA AT HEATH BROOK 352/369-4610

SAVE Extended Stay Hotel. **Address:** 4610 SW 49th Rd 34474

AAA Benefit: Members save 5% or more!

QUALITY INN OCALA 352/854-3200

Hotel. **Address:** 3434 SW College Rd 34474

RESIDENCE INN BY MARRIOTT OCALA 352/547-1600

Extended Stay Hotel

Residence INN **AAA Benefit:** Members save 5% or more!

Address: 3610 SW 38th Ave 34474 **Location:** I-75 exit 350, just w on SR 200 (SW College Rd), then n. **Facility:** 87 units, some two bedrooms, efficiencies and kitchens. 3 stories, interior corridors. **Terms:** check-in 4 pm. **Pool:** heated outdoor. **Activities:** hot tub, exercise room. **Guest Services:** valet and coin laundry. **Featured Amenity: full hot breakfast.**

   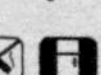

/ SOME UNITS

SLEEP INN & SUITES 352/347-8383

Hotel. **Address:** 13600 SW 17th Ct 34473

SPRINGHILL SUITES BY MARRIOTT OCALA 352/500-0501

SAVE Hotel. **Address:** 4100 SW 40th St 34474

AAA Benefit: Members save 5% or more!

WHERE TO EAT

AKI JAPANESE SUSHI RESTAURANT 352/369-3388

Japanese Sushi. Casual Dining. **Address:** 303 SE 17th St, Suite 306 34471

CHINA LEE BUFFET 352/671-1888

Chinese. Quick Serve. **Address:** 3743 E Silver Springs Blvd 34470

CODY'S ORIGINAL ROADHOUSE 352/237-8182

American. Casual Dining. **Address:** 2505 SW College Rd 34471

CRAFT CUISINE 352/237-7300

American. Fine Dining. **Address:** 2237 SW 19th Ave 34471

HARRY'S SEAFOOD BAR & GRILLE 352/840-0900

Cajun Seafood. Casual Dining. **Address:** 24 SE First Ave 34471

HORSE & HOUNDS RESTAURANT & PUB 352/620-2500

Steak Seafood. Casual Dining. **Address:** 6998 NW US 27 34482

IPANEMA BRAZILIAN STEAK HOUSE 352/622-1741

Brazilian Steak. Casual Dining. **Address:** 2023 S Pine Ave 34474

MARK'S PRIME STEAKHOUSE & SEAFOOD 352/402-0097

Steak Seafood. Fine Dining. **Address:** 30 S Magnolia Ave 34471

THE MOJO GRILL & CATERING CO. 352/291-6656

American. Casual Dining. **Address:** 4620 E Silver Springs Blvd 34471

THE MOJO GRILL & CATERING CO. 352/369-6656

American. Casual Dining. **Address:** 2015 SW 17th St 34471

ROYAL ORCHID THAI CUISINE 352/237-4949

Thai. Casual Dining. **Address:** 3131 SW College Rd 34474

SCRAMBLES CAFE 352/694-4405

American. Casual Dining. **Address:** 3233 SE Maricamp Rd 34471

SONNY'S REAL PIT BAR-B-Q

Barbecue. Casual Dining.

LOCATIONS:

Address: 4102 E Silver Springs Blvd 34470 **Phone:** 352/236-1012

Address: 1794 SW CR 484 34473 **Phone:** 352/245-5595

Address: 1845 SW College Rd 34474 **Phone:** 352/629-2663

TACO 'N MADRE RESTAURANTE MEXICANO 352/671-5277

Mexican. Quick Serve. **Address:** 80 N Pine Ave 34475

TONY'S SUSHI 352/237-3151

Japanese. Casual Dining. **Address:** 3405 SW College Rd, Suite 103 34474

OCALA NATIONAL FOREST (E-3)

Elevations in the forest range from 10 ft. to 125 ft.

In central Florida, the 383,573-acre forest contains numerous plant species of vegetation and clear lakes, springs and streams. The forest is said to have the world's largest stand of sand pine. Other predominant trees types include longleaf and slash pine, cypress and hardwood. In addition to several shorter trails, a well-traveled section of the Florida National Scenic Trail winds through the forest and is popular with hikers. Hunting is allowed by permit from the Florida Fish and Wildlife Conservation Commission *(see Good Facts To Know)*.

Developed recreation sites include Alexander Springs, Juniper Springs, Lake Dorr, Fore Lake, Mill Dam, Clearwater Lake, Salt Springs and Silver Glen Springs. Juniper Prairie Wilderness is home to Pat's Island, where parts of the 1946 movie "The Yearling" were filmed. Juniper Springs was constructed in 1935 by the Civilian Conservation Corps. *See Recreation Areas Chart.*

Brochures and information on forest recreational opportunities are available at Ocklawaha Visitor Center on SR 40 at 3199 N.E. CR 315, between Silver Springs and the Ocklawaha River. The center is open daily 9-4 (based on staff availability); phone (352) 236-0288.

OCOEE pop. 35,579

• **Hotels & Restaurants map & index p. 188**
• **Part of Orlando area — see map p. 2**

GATOR'S DOCKSIDE 407/521-5545

American. Casual Dining. **Address:** 8969 W Colonial Dr 34761

RUSTEAK RESTAURANT & WINE BAR 407/614-3765 (143)

New American. Gastropub. **Address:** 1568 Maguire Rd 34761

OKEECHOBEE (I-5) pop. 5,621, elev. 29'

At the crossroads of SR 70, US 98 and US 441, Okeechobee serves as a center for such outdoor activities as boating, fishing, camping and airboat rides. The town also is a commercial center for cattle, which is evident in the several festivals and rodeos that take place throughout the year.

Chamber of Commerce of Okeechobee County: 55 S. Parrott Ave., Okeechobee, FL 34974. **Phone:** (863) 467-6246.

BEST WESTERN LAKE OKEECHOBEE 863/357-7100

Hotel

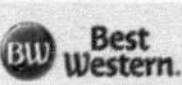

AAA Benefit: Members save up to 15% and earn bonus points!

Address: 3975 US Hwy 441 S 34974 **Location:** US 98/441, 2.5 mi s of jct SR 70; 0.7 mi n of Lake Okeechobee and jct SR 78. **Facility:** 44 units. 2 stories (no elevator), exterior corridors. **Pool:** outdoor. **Guest Services:** coin laundry. **Featured Amenity: breakfast buffet.**

SAVE CALL BIZ HS / SOME UNITS

HOLIDAY INN EXPRESS & SUITES LAKE OKEECHOBEE 863/357-3529

Hotel. **Address:** 3101 US Hwy 441 S 34974

WHERE TO EAT

COWBOYS BAR-B-Q & STEAK CO. 863/467-0321

Barbecue. Casual Dining. **Address:** 202 NE 7th Ave 34974

OLDSMAR pop. 13,591

• **Hotels & Restaurants map & index p. 286**
• **Part of St. Petersburg-Clearwater and Beaches area — see map p. 275**

COURTYARD BY MARRIOTT TAMPA-OLDSMAR 813/925-8887 (12)

Hotel

COURTYARD **AAA Benefit:** Members save 5% or more!

Address: 4014 Tampa Rd 34677 **Location:** On SR 580, jct St. Petersburg Dr. **Facility:** 99 units. 4 stories, interior corridors. **Amenities:** video games. **Pool:** heated outdoor. **Activities:** hot tub, health club. **Guest Services:** valet and coin laundry, boarding pass kiosk.

SAVE ECO CALL

BIZ HS

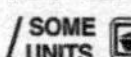

/ SOME UNITS

HAMPTON INN & SUITES TAMPA-NORTHWEST-OLDSMAR 813/818-7202 (9)

SAVE Hotel. **Address:** 4017 Tampa Rd 34677

AAA Benefit: Members save 5% or more!

HILTON GARDEN INN TAMPA NORTHWEST/OLDSMAR 813/891-9990 (11)

SAVE Hotel. **Address:** 4052 Tampa Rd 34677

AAA Benefit: Members save 5% or more!

HOLIDAY INN EXPRESS HOTEL & SUITES TAMPA-ODSMAR 813/854-5080 (10)

Hotel. **Address:** 3990 Tampa Rd 34677

RESIDENCE INN BY MARRIOTT TAMPA/OLDSMAR 813/818-9400 (13)

Extended Stay Hotel

Residence INN **AAA Benefit:** Members save 5% or more!

Address: 4012 Tampa Rd 34677 **Location:** On SR 580, jct St. Petersburg Dr. **Facility:** 78 kitchen units, some two bedrooms. 4 stories, interior corridors. **Terms:** check-in 4 pm. **Pool:** heated outdoor. **Activities:** hot tub, exercise room. **Guest Services:** valet and coin laundry.

SAVE ECO CALL

BIZ HS / SOME UNITS

WHERE TO EAT

FLAMESTONE AMERICAN GRILL 813/814-7778 (14)

American. Casual Dining. **Address:** 4009 Tampa Rd 34677

GREEN MARKET CAFE 727/787-5494

Sandwiches Natural/Organic. Quick Serve. **Address:** 3150 Tampa Rd 34677

ORANGE CITY (F-4) pop. 10,599, elev. 43'

• **Hotels p. 158 • Restaurants p. 158**

Orange City's early residents were the Timucuan Indians, who lived along the St. Johns River and ate the snails that inhabited the river's sandbars. The mound formed by the accumulation of centuries of snail shells later served as a foundation for the area's first permanent home, the 1872 Thursby House. Today the residence is preserved in Blue Spring State Park, a winter habitat of the endangered manatee.

BLUE SPRING STATE PARK, 2 mi. w. off US 17/92 on W. French Ave., contains a spring run that maintains a temperature of 73 degrees Fahrenheit. Manatees come here mid-November through March to escape the cooler waters of the St. Johns River. Viewing platforms, ranger interpretation programs and a video presentation introduce visitors to these gentle creatures. While visitors may not swim with or feed the manatees, swimming is allowed from mid-March to mid-November as long as manatees are not present. Campsites, interpretative river cruises and canoe and kayak rentals are available. A trailhead to the Spring-to-Spring trail is located within the park. *See Recreation Areas Chart.*

Time: Allow 2 hours minimum. **Hours:** Park daily 8-dusk. Video presentation shown daily at 1:30, 2:30 and 3:30, mid-Nov. to mid-Mar. **Cost:** $6 (per private vehicle with two to eight people); $4 (per motorcyclist or single-occupancy private vehicle); $2 (per additional passenger or person arriving by bicycle or on foot). **Phone:** (386) 775-3663.

St. Johns River Cruises, in Blue Spring State Park at 2100 W. French Ave., offers 2-hour narrated cruises and nature tours aboard *Native II* along the St. Johns River. Guided Segway and kayak tours also are available as well as rental canoes and kayaks. **Time:** Allow 2 hours minimum. **Hours:** Cruises depart daily at 10 and 1 (also at 3:30, Jan.-Apr.; minimum of 10 adults required). **Cost:** $25; $23 (ages 60+); $18 (ages 3-12). Blue Spring State Park admission $6 (per private vehicle with two to eight people); $4 (per motorcyclist or single-occupancy private vehicle); $2 (per additional passenger or person arriving by bicycle or on foot). Reservations are recommended for cruises; reservations are required for Segway and kayak tours. **Phone:** (407) 330-1612 or (386) 917-0724. GT

HOLIDAY INN EXPRESS & SUITES ORANGE CITY
386/917-0004

Hotel

Address: 1330 Saxon Blvd 32763 **Location:** I-4 exit 111B, just w. **Facility:** 114 units. 5 stories, interior corridors. **Amenities:** safes. **Pool:** outdoor. **Activities:** hot tub, exercise room. **Guest Services:** coin laundry. **Featured Amenity: breakfast buffet.**

WHERE TO EAT

MI TIERRA 386/774-1438
Mexican. Casual Dining. **Address:** 2235 S Volusia Ave 32763

SONNY'S REAL PIT BAR-B-Q 386/775-9900
Barbecue. Casual Dining. **Address:** 1024 Saxon Blvd 32763

ORANGE PARK pop. 8,412

• Hotels & Restaurants map & index p. 92
• Part of Jacksonville area — see map p. 84

DAYS INN ORANGE PARK 904/269-8887 75
Motel. **Address:** 4280 Eldridge Loop 32073

HAMPTON INN & SUITES JACKSONVILLE - ORANGE PARK 904/278-6140 76
SAVE Hotel. **Address:** 141 Park Ave 32073

AAA Benefit: Members save 5% or more!

HILTON GARDEN INN 904/458-1577 77
SAVE Hotel. **Address:** 145 Park Ave 32073

AAA Benefit: Members save 5% or more!

HOLIDAY INN & SUITES ORANGE PARK
904/562-7400 78

Hotel

Address: 620 Wells Rd 32073 **Location:** I-295 exit 10 (US 17), 0.9 mi s to Eldridge Ave, just w to Wells Rd, then just n. **Facility:** 134 units. 6 stories, interior corridors. **Pool:** outdoor. **Activities:** hot tub, exercise room. **Guest Services:** valet and coin laundry.

WHERE TO EAT

4 RIVERS SMOKEHOUSE 844/474-8377
Barbecue. Quick Serve. **Address:** 220 Park Ave 32073

THE HILLTOP 904/272-5959 96
American. Casual Dining. **Address:** 2030 Wells Rd 32073

OP FISH HOUSE AND OYSTER BAR 904/579-3931 97
Seafood. Casual Dining. **Address:** 636 Kingsley Ave 32073

Hands-Free
IS NOT Risk-Free
Use hands-free systems cautiously and keep your focus on the road when driving.
AAA.com/Distraction

Orlando

Then & Now

Walt Disney World® Resort shaped the young city of Orlando into one of the world's most popular leisure travel destinations. On average, nearly two-thirds of the domestic visitors head for the theme parks. But while Disney is the centerpiece of Orlando's appeal, the City Beautiful delivers more than fantasy and fast rides.

There are dozens of county and state parks in which to hike, bike or engage in water sports, and wild Florida, in all its natural splendor, is closer than you think. Nature-oriented diversions such as botanical gardens, meandering waterways and swampy wetlands with exotic wildlife were tourist draws in the early years, and still are. Since 1949, Gatorland has thrilled onlookers with dangerous stunts pitting man against reptile.

The city began as a small settlement with one cattle ranch and a trading post; by 1890 the "cow town" had become a real town, with all the trappings of 19th-century success. The postwar period ushered in the region's most dynamic growth. Kennedy Space Center created new jobs, and the resulting economic activity spawned numerous supporting businesses, attracting a tremendous influx of new residents. With the opening of a visitors complex in 1967, KSC officially entered the tourism race, taking its first small step towards becoming a major attraction.

AAA.com/travelguides—
more ways to look, book and save

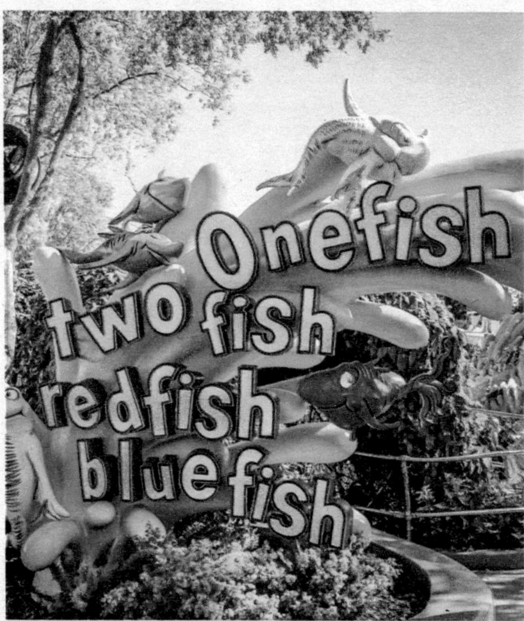

Universal Studios Florida™

Central Florida's Disney story began in the mid-1960s, when visionary "Uncle Walt" Disney paid a series of hush-hush visits to the swamplands of southwest Orange County. Secretive property deals soon followed, sparking questions about the mysterious doings south of town. The answer came in 1971 when Magic Kingdom® Park became Orlando's first theme park. In the decades since then, expansions have presented Epcot®, Disney's Hollywood Studios®, Disney's Animal Kingdom® Theme Park and two water parks. Also adding convenience are hotel accommodations, restaurants, entertainment areas and golf courses.

Bolstered by Walt Disney World® Resort's success, Orlando evolved into a theme park mecca. On the heels of triumphs in San Diego, Calif., and Aurora, Ohio, SeaWorld creators opened a third park in Florida in 1973. Decades later, SeaWorld Orlando gained two sister parks: Discovery Cove Orlando, an interactive dolphin encounter, and Aquatica, a water park. Universal Studios Florida

(Continued on p. 161.)

Destination Orlando

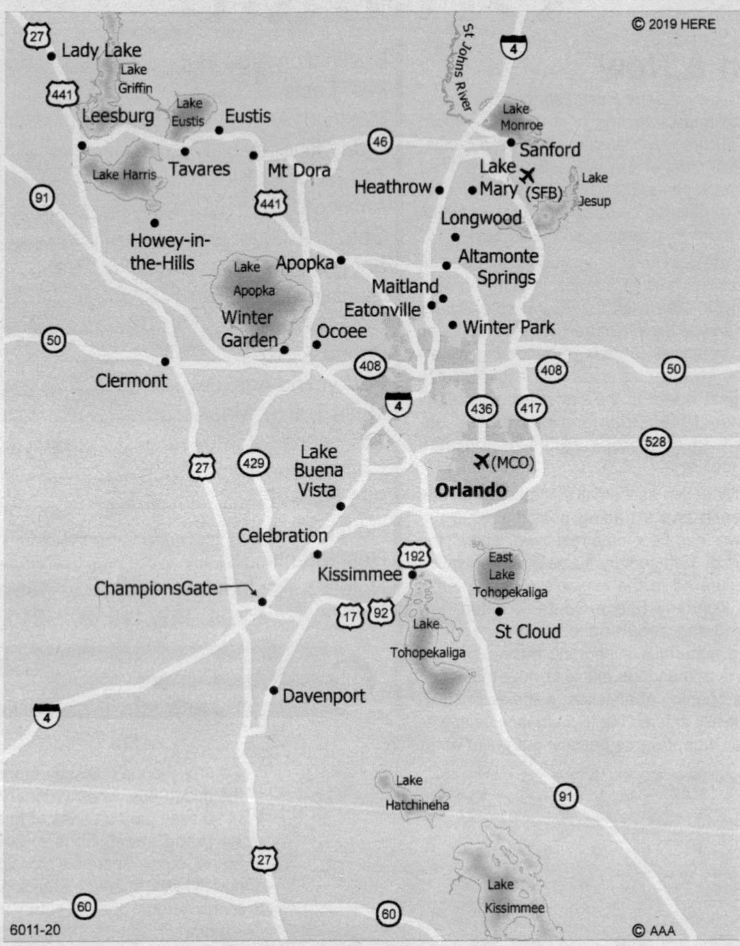

This map shows cities in the Orlando vicinity where you will find attractions, hotels and restaurants. Cities are listed alphabetically in this book on the following pages.

Fast Facts

ABOUT THE CITY

POP: 238,300 ▪ **ELEV:** 111 ft.

MONEY

SALES TAX: In Orange County the sales tax is 6.5 percent; in Lake and Seminole counties it is 7 percent; Osceola sales tax is 7.5 percent. Orange and Osceola counties levy a 6 percent resort tax, while Seminole County imposes a 5 percent tax and Lake County 4 percent.

WHOM TO CALL

EMERGENCY: 911

POLICE (non-emergency): (321) 235-5300 ▪ Sheriff (407) 836-4357

FIRE (non-emergency): (407) 246-3473

TIME AND TEMPERATURE: (407) 646-3131

HOSPITALS: Dr. P. Phillips Hospital, (407) 351-8500 ▪ AdventHealth East Orlando, (407) 303-8110 ▪ AdventHealth Orlando, (407) 303-5600 ▪ Orlando Health Orlando Regional Medical Center, (321) 841-5111.

VISITOR INFORMATION

Orlando, Inc. (Orlando Regional Chamber of Commerce): 301 E. Pine St., Orlando, FL 32801. **Phone:** (407) 425-1234 Mon.-Fri. 9-5.

Visit Orlando: 8102 International Dr., Orlando, FL 32819. **Phone:** (407) 363-5872 or (800) 972-3304.

The bureau distributes a variety of information daily 8 a.m.-9 p.m. Closed Christmas.

TRANSPORTATION

AIR TRAVEL: The Orlando area is served by two airports: Orlando International Airport (MCO), at SR 436 and the Beachline Expressway, and Orlando-Sanford International Airport (SFB) in Sanford, which serves commercial and private aircraft. *See Arriving, Air Travel.*

RENTAL CARS: Orlando is served by several major rental car agencies. Arrangements should be made before you depart, especially during peak seasons. Your local AAA club can provide this service or additional information. Hertz, (407) 859-8400 or (800) 654-3080, offers discounts to AAA members.

Book and save at AAA.com/hertz

RAIL SERVICE: Amtrak provides train service to four stations in the metro area. Passenger-only trains stop at the stations at 1400 Sligh Blvd. in downtown Orlando and 148 W. Morse Blvd. in downtown Winter Park; Kissimmee's passenger station is at 111 E. Dakin Ave. The Auto Train, which runs round-trip from Lorton, Va., stops at the Sanford station at 600 S. Persimmon Ave. Phone (800) 872-7245 for both rail services.

Virgin Trains USA, a high-speed passenger train, connects Fort Lauderdale, West Palm Beach and Miami. Service to or from Orlando International Airport's South Intermodal Center will occur around 2022; phone (305) 521-4800 for customer service.

BUSES: A Greyhound Lines Inc. terminal, (407) 292-3422 for customer service, (407) 292-3424 for tickets or (800) 531-5332 for Spanish-speaking persons, is off West SR 50 (Colonial Drive) at 555 N. John Young Pkwy.

TAXIS: Local taxis are metered and charge $4.20-$5.40 for the first mile and $2.65 for each additional mile plus 60c for each 80 seconds of waiting time. Major cab companies are Ace Metro, (407) 855-1111 ▪ Diamond Cab Co., (407) 523-3333 ▪ Quick Cab, (407) 447-1444 ▪ Town & Country, (407) 828-3036 ▪ and Orlando Taxi, (407) 422-2222.

Limousine service is available throughout most of the city; the ride from the airport to downtown Orlando or International Drive is about $50-$90 plus tax and a 20 percent tip but can vary depending on company and other factors.

PUBLIC TRANSPORTATION: Transportation by bus, trolley or rail is available in Orlando. *See Getting Around, Public Transportation.*

(Continued from p. 159.)

debuted in the summer of 1990. Within 10 years, Universal made the leap from single theme park to Universal Orlando Resort, a multifaceted family vacation destination with hotels, restaurants and nightlife.

Those who think a trip to Orlando is all about being a kid are in for a surprise. All-inclusive spa resorts and celebrity chef-helmed restaurants attract a sophisticated clientele. The city plays host to such exciting sports events as basketball games by the Orlando Magic, soccer games by the Orlando Pride and Orlando City Soccer Club, arena football games by the Orlando Predators, and the PGA's prestigious Arnold Palmer Invitational, which takes place at the legend's own Bay Hill Club. Orlando's cosmopolitan population also supports a milieu of cultural museums that visitors will want to add to their agendas.

Must Do: AAA Editor's Picks

- Add some excitement to your vacation by traveling to Orlando, Fla. Pose for a picture between the massive alligator jaws at **Gatorland** (14501 S. Orange Blossom Tr.), and continue snapping away inside the longtime Orlando favorite. Since 1949, the attraction has provided a way to (safely) view Florida's famous reptiles. A secondary site—a collaboration with **Fun Spot America** (5700 Fun Spot Way) called Gator Spot—adds more gators to the mix, including a white one!
- Ready to travel to an out-of-this-world destination? Set a course for **Kennedy Space Center,** 11 mi. e. of I-95 on SR 405, for an interstellar daytrip to the Space Coast. Options include tours of launch headquarters, exhibits about space and a simulated space shuttle launch. If reliving Neil Armstrong's historic moon landing isn't enough, then plan to meet a real astronaut.
- Splash around at a thrilling water park to beat the heat. Top picks include **Aquatica** (5800 Water Play Way), **Disney's Blizzard Beach Water Park** (1500 W. Buena Vista Dr.), **Disney's Typhoon Lagoon Water Park** (1195 E. Buena Vista Dr.) and **Universal's Volcano Bay™** (6000 Universal Blvd.).
- There is no shortage of things for couples to do in the area. Visit postcard-worthy **Lake Eola Park** (195 N. Rosalind St.). A band shell, amphitheater and lighted fountain punctuate the City Beautiful's 43-acre downtown oasis, a landmark since 1888. Pedal a swan boat across the lake or plop down on a shaded bench to savor the serenity.
- See Florida animals during your trip. Observe alligators, eagles, turtles and other creatures in their native habitat by taking an airboat through wetlands and across the headwaters of the Everglades. **Boggy Creek Airboat Rides** (2001 E. Southport Rd.) offers a thrilling "wild Florida" encounter in Kissimmee; then head northeast on John Young Pkwy. and I-4 for a charming detour to **Winter Park**.
- Stroll along Winter Park's refined Park Avenue, which features designer boutiques, sidewalk cafés, cozy local restaurants, shops with high-end home décor and a centrally located park. At **The Charles Hosmer Morse Museum of American Art** (445 N. Park Ave.), bask in the aura of Louis Comfort Tiffany's stunning stained-glass creations, a renowned collection that has no equal. Lovely lakeside residences and natural tropical scenery are highlights of a narrated cruise on Winter Park's chain of lakes and canals, offered by **Scenic Boat Tours** (312 E. Morse Blvd.).
- Venture out to the quaint village of **Mount Dora,** central Florida's antiques and collectibles capital, by driving west on SR 414. This small town overlooking Lake Dora draws quite a crowd on weekends because there are so many fun things to do. Make sure you arrive early to get a good parking spot. Later, take in a play or a musical at the **Sonnentag Theatre at the IceHouse** (100 N. Unser St.), where you can see shows like "Bye-Bye Birdie" and "Miracle on 34th Street" performed by local thespians. Mount Dora also holds a plethora of activities throughout the year, such as art and music festivals, a sailboat regatta and craft shows.
- There are many fun things to do with friends, especially if you like adventure and the outdoors. Drive west on I-4 to **Blue Spring State Park** (2100 W. French Ave.), in **Orange City,** for the annual winter migration of manatees—mid-November through March—from the cool waters of the St. Johns River to the park's warm spring. Enjoy a picnic lunch and a myriad of water sports during your adventure travel experience, including snorkeling, swimming, canoeing and kayaking. Let **St. Johns River Cruises** (also at 2100 W. French Ave.) show you more of the state's longest river and its wild residents, including alligators, deer and birds. You'll never have a lack of things to do while you're here.

Kennedy Space Center Visitor Complex

Orlando 1-day Itinerary

AAA editors suggest these activities for a great short vacation experience. Those staying in the area for a longer visit can access a 3-day itinerary at AAA.com/TravelGuides.

Millions vacation in Orlando each year. If you're among the park-hopping majority, you've probably arrived clutching multiday tickets to **Walt Disney World® Resort** (3111 World Dr.), **Universal Orlando Resort™** (1000 Universal Studios Plaza) or **SeaWorld Orlando** (7007 SeaWorld Dr.)—or all of the above. Why not set aside some time to discover greater Orlando's other assets?

Morning

- Start early in **Ivanhoe Village,** a historic section of Orlando along Lake Ivanhoe featuring one-of-a-kind shops and places to eat. Open since 1991, the **White Wolf Café** (1829 N. Orange Ave.) remains a time-honored choice for breakfast, offering gourmet coffee and gooey cinnamon rolls to name a few favorites. If you love antiques and stylish decorative items, then walk down the street to **1618 Something Different Retro** and **A T Furniture & Antiques.**
- **Orlando Loch Haven Park** (777 E. Princeton St.) contains several cultural institutions, including **The Mennello Museum of American Art,** 900 E. Princeton St., and **Orlando Science Center,** 777 E. Princeton St.
- Consider spending some time outdoors, particularly when the weather is nice. The **Harry P. Leu Gardens** (1920 N. Forest Ave.) provides a peaceful retreat, especially when the flowers are in bloom.

Afternoon

- Drop by **East End Market** (3201 Corrine Dr.), a two-story building with garden beds out front. This destination, a love letter to all things local, features several independent businesses, including restaurants and shops.
- If inspired by greenery, consider a plant-based meal at **Ethos Vegan Kitchen Inc.** The restaurant in nearby **Winter Park** serves hearty fare—minus the meat and dairy. It's also a local hangout with a bar and mouthwatering desserts. If you decide to skip the special of the day, then try the sheep's pie with an orange cookie.
- Next, you'll want to stroll down the imminently walkable **Park Avenue** and indulge in some window shopping. Well-known clothing retailers include Eileen Fisher and Lilly Pulitzer. Another interesting place to browse is **Kathmandu** (352 N. Park Ave.), which contains everything from incense to jewelry.
- **The Charles Hosmer Morse Museum of American Art** (445 N. Park Ave.), which holds the largest collection of art by Louis Comfort Tiffany and his associates. One of the most impressive works in the collection is the 1893 Tiffany Chapel.

The Charles Hosmer Morse Museum of American Art

Evening

- Are you ready to experience nightlife at an Orlando theme park? Head toward **Universal CityWalk™** (6000 Universal Blvd.), where you can see a show (Blue Man Group) or grab dinner. Happening spots include **The Cowfish Sushi Burger Bar,** an unconventional restaurant where you can pair a burger with sushi ("burgushi," anyone?), and **Jimmy Buffett's Margaritaville** (both at 6000 Universal Blvd.). Finish the night at **Pat O'Brien's** piano bar.
- Another option is **ICON Park** (8375 International Dr.); **The Wheel** catches the eye after sunset when it's aglow. If you're wondering where to eat, **Tapa Toro** offers flavorful Spanish cuisine and nightly flamenco dancing. Then walk to one of the other attractions, such as **Madame Tussauds Orlando Wax Attraction**, **SEA LIFE Orlando Aquarium** or **SKELETONS: Museum of Osteology,** which are open late.
- **Lake Buena Vista** also provides magical choices for shopping, dining and nightlife, especially if you are staying at **Walt Disney World® Resort.** Catch a set at the **House of Blues** (1478 E. Buena Vista Dr.) in **Disney Springs™** (1486 Buena Vista Dr.). Make reservations in advance for restaurants such as **Morimoto Asia**, 1600 E. Buena Vista Dr., known for its Peking duck. Afterward, plan to strike **Splitsville Luxury Lanes**, 1494 E. Buena Vista Dr., and end the night with a win.

Top Picks for Kids

Under 13

- Disney parks offer loads of fun things to do for all ages! Talk to your AAA travel agent about how to save money with cheap airline flights and travel packages. At the **Magic Kingdom® Park** (3111 World Dr.) in Lake Buena Vista, kids soar into the sky on Dumbo the Flying Elephant®, spin their teacup in the Mad Tea Party and scream as loud as they want on the Seven Dwarfs Mine Train.
- More of Orlando's special brand of magic awaits at **Universal's Islands of Adventure™** (1000 Universal Studios Plaza). There are many fun places to go in this part of the park.
- At Winter Haven's **LEGOLAND Florida Resort** (One LEGOLAND Way), kids will feel like Gulliver as they travel through cities like San Francisco, New York City and Las Vegas in Miniland USA, made from countless of LEGO bricks. Activities and shows include roller coasters; DUPLO Village, a toddler play area; and a water-skiing stunt show.
- When you're tired of being on your feet all day, there are plenty of relaxing and interesting things to do in Orlando. Venture outside the theme parks to feed the swans or ride paddleboat likenesses in downtown Orlando's centerpiece, **Lake Eola Park** (195 N. Rosalind St.), where locals stroll and relax. This photogenic beauty has a landscaped walkway, shade trees, a lighted fountain and an amphitheater.

Gatorland

Teens

- Experience the movies as never before at **Universal Studios Florida™** (1000 Universal Studios Plaza) on such rides as Shrek 4-D, E.T. Adventure and 3-D Terminator 2. The heart-pounding drops on the Hollywood Rip Ride Rockit or Revenge of the Mummy roller coasters are perfect for those with nerves of steel. Learn the secrets of monsterish makeup at the Horror Make-Up Show, or outmaneuver other contestants at Fear Factor Live.
- Encounter the snapping jaws of live alligators at **Gatorland** (14501 S. Orange Blossom Tr.), one of the area's oldest attractions. Climb the observation tower for a view of the breeding marsh where 130 gators live. At the Gator Jumparoo brave trainers let the reptiles snatch meat from their hands; it's a must-see.
- Discover more of natural Florida with **Boggy Creek Airboat Rides** (2001 E. Southport Rd.) in nearby **Kissimmee**. From a dock on East Lake Tohopekaliga, your airboat skims across the Everglades headwaters on a river of grass while you watch for gators, birds and native wildlife.

All Ages

- Experience the wondrous world of science at **WonderWorks** (9067 International Dr.). Try to stand in 71-mph hurricane winds, feel an earthquake measuring 5.3 on the Richter scale, climb inside a replica of the Mercury space capsule, lie on a bed of nails and use EEG technology to move a ball.
- At **Disney's Animal Kingdom® Theme Park** (2901 Osceola Pkwy.), try to find the 300 different animals carved into the 14-story Tree of Life®. Watch out for geysers and waterfalls while drifting through a lush rain forest with your family on the Kali River Rapids®. Go on safari through an African savanna and spot lions, giraffes, zebras and hippos on Kilimanjaro Safaris®.
- Have a blast on the Twilight Zone Tower of Terror® and the Rock 'n' Roller Coaster® Starring Aerosmith at **Disney's Hollywood Studios®** (50 Animation Dr.). Then there are Toy Story Mania!® and Star Tours®—The Adventures Continue. But don't miss Fantasmic!, an entrancing nighttime show led by Sorcerer Mickey that will have you oohing and aahing as pyrotechnics and lasers light up the sky.
- There are many delicious places to eat in Orlando theme parks. If you're traveling with kids, be sure to check out **Disney Springs®** (1486 Buena Vista Dr.) for kid-friendly themed restaurants. **T-Rex** (1676 Buena Vista Dr.) features meteor showers with flashing lights, thunder and misting water. Waterfalls, a volcano, tropical greenery and animatronic animals surround you at the **Rainforest Cafe®** (1800 E. Buena Vista Dr.) while the menu will please every appetite with its wide variety of dishes.

Arriving

By Car

Orlando is laced with busy thoroughfares. Primary among these is I-4, a trans-Florida route that combines direct travel through the city with strategic controlled access. From the Daytona Beach area it forks off I-95 and enters Orlando on the northeast side; from the Gulf Coast it comes from Tampa, passing Walt Disney World® Resort and entering town from the southwest.

Florida's Turnpike (toll) links Orlando with the resort areas of southeastern Florida. About 35 miles to the northwest it connects with I-75, a major north-south freeway. Florida's Turnpike interchanges with I-4 at the southwestern city limits.

I-4 and Florida's Turnpike form an X across central Florida. Two older routes, US 17/92 and US 441, also cross at Orlando, traversing different portions of the area.

SR 528, more commonly known as the Beachline Expressway (toll), passes south of the city. It channels traffic between Orlando and the Cape Canaveral area and connects with routes leading to a downtown destination.

SR 50 (Colonial Drive) is an east-west route that passes through downtown and connects smaller communities near the Gulf with Atlantic coast areas. To avoid traffic an alternative is SR 408, the East-West Expressway (toll), which links with SR 50 both east and west of downtown. The expressway also connects with the Central Florida Greeneway (SR 417) just south of SR 50. An expansion to the eastern terminus brings the toll road to US 17/92 in Sanford; other eastern and western expansions are planned and sections of the expressway may be undergoing construction.

SR 436 (Semoran Boulevard) swings in a wide northwesterly arc from the airport and SR 528 (Beachline Expressway) southeast of town to US 441 northwest at Apopka and offers an alternative—although often busy—route to I-4.

Air Travel

Several airlines serve the Orlando area using one of the city's two airports: Orlando International Airport (MCO), at SR 436 (Semoran Boulevard) and SR 528 (the Beachline Expressway), and Orlando Sanford International Airport (SFB) in Sanford, which serves commercial and private aircraft. OIA, about 15 miles from both downtown and the tourist district, is a primary destination for many major domestic and international airlines. Serving more than 35 million passengers a year, it is one of the world's fastest-growing major airports. Its four satellite terminals are linked to the main terminal by automated people movers, making it easy to navigate; a south terminal is planned to open by 2019. Use AAA, one of the top travel websites, to find cheap airfare to the Sunshine State. (**Note:** Orlando's tourist volume often leads to traffic congestion during peak vacation seasons. When planning your trip, allow plenty

Florida's Turnpike

of transit time—coming and going—between the airport and your destination.)

To reach downtown Orlando, follow Airport Boulevard north as it merges into SR 436. Though heavily traveled, SR 436 offers direct access to central, east and north Orlando via SRs 50 or 408 (toll). To reach the International Drive area, take Airport Boulevard to SR 528 (toll), then head west to SR 482, which intersects International just east of I-4. Take Airport Boulevard south to SR 417 (toll) to go to the Walt Disney World® Resort via SR 536 or to reach Kissimmee via US 17/92/441.

Cab fares from the Orlando airport to downtown or International Drive run about $35-$39; limousines cost about $50-$90 plus tax and a 20 percent tip but can vary depending on the company and other factors; shuttle vans are $19-$20 one way, or $31-$32 round-trip; and bus transportation is $2. Cab fare to the Disney resort averages $60. Many hotels have courtesy shuttle service.

Orlando is served by several major rental car agencies. Arrangements should be made before you depart, especially during peak seasons. Your local AAA club can provide this service or additional information. Hertz, (407) 859-8400 or (800) 654-3080, offers discounts to AAA members.

Getting Around

Street System

Because much of Orlando's growth occurred during the 1960s and '70s, the city is remarkably car-friendly. Roads are generally in good shape, although construction caused by near-constant expansion is a fact of life around the tourist district and downtown. Points of interest are usually on or near the main thoroughfares, most of which are accessible via I-4. For a small city, Orlando has surprisingly lengthy rush-hour periods, 6:30-9 a.m. and 4-6:30 p.m. Try to avoid traveling on I-4, US 17/92, SR 50 and SR 436 during these times.

Downtown Orlando is basically a grid, with several one-way streets. All street numbering begins at the intersection of Central Boulevard and Orange Avenue, the main strip through downtown. Orange is a one-way road south through the downtown core; its northbound counterpart is Rosalind Avenue. East-west roads accessing important downtown sites include Livingston Street (Bob Carr Performing Arts Centre), Robinson Street (Lake Eola), Central (Orlando Public Library, Lake Eola), Church Street (Amway Center, Church Street Market) and South Street (City Hall).

International Drive, the heart of the tourist area, is south Orlando's busiest road. A profusion of hotels, shopping centers, outlet stores, restaurants, strolling vacationers and cruising teenagers usually combine to create crowded conditions and frequent delays.

Unless otherwise posted, the speed limit on most streets is 30 mph. Unless otherwise posted, right turns are permitted on red after a complete stop.

Parking

Metered street parking downtown is available at $1 per hour, but spaces are generally hard to find at peak periods, which are on weekdays and weekend evenings. Meter enforcement hours are Mon.-Sat. 8-6 except on city holidays. Downtown parking also is available in several open-air lots underneath I-4 between Hughey and Garland avenues, near Amway Center. These lots cost $1 per hour except during events, when the fee is $10 for an evening.

Orlando International Airport

Nearly a dozen municipal garages can be found throughout downtown, including at W. Amelia Street, between Revere and N. Hughey avenues; E. Amelia Street next to the Orange County Courthouse, between N. Magnolia and N. Orange avenues; W. Pine Street, between Garland and Orange avenues; three adjacent lots between W. Jefferson to the north and W. Central Boulevard to the south (between N. Garland and Orange avenues); E. Central Boulevard, between Rosalind and Magnolia avenues; and the garage by the Orange County Administration Building at the intersection of Liberty Avenue and E. Jackson Street (this will service the new Dr. P. Phillips Center for the Performing Arts). Rates are $2 per hour or $15 per day. Event parking costs $10 for an evening. For more details, contact the City of Orlando Parking Division at (407) 246-2155.

The city of Winter Park has free parking along Park Avenue, but spaces can be hard to come by during peak hours. Fortunately, several free public lots are located just a few blocks east and west off Park Avenue.

Most attractions and shopping centers have ample parking, but parking fees for the major theme parks can run as high as $15-$20 per day. Check with your hotel to see if it offers free shuttle service to the theme parks.

Public Transportation

Brightly painted buses are a colorful sight in the metro area, thanks to LYNX, the transit authority for Orange, Osceola and Seminole counties, which operates more than 300 buses on 88 routes.

Bus stops, called Links, are marked by fuchsia paw-print signs listing all the routes that are immediately accessible from that stop. The system serves most of the city, including downtown, the tourist district and major shopping centers. Main routes are Links 107 and 108, between downtown Orlando and Kissimmee; 10, through Kissimmee to St. Cloud; 38, downtown to the International Drive area; 436S, between SR 436 and the airport; 42, between International Drive and the airport; and 50, between downtown to the Walt Disney World® Resort.

LYNX fare is $2; transfers are free. Xpress service is $3.50. Exact change is required. Bus passes in daily, weekly and monthly increments also are available. Buses run Mon.-Fri. 4:15 a.m.-3:05 a.m., Sat. 4:45 a.m.-1:05 a.m., Sun. 4:45 a.m.-10:35 p.m.; holiday schedules may vary. For additional information about routes and schedules phone (407) 841-5969.

LYNX offers LYMMO, four limited fare-free bus routes that primarily use a bus-only lane to transport passengers throughout the downtown area. LYMMO runs Mon.-Thurs. 6 a.m.-10:45 p.m., Fri. 6 a.m.-midnight, Sat. 10 a.m.-midnight, Sun. 10 a.m.-10 p.m.

LYNX—routes 8, 107 and 441—also connects to Megabus, a low-cost bus service that arrives to and departs from Orlando, at 4504 S. Orange Blossom Tr. Fares, available in Suite 4652 in the Orange Blossom Center, start at $1.

I-Ride Trolleys cater exclusively to tourist traffic along International Drive 8 a.m.-10:30 p.m.; the wait is about 20 minutes. The Red Line runs along International Drive while the Green Line starts in the business district and runs along Universal Boulevard and South International Drive. Trolley fare is $2; $1 (ages 3-9 with adult); 25c (ages 65+); $5 (all-day pass); $7 (3-day pass); $9 (5-day pass); $12 (7-day pass); $18 (14-day pass). Transfers are free. Exact change is required. Passes also may be purchased at various locations; phone (866) 243-7483.

SunRail, a commuter train operating Mon.-Fri., links DeBary in Volusia County to Sand Lake Road, south of the City of Orlando. There are 16 stations along the 49-mile route, including stops in Sanford, Altamonte Springs, Winter Park, four stops in downtown Orlando, Meadow Woods in Orange County and three stations in Osceola County—the Tupperware Station (at Osceola Parkway), Kissimmee at downtown Kissimmee and Poinciana. A round-trip ticket for the longest route (DeBary to Poinciana) costs $9.50; $4.75 (ages 7-18, ages 65+ and the physically impaired). An expansion is in the works to connect Orlando International Airport. Though there's service during the morning, midday and evening on weekdays, the train's schedule may fluctuate depending on special events and demand; SunRail is closed major holidays. Phone (855) 724-5411 for additional details.

Virgin Trains USA—an express, inter-city high-speed passenger train connecting Orlando (adjacent to Orlando International Airport), Fort Lauderdale, West Palm Beach and Miami—is under construction at press time. A Miami-to-West Palm Beach route is available. Service to and from Orlando is scheduled to start by 2022; phone ahead (305) 521-4800 to confirm schedules and fares.

Shopping

Orlando is a shopper's wonderland. You can buy mouse ears, T-shirts and, ironically enough, snow globes, to your heart's content in Orlando, but the city has so much more to offer both bargain hunters and lovers of luxury goods than just ordinary souvenirs. You just have to know where to find it all when you travel there.

Antiques

Escape the stifling heat and bustling theme parks with a leisurely amble through one of Orlando's antique districts. Shopping for antiques is always a good idea if you're looking for fun things to do with friends. Wander in and out of air-conditioned emporiums in the **North Orange Avenue Antiques District** downtown, running south from the 2900 block to the 1600 block. Shops are packed to the rafters with one-of-a-kind finds; excavate for such relics as a 1930s RCA Victor radio, an 18th-century French buffet or vintage threads. Pop into **Rock & Roll Heaven,** 1814 N. Orange Ave., where they have a heck of a band (on vinyl and CDs, anyway); the selection of rare and collectible music ranges from Miles Davis and Elvis to The Mothers of Invention and Devo. Discover even more charming shops just down the street on **Ivanhoe Row,** along the 1200 block across from Lake Ivanhoe. If you like antiques and decorative items, stop at **1618 Something Different Retro** and **A T Furniture & Antiques**, which are next to each other on North Orange Avenue.

Park Avenue

Ritzy **Park Avenue,** in Winter Park to the north, has a handful of antique shops where you may unearth that perfect Art Deco brooch or turn-of-the-20th-century Tiffany lamp. Save money on your overall vacation costs by purchasing affordable vacation packages and you'll have a little extra to spend on fancy antique treasures.

Take a side trip to historic **Mount Dora,** a half-hour northwest of Orlando, and while away the day visiting its quaint antique shops. Rummage through the wares of the hundreds of dealers who gather each weekend at **Renninger's Florida Twin Markets** on SR 441, also in Mount Dora. Lovers of antiquities also can hunt for treasure at the antique boutiques on First Street in downtown **Sanford.**

Malls

Orlando is a mall rat's delight, and the *crème de la crème* is **The Mall at Millenia,** off I-4 at 4200 Conroy Rd. Feast your eyes on its upscale shops including Bloomingdale's, Chanel, Gucci, Neiman Marcus, Lilly Pulitzer and Tiffany & Co., as well as more than 150 retailers, services and eateries. With its luxe design—intricate mosaic floors, leaping fountains, modern décor, sculptures and fashion shows broadcast on 35-foot-high LED screens—the mall is a sight to behold. Despite its opulent look, the mall also appeals to those without deep pockets with such mall standards as Banana Republic, Express, Forever 21, Gap, Macy's and Urban Outfitters. Bonus: **IKEA** is next to the mall.

More than 250 shops occupy one of the largest malls in Florida, so it's the perfect destination for shoppers who value variety. **The Florida Mall,** 8001 S. Orange Blossom Tr. in south Orlando, is anchored by major retailers Dillard's, JCPenney, Macy's and Sears. A number of smaller stores impress as well, including apparel store BoxLunch, where every purchase above $10 goes toward feeding a hungry person through Feeding America. Kid-friendly M&M's World Orlando, American Girl's specialty doll store, and The Crayola Store with its accompanying **Crayola Experience** *(see attraction listing p. 177)*, add even more options. That's why international tourists arrive by the busful, joining the sea of shoppers who invade this mall regularly. There's also an attached hotel, so intrepid bargain hunters can drop bags off in their rooms and stay overnight.

Not enough malls for you? Shop all you want: Greater Orlando's got more. Most malls contain an assortment of heavyweight anchors such as Belk, Dillard's, JCPenney, Macy's and Sears as well as mall stalwarts including Aéropostale, Banana Republic and Gap—with food courts to provide fuel for more shopping. Take your pick from the following list.

Lake Buena Vista Factory Stores

Altamonte Mall, on 451 E. Altamonte Dr. in Altamonte Springs, offers 2 floors containing 150 boutiques. To the east is **Oviedo Mall,** 1700 Oviedo Mall Blvd., with more than 50 retailers as well as a kid's learning and fitness entertainment center. Northeast of Orlando's downtown is **Orlando Fashion Square,** 3201 E. Colonial Dr.; it houses more than 65 shops and services. Sanford's **Seminole Towne Center,** 200 Towne Center Cir., is the northernmost of the malls, while west of downtown in Ocoee is **West Oaks Mall** at 9401 W. Colonial Dr. (SR 50); both have more than 100 businesses.

Outlets

Looking for cheap things to do? **International Drive** is a mecca for bargain hunters and fashionistas. Souvenir shops abound, of course, especially in this part of Orlando, but the outlet stores are the true treasure troves. It's not a boast to say that whatever you're looking for, you'll find it at one of the outlet malls, and you'll save a bundle. From electronics to cookware and designer fashions to luggage, you won't be able to leave Orlando empty-handed.

Orlando Premium Outlets—Vineland Avenue offers name brand and luxury brand shops in a Mediterranean village atmosphere at 8200 Vineland Ave., which connects International Drive and SR 535 (or off I-4 exit 68). The lineup of 160 outlet stores includes Banana Republic, Burberry, DKNY, Forever 21, Motherhood Maternity, Nike, OshKosh B'gosh, Polo Ralph Lauren, Prada, Steve Madden and Tommy Hilfiger. Covered outdoor walkways offer protection from the Florida sun. Amenities include parcel lockers and a currency exchange. **Note:** Premium parking, such as the on-site garage, costs $10.

At 4951 International Dr. is **Orlando International Premium Outlets,** featuring apparel, electronics, fine jewelry, shoes, housewares and other items from 180 vendors, including BCBG Max Azria, Carter's, Kitchen Collection, Michael Kors, Saks Fifth Avenue OFF 5th, Skechers, Sunglass Hut, Swarovski and Vera Bradley. Not your ordinary outlet mall, the center is an elegant outdoor marketplace with beautiful landscaping and Mediterranean styling. Both Premium Outlets locations offer many of the same stores. **Note:** Premium parking spaces cost $10.

Lake Buena Vista Factory Stores, 15657 S. Apopka Vineland Rd. (SR 535), is a rare jewel in the crown of Orlando outlets. With roughly 50 stores and a new expansion, this venue offers a much different shopping experience compared to the Premium outlets but still features bargains galore. You'll find Aéropostale, Crocs, Eddie Bauer, Gap, Levi's, Old Navy, Reebok, Under Armour and Van Heusen. There are shops that cater to both men and women, so shopping here is one of the most enjoyable things for couples to do.

Specialty Districts

Large malls and outlets aren't the only games in town—follow the lead of Orlandoans and check out the following independent and themed shopping districts. Some are tucked in among the nightclubs, business offices and local restaurants in **Downtown Orlando** within a few blocks of Lake Eola Park.

The **Orange County Regional History Center Emporium** at 65 E. Central Blvd., is a fun place to go for gifts thanks to its shelves stocked with toys and books as well as items representative of Central Florida history.

Gentlemen can check out **Siegel's Clothing Co.,** 130 S. Orange Ave., for fine suits and sportswear; they also carry a good selection of attire for women. (A second location for **Siegel's** can be found on Winter Park's Park Avenue.) When only the most current styles will do, head a few blocks east to **Zou Zou Boutique,** 2 N. Summerlin Ave. (near the Thornton Park neighborhood), for designer fashions by the likes of Ella Moss, Milly, J Brand jeans and Sam Edelman shoes; this trés chic women's shop has another location at 7988 Via Dellagio Way in the Bay Hill area.

The **College Park** neighborhood, located near the intersection of Edgewater Drive and Princeton Street, offers a small selection of stores and is a nice location for browsing. If you're on the hunt for home décor, a bicycle, jewelry, a new outfit or a gift, try College Park. The dining scene is good as well.

Get your local produce, specialty foods, baking supplies and a foodie education at **East End Market,** 3201 Corrine Dr. The market—not a typical farmers market but rather a cultural food hub—features a garden, a demonstration kitchen, stores, offices, restaurants and event space in a two-story building in Orlando's **Audubon Park Garden District.**

There are several other markets worth checking out. Sundays at Lake Eola Park's **Orlando Farmers Market**, corner at E. Central Blvd. and N. Eola Dr., are especially nice. From 10-4 vendors sell produce, plants, art and handmade crafts, and there often is live entertainment. On Monday nights, head to the parking lot of Stardust Video and Coffee at 1842 E. Winter Park Rd. for the **Audubon Park Community Market.** This one is small, but hip.

Beyond Orlando, there is the **Maitland Farmers Market** at Lake Lily Park, 701 Lake Lily Dr., in Maitland, which features nearly three dozen vendors and live music every Sunday 9-2. On Saturday mornings, locals make tracks to the **Winter Park Farmers Market** in a refurbished train depot at 200 W. New England Ave. for the freshest produce, herbs, baked treats and cheeses.

Where to Eat and Shop

One block east is Winter Park's heart and soul, **Park Avenue.** An eclectic assortment of upscale, preppy and trendy boutiques, galleries and bistros line this lengthy European-flavored street near Rollins College, perfect for shopping, people watching or just taking a stroll. Brick-paved alleys provide a taste of the old country with hidden courtyards and gardens. **Kathmandu,** 352 N. Park Ave., in Winter

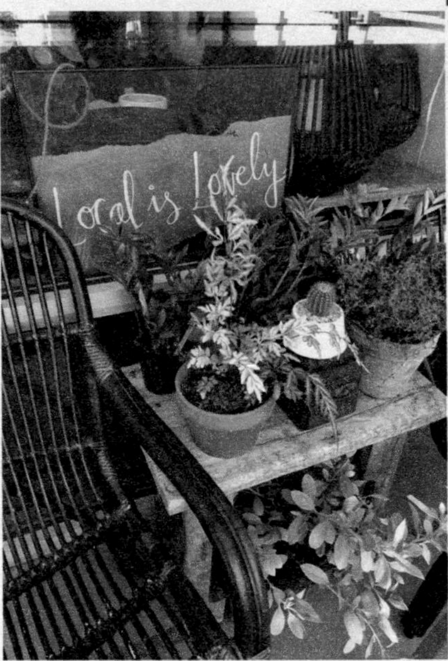

East End Market

Park, will ensure you go home with a unique treasure from its collection of items from different countries. When you get hungry, there are plenty of places to eat nearby that will satisfy your appetite and your palate.

Running out of steam? Relax your weary dogs under a century-old oak in shady **Central Park,** or sip ice-cold chardonnay at a sidewalk café. Speaking of dogs, bring yours or enjoy the parade as locals show off their purebreds; shop owners thoughtfully set out bowls of water for parched pups.

Disney Springs®, centered around 1486 Buena Vista Dr. in Lake Buena Vista, features tons of shopping venues along the shores of Buena Vista Lagoon. In The Landing, you can ease into the charming rustic vibe of the waterside district by shopping at a trendy boutique. In Town Center, you can stroll the day away shopping at boutiques and one-of-a-kind flagship stores along the Mediterranean-inspired Florida streets. Featuring amazing crystal glass coaches to sportswear with a Disney flair, The Marketplace remains one of the hippest shopping experiences around. However, the go-to destination for Disney souvenir gifts remains **World of Disney**, the world's largest Disney character and memorabilia shop.

Farther south, near the intersection of I-4 and US 192, is the **Town of Celebration;** its picturesque downtown offers nearly two dozen shops and restaurants. Celebration evokes a turn-of-the-20th-century small town with brick streets. It's not too old-fashioned, though; you'll still find signs of the 21st century, including the requisite Starbucks.

Nightlife

Orlando's evening scene is all over the map, literally, but the greatest concentrations of fun things to do are downtown and along I-Drive. For those who want a theme to go with their nightlife, the entertainment zones at Universal Orlando Resort and Walt Disney World Resort® are packed with diverse nightspots. Here, clubbers can hop from one dance floor to another within a short distance.

Disney Springs

One of the four fascinating neighborhoods at Disney Springs®, the West Side, is a neighborhood with a vibe all its own. There, the air is mixed with the sound of applause for world-renowned entertainment and tempting aromas that will ignite your senses. Or, head over to The Landing, where the wharf-side eateries offer everything from artisanal cocktails crafted at the edge of your stage-side table to a sushi bar. The most difficult decision you'll make when you're here is choosing where to eat. There are so many great restaurants here that serve mouth-watering dishes in a fun and energetic atmosphere.

Some of the best national recording acts perform at **House of Blues®** (1490 Buena Vista Dr.); past acts include Jane's Addiction, The Used, Flogging Molly, Colbie Caillat and Jerry Lee Lewis. The club has a warm and homey feel, with folk art everywhere you look. A large floor in front of the stage gives you plenty of room to dance and get close to your favorite rock star; there are seating areas for those who would rather spectate.

Get your jig on at **Raglan Road Irish Pub and Restaurant** (1640 Buena Vista Dr.), where live Irish music and Irish dancers await nightly and everyone becomes Irish as soon as they step inside. The entire pub, bar and all, was made in Ireland and shipped here for a true Gaelic experience. The fully stocked bar is a beer lover's dream, with a wide variety of Irish imports, craft beers, stouts and ales as well as a selection of specialty drinks, wine and Irish whiskeys. Sampling the various alcoholic beverages is one of the most fun things to do with friends while you're here.

House of Blues®

Downtown Orlando

For concerts by today's biggest names in music, hit the **Amway Center,** 400 W. Church St., where recording artists such as Bruno Mars and Ed Sheeran have recently played. This arena holds 20,000 concertgoers, so be prepared for large crowds. This is a great place to go if you're on a group travel vacation and can't cram your entire party into a small club.

The **Church Street Entertainment** complex, 33 W. Church St., is home to **Chillers,** a typical party bar; and **Latitudes,** an outdoor rooftop bar. Behind the building is **Rok Room,** a local favorite that features guest DJs. If you're looking for fun and energetic things to do in Orlando, this bar is the perfect destination.

Shhh, Orlando has a secret—speakeasy, that is. A handcrafted product awaits you at **Hanson's Shoe Repair,** 27 E. Pine St., but only with the right password; phone (407) 476-9446. A text back means an "in," so tread wisely.

For a pint of Guinness and some *craic* (aka fun), there's **Harp and Celt,** 25 S. Magnolia Ave. The Celt Irish Pub not only features classic Irish music but also the latest soccer and rugby matches.

Get into the holiday spirit at any time of year at **Frosty's Christmastime Lounge** (50 E. Central Blvd.). This is where to grab a drink and express some holiday cheer year-round in Orlando.

The renovated old Beacham Theater, 46 N. Orange Ave., houses **The Beacham,** an upscale hot spot popular for its mix of hip-hop, high-energy and Top 40 tunes—and for its VIP clientèle and celebrity performers. However, Orange Avenue also is the main strip for less-formal dance clubs that typically belt alternative, punk, funk, rock and indie music. Casually dressed twentysomethings frequent **Independent Bar** (aka IBar), 70 N. Orange Ave., which has three bars and two dance floors. **The Social,** 54 N. Orange Ave., is a small (400-person capacity) indie music venue.

Party on at **Wall Street Plaza**, a side street in the heart of downtown Orlando where you'll find **Wall Street Cantina, Shine, Hen House, Hooch, Waitiki, Monkey Bar** and **Sideshow**. These clubs and bars line each side of the street and there are outdoor tables and chairs to enjoy balmy Florida evenings and musical acts that sometimes perform outside. You also can get a bite to eat until 11 p.m. or dine at one of the nearby restaurants. The street is closed off often for block parties, and holidays like New Year's Eve, St. Patrick's Day and Cinco de Mayo as well as other special events are done up big here.

International Drive

The house bands at **B.B. King's Blues Club** at Pointe Orlando, 9101 International Dr., play everything from blues to Motown to classic rock on an elevated stage right in the middle of this restaurant/nightclub with a supper club feel. Do your best jitterbug on the checkered dance floor, and if you feel the need for a tropical breeze, step outside onto the patio.

Blue Martini, also at Pointe Orlando at 9101 International Dr., is a happening spot with upscale décor and drink prices to match (but worth every penny). A quality martini menu includes concoctions like Lemon Drop, Masterpiece Bleu and the Blue Martini (served with a glow stick). Snack on appetizers from the limited menu, and when the feeling strikes, get down and shake it up on the small dance floor.

3NINE, tucked away in the Rosen Plaza Hotel at 9700 International Dr., features DJs most nights, comedy on Wednesday and karaoke on Thursday; the sports bar area has dart boards, pool tables and large TVs. Need something hotter? **FIRE Lounge,** 8967 International Dr., draws a diverse bump-n-grind crowd and the DJs mostly spin hip-hop and top 40 tunes. Neighboring **ICEBAR Orlando,** on the other hand, will make you feel like an extra from "Dr. Zhivago" after you pull on borrowed parkas and gloves for an adventure in a chilly setting (27 degrees Fahrenheit) made from carved ice and enhanced with lights and music. Warm up with shots served in glasses made of ice.

For something a little different, where you can belt out pop tunes, commercial jingles, and songs you forgot you knew under the direction of dueling piano players, visit **Howl at the Moon,** 8815 International Dr.

Universal CityWalk

Bustling crowds, bright lights and variety at a single location make this a popular destination for park visitors and locals.

At the entrance to Universal Orlando Resort is **Universal CityWalk™,** 6000 Universal Blvd., which features an eye-catching promenade of shops, restaurants, clubs and a 20-screen movie theater. There's something here to satisfy any age group or music sensibility. Before you start your evening, inquire about opening times and cover charges at various restaurants and clubs. You can save a bundle by purchasing a CityWalk Party Pass at guest services.

Jump-start your evening with happy-hour mojitos or martinis at the **Red Coconut Club.** With its retro-style furnishings, banquette seating, conga drums, fake palm trees, velvet-roped VIP areas and intimate dance floor, this lounge-style dance club looks like an updated version of an early Vegas nightclub.

Reggae rules at **Bob Marley-A Tribute to Freedom,** which is housed in a replica of Marley's former home in Jamaica. A reggae band and a DJ in the interior courtyard accompany dinner or just drinks every evening.

Hard Rock Live

Speaking of courtyards, **Pat O'Brien's,** next door, is a carbon copy of the New Orleans landmark, right down to the meticulously re-created carriageway entrance with arched rifles overhead. The main bar exudes the character of a vintage New Orleans neighborhood watering hole, while a secluded patio surrounded by worn brick walls features faithful appointments such as slate floors, ironwork fencing, huge planters of greenery and the famous flaming fountain. Pianos duel it out in the club's raucous third bar. The signature Hurricane drink, served in a souvenir glass, looks like punch and really packs one. You've been warned.

Hard Rock Live is a concert venue with a full bar where you can catch national recording artists like BB King; Crosby, Stills & Nash; Earth, Wind & Fire; Elvis Costello; Florence and the Machine; The Fray; and Neon Trees as well as well-known comedians. Before the show, check out the rare music memorabilia that decks the walls. Right next door is the SAVE **Hard Rock Cafe,** where you can have a burger or steak before the show and gaze at walls blanketed with hundreds of rock artifacts.

Several wildly decorated intimate lounges offer retreats from the pounding beat on the dance floor at **the groove,** where DJs play Top 40, hip-hop, R&B and pop hits nightly. And when your dancing machine runs out of steam, decide if you want to be the entertainment at **CityWalk's Rising Star.** This innovative karaoke club rewards daring performers with a live band and backup singers. There's nothing cliché about the district's newest nightspot.

Don't overlook nocturnal happenings at the on-site hotels, all of which can easily be reached via the water taxi. **Velvet Bar,** inside Hard Rock Hotel, 5800 Universal Blvd., at Universal Orlando, is best known for its monthly Velvet Sessions (the last Thursday of the month, January-October), a themed cocktail party featuring a live band. Cabana Bay Beach Resort, 6550 Adventure Way, offers a blast from the past (and classic cocktails) at the poolside **Atomic Tonic** or **Hideaway Bar & Grille** near the lazy river. Head over to Loews Royal Pacific Resort, 6300 Hollywood Way, at Universal Orlando for **Jake's American Bar,** featuring live entertainment on select nights, and **Orchid Court Lounge & Sushi Bar,** providing a serene setting to sip cocktails among orchids and fountains. Loews Portofino Bay Hotel, 5601 Universal Blvd., at Universal Orlando is home to two watering holes. **The Thirsty Fish** is a casual dockside bar offering great sunset views and live jazz three nights a week. If cocktails and conversation are more your speed, grab a seat at swanky **Bar American.**

Big Events

On New Year's Day two top college football teams test their skills during the **VRBO Citrus Bowl**. A parade and other related activities precede the big game. For suggestions of things to do during your stay, talk to your AAA travel agent about events and activities that are scheduled during your visit.

In late January the **Zora Neale Hurston Festival of the Arts and Humanities** celebrates the life of the noted interpreter of Southern rural African American culture. The African American writer grew up in Eatonville, a community just north of Orlando that holds the distinction of being the nation's oldest incorporated black municipality; this is where the event takes place. Renowned African American musicians, vocalists, authors, educators and artisans celebrate Zora's legacy and Eatonville's heritage with this 10-day precursor to Black History Month. This energetic event is a great option if you're looking for fun things to do with friends.

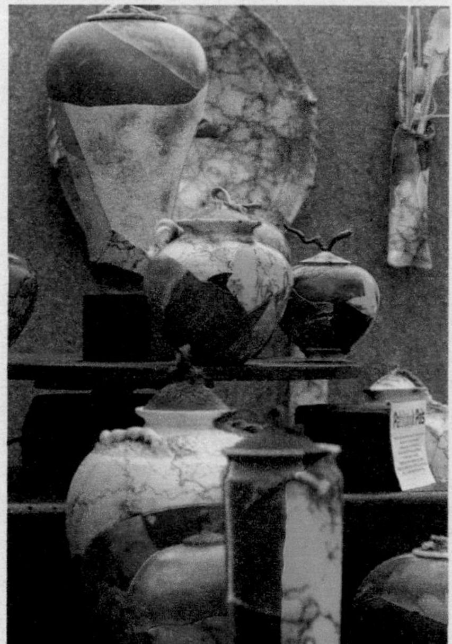

Winter Park Sidewalk Art Festival

Orlando's moderate temperatures are ideal for art festivals. Most popular are the **Mount Dora Arts Festival** in early February and the **Winter Park Sidewalk Art Festival** on the third weekend in March. **Spring Fiesta in the Park** and **Fall Fiesta in the Park** celebrations take place in April and November on the shores of **Lake Eola.**

In March PGA's **Arnold Palmer Invitational** is held at **Arnold Palmer's Bay Hill Club & Lodge.** Golf's top contenders drive, putt and birdie their way across a challenging championship course.

Cultural festivals explore the visual and performing arts. Held in April, the **Florida Film Festival** highlights cutting-edge current cinema from more than 30 countries at selected theaters. For 2 weeks in May, entertainers from around the world converge on downtown Orlando, treating theatergoers to a variety of unusual and cutting-edge performances as part of the **Orlando International Fringe Theatre Festival.** The event nurtures "outsider-artist" expressionism with uncensored genre performances ranging from comedy improv to dramedy to musical cabaret. The name says it all. This is nontraditional theater at large. Pencil it into your group travel itinerary and enjoy top-rate entertainment with your fellow travelers.

Pay tribute to our nation's anniversary at early July's **Lake Eola Park Fireworks at the Fountain.** This picture-perfect setting downtown features a colorful fountain in the lake, but the true show is the spectacular fireworks display that takes place after dark. Live bands fill the park with music, and you can supplement your picnic with a cold one from the beer garden.

The horror, the horror! At **Halloween Horror Nights** at **Universal Studios Florida,** don't be surprised if you hear yourself screaming this out loud as zombies pop out of the woodwork in haunted houses and scare zones, complete with terrifying sound effects, strobe lights and fog. This may be the Halloween party of your dreams (or nightmares, as the case may be). If you love adventure travel, it doesn't get much more adventurous than this! This activity may not be ideal for the faint of heart. You've been warned.

Orlando's holiday season unofficially kicks off with mid-November's **Festival of Trees** at the **Orlando Museum of Art.** Eyeball a large array of stunning Christmas trees, wreaths and gingerbread villages and gather ideas for your own holiday decorating. Kids can get crafty in Toyland Town and meet Santa, and everyone can treat themselves to treasures and trinkets in the holiday boutique. If you love shopping, this is one of the most fun things to do while you're here.

Change your blah "Bah Humbug" to a merry "Ho, Ho, Ho" with a visit to **Light Up UCF** mid-November through late December at the Addition Financial Arena. Hit the ice on an outdoor skating rink, marvel at a dazzling light show, take in holiday films, tap your toes to live music, glide down an icy slide and take joy rides on a Santa Train, Ferris wheel and carousel. Complete your evening by warming up with a fresh-cooked meal from one of the nearby restaurants.

The city of **Winter Park** rings in the holiday season with **Christmas in the Park,** which combines a concert by the Bach Festival Choir and stunning outdoor displays of lighted Tiffany windows on loan from The Charles Hosmer Morse Museum of American Art.

Sports & Rec

Looking for a vacation destination for sports lovers? Orlando will not disappoint! From downtown Orlando to Walt Disney World® Resort, locals have several venues to choose from when it comes to the city's various professional sports offerings. Orlando's Amway Center, 400 W. Church St., hosts basketball and hockey games, while the renovated Camping World Stadium, One Citrus Bowl Pl., features college football games.

Area residents also make the most of central Florida's lengthy summers and mild winters, which create ideal recreation conditions year-round. The area's many waterways host a wide variety of activities, and drier pastimes abound as well. Phone the Orange County Parks & Recreation Division at (407) 836-6200, or (407) 836-6280 for the event information line.

Baseball The **Florida Fire Frogs** (formerly the Brevard County Manatees), a Class A affiliate of the Atlanta Braves, play at **Osceola County Stadium,** 631 Heritage Park Way in Kissimmee; phone (321) 697-3220.

Basketball Orlando basketball enthusiasts fill **Amway Center** to watch he NBA's **Orlando Magic;** for schedule and ticket information phone (407) 896-2442.

Orlando's **University of Central Florida Knights'** men's and women's basketball teams play at **Addition Financial Arena,** (407) 823-6006, which seats more than 10,000. Nearby Winter Park's **Rollins College** also has men's and women's basketball teams; they play at **Alfond Sports Center,** (407) 646-2000.

Football The **UCF Knights** play at the 45,000-seat **Spectrum Stadium,** (407) 823-1000.

The **Camping World Stadium** hosts college football games, including the annual Camping World Bowl and the VRBO Citrus Bowl, (407) 440-5700.

The **Amway Center** is once again home to arena football's Orlando Predators. The season runs mid-March to early August.

Kraft Azalea Garden

Soccer Home to the **Orlando City Lions** as well as the **Orlando Pride**, a National Women's Soccer League expansion franchise, the new Exploria Stadium, 655 W. Church St., seats at least 25,500 fans. Orlando City B (OCB), a United Soccer League club, also plays home games at the new stadium in the Parramore neighborhood. For tickets phone (855) 675-2489.

Greyhound Racing Dog racing is a year-round diversion. Watching it in action is one of the most unique and fun things to do with friends while you're here. **Sanford Orlando Kennel Club,** (407) 831-1600, at 301 Dog Track Rd. in Longwood, holds matinee and evening races.

Note: Policies concerning admittance of children to pari-mutuel betting facilities vary. Phone for information.

Jai-Alai Played in only a few states, jai-alai is one of Orlando's most unusual offerings. The game is similar to handball, except the athletes field the ball not with their bare hands, but with a curved basket worn on one arm. Pari-mutuel betting adds to the excitement of this fast-paced sport at **Orlando Jai-Alai & Race Book,** (407) 339-6221, in Fern Park at 6405 US 17/92. The live jai-alai season in Orlando is February through April, although the facility is open year-round for televised jai-alai and racing events. The sport and facility aren't as popular as they once were, so expect small crowds in this 1960s facility.

Note: Policies concerning admittance of children to pari-mutuel betting facilities vary. Phone for information.

Bicycling Bicycling is a great option if you're looking for fun things to do that will help you stay active during your vacation. While it's a fun and entertaining way to see the city, traffic is always a concern. Exercise caution and obey all traffic laws when bicycling on the street. If possible, ride in a park—both **Bill Frederick at Turkey Lake** and **Lake Underhill** parks offer trails—or other specially designated area. The **Walt Disney World® Resort** offers a variety of trails as well as bicycle rentals.

Locals enjoy the quiet, tree-lined streets of **Rollins College** (in nearby Winter Park), **College Park** and **downtown Orlando.** Many points of interest can be seen along the **Orlando Urban Trail**, which runs from downtown along Orange Avenue to Loch Haven Park and Winter Park's Mead Botanical Garden.

The **Little Econ Greenway,** about 8 miles, begins at the intersection of Alafaya and Lokanotosa trails and runs alongside the Little Econlockhatchee River through Jay Blanchard Park to Forsyth Road. There's also a butterfly garden about halfway through near Union Park Middle School. For trail information phone (407) 254-9030.

Just north of Orlando in Seminole County, home to Orlando's bedroom communities, are the 23-mile **Cross Seminole Trail** and the 14-mile **Seminole Wekiva Trail.** Sections of these trails are part of the **Florida National Scenic Trail.** The Cross Seminole Trail begins in Casselberry at the intersection of Howell Branch Road and Aloma Avenue, runs through the Spring Hammock Preserve, then ends in Lake Mary at the pedestrian bridge, where it joins the Seminole Wekiva Trail. Built on the Orange Belt Railway, the Seminole Wekiva Trail runs south to Altamonte Springs. Phone (407) 665-2001 for more information.

Wekiwa Springs State Park

Many jogging/walking sites also cater to bicyclists; see the next section.

Jogging and Walking Orlando boasts two scenic, paved recreation trails built on old railway beds. Active people who love adventure travel can see the city from a whole new light while walking along the many beautiful walking trails. Prefer to explore the trails at a faster pace? Try jogging or bicycling. The 22-mile **West Orange Trail** runs between the Killarney Station in Oakland to Apopka; phone (407) 654-1108. A 10-mile portion of the trail also is open to equestrians.

Closer to downtown Orlando, the 7.2-mile **Cady Way Trail** connects Orlando Fashion Square Mall with Winter Park, where it connects to the Cross Seminole Trail; phone (407) 254-9025. The 3-mile **Orlando Urban Trail** runs along a rail line downtown from the intersection of Magnolia Avenue and Weber Street north to Winter Park's **Mead Botanical Garden,** which is a nice place to stroll through nature trails and the freshwater creek. For additional information contact the Orange County Parks and Recreation Division at (407) 836-6200.

Downtown Orlando features **Lake Eola Park** (E. Central Boulevard), noted for the Linton Allen Memorial Fountain, as well as **Mayor Carl T. Langford Park** on Central Boulevard. Just outside downtown are the charming streets of **College Park** and the serene oasis of Lake Ivanhoe's **Gaston Edwards Park. Cypress Grove Park** on Holden Avenue is a nice sport for walking and biking and has playgrounds and a lake; each holiday season the park puts on a Christmas light drive-through show.

Orlando Loch Haven Park *(see attraction listing p. 180)*, home to two art museums and the Orlando Science Center, is a nice place to spend some time outdoors among the sculptures at this cultural hub.

Orlando's beautiful, upscale Baldwin Park neighborhood (about 3 miles from downtown) features a 2.5-mile walking/biking trail around **Lake Baldwin.**

Winter Park is a good place for a stroll, particularly along popular **Park Avenue** or on the **Rollins College** campus. Other appealing sites include **Kraft Azalea Garden** in Winter Park as well as **Harry P. Leu Gardens** *(see attraction listing p. 177)* in Orlando. Due to the relentless Florida sun, early morning and late afternoon are the best times for either activity.

For a more rural destination, head about 25 miles east of Orlando to Christmas' **Orlando Wetlands Park**, where you can walk, jog and bike; phone (407) 568-1706.

Fishing With hundreds of lakes and several rivers to choose from, anglers will have no problem finding a place to cast their lines—bass, bream and catfish are among the available catches. Some favorite spots are **Bill Frederick Park at Turkey Lake**

and **Lake Cane/Marsha Park,** both just off Conroy-Windermere Rd.; **Gaston Edwards Park** on **Lake Ivanhoe** near downtown; **Lake Fairview,** north of College Park; **Lake Tohopekaliga** in Kissimmee, south of US 192; **Lake Underhill Park,** east of town off Conway Road; and **Wekiwa Springs State Park** in northwest Orange County. Walt Disney World® Resort also affords angling opportunities for tourists and residents alike.

Deep-sea fishing is a popular pastime, and charters are available in many beachfront towns. Anglers age 16 and over must purchase freshwater or saltwater licenses, which are available at many bait and tackle shops, most Wal-Marts and Bass Pro Shops and at all tax assessors' offices. For further information phone the Florida Fish and Wildlife Conservation Commission, (888) 347-4356.

Golf For many Orlando residents, golf is a way of life, and there are numerous ways to play. One of the newest facilities is the 65,000-square-foot Topgolf Orlando, 9395 Universal Blvd., which features 102 hitting bays.

An abundance of courses—more than 175—also grace the metropolitan area, from the city-bound links of small municipal properties to the spectacular settings of the luxury resorts. All of the following courses offer at least 18 holes and are open to the public year round: **Casselberry Golf Club,** (407) 699-9310, 300 S. Triplet Lake Dr. in Casselberry; **Celebration Golf Club,** (407) 566-4653, 701 Golfpark Dr. in Celebration; **Dubsdread,** (407) 246-2551, 549 W. Par St.; **EastWood Golf Club,** (407) 281-4653, 13950 Golfway Blvd.; **Hunter's Creek,** (407) 240-4653, 14401 Sports Club Way; **Mayfair Country Club,** (407) 322-2531, 3536 Country Club Rd. in Sanford; **MetroWest Golf Club,** (407) 299-1099, 2100 S. Hiawassee Rd.; **Stoneybrook East Golf Club,** (407) 384-6888, 2900 Northampton Ave.; **Walt Disney World** golf courses, (407) 939-4653, in Lake Buena Vista; and **Wedgefield Golf and Country Club,** (407) 568-2116, 20550 Maxim Pkwy.

Hot Air Ballooning The following offer aerial views of the Orlando area: **Aerostat Adventures,** (407) 476-7101 or (877) 495-7433; **Bob's Balloon Charters,** (407) 466-6380 or (877) 824-4606; **Magic Sunrise Ballooning,** (866) 606-7433; **Orlando Balloon Adventures,** (407) 786-7473 or (321) 229-4213; and **Orlando Balloon Rides,** (407) 894-5040. Some trips include champagne.

Tennis In metropolitan Orlando, tennis courts are nearly as numerous as lakes, with more than 600 offering tennis programs. Some have national-level recognition. The United States Tennis Association features at least 100 courts at the new 63-acre **USTA National Campus** in Lake Nona and supports tennis players ranging from beginner to professional; phone (914) 675-2500.

Many hotels offer court privileges to their guests. The courts at county parks are always open to the general public; for further details phone the City of Orlando Recreation Bureau, (407) 246-4300, or the Orange County Parks and Recreation Division, (407) 836-6200. Some resorts offer public access, including **Grand Cypress Tennis and Racquet Club,** 55 Grand Cypress Blvd., (407) 239-1234 (making reservations 24 hours in advance is recommended).

Water Sports The abundance of lakes in central Florida—more than 2,000 by some counts—provides endless opportunities for water sports of all kinds, including boating, canoeing, paddleboarding, swimming, water skiing and windsurfing. Some of the most popular sites include **Lake Ivanhoe; Lake Underhill;** and the **Butler Chain of Lakes** and **Winter Park Chain of Lakes.** For more information contact the Orange County Parks and Recreation Division at (407) 836-6200 or the City of Orlando Recreation Bureau at (407) 246-4300. For information about the Winter Park Chain of Lakes, phone (407) 599-3334.

Just north of Orlando in Apopka is **Wekiwa Springs State Park** *(see Recreation Areas Chart),* where swimming in the crystal clear spring water is popular. The **Wekiva River** is considered one of the state's best canoeing rivers; canoe and kayak rental information is available at the marina, (407) 884-4311.

Boating is a favorite recreation; residents have their choice of several inland waterways to explore. The Butler and Winter Park Chain of Lakes are groupings of connected lakes. The Rollins College campus and beautiful homes line the shores of the lakes in Winter Park's chain, and boat tours are available *(see place listing p. 370).* Another active waterway, the **St. Johns River,** connects nearby Sanford with Jacksonville. Houseboats can be rented in DeLand, allowing visitors to navigate the river in comfort. With such a wide variety of recreational options available, you'll never have to wonder what to do while you're here.

Performing Arts

The strength of Orlando's appeal lies mainly with its family attractions and entertainment. While this is good news for the folks at Disney and Universal, it has detracted some focus from the city's cultural scene. Arts enthusiasts need not despair, though—local arts groups have begun to expand their presence. Theater offers the most varied slate, with dance and music filling in the gaps. Performing arts lovers around the world think of Orlando as a prime destination for dance, film, music and theater.

The **Dr. P. Phillips Center for the Performing Arts,** 445 S. Magnolia Ave., adds even more options to the ever-evolving arts scene. The venue, which covers two blocks, features several individual theaters as well as an outdoor plaza and performance space. Phone (844) 513-2014 for the box office.

Opened in 1927, the historic **Bob Carr Theater,** 401 W. Livingston St., is nestled in the heart of Orlando and serves as the primary arts and cultural destination for the Orlando Philharmonic and concerts. Phone (407) 246-4262.

Orlando Amphitheater at the Central Florida Fairgrounds, 4603 W. Colonial Dr., draws a variety of performers. The open-air venue has no seats but can accommodate some 10,000 guests. If you're a fan of group travel and are looking for fun things to do that can accommodate large groups, squeeze a show at this amphitheater into your itinerary. Phone (407) 295-3247. Check with your travel agency to see if any performing arts tickets are offered with select travel packages.

Dance The **Orlando Ballet** produces year-round main stage productions. Concerts and programs ranging from classical to modern are featured. The Nutcracker ballet is performed in December, accompanied by a live orchestra of local musicians. Orlando Ballet performances generally are held at the Dr. Phillips Center for the Performing Arts' Walt Disney Theater. Once the new Steinmetz Hall at the Dr. Phillips Center opens sometime in 2020, the Orlando Ballet's performances will likely take place in the new 1,700-seat theater. For information phone (844) 513-2014.

Rollins College brings in some of the dance world's brightest stars, such as the Alvin Ailey Repertory and Pilobolus, to the **Annie Russell Theatre** to supplement the **Rollins Dance** student program; phone (407) 646-2145.

Film Alternative cinema finds a home at the **Enzian Theater,** 1300 S. Orlando Ave., offering filmgoers a varied menu of critically acclaimed American independent and foreign films. The Enzian also produces the annual Florida Film Festival. The theater itself is unusual—it is set in an old house, with audience seating at tables rather than in an auditorium. For information phone (407) 629-0054.

Enzian Theater

Music Orlando has a variety of groups dedicated to making beautiful music. The **Orlando Philharmonic Orchestra** gives four concert series during the year. It's one of the most romantic things for couples to do during their vacation. Performances are held at the Bob Carr Theater, but the orchestra is scheduled to move to the planned 1,700-seat Steinmetz Hall at the Dr. Phillips Center in 2020. For additional information phone (407) 770-0071 for the box office.

Central Florida Community Arts, 250 S.W. Ivanhoe Blvd., performs concerts appropriate for most audiences, such as Broadway-style musicals, community chorus and symphony orchestra, at various locations in the area. For additional information phone (407) 937-1800.

Blue Bamboo Center for the Arts hosts live performances, such as classical, jazz, world music and spoken word, in Winter Park's South on Fairbanks Avenue (SOFA) district at 1905 Kentucky Ave. For tickets phone (407) 636-9951; reservations are recommended. When you're done soaking up the music, head to one of the nearby restaurants for delicious local food.

A favorite local event is the **Bach Festival,** a celebration of masterworks by Bach and other major composers. Held in late February or early March, the program is performed by the **Bach Festival Society of Winter Park,** which also offers the Visiting Artists and Choral Masterworks series. The group performs at the **Knowles Memorial Chapel** at **Rollins College;** phone (407) 646-2115 for the chapel or (407) 646-2182 for ticket information.

Theater A local favorite is the **Broadway Across America-Orlando** series, which brings touring Broadway shows to the Dr. Phillips Center. The season runs December through June, and tickets for the biggest hits often require several weeks' notice; phone (800) 448-6322.

One of the area's most popular theaters for families is the **Orlando Repertory Theatre,** 1001 E. Princeton St., (407) 896-7365. The **Mad Cow Theatre,** (407) 297-8788, 54 W. Church St., offers avant-garde and mainstream works; phone ahead. If you're looking for fun things to do with friends, purchase your tickets to popular shows in advance.

The play's the thing at **Orlando Shakes,** in partnership with UCF, which is dedicated to staging the bard's timeless plays in innovative ways at the John and Rita Lowndes Shakespeare Center at Loch Haven Park, 812 E. Rollins St.; phone (407) 447-1700. The organization produces works throughout the year, from classically inspired independent pieces to Broadway productions to the **PlayFest Series,** a three-day festival of experimental plays.

The University of Central Florida features a full season of performances through **Theatre UCF,** (407) 823-1500. Rollins College also mounts a full season, with four productions at the Annie Russell

Theatre, 1000 Holt Ave. in Winter Park, running the gamut of theatrical genres; phone (407) 646-2145.

ATTRACTIONS

For a complete list of attractions, visit AAA.com/travelguides/attractions

CRAYOLA EXPERIENCE is in The Florida Mall at 8001 S. Orange Blossom Tr. The 26 stations, including places to color and sculpt, allow children and adults to play and create works of art. Creating a personalized crayon label as well as using melted wax to paint or splatter in drip art are among the highlights. In the Adventure Lab, kids can go on digital and physical quests. Toddler- and kid-oriented playgrounds are on-site. **Time:** Allow 3 hours minimum. **Hours:** Mon.-Fri. 10-6, Sat.-Sun. 10-8. Hours may vary; phone ahead. **Cost:** $24.99 (ages 3+). Additional fees for some specialty crafts (wax hands and glitter tattoos). **Phone:** (407) 757-1700.

DISNEY'S ANIMAL KINGDOM THEME PARK—see Lake Buena Vista p. 116.

DISNEY'S HOLLYWOOD STUDIOS—see Lake Buena Vista p. 117.

EPCOT—see Lake Buena Vista p. 117.

FUN SPOT AMERICA, 5700 Fun Spot Way, offers roller coasters (one of which is wooden), several thrill rides and more than a dozen family and children's rides as well as an arcade, a midway and four go-cart tracks. The 15,000-square-foot Gator Spot portion features birds, snakes, lizards and, of course, alligators. **Hours:** Daily 10 a.m.-midnight, mid-Feb. through Labor Day; Mon.-Fri. 2 p.m.-midnight, Sat.-Sun. 10 a.m.-midnight, rest of year. Phone ahead to confirm schedule. **Cost:** $49.95; free (spectators only). Gator Spot $6. Arcade games and Midway are additional fees. **Phone:** (407) 363-3867.

GATORLAND is 6 mi. s. of the Beachline Expwy. (SR 528) on US 17/92/441 at 14501 S. Orange Blossom Tr. Opened as a roadside attraction in 1949, the park and wildlife preserve is home to thousands of alligators, crocodiles, snakes and other reptiles. Highlights include the Stompin' Gator Off-Road Adventure, a children's petting zoo, a train ride, an aviary, a breeding marsh with observation tower, Gator Gauntlet Zip Line and the Screamin' Gator Zip Line. Daily shows include Gator Wrestlin', Gator Jumparoo and Up-Close Encounters. Gator Gully Splash Park includes more than a quarter acre of dueling water guns, a bucket tree and a splash fountain.

Rental strollers and wheelchairs are available. **Time:** Allow 3 hours minimum. **Hours:** Daily 10-5. Closing times may vary; phone ahead. **Cost:** $26.99; $18.99 (ages 3-12). Gatorland and Stompin' Gator Off-Road Adventure $36.99; $28.99. Gatorland and Screamin' Gator Zip Line $69.99. Reservations are recommended for zipline tour; height and age restrictions apply. **Phone:** (407) 855-5496 or (800) 393-5297. GT

HARRY P. LEU GARDENS is at 1920 N. Forest Ave.; I-4 exit 85 to Princeton Ave., s. on Mills Ave., then .5 mi. e. via Virginia Dr. Stop and smell the roses at this 50-acre botanical garden sheltering camellias, vegetable and herb plots, and a colorful butterfly garden. The site also boasts 10 "idea" gardens designed to inspire weekend horticulturists as well as a tropical stream garden ornamented by banana and palm trees, ginger plants and bamboo. Guided tours lasting approximately 30 minutes showcase the Leu House Museum, a two-story farmhouse dating from the 1880s.

Time: Allow 1 hour, 30 minutes minimum. **Hours:** Gardens open daily 9-5. House tours are given daily 10-3:30. Closed Christmas. **Cost:** $10; $5 (ages 4-17). Prices may vary; phone ahead. **Phone:** (407) 246-2620. GT

ICON PARK, 8387-8449 International Dr., offers entertainment, dining and shopping around The Wheel, a 400-foot tall observation wheel. The complex features The Wheel, Madame Tussauds, SEA LIFE Orlando, SKELETONS: Museum of Osteology and Wheelhouse Market, as well as a central lawn with water features, including a colorful water show choreographed to music. Special events also are held throughout the year.

Note: The Orlando Gyro Drop Tower and Orlando Slingshot are under construction until 2020; phone ahead to confirm schedules. **Hours:** Daily 10 a.m.-2 a.m. **Cost:** Free. Attraction admissions, including combination attraction admissions, may vary; phone ahead. **Phone:** (407) 999-9985.

Madame Tussauds Orlando Wax Attraction is at 8387 International Dr., part of ICON Park, home of The Wheel. This international franchise features representations of A-listers, historical figures, sports legends, famous artists, tech icons, pop stars and even local celebrities.

Hours: Sun.-Thurs. 10-10, Fri.-Sat. 10 a.m.-11 p.m. Last admission 1 hour before closing. **Cost:** $28; $22.50 (ages 3-12). Combination tickets are available. Admission and schedule may vary; phone ahead. **Phone:** (407) 999-9985.

SEA LIFE Orlando Aquarium is at 8449 International Dr., part of ICON Park, home of The Wheel. The stunning walk-through tunnel offers a 360-degree view of fish and sea creatures such as sharks, rays and turtles. Other displays include jellyfish, colorful fish and seahorses. The facility also offers a hands-on rock pool experience. Daily educational talks aim to inspire visitors to help in the important work of conservation.

Time: Allow 30 minutes minimum. **Hours:** Daily 10-9. Last admission 1 hour before closing. **Cost:**

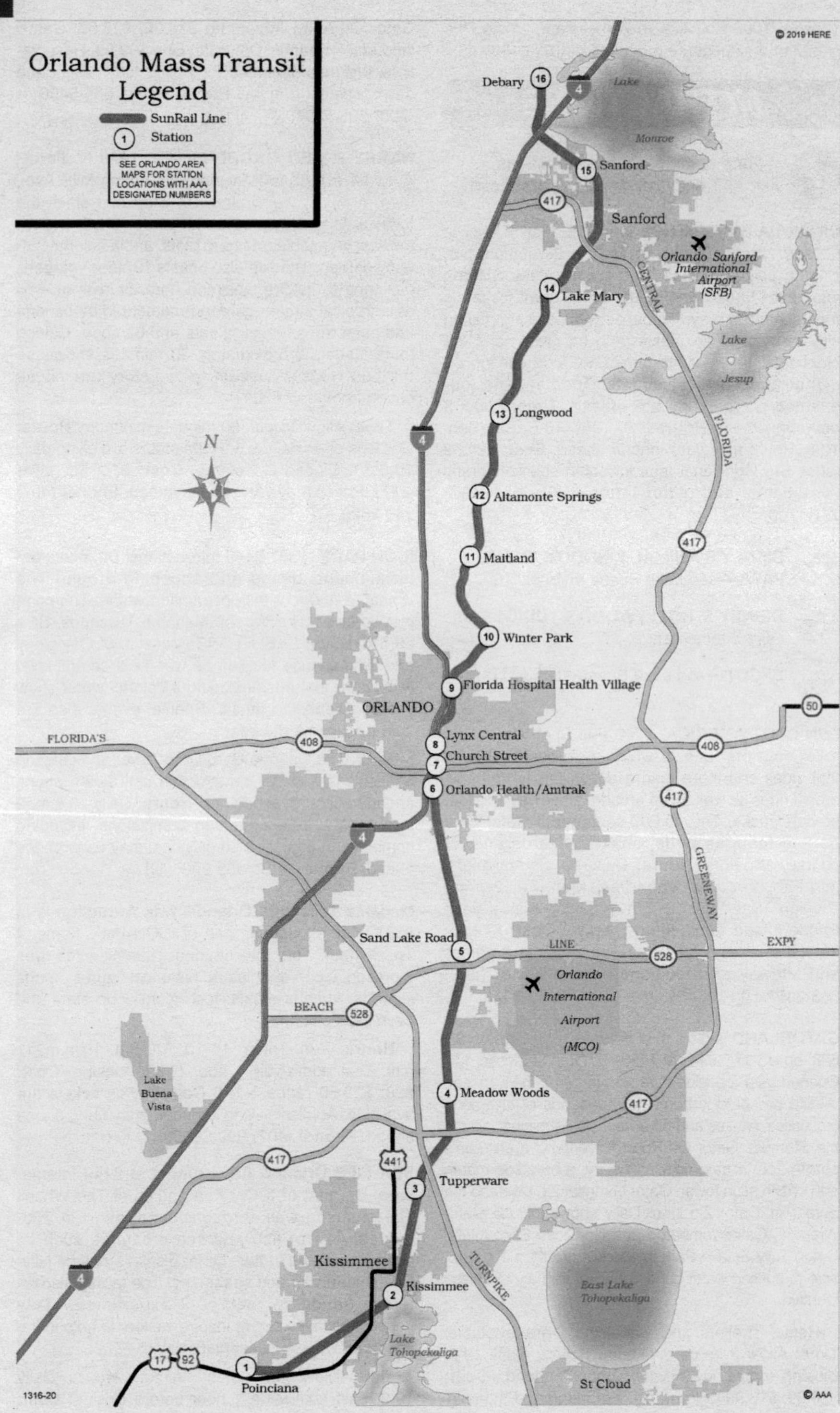

Orlando Mass Transit Legend
SunRail Line
Station
SEE ORLANDO AREA MAPS FOR STATION LOCATIONS WITH AAA DESIGNATED NUMBERS
© 2019 HERE
N
Debary
Lake Monroe
Sanford
Orlando Sanford International Airport (SFB)
Lake Mary
Lake Jesup
CENTRAL FLORIDA GREENEWAY
Longwood
Altamonte Springs
Maitland
Winter Park
Florida Hospital Health Village
ORLANDO
FLORIDA'S
Lynx Central
Church Street
Orlando Health/Amtrak
Sand Lake Road
LINE
EXPY
BEACH
Orlando International Airport (MCO)
Lake Buena Vista
Meadow Woods
Tupperware
Kissimmee
TURNPIKE
East Lake Tohopekaliga
Lake Tohopekaliga
Poinciana
St Cloud
1316-20
© AAA

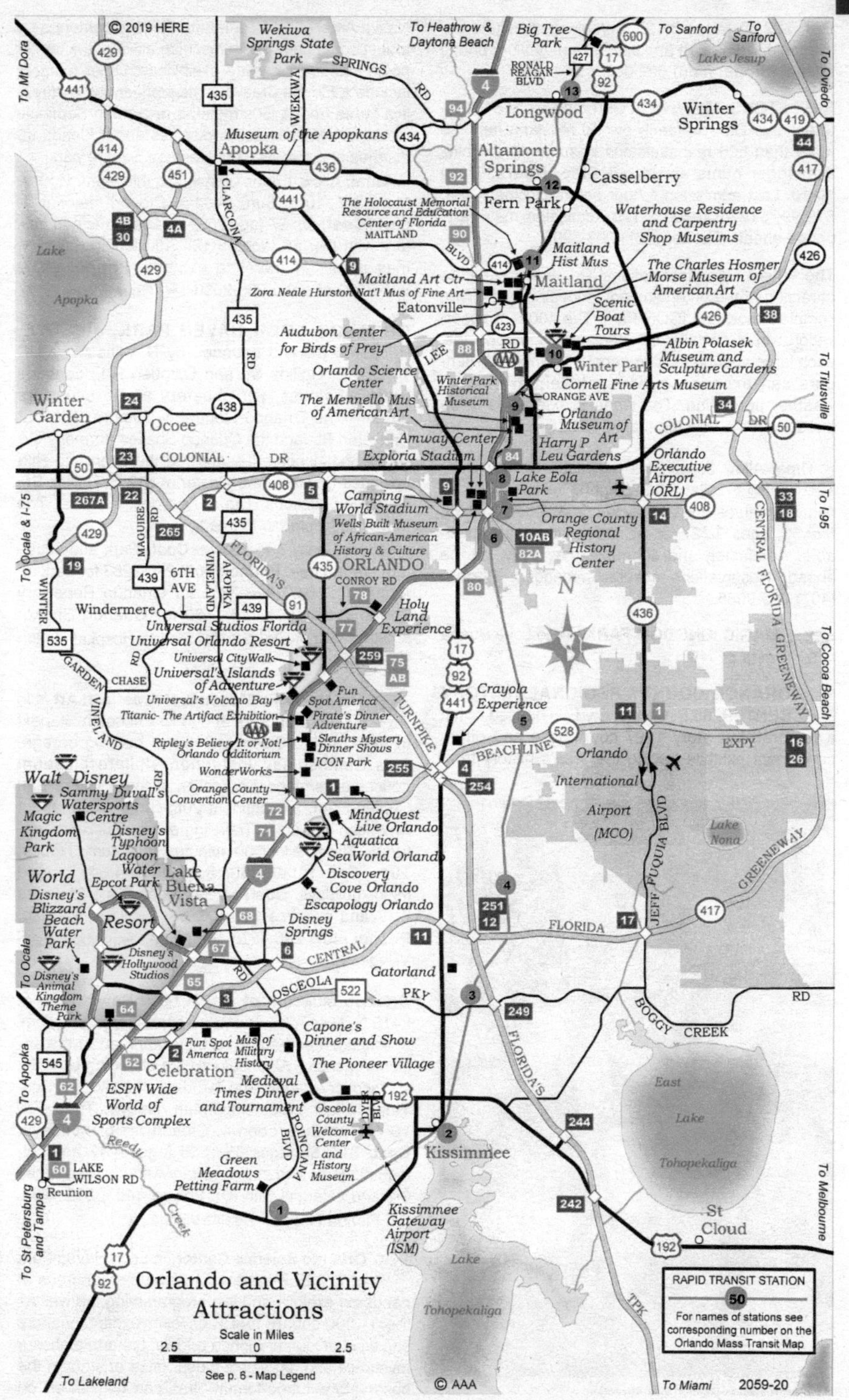
© 2019 HERE
Orlando and Vicinity Attractions
Scale in Miles
2.5 0 2.5
See p. 6 - Map Legend
RAPID TRANSIT STATION
50
For names of stations see corresponding number on the Orlando Mass Transit Map
© AAA
2059-20
Wekiwa Springs State Park
Museum of the Apopkans
Apopka
Longwood
Winter Springs
Altamonte Springs
Casselberry
Fern Park
The Holocaust Memorial Resource and Education Center of Florida
Waterhouse Residence and Carpentry Shop Museums
Maitland Hist Mus
Maitland
Maitland Art Ctr
Zora Neale Hurston Nat'l Mus of Fine Art
Eatonville
The Charles Hosmer Morse Museum of American Art
Scenic Boat Tours
Audubon Center for Birds of Prey
Albin Polasek Museum and Sculpture Gardens
Orlando Science Center
Winter Park
Winter Park Historical Museum
Cornell Fine Arts Museum
The Mennello Mus of American Art
Orlando Museum of Art
Harry P Leu Gardens
Amway Center
Exploria Stadium
Winter Garden
Ocoee
Lake Eola Park
Orlando Executive Airport (ORL)
Camping World Stadium
Wells Built Museum of African-American History & Culture
Orange County Regional History Center
ORLANDO
Windermere
Holy Land Experience
Universal Studios Florida
Universal Orlando Resort
Universal CityWalk
Universal's Islands of Adventure
Universal's Volcano Bay
Fun Spot America
Crayola Experience
Titanic- The Artifact Exhibition
Pirate's Dinner Adventure
Ripley's Believe It or Not! Orlando Odditorium
Sleuths Mystery Dinner Shows
ICON Park
WonderWorks
Orlando International Airport (MCO)
Orange County Convention Center
Walt Disney World Resort
Sammy Duvall's Watersports Centre
Magic Kingdom Park
MindQuest Live Orlando
Aquatica
Disney's Typhoon Lagoon Water Park
SeaWorld Orlando
Discovery Cove Orlando
Lake Buena Vista
Epcot Park
Escapology Orlando
Disney's Blizzard Beach Water Park
Disney Springs
Disney's Hollywood Studios
Gatorland
Disney's Animal Kingdom Theme Park
Capone's Dinner and Show
Fun Spot America
Mus of Military History
The Pioneer Village
Celebration
ESPN Wide World of Sports Complex
Medieval Times Dinner and Tournament
Osceola County Welcome Center and History Museum
Kissimmee
Green Meadows Petting Farm
Kissimmee Gateway Airport (ISM)
St Cloud
Reunion
Big Tree Park
To Heathrow & Daytona Beach
To Sanford
To Mt Dora
To Oviedo
To Titusville
To I-95
To Cocoa Beach
To Melbourne
To Miami
To Lakeland
To St Petersburg and Tampa
To Apopka
To Ocala
To Ocala & I-75
Lake Apopka
Lake Jesup
East Lake Tohopekaliga
Lake Tohopekaliga
Lake Nona
Reedy Creek
COLONIAL DR
FLORIDA'S TURNPIKE
BEACHLINE EXPY
CENTRAL FLORIDA GREENEWAY
OSCEOLA PKY
BOGGY CREEK RD
JEFF FUQUIA BLVD
LAKE WILSON RD
POINCIANA BLVD
CONROY RD
RONALD REAGAN BLVD
ORANGE AVE
SPRINGS RD
N

$28; $22.50 (ages 3-12). Combination tickets are available. Admission and schedule may vary; phone ahead. **Phone:** (866) 622-0607.

SKELETONS: Museum of Osteology is at 8441 International Dr. The family-owned museum features more than 500 real skeletons in some 40 exhibits, scavenger hunts and a gift shop. **Hours:** Daily 10-10. Last admission 1 hour before closing. **Cost:** $19.99; $12.99 (ages 3-11). Admission may vary; phone ahead. **Phone:** (407) 203-6999.

The Wheel, 8445 International Dr., is the signature attraction of the entertainment, shopping and dining complex known as ICON Park. The 400-foot observation wheel contains 30 air-conditioned capsules, each large enough to fit 15 people, is where passengers can experience views of Central Florida, weather permitting. The wheel's exterior is lit up throughout the evening thanks to LED lights.

Time: Allow 30 minutes minimum. **Hours:** Daily 10-10 (also Fri.-Sat. 10-midnight). Visitors must arrive 15 minutes ahead of ticket time. **Cost:** $27.99; $22.50 (ages 3-12). Combination tickets are available. Admission and schedule may vary; phone ahead. Reservations are recommended. **Phone:** (407) 999-9985.

GEM **MAGIC KINGDOM PARK**—see Lake Buena Vista p. 119.

SAVE **ORANGE COUNTY REGIONAL HISTORY CENTER,** 65 E. Central Blvd., is housed within a restored five-story 1927 courthouse and offers permanent exhibits tracing the area's history from Native American settlement to its development as a tourist community. A Smithsonian affiliate, the center hosts biannual traveling exhibitions. Other features include a Florida Cracker-style pioneer cabin, a replica tepee from a '50s motel, a re-created Seminole Indian village, interactive displays about Florida industries and the adjacent Heritage Square park.

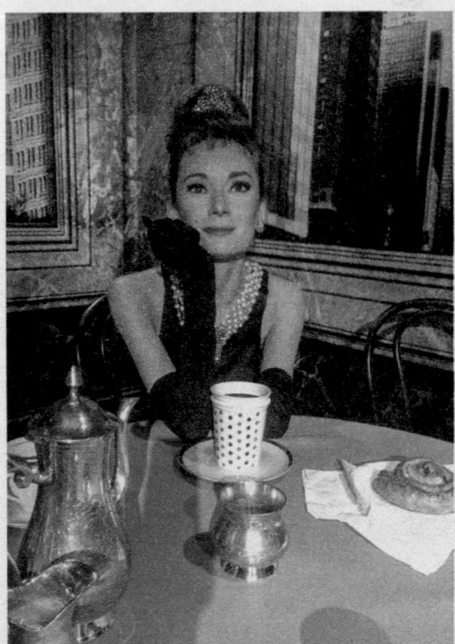

Madame Tussauds Orlando Wax Attraction

Time: Allow 1 hour, 30 minutes minimum. **Hours:** Mon.-Sat. 10-5, Sun. noon-5. Closed major holidays. **Cost:** $8; $7 (ages 55+ and students and military with ID); $6 (ages 5-12). Additional admission may apply for traveling exhibits. **Phone:** (407) 836-8500 or (800) 965-2030. Church Street, 7

ORLANDO LOCH HAVEN PARK, at 777 E. Princeton St. and bounded by N. Mills Ave. (US 17/92), E. Rollins St. and Camden Rd., contains three museums, two theaters and a sculpture garden. The Orlando Repertory Theatre, 1001 E. Princeton St., and the Orlando Shakes (formerly Orlando Shakespeare Theater), in the John and Rita Lowndes Shakespeare Center at 812 E. Rollins St., stages productions. The city's oldest oak tree, The Mayor, is located in the park.

Hours: Daily 5 to sunset. **Cost:** Park and sculpture garden free. **Phone:** (407) 246-2283 for park information, (407) 896-7365 for Orlando Repertory Theatre, or (407) 447-1700 for Orlando Shakespeare Theater. Florida Hospital Health Village, 9

SAVE **The Mennello Museum of American Art** is in Loch Haven Park at 900 E. Princeton St. next to the Orlando Science Center's parking garage. This Smithsonian Institution affiliate museum houses a permanent collection of the works of Earl Cunningham, a prominent 20th-century self-taught American folk artist. Traveling exhibits also are featured. **Time:** Allow 30 minutes minimum. **Hours:** Tues.-Sat. 10:30-4:30, Sun. noon-4:30. Closed major holidays. **Cost:** $5; $4 (ages 60+); $1 (ages 6-17 and students with ID); free (military with ID). **Phone:** (407) 246-4278. Florida Hospital Health Village, 9

Orlando Museum of Art, in Loch Haven Park at 2416 N. Mills Ave., maintains permanent collections of American and African art, including art of the ancient Americas. Also featured are changing exhibits, a discovery center and hands-on family activities. **Time:** Allow 1 hour minimum. **Hours:** Tues.-Fri. 10-4, Sat.-Sun. noon-4. Closed major holidays. **Cost:** $15; $8 (ages 65+); $5 (ages 4-17 and college students and active military with ID); free (ages 0-3 and veterans with ID). **Phone:** (407) 896-4231. Florida Hospital Health Village, 9

SAVE **Orlando Science Center,** in Loch Haven Park at 777 E. Princeton St., features hundreds of hands-on exhibits and live programming, as well as the 11,000-square-foot KidsTown exhibit. Visitors can also encounter Florida wildlife, unearth dinosaur mysteries and, on select dates, gaze at stars in the observatory. Large-format films can be viewed on the eight-story screen in the Dr. Phillips CineDome while feature films play in the Digital Adventure Theater.

Time: Allow 2 hours minimum. **Hours:** Sun.-Tues. and Thurs.-Sat. 10-5 year-round; also 10-5 every Wed. June-Aug. and first Wed. of month Sept.-May. Phone ahead for observatory hours. Closed Easter, Thanksgiving, Christmas Eve and Christmas. Phone ahead to confirm schedule. **Cost:** $20.95; $18.95 (ages 55+ and students with ID); $14.95 (ages 3-11). Prices may vary during special exhibitions. **Parking:** $5. **Phone:** (407) 514-2000. Florida Hospital Health Village, 9

PIRATE'S DINNER ADVENTURE is .25 mi. s. of International Dr. at 6400 Carrier Dr. Guests at this interactive dinner show enjoy a feast while musical comedy, swashbuckling stunts and live-action performances take place aboard a pirate galleon. After the show, guests may attend the Buccaneer Bash dance party. **Hours:** Sun.-Thurs. at 7:30, Fri. at 8:30, Sat. at 5:30 and 8:30. Phone ahead to confirm schedule. **Cost:** $67.95; $41.45 (ages 3-12). Prices may vary; phone ahead. Reservations are recommended. **Phone:** (407) 206-5102 or (800) 866-2469.

RIPLEY'S BELIEVE IT OR NOT! ORLANDO ODDITORIUM is .5 mi. s.e. of I-4 exit 74A (Sand Lake Rd.) at 8201 International Dr. Odd and unusual exhibits and video presentations from around the world are featured in 16 themed galleries that include interactive illusions, human and animal oddities, weird art and dinosaurs and fossils. **Time:** Allow 1 hour minimum. **Hours:** Daily 9 a.m.-midnight. Last admission 1 hour before closing. Phone ahead to confirm schedule. **Cost:** $19.99; $13.99 (ages 4-11). **Phone:** (407) 345-0501.

SEAWORLD PARKS ORLANDO, jct. I-4 and SR 528 (Beachline Expwy.), offers South Sea islands-inspired water fun at Aquatica, unforgettable encounters with marine life at Discovery Cove Orlando and sea-themed shows, exhibits and rides at SeaWorld Orlando.

Rental strollers and wheelchairs are available. **Hours:** Aquatica opens daily at 9 or 10; closing times vary. Discovery Cove Orlando daily 8-5:30. SeaWorld Orlando opens daily at 9; closing times vary. Phone ahead to confirm park schedules.

Cost: Aquatica $59.99; $54.99 (ages 3-9). Discovery Cove Orlando Dolphin Swim Day Resort Package starts at $339; Day Resort Package starts at $199; free (ages 0-2). Discovery Cove Orlando admission includes 14 consecutive days admission to Aquatica and SeaWorld Orlando, breakfast and lunch, all snacks and beverages throughout the day and all swim gear. Reservations are required for Discovery Cove Orlando. SeaWorld Orlando $99.99; free (ages 0-2). Combination tickets are available at all parks. Park prices may vary; phone ahead. Discounted tickets are available in advance from the attraction's website. **Parking:** $15 (Aquatica); $20 (SeaWorld Orlando); free (Discovery Cove Orlando). **Phone:** (888) 800-5447 for SeaWorld, or (407) 545-5550 for Aquatica.

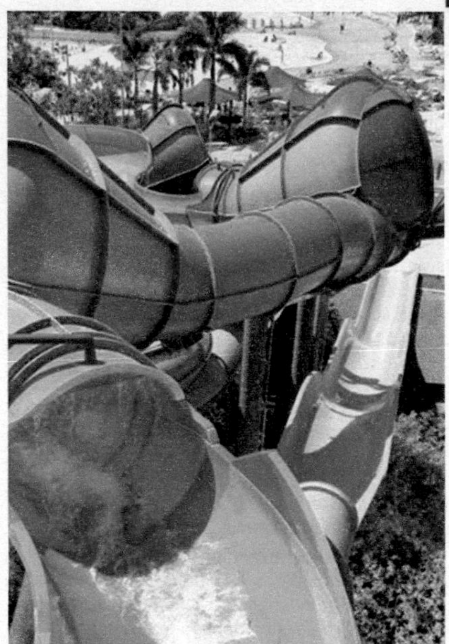

Aquatica

Aquatica is at 5800 Water Play Way next to SeaWorld Orlando. The whimsical water park, inspired by the colors, flora and personality of South Sea islands, combines thrill rides; vast, sandy beaches with exotic trees and personal cabanas; and an opportunity for up-close animal experiences. Dolphin Plunge, a park highlight, is a clear tube ride that sends riders plunging through a lagoon inhabited by Commerson's dolphins. Ihu's Breakaway Falls features slides that drop riders 80 feet. Twisting rivers, raft rides and side-by-side wave pools add to the fun.

Height restrictions apply on some rides. Cabanas, lockers and towels can be rented. Allow a full day. **Hours:** Opens daily at 9 or 10; closing times vary. Phone ahead to confirm schedule. **Cost:** $59.99; $54.99 (ages 3-9). **Parking:** $15; $20 (RVs). **Phone:** (888) 800-5447.

GEM **Discovery Cove Orlando** is at 6000 Discovery Cove Way next to SeaWorld Orlando. The all-inclusive day resort allows guests, at their own pace, to encounter a variety of animals up-close and in a lush island resort setting. You can touch and swim with dolphins, meet otters and marmosets, swim with sharks, snorkel in waters inhabited by mysterious stingrays and schools of tropical fish, view hundreds of exotic birds in a free-flight aviary, drift down a lazy river and lounge on powdery beaches.

Allow a full day. **Hours:** Daily 8-5:30. **Cost:** Dolphin Swim Day Resort Package starts at $245; Day Resort Package starts at $195; free (ages 0-2). Discovery Cove Orlando admission includes 14 consecutive days admission to Aquatica and SeaWorld Orlando, breakfast and lunch at Laguna Grill, all snacks and beverages throughout the day and all swim gear. Prices vary seasonally; phone ahead. Children under 6 are not permitted to interact with the dolphins. Reservations are required. **Phone:** (407) 513-4600 for general information.

GEM **SeaWorld Orlando** is at 7007 SeaWorld Dr., at jct. I-4 and SR 528 (Beachline Expwy.). This marine life adventure park has themed shows; up-close animal encounters; attractions; and rides, including the face-down flying coaster Manta, the floorless coaster Kraken Unleashed and the water coaster Journey to Atlantis.

At 200 feet tall and running up to 73 mph, the Mako roller coaster is reportedly the highest and fastest coaster in Orlando. Kraken Unleashed, now a virtual reality coaster, transports guests into Kraken's lair in the deep ocean.

Climb aboard your raft and prepare to get soaked while reaching peak excitement on Infinity Falls. Enjoy roaring rapids, thrilling chutes and splashing turns before plunging down the tallest drop of its kind into churning whitewater.

Shows include Dolphin Days, with dolphins, trainers and exotic birds in an educational production; Pets Ahoy, highlighting the talents of rescued four-legged friends; and "Clyde & Seamore's Sea Lion High," featuring comical sea lions and otters.

The Antarctica: Empire of the Penguin exhibit—complete with chilly temps, simulated snowstorms, imitation ice formations, a penguin-themed family ride and 250 live penguins—provides a glimpse into the fascinating lives of the tuxedoed cold-weather creatures. At the TurtleTrek exhibit, guests visit a manatee and sea turtle habitat before stepping into a huge dome theater for a 360-degree 3-D film experience.

Take a stroll down Sesame Street and visit your favorite furry friends. Stop by the famous stoop at 123. Explore the inside of Hooper's Store and Big Bird's Nest. Come and play with Elmo, Cookie Monster, Abby and all the gang. Also enjoy an award-winning parade and rides at Sesame Street Land.

Dolphin Nursery, Stingray Lagoon and Shark Encounter. On Behind-the-Scenes Tours, guests can interact with a penguin, touch a shark and learn how animal experts care for rescued manatees and sea turtles. Several other guided tours are offered.

If you happen to get went at Infinity Falls, you'll be able to dry off in no time at dryers for a small fee. Kennels, strollers, wheelchairs and lockers can be rented. Allow a full day. **Hours:** Opens daily at 9; closing times vary. **Cost:** $99.99; free (ages 0-2). There is an additional fee for VIP tours. Dine with Shamu reservations are required; visit Guest Relations for details. **Parking:** $25; $30 (RVs, trailers, semitrucks and preferred). **Phone:** (888) 800-5447. GT

SAVE **SLEUTHS MYSTERY DINNER SHOWS** is at 8267 International Dr. Guests become detectives to help solve a crime in these comedy-mystery dinner shows. **Time:** Allow 3 hours minimum. **Hours:** Shows nightly; seating times vary with the show. Phone ahead to confirm schedule. **Cost:** $64.95; $29.95 (ages 3-11). Reservations are required. **Phone:** (407) 363-1985 or (800) 393-1985.

GEM **UNIVERSAL ORLANDO RESORT™** is off I-4 exit 75A (eastbound) or 74B (westbound), following signs to the parking garages at 6000 Universal Blvd.

At Universal Orlando Resort™, three amazing theme parks let you immerse yourself in the next generation of blockbuster entertainment, journey through the legendary worlds of incredible heroes, and enjoy the thrills and relaxation of a tropical paradise. You can script an incredible day of fun at Universal Studios Florida™, a real working film and TV studio that features rides, shows and attractions that puts you right in the middle of the action. Next door you'll step right into powerful stories, myths and legends at Universal's Islands of Adventure™. At Universal's Volcano Bay™ water theme park, you'll find an oasis of excitement along with laid-back luxuries.

Don't forget to savor the unforgettable dining and entertainment of Universal CityWalk™, home to an array of themed restaurants, clubs, concert venues, movies, shops, miniature golf and more. Unwind at your choice of six on-site hotels featuring a range of accommodations, amenities, recreation and special theme park benefits.

Strollers, wheelchairs, electric carts and air-conditioned kennels can be rented. Vehicles can leave the garage and return the same day by stopping at the toll plaza upon re-entry and presenting their parking ticket. **Hours:** The theme parks generally open daily at 9 a.m.; closing times vary by season. Universal CityWalk™ is open daily 11 a.m.-2 a.m. Theme park and CityWalk™ hours may vary; phone ahead.

Cost: A 1-Day Anytime ticket to Universal's Volcano Bay™ starting from $70; $65 (ages 3-9). A 1-Park Base ticket, which allows access to either Universal Studios Florida™ or Universal's Islands of Adventure™, starting from $115; $110 (ages 3-9). A 2-Park 1-Day ticket, which allows same-day access to both Universal Studios Florida™ and Universal's Islands of Adventure™ starting from $170; $165 (ages 3-9). A 3-Park ticket (valid at Universal Studios Florida™, Universal's Islands of Adventure™ and Universal's Volcano Bay™) starting from $279; $269 (ages 3-9). Additional combination options are available. All multi-day park tickets include admission to select live entertainment venues at Universal CityWalk™. Special advance purchase discount tickets are available at participating AAA/CAA offices. Members who pre-purchase admission through their AAA/CAA branch will receive discounts at select restaurant and merchandise locations within the resort (excludes purchases at food or merchandise carts and purchases of alcohol, tobacco, candy, film, collectibles, sundry items, tattoos and services). Phone ahead to confirm admission and schedule. **Parking:** $25; free (after 6 p.m.; not valid during Halloween Horror Nights™). Bus and RV $30; Prime $35. Valet parking $25-$65.

Phone: (407) 363-8000.

SAVE **Universal CityWalk™,** off I-4 exit 75A (eastbound) or 74B (westbound), following signs to the parking garages at 6000 Universal Blvd., is an entertainment complex featuring specialty shopping, the 20-screen AMC Universal Cineplex 20 movie theater, nightclubs, two miniature putt-putt golf courses, and casual and fine dining in themed restaurants that cater to every member of the family. The complex is located between Universal's Islands of Adventure™ and Universal Studios™ and within walking distance of each on-site hotel. **Note:** Vehicles can leave the garage and return the same day by stopping at the toll plaza upon re-entry and presenting their parking ticket. **Hours:** Daily 11 a.m.-2 a.m. **Cost:** CityWalk™ complex free. Evening cover charges vary by venue. Age restrictions apply for certain venues. Phone ahead to confirm admission and schedule. **Parking:** $25; free (after 6 p.m.; not valid during Halloween Horror Nights™). Bus and RV $30; Prime $35. Valet parking $25-$65. **Phone:** (407) 363-8000, or (407) 258-3626 for Blue Man Group tickets.

GEM SAVE **Universal's Islands of Adventure™** is off I-4 exit 75A (eastbound) or 74B (westbound), following signs to the parking garages at 6000 Universal Blvd.

Journey through the legendary worlds of incredible heroes at Universal's Islands of Adventure™, where you'll step into powerful stories, myths and legends during thrilling rides and attractions.

Encompassing 20 acres, The Wizarding World of Harry Potter is home to Harry Potter and the Forbidden Journey, a state-of-the-art attraction that brings the magic, characters and stories of Harry Potter to life. The Flight of the Hippogriff coaster provides thrills for all ages. Note: Only guests with Park-to-Park admission tickets are eligible to ride the Hogwarts Express to the Wizarding World of Harry Potter-Diagon Alley at Universal Studios Florida.

Marvel Super Hearo Island puts you in the middle of a comic book where you'll find the 3D thrill ride The Amazing Adventures of Spider-Man, The Incredible Hulk Coaster, the gravity-defying Doctor Doom's Fearfall and Storm Force Accelatron.

Based on cartoons and comic strips, Toon Lagoon's attractions include Dudley Do-Right's Ripsaw Falls log flume ride and Popeye & Bluto's Bilge-Rat Barges white-water raft ride. Children can explore all three decks of Popeye's boat, *Me Ship, The Olive.*

Universal's Islands of Adventure™

Then there's Skull Island: Reign of Kong, which allows visitors to go on expedition to the mysterious island.

Jurassic Park brings to life a land inhabited by prehistoric creatures. Jurassic Park River Adventures features a narrow from an hungry T-rex. Visitors unearth mysteries from the past at the Jurassic Park Discovery Center. Camp Jurassic is an interactive children's play area which also features the Pteranodon Flyers, an attraction made especially for kids.

Dr. Seuss' stories and characters come to life at Seuss Landing. The Cat in the Hat takes visitors on a ride through the classic children's book, and a menagerie of Dr. Seuss characters serves as steeds on the Caro-Seuss-el. Other attractions include the If I Ran The Zoo play area, The High in The Sky Seuss Trolley Train Ride! And the One Fish, Two Fish, Rd Fish, Blue Fish ride. **Note:** Vehicles can leave the garage and return the same day by stopping at the toll plaza upon re-entry and presenting their parking ticket. **Hours:** Generally opens daily at 9 a.m.; closing times vary according to season. Phone ahead to confirm schedule. **Cost:** A 1-Day Anytime ticket to Universal's Volcano Bay™ starting from $70; $65 (ages 3-9). A 1-Park Base ticket, which allows access to either Universal Studios Florida™ or Universal's Islands of Adventure™, starting from $115; $110 (ages 3-9). A 2-Park 1-Day ticket, which allows same-day access to both Universal Studios Florida™ and Universal's Islands of Adventure™ starting from $170; $165 (ages 3-9). A 3-Park ticket (valid at Universal Studios Florida™, Universal's Islands of Adventure™ and Universal's Volcano

Bay™) starting from $279; $269 (ages 3-9). Additional combination options are available. All multi-day park tickets include admission to select live entertainment venues at Universal CityWalk™. Special advance purchase discount tickets are available at participating AAA/CAA offices. Members who pre-purchase admission through their AAA/CAA branch will receive discounts at select restaurant and merchandise locations within the resort (excludes purchases at food or merchandise carts and purchases of alcohol, tobacco, candy, film, collectibles, sundry items, tattoos and services). Phone ahead to confirm admission and schedule. **Parking:** $25; free (after 6 p.m.; not valid during Halloween Horror Nights™). Bus and RV $30; Prime $35. Valet parking $25-$65.

Phone: (407) 363-8000.

GEM SAVE **Universal Studios Florida™** is off I-4 exit 75A (eastbound) or 74B (westbound), following signs to the parking garages at 6000 Universal Blvd.

Immerse yourself in the next generation of blockbuster entertainment at Universal Studios™. You'll script a day of fun at this real working film and TV studio that features rides, shows and attractions that put you in the middle of the action.

Hollywood Rip Ride Rockit is a multimedia roller coaster that lets you pick your own music and download a video of your experience. Transformers: The Ride 3-D includes high-tech, action-packed fun.

Join Homer, Marge, Bart, Lisa and Maggie on The Simpsons Ride as they visit the Krustyland theme park. Riders are plunged into darkness in Revenge of the Mummy. Guests see, hear and feel the action courtesy of Ogrevision in Shrek 4-D. Despicable Me Minion Mayhem is a 3-D motion-simulator ride through Gru's secret laboratory.

The interactive ride MEN IN BLACK Alien Attack allows visitors to save the galaxy by zapping creatures as the ride moves through city streets. The seasonal Fear Factor Live is an audience participation stunt show based on the reality TV program.

At Race Through New York Starring Jimmy Fallon it's you versus Jimmy in a fun-filled race around New York City landmarks. Fast & Furious – Supercharged Universal takes you into an amazing recreation of the crew's headquarters filled with movie props and supercharged vehicles you've only seen on the big screen. Orlando's Horror Make-Up Show offers an in-depth look at the creation of horror movie characters.

Woody Woodpecker's KidZone features Animal Actors on Location!, E.T. Adventure and Woody Woodpecker's Nuthouse Coaster.

The Wizarding World of Harry Potter–Diagon Alley is an expansion of Universal's Islands of Adventure's The Wizarding World of Harry Potter–Hogsmeade. Climb aboard a mind-blowing, multidimensional ride Harry Potter and the Escape from Gringotts. The Hogwarts Express allows guests with Park to Park tickets to experience this adventure, connecting King's Cross Station in London to Hogsmeade.

Note: Vehicles can leave the garage and return the same day by stopping at the toll plaza upon re-entry and presenting their parking ticket. **Hours:** Generally opens daily at 9 a.m.; closing times vary according to season. Phone ahead to confirm schedule. **Cost:** A 1-Park Base ticket, which allows access to either Universal Studios Florida™ or Universal's Islands of Adventure™, starting from $115; $110 (ages 3-9). A 2-Park 1-Day ticket, which allows same-day access to both Universal Studios Florida™ and Universal's Islands of Adventure™ starting from $170; $165 (ages 3-9). A 3-Park ticket (valid at Universal Studios Florida™, Universal's Islands of Adventure™ and Universal's Volcano Bay™) starting from $279; $269 (ages 3-9). Additional combination options are available. All multi-day park tickets include admission to select live entertainment venues at Universal CityWalk™. Special advance purchase discount tickets are available at participating AAA/CAA offices. Members who pre-purchase admission through their AAA/CAA branch will receive discounts at select restaurant and merchandise locations within the resort (excludes purchases at food or merchandise carts and purchases of alcohol, tobacco, candy, film, collectibles, sundry items, tattoos and services). Phone ahead to confirm admission and schedule.

Parking: $25; free (after 6 p.m.; not valid during Halloween Horror Nights™). Bus and RV $30; Prime $35. Valet parking $25-$65. **Phone:** (407) 363-8000.

SAVE **Universal's Volcano Bay™** is off I-4 exit 75A (eastbound) or 74B (westbound), following signs to the parking garages at 6000 Universal Blvd. An adventure-drenched water theme park, the third at Universal Orlando Resort™, is filled with both thrilling rides and relaxing indulges.

Ride the Ko'okiri Body Plunge, featuring a 70-degree fall through a drop door and 125 feet of white-knuckle fun, or brave the rope bridge and take the plunge down the Ohno and Ohva Slides, serpentine adventures that each end several feet above the pool below. Whether plummeting down Krakatau™ Aqua Coaster or catapulting into pools of blue water, thrill seekers will have plenty to do day and night. Calming lagoons, leisure pools, secluded waterfalls and lazily winding rivers make the water theme park a place of thrills and relaxation.

Two-story cabanas, concierge services and resortlike amenities also are available. Vehicles can leave the garage and return the same day by stopping at the toll plaza upon re-entry and presenting their parking ticket. **Hours:** Generally opens daily at 9 a.m.; closing times vary by season.

Cost: 1-Park ticket for Volcano Bay starting from $70; A 1-Park Base ticket, which allows access to either Universal Studios Florida™ or Universal's Islands of Adventure™, starting from $115; $110 (ages 3-9). A 2-Park 1-Day ticket, which allows same-day access to both Universal Studios Florida™ and Universal's Islands of Adventure™ starting from $170; $165 (ages 3-9). A 3-Park ticket (valid at Universal Studios Florida™, Universal's Islands of Adventure™ and Universal's Volcano Bay™) starting from $279; $269 (ages 3-9). Additional combination options are available. All multi-day park tickets include admission to select live entertainment venues at Universal CityWalk™. Special advance purchase discount tickets are available at participating AAA/CAA offices. Members who pre-purchase admission through their AAA/CAA branch will receive discounts at select restaurant and merchandise locations within the resort (excludes purchases at food or merchandise carts and purchases of alcohol, tobacco, candy, film, collectibles, sundry items, tattoos and services). Phone ahead to confirm admission and schedule.

Parking: $25; free (after 6 p.m.; not valid during Halloween Horror Nights™). Bus and RV $30; Prime $35. Valet parking $25-$65. **Phone:** (407) 363-8000.

GEM **WALT DISNEY WORLD RESORT**—see Lake Buena Vista p. 115.

WELLS' BUILT MUSEUM OF AFRICAN-AMERICAN HISTORY & CULTURE is at 511 W. South St. Orlando's African American history is depicted through photographs, artifacts and multimedia exhibits. The structure was originally a hotel built by Dr. William Monroe Wells, one of the area's first black physicians. **Time:** Allow 45 minutes minimum. **Hours:** Mon.-Fri. 9-5; (also Sat. 9-5, Sun. noon-5, second weekend of the month); by appointment rest of year. Closed major holidays. Phone ahead to confirm schedule. **Cost:** $5; $3 (students with ID). **Phone:** (407) 245-7535.

Church Street, 7

WONDERWORKS is .8 mi. n. of SR 528 at 9067 International Dr. An upside-down building contains this interactive attraction, which features more than 100 hands-on exhibits and a laser tag arena. Virtual reality technology and simulations enable visitors to experience an earthquake and hurricane force winds, design and ride their own roller-coaster, explore a replica of a Mercury space capsule, play virtual sports and land a space shuttle. Also of interest is a three-story, glow-in-the-dark ropes course (height and weight restrictions apply; closed-toe shoes are required) and the 4D Motion Theater. The Outta Control Magic Comedy dinner show is offered nightly.

Time: Allow 1 hour minimum. **Hours:** Daily 9 a.m.-midnight. Dinner show at 6 and 8 p.m. **Cost:** All-Access (includes exhibits, 4D theater, ropes course and a laser tag game) $33.99; $24.99 (ages 4-12 and 60+). VIP Access (includes exhibits, 4D theater, ropes course, a laser tag game and the dinner show) $59.99; $41.99 (ages 4-12 and 60+). Dinner show only $31.99; $21.99 (ages 4-12 and 60+). **Parking:** $4 (first 2 hours); $2 (each additional hour); $10 (all day) at Pointe Orlando Parking Garage. **Phone:** (407) 351-8800.

Sightseeing

Looking for group travel activities that are both affordable and entertaining? Go Orlando pass is an all-access digital pass to more than 25 area attractions. There are different passes to suit, whether you want to choose the number of days or attractions to visit. Attractions include Boggy Creek Airboats, Fun Spot America, Gatorland, Kennedy Space Center, LEGOLAND Florida Resort, SEA LIFE Orlando Aquarium, Wheel at ICON Park and WonderWorks as well as other popular activities and sightseeing tours. The Go Orlando pass is available online, or by phone (800) 887-9103.

Bus and Van Tours

There are a variety of bus and van tours available to take you to any destination in Orlando. Bus and van tours are a great way to save money while visiting popular travel sites.

Let Your Voice Be Heard

- Tell us if a listed establishment doesn't meet your expectations.
- Recommend a favorite hotel or restaurant for inspection.

AAA.com/MemberFeedback

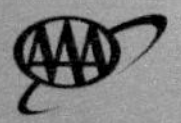

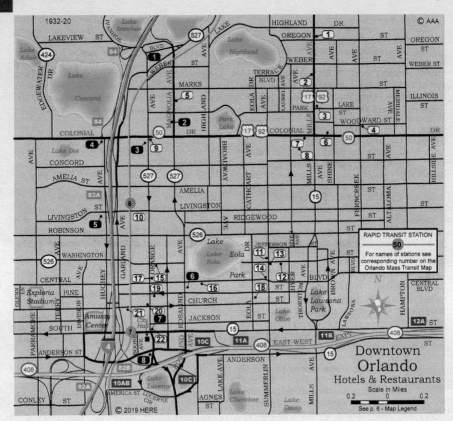

Downtown Orlando

This index helps you "spot" where approved hotels and restaurants are located on the corresponding detailed maps. Restaurant price range is a combination of lunch and/or dinner. Turn to the listing page for more information and consult display ads for special promotions.

For more details, rates and reservations: AAA.com/travelguides/hotels

DOWNTOWN ORLANDO

Map Page	Hotels	Diamond Rated	Member Savings	Page
1 this page	**DoubleTree by Hilton Orlando Downtown**	♦♦♦	✔	217
2 this page	**Courtyard by Marriott Orlando Downtown** *(See ad p. 217.)*	♦♦♦	✔	217
3 this page	**Residence Inn by Marriott Orlando Downtown**	♦♦♦	✔	218
4 this page	Crowne Plaza Orlando-Downtown	♦♦♦		217
5 this page	**Marriott Orlando Downtown**	♦♦♦	✔	218
6 this page	**Embassy Suites by Hilton Orlando-Downtown**	♦♦♦	✔	217
7 this page	**The Grand Bohemian Hotel Orlando, Autograph Collection**	♦♦♦♦	✔	218
8 this page	**Aloft Orlando Downtown**	♦♦♦	✔	217

Map Page	Restaurants	Diamond Rated	Cuisine	Price Range	Page
1 this page	Hawkers Asian Street Fare	♦♦	Asian Small Plates	$4-$10	218
2 this page	Tako Cheena	♦	Asian Fusion	$4-$11	218

Map Page	Restaurants (cont'd)	Diamond Rated	Cuisine	Price Range	Page
3 p. 186	The Strand	◆◆◆	American	$10-$27	218
4 p. 186	The Sanctum Cafe	◆◆	Vegetarian Small Plates	$6-$15	218
5 p. 186	Cafe Trastevere	◆◆	Italian	$12-$30	218
6 p. 186	Mamak	◆◆	Asian Fusion Small Plates	$4-$13	218
7 p. 186	Little Saigon Restaurant	◆◆	Vietnamese	$7-$19	218
8 p. 186	Dandelion Community Cafe	◆	Vegetarian	$6-$10	218
9 p. 186	New York Deli	◆	Deli	$4-$9	218
10 p. 186	DoveCote Brasserie	◆◆◆	French	$16-$32	218
11 p. 186	Anthony's Pizzeria & Italian Restaurant	◆◆	Italian Pizza	$9-$22	218
12 p. 186	Dexter's	◆◆◆	New American	$8-$25	218
13 p. 186	Graffiti Junktion	◆◆	Burgers	$6-$15	218
14 p. 186	Soco	◆◆◆	New Southern	$11-$33	218
15 p. 186	Gringos Locos	◆	Mexican	$3-$10	218
16 p. 186	310 Lakeside	◆◆	New American	$11-$34	218
17 p. 186	Wall Street Cantina	◆◆	Mexican	$8-$18	218
18 p. 186	The Menagerie Eatery & Bar	◆◆	Southern	$14-$20	218
19 p. 186	Artisan's Table	◆◆◆	American	$6-$29	218
20 p. 186	Kres ChopHouse	◆◆◆	Steak	$29-$59	218
21 p. 186	Hamburger Mary's Bar & Grille	◆◆	American	$8-$16	218
22 p. 186	The Boheme	◆◆◆	New American	$11-$49	218

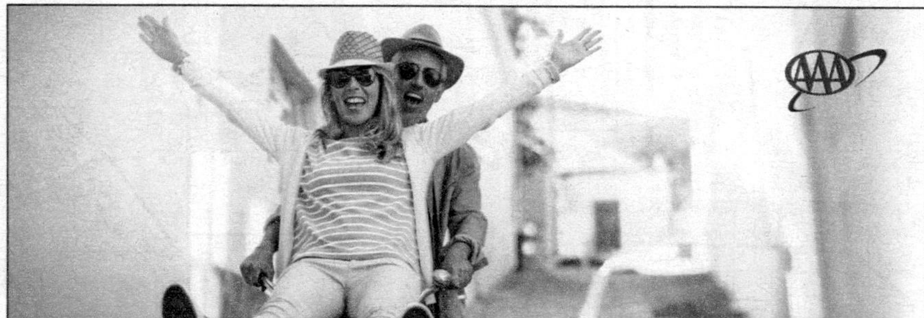

Hit the Road with Financial Services

Providing peace-of-mind benefits for members.

Visit your local AAA office or online at

AAA.com/Financial

All products not available at all locations.

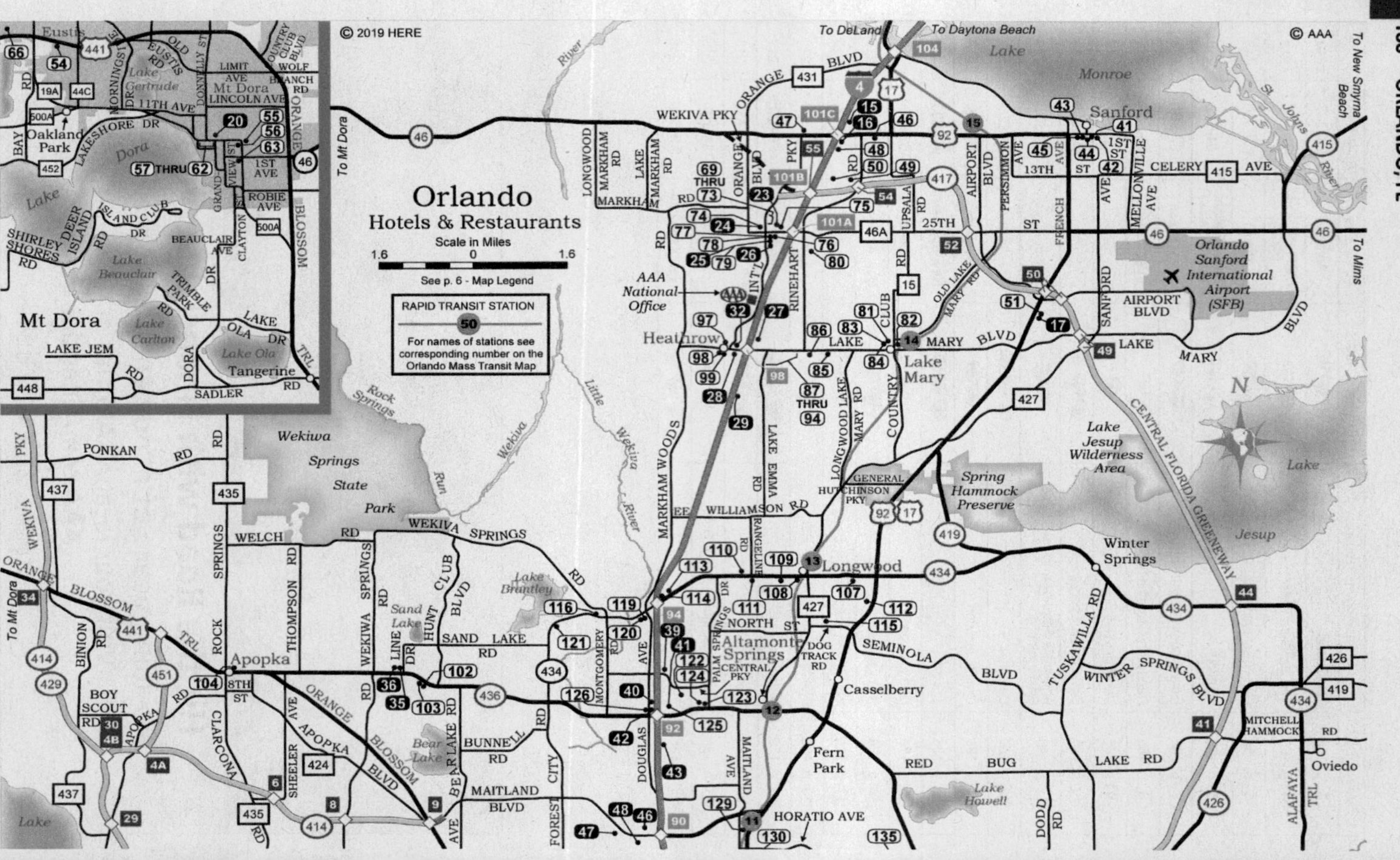
Orlando
Hotels & Restaurants
Scale in Miles
1.6
0
1.6
See p. 6 - Map Legend
RAPID TRANSIT STATION
50
For names of stations see corresponding number on the Orlando Mass Transit Map
© AAA
© 2019 HERE
To New Smyrna Beach
To Mims
To Daytona Beach
To DeLand
To Mt Dora
Sanford
Lake Monroe
St Johns River
Orlando Sanford International Airport (SFB)
Lake Jesup
Lake Jesup Wilderness Area
Spring Hammock Preserve
Winter Springs
Oviedo
Lake Mary
Longwood
Heathrow
AAA National Office
Altamonte Springs
Casselberry
Fern Park
Lake Howell
Lake Brantley
Sand Lake
Bear Lake
Apopka
Wekiwa Springs State Park
Rock Springs Run
Little Wekiva River
Wekiva River
CENTRAL FLORIDA GREENEWAY
CELERY AVE
MELLONVILLE AVE
SANFORD AVE
FRENCH AVE
PERSIMMON AVE
AIRPORT BLVD
LAKE MARY BLVD
OLD LAKE MARY RD
UPSALA RD
25TH ST
COUNTRY CLUB RD
LONGWOOD LAKE MARY RD
GENERAL HUTCHINSON PKY
RINEHART RD
INT'L PKY
LAKE EMMA RD
MARKHAM WOODS RD
ORANGE BLVD
WEKIVA PKY
LONGWOOD MARKHAM RD
LAKE MARKHAM RD
WILLIAMSON RD
RANGELINE RD
NORTH ST
DOG TRACK RD
CENTRAL PKY
PALM SPRINGS DR
TUSKAWILLA RD
WINTER SPRINGS BLVD
SEMINOLA BLVD
RED BUG LAKE RD
DODD RD
MITCHELL HAMMOCK RD
ALAFAYA TRL
HORATIO AVE
MAITLAND AVE
MAITLAND BLVD
DOUGLAS AVE
MONTGOMERY RD
FOREST CITY RD
BUNNELL RD
BEAR LAKE RD
HUNT CLUB BLVD
SAND LAKE RD
LINE DR
WEKIVA SPRINGS RD
WEKIWA SPRINGS RD
THOMPSON RD
WELCH RD
ROCK SPRINGS RD
PONKAN RD
8TH ST
CLARCONA RD
ORANGE BLOSSOM TRL
APOPKA BLVD
SHEELER AVE
BOY SCOUT RD
BINION RD
WEKIVA PKY
Mt Dora
Eustis
Lake Gertrude
Lake Dora
Lake Beauclair
Lake Carlton
Lake Ola
Tangerine
Oakland Park
Trimble Park
ORANGE BLOSSOM
LIMIT AVE
LINCOLN AVE
DONNELLY ST
OLD EUSTIS RD
11TH AVE
MORNINGSIDE DR
LAKESHORE DR
ISLAND CLUB DR
DEER ISLAND RD
SHIRLEY SHORES RD
BAY RD
LAKE JEM RD
SADLER RD
DORA DR
BEAUCLAIR DR
CLAYTON ST
ROBIE AVE
1ST AVE
WOLF BRANCH RD
COUNTRY CLUB BLVD
LAKE OLA DR
TANGERINE TRL

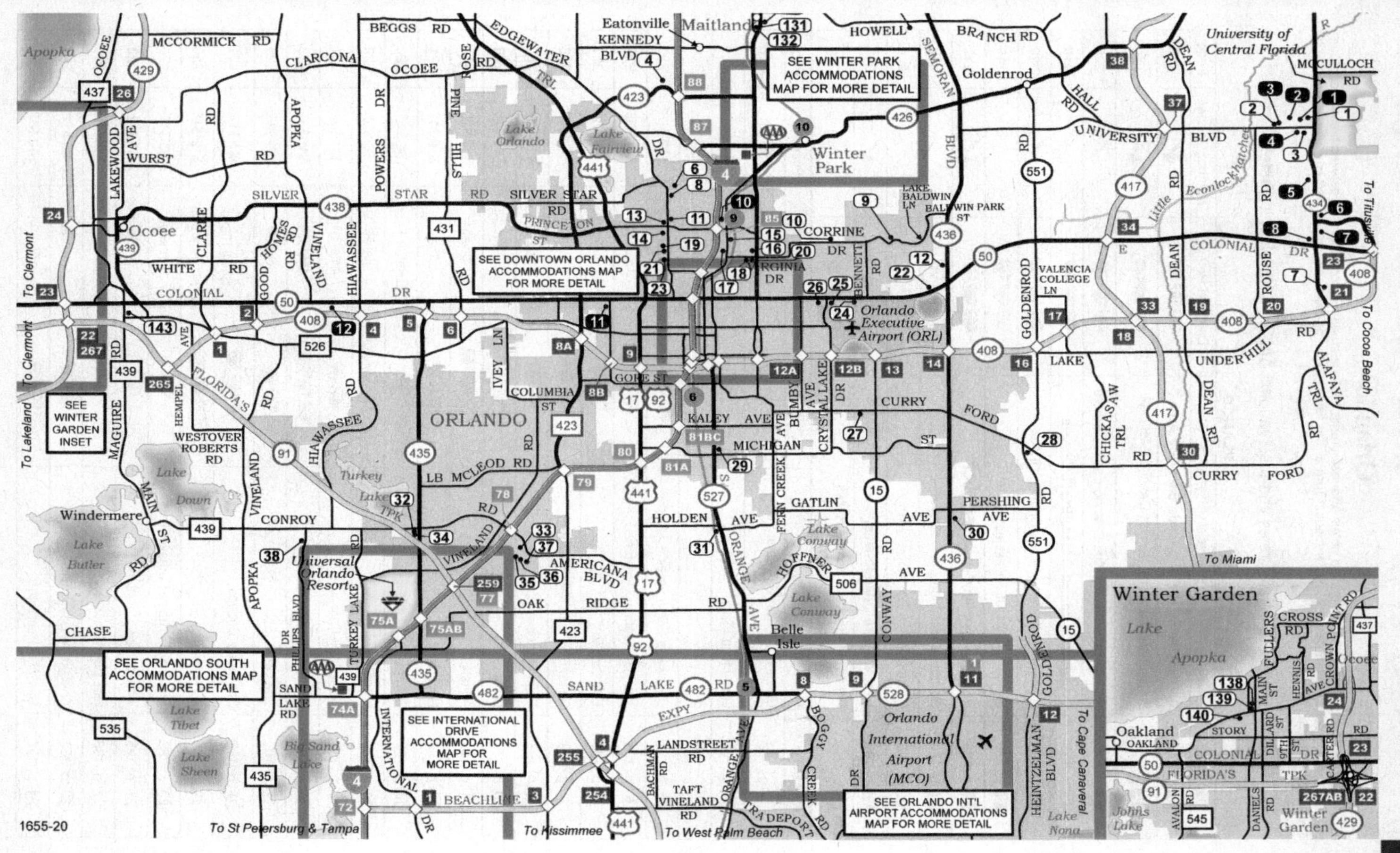
University of Central Florida
To Titusville
To Cocoa Beach
Maitland
Eatonville
Goldenrod
SEE WINTER PARK ACCOMMODATIONS MAP FOR MORE DETAIL
Winter Park
Lake Orlando
Lake Fairview
Ocoee
To Clermont
To Lakeland
SEE DOWNTOWN ORLANDO ACCOMMODATIONS MAP FOR MORE DETAIL
Orlando Executive Airport (ORL)
ORLANDO
SEE WINTER GARDEN INSET
Lake Down
Windermere
Lake Butler
Turkey Lake
Universal Orlando Resort
Lake Conway
Belle Isle
To Miami
Winter Garden
Lake Apopka
Oakland
Johns Lake
Winter Garden
SEE ORLANDO SOUTH ACCOMMODATIONS MAP FOR MORE DETAIL
Lake Tibet
Lake Sheen
Big Sand Lake
SEE INTERNATIONAL DRIVE ACCOMMODATIONS MAP FOR MORE DETAIL
Orlando International Airport (MCO)
SEE ORLANDO INT'L AIRPORT ACCOMMODATIONS MAP FOR MORE DETAIL
To Cape Canaveral
Lake Nona
1655-20
To St Petersburg & Tampa
To Kissimmee
To West Palm Beach

Orlando

This index helps you "spot" where approved hotels and restaurants are located on the corresponding detailed maps. Restaurant price range is a combination of lunch and/or dinner. Turn to the listing page for more information and consult display ads for special promotions.

For more details, rates and reservations: **AAA.com/travelguides/hotels**

ORLANDO

Map Page	Hotels	Diamond Rated	Member Savings	Page
1 p. 188	**DoubleTree by Hilton Orlando East-UCF Area**	◆◆◆	✔	219
2 p. 188	TownePlace Suites by Marriott-Orlando East/UCF Area	◆◆◆	✔	220
3 p. 188	Residence Inn by Marriott-Orlando East/UCF Area	◆◆◆	✔	220
4 p. 188	Courtyard by Marriott-Orlando East/UCF Area	◆◆◆	✔	219
5 p. 188	Homewood Suites by Hilton Orlando-UCF Area	◆◆◆	✔	220
6 p. 188	Comfort Suites UCF/Research Park	◆◆◆		219
7 p. 188	**Hilton Garden Inn-Orlando East/UCF**	◆◆◆	✔	219
8 p. 188	Holiday Inn Orlando East-UCF Area	◆◆◆		219
10 p. 188	Comfort Suites Downtown Orlando	◆◆		219
11 p. 188	**Best Western Orlando West**	◆◆	✔	219
12 p. 188	Holiday Inn Express Hotel & Suites Orlando-Ocoee East	◆◆◆		219

Map Page	Restaurants	Diamond Rated	Cuisine	Price Range	Page
1 p. 188	Giovanni's Italian Restaurant & Pizzeria	◆◆	Italian Pizza	$9-$31	220
2 p. 188	Lazy Moon Pizza	◆	Pizza	$6-$27	220
3 p. 188	Pita Pit	◆	Sandwiches	$5-$8	220
4 p. 188	Christner's Prime Steak & Lobster	◆◆◆	Steak Seafood	$32-$75	220
6 p. 188	The Tap Room at Dubsdread	◆◆	American	$11-$38	221
7 p. 188	Thai Singha	◆◆	Thai Sushi	$8-$22	221
8 p. 188	Ragazzi's Pizza & Restaurant	◆◆	Italian	$9-$22	220
9 p. 188	Colibri Mexican Cuisine	◆◆	Mexican	$10-$21	220
10 p. 188	Domu	◆◆	Asian Noodles	$10-$16	220
11 p. 188	Adriatico Trattoria Italiana	◆◆◆	Italian	$11-$35	220
12 p. 188	Royal Thai	◆◆	Thai	$10-$17	221
13 p. 188	College Park Cafe	◆	Comfort Food	$6-$12	220
14 p. 188	Kingfish Grill	◆◆	Italian	$8-$20	220
15 p. 188	White Wolf Cafe	◆◆	American	$11-$24	221
16 p. 188	Firebirds Wood Fired Grill	◆◆◆	American	$11-$35	220
17 p. 188	The Greek Corner Restaurant	◆◆	Greek	$8-$25	220
18 p. 188	Santiago's Bodega	◆◆◆	International Small Plates	$7-$17	221
19 p. 188	K Restaurant	◆◆◆	New American	$12-$48	220
20 p. 188	Pig Floyd's Urban Barbakoa	◆	Barbecue	$3-$18	220
21 p. 188	Infusion Tea	◆	Natural/Organic	$7-$12	220
22 p. 188	**Hot Dog Heaven**	◆	Hot Dogs	$4-$8	220
23 p. 188	Shakers American Cafe	◆◆	American	$5-$11	221
24 p. 188	Sea Thai Restaurant	◆◆	Thai	$10-$18	221

Map Page	Restaurants (cont'd)	Diamond Rated	Cuisine	Price Range	Page
25 p. 188	Kabooki Sushi	◆◆◆	New Japanese Sushi Fusion	$8-$45	220
26 p. 188	Se7en Bites	◆	Southern American	$6-$14	221
27 p. 188	Pizza Bruno	◆◆	Pizza	$10-$17	220
28 p. 188	Jack and Mary's	◆	Breakfast Sandwiches	$3-$10	220
29 p. 188	Numero Uno Cuban Restaurant	◆◆	Cuban	$6-$26	220
30 p. 188	High Tide Harry's	◆◆	Seafood	$7-$30	220
31 p. 188	Le Coq au Vin	◆◆◆	French	$18-$45	220
32 p. 188	Bubbalou's Bodacious Bar-B-Que	◆	Barbecue	$5-$17	220
33 p. 188	Greens & Grille	◆	Sandwiches	$7-$12	220
34 p. 188	Agave Azul	◆◆	Mexican	$11-$20	220
35 p. 188	P.F. Chang's China Bistro	◆◆◆	Chinese	$11-$28	220
36 p. 188	The Cheesecake Factory	◆◆◆	International	$10-$30	220
37 p. 188	Brio Tuscan Grille	◆◆◆	Italian	$12-$30	220
38 p. 188	Le Cafe de Paris	◆◆	French	$7-$15	220

SANFORD

Map Page	Hotels	Diamond Rated	Member Savings	Page
15 p. 188	**Comfort Inn & Suites North Orlando/Sanford**	◆◆◆	✔	295
16 p. 188	**SpringHill Suites by Marriott-Orlando North/ Sanford**	◆◆◆	✔	295
17 p. 188	**Best Western Plus Sanford Airport/Lake Mary**	◆◆	✔	295

Map Page	Restaurants	Diamond Rated	Cuisine	Price Range	Page
41 p. 188	Hollerbach's Willow Tree Cafe	◆◆	German	$9-$20	295
42 p. 188	The Old Jailhouse Kitchen & Spirits	◆◆◆	American	$12-$23	296
43 p. 188	The Corner Cafe Home of Gourmet2go	◆	Deli	$7-$13	295
44 p. 188	Colonial Room Restaurant	◆	Comfort Food	$4-$11	295
45 p. 188	The Tennessee Truffle	◆◆	Southern	$9-$26	296
46 p. 188	LaSpadas Original Philly Cheese Steaks	◆	Sandwiches	$4-$13	295
47 p. 188	Riverwalk Pizzeria	◆◆	Italian Pizza	$2-$40	296
48 p. 188	Maru Sushi & Grill	◆◆	Asian	$6-$30	296
49 p. 188	Caffe Positano	◆◆	Italian Pizza	$8-$22	295
50 p. 188	Chianti's Pizza & Pasta	◆◆	Italian	$9-$24	295
51 p. 188	Mel's Family Diner	◆◆	Comfort Food	$5-$14	296

MOUNT DORA

Map Page	Hotel	Diamond Rated	Member Savings	Page
20 p. 188	Adora Inn	◆◆◆		153

Map Page	Restaurants	Diamond Rated	Cuisine	Price Range	Page
54 p. 188	Froggers Grill & Bar	◆◆	American	$7-$15	153
55 p. 188	Jeremiah's	◆◆	American	$9-$22	153
56 p. 188	Lake House Bar & Grill	◆◆	American	$10-$20	153
57 p. 188	One Flight Up Café	◆	Sandwiches	$8-$10	153
58 p. 188	Fiesta Grande Mexican Grill	◆◆	Mexican	$8-$14	153

Map Page	Restaurants (cont'd)	Diamond Rated	Cuisine	Price Range	Page
59 p. 188	1921	♦♦♦	New American	$16-$55	153
60 p. 188	Pisces Rising	♦♦♦	Seafood Steak	$15-$45	153
61 p. 188	The Windsor Rose Restaurant & English Tea Room	♦♦	English	$8-$18	153
62 p. 188	The Goblin Market	♦♦	American	$10-$39	153
63 p. 188	The Highland St Cafe	♦♦	Comfort Food	$6-$10	153

LAKE MARY

Map Page	Hotels	Diamond Rated	Member Savings	Page
23 p. 188	Hampton Inn & Suites Lake Mary at Colonial TownPark	♦♦♦	✔	140
24 p. 188	**The Westin Lake Mary, Orlando North**	♦♦♦	✔	141
25 p. 188	**Orlando Marriott Lake Mary** *(See ad p. 141.)*	♦♦♦	✔	141
26 p. 188	Residence Inn by Marriott-Orlando Lake Mary	♦♦♦	✔	141
27 p. 188	**Hilton Garden Inn Orlando North/Lake Mary**	♦♦♦	✔	140
28 p. 188	**Hyatt Place Lake Mary/Orlando-North**	♦♦♦	✔	140
29 p. 188	Candlewood Suites Lake Mary	♦♦		140

Map Page	Restaurants	Diamond Rated	Cuisine	Price Range	Page
69 p. 188	Papa Joe's Pizza - Colonial TownPark	♦♦	Italian Pizza	$7-$25	142
71 p. 188	The Vineyard Wine Company	♦♦♦	New American	$11-$43	142
72 p. 188	Amura	♦♦	Japanese Sushi	$9-$45	141
73 p. 188	Liam Fitzpatrick's Irish Restaurant & Pub	♦♦	Irish	$11-$38	142
74 p. 188	Shula's 347	♦♦♦	Steak	$10-$35	142
75 p. 188	Ruth's Chris Steak House	♦♦♦	Steak	$32-$124	142
76 p. 188	FishBones	♦♦♦	Seafood Steak	$22-$47	142
77 p. 188	Terramia Brick Oven Pizza	♦♦	Italian Pizza	$8-$22	142
78 p. 188	F&D Kitchen & Bar	♦♦♦	New American	$11-$38	142
79 p. 188	Bistro 1501	♦♦♦	New American	$15-$50	141
80 p. 188	Giovanni's Italian Restaurant & Pizzeria	♦♦	Italian	$9-$31	142
81 p. 188	Krazy Greek Kitchen	♦♦	Greek	$12-$23	142
82 p. 188	Dalli's Restaurant & Pizzeria	♦♦	Italian Pizza	$5-$27	141
83 p. 188	4th Street Grill	♦♦	American	$11-$24	141
84 p. 188	Lonnies Fusion Cuisine	♦♦♦	Regional American	$10-$36	142
85 p. 188	Appleton's Cafe	♦♦	Comfort Food	$6-$11	141
86 p. 188	Grato Italian Grill & Pizzeria	♦♦	Italian Pizza	$8-$33	142
87 p. 188	Papa Joe's Pizza	♦♦	Italian Pizza	$7-$25	142
88 p. 188	Keller's Real Smoked Bar-B-Q	♦♦	Barbecue	$7-$17	142
89 p. 188	Digino's Pizza	♦	Pizza Sandwiches	$8-$23	142
90 p. 188	Don Julio	♦♦	Mexican	$8-$29	142
91 p. 188	La Antioquena Restaurant	♦♦	Colombian	$10-$20	142
92 p. 188	Cheng's Chinese Restaurant	♦♦	Chinese	$6-$18	141
93 p. 188	**Thai Corner Restaurant**	♦♦	Thai	$9-$19	142

Map Page	Restaurants (cont'd)	Diamond Rated	Cuisine	Price Range	Page
94 p. 188	The Greek Village Restaurant	♦♦	Greek	$9-$22	142

HEATHROW

Map Page	Hotel	Diamond Rated	Member Savings	Page
32 p. 188	Courtyard by Marriott-Orlando Lake Mary/North	♦♦♦	✔	79

Map Page	Restaurants	Diamond Rated	Cuisine	Price Range	Page
97 p. 188	Samurai Sushi Japanese Cuisine & Sushi Bar	♦♦	Japanese Sushi	$10-$20	81
98 p. 188	Peach Valley Cafe	♦♦	Breakfast Sandwiches	$4-$13	81
99 p. 188	Stonewood Grill & Tavern	♦♦♦	American	$11-$36	81

APOPKA

Map Page	Hotels	Diamond Rated	Member Savings	Page
35 p. 188	Holiday Inn Express & Suites Orlando-Apopka	♦♦♦		32
36 p. 188	Hampton Inn & Suites Orlando-Apopka	♦♦♦	✔	32

Map Page	Restaurants	Diamond Rated	Cuisine	Price Range	Page
102 p. 188	1-6-8 Chinese Restaurant	♦♦	Chinese	$9-$22	32
103 p. 188	Caffé Positano	♦♦	Italian	$9-$25	32
104 p. 188	Catfish Place of Apopka	♦♦	Seafood	$12-$23	32

ALTAMONTE SPRINGS

Map Page	Hotels	Diamond Rated	Member Savings	Page
39 p. 188	Hawthorn Suites by Wyndham-Altamonte Springs	♦♦		29
40 p. 188	**Hampton Inn & Suites Orlando-North/Altamonte Springs**	♦♦♦	✔	29
41 p. 188	**Embassy Suites by Hilton Orlando North**	♦♦♦	✔	29
42 p. 188	**TownePlace Suites by Marriott Orlando Altamonte Springs/Maitland**	♦♦♦	✔	29
43 p. 188	**Hilton Orlando/Altamonte Springs**	♦♦♦	✔	29

Map Page	Restaurants	Diamond Rated	Cuisine	Price Range	Page
119 p. 188	Terramia Wine Bar & Trattoria	♦♦♦	Italian Pizza	$8-$26	30
120 p. 188	Santiago's Bodega	♦♦♦	International Small Plates	$7-$17	29
121 p. 188	Mr. Margarita Mexican Kitchen & Tequila Bar	♦♦	Mexican	$10-$26	29
122 p. 188	Cafe Murano	♦♦♦	Italian	$11-$36	29
123 p. 188	Bahama Breeze Island Grille	♦♦♦	Caribbean	$10-$25	29
124 p. 188	Seasons 52 Fresh Grill	♦♦♦	New American	$15-$33	30
125 p. 188	Omaha Steakhouse	♦♦♦	Steak	$10-$22	29
126 p. 188	Kohinoor Indian Restaurant	♦♦	Indian	$13-$22	29

MAITLAND

Map Page	Hotels	Diamond Rated	Member Savings	Page
46 p. 188	**Sheraton Orlando North**	♦♦♦	✔	147
47 p. 188	**Courtyard by Marriott Orlando-Altamonte Springs/Maitland**	♦♦	✔	147
48 p. 188	Homewood Suites by Hilton-Orlando North/ Maitland	♦♦♦	✔	147

Map Page	Restaurants	Diamond Rated	Cuisine	Price Range	Page
129 p. 188	Kappy's	♦	American	$5-$11	147
130 p. 188	Francesco's Ristorante & Pizzeria	♦♦♦	Italian	$13-$21	147

Map Page	Restaurants (cont'd)	Diamond Rated	Cuisine	Price Range	Page
131 p. 188	Antonio's Market & Cafe Downstairs	◆◆	Italian	$8-$39	147
132 p. 188	Antonio's Upstairs	◆◆◆	Italian	$11-$37	147

EUSTIS

Map Page	Restaurant	Diamond Rated	Cuisine	Price Range	Page
66 p. 188	Haystax Restaurant	◆◆	Comfort Food	$5-$15	72

LONGWOOD

Map Page	Restaurants	Diamond Rated	Cuisine	Price Range	Page
107 p. 188	Gateway To India	◆◆	Northern Indian	$12-$20	145
108 p. 188	Cafe Paisano	◆◆	Italian	$6-$30	145
109 p. 188	Thailicious	◆◆	Thai	$11-$19	145
110 p. 188	Korea House	◆◆	Korean	$12-$35	145
111 p. 188	Bayridge Sushi	◆◆	Japanese Sushi	$8-$33	145
112 p. 188	Enzo's On The Lake	◆◆◆	Regional Italian	$23-$40	145
113 p. 188	Bonefish Grill	◆◆◆	Seafood	$15-$34	145
114 p. 188	Pickles Authentic New York Delicatessen	◆◆	Deli Sandwiches	$6-$14	145
115 p. 188	Victorio's Oyster Bar & Grille	◆◆	American	$8-$27	145
116 p. 188	Hurricane Grill & Wings	◆◆	American	$8-$20	145

WINTER PARK

Map Page	Restaurant	Diamond Rated	Cuisine	Price Range	Page
135 p. 188	Boardwalk Pizza	◆◆	Italian	$3-$26	371

WINTER GARDEN

Map Page	Restaurants	Diamond Rated	Cuisine	Price Range	Page
138 p. 188	Thai Blossom Restaurant	◆◆	Thai	$9-$20	369
139 p. 188	The Chef's Table at the Edgewater and Tasting Room	◆◆◆	American	$59	369
140 p. 188	4 Locos Tacos	◆	Mexican	$3-$11	369

OCOEE

Map Page	Restaurant	Diamond Rated	Cuisine	Price Range	Page
143 p. 188	RusTeak Restaurant & Wine Bar	◆◆◆	New American	$10-$34	157

Circle the globe! Enjoy up to 20% savings with our exclusive offers on hotels, up to 20% on car rentals, and out-of-this-world deals on complete vacation packages. With a website that's easy to navigate and customer support you can trust, expect something more when you travel with AAA and CAA.

Plan it, book it and save at AAA.com/travel or CAA.ca/travel

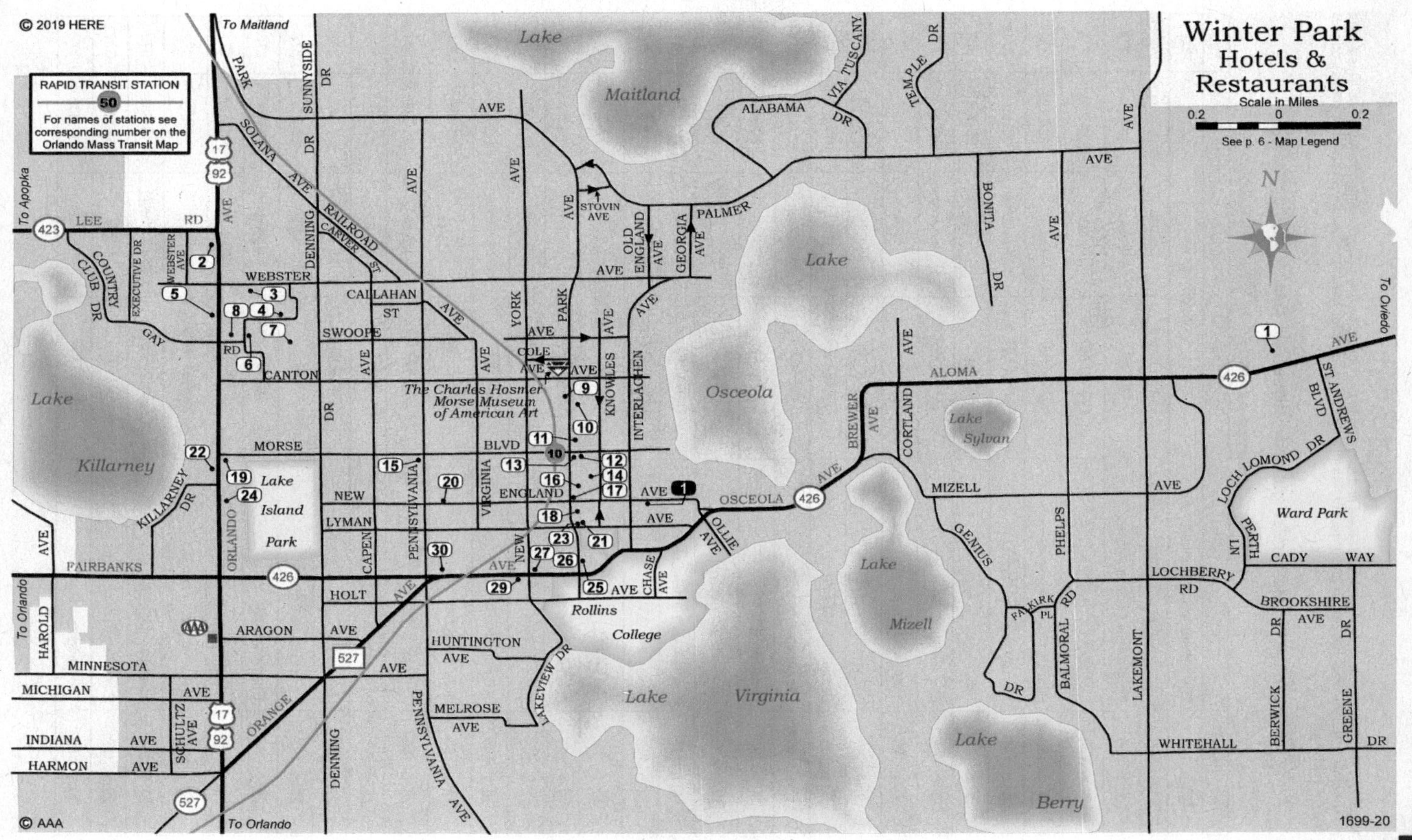
Winter Park
Hotels & Restaurants
Scale in Miles
0.2 0 0.2
See p. 6 - Map Legend
N
RAPID TRANSIT STATION
50
For names of stations see corresponding number on the Orlando Mass Transit Map
© 2019 HERE
© AAA
1699-20
To Oviedo
To Maitland
To Apopka
To Orlando
Lake Maitland
Lake Osceola
Lake Virginia
Lake Mizell
Lake Sylvan
Lake Berry
Lake Killarney
Ward Park
Lake Island Park
Rollins College
The Charles Hosmer Morse Museum of American Art

Winter Park

This index helps you "spot" where approved hotels and restaurants are located on the corresponding detailed maps. Restaurant price range is a combination of lunch and/or dinner. Turn to the listing page for more information and consult display ads for special promotions.

For more details, rates and reservations: AAA.com/travelguides/hotels

WINTER PARK

Map Page	Hotel	Diamond Rated	Member Savings	Page
1 p. 195	**The Alfond Inn at Rollins**	◆◆◆◆	✔	371

Map Page	Restaurants	Diamond Rated	Cuisine	Price Range	Page
1 p. 195	Tibby's New Orleans Kitchen	◆◆	Cajun	$9-$17	372
2 p. 195	Fleming's Prime Steakhouse & Wine Bar	◆◆◆	Steak	$38-$89	372
3 p. 195	Ruth's Chris Steak House	◆◆◆	Steak	$32-$124	372
4 p. 195	The Cheesecake Factory	◆◆◆	International	$8-$31	371
5 p. 195	Thai Place	◆◆	Thai	$9-$22	372
6 p. 195	Brio Tuscan Grille	◆◆◆	Italian	$11-$45	371
7 p. 195	Pizzeria Valdiano	◆	Pizza	$9-$21	372
8 p. 195	P.F. Chang's China Bistro	◆◆◆	Chinese	$11-$28	372
9 p. 195	Orchid Thai Cuisine	◆◆◆	Thai	$14-$38	372
10 p. 195	The Briarpatch	◆◆	American	$14-$18	371
11 p. 195	Prato	◆◆◆	Italian	$9-$34	372
12 p. 195	Croissant Gourmet	◆	Breads/Pastries Breakfast	$6-$12	372
13 p. 195	Bosphorous Turkish Cuisine	◆◆◆	Turkish	$10-$28	371
14 p. 195	Cocina 214	◆◆◆	Tex-Mex	$13-$28	371
15 p. 195	The Coop	◆	Southern Comfort Food	$7-$37	371
16 p. 195	Pannullo's Italian Restaurant	◆◆	Italian	$7-$22	372
17 p. 195	Luma on Park	◆◆◆◆	New American	$12-$42	372
18 p. 195	310 Park South	◆◆	New American	$11-$34	371
19 p. 195	Bulla Gastrobar	◆◆◆	Spanish Small Plates	$6-$39	371
20 p. 195	Armando's Cucina Italiana & Pizzeria	◆◆	Italian	$8-$26	371
21 p. 195	Park Avenue Pizza	◆	Italian Pizza	$7-$24	372
22 p. 195	Hillstone	◆◆◆	American	$15-$46	372
23 p. 195	Power House Cafe	◆	Sandwiches	$8-$16	372
24 p. 195	The Glass Knife	◆◆	Desserts	$7-$14	372
25 p. 195	Cafe De France	◆◆◆	French	$10-$32	371
26 p. 195	Umi	◆◆◆	Japanese Fusion	$8-$28	372
27 p. 195	Scratch	◆◆◆	Small Plates	$12-$35	372
29 p. 195	Ethos Vegan Kitchen Inc	◆◆	Vegan	$7-$14	372
30 p. 195	The Ravenous Pig	◆◆◆	American	$17-$32	372

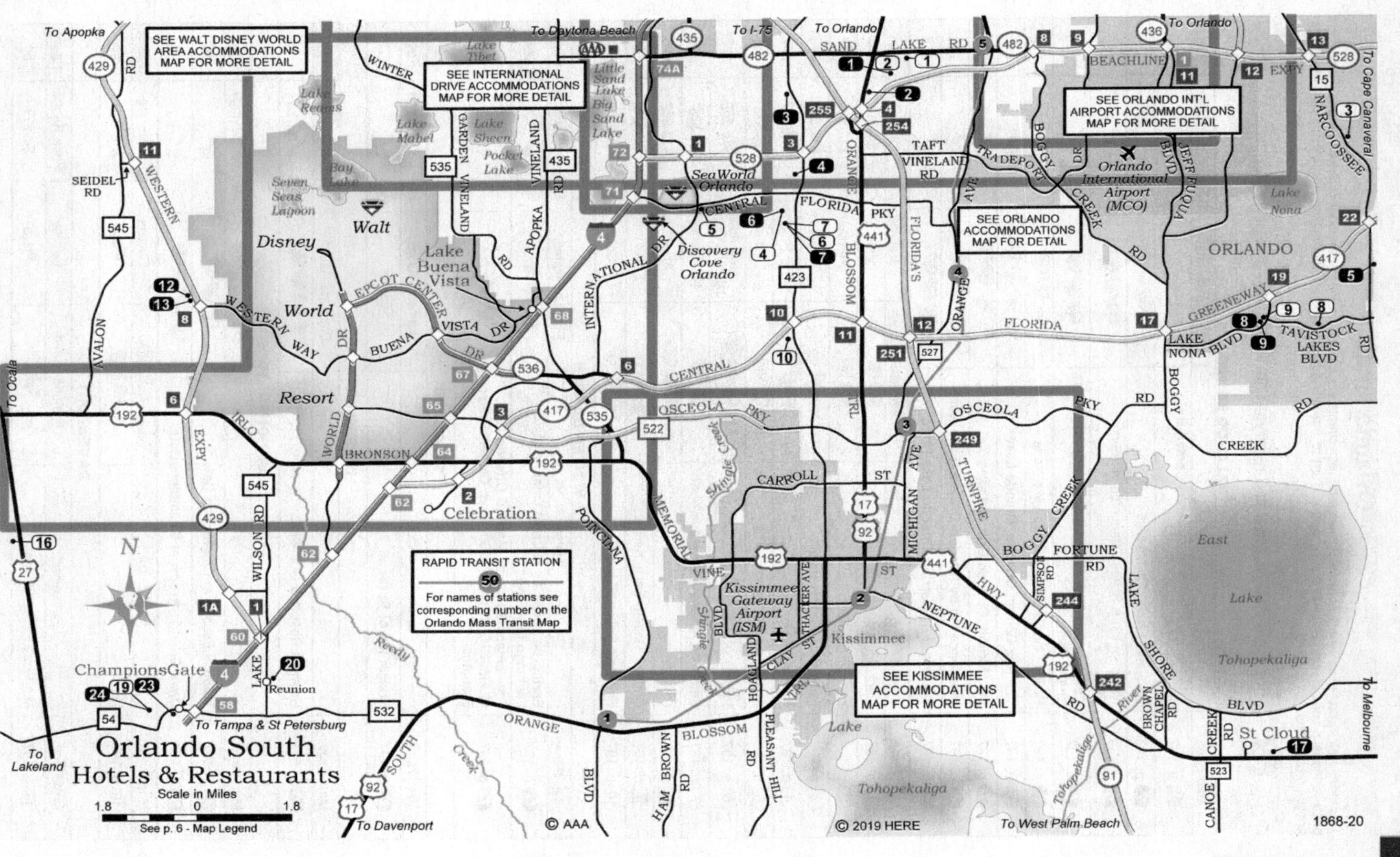
Orlando South
Hotels & Restaurants
SEE WALT DISNEY WORLD AREA ACCOMMODATIONS MAP FOR MORE DETAIL
SEE INTERNATIONAL DRIVE ACCOMMODATIONS MAP FOR MORE DETAIL
SEE ORLANDO ACCOMMODATIONS MAP FOR DETAIL
SEE ORLANDO INT'L AIRPORT ACCOMMODATIONS MAP FOR MORE DETAIL
SEE KISSIMMEE ACCOMMODATIONS MAP FOR MORE DETAIL
RAPID TRANSIT STATION
For names of stations see corresponding number on the Orlando Mass Transit Map
Walt Disney World Resort
Celebration
Lake Buena Vista
SeaWorld Orlando
Discovery Cove Orlando
Orlando International Airport (MCO)
Kissimmee Gateway Airport (ISM)
Kissimmee
St Cloud
East Lake Tohopekaliga
Lake Tohopekaliga
Lake Nona
ORLANDO
ChampionsGate
Reunion
To Apopka
To Ocala
To Lakeland
To Tampa & St Petersburg
To Davenport
To West Palm Beach
To Melbourne
To Cape Canaveral
To Orlando
To Daytona Beach
To I-75
Scale in Miles
See p. 6 - Map Legend
© 2019 HERE
© AAA
1868-20

Orlando South

This index helps you "spot" where approved hotels and restaurants are located on the corresponding detailed maps. Restaurant price range is a combination of lunch and/or dinner. Turn to the listing page for more information and consult display ads for special promotions.

For more details, rates and reservations: AAA.com/travelguides/hotels

ORLANDO SOUTH

Map Page	Hotels	Diamond Rated	Member Savings	Page
1 p. 197	**The Florida Hotel & Conference Center, BW Premier Collection**	◆◆◆	✔	230
2 p. 197	Ramada Orlando Florida Mall	◆◆		238
3 p. 197	Hampton Inn & Suites Orlando-John Young Pkwy/S Park	◆◆◆	✔	230
4 p. 197	**Courtyard by Marriott Orlando South John Young Parkway**	◆◆◆	✔	226
5 p. 197	Holiday Inn Express & Suites Lake Nona	◆◆◆		233
6 p. 197	**The Ritz-Carlton Orlando, Grande Lakes**	◆◆◆◆	✔	240
7 p. 197	**JW Marriott, Orlando Grande Lakes**	◆◆◆◆	✔	237
8 p. 197	**Residence Inn by Marriott-Orlando Lake Nona**	◆◆◆	✔	240
9 p. 197	**Courtyard by Marriott-Orlando Lake Nona**	◆◆◆	✔	225

Map Page	Restaurants	Diamond Rated	Cuisine	Price Range	Page
1 p. 197	Garibaldi Mexican Cuisine	◆◆	Mexican	$9-$19	247
2 p. 197	Memories of Peru	◆◆	Peruvian	$12-$31	247
3 p. 197	Nona Blue Modern Tavern	◆◆◆	American	$11-$44	247
4 p. 197	Highball & Harvest	◆◆◆	New Southern	$16-$47	247
5 p. 197	Thai Thani Restaurant	◆◆	Thai	$8-$25	248
6 p. 197	Primo	◆◆◆◆	New Italian Natural/Organic	$16-$69	247
7 p. 197	Citron, An American Brasserie	◆◆	New American	$8-$32	246
8 p. 197	Canvas	◆◆◆	American	$13-$32	246
9 p. 197	Chroma Modern Bar + Kitchen	◆◆◆	Small Plates	$8-$18	246
10 p. 197	Padrino's Cuban Cuisine	◆◆◆	Cuban	$8-$23	247

WINTER GARDEN

Map Page	Hotels	Diamond Rated	Member Savings	Page
12 p. 197	**SpringHill Suites by Marriott Orlando at Flamingo Crossings**	◆◆◆	✔	368
13 p. 197	**TownePlace Suites by Marriott Orlando at FLAMINGO CROSSINGS® Town Center/Western Entrance**	◆◆◆	✔	369

ST. CLOUD

Map Page	Hotel	Diamond Rated	Member Savings	Page
17 p. 197	**Budget Inn of St Cloud**	◆◆	✔	272

KISSIMMEE

Map Page	Hotel	Diamond Rated	Member Savings	Page
20 p. 197	**Reunion Resort & Golf Club**	◆◆◆◆	✔	114

CHAMPIONSGATE

Map Page	Hotels	Diamond Rated	Member Savings	Page
23 p. 197	**Tropical Escape at Champions Gate**	◆◆◆	✔	40
24 p. 197	**Omni Orlando Resort at ChampionsGate**	◆◆◆◆	✔	40

Map Page	Restaurant	Diamond Rated	Cuisine	Price Range	Page
19 p. 197	Zen	◆◆◆	Asian	$18-$40	40

DAVENPORT

Map Page	Restaurant	Diamond Rated	Cuisine	Price Range	Page
16 p. 197	Mia Pizza Pasta Kitchen	◆	Pizza	$6-$19	54

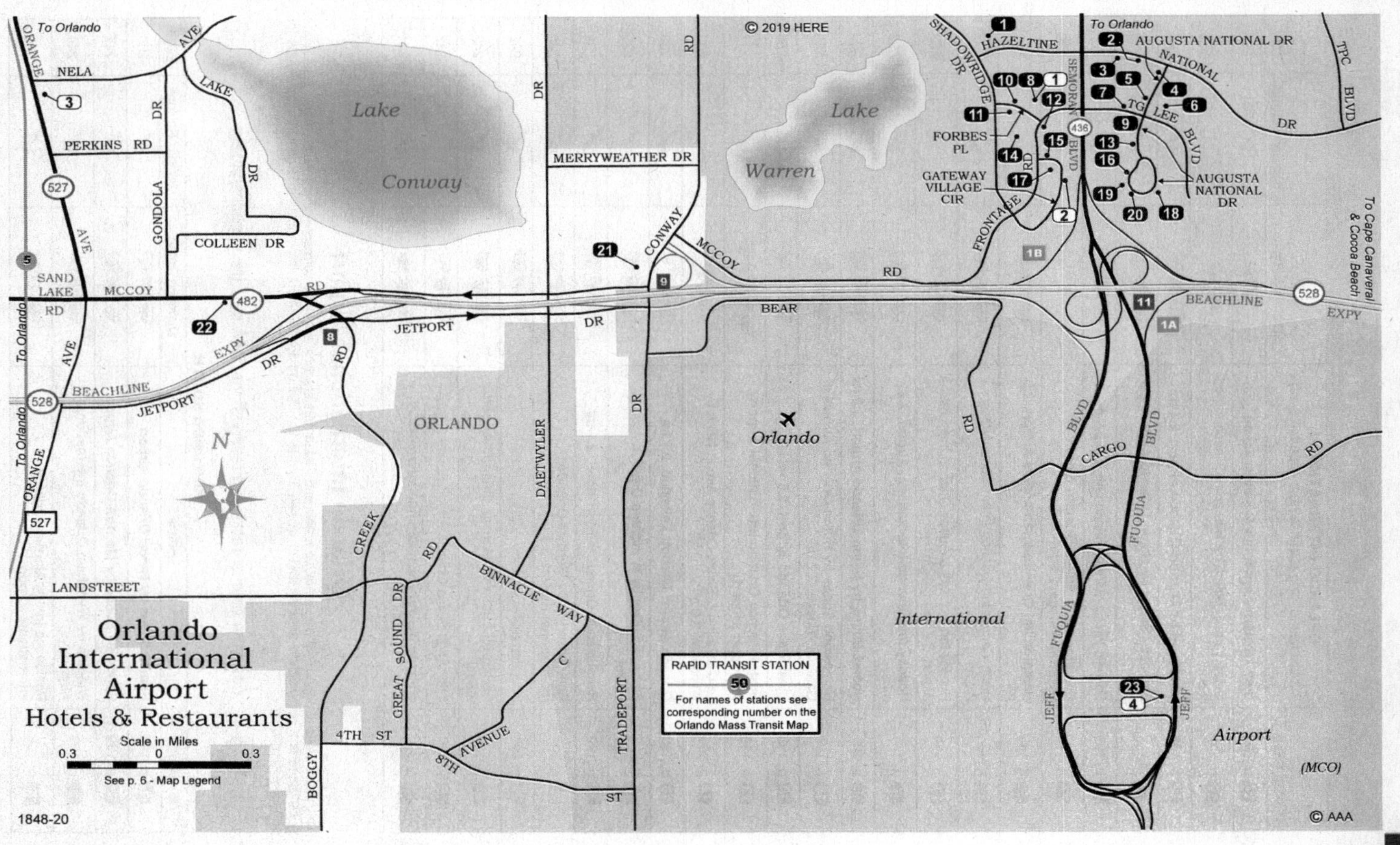
Orlando International Airport
Hotels & Restaurants
Scale in Miles
0.3
0
0.3
See p. 6 - Map Legend
1848-20
© 2019 HERE
© AAA
RAPID TRANSIT STATION
For names of stations see corresponding number on the Orlando Mass Transit Map
Orlando International Airport
(MCO)
ORLANDO
To Orlando
To Cape Canaveral & Cocoa Beach
Lake Conway
Lake Warren
ORANGE AVE
NELA
PERKINS RD
GONDOLA
COLLEEN DR
LAKE DR
SAND LAKE RD
MCCOY RD
BEACHLINE EXPY
JETPORT DR
LANDSTREET
BOGGY CREEK RD
4TH ST
GREAT SOUND DR
8TH AVENUE
BINNACLE WAY
DAETWYLER DR
TRADEPORT DR
CONWAY RD
MERRYWEATHER DR
BEAR RD
FRONTAGE RD
GATEWAY VILLAGE CIR
FORBES PL
SHADOWRIDGE DR
HAZELTINE
SEMORAN BLVD
AUGUSTA NATIONAL DR
TPC BLVD
TG LEE BLVD
CARGO RD
JEFF FUQUIA BLVD

Airport Hotels

Map Page	**ORLANDO INTERNATIONAL** (Maximum driving distance from airport: 5.0 mi)	Diamond Rated	Member Savings	Page
22 p. 199	**Best Western Airport Inn & Suites, 5.0 mi**	◆◆	✔	221
11 p. 199	Country Inn & Suites By Radisson-Orlando Airport, 2.5 mi	◆◆		225
12 p. 199	**Courtyard by Marriott-Orlando Airport, 2.4 mi**	◆◆◆	✔	225
6 p. 199	**Embassy Suites by Hilton Orlando-Airport, 2.5 mi**	◆◆◆	✔	229
5 p. 199	Fairfield Inn by Marriott-Orlando Airport, 2.5 mi	◆◆◆	✔	229
17 p. 199	**Hampton Inn & Suites-Orlando Airport at Gateway Village, 2.6 mi**	◆◆◆	✔	230
7 p. 199	**Hampton Inn Orlando-International Airport, 2.9 mi**	◆◆◆	✔	232
13 p. 199	Hilton Garden Inn-Orlando International Airport, 2.5 mi	◆◆◆	✔	233
21 p. 199	Holiday Inn Express & Suites Orlando International Airport, 3.7 mi	◆◆◆		233
9 p. 199	**Holiday Inn Orlando-International Airport, 2.4 mi**	◆◆◆	✔	233
1 p. 199	**Home2 Suites by Hilton Orlando Airport, 3.0 mi**	◆◆◆	✔	235
15 p. 199	**Homewood Suites by Hilton-Orlando Airport at Gateway Village, 2.7 mi**	◆◆◆	✔	235
10 p. 199	**Hyatt Place Orlando Airport, 2.5 mi**	◆◆◆	✔	236
23 p. 199	**Hyatt Regency Orlando International Airport, on airport property**	◆◆◆◆	✔	237
14 p. 199	La Quinta Inn & Suites Orlando Airport North by Wyndham, 3.0 mi	◆◆		237
18 p. 199	**Orlando Airport Marriott Lakeside, 2.7 mi**	◆◆◆	✔	238
19 p. 199	**Ramada Suites by Wyndham Orlando Airport, 2.7 mi**	◆◆◆	✔	239
8 p. 199	**Renaissance Orlando Airport Hotel, 2.5 mi**	◆◆◆	✔	239
4 p. 199	**Residence Inn by Marriott-Orlando International Airport, 2.6 mi**	◆◆◆	✔	240
20 p. 199	Sheraton Suites Orlando Airport, 2.7 mi	◆◆◆	✔	242
2 p. 199	**SpringHill Suites by Marriott-Orlando Airport, 2.6 mi**	◆◆◆	✔	242
16 p. 199	Staybridge Suites Orlando Airport South, 2.6 mi	◆◆◆		243
3 p. 199	**Wingate by Wyndham Orlando International Airport, 2.6 mi**	◆◆◆	✔	244

Orlando International Airport

This index helps you "spot" where approved hotels and restaurants are located on the corresponding detailed maps. Restaurant price range is a combination of lunch and/or dinner. Turn to the listing page for more information and consult display ads for special promotions.

For more details, rates and reservations: **AAA.com/travelguides/hotels**

ORLANDO SOUTH

Map Page	Hotels	Diamond Rated	Member Savings	Page
1 p. 199	**Home2 Suites by Hilton Orlando Airport**	◆◆◆	✔	235
2 p. 199	**SpringHill Suites by Marriott-Orlando Airport**	◆◆◆	✔	242
3 p. 199	**Wingate by Wyndham Orlando International Airport**	◆◆◆	✔	244
4 p. 199	**Residence Inn by Marriott-Orlando International Airport**	◆◆◆	✔	240

ORLANDO SOUTH (cont'd)

Map Page	Hotels (cont'd)	Diamond Rated	Member Savings	Page
5 p. 199	Fairfield by Marriott-Orlando Airport	◆◆◆	✔	229
6 p. 199	**Embassy Suites by Hilton Orlando-Airport** *(See ad p. 228.)*	◆◆◆	✔	229
7 p. 199	**Hampton Inn Orlando-International Airport**	◆◆◆	✔	232
8 p. 199	**Renaissance Orlando Airport Hotel**	◆◆◆	✔	239
9 p. 199	**Holiday Inn Orlando-International Airport**	◆◆◆	✔	233
10 p. 199	**Hyatt Place Orlando Airport**	◆◆◆	✔	236
11 p. 199	Country Inn & Suites By Radisson-Orlando Airport	◆◆		225
12 p. 199	**Courtyard by Marriott-Orlando Airport**	◆◆◆	✔	225
13 p. 199	Hilton Garden Inn-Orlando International Airport	◆◆◆	✔	233
14 p. 199	La Quinta Inn & Suites Orlando Airport North by Wyndham	◆◆		237
15 p. 199	**Homewood Suites by Hilton-Orlando Airport at Gateway Village**	◆◆◆	✔	235
16 p. 199	Staybridge Suites Orlando Airport South	◆◆◆		243
17 p. 199	**Hampton Inn & Suites-Orlando Airport at Gateway Village**	◆◆◆	✔	230
18 p. 199	**Orlando Airport Marriott Lakeside**	◆◆◆	✔	238
19 p. 199	**Ramada Suites by Wyndham Orlando Airport**	◆◆◆	✔	239
20 p. 199	Sheraton Suites Orlando Airport	◆◆◆	✔	242
21 p. 199	Holiday Inn Express & Suites Orlando International Airport	◆◆◆		233
22 p. 199	**Best Western Airport Inn & Suites**	◆◆	✔	221
23 p. 199	**Hyatt Regency Orlando International Airport**	◆◆◆◆	✔	237

Map Page	Restaurants	Diamond Rated	Cuisine	Price Range	Page
1 p. 199	Fresco Moderne Brasserie	◆◆	American	$9-$32	247
2 p. 199	Bonefish Grill	◆◆◆	Seafood	$15-$34	246
3 p. 199	Dixie Belle's Cafe	◆◆	Breakfast	$6-$12	247
4 p. 199	Hemisphere	◆◆◆	Steak Seafood	$28-$50	247

Save time and stay secure year-round

Continue receiving the benefits you know and love. Renew your AAA membership or inquire about auto renewal.

Renew your membership today:
- Online at AAA.com/membership
- Visit your local club office
- Call 800-Join-AAA (564-6222)

AAA

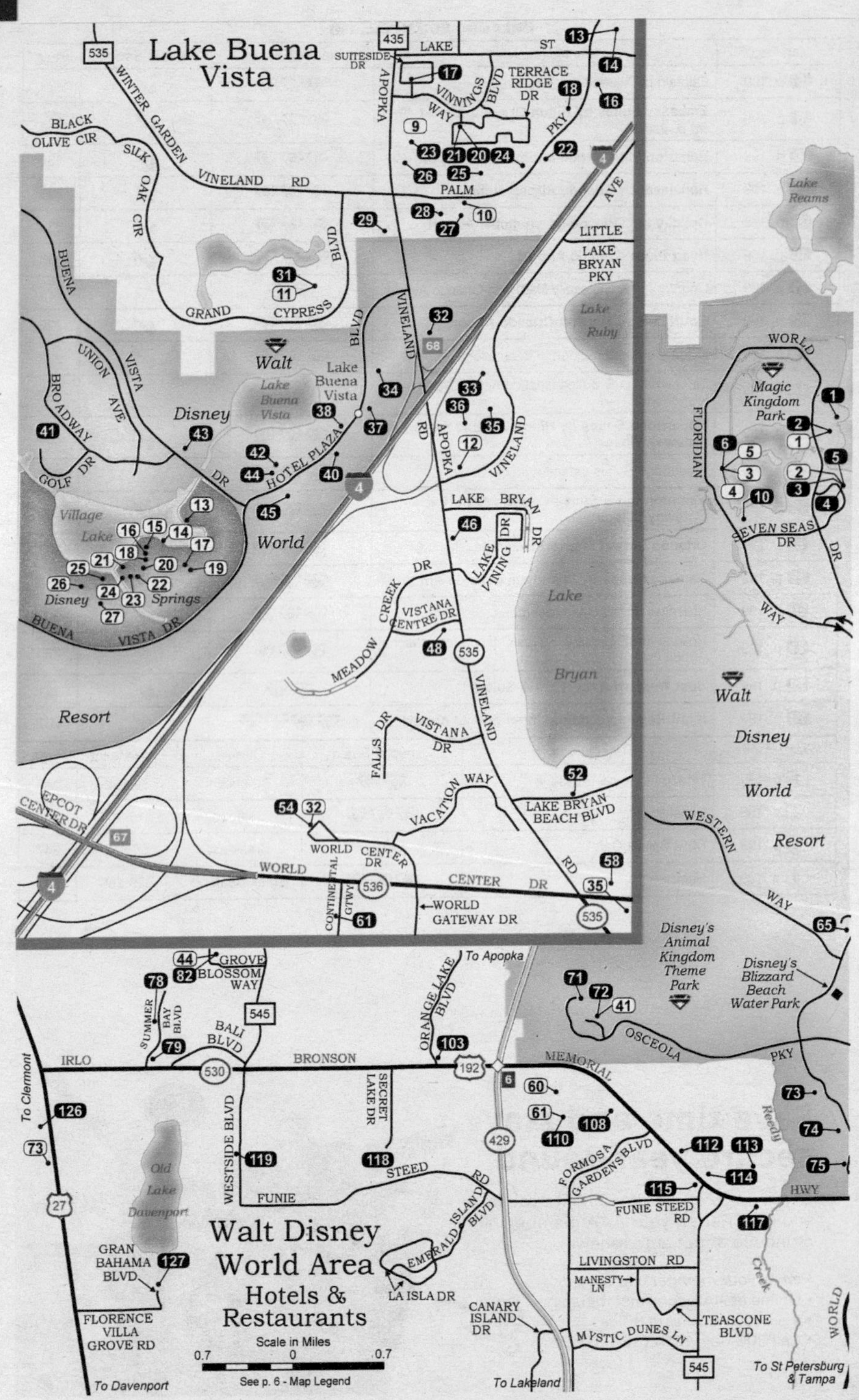

Lake Buena Vista
Walt Disney World Resort
Village Lake
Disney Springs
Magic Kingdom Park
Disney's Animal Kingdom Theme Park
Disney's Blizzard Beach Water Park
Lake Bryan
Lake Ruby
Lake Reams
Old Lake Davenport
To Clermont
To Apopka
To Davenport
To Lakeland
To St Petersburg & Tampa
Walt Disney World Area
Hotels & Restaurants
Scale in Miles
0.7
0
0.7
See p. 6 - Map Legend

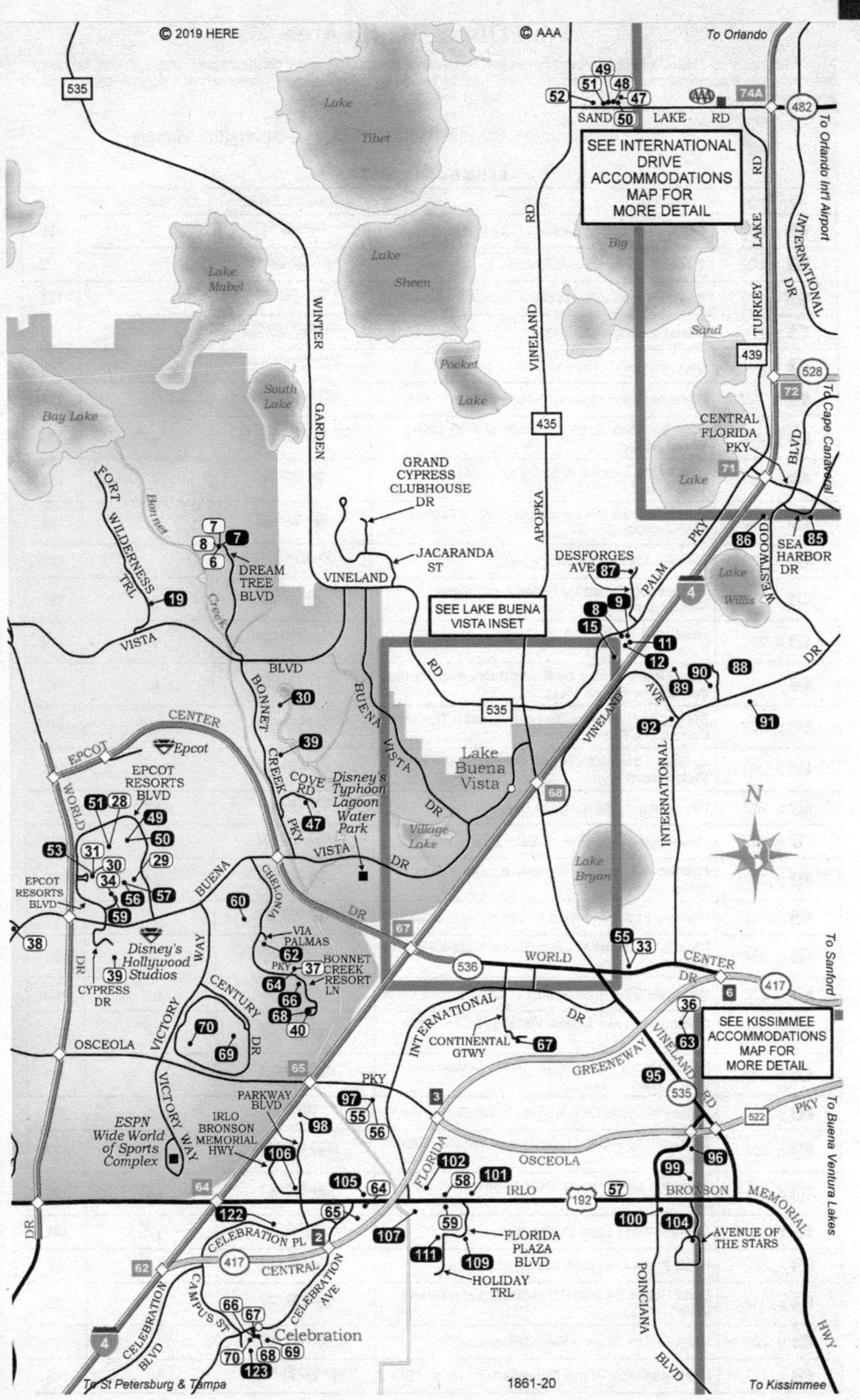
© 2019 HERE
© AAA
To Orlando
SEE INTERNATIONAL DRIVE ACCOMMODATIONS MAP FOR MORE DETAIL
To Orlando Int'l Airport
To Cape Canaveral
SEE LAKE BUENA VISTA INSET
SEE KISSIMMEE ACCOMMODATIONS MAP FOR MORE DETAIL
To Sanford
To Buena Ventura Lakes
To St Petersburg & Tampa
To Kissimmee
1861-20
Lake Tibet
Lake Sheen
Lake Mabel
Pocket Lake
South Lake
Bay Lake
Big Sand Lake
Lake Willis
Lake Bryan
Village Lake
Lake Buena Vista
Epcot
Disney's Typhoon Lagoon Water Park
Disney's Hollywood Studios
ESPN Wide World of Sports Complex
Celebration
SAND LAKE RD
WINTER GARDEN VINELAND RD
APOPKA VINELAND RD
TURKEY LAKE RD
INTERNATIONAL DR
CENTRAL FLORIDA PKY
GRAND CYPRESS CLUBHOUSE DR
JACARANDA ST
DESFORGES AVE
PALM PKY
WESTWOOD BLVD
SEA HARBOR DR
FORT WILDERNESS TRL
DREAM TREE BLVD
VISTA BLVD
BONNET CREEK PKY
BUENA VISTA DR
EPCOT CENTER DR
EPCOT RESORTS BLVD
WORLD DR
COVE RD
VINELAND AVE
WORLD CENTER DR
CHELONIA
VIA PALMAS
BONNET CREEK RESORT LN
CYPRESS DR
CENTURY DR
VICTORY WAY
OSCEOLA PKY
INTERNATIONAL DR
CONTINENTAL GTWY
GREENEWAY
VINELAND RD
PARKWAY BLVD
IRLO BRONSON MEMORIAL HWY
FLORIDA PKY
CELEBRATION PL
CENTRAL
CELEBRATION AVE
CAMPUS ST
CELEBRATION BLVD
FLORIDA PLAZA BLVD
HOLIDAY TRL
POINCIANA BLVD
AVENUE OF THE STARS

Walt Disney World Area

This index helps you "spot" where approved hotels and restaurants are located on the corresponding detailed maps. Restaurant price range is a combination of lunch and/or dinner. Turn to the listing page for more information and consult display ads for special promotions.

For more details, rates and reservations: AAA.com/travelguides/hotels

LAKE BUENA VISTA

Map Page	Hotels	Diamond Rated	Member Savings	Page
1 p. 202	Bay Lake Tower at Disney's Contemporary Resort	◆◆◆		120
2 p. 202	Disney's Contemporary Resort	◆◆◆◆		122
3 p. 202	Boulder Ridge Villas at Disney's Wilderness Lodge	◆◆◆		121
4 p. 202	Disney's Wilderness Lodge	◆◆◆◆		123
5 p. 202	Copper Creek Villas and Cabins	◆◆◆◆		122
6 p. 202	Disney's Grand Floridian Resort & Spa	◆◆◆◆		122
7 p. 202	**Four Seasons Resort Orlando at Walt Disney World Resort**	◆◆◆◆◆	✔	123
8 p. 202	Holiday Inn Express & Suites Orlando -Lk Buena Vista Area	◆◆◆		126
9 p. 202	**Hilton Garden Inn Lake Buena Vista/Orlando** *(See ad p. 124.)*	◆◆◆	✔	124
10 p. 202	Disney's Polynesian Village Resort	◆◆◆◆		123
11 p. 202	**Homewood Suites by Hilton Lake Buena Vista/Orlando** *(See ad p. 124.)*	◆◆◆	✔	126
12 p. 202	Residence Inn by Marriott Orlando Lake Buena Vista	◆◆◆	✔	129
13 p. 202	**TownePlace Suites by Marriott Orlando Theme Parks/Lake Buena Vista**	◆◆◆	✔	131
14 p. 202	**SpringHill Suites by Marriott Orlando Theme Parks/Lake Buena Vista**	◆◆◆	✔	131
15 p. 202	**Embassy Suites by Hilton Orlando-Lake Buena Vista Resort**	◆◆◆	✔	123
16 p. 202	Hampton Inn Orlando-Lake Buena Vista	◆◆◆	✔	123
17 p. 202	Staybridge Suites-Orlando/Lake Buena Vista	◆◆◆		131
18 p. 202	**Hawthorn Suites by Wyndham Lake Buena Vista**	◆◆◆	✔	123
19 p. 202	Disney's Fort Wilderness Resort & Campground	◆◆◆		122
20 p. 202	**Blue Tree Resort at Lake Buena Vista-SPM Resorts**	◆◆◆	✔	121
21 p. 202	**Westgate Blue Tree Resort at Lake Buena Vista**	◆◆◆	✔	133
22 p. 202	**Clarion Inn Lake Buena Vista, a Rosen Hotel** *(See ad p. 224.)*	◆◆◆	✔	122
23 p. 202	Fairfield Inn & Suites by Marriott Orlando-Lake Buena Vista	◆◆◆	✔	123
24 p. 202	Legacy Vacation Club Resorts- Lake Buena Vista	◆◆		129
25 p. 202	Courtyard by Marriott Lake Buena Vista @ Vista Centre	◆◆◆	✔	122
26 p. 202	**Sheraton Lake Buena Vista Resort** *(See ad p. 131.)*	◆◆◆	✔	129
27 p. 202	**Crowne Plaza Lake Buena Vista**	◆◆	✔	122
28 p. 202	**Hyatt Place Orlando/Lake Buena Vista**	◆◆◆	✔	129
29 p. 202	**Delta Hotels by Marriott Orlando Lake Buena Vista**	◆◆◆	✔	122
30 p. 202	Disney's Port Orleans Resort-Riverside	◆◆◆		123
31 p. 202	**Hyatt Regency Grand Cypress** *(See ad p. 130.)*	◆◆◆◆	✔	129

LAKE BUENA VISTA (cont'd)

Map Page	Hotels (cont'd)	Diamond Rated	Member Savings	Page
32 p. 202	Radisson Hotel Orlando-Lake Buena Vista	◆◆◆		129
33 p. 202	**SpringHill Suites by Marriott at The Marriott Village Lake Buena Vista**	◆◆◆	✔	131
34 p. 202	**DoubleTree Suites by Hilton Hotel Orlando in the Walt Disney World Resort**	◆◆◆	✔	123
35 p. 202	**Courtyard by Marriott Orlando Lake Buena Vista in the Marriott Village**	◆◆◆	✔	122
36 p. 202	**Fairfield Inn & Suites by Marriott Orlando Lake Buena Vista in the Marriott Village**	◆◆◆	✔	123
37 p. 202	B Resort & Spa Lake Buena Vista	◆◆◆		121
38 p. 202	**Best Western Lake Buena Vista Resort Hotel**	◆◆	✔	120
39 p. 202	Disney's Port Orleans Resort-French Quarter	◆◆◆		123
40 p. 202	**Holiday Inn Orlando-Disney Springs Area**	◆◆◆	✔	126
41 p. 202	Disney's Saratoga Springs Resort & Spa	◆◆◆		123
42 p. 202	**Wyndham Garden Lake Buena Vista Disney Springs Resort Area** *(See ad on inside front cover, p. 134.)*	◆◆◆	✔	133
43 p. 202	**Hilton Orlando Buena Vista Palace, Disney Springs Resort** *(See ad p. 125, p. 127.)*	◆◆◆	✔	126
44 p. 202	**Wyndham Lake Buena Vista Disney Springs Resort Area** *(See ad on inside front cover, p. 134.)*	◆◆◆	✔	135
45 p. 202	**Hilton Orlando Lake Buena Vista** *(See ad p. 127.)*	◆◆◆	✔	126
46 p. 202	**Holiday Inn Resort Orlando-Lake Buena Vista** *(See ad p. 224.)*	◆◆◆	✔	126
47 p. 202	Disney's Old Key West Resort	◆◆◆		122
48 p. 202	Sheraton's Vistana Resort Villas, Lake Buena Vista/Orlando	◆◆◆	✔	129
49 p. 202	Disney's Beach Club Resort	◆◆◆◆		122
50 p. 202	Disney's Beach Club Villas	◆◆◆		122
51 p. 202	Disney's Yacht Club Resort	◆◆◆◆		123
52 p. 202	Grand Beach Resort	◆◆◆		123
53 p. 202	**Walt Disney World Dolphin**	◆◆◆◆	✔	132
54 p. 202	**Orlando World Center Marriott**	◆◆◆◆	✔	129
55 p. 202	**Caribe Royale Orlando**	◆◆◆	✔	121
56 p. 202	Disney's BoardWalk Villas	◆◆◆		122
57 p. 202	Disney's BoardWalk Inn	◆◆◆◆		122
58 p. 202	**Buena Vista Suites**	◆◆◆	✔	121
59 p. 202	**Walt Disney World Swan Resort**	◆◆◆◆	✔	133
60 p. 202	Disney's Caribbean Beach Resort	◆◆◆		122
61 p. 202	**Holiday Inn Resort Orlando Suites-Waterpark** *(See ad p. 128.)*	◆◆◆	✔	126
62 p. 202	**Wyndham Bonnet Creek Resort**	◆◆◆	✔	133
63 p. 202	**Lake Buena Vista Resort Village & Spa**	◆◆◆	✔	129
64 p. 202	**Wyndham Grand Orlando Resort Bonnet Creek** *(See ad p. 134.)*	◆◆◆◆	✔	133
65 p. 202	Disney's Coronado Springs Resort	◆◆◆◆		122
66 p. 202	**Hilton Orlando Bonnet Creek** *(See ad p. 125.)*	◆◆◆◆	✔	124

LAKE BUENA VISTA (cont'd)

Map Page	Hotels (cont'd)	Diamond Rated	Member Savings	Page
67 p. 202	WorldQuest Resort	◆◆◆		133
68 p. 202	**Waldorf Astoria Orlando** *(See ad p. 132.)*	◆◆◆◆	✔	132
69 p. 202	Disney's Pop Century Resort	◆◆◆		123
70 p. 202	Disney's Art of Animation Resort	◆◆◆		122
71 p. 202	Disney's Animal Kingdom Villas-Kidani Village	◆◆◆◆		122
72 p. 202	Disney's Animal Kingdom Villas-Jambo House	◆◆◆◆		122
73 p. 202	Disney's All-Star Sports Resort	◆◆		122
74 p. 202	Disney's All-Star Music Resort	◆◆		122
75 p. 202	Disney's All-Star Movies Resort	◆◆		122

Map Page	Restaurants	Diamond Rated	Cuisine	Price Range	Page
1 p. 202	California Grill	◆◆◆	Regional American	$36-$53	135
2 p. 202	Artist Point	◆◆◆	Regional American	$35-$60	135
3 p. 202	Citricos	◆◆◆	Southern Mediterranean	$35-$60	135
4 p. 202	**Victoria & Albert's**	◆◆◆◆◆	New American	$185-$250	136
5 p. 202	Narcoossee's	◆◆◆	Seafood	$39-$69	136
6 p. 202	Capa	◆◆◆◆	Basque	$10-$68	135
7 p. 202	Ravello	◆◆◆	Italian	$11-$59	136
8 p. 202	PB & G	◆◆	Comfort Food	$17-$36	136
9 p. 202	El Patron Mexican Restaurant & Cantina	◆◆	Mexican	$13-$22	135
10 p. 202	Havana's Cafe	◆◆	Cuban	$9-$32	135
11 p. 202	Hemingway's	◆◆◆	Seafood	$22-$60	135
12 p. 202	Bahama Breeze Island Grille	◆◆◆	Caribbean	$10-$25	135
13 p. 202	Rainforest Cafe	◆◆	American	$15-$35 SAVE	136
14 p. 202	Paddlefish	◆◆◆	Seafood	$15-$60	136
15 p. 202	Morimoto Asia	◆◆◆	Asian Dim Sum Sushi	$11-$39	136
16 p. 202	Wine Bar George	◆◆	American	$8-$59	136
17 p. 202	T-Rex Cafe	◆◆	American	$15-$36	136
18 p. 202	Raglan Road Irish Pub and Restaurant	◆◆	Irish	$10-$29	136
19 p. 202	The Polite Pig	◆◆	Barbecue	$11-$23	136
20 p. 202	The BOATHOUSE Waterfront Dining	◆◆◆	Seafood Steak	$14-$55	135
21 p. 202	The Edison	◆◆◆	American	$16-$34	135
22 p. 202	Homecomin' Kitchen	◆◆	Southern Comfort Food	$32	135
23 p. 202	STK Orlando	◆◆◆	Steak	$28-$128	136
24 p. 202	Enzo's Hideaway Tunnel Bar	◆◆◆	Italian	$17-$43	135
25 p. 202	Bongos Cuban Cafe Orlando	◆◆	Cuban	$9-$45	135
26 p. 202	Splitsville Luxury Lanes	◆◆	American	$14-$25	136
27 p. 202	Paradiso 37 Taste Of The Americas	◆◆	Continental	$17-$29	136
28 p. 202	Yachtsman Steakhouse	◆◆◆	Steak	$34-$63	136

Map Page	Restaurants (cont'd)	Diamond Rated	Cuisine	Price Range	Page
29 p. 202	Flying Fish Cafe	◆◆◆	Seafood	$37-$59	135
30 p. 202	Todd English's bluezoo	◆◆◆◆	Seafood	$14-$60	136
31 p. 202	Shula's America's Steak House	◆◆◆	Steak	$28-$130	136
32 p. 202	Latitude and Longitude	◆◆◆	American	$16-$34	135
33 p. 202	**The Venetian Chop House**	◆◆◆◆	Continental	$36-$43	136
34 p. 202	Il Mulino	◆◆◆	Italian	$17-$48	135
35 p. 202	Gourmeto's NY Pizza & Classic Italian Cuisine	◆	Italian	$9-$26	135
36 p. 202	Frankie Farrell's Irish Pub & Grille	◆◆	Irish	$10-$33	135
37 p. 202	**deep blu Seafood Grille**	◆◆◆◆	Seafood	$28-$78	135
38 p. 202	Toledo	◆◆◆	Steak Seafood	$28-$60	136
39 p. 202	The Hollywood Brown Derby	◆◆◆	American	$15-$49	135
40 p. 202	Bull & Bear Restaurant	◆◆◆◆	New Steak Seafood	$45-$75	135
41 p. 202	Jiko-The Cooking Place	◆◆◆	African	$30-$49	135

CLERMONT

Map Page	Hotels	Diamond Rated	Member Savings	Page
78 p. 202	Summer Bay Orlando By Exploria Resorts	◆◆◆		48
79 p. 202	Exploria Express by Exploria Resorts	◆◆		48

WINTER GARDEN

Map Page	Hotel	Diamond Rated	Member Savings	Page
82 p. 202	**The Grove Resort Orlando**	◆◆◆	✔	368

Map Page	Restaurant	Diamond Rated	Cuisine	Price Range	Page
44 p. 202	Valencia Restaurant	◆◆◆	Continental	$10-$34	369

ORLANDO SOUTH

Map Page	Hotels	Diamond Rated	Member Savings	Page
85 p. 202	Hilton Grand Vacations at SeaWorld	◆◆◆	✔	233
86 p. 202	**Residence Inn by Marriott-Orlando at SeaWorld**	◆◆◆	✔	239
87 p. 202	Parc Soleil by Hilton Grand Vacations Club	◆◆◆	✔	238
88 p. 202	Bluegreen Vacations The Fountains, an Ascend Resort Collection Member	◆◆◆		223
89 p. 202	Home2 Suites by Hilton Orlando International Drive South	◆◆◆	✔	235
90 p. 202	**Floridays Resort Orlando**	◆◆◆	✔	230
91 p. 202	Sheraton Vistana Villages	◆◆◆	✔	242
92 p. 202	Hilton Grand Vacations Club at Tuscany Village	◆◆◆	✔	233

Map Page	Restaurants	Diamond Rated	Cuisine	Price Range	Page
47 p. 202	Urbain 40	◆◆◆	American	$18-$65	248
48 p. 202	Fleming's Prime Steakhouse & Wine Bar	◆◆◆	Steak	$38-$89	247
49 p. 202	Big Fin Seafood Kitchen	◆◆◆	Seafood	$15-$60	246
50 p. 202	Dragonfly Robata Grill-Sushi Lounge	◆◆◆	Japanese Small Plates Sushi	$9-$78	247
51 p. 202	Pharmacy	◆◆◆	New American	$17-$32	247
52 p. 202	Slate	◆◆◆	New American	$10-$39	247

KISSIMMEE

Map Page	Hotels	Diamond Rated	Member Savings	Page
95 p. 202	**Best Western Plus Kissimmee Lake Buena Vista South Inn and Suites**	◆◆◆	✔	107
96 p. 202	**Holiday Inn Express & Suites Orlando-South Lake Buena Vista**	◆◆◆	✔	112
97 p. 202	**Gaylord Palms Resort & Convention Center**	◆◆◆◆	✔	112
98 p. 202	Wingate by Wyndham Kissimmee at Celebration	◆◆◆		114
99 p. 202	**Fantasy World Resort**	◆◆◆	✔	111
100 p. 202	Red Lion Hotel Lake Buena Vista South	◆◆◆		113
101 p. 202	**Holiday Inn Orlando SW-Celebration Area**	◆◆	✔	113
102 p. 202	Super 8 Maingate	◆◆		114
103 p. 202	**Holiday Inn Club Vacations at Orange Lake Resort** *(See ad p. 233.)*	◆◆◆	✔	112
104 p. 202	Star Island Resort & Club	◆◆◆		114
105 p. 202	**Fairfield Inn & Suites by Marriott Orlando Kissimmee/Celebration** *(See ad p. 111.)*	◆◆◆	✔	111
106 p. 202	**Grand Orlando Resort at Celebration**	◆◆◆	✔	112
107 p. 202	**Staybridge Suites Royale Parc**	◆◆	✔	114
108 p. 202	**Clarion Suites Maingate** *(See ad p. 111.)*	◆◆	✔	110
109 p. 202	**Comfort Suites Maingate East at Old Town** *(See ad p. 109.)*	◆◆◆	✔	110
110 p. 202	**Margaritaville Resort Orlando** *(See ad p. 113.)*	◆◆◆◆	✔	113
111 p. 202	Barefoot Suites	◆◆◆		107
112 p. 202	**Comfort Inn Maingate**	◆◆	✔	110
113 p. 202	Hawthorn Suites by Wyndham Maingate Kissimmee	◆◆◆		112
114 p. 202	**Galleria Palms Hotel**	◆◆	✔	112
115 p. 202	**Westgate Towers Resort**	◆◆	✔	114
117 p. 202	**Red Lion Hotel Orlando/Kissimmee Maingate**	◆◆	✔	113
118 p. 202	**Encantada Resort**	◆◆◆	✔	110
119 p. 202	**Caribe Cove Resort By Wyndham Vacation Rentals** *(See ad p. 108.)*	◆◆◆	✔	110

Map Page	Restaurants	Diamond Rated	Cuisine	Price Range	Page
55 p. 202	Villa De Flora	◆◆	Continental	$18-$38	115
56 p. 202	Moor	◆◆◆	Caribbean	$16-$45	114
57 p. 202	Ichiban Chinese & Japanese Buffet	◆◆	Chinese	$8-$12	114
58 p. 202	Pacino's Italian Ristorante	◆◆◆	Italian	$8-$35	114
59 p. 202	Flippers Pizzeria	◆◆	Pizza Sandwiches	$9-$22	114
60 p. 202	Ford's Garage	◆◆	American	$7-$19	114
61 p. 202	On Vacation	◆◆	Regional American	$9-$25	114

CELEBRATION

Map Page	Hotels	Diamond Rated	Member Savings	Page
122 p. 202	**Melia Orlando Suite Hotel at Celebration** *(See ad p. 39, p. 120.)*	◆◆◆	✔	39
123 p. 202	Bohemian Hotel Celebration, Autograph Collection	◆◆◆	✔	39

Map Page	Restaurants	Diamond Rated	Cuisine	Price Range	Page
64 p. 202	Joe's Crab Shack	♦♦	Seafood	$11-$39 SAVE	39
65 p. 202	Le China Chinese Restaurant	♦♦	Chinese	$7-$18	39
66 p. 202	Sweet Escape	♦	Sandwiches Desserts	$4-$10	39
67 p. 202	Thai Thani	♦♦	Thai	$13-$30	39
68 p. 202	Cafe D'Antonio	♦♦♦	Italian	$8-$35	39
69 p. 202	Columbia Restaurant	♦♦♦	Spanish	$8-$30	39
70 p. 202	Market Street Cafe	♦♦	American	$8-$18	39

DAVENPORT

Map Page	Hotels	Diamond Rated	Member Savings	Page
126 p. 202	**Holiday Inn Club Vacations Orlando Breeze Resort**	♦♦♦	✔	54
127 p. 202	**Bahama Bay Resort & Spa** *(See ad p. 108.)*	♦♦♦	✔	54

Map Page	Restaurant	Diamond Rated	Cuisine	Price Range	Page
73 p. 202	Diromio's Pizza & Grill	♦♦	Italian	$9-$32	54

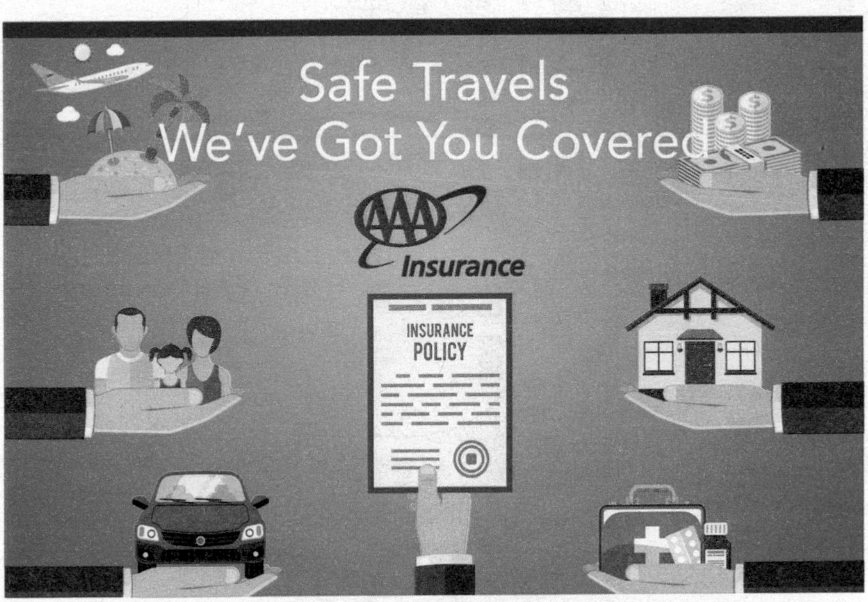

From vacations to recreation, downtime should be worry free. Trust your knowledgeable AAA insurance representative to help you get the right coverage for every phase of life. Enjoy quality products at competitive rates.

Stop by your local AAA office or visit us online.

AAA.com/Insurance

Auto • Home • Life & Other Insurance Products

Product availability may vary by AAA club.

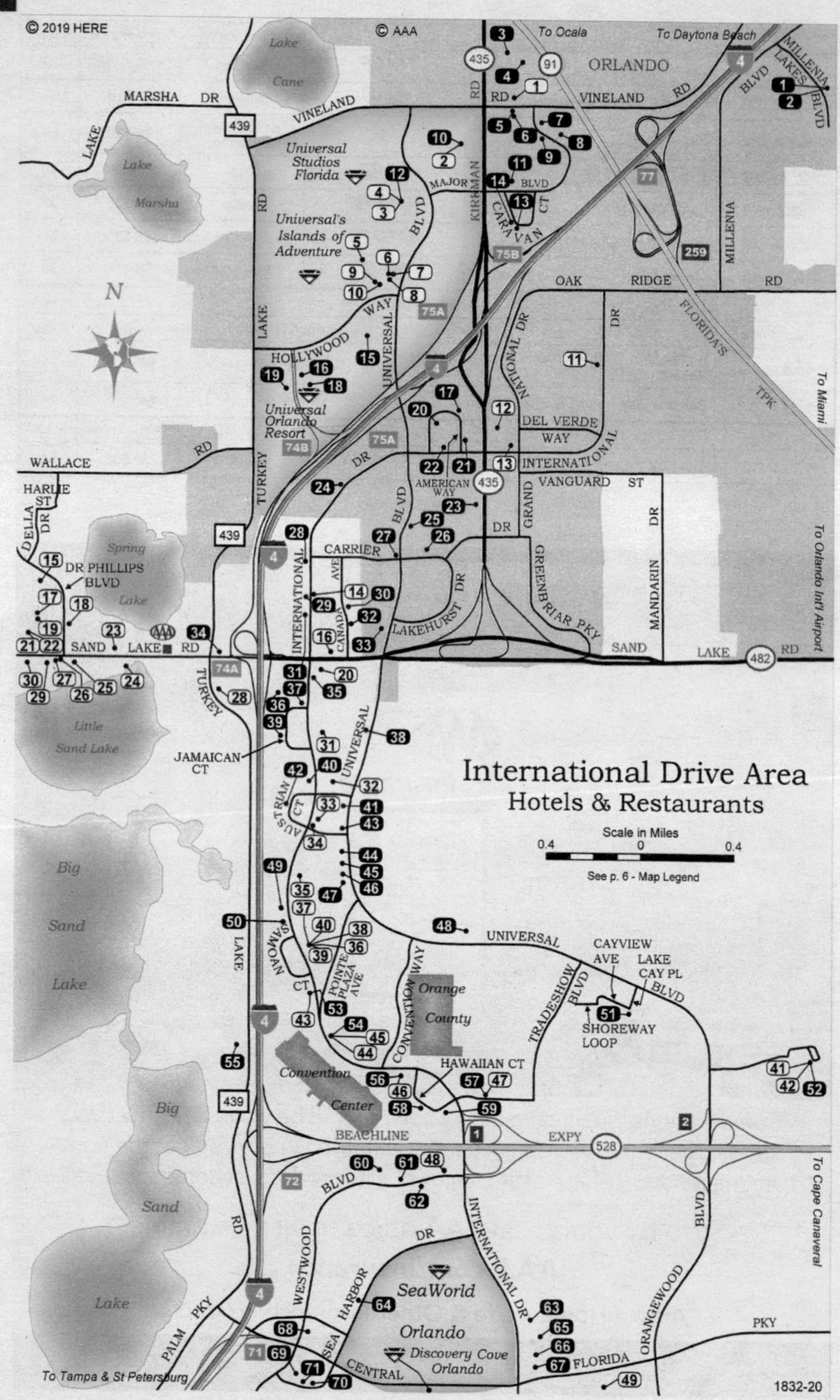

© 2019 HERE
© AAA
International Drive Area
Hotels & Restaurants
Scale in Miles
0.4 0 0.4
See p. 6 - Map Legend
To Ocala
To Daytona Beach
ORLANDO
To Miami
To Orlando Int'l Airport
To Cape Canaveral
To Tampa & St Petersburg
Universal Studios Florida
Universal's Islands of Adventure
Universal Orlando Resort
Convention Center
Orange County
SeaWorld Orlando
Discovery Cove Orlando
Lake Cane
Lake Marsha
Spring Lake
Little Sand Lake
Big Sand Lake
1832-20

International Drive Area

This index helps you "spot" where approved hotels and restaurants are located on the corresponding detailed maps. Restaurant price range is a combination of lunch and/or dinner. Turn to the listing page for more information and consult display ads for special promotions.

For more details, rates and reservations: AAA.com/travelguides/hotels

ORLANDO SOUTH

Map Page	Hotels	Diamond Rated	Member Savings	Page
1 p. 210	**SpringHill Suites by Marriott Orlando at Millenia**	◆◆◆	✔	243
2 p. 210	**Residence Inn by Marriott Orlando at Millenia**	◆◆◆	✔	239
3 p. 210	Wingate by Wyndham at Universal Studios & Convention Center	◆◆◆		244
4 p. 210	**Hampton Inn closest to Universal Orlando**	◆◆◆	✔	232
5 p. 210	Fairfield Inn & Suites by Marriott Orlando-Near Universal Orlando Resort	◆◆◆	✔	229
6 p. 210	**Best Western Plus Universal Inn**	◆◆	✔	223
7 p. 210	Holiday Inn Express & Suites Nearest Universal Orlando	◆◆		233
8 p. 210	Comfort Suites Nearest Universal Orlando	◆◆◆		225
9 p. 210	**Residence Inn by Marriott Near Universal Orlando**	◆◆◆	✔	239
10 p. 210	**Loews Portofino Bay Hotel at Universal Orlando™**	◆◆◆◆	✔	237
11 p. 210	**DoubleTree by Hilton Hotel at the Entrance to Universal Orlando** *(See ad p. 226.)*	◆◆◆	✔	226
12 p. 210	**Hard Rock Hotel® at Universal Orlando™**	◆◆◆◆	✔	232
13 p. 210	**Hyatt Place across from Universal Orlando Resort™**	◆◆◆	✔	236
14 p. 210	**Hyatt House across from Universal Orlando Resort**	◆◆◆	✔	235
15 p. 210	**Loews Royal Pacific Resort at Universal Orlando™**	◆◆◆◆	✔	237
16 p. 210	**Loews Sapphire Falls Resort at Universal Orlando™**	◆◆◆◆	✔	237
17 p. 210	**SUNSOL International Drive**	◆◆	✔	243
18 p. 210	**Universal's Aventura Hotel**	◆◆◆	✔	243
19 p. 210	**Universal's Cabana Bay Beach Resort**	◆◆◆	✔	244
20 p. 210	Home2 Suites by Hilton Orlando Near Universal	◆◆◆	✔	235
21 p. 210	**La Quinta Inn-Orlando International Drive North**	◆◆	✔	237
22 p. 210	**Four Points by Sheraton Orlando International Drive**	◆◆◆	✔	230
23 p. 210	**Hampton Inn by Hilton Orlando Near Universal Blvd/International Drive** *(See ad p. 232.)*	◆◆◆	✔	230
24 p. 210	**Rosen Inn** *(See ad p. 240.)*	◆◆◆	✔	241
25 p. 210	**Best Western Orlando Gateway Hotel** *(See ad p. 223.)*	◆◆	✔	221
26 p. 210	**The Point Hotel & Suites**	◆◆◆	✔	238
27 p. 210	**Westgate Palace Resort**	◆◆◆	✔	244
28 p. 210	**Holiday Inn Express & Suites Orlando-International Drive**	◆◆◆	✔	233
29 p. 210	Hampton Inn & Suites Orlando-International Dr. North	◆◆◆	✔	230
30 p. 210	**Comfort Inn & Suites near Universal Orlando Resort** *(See ad p. 225.)*	◆◆	✔	225
31 p. 210	**Rosen Inn International** *(See ad p. 242.)*	◆◆◆	✔	241

ORLANDO SOUTH (cont'd)

Map Page	Hotels (cont'd)	Diamond Rated	Member Savings	Page
32 p. 210	**staySky Suites I-Drive Orlando**	◆◆	✔	243
33 p. 210	Crowne Plaza Orlando-Universal Blvd	◆◆◆		226
34 p. 210	Drury Inn & Suites near Universal Orlando Resort	◆◆◆		229
35 p. 210	**Wyndham Orlando Resort International Drive** *(See ad p. 245.)*	◆◆◆	✔	244
36 p. 210	**Comfort Inn International Drive Orlando**	◆◆	✔	225
37 p. 210	**Best Western International Drive-Orlando**	◆◆	✔	221
38 p. 210	Fairfield Inn & Suites by Marriott Orlando International Drive/Convention Center	◆◆◆	✔	229
39 p. 210	**Quality Inn at International Drive**	◆◆	✔	238
40 p. 210	**Sonesta ES Suites Orlando – International Drive**	◆◆◆	✔	242
41 p. 210	La Quinta by Wyndham Orlando I Drive/Conv Center	◆◆		237
42 p. 210	Courtyard by Marriott Orlando International Drive/Convention Center	◆◆◆	✔	225
43 p. 210	**Castle Hotel, Autograph Collection**	◆◆◆◆	✔	223
44 p. 210	**Hyatt Place Orlando/Convention Center**	◆◆◆	✔	236
45 p. 210	**Residence Inn by Marriott-Orlando Convention Center**	◆◆◆	✔	240
46 p. 210	**SpringHill Suites by Marriott-Orlando Convention Center/International Drive Area**	◆◆◆	✔	243
47 p. 210	Hampton Inn Orlando-International Drive/Convention Center	◆◆◆	✔	232
48 p. 210	Las Palmeras, a Hilton Grand Vacations Club	◆◆◆◆	✔	237
49 p. 210	**Embassy Suites by Hilton Orlando International Drive-Convention Center**	◆◆◆	✔	229
50 p. 210	**Rosen Inn at Pointe Orlando** *(See ad p. 241.)*	◆◆◆	✔	241
51 p. 210	**Vista Cay Resort by Millenium**	◆◆◆	✔	244
52 p. 210	**Rosen Shingle Creek**	◆◆◆◆	✔	242
53 p. 210	**Rosen Plaza Hotel**	◆◆◆	✔	242
54 p. 210	**Hyatt Regency Orlando**	◆◆◆◆	✔	236
55 p. 210	**Westgate Lakes Resort & Spa**	◆◆◆	✔	244
56 p. 210	**Rosen Centre Hotel**	◆◆◆	✔	241
57 p. 210	**Hilton Orlando** *(See ad p. 234, p. 116.)*	◆◆◆◆	✔	233
58 p. 210	**MidPointe Hotel by Rosen Hotels & Resorts** *(See ad p. 238.)*	◆◆	✔	238
59 p. 210	**Days Inn Orlando Convention Center**	fyi	✔	226
60 p. 210	Four Points by Sheraton Orlando Convention Center	◆◆◆	✔	230
61 p. 210	**Best Western Plus Orlando Convention Center Hotel**	◆◆	✔	221
62 p. 210	**DoubleTree by Hilton Orlando at SeaWorld** *(See ad p. 227.)*	◆◆◆	✔	229
63 p. 210	**TownePlace Suites by Marriott Orlando at SeaWorld**	◆◆◆	✔	243
64 p. 210	**Renaissance Orlando at SeaWorld**	◆◆◆◆	✔	239
65 p. 210	**Holiday Inn Express at SeaWorld**	◆◆◆	✔	233
66 p. 210	**SpringHill Suites by Marriott Orlando at SeaWorld**	◆◆◆	✔	243

ORLANDO SOUTH (cont'd)

Map Page	Hotels (cont'd)	Diamond Rated	Member Savings	Page
67 p. 210	**Fairfield Inn & Suites by Marriott Orlando at SeaWorld**	♦♦♦	✔	229
68 p. 210	**Hilton Garden Inn Orlando at SeaWorld**	♦♦♦	✔	232
69 p. 210	**Homewood Suites by Hilton Orlando Theme Parks** *(See ad p. 235.)*	♦♦♦	✔	235
70 p. 210	**Staybridge Suites Orlando at SeaWorld**	♦♦♦	✔	243
71 p. 210	Hampton Inn & Suites Orlando at SeaWorld	♦♦♦	✔	230

Map Page	Restaurants	Diamond Rated	Cuisine	Price Range	Page
1 p. 210	Border Grill	♦	Mexican	$5-$11	246
2 p. 210	Bice Ristorante	♦♦♦	Northern Italian	$23-$90	246
3 p. 210	The Kitchen	♦♦♦	New American	$14-$42	247
4 p. 210	The Palm Restaurant	♦♦♦	American	$26-$62	247
5 p. 210	Hard Rock Cafe	♦♦	American	$13-$40 SAVE	247
6 p. 210	The Cowfish Sushi Burger Bar	♦♦	Burgers Sushi	$10-$28	246
7 p. 210	Bob Marley-A Tribute to Freedom	♦♦	Jamaican	$12-$22	246
8 p. 210	Pat O'Brien's	♦♦	Cajun	$10-$18	247
9 p. 210	Jimmy Buffett's Margaritaville	♦♦	American	$15-$31	247
10 p. 210	Antojito's Authentic Mexican Cuisine	♦♦	Mexican	$13-$18	246
11 p. 210	Texas de Brazil	♦♦♦	Brazilian Steak	$30-$50	247
12 p. 210	Thai Silk Restaurant	♦♦	Thai	$12-$32	248
13 p. 210	Kosher Grill	♦♦	Kosher	$10-$30	247
14 p. 210	New Punjab Indian Restaurant	♦♦	Indian	$11-$22	247
15 p. 210	The H Cuisine	♦♦♦	Mediterranean	$30-$55	247
16 p. 210	FishBones	♦♦♦	Seafood Steak	$22-$47	247
17 p. 210	bartaco	♦♦	Specialty	$3-$11	246
18 p. 210	Chatham's Place Restaurant	♦♦♦	Continental	$25-$88	246
19 p. 210	**Christini's Ristorante Italiano**	♦♦♦♦	Northern Italian	$25-$68	246
20 p. 210	Cooper's Hawk Winery & Restaurant	♦♦♦	American	$12-$42	246
21 p. 210	Bosphorous Turkish Cuisine	♦♦	Turkish	$11-$33	246
22 p. 210	Nagoya Sushi	♦♦	Japanese Sushi	$10-$35	247
23 p. 210	MoonFish	♦♦♦	Seafood Steak	$11-$65	247
24 p. 210	Eddie V's Prime Seafood	♦♦♦	Seafood	$29-$98	247
25 p. 210	Seasons 52 Fresh Grill	♦♦♦	New American	$15-$33	247
26 p. 210	Cedar's Restaurant	♦♦	Lebanese	$11-$35	246
27 p. 210	Saffron Indian Cuisine	♦♦	Indian	$12-$35	247
28 p. 210	Seito Sushi	♦♦♦	New Japanese Sushi	$12-$92	247
29 p. 210	Roy's	♦♦♦	Pacific Rim Fusion	$13-$59	247
30 p. 210	Bonefish Grill	♦♦♦	Seafood	$15-$34	246
31 p. 210	Charley's Steakhouse	♦♦♦	Steak	$24-$79	246
32 p. 210	Tapa Toro	♦♦♦	Spanish	$15-$35	247
33 p. 210	Cafe Tu Tu Tango	♦♦♦	Small Plates	$6-$12	246

Map Page	Restaurants (cont'd)	Diamond Rated	Cuisine	Price Range	Page
34 p. 210	Vito's Chop House	◆◆◆	Steak Seafood	$24-$69	248
35 p. 210	Bahama Breeze Island Grille	◆◆◆	Caribbean	$10-$25	246
36 p. 210	Copper Canyon Grill	◆◆◆	American	$15-$39	246
37 p. 210	Maggiano's Little Italy	◆◆◆	Italian	$13-$48	247
38 p. 210	Taverna Opa	◆◆	Greek	$15-$42	247
39 p. 210	Cuba Libre Restaurant & Rum Bar	◆◆◆	New Cuban	$20-$37	246
40 p. 210	The Oceanaire Seafood Room	◆◆◆	Seafood	$29-$69 SAVE	247
41 p. 210	**A Land Remembered**	◆◆◆◆	Steak Seafood	$26-$60	246
42 p. 210	**Cala Bella**	◆◆◆◆	Regional Italian	$23-$45	246
43 p. 210	Jack's Place	◆◆◆	Steak Seafood	$28-$48	247
44 p. 210	Fiorenzo	◆◆◆	Italian	$28-$64	247
45 p. 210	B-Line Diner	◆◆	American	$11-$25	246
46 p. 210	Everglades Restaurant	◆◆◆	Regional Seafood Steak	$22-$50	247
47 p. 210	Spencer's for Steaks & Chops	◆◆◆	Steak	$30-$69	247
48 p. 210	Ciao Italia Ristorante Italiano	◆◆◆	Italian	$15-$35	246
49 p. 210	Fama's Ristorante Italiano & Pizzeria	◆◆	Italian Pizza	$10-$23	247

Enjoy AAA membership discounts and benefits wherever you go.*

Up to 20% off the base rate

Free Additional Driver

$6.99 NeverLost® GPS

10% off tank of gas

Click: AAA.com/hertz | Call: 1-800-654-3080 | Visit: Your local AAA branch

*Discount applies to pay later base rate. Taxes and fees excluded. Benefits available at participating Hertz locations in the U.S., Canada and Puerto Rico. Gas savings is only valid when prepaid fuel option is purchased. No charge for additional drivers who are also AAA members, have a credit card in their own name and meet standard rental qualifications. Additional terms apply. © 2019 Hertz System, Inc. All rights reserved.

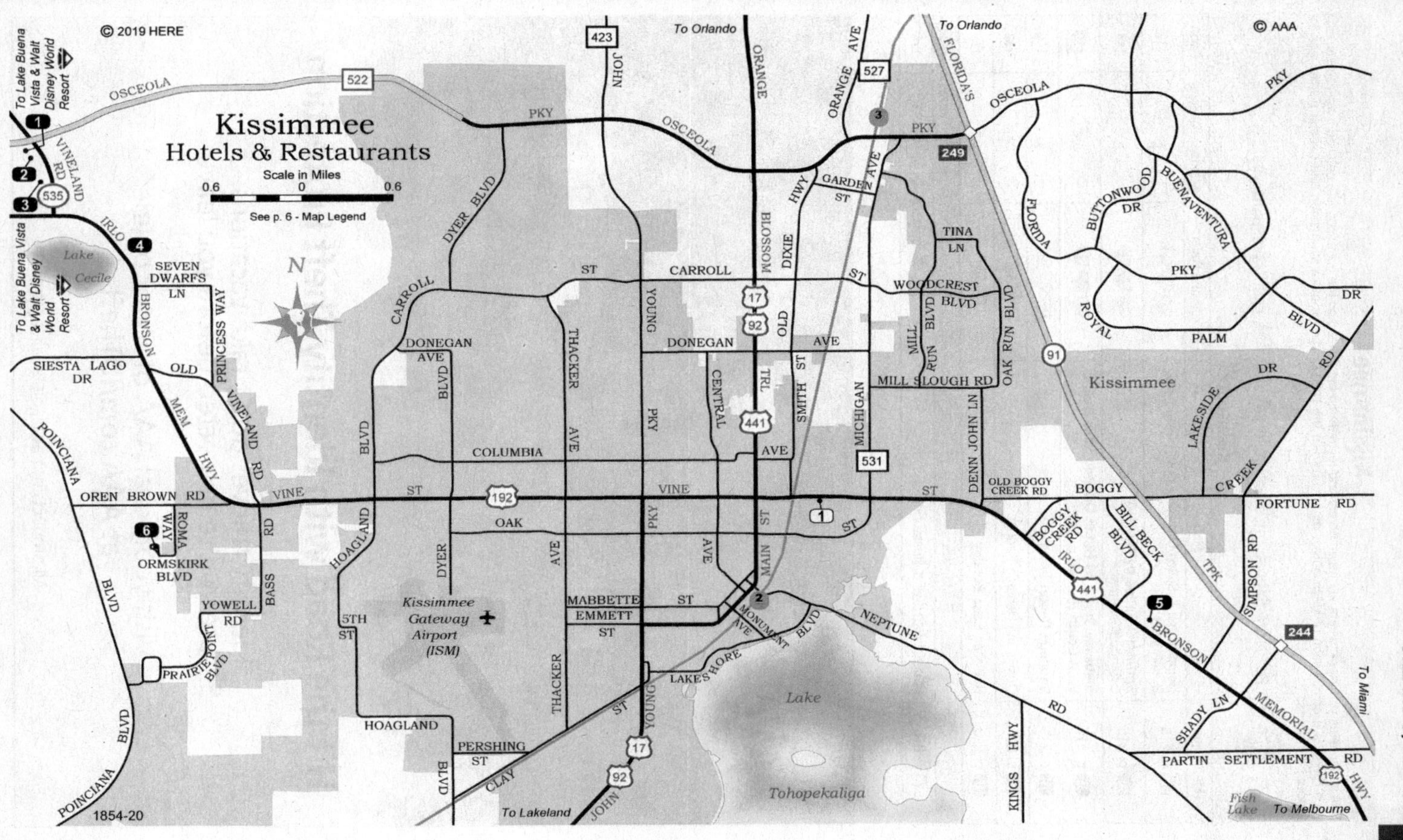
Kissimmee
Hotels & Restaurants
Scale in Miles
0.6
0
0.6
See p. 6 - Map Legend
N
© 2019 HERE
© AAA
1854-20
To Orlando
To Miami
To Melbourne
To Lakeland
To Lake Buena Vista & Walt Disney World Resort
Lake Tohopekaliga
Lake Cecile
Fish Lake
Kissimmee
Kissimmee Gateway Airport (ISM)
FLORIDA'S TPK
OSCEOLA PKY
ORANGE BLOSSOM TRL
IRLO BRONSON MEM HWY
JOHN YOUNG PKY
VINE ST
MAIN ST
THACKER AVE
CENTRAL AVE
DONEGAN AVE
CARROLL ST
COLUMBIA AVE
OAK ST
DYER BLVD
HOAGLAND BLVD
POINCIANA BLVD
OREN BROWN RD
VINELAND RD
BOGGY CREEK RD
OLD BOGGY CREEK RD
DENN JOHN LN
MICHIGAN AVE
SMITH ST
OLD DIXIE HWY
GARDEN ST
NEPTUNE RD
KINGS HWY
SHADY LN
SIMPSON RD
FORTUNE RD
LAKESIDE DR
CREEK
PALM
ROYAL PALM PKY
BUENAVENTURA BLVD
BUTTONWOOD DR
FLORIDA PKY
BILL BECK BLVD
OAK RUN BLVD
MILL RUN BLVD
MILL SLOUGH RD
WOODCREST BLVD
TINA LN
MONUMENT AVE
LAKESHORE BLVD
MABBETTE ST
EMMETT ST
PERSHING ST
CLAY ST
5TH ST
BASS RD
YOWELL RD
PRAIRIE POINT BLVD
ROMA WAY
ORMSKIRK BLVD
SIESTA LAGO DR
SEVEN DWARFS LN
PRINCESS WAY
PARTIN SETTLEMENT RD
MEMORIAL HWY
244
249
522
527
423
531
535
91
441
17
92
192

Kissimmee

This index helps you "spot" where approved hotels and restaurants are located on the corresponding detailed maps. Restaurant price range is a combination of lunch and/or dinner. Turn to the listing page for more information and consult display ads for special promotions.

For more details, rates and reservations: **AAA.com/travelguides/hotels**

KISSIMMEE

Map Page	Hotels	Diamond Rated	Member Savings	Page
1 p. 215	Hampton Inn & Suites Orlando - South Lake Buena Vista	◆◆◆	✔	112
2 p. 215	**SpringHill Suites by Marriott Orlando/Kissimmee**	◆◆◆	✔	114
3 p. 215	**Embassy Suites by Hilton Orlando Lake Buena Vista South** *(See ad p. 228.)*	◆◆◆	✔	110
4 p. 215	**Saratoga Resort Villas** *(See ad p. 121.)*	◆◆◆	✔	114
5 p. 215	Quality Inn Heritage Park	◆◆		113
6 p. 215	**Hapimag Lake Berkley**	◆◆	✔	112

Map Page	Restaurant	Diamond Rated	Cuisine	Price Range	Page
1 p. 215	Paul's Italian Deli & Restaurant	◆	Sandwiches	$5-$9	115

Hit the Road with Identity Theft Protection

Identity thieves don't take vacations.
Ensure you're protected before you leave.

Visit your local AAA office or online
at **AAA.com/IDTheft**

All products not available at all locations.

DOWNTOWN ORLANDO

• Restaurants p. 218
• Hotels & Restaurants map & index p. 186

ALOFT ORLANDO DOWNTOWN 407/380-3500 8

Historic Boutique Hotel

AAA Benefit: Members save 5% or more!

Address: 500 S Orange Ave 32801 **Location:** On SR 527 (Orange Ave), just s of Anderson St. Across from Dr. Phillips Center for the Performing Arts. Church Street, 7. **Facility:** Functional-style rooms at the trendy hotel feature comfortable beds and limited seating. Spend downtime playing a game of pool, enjoying refreshments from the bar or chilling out at the inviting pool. 118 units. 8 stories, interior corridors. *Bath:* shower only. **Parking:** valet only. **Amenities:** safes. **Pool:** heated outdoor. **Activities:** exercise room. **Guest Services:** valet and coin laundry.

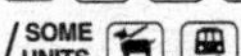

SAVE BIZ HS / SOME UNITS

COURTYARD BY MARRIOTT ORLANDO DOWNTOWN 407/996-1000 2

Hotel

COURTYARD **AAA Benefit:** Members save 5% or more!

Address: 730 N Magnolia Ave 32803 **Location:** I-4 exit 83A, just e on SR 50 (Colonial Dr) to Magnolia Ave, then just n. Lynx Central, 8. **Facility:** 200 units. 6 stories, interior corridors. **Parking:** on-site (fee). **Amenities:** safes. **Pool:** heated outdoor. **Activities:** exercise room. **Guest Services:** valet and coin laundry, boarding pass kiosk, area transportation. *(See ad this page.)*

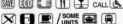

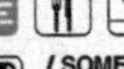

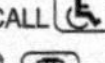

SAVE ECO CALL BIZ / SOME UNITS

CROWNE PLAZA ORLANDO-DOWNTOWN 407/843-8700 4

Hotel. **Address:** 304 W Colonial Dr 32801

DOUBLETREE BY HILTON ORLANDO DOWNTOWN 407/425-4455 1

Hotel

AAA Benefit: Members save 5% or more!

Address: 60 S Ivanhoe Blvd 32804 **Location:** I-4 exit 83A, 0.3 mi e on Colonial Dr/SR 50 to Magnolia Ave, 0.5 mi n to Ivanhoe Blvd, then just w. Lynx Central, 8. **Facility:** 342 units. 15 stories, interior corridors. **Parking:** on-site (fee) and valet. **Terms:** check-in 4 pm. **Amenities:** safes. **Pool:** heated outdoor. **Activities:** exercise room, massage. **Guest Services:** valet laundry, area transportation.

SAVE BIZ

EMBASSY SUITES BY HILTON ORLANDO-DOWNTOWN 407/841-1000 6

Hotel

AAA Benefit: Members save 5% or more!

Address: 191 E Pine St 32801 **Location:** SR 408 exit 11A to South St, just w to Rosalind Ave, then just e to Pine St. Church Street, 7. **Facility:** 167 units. 7 stories, interior corridors. **Parking:** valet only. **Terms:** check-in 4 pm. **Amenities:** safes. **Pool:** heated outdoor. **Activities:** exercise room. **Guest Services:** complimentary and valet laundry, area transportation. **Featured Amenity: full hot breakfast.**

SAVE ECO BIZ sHS

Dreaming of s'mores and starry nights?

AAA.com/campgrounds

▼ *See AAA listing this page* ▼

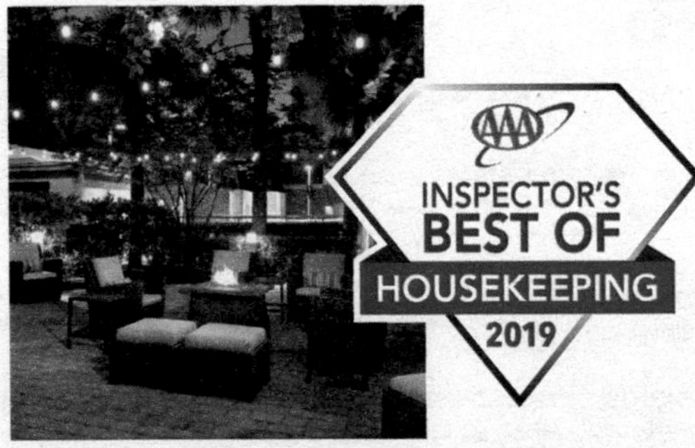

COURTYARD BY MARRIOTT
ORLANDO DOWNTOWN

730 N Magnolia Ave
Orlando, FL 32803
407-996-1000

(See map & index p. 186.)

THE GRAND BOHEMIAN HOTEL ORLANDO, AUTOGRAPH COLLECTION 407/313-9000 7

Boutique Hotel

AUTOGRAPH COLLECTION HOTELS **AAA Benefit:** Members save 5% or more!

Address: 325 S Orange Ave 32801 **Location:** I-4 exit 82B, just e on South St to Orange Ave, then just s. Church Street, 7. **Facility:** Luxury awaits in cozy rooms with soft teal accents, custom furnishings and plush bedding. Art lovers will be jazzed here. A wealth of art and a rare Imperial Grand Bosendorfer piano are on display. 247 units. 15 stories, interior corridors. **Parking:** valet only. **Terms:** check-in 4 pm. **Amenities:** safes. **Dining:** The Boheme, see separate listing. **Pool:** heated outdoor. **Activities:** hot tub, exercise room, spa. **Guest Services:** valet laundry.

SAVE ECO CALL BIZ / SOME UNITS HS

MARRIOTT ORLANDO DOWNTOWN 407/868-8686 5

Hotel

MARRIOTT **AAA Benefit:** Members save 5% or more!

Address: 400 W Livingston St 32801 **Location:** From SR 50 (Colonial Dr) 0.4 mi s on Hughey Ave, then just w. Lynx Central, 8. **Facility:** 297 units. 15 stories, interior corridors. **Parking:** valet only. **Amenities:** safes. **Activities:** exercise room. **Guest Services:** valet laundry.

SAVE ECO CALL BIZ sHS

RESIDENCE INN BY MARRIOTT ORLANDO DOWNTOWN 407/482-1500 3

Extended Stay Hotel

Residence INN. **AAA Benefit:** Members save 5% or more!

Address: 680 N Orange Ave 32801 **Location:** I-4 exit 83A, just n to US 92/SR 50, just e to Orange Ave, then just s. Lynx Central, 8. **Facility:** 138 kitchen units, some two bedrooms. 7 stories, interior corridors. **Parking:** on-site (fee). **Terms:** check-in 4 pm. **Pool:** heated indoor. **Activities:** exercise room. **Guest Services:** valet and coin laundry. **Featured Amenity: full hot breakfast.**

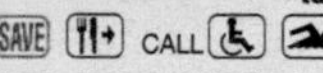

SAVE CALL BIZ HS / SOME UNITS

WHERE TO EAT

310 LAKESIDE 407/373-0310 16
New American. Dinner Theatre. **Address:** 301 E Pine St 32801

ANTHONY'S PIZZERIA & ITALIAN RESTAURANT 407/648-0009 11
Italian Pizza. Casual Dining. **Address:** 100 N Summerlin Ave 32801

ARTISAN'S TABLE 407/720-9542 19
American. Casual Dining. **Address:** 22 E Pine St 32801

THE BOHEME 407/313-9000 22
New American. Fine Dining. **Address:** 325 S Orange Ave 32801

CAFE TRASTEVERE 407/839-0235 5
Italian. Casual Dining. **Address:** 825 N Magnolia Ave 32803

DANDELION COMMUNITY CAFE 407/362-1864 8
Vegetarian. Casual Dining. **Address:** 618 N Thornton Ave 32803

DEXTER'S 407/648-2777 12
New American. Casual Dining. **Address:** 808 E Washington St 32801

DOVECOTE BRASSERIE 407/930-1700 10
French. Fine Dining. **Address:** 390 N Orange Ave, Suite 110 32801

GRAFFITI JUNKTION 321/424-5800 13
Burgers. Casual Dining. **Address:** 700 E Washington St 32801

GRINGOS LOCOS 407/841-5626 15
Mexican. Quick Serve. **Address:** 22 E Washington St 32801

HAMBURGER MARY'S BAR & GRILLE 321/319-0600 21
American. Casual Dining. **Address:** 110 W Church St 32801

HAWKERS ASIAN STREET FARE 407/237-0606 1
Asian Small Plates. Casual Dining. **Address:** 1103 N Mills Ave 32803

KRES CHOPHOUSE 407/447-7950 20
Steak. Casual Dining. **Address:** 17 W Church St 32801

LITTLE SAIGON RESTAURANT 407/423-8539 7
Vietnamese. Casual Dining. **Address:** 1106 E Colonial Dr 32801

MAMAK 407/270-4688 6
Asian Fusion Small Plates. Casual Dining. **Address:** 1231 E Colonial Dr 32803

THE MENAGERIE EATERY & BAR 407/843-9676 18
Southern. Casual Dining. **Address:** 101 S Eola Dr 32801

NEW YORK DELI 407/649-4900 9
Deli. Quick Serve. **Address:** 693 N Orange Ave 32801

THE SANCTUM CAFE 407/757-0346 4
Vegetarian Small Plates. Casual Dining. **Address:** 715 N Fern Creek Ave 32803

SOCO 407/849-1800 14
New Southern. Casual Dining. **Address:** 629 E Central Blvd 32801

THE STRAND 407/920-7744 3
American. Casual Dining. **Address:** 807 N Mills Ave 32803

TAKO CHEENA 407/757-0626 2
Asian Fusion. Casual Dining. **Address:** 932 N Mills Ave 32806

WALL STREET CANTINA 407/420-1515 17
Mexican. Casual Dining. **Address:** 19 N Orange Ave 32801

ORLANDO

• Restaurants p. 220
• Hotels & Restaurants map & index p. 188

BEST WESTERN ORLANDO WEST 407/841-8600 11

Hotel

AAA Benefit: Members save up to 15% and earn bonus points!

Address: 2014 W Colonial Dr 32804 **Location:** I-4 exit 83A, just n to SR 50 (Colonial Dr), then 1.5 mi w. **Facility:** 107 units. 2 stories, interior corridors. **Terms:** check-in 4 pm. **Amenities:** safes. **Pool:** outdoor. **Guest Services:** coin laundry. **Featured Amenity: breakfast buffet.**

 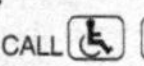  
 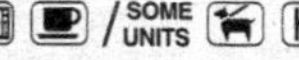 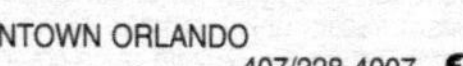
SAVE CALL / SOME UNITS HS

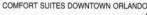

COMFORT SUITES DOWNTOWN ORLANDO 407/228-4007 10
Hotel. **Address:** 2416 N Orange Ave 32804

COMFORT SUITES UCF/RESEARCH PARK 407/737-7303 6
Hotel. **Address:** 12101 Challenger Pkwy 32826

COURTYARD BY MARRIOTT-ORLANDO EAST/UCF AREA 407/277-7676 4
SAVE Hotel. **Address:** 12000 Collegiate Way 32817

AAA Benefit: Members save 5% or more!

DOUBLETREE BY HILTON ORLANDO EAST-UCF AREA 407/275-9000 1

Hotel

AAA Benefit: Members save 5% or more!

Address: 12125 High Tech Ave 32817 **Location:** SR 417 exit 37A (University Blvd), 2.2 mi e to Systems Way, then just n. **Facility:** 242 units. 6 stories, interior corridors. **Amenities:** safes. **Pool:** outdoor. **Activities:** trails, exercise room. **Guest Services:** valet and coin laundry.

  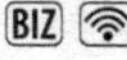
SAVE ECO BIZ / SOME UNITS HS

HILTON GARDEN INN-ORLANDO EAST/UCF 407/992-5000 7

Hotel

AAA Benefit: Members save 5% or more!

Address: 1959 N Alafaya Tr 32826 **Location:** SR 408 exit 21 (Alafaya Tr), 1.6 mi n. **Facility:** 122 units. 3 stories, interior corridors. **Pool:** heated outdoor. **Activities:** hot tub, exercise room. **Guest Services:** valet and coin laundry.

  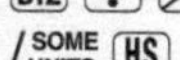
SAVE CALL BIZ / SOME UNITS HS

HOLIDAY INN EXPRESS HOTEL & SUITES ORLANDO-OCOEE EAST 407/290-2710 12
Hotel. **Address:** 7474 W Colonial Dr 32818

HOLIDAY INN ORLANDO EAST-UCF AREA 407/658-9008 8
Hotel. **Address:** 1724 N Alafaya Tr 32826

For highways, byways and more: AAA.com/maps

▼ *See AAA listing p. 82* ▼

Perfect for a relaxing vacation or sportsman's getaway
2 GOLF COURSES • TENNIS • SPA • MARINA • TRAP & SKEET • 4 RESTAURANTS
AAA SAVE UP TO 30%
800-874-9053 | MissionInnResort.com | *35 minutes N.W. of Orlando*

(See map & index p. 188.)

HOMEWOOD SUITES BY HILTON ORLANDO-UCF AREA 407/282-0067 (5)

Extended Stay Hotel. **Address:** 3028 N Alafaya Tr 32826

AAA Benefit: Members save 5% or more!

RESIDENCE INN BY MARRIOTT-ORLANDO EAST/UCF AREA 407/513-9000 (3)

Extended Stay Hotel. **Address:** 11651 University Blvd 32817

AAA Benefit: Members save 5% or more!

TOWNEPLACE SUITES BY MARRIOTT-ORLANDO EAST/UCF AREA 407/243-6100 (2)

Extended Stay Hotel. **Address:** 11801 High Tech Ave 32817

AAA Benefit: Members save 5% or more!

WHERE TO EAT

ADRIATICO TRATTORIA ITALIANA 407/428-0044 (11)

Italian. Casual Dining. **Address:** 2417 Edgewater Dr 32804

AGAVE AZUL 407/704-6930 (34)

Mexican. Casual Dining. **Address:** 4750 S Kirkman Rd 32811

BRIO TUSCAN GRILLE 407/351-8909 (37)

Italian. Fine Dining. **Address:** 4200 Conroy Rd, Suite 154 32839

BUBBALOU'S BODACIOUS BAR-B-QUE 407/423-1212

Barbecue. Quick Serve. **Address:** 12100 Challenger Pkwy 32826

BUBBALOU'S BODACIOUS BAR-B-QUE 407/295-1212 (32)

Barbecue. Casual Dining. **Address:** 5818 Conroy Rd 32835

THE CHEESECAKE FACTORY 407/226-0333 (36)

International. Casual Dining. **Address:** 4200 Conroy Rd, Suite SP A148 32839

CHRISTNER'S PRIME STEAK & LOBSTER 407/645-4443 (4)

Steak Seafood. Fine Dining. **Address:** 729 Lee Rd 32810

COLIBRI MEXICAN CUISINE 407/629-6601 (9)

Mexican. Casual Dining. **Address:** 4963 New Broad St 32814

COLLEGE PARK CAFE 407/420-9892 (13)

Comfort Food. Casual Dining. **Address:** 2304 Edgewater Dr 32804

DOMU 407/960-1228 (10)

Asian Noodles. Casual Dining. **Address:** 3201 Corrine Dr, Suite 100 32803

FIREBIRDS WOOD FIRED GRILL 407/581-9861 (16)

American. Casual Dining. **Address:** 1562 N Mills Ave 32803

GATOR'S DOCKSIDE 407/249-9444

American. Casual Dining. **Address:** 12448 Lake Underhill Rd 32829

GIOVANNI'S ITALIAN RESTAURANT & PIZZERIA 407/359-5900 (1)

Italian Pizza. Casual Dining. **Address:** 4250 AlafayaTr, Suite 132 32765

THE GREEK CORNER RESTAURANT 407/228-0303 (17)

Greek. Casual Dining. **Address:** 1600 N Orange Ave 32804

GREENS & GRILLE 407/770-1407 (33)

Sandwiches. Quick Serve. **Address:** 4104 Millenia Blvd, Suite 114 32839

HIGH TIDE HARRY'S 407/273-4422 (30)

Seafood. Casual Dining. **Address:** 4645 S Semoran Blvd 32822

HOT DOG HEAVEN 407/282-5746 (22)

Hot Dogs Quick Serve

$4-$8

AAA Inspector Notes: Easily identified from the road by its landmark sign, the small spot sources products directly from Chicago and have been serving up authentic Chicago hot dogs since 1987. Patrons can choose a dog with a chili-cheese combo or they can pile on the sauerkraut. I suggest the Great Chicago Fire dog topped with mustard, relish, onion, tomato, pickle and hot peppers. Cap off the meal with a cup or cone of ice cream or a refreshing rootbeer float. **Features:** patio dining. **Address:** 5355 E Colonial Dr 32807 **Location:** SR 50 (Colonial Dr), just w of jct SR 436 (Semoran Blvd). (L)

INFUSION TEA 407/999-5255 (21)

Natural/Organic. Quick Serve. **Address:** 1600 Edgewater Dr 32804

JACK AND MARY'S 407/281-1113 (28)

Breakfast Sandwiches. Casual Dining. **Address:** 2323 S Goldenrod Rd 32822

KABOOKI SUSHI 407/228-3839 (25)

New Japanese Sushi Fusion. Fine Dining. **Address:** 3122 E Colonial Dr 32803

KINGFISH GRILL 407/367-7992 (14)

Italian. Casual Dining. **Address:** 2124 Edgewater Dr 32804

K RESTAURANT 407/872-2332 (19)

New American. Fine Dining. **Address:** 1710 Edgewater Dr 32804

LAZY MOON PIZZA 407/658-2396 (2)

Pizza. Casual Dining. **Address:** 11551 University Blvd 32817

LE CAFE DE PARIS 407/293-2326 (38)

French. Casual Dining. **Address:** 5170 Dr. Phillips Blvd 32819

LE COQ AU VIN 407/851-6980 (31)

French. Fine Dining. **Address:** 4800 S Orange Ave 32806

NUMERO UNO CUBAN RESTAURANT 407/841-3840 (29)

Cuban. Casual Dining. **Address:** 2499 S Orange Ave 32806

P.F. CHANG'S CHINA BISTRO 407/345-2888 (35)

Chinese. Fine Dining. **Address:** 4200 Conroy Pl 32839

PIG FLOYD'S URBAN BARBAKOA 407/203-0866 (20)

Barbecue. Quick Serve. **Address:** 1326 N Mills Ave 32803

PITA PIT 407/380-2333 (3)

Sandwiches. Quick Serve. **Address:** 12140 Collegiate Way 32817

PIZZA BRUNO 407/440-3894 (27)

Pizza. Casual Dining. **Address:** 3990 Curry Ford Rd 32806

RAGAZZI'S PIZZA & RESTAURANT 407/999-9973 (8)

Italian. Casual Dining. **Address:** 3201 Edgewater Dr 32804

(See map & index p. 188.)

ROYAL THAI 407/275-0776 (12)

Thai. Casual Dining. **Address:** 1202 N Semoran Blvd 32807

SANTIAGO'S BODEGA 407/412-6979 (18)

International Small Plates. Casual Dining. **Address:** 802 Virginia Dr 32803

SE7EN BITES 407/203-0727 (26)

Southern American. Quick Serve. **Address:** 617 N Primrose Dr 32803

SEA THAI RESTAURANT 407/895-0985 (24)

Thai. Casual Dining. **Address:** 3812 E Colonial Dr 32803

SHAKERS AMERICAN CAFE 407/422-3534 (23)

American. Casual Dining. **Address:** 1308 Edgewater Dr 32804

SONNY'S REAL PIT BAR-B-Q 407/482-0888

Barbecue. Casual Dining. **Address:** 310 S Alafaya Tr 32825

THE TAP ROOM AT DUBSDREAD 407/650-0100 (6)

American. Casual Dining. **Address:** 549 W Par St 32804

THAI SINGHA 407/382-8201 (7)

Thai Sushi. Casual Dining. **Address:** 863 N Alafaya Tr 32828

TIJUANA FLATS 407/822-4257

Tex-Mex. Quick Serve. **Address:** 2320 S Kirkman Rd 32811

TOOJAY'S GOURMET DELI

American. Casual Dining.

LOCATIONS:

Address: 715 N Alafaya Tr 32828 **Phone:** 407/249-9475

Address: 2400 E Colonial Dr 32801 **Phone:** 407/894-1718

WHITE WOLF CAFE 407/895-9911 (15)

American. Casual Dining. **Address:** 1829 N Orange Ave 32804

ORLANDO SOUTH

• **Restaurants p. 246**
• **Hotels & Restaurants map & index p. 197, 199, 202, 210**

BEST WESTERN AIRPORT INN & SUITES

407/581-2800 (22)

Hotel

AAA Benefit: Members save up to 15% and earn bonus points!

Address: 8101 Aircenter Ct 32809 **Location:** SR 528 (Beachline Expwy) exit 8, just e on Jetport Rd to Boggy Creek Rd, then 0.4 mi w. Sand Lake Road, 5. **Facility:** 100 units. 5 stories, interior corridors. **Pool:** outdoor. **Activities:** exercise room. **Guest Services:** valet and coin laundry, area transportation. **Featured Amenity: full hot breakfast.**

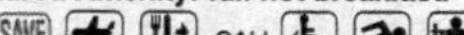

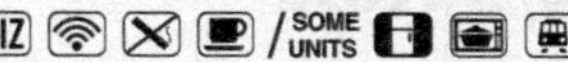

BEST WESTERN INTERNATIONAL DRIVE-ORLANDO

407/345-1172 (37)

Hotel

AAA Benefit: Members save up to 15% and earn bonus points!

Address: 8222 Jamaican Ct 32819 **Location:** I-4 exit 74A (Sand Lake Rd), 0.3 mi e to International Dr, just s to Jamaican Ct, then just e. **Facility:** 125 units. 4 stories, exterior corridors. **Amenities:** safes. **Pool:** heated outdoor. **Activities:** picnic facilities, exercise room. **Guest Services:** coin laundry, area transportation. **Featured Amenity: breakfast buffet.**

SAVE CALL BIZ

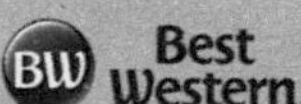

Best Western — **Your home away from home. Located in the heart of International Drive.**

BEST WESTERN ORLANDO GATEWAY HOTEL

407/351-5009 (25)

Hotel

Best Western. **AAA Benefit:** Members save up to 15% and earn bonus points!

Address: 7299 Universal Blvd 32819 **Location:** I-4 exit 74A (Sand Lake Rd), 0.7 mi e to Universal Blvd, then 0.6 mi n. **Facility:** 297 units. 7-8 stories, interior corridors. **Terms:** check-in 4 pm. **Amenities:** safes. **Dining:** 2 restaurants. **Pool:** heated outdoor. **Activities:** hot tub, game room, exercise room. **Guest Services:** valet and coin laundry, boarding pass kiosk, rental car service, area transportation. *(See ad p. 223.)*

SAVE CALL BIZ

BEST WESTERN PLUS ORLANDO CONVENTION CENTER HOTEL

407/313-4100 (61)

Hotel

AAA Benefit: Members save up to 15% and earn bonus points!

Address: 6301 Westwood Blvd 32821 **Location:** I-4 exit 72, 1.1 mi e to exit 1 (International Dr), just s to Westwood Blvd, then just w. **Facility:** 93 units. 4 stories, interior corridors. **Amenities:** safes. **Pool:** outdoor. **Activities:** exercise room. **Guest Services:** valet and coin laundry, area transportation. **Featured Amenity: breakfast buffet.**

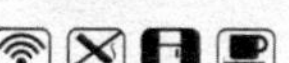

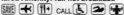

Discover member savings around the world: AAA.com/discounts

PARADISE.
MAKE IT YOURS.

Get away to paradise. Come play on miles of white-sand beaches, splash in turquoise waters and explore endless family fun, eco-adventures, nonstop thrills and romantic escapes. Exhilaration awaits. Make it yours.

VISIT NOW
VISITPANAMACITYBEACH.COM/MAKE-IT-YOURS

(See maps & indexes p. 197, 199, 202, 210.)

Get an expert view from AAA inspectors:

AAA.com/travelguides/hotels

(See maps & indexes p. 197, 199, 202, 210.)

BEST WESTERN PLUS UNIVERSAL INN
407/226-9119 6

Hotel

AAA Benefit: Members save up to 15% and earn bonus points!

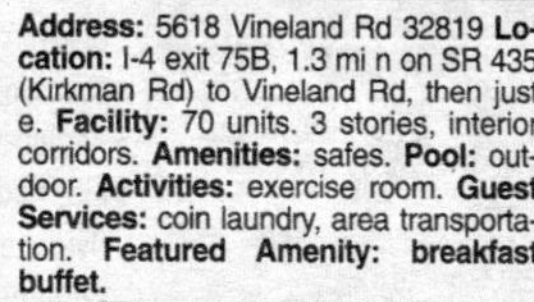

Address: 5618 Vineland Rd 32819 **Location:** I-4 exit 75B, 1.3 mi n on SR 435 (Kirkman Rd) to Vineland Rd, then just e. **Facility:** 70 units. 3 stories, interior corridors. **Amenities:** safes. **Pool:** outdoor. **Activities:** exercise room. **Guest Services:** coin laundry, area transportation. **Featured Amenity:** breakfast buffet.

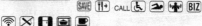

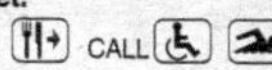

SAVE CALL BIZ

BLUEGREEN VACATIONS THE FOUNTAINS, AN ASCEND RESORT COLLECTION MEMBER 407/905-4100 88

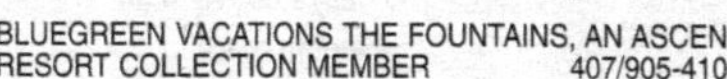
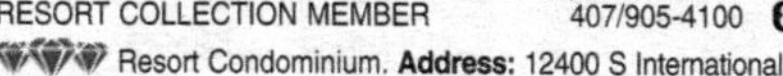

Resort Condominium. **Address:** 12400 S International Dr 32821

CASTLE HOTEL, AUTOGRAPH COLLECTION
407/345-1511 43

Boutique Hotel

AUTOGRAPH COLLECTION HOTELS

AAA Benefit: Members save 5% or more!

Address: 8629 International Dr 32819 **Location:** I-4 exit 74A (Sand Lake Rd), 0.5 mi e to International Dr, then 0.5 mi s. **Facility:** The unique hotel is upscale in design with exquisite art pieces and furnishings that are castle worthy. Highlights include on-site restaurants, a well-equipped gym and an inviting pool area. 214 units. 9 stories, interior corridors. **Parking:** on-site (fee) and valet. **Terms:** check-in 4 pm. **Amenities:** safes. **Dining:** 4 restaurants, also, Cafe Tu Tu Tango, Vito's Chop House, see separate listings. **Pool:** heated outdoor. **Activities:** hot tub, cabanas, exercise room, massage. **Guest Services:** valet and coin laundry.

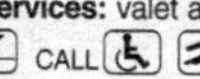

SAVE CALL BIZ / SOME UNITS

▼ See AAA listing p. 221 ▼

BW Best Western.

AAA Discounts Available

EXPLORE ORLANDO HERE

Free Wi-Fi • Restaurant Deli • Heated Pool • Basketball Court
Fitness Center • Business Center • Modern Rooms

Orlando Gateway Hotel
800-445-7299 | 407-351-5009 | bworlando.com
7299 Universal Blvd. Orlando, FL 32819

Book and save at AAA.com/hertz

▼ See AAA listing p. 126 ▼

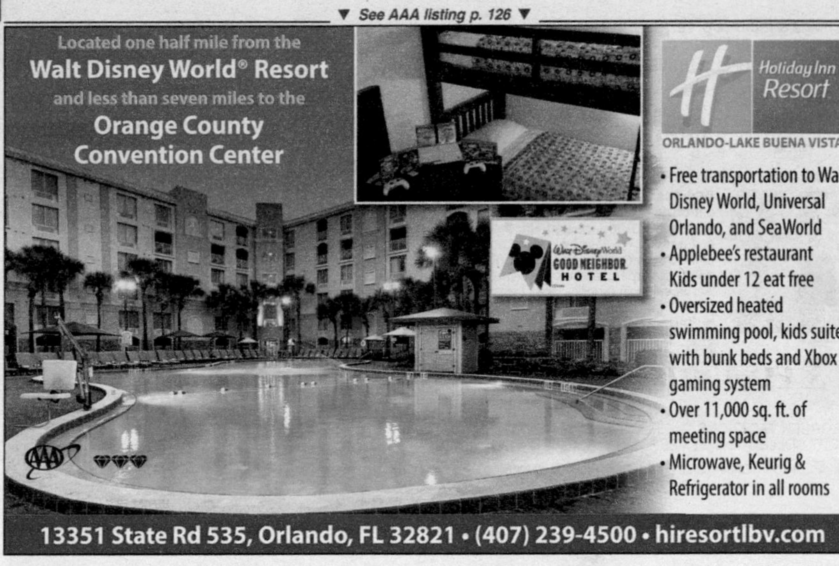

Located one half mile from the

and less than seven miles to the

• Applebee's restaurant Kids under 12 eat free
• Oversized heated swimming pool, kids suite with bunk beds and Xbox gaming system

13351 State Rd 535, Orlando, FL 32821 • (407) 239-4500 • hiresortlbv.com

(See maps & indexes p. 197, 199, 202, 210.)

▼ See AAA listing p. 122 ▼

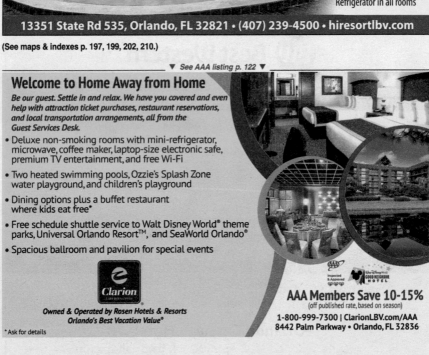

Welcome to Home Away from Home

Be our guest. Settle in and relax. We have you covered and even help with attraction ticket purchases, restaurant reservations, and local transportation arrangements, all from the Guest Services Desk.

- Deluxe non-smoking rooms with mini-refrigerator, microwave, coffee maker, laptop-size electronic safe, premium TV entertainment, and free Wi-Fi
- Two heated swimming pools, Ozzie's Splash Zone water playground, and children's playground
- Dining options plus a buffet restaurant where kids eat free*
- Free schedule shuttle service to Walt Disney World® theme parks, Universal Orlando Resort™, and SeaWorld Orlando®
- Spacious ballroom and pavilion for special events

Clarion

Owned & Operated by Rosen Hotels & Resorts
Orlando's Best Vacation Value®

*Ask for details

AAA Members Save 10-15%
(off published rate, based on season)

1-800-999-7300 | ClarionLBV.com/AAA
8442 Palm Parkway • Orlando, FL 32836

From simple to spectacular:

AAA.com/travelguides/restaurants

(See maps & indexes p. 197, 199, 202, 210.)

COMFORT INN & SUITES NEAR UNIVERSAL ORLANDO RESORT 407/351-7000 **30**

Hotel

Address: 7495 Canada Ave 32819 **Location:** I-4 exit 74A (Sand Lake Rd), just e to Canada Ave, then 0.3 mi n. **Facility:** 200 units. 5 stories, interior corridors. **Pool:** outdoor. **Activities:** hot tub, exercise room. **Guest Services:** valet and coin laundry, area transportation. **Featured Amenity: breakfast buffet.** *(See ad this page.)*

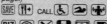

SAVE CALL BIZ

COMFORT INN INTERNATIONAL DRIVE ORLANDO 407/313-4000 **36**

Hotel

Address: 8134 International Dr 32819 **Location:** I-4 exit 74A, just e on SR 482 (Sand Lake Rd), then just s. **Facility:** 112 units. 6 stories, interior corridors. **Amenities:** safes. **Pool:** outdoor. **Activities:** exercise room. **Guest Services:** valet and coin laundry, area transportation. **Featured Amenity: breakfast buffet.**

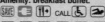

SAVE CALL BIZ HS

Comfort™ International Drive

Convenience and comfort all rolled into one. Located in the heart of International Drive.

COMFORT SUITES NEAREST UNIVERSAL ORLANDO 407/363-1967 **8**

Hotel. **Address:** 5617 Major Blvd 32819

COUNTRY INN & SUITES BY RADISSON-ORLANDO AIRPORT 407/856-8896 **11**

Hotel. **Address:** 5440 Forbes Pl 32812

COURTYARD BY MARRIOTT-ORLANDO AIRPORT 407/240-7200 **12**

Hotel

COURTYARD® **AAA Benefit:** Members save 5% or more!

Address: 7155 N Frontage Rd 32812 **Location:** SR 528 (Beachline Expwy) exit 11 (Semoran Blvd/SR 436), 1 mi n to Frontage Rd, then just w. **Facility:** 149 units. 3 stories, interior corridors. **Pool:** heated outdoor. **Activities:** exercise room. **Guest Services:** valet and coin laundry, boarding pass kiosk, area transportation.

SAVE CALL BIZ / SOME UNITS

COURTYARD BY MARRIOTT ORLANDO INTERNATIONAL DRIVE/CONVENTION CENTER 407/351-2244 **42**

SAVE Hotel. **Address:** 8600 Austrian Ct 32819

AAA Benefit: Members save 5% or more!

COURTYARD BY MARRIOTT-ORLANDO LAKE NONA 407/856-9165 **9**

Hotel

COURTYARD® **AAA Benefit:** Members save 5% or more!

Address: 6955 Lake Nona Blvd 32827 **Location:** Jct Florida's Turnpike and Central Florida GreeneWay; 2.7 mi e; then 0.5 mi s. **Facility:** 102 units. 7 stories, interior corridors. **Pool:** heated outdoor. **Activities:** bicycles, exercise room. **Guest Services:** valet and coin laundry, boarding pass kiosk, area transportation.

SAVE CALL

BIZ

▼ *See AAA listing this page* ▼

In the heart of the International Drive Resort Area AAA

BY CHOICE HOTELS

Comfort Inn & Suites
near Universal Orlando Resort™
7495 Canada Ave.
Orlando, FL 32819
407-351-7000

- Free hot breakfast buffet • Free Attractions & Shopping Shuttle
- Free Wi-Fi • I-Ride Trolley Stop • Mini fridge & microwave in all rooms
- Double Queen Suites available that sleep up to 6 people
- One mile from Universal Studios

choicehotels.com/flc02

(See maps & indexes p. 197, 199, 202, 210.)

COURTYARD BY MARRIOTT ORLANDO SOUTH JOHN YOUNG PARKWAY 407/351-2661 **4**

Hotel

COURTYARD **AAA Benefit:** Members save 5% or more!

Address: 4120 W Taft Vineland Rd 32837 **Location:** I-4 exit 71, 2.9 mi e at jct Central Florida Pkwy and S John Young Pkwy, then just n. **Facility:** 128 units. 6 stories, interior corridors. **Pool:** heated outdoor. **Activities:** exercise room. **Guest Services:** valet and coin laundry, boarding pass kiosk.

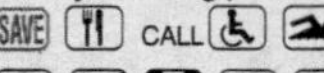

CROWNE PLAZA ORLANDO-UNIVERSAL BLVD 407/355-0550 **33**

Hotel. **Address:** 7800 Universal Blvd 32819

DAYS INN ORLANDO CONVENTION CENTER 407/352-8700 **59**

fyi

Hotel

Under major renovation, call for details. **Last Rated:** ♦♦ **Address:** 9990 International Dr 32819 **Location:** I-4 exit 72, just e on SR 528 (Beachline Expwy) exit 1, just n. **Facility:** 219 units. 4 stories, exterior corridors. **Terms:** check-in 4 pm. **Amenities:** safes. **Pool:** outdoor. **Activities:** limited exercise equipment. **Guest Services:** valet and coin laundry, area transportation.

DOUBLETREE BY HILTON HOTEL AT THE ENTRANCE TO UNIVERSAL ORLANDO 407/351-1000 **11**

Hotel

AAA Benefit: Members save 5% or more!

Address: 5780 Major Blvd 32819 **Location:** I-4 exit 75B, 0.7 mi n to Major Blvd, then just e. Opposite main entrance to Universal Studios. **Facility:** 742 units, some two bedrooms. 18-19 stories, interior corridors. **Parking:** on-site (fee) and valet. **Terms:** check-in 4 pm. **Amenities:** safes. **Dining:** 3 restaurants. **Pool:** heated outdoor. **Activities:** hot tub, game room, exercise room. **Guest Services:** valet and coin laundry, boarding pass kiosk, rental car service, area transportation. *(See ad this page.)*

GET THE APP

Download today.
Connect every day.
AAA.com/mobile
CAA.ca/mobile

▼ *See AAA listing this page* ▼

WELCOME TO DOUBLETREE UNIVERSAL

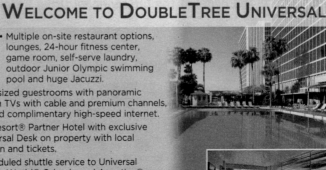

- Multiple on-site restaurant options, lounges, 24-hour fitness center, game room, self-serve laundry, outdoor Junior Olympic swimming pool and huge Jacuzzi.
- 742 luxuriously oversized guestrooms with panoramic views, 50" flat screen TVs with cable and premium channels, mini-refrigerators and complimentary high-speed internet.
- Universal Orlando Resort® Partner Hotel with exclusive benefits and a Universal Desk on property with local attraction information and tickets.
- Complimentary scheduled shuttle service to Universal Orlando Resort®, Sea World® Orlando and Aquatica® Orlando.
- 62,800 square feet of flexible meeting space for up to 2,000 attendees, on-site professional A/V company, and professional meeting planners.

5780 Major Boulevard, Orlando, FL 32819 • (407) 351-1000 • DoubleTree.com

Call the dedicated DoubleTree AAA number, **1-877-655-5697** or your local AAA travel office.

▼ See AAA listing p. 229 ▼

AN OASIS IN THE CENTER OF IT ALL

Offers spacious accommodations, two sparkling pools, delicious dining options, complimentary transportation to most of the major theme parks and abundant recreational amenities for the entire family. The DoubleTree by Hilton Orlando is an Official SeaWorld Hotel.

10100 International Drive, Orlando, FL 32821
DoubleTreeOrlandoSeaWorld.com
407-352-1100

(See maps & indexes p. 197, 199, 202, 210.)

For exclusive AAA member savings and benefits: AAA.com/hertz

▼ See AAA listing p. 110 ▼

Embassy Suites by Hilton Orlando Lake Buena Vista South

*Service of alcohol subject to state and local laws. Must be of legal drinking age. ©2016 Hilton Worldwide. ™ indicates a trademark of Hilton Worldwide.

When you stay at the Embassy Suites Orlando Lake Buena Vista South, you get a spacious two-room suite, free made-to-order breakfast and complimentary drinks at our Evening Reception. Located 3.5 miles from Walt Disney World® Resort theme parks. Golf, shopping and dining nearby.

EMBASSY SUITES by Hilton™

Orlando Lake Buena Vista South

No Resort Fees

orlandolakebuenavistasouth.embassysuites.com

407-597-4000

(See maps & indexes p. 197, 199, 202, 210.)

▼ See AAA listing p. 229 ▼

AAA
INSPECTOR'S
BEST OF
HOUSEKEEPING
2019

EMBASSY SUITES by HILTON™

Orlando Airport

5835 T.G. Lee Boulevard
Orlando, Florida 32822
407-888-9339

Make the Connection

Find this symbol for places to look, book and save on AAA.com.

iStockphoto.com_shapecharge

(See maps & indexes p. 197, 199, 202, 210.)

DOUBLETREE BY HILTON ORLANDO AT SEAWORLD
407/352-1100 62

Resort Hotel

AAA Benefit: Members save 5% or more!

Address: 10100 International Dr 32821 **Location:** I-4 exit 72, 0.5 mi e on SR 528 (Beachline Expwy) exit 1 (International Dr), just e. **Facility:** The resort's 28 lushly landscaped acres offer a tranquil setting within the busy International Drive area. Rooms and bathrooms offer upgraded accommodations and décor elements. 1019 units. 2-17 stories, interior/exterior corridors. **Parking:** on-site (fee) and valet. **Amenities:** safes. **Dining:** 3 restaurants. **Pool:** heated outdoor. **Activities:** hot tub, miniature golf, recreation programs, kids club, playground, lawn sports, exercise room. **Guest Services:** valet and coin laundry, rental car service, area transportation. *(See ad p. 227.)*

SAVE ECO CALL

BIZ / SOME UNITS

An Official SeaWorld Hotel with complimentary shuttle, 2 pools, dining, and recreational amenities.

DRURY INN & SUITES NEAR UNIVERSAL ORLANDO RESORT
407/354-1101 34

Hotel. **Address:** 7301 W Sand Lake Rd 32819

EMBASSY SUITES BY HILTON ORLANDO-AIRPORT
407/888-9339 6

Hotel

AAA Benefit: Members save 5% or more!

Address: 5835 T.G. Lee Blvd 32822 **Location:** SR 528 (Beachline Expwy) exit 11 (Semoran Blvd/SR 436), 1 mi n to T.G. Lee Blvd, then just e. **Facility:** 174 units. 7 stories, interior corridors. **Parking:** on-site (fee). **Amenities:** safes. **Pool:** heated outdoor. **Activities:** hot tub, exercise room. **Guest Services:** valet and coin laundry, area transportation. **Featured Amenity: full hot breakfast.** *(See ad p. 228.)*

SAVE ECO CALL BIZ

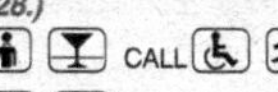

EMBASSY SUITES BY HILTON ORLANDO INTERNATIONAL DRIVE-CONVENTION CENTER
407/352-1400 49

Hotel

AAA Benefit: Members save 5% or more!

Address: 8978 International Dr 32819 **Location:** I-4 exit 74A (Sand Lake Rd), just e to International Dr, then just s. **Facility:** 244 units, some two bedrooms. 8 stories, interior corridors. **Parking:** on-site (fee) and valet. **Terms:** check-in 4 pm. **Amenities:** safes. **Pool:** heated outdoor, heated indoor. **Activities:** hot tub, exercise room. **Guest Services:** valet and coin laundry, rental car service, area transportation. **Featured Amenity: full hot breakfast.**

SAVE ECO CALL BIZ

/ SOME UNITS

FAIRFIELD INN & SUITES BY MARRIOTT ORLANDO AT SEAWORLD
407/354-1139 67

Hotel

Fairfield **AAA Benefit:** Members save 5% or more!

Address: 10815 International Dr 32821 **Location:** I-4 exit 71, 1.1 mi e on Central Florida Pkwy. **Facility:** 200 units. 6 stories, interior corridors. **Parking:** on-site (fee). **Terms:** check-in 4 pm. **Pool:** heated outdoor. **Activities:** hot tub, game room, exercise room. **Guest Services:** valet and coin laundry, boarding pass kiosk, area transportation. **Featured Amenity: breakfast buffet.**

SAVE BIZ HS

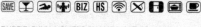

FAIRFIELD INN & SUITES BY MARRIOTT ORLANDO INTERNATIONAL DRIVE/CONVENTION CENTER
407/581-9001 38

SAVE Hotel. **Address:** 8214 Universal Blvd 32819

AAA Benefit: Members save 5% or more!

FAIRFIELD INN & SUITES BY MARRIOTT ORLANDO-NEAR UNIVERSAL ORLANDO RESORT
407/581-5600 5

SAVE Hotel. **Address:** 5614 Vineland Rd 32819

AAA Benefit: Members save 5% or more!

FAIRFIELD INN BY MARRIOTT-ORLANDO AIRPORT
407/888-2666 5

SAVE Hotel. **Address:** 7100 Augusta National Dr 32822

AAA Benefit: Members save 5% or more!

AAA.com/maps—Dream, plan, go with AAA travel planning tools

(See maps & indexes p. 197, 199, 202, 210.)

THE FLORIDA HOTEL & CONFERENCE CENTER, BW PREMIER COLLECTION 407/859-1500 **1**

Hotel

BW Premier COLLECTION by BEST WESTERN **AAA Benefit:** Members save up to 15% and earn bonus points!

Address: 1500 Sand Lake Rd 32809 **Location:** Jct Sand Lake Rd and S Orange Blossom Tr, just s. Located in The Florida Mall, south side. **Facility:** 511 units. 11 stories, interior corridors. **Parking:** on-site (fee). **Terms:** check-in 4 pm. **Amenities:** safes. **Dining:** 2 restaurants. **Pool:** heated outdoor. **Activities:** hot tub, exercise room, massage. **Guest Services:** valet laundry, boarding pass kiosk.

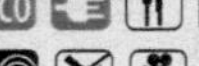   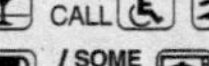

SAVE ECO CALL BIZ sHS / SOME UNITS

FLORIDAYS RESORT ORLANDO 407/238-7700 **90**

Extended Stay Hotel

Address: 12562 International Dr 32821 **Location:** I-4 exit 72, 1.3 mi e on SR 528 exit 1, then 3.2 mi s. **Facility:** 432 kitchen units, some two and three bedrooms. 6 stories, exterior corridors. **Terms:** check-in 4 pm. **Amenities:** safes. **Pool:** heated outdoor. **Activities:** hot tub, recreation programs, game room, exercise room. **Guest Services:** complimentary laundry, area transportation.

  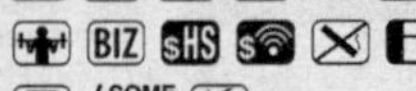

SAVE ECO CALL BIZ sHS / SOME UNITS

FOUR POINTS BY SHERATON ORLANDO CONVENTION CENTER 407/351-6600 **60**

SAVE Hotel. **Address:** 6435 Westwood Blvd 32821

AAA Benefit: Members save 5% or more!

FOUR POINTS BY SHERATON ORLANDO INTERNATIONAL DRIVE 407/351-2100 **22**

Hotel

FOUR POINTS BY SHERATON **AAA Benefit:** Members save 5% or more!

Address: 5905 International Dr 32819 **Location:** I-4 exit 75A, 0.6 mi s to International Dr, then just w. **Facility:** 301 units. 21 stories, interior corridors. **Amenities:** safes. **Dining:** 2 restaurants. **Pool:** heated outdoor. **Activities:** exercise room. **Guest Services:** valet and coin laundry, rental car service, area transportation.

 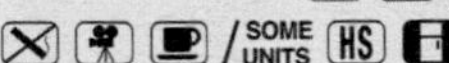

SAVE BIZ / SOME UNITS HS

HAMPTON INN & SUITES-ORLANDO AIRPORT AT GATEWAY VILLAGE 407/857-2830 **17**

Hotel

AAA Benefit: Members save 5% or more!

Address: 5460 Gateway Village Cir 32812 **Location:** SR 528 exit 11 (Semoran Blvd/SR 436), just n. **Facility:** 180 units. 8 stories, interior corridors. **Pool:** heated outdoor. **Activities:** exercise room. **Guest Services:** valet and coin laundry, area transportation.

SAVE CALL BIZ HS / SOME UNITS

HAMPTON INN & SUITES ORLANDO AT SEAWORLD 407/778-5900 **71**

SAVE Hotel. **Address:** 7003 Sea Harbor Dr 32821

AAA Benefit: Members save 5% or more!

HAMPTON INN & SUITES ORLANDO-INTERNATIONAL DR. NORTH 407/313-3030 **29**

SAVE Hotel. **Address:** 7448 N International Dr 32819

AAA Benefit: Members save 5% or more!

HAMPTON INN & SUITES ORLANDO-JOHN YOUNG PKWY/S PARK 407/226-3999 **3**

SAVE Contemporary Hotel. **Address:** 7500 Futures Dr 32819

AAA Benefit: Members save 5% or more!

HAMPTON INN BY HILTON ORLANDO NEAR UNIVERSAL BLVD/INTERNATIONAL DRIVE 407/345-1112 **23**

Hotel

AAA Benefit: Members save 5% or more!

Address: 7110 S Kirkman Rd 32819 **Location:** I-4 exit 75B, just s. **Facility:** 169 units. 8 stories, interior corridors. **Pool:** outdoor. **Activities:** exercise room. **Guest Services:** valet and coin laundry, area transportation. **Featured Amenity: breakfast buffet.** *(See ad p. 232.)*

SAVE CALL BIZ

For getaways off the beaten path, visit **AAA.com/campgrounds** or **AAA.com/maps** for thousands of places to camp.

THE PERFECT ESCAPE

We have something for everyone! Find your sanctuary at our resorts, each with their own personality. Vacation in comfort with *Endless Privileges*® and *Unlimited-Luxury*® — where everything is included. Experience the highest levels of boutique wellness retreats, all-adult romantic getaways, escapes for the socially sophisticated and fun-packed vacations for families.

AAA members save more with AMResorts.
Contact your local agent for offers or call us directly at 1-800-597-4761.

AMResorts.com

THE **AMRESORTS**® COLLECTION

COSTA RICA | **CURAÇAO** | **DOMINICAN REPUBLIC:** CAP CANA • LA ROMANA • PUERTO PLATA • PUNTA CANA **JAMAICA:** MONTEGO BAY | **MEXICO:** ACAPULCO • AKUMAL • CANCUN • COZUMEL • HUATULCO • ISLA MUJERES • IXTAPA LOS CABOS • NUEVO VALLARTA • PLAYA MUJERES • PUERTO AVENTURAS • PUERTO VALLARTA • RIVIERA CANCUN • RIVIERA MAYA • TULUM | **PANAMA** | **SPAIN:** FUERTEVENTURA • IBIZA • LANZAROTE • MALLORCA • TENERIFE | **ST. MARTIN** (2020)

(See maps & indexes p. 197, 199, 202, 210.)

HAMPTON INN CLOSEST TO UNIVERSAL ORLANDO
407/351-6716 **4**

Hotel

AAA Benefit: Members save 5% or more!

Address: 5621 Windhover Dr 32819 **Location:** I-4 exit 75B, 1.5 mi n on SR 435 (Kirkman Rd) to Windhover Dr, then just e. **Facility:** 120 units. 5 stories, interior corridors. **Amenities:** safes. **Pool:** heated outdoor. **Activities:** limited exercise equipment. **Guest Services:** valet laundry, area transportation. **Featured Amenity: full hot breakfast.**

SAVE CALL BIZ

HAMPTON INN ORLANDO-INTERNATIONAL AIRPORT
407/888-2995 **7**

Hotel

AAA Benefit: Members save 5% or more!

Address: 5767 T.G. Lee Blvd 32822 **Location:** SR 528 (Beachline Expwy) exit 11 (Semoran Blvd/SR 436), 0.5 mi n on T.G. Lee Blvd, then just e. **Facility:** 123 units. 7 stories, interior corridors. **Pool:** outdoor. **Activities:** exercise room. **Guest Services:** valet and coin laundry, area transportation. **Featured Amenity: breakfast buffet.**

SAVE   BIZ 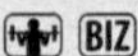

HAMPTON INN ORLANDO-INTERNATIONAL DRIVE/CONVENTION CENTER 407/354-4447 **47**

SAVE Hotel. **Address:** 8900 Universal Blvd 32819

AAA Benefit: Members save 5% or more!

HARD ROCK HOTEL® AT UNIVERSAL ORLANDO™
407/503-2000 **12**

Resort Hotel

Address: 5800 Universal Blvd 32819 **Location:** I-4 exit 74B; exit 75A eastbound, 1.3 mi n to Vineland Rd, just w to Universal Blvd, then just s. **Facility:** Enjoy contemporary comfort in tastefully designed rooms that showcase the latest hip industry styles and feature upscale bedding packages. The cabanas and sandy beach will draw you into the pool area. 650 units. 7 stories, interior corridors. **Parking:** on-site (fee) and valet. **Terms:** check-in 4 pm. **Amenities:** safes. **Dining:** 5 restaurants, also, The Kitchen, The Palm Restaurant, see separate listings, entertainment. **Pool:** heated outdoor. **Activities:** sauna, hot tub, steamroom, cabanas, recreation programs, kids club, game room, health club, massage. **Guest Services:** valet and coin laundry, boarding pass kiosk, rental car service, area transportation.

SAVE ECO CALL BIZ / SOME UNITS

HILTON GARDEN INN ORLANDO AT SEAWORLD
407/354-1500 **68**

Hotel

Hilton Garden Inn **AAA Benefit:** Members save 5% or more!

Address: 6850 Westwood Blvd 32821 **Location:** I-4 exit 72, 1 mi e to exit 1 (International Dr), then 0.6 mi w. **Facility:** 224 units. 8 stories, interior corridors. **Terms:** check-in 4 pm. **Pool:** heated outdoor. **Activities:** hot tub, exercise room. **Guest Services:** valet and coin laundry, area transportation.

SAVE ECO CALL BIZ / SOME UNITS HS

▼ See AAA listing p. 230 ▼

Hampton Inn Orlando Near Universal Blv/International Dr

7110 S. Kirkman Road
Orlando, FL 32819
407-345-1112

For more details, rates and reservations: AAA.com/travelguides/hotels

(See maps & indexes p. 197, 199, 202, 210.)

HILTON GARDEN INN-ORLANDO INTERNATIONAL AIRPORT
407/240-3725 13

SAVE Hotel. **Address:** 7300 Augusta National Dr 32822

AAA Benefit: Members save 5% or more!

HILTON GRAND VACATIONS AT SEAWORLD
407/239-0100 85

SAVE Resort Condominium. **Address:** 6924 Grand Vacations Way 32821

AAA Benefit: Members save 5% or more!

HILTON GRAND VACATIONS CLUB AT TUSCANY VILLAGE
407/465-2600 92

SAVE Resort Condominium. **Address:** 8122 Arrezzo Way 32821

AAA Benefit: Members save 5% or more!

HILTON ORLANDO 407/313-4300 57

Resort Hotel

AAA Benefit: Members save 5% or more!

Address: 6001 Destination Pkwy 32819 **Location:** SR 528 (Beachline Expwy) exit 1 (International Dr), just n to Destination Pkwy. **Facility:** Rooms feature modern décor with custom bedding, big desks and soothing colors. Two pools, a lazy river, a waterslide, a well-equipped health club, a basketball court and tennis courts are stand outs. 1424 units. 19 stories, interior corridors. **Parking:** on-site (fee) and valet. **Amenities:** safes. **Dining:** 5 restaurants, also, Spencer's for Steaks & Chops, see separate listing. **Pool:** heated outdoor. **Activities:** hot tub, steamroom, cabanas, tennis, recreation programs, health club, spa. **Guest Services:** valet laundry, boarding pass kiosk, rental car service. *(See ad p. 234, p. 116.)*

SAVE CALL BIZ SHS

Hilton Orlando

Lazy River, Two Pools, Water Slide, Splash Zone, Cabanas, Spa & more. Minutes from the theme parks.

HOLIDAY INN EXPRESS & SUITES LAKE NONA
407/207-7001 5

Hotel. **Address:** 10115 William Carey Dr 32832

HOLIDAY INN EXPRESS & SUITES NEAREST UNIVERSAL ORLANDO
407/363-1333 7

Hotel. **Address:** 5605 Major Blvd 32819

HOLIDAY INN EXPRESS & SUITES ORLANDO INTERNATIONAL AIRPORT
407/581-7900 21

Hotel. **Address:** 7900 S Conway Rd 32812

HOLIDAY INN EXPRESS & SUITES ORLANDO-INTERNATIONAL DRIVE 407/535-4100 28

Hotel

Address: 7276 International Dr 32819 **Location:** I-4 exit 74A (Sand Lake Rd), just e to International Dr, then 0.4 mi n. **Facility:** 156 units, some two bedrooms. 6 stories, interior corridors. **Amenities:** safes. **Pool:** outdoor. **Activities:** hot tub, exercise room. **Guest Services:** valet and coin laundry, area transportation. **Featured Amenity: continental breakfast.**

SAVE CALL BIZ

HOLIDAY INN EXPRESS AT SEAWORLD
407/996-4100 65

Hotel

Address: 10771 International Dr 32821 **Location:** I-4 exit 71, 1.1 mi e on Central Florida Pkwy, then just n. **Facility:** 181 units. 6 stories, interior corridors. **Pool:** heated outdoor. **Activities:** exercise room. **Guest Services:** coin laundry.

SAVE CALL BIZ

HOLIDAY INN ORLANDO-INTERNATIONAL AIRPORT
407/851-6400 9

Hotel

Address: 5750 T.G. Lee Blvd 32822 **Location:** SR 528 (Beachline Expwy) exit 11 (Semoran Blvd/SR 436), 1 mi n to T.G. Lee Blvd, then just e. **Facility:** 288 units. 7 stories, interior corridors. **Parking:** on-site (fee) and valet. **Pool:** heated outdoor. **Activities:** hot tub, tennis, lawn sports, exercise room. **Guest Services:** valet and coin laundry, boarding pass kiosk, rental car service, area transportation.

SAVE ECO CALL BIZ

▼ See AAA listing p. 112 ▼

More than a place to stay.
A place to play!

Enjoy all this close to the Walt Disney World® Theme Parks:

- Seven pools and watersports
- Four golf courses and mini golf
- Nine restaurants
- Free parking and Wi-Fi

Save up to 15% with your AAA member discount! Call **(866) 892-5890** and mention code **IDAAA** or visit **discoverhcv.com/stay-and-play**

18-MRP-0487

SWIM, SPLASH, SLEEP, Save

Everyone will love our AAA Four Diamond Award-winning hotel, centrally located to all major theme-parks and attractions and just minutes from International Drive.

Hilton Orlando sits on over 26 acres of lush landscaping and tropical inspirations, offering an experience of its own. It's in our two pools, lazy river, Splash Zone, waterslide, poolside cabanas, fire pits, signature spa and seven unique dining outlets where unforgettable memories are made. Experience Orlando like never before.

SAVE EXTRA WITH YOUR AAA MEMBERSHIP*

Visit www.theHiltonOrlando.com
(407) 313-4300
6001 Destination Pkwy, Orlando

**Based on availability. Proof of AAA membership required.*
Offer cannot be combined with any other discount and is not applicable to group rates. © 2019 Hilton

(See maps & indexes p. 197, 199, 202, 210.)

HOME2 SUITES BY HILTON ORLANDO AIRPORT
407/852-0844 **1**

Extended Stay Hotel

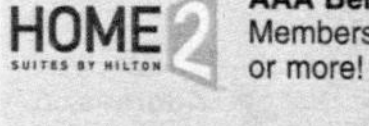

Address: 5445 Hazeltine National Dr 32812 **Location:** SR 528 (Beachline Expwy) exit 11 (Semoran Blvd/SR 436), 1.3 mi n, then just w. **Facility:** 128 kitchen units. 5 stories, interior corridors. **Pool:** outdoor. **Activities:** exercise room. **Guest Services:** valet and coin laundry, area transportation. **Featured Amenity: full hot breakfast.**

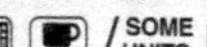 
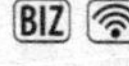   / SOME UNITS

HOME2 SUITES BY HILTON ORLANDO INTERNATIONAL DRIVE SOUTH
407/944-1705 **89**

SAVE Extended Stay Hotel. **Address:** 12107 Regency Village Dr 32821

AAA Benefit: Members save 5% or more!

HOME2 SUITES BY HILTON ORLANDO NEAR UNIVERSAL
407/519-3151 **20**

SAVE Extended Stay Hotel. **Address:** 5910 American Way 32819

AAA Benefit: Members save 5% or more!

HOMEWOOD SUITES BY HILTON-ORLANDO AIRPORT AT GATEWAY VILLAGE
407/857-5791 **15**

Extended Stay Hotel

AAA Benefit: Members save 5% or more!

Address: 5425 Gateway Village Cir 32812 **Location:** SR 528 exit 11 (Semoran Blvd/SR 436), just n. **Facility:** 128 kitchen units, some two bedrooms. 4 stories, interior corridors. **Terms:** check-in 4 pm. **Pool:** heated outdoor. **Activities:** recreation programs, exercise room. **Guest Services:** valet and coin laundry, area transportation.

 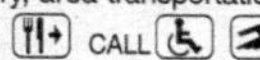
 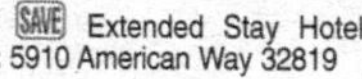 / SOME UNITS

HOMEWOOD SUITES BY HILTON ORLANDO THEME PARKS
407/778-5888 **69**

Extended Stay Hotel

AAA Benefit: Members save 5% or more!

Address: 6940 Westwood Blvd 32821 **Location:** I-4 exit 71, just e on Central Florida Pkwy, then just s. **Facility:** 133 kitchen units, some two bedrooms. 7 stories, interior corridors. **Terms:** check-in 4 pm. **Amenities:** safes. **Pool:** heated outdoor. **Activities:** exercise room. **Guest Services:** valet and coin laundry, area transportation. *(See ad this page.)*

 CALL    

HYATT HOUSE ACROSS FROM UNIVERSAL ORLANDO RESORT
407/352-5660 **14**

Extended Stay Hotel

AAA Benefit: Members save up to 10%!

Address: 5915 Caravan Ct 32819 **Location:** I-4 exit 75B, 0.6 mi n to Major Blvd, just e to Caravan Ct, then just s. **Facility:** 168 units, some kitchens. 9 stories, interior corridors. **Amenities:** safes. **Pool:** heated outdoor. **Activities:** exercise room. **Guest Services:** valet and coin laundry. **Featured Amenity: breakfast buffet.**

An official Universal Partner Hotel. Within walking distance to Universal Orlando Resort™

Save on travel, shopping and more: AAA.com/discounts

▼ *See AAA listing this page* ▼

6940 Westwood Blvd.
Orlando, FL 32821
407-778-5888

(See maps & indexes p. 197, 199, 202, 210.)

HYATT PLACE ACROSS FROM UNIVERSAL ORLANDO RESORT™ 407/351-0627 **13**

Hotel

AAA Benefit: Members save up to 10%!

Address: 5895 Caravan Ct 32819 **Location:** I-4 exit 75B, 0.6 mi n to Major Blvd, just e to Caravan Ct, then just s. **Facility:** 150 units. 7 stories, interior corridors. **Amenities:** safes. **Pool:** heated outdoor. **Activities:** exercise room. **Guest Services:** valet and coin laundry, area transportation. **Featured Amenity:** breakfast buffet.

SAVE CALL BIZ / SOME UNITS HS

HYATT PLACE

An official Universal Partner Hotel Within walking distance to Universal Orlando Resort™

HYATT PLACE ORLANDO AIRPORT 407/816-7800 **10**

Hotel

AAA Benefit: Members save up to 10%!

Address: 5435 Forbes Pl 32812 **Location:** SR 528 (Beachline Expwy) exit 11 (Semoran Blvd/SR 436), 1.1 mi n to Frontage Rd, then just w. **Facility:** 134 units. 6 stories, interior corridors. **Pool:** heated outdoor. **Activities:** exercise room. **Guest Services:** area transportation. **Featured Amenity:** breakfast buffet.

SAVE CALL BIZ / SOME UNITS HS

HYATT PLACE

5 mins to MCO Airport. 30 mins to Downtown and Port Canaveral. ParkStayFly & Cruise Pkg available.

HYATT PLACE ORLANDO/CONVENTION CENTER 407/370-4720 **44**

Hotel

AAA Benefit: Members save up to 10%!

Address: 8741 International Dr 32819 **Location:** I-4 exit 74A (Sand Lake Rd), just e to International Dr, then 0.8 mi s. **Facility:** 150 units. 7 stories, interior corridors. **Amenities:** safes. **Pool:** heated outdoor. **Activities:** exercise room. **Guest Services:** valet and coin laundry. **Featured Amenity:** breakfast buffet.

SAVE BIZ / SOME UNITS

HYATT PLACE

Within walking distance to the Convention Center.

HYATT REGENCY ORLANDO 407/352-4000 **54**

Resort Hotel

HYATT REGENCY

AAA Benefit: Members save up to 10%!

Address: 9801 International Dr 32819 **Location:** I-4 exit 72 (SR 528), 1.1 mi e to exit 1 (International Dr), then 1 mi nw. Adjacent Orange County Convention Center. **Facility:** The expansive resort is attached to the Orange County Convention Center and features abundant recreational amenities, upscale rooms with plush bedding and scenic views, and a world class spa on site. 1641 units, some two bedrooms. 31-32 stories, interior corridors. **Parking:** on-site (fee) and valet. **Amenities:** safes. **Dining:** 3 restaurants, also, B-Line Diner, Fiorenzo, see separate listings, entertainment. **Pool:** heated outdoor. **Activities:** sauna, hot tub, steamroom, cabanas, tennis, recreation programs, bicycles, health club, spa. **Guest Services:** valet laundry, boarding pass kiosk, rental car service.

SAVE ECO CALL BIZ HS / SOME UNITS

AAA DISCOUNTS»REWARDS

DISCOUNTS WITHOUT LIMITS

AAA.com/discounts

(See maps & indexes p. 197, 199, 202, 210.)

HYATT REGENCY ORLANDO INTERNATIONAL AIRPORT 407/825-1234 23

Hotel

AAA Benefit: Members save up to 10%!

Address: 9300 Jeff Fuqua Blvd (Airport Blvd) 32827 **Location:** SR 528 (Beachline Expwy) exit 11, 1.4 mi se, enter via Terminal B; at Orlando International Airport. **Facility:** Forget shuttle buses- this beautiful hotel is actually within the airport, only an elevator ride from the terminal. Updated rooms have upscale décor and oversize TVs, and the rooftop pool is a plus. 445 units, some two bedrooms. 10 stories, interior corridors. **Parking:** on-site (fee) and valet. **Terms:** check-in 4 pm. **Amenities:** safes. **Dining:** Hemisphere, see separate listing. **Pool:** heated outdoor. **Activities:** exercise room, massage. **Guest Services:** valet laundry, boarding pass kiosk, rental car service, luggage security pick-up.

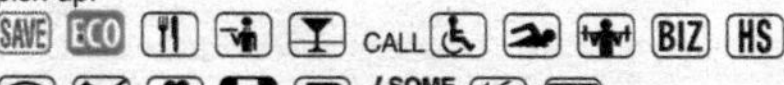

JW MARRIOTT, ORLANDO GRANDE LAKES 407/206-2300 7

Resort Hotel

AAA Benefit: Members save 5% or more!

Address: 4040 Central Florida Pkwy 32837 **Location:** I-4 exit 71, 2.8 mi e. **Facility:** Elegant throughout, the property offers spacious rooms with soft tones that create a sense of serenity. Enjoy leisure time in the expansive and inviting pool area. Balcony rooms offer great views. 998 units. 26 stories, interior corridors. **Parking:** on-site (fee) and valet. **Terms:** check-in 4 pm. **Amenities:** safes. **Dining:** 4 restaurants, also, Citron, An American Brasserie, Primo, see separate listings. **Pool:** heated outdoor. **Activities:** sauna, hot tub, steamroom, self-propelled boats, fishing, regulation golf, tennis, recreation programs, kids club, bicycles, playground, game room, lawn sports, trails, health club, spa. **Guest Services:** valet and coin laundry, boarding pass kiosk, rental car service, area transportation.

LA QUINTA BY WYNDHAM ORLANDO I DRIVE/CONV CENTER 407/345-1365 41

Hotel. **Address:** 8504 Universal Blvd 32819

LA QUINTA INN & SUITES ORLANDO AIRPORT NORTH BY WYNDHAM 407/240-5000 14

Hotel. **Address:** 7160 N Frontage Rd 32812

LA QUINTA INN-ORLANDO INTERNATIONAL DRIVE NORTH 407/351-4100 21

Hotel

Address: 5825 International Dr 32819 **Location:** I-4 exit 75A, 0.6 mi s to International Dr, then just w. **Facility:** 156 units. 2 stories (no elevator), interior corridors. **Amenities:** safes. **Pool:** outdoor. **Activities:** limited exercise equipment. **Guest Services:** valet and coin laundry, area transportation. **Featured Amenity: continental breakfast.**

LAS PALMERAS, A HILTON GRAND VACATIONS CLUB 407/233-2200 48

Hotel. **Address:** 9501 Universal Blvd 32819

AAA Benefit: Members save 5% or more!

LOEWS PORTOFINO BAY HOTEL AT UNIVERSAL ORLANDO™ 407/503-1000 10

Resort Hotel

Address: 5601 Universal Blvd 32819 **Location:** I-4 exit 74B westbound; exit 75A eastbound, 1 mi n. **Facility:** Resembling a small town on the Italian Riviera, the hotel features a small bay, gardens, piazzas and multiple pools. Luxurious, custom furnishings and marble accents create cozy, inviting rooms. 750 units, some two bedrooms. 6 stories, interior corridors. **Parking:** on-site (fee) and valet. **Terms:** check-in 4 pm. **Amenities:** safes. **Dining:** 9 restaurants, also, Bice Ristorante, see separate listing, entertainment. **Pool:** heated outdoor. **Activities:** sauna, hot tub, steamroom, cabanas, recreation programs, kids club, playground, game room, trails, health club, spa. **Guest Services:** valet laundry, boarding pass kiosk, rental car service, area transportation.

LOEWS ROYAL PACIFIC RESORT AT UNIVERSAL ORLANDO™ 407/503-3000 15

Resort Hotel

Address: 6300 Hollywood Way 32819 **Location:** I-4 exit 74A, just w to Turkey Lake Rd, 1.3 mi n to Hollywood Way, then just e. **Facility:** Aloha! With its tropical gardens, towering palms and soothing water features, the South Pacific-themed hotel exudes an island ambience. The inviting rooms are designed with gray hues and cozy bedding. 1000 units, some two bedrooms. 7 stories, interior corridors. **Parking:** on-site (fee) and valet. **Terms:** check-in 4 pm. **Amenities:** video games, safes. **Dining:** 4 restaurants, entertainment. **Pool:** heated outdoor. **Activities:** sauna, hot tub, steamroom, cabanas, recreation programs, kids club, playground, game room, trails, health club, massage. **Guest Services:** valet and coin laundry, boarding pass kiosk, rental car service, area transportation.

LOEWS SAPPHIRE FALLS RESORT AT UNIVERSAL ORLANDO™ 407/503-5000 16

Resort Hotel

Address: 6601 Adventure Way 32819 **Location:** I-4 exit 75A, 0.5 mi n on Universal Blvd to Hollywood Way, just w to Adventure Way, then just s. **Facility:** You'll be swept away to the Caribbean at this island-inspired resort which features bright designs, cascading waterfalls and lush landscaping. Rooms have modern amenities and an upscale island feel. 1000 units, some two and three bedrooms. 8 stories, interior corridors. **Parking:** on-site (fee) and valet. **Terms:** check-in 4 pm. **Amenities:** safes. **Dining:** 3 restaurants, entertainment. **Pool:** heated outdoor. **Activities:** sauna, hot tub, cabanas, recreation programs, game room, health club. **Guest Services:** valet and coin laundry, boarding pass kiosk, rental car service, area transportation.

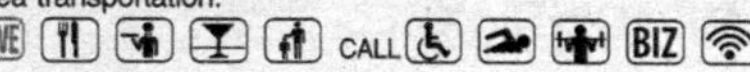

(See maps & indexes p. 197, 199, 202, 210.)

MIDPOINTE HOTEL BY ROSEN HOTELS & RESORTS 407/352-1507 58

Hotel

Address: 9956 Hawaiian Ct 32819 **Location:** SR 528 (Beachline Expwy) exit 1 (International Dr), 0.5 mi n to Hawaiian Ct, then just s. **Facility:** 356 units. 2 stories (no elevator), interior/exterior corridors. **Terms:** check-in 4 pm. **Amenities:** safes. **Pool:** outdoor. **Activities:** hot tub, exercise room. **Guest Services:** valet and coin laundry, area transportation. *(See ad this page.)*

SAVE CALL BIZ

/ SOME UNITS

ORLANDO AIRPORT MARRIOTT LAKESIDE 407/851-9000 18

Hotel

MARRIOTT **AAA Benefit:** Members save 5% or more!

Address: 7499 Augusta National Dr 32822 **Location:** SR 528 (Beachline Expwy) exit 11 (Semoran Blvd/SR 436), 1 mi n to T.G. Lee Blvd, just e to Augusta National Dr, then just s. **Facility:** 485 units. 9 stories, interior corridors. **Parking:** on-site (fee) and valet. **Dining:** 3 restaurants. **Pool:** heated outdoor, heated indoor. **Activities:** hot tub, bicycles, trails, exercise room, massage. **Guest Services:** valet and coin laundry, boarding pass kiosk, rental car service, area transportation.

SAVE ECO BIZ SHS

/ SOME UNITS

PARC SOLEIL BY HILTON GRAND VACATIONS CLUB 407/465-4000 87

SAVE Resort Condominium. **Address:** 11272 Desforges Ave 32836

AAA Benefit: Members save 5% or more!

THE POINT HOTEL & SUITES 407/956-2000 26

Hotel

Address: 7389 Universal Blvd 32819 **Location:** I-4 exit 74A (Sand Lake Rd), 0.5 mi e to Universal Blvd, then 0.4 mi n. **Facility:** 240 units, some kitchens. 12 stories, interior corridors. **Parking:** on-site (fee). **Terms:** check-in 4 pm. **Amenities:** safes. **Dining:** 2 restaurants. **Pool:** heated outdoor. **Activities:** hot tub, exercise room, massage. **Guest Services:** valet laundry, area transportation.

SAVE BIZ

QUALITY INN AT INTERNATIONAL DRIVE 407/351-1660 39

Hotel

Address: 8300 Jamaican Ct 32819 **Location:** I-4 exit 74A (Sand Lake Rd), 0.3 mi e to International Dr, just s to Jamaican Ct, then just w. **Facility:** 200 units. 4 stories, exterior corridors. **Pool:** heated outdoor. **Activities:** hot tub. **Guest Services:** valet and coin laundry, area transportation. **Featured Amenity: full hot breakfast.**

SAVE CALL BIZ

/ SOME UNITS

Free Shuttle to Theme Parks, Free Hot Breakfast Bar, Free WIFI, Outdoor Pool, Kiddie Pool & Hot Tub

RAMADA ORLANDO FLORIDA MALL 407/859-4100 2

Hotel. **Address:** 8601 S Orange Blossom Tr 32809

▼ *See AAA listing this page* ▼

A Sweet Stay in the Convention Center Area

Discover this sweet stay right across the street from the Orange County Convention Center. Nearby shopping, dining and entertainment along International Drive.

- Deluxe non-smoking rooms with mini-refrigerator, coffee maker, laptop-size electronic safe and premium TV entertainment
- Two swimming pools, two hot tubs and fitness center
- Free scheduled shuttles to Universal Orlando Resort, Sea World Orlando and Aquatica Waterpark
- Free parking, Free Wi-Fi & No Resort Fees!
- Spacious meeting rooms for special events

Visit our guest services desk to purchase attraction tickets.

Owned & Operated by Rosen Hotels & Resorts Orlando's Best Vacation Value

AAA MEMBERS SAVE 10 - 15% (based on season)

1-833-527-4349 | MidpointeHotel.com
9956 Hawaiian Court, Orlando, FL 32819

(See maps & indexes p. 197, 199, 202, 210.)

RAMADA SUITES BY WYNDHAM ORLANDO AIRPORT
407/240-3939 19

Hotel

Address: 7500 Augusta National Dr 32822 **Location:** SR 528 (Beachline Expwy) exit 11 (Semoran Blvd/SR 436), 0.6 mi n to T.G. Lee Blvd, just e to Augusta National Dr, then just s. **Facility:** 128 units. 4 stories, interior corridors. **Terms:** check-in 4 pm. **Amenities:** safes. **Pool:** outdoor. **Activities:** exercise room. **Guest Services:** valet and coin laundry, area transportation. **Featured Amenity: full hot breakfast.**

RENAISSANCE ORLANDO AIRPORT HOTEL
407/240-1000 8

Hotel

AAA Benefit: Members save 5% or more!

Address: 5445 Forbes Pl 32812 **Location:** SR 528 (Beachline Expwy) exit 11 (Semoran Blvd/SR 436), 1 mi n to Frontage Rd, then just w. **Facility:** 297 units. 9 stories, interior corridors. **Parking:** on-site (fee) and valet. **Amenities:** safes. **Dining:** Fresco Moderne Brasserie, see separate listing. **Pool:** heated outdoor. **Activities:** hot tub, cabanas, exercise room, massage. **Guest Services:** valet laundry, boarding pass kiosk.

RENAISSANCE ORLANDO AT SEAWORLD
407/351-5555 64

Resort Hotel

AAA Benefit: Members save 5% or more!

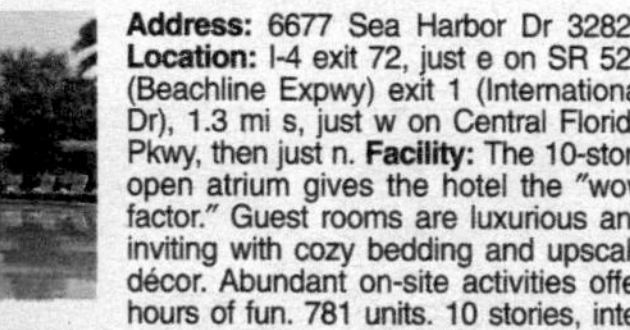

Address: 6677 Sea Harbor Dr 32821 **Location:** I-4 exit 72, just e on SR 528 (Beachline Expwy) exit 1 (International Dr), 1.3 mi s, just w on Central Florida Pkwy, then just n. **Facility:** The 10-story open atrium gives the hotel the "wow factor." Guest rooms are luxurious and inviting with cozy bedding and upscale décor. Abundant on-site activities offer hours of fun. 781 units. 10 stories, interior corridors. **Parking:** on-site (fee) and valet. **Terms:** check-in 4 pm. **Amenities:** safes. **Dining:** 4 restaurants. **Pool:** heated outdoor. **Activities:** hot tub, steamroom, recreation programs in season, game room, lawn sports, trails, exercise room, spa. **Guest Services:** valet and coin laundry, boarding pass kiosk, rental car service, area transportation.

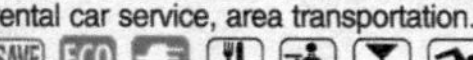

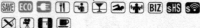

RESIDENCE INN BY MARRIOTT NEAR UNIVERSAL ORLANDO
407/313-1234 9

Extended Stay Hotel

Residence INN. **AAA Benefit:** Members save 5% or more!

Address: 5616 Major Blvd 32819 **Location:** I-4 exit 75B, 1.3 mi n on SR 435 (Kirkman Rd) to Vineland Rd, then just e. **Facility:** 195 kitchen units, some two bedrooms. 5 stories, interior corridors. **Terms:** check-in 4 pm. **Pool:** outdoor. **Activities:** exercise room. **Guest Services:** valet and coin laundry, area transportation. **Featured Amenity: breakfast buffet.**

SAVE CALL BIZ HS

SOME UNITS

RESIDENCE INN BY MARRIOTT ORLANDO AT MILLENIA
407/352-2700 2

Extended Stay Hotel

Residence INN. **AAA Benefit:** Members save 5% or more!

Address: 5403 Millenia Lakes Blvd 32839 **Location:** I-4 exit 78 (Conroy Rd), just e; near The Mall at Millenia. **Facility:** 120 kitchen units. 6 stories, interior corridors. **Pool:** heated outdoor. **Activities:** exercise room. **Guest Services:** valet and coin laundry.

SAVE CALL BIZ SOME UNITS

RESIDENCE INN BY MARRIOTT-ORLANDO AT SEAWORLD
407/313-3600 86

Extended Stay Hotel

Residence INN. **AAA Benefit:** Members save 5% or more!

Address: 11000 Westwood Blvd 32821 **Location:** I-4 exit 71, just e on Central Florida Pkwy, then just s. **Facility:** 350 units, some two bedrooms, efficiencies and kitchens. 6 stories, interior corridors. **Parking:** on-site (fee). **Terms:** check-in 4 pm. **Pool:** heated outdoor. **Activities:** hot tub, lawn sports, picnic facilities, exercise room. **Guest Services:** valet and coin laundry, area transportation. **Featured Amenity: breakfast buffet.**

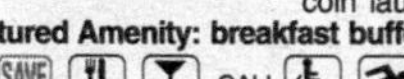
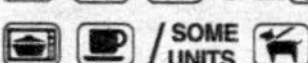

For complete hotel, dining and attraction listings: AAA.com/travelguides

(See maps & indexes p. 197, 199, 202, 210.)

RESIDENCE INN BY MARRIOTT-ORLANDO CONVENTION CENTER

407/226-0288 45

Extended Stay Hotel

Residence INN **AAA Benefit:** Members save 5% or more!

Address: 8800 Universal Blvd 32819 **Location:** I-4 exit 74A (Sand Lake Rd), 0.5 mi e to Universal Blvd, then 0.9 mi s. **Facility:** 124 units, some two bedrooms, efficiencies and kitchens. 5 stories, interior corridors. **Terms:** check-in 4 pm. **Pool:** heated outdoor. **Activities:** hot tub, exercise room. **Guest Services:** valet and coin laundry, area transportation. **Featured Amenity:** breakfast buffet.

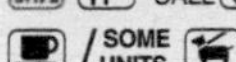

SAVE CALL BIZ / SOME UNITS

RESIDENCE INN BY MARRIOTT-ORLANDO INTERNATIONAL AIRPORT

407/856-2444 4

Extended Stay Hotel

Residence INN **AAA Benefit:** Members save 5% or more!

Address: 7024 Augusta National Dr 32822 **Location:** SR 528 (Beachline Expwy) exit 11 (Semoran Blvd/SR 436), 1.2 mi n to Hazeltine Dr, just e to Augusta National Dr, then just s. **Facility:** 132 units, some two bedrooms, efficiencies and kitchens. 6 stories, interior corridors. **Amenities:** safes. **Pool:** heated outdoor. **Activities:** hot tub, exercise room. **Guest Services:** valet and coin laundry, area transportation. **Featured Amenity:** breakfast buffet.

 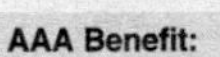

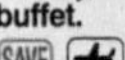   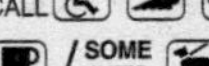 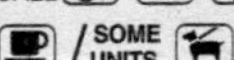

SAVE CALL BIZ HS / SOME UNITS

RESIDENCE INN BY MARRIOTT-ORLANDO LAKE NONA

407/888-9974 8

Extended Stay Hotel

Residence INN **AAA Benefit:** Members save 5% or more!

Address: 6955 Lake Nona Blvd 32827 **Location:** Jct Florida's Turnpike and Central Florida GreeneWay; 2.7 mi e; then 0.5 mi s. **Facility:** 102 units, some kitchens. 7 stories, interior corridors. **Pool:** heated outdoor. **Activities:** bicycles, exercise room. **Guest Services:** valet and coin laundry, area transportation.

SAVE CALL BIZ / SOME UNITS

THE RITZ-CARLTON ORLANDO, GRANDE LAKES

407/206-2400 6

Resort Hotel

THE RITZ-CARLTON **AAA Benefit:** Unequaled service at special member savings!

Address: 4012 Central Florida Pkwy 32837 **Location:** I-4 exit 71, 2.8 mi e. **Facility:** Manicured grounds, lush foliage and a winding road create a great first impression. Posh rooms with custom furniture and fine amenities ensure a luxurious stay. Expect first-class service. 582 units, some two bedrooms. 14 stories, interior corridors. **Parking:** on-site (fee) and valet. **Terms:** check-in 4 pm. **Amenities:** safes. **Dining:** 6 restaurants, also, Highball & Harvest, see separate listing. **Pool:** heated outdoor. **Activities:** sauna, hot tub, steamroom, cabanas, self-propelled boats, fishing, regulation golf, tennis, recreation programs, kids club, bicycles, playground, game room, lawn sports, trails, health club, spa. **Guest Services:** valet laundry, boarding pass kiosk, rental car service, area transportation.

 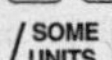   

SAVE ECO BIZ SHS / SOME UNITS

▼ See AAA listing p. 241 ▼

A Universe of Fun Just Minutes Away

Yet everything you need is right here. We even help with attraction ticket purchases, restaurant reservations, and local transportation arrangements, all from the Guest Services Desk.

- Less than a mile from Universal Orlando Resort™
- Deluxe non-smoking rooms with mini-refrigerator, microwave, coffee maker, laptop-size electronic safe, premium TV entertainment, and free Wi-Fi
- Heated swimming pool, video arcade game room, fitness center, 24/7 mini market and deli
- Shogun Authentic Japanese Steakhouse, Sakura Sushi, and breakfast buffet where kids eat free*
- Free scheduled shuttles to Universal Orlando Resort™ and SeaWorld Orlando®

Owned & Operated by Rosen Hotels & Resorts
Orlando's Best Vacation Value®

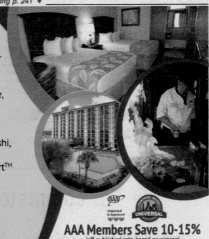

AAA Members Save 10-15%
(off published rate, based on season)
1-800-999-6327 | RosenInn6327.com/AAA
6327 International Dr., Orlando, FL 32819

* Ask for details

(See maps & indexes p. 197, 199, 202, 210.)

ROSEN CENTRE HOTEL 407/996-9840 56

Address: 9840 International Dr 32819 **Location:** I-4 exit 72 (SR 528), 1.1 mi e to exit 1 (International Dr), then 0.5 mi n; adjacent to Orange County Convention Center. **Facility:** 1334 units, some two bedrooms. 24 stories, interior corridors. **Parking:** on-site (fee) and valet. **Amenities:** safes. **Dining:** 5 restaurants, also, Everglades Restaurant, see separate listing. **Pool:** heated outdoor. **Activities:** hot tub, health club, spa. **Guest Services:** valet and coin laundry, boarding pass kiosk, rental car service, area transportation.

  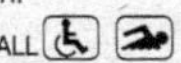 

ROSEN INN AT POINTE ORLANDO 407/996-8585 50

Address: 9000 International Dr 32819 **Location:** I-4 exit 74A (Sand Lake Rd), just e to International Dr, then 1.1 mi s. **Facility:** 1020 units. 4-10 stories, exterior corridors. **Terms:** check-in 4 pm. **Amenities:** safes. **Dining:** 2 restaurants, entertainment. **Pool:** outdoor, heated outdoor. **Activities:** playground, game room, exercise room. **Guest Services:** valet and coin laundry, area transportation. *(See ad this page.)*

   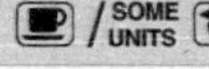

ROSEN INN 407/996-4444 24

Address: 6327 International Dr 32819 **Location:** I-4 exit 74A (Sand Lake Rd), just e to International Dr, then 0.7 mi n. **Facility:** 315 units. 4-9 stories, interior/exterior corridors. **Terms:** check-in 4 pm. **Amenities:** safes. **Dining:** 3 restaurants. **Pool:** heated outdoor. **Activities:** game room, exercise room. **Guest Services:** valet and coin laundry, area transportation. *(See ad p. 240.)*

 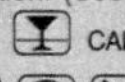   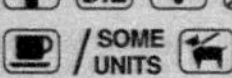

ROSEN INN INTERNATIONAL 407/996-1600 31

Address: 7600 International Dr 32819 **Location:** I-4 exit 74A (Sand Lake Rd), just e to International Dr, then just n. **Facility:** 728 units. 2-6 stories, exterior corridors. **Terms:** check-in 4 pm. **Amenities:** safes. **Pool:** heated outdoor. **Activities:** playground, game room, exercise room. **Guest Services:** valet and coin laundry, area transportation. *(See ad p. 242.)*

▼ See AAA listing this page ▼

Luxury at a Price that's On Point

Ideally located close to the theme parks and walking distance to shopping, dining, and entertainment at Pointe Orlando.

- Deluxe non-smoking rooms with mini-refrigerator, microwave, laptop-size electronic safe, premium TV entertainment, and free Wi-Fi
- Three swimming pools (two heated seasonally), playground, and video arcade game room
- Buffet restaurant with kids eat free program*, sports bar & grille, and 24-hour mini market
- Free scheduled shuttles to Universal Orlando Resort™ and SeaWorld Orlando®
- Spacious meeting rooms for special events

Visit our guest services desk to purchase attraction tickets, make restaurant reservations, and arrange transportation.

ROSEN INN
AT POINTE ORLANDO

Owned & Operated by Rosen Hotels & Resorts
Orlando's Best Vacation Value®

* Ask for details

AAA Members Save 10-15%
(off published rate, based on season)

1-800-999-8585 | RosenInn9000.com/AAA
9000 International Dr., Orlando, FL 32819

(See maps & indexes p. 197, 199, 202, 210.)

ROSEN PLAZA HOTEL 407/996-9700 53

Hotel

Address: 9700 International Dr 32819 **Location:** I-4 exit 74A (Sand Lake Rd), just e to International Dr, then 1.5 mi s. **Facility:** 800 units. 14 stories, interior corridors. **Parking:** on-site (fee) and valet. **Amenities:** safes. **Dining:** 3 restaurants, also, Jack's Place, see separate listing, nightclub, entertainment. **Pool:** heated outdoor. **Activities:** hot tub, exercise room. **Guest Services:** valet and coin laundry, boarding pass kiosk, area transportation.

SAVE ECO CALL BIZ HS / SOME UNITS

ROSEN SHINGLE CREEK 407/996-9939 52

Resort Hotel

Address: 9939 Universal Blvd 32819 **Location:** I-4 exit 72 (SR 528), 1.7 mi e to exit 2 (Orangewood Blvd), then 0.5 mi n. **Facility:** The sprawling 230-acre retreat offers upscale rooms with custom design elements, numerous dining and lounge outlets, a championship 18-hole golf course and extensive spa and recreational facilities. 1501 units, some two bedrooms. 14 stories, interior corridors. **Parking:** on-site (fee) and valet. **Amenities:** safes. **Dining:** 10 restaurants, also, A Land Remembered, Cala Bella, see separate listings. **Pool:** heated outdoor. **Activities:** sauna, hot tub, steamroom, cabanas, fishing, regulation golf, tennis, recreation programs in season, game room, lawn sports, trails, health club, spa. **Guest Services:** valet and coin laundry, boarding pass kiosk, rental car service, area transportation.

SAVE ECO CALL BIZ HS / SOME UNITS

SHERATON SUITES ORLANDO AIRPORT 407/240-5555 20

SAVE Hotel. **Address:** 7550 Augusta National Dr 32822

AAA Benefit: Members save 5% or more!

SHERATON VISTANA VILLAGES 407/238-5000 91

SAVE Resort Condominium. **Address:** 12401 International Dr 32821

AAA Benefit: Members save 5% or more!

SONESTA ES SUITES ORLANDO – INTERNATIONAL DRIVE 407/352-2400 40

Extended Stay Hotel

Address: 8480 International Dr 32819 **Location:** I-4 exit 74A (Sand Lake Rd), just e to International Dr, then 0.5 mi s. **Facility:** 146 units, some two bedrooms, efficiencies and kitchens. 5 stories, exterior corridors. **Terms:** check-in 4 pm. **Amenities:** safes. **Pool:** heated outdoor. **Activities:** hot tub, game room, picnic facilities, exercise room. **Guest Services:** valet and coin laundry, area transportation. **Featured Amenity:** **breakfast buffet.**

SAVE BIZ

SPRINGHILL SUITES BY MARRIOTT-ORLANDO AIRPORT 407/816-5533 2

Hotel

SPRINGHILL SUITES MARRIOTT **AAA Benefit:** Members save 5% or more!

Address: 5828 Hazeltine National Dr 32822 **Location:** SR 528 (Beachline Expwy) exit 11 (Semoran Blvd/SR 436), 1.2 mi n to Hazeltine National Dr, then just e. **Facility:** 130 units. 6 stories, interior corridors. **Amenities:** safes. **Pool:** outdoor. **Activities:** exercise room. **Guest Services:** valet and coin laundry, area transportation. **Featured Amenity:** **breakfast buffet.**

SAVE BIZ HS

▼ See AAA listing p. 241 ▼

Internationally Known, Local Value

Guests from across the world and from across state lines know we are the real deal.

- Deluxe non-smoking rooms with mini-refrigerator, microwave, coffee maker, laptop-size electronic safe, premium TV entertainment, and free Wi-Fi
- Two heated swimming pools, fitness center, children's wading pool, video arcade game room, and playground
- Dining options plus a buffet restaurant where kids eat free*
- Free scheduled shuttles to Universal Orlando Resort™ and SeaWorld Orlando®

Visit our guest services desk to purchase attraction tickets, make restaurant reservations, and arrange transportation.

Owned & Operated by Rosen Hotels & Resorts
Orlando's Best Vacation Value®

* Ask for details

AAA Members Save 10-15%
(off published rate, based on season)

1-855-887-7600 | RosenInn7600.com/AAA
7600 International Dr., Orlando, FL 32819

(See maps & indexes p. 197, 199, 202, 210.)

SPRINGHILL SUITES BY MARRIOTT ORLANDO AT MILLENIA 407/352-2500 1

Hotel

SPRINGHILL SUITES MARRIOTT **AAA Benefit:** Members save 5% or more!

Address: 5403 Millenia Lakes Blvd 32839 **Location:** I-4 exit 78 (Conroy Rd), just e; near The Mall at Millenia. **Facility:** 134 units. 6 stories, interior corridors. **Pool:** heated outdoor. **Activities:** exercise room. **Guest Services:** valet and coin laundry.

 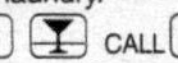 CALL 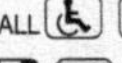 

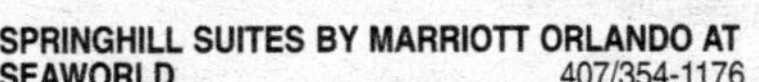

SPRINGHILL SUITES BY MARRIOTT ORLANDO AT SEAWORLD 407/354-1176 66

Hotel

SPRINGHILL SUITES MARRIOTT **AAA Benefit:** Members save 5% or more!

Address: 10801 International Dr 32821 **Location:** I-4 exit 72 westbound; exit 71 eastbound to SR 528 (Beachline Expwy), exit 1, then 0.8 mi s. **Facility:** 200 units. 6 stories, interior corridors. **Parking:** on-site (fee). **Terms:** check-in 4 pm. **Pool:** heated outdoor. **Activities:** hot tub, exercise room. **Guest Services:** valet and coin laundry, boarding pass kiosk, area transportation.

  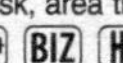   

SPRINGHILL SUITES BY MARRIOTT-ORLANDO CONVENTION CENTER/INTERNATIONAL DRIVE AREA 407/345-9073 46

Hotel

SPRINGHILL SUITES MARRIOTT **AAA Benefit:** Members save 5% or more!

Address: 8840 Universal Blvd 32819 **Location:** I-4 exit 74A (Sand Lake Rd), 0.5 mi e on SR 482 (Sand Lake Rd), then 0.8 mi s. **Facility:** 167 units. 7 stories, interior corridors. **Pool:** outdoor. **Activities:** exercise room. **Guest Services:** valet and coin laundry, area transportation. **Featured Amenity: breakfast buffet.**

 CALL

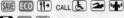

STAYBRIDGE SUITES ORLANDO AIRPORT SOUTH 407/438-2121 16

Extended Stay Hotel. **Address:** 7450 Augusta National Dr 32822

STAYBRIDGE SUITES ORLANDO AT SEAWORLD 407/917-9200 70

Extended Stay Hotel

Address: 6985 Sea Harbor Dr 32821 **Location:** Just e on SR 528 (Beachline Expwy) exit 1 (International Dr), 1.3 mi s, just w on Central Florida Pkwy, then just s. **Facility:** 89 kitchen units, some two bedrooms. 6 stories, interior corridors. **Pool:** outdoor. **Activities:** exercise room. **Guest Services:** complimentary and valet laundry.

STAYSKY SUITES I-DRIVE ORLANDO 407/581-2151 32

Hotel

Address: 7601 Canada Ave 32819 **Location:** I-4 exit 74A (Sand Lake Rd), just e to Canada Ave, then just n. **Facility:** 153 units, some kitchens. 6 stories, interior corridors. **Amenities:** *Some:* safes. **Pool:** heated outdoor. **Activities:** hot tub, game room, picnic facilities, exercise room. **Guest Services:** valet and coin laundry, area transportation. **Featured Amenity: full hot breakfast.**

/ SOME UNITS

SUNSOL INTERNATIONAL DRIVE 407/203-2664 17

Hotel

Address: 5859 American Way 32819 **Location:** I-4 exit 75B, just s to International Dr, just e to American Way, then just n. **Facility:** 192 units. 4 stories, exterior corridors. **Parking:** on-site (fee). **Amenities:** safes. **Pool:** heated outdoor. **Activities:** playground, picnic facilities. **Guest Services:** area transportation.

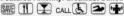

TOWNEPLACE SUITES BY MARRIOTT ORLANDO AT SEAWORLD 407/996-3400 63

Extended Stay Hotel

TOWNEPLACE SUITES MARRIOTT **AAA Benefit:** Members save 5% or more!

Address: 10731 International Dr 32821 **Location:** I-4 exit 71, 1.1 mi e on Central Florida Pkwy, then just n. **Facility:** 188 kitchen units. 6 stories, interior corridors. **Terms:** check-in 4 pm. **Pool:** heated outdoor. **Activities:** exercise room. **Guest Services:** coin laundry. **Featured Amenity: breakfast buffet.**

  CALL 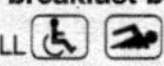

 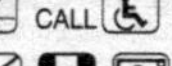

 SOME UNITS

UNIVERSAL'S AVENTURA HOTEL 407/503-6000 18

Hotel

Address: 6725 Adventure Way 32819 **Location:** I-4 exit 75A, 0.5 mi n on Universal Blvd to Hollywood Way, just w to Adventure Way, then just s. **Facility:** 600 units. 17 stories, interior corridors. **Parking:** on-site (fee). **Terms:** check-in 4 pm. **Amenities:** safes. **Dining:** 4 restaurants. **Pool:** heated outdoor. **Activities:** hot tub, recreation programs, game room, lawn sports, exercise room. **Guest Services:** valet and coin laundry, boarding pass kiosk, rental car service, area transportation.

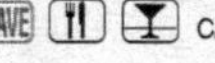 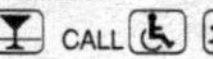 CALL 

(See maps & indexes p. 197, 199, 202, 210.)

UNIVERSAL'S CABANA BAY BEACH RESORT 407/503-4000 **19**

Retro Resort Hotel

Address: 6550 Adventure Way 32819 **Location:** I-4 exit 75A, 0.5 mi n on Universal Blvd to Hollywood Way, just w to Adventure Way, then just s. **Facility:** Close to popular Universal Studios attractions and just steps from Volcano Bay water park, the hotel features a '50s and '60s theme. Rooms are vibrant, some have great views of Volcano Bay. 2200 units. 2-11 stories, interior/exterior corridors. **Parking:** on-site (fee). **Terms:** check-in 4 pm. **Amenities:** safes. **Dining:** 4 restaurants. **Pool:** heated outdoor. **Activities:** hot tub, cabanas, game room, health club. **Guest Services:** valet and coin laundry, rental car service, area transportation. Affiliated with Loews Hotels.

VISTA CAY RESORT BY MILLENIUM 407/313-6501 **51**

Vacation Rental Hotel

Address: 4874 Cayview Ave 32819 **Location:** Waterfront. I-4 exit 74A (Sand Lake Rd), 0.5 mi e to Universal Blvd, then 2.3 mi se. **Facility:** Serenely situated on Lake Cay, the property features two-bedroom condos and three-bedroom townhomes. Major attractions and the Orlando Convention Center are just minutes away. 228 condominiums. 3-4 stories, interior/exterior corridors. **Parking:** on-site (fee). **Terms:** check-in 4 pm. **Amenities:** safes. **Pool:** heated outdoor. **Activities:** hot tub, game room, picnic facilities, trails, exercise room. **Guest Services:** complimentary laundry.

WESTGATE LAKES RESORT & SPA 407/345-0000 **55**

Resort Hotel

Address: 9500 Turkey Lake Rd 32819 **Location:** Waterfront. I-4 exit 74A (Sand Lake Rd), 1.1 mi s to Sand Lake Rd, just w to Turkey Lake Rd, then 2.1 mi s. **Facility:** Nestled serenely on Big Sand Lake, the multifaceted resort is spread out over nearly 100 acres and is comprised of several buildings. Multiple room types are offered, most feature a balcony or patio. 2166 units, some two bedrooms, three bedrooms, efficiencies and kitchens. 6 stories, interior/exterior corridors. **Parking:** on-site and valet. **Terms:** check-in 4 pm. **Amenities:** safes. **Dining:** 3 restaurants. **Pool:** heated outdoor. **Activities:** sauna, hot tub, steamroom, motor boats, self-propelled boats, marina, fishing, miniature golf, tennis, recreation programs, kids club, bicycles, playground, game room, lawn sports, picnic facilities, health club, spa. **Guest Services:** complimentary and valet laundry, area transportation.

WESTGATE PALACE RESORT 407/996-6000 **27**

Condominium

Address: 6145 Carrier Dr 32819 **Location:** Waterfront. I-4 exit 74A, 0.3 mi e to International Dr, 0.4 mi n to Carrier Dr, then just e. **Facility:** Condo-style rooms are spacious and some offer scenic views of the surrounding areas and a small lake below. Numerous on-site activities keep guests entertained for days. Major attractions are nearby. 403 two-bedroom kitchen units. 19 stories, interior corridors. **Terms:** check-in 4 pm. **Amenities:** safes. **Pool:** heated outdoor. **Activities:** hot tub, cabanas, self-propelled boats, fishing, recreation programs, playground, game room, picnic facilities, exercise room. **Guest Services:** complimentary and valet laundry, area transportation.

WINGATE BY WYNDHAM AT UNIVERSAL STUDIOS & CONVENTION CENTER 407/226-0900 **3**

Hotel. **Address:** 5661 Windhover Dr 32819

WINGATE BY WYNDHAM ORLANDO INTERNATIONAL AIRPORT 407/826-5258 **3**

Hotel

Address: 5750 Hazeltine National Dr 32822 **Location:** SR 528 (Beachline Expwy) exit 11 (Semoran Blvd), 1.2 mi n to Hazeltine National Dr, then just e. **Facility:** 108 units. 5 stories, interior corridors. **Terms:** check-in 4 pm. **Amenities:** safes. **Pool:** outdoor. **Activities:** hot tub, exercise room. **Guest Services:** valet and coin laundry, area transportation.

WYNDHAM ORLANDO RESORT INTERNATIONAL DRIVE 407/351-2420 **35**

Hotel

Address: 8001 International Dr 32819 **Location:** I-4 exit 74A (Sand Lake Rd), just e. **Facility:** 613 units. 2 stories (no elevator), interior/exterior corridors. **Terms:** check-in 4 pm. **Amenities:** safes. **Pool:** heated outdoor. **Activities:** sauna, hot tub, steamroom, exercise room. **Guest Services:** valet laundry, boarding pass kiosk, rental car service, area transportation. *(See ad p. 245.)*

Use the free travel planning tools at AAA.com/maps

▼ See AAA listing p. 244 ▼

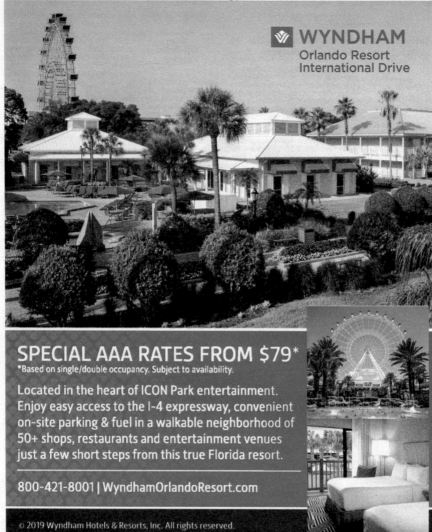

WYNDHAM
Orlando Resort
International Drive

SPECIAL AAA RATES FROM $79*
*Based on single/double occupancy. Subject to availability.

Located in the heart of ICON Park entertainment. Enjoy easy access to the I-4 expressway, convenient on-site parking & fuel in a walkable neighborhood of 50+ shops, restaurants and entertainment venues just a few short steps from this true Florida resort.

800-421-8001 | WyndhamOrlandoResort.com

© 2019 Wyndham Hotels & Resorts, Inc. All rights reserved.

(See maps & indexes p. 197, 199, 202, 210.)

For complete hotel, dining and attraction listings: AAA.com/travelguides

(See maps & indexes p. 197, 199, 202, 210.)

WHERE TO EAT

A LAND REMEMBERED 407/996-9939 (41)

Steak Seafood Fine Dining $26-$60

AAA Inspector Notes: Bearing the name of the iconic book by Patrick D. Smith, the restaurant offers patrons an evening to remember with excelled service, an elegant ambience and picturesque views of an expansive golf course. The menu is steeped in delicious, high-quality items, such as goat cheese fritters, Black Angus aged beef, Chilean sea bass and a tempting broiled seafood platter. The award-winning desserts created by the pastry chef should not be missed. **Features:** full bar, patio dining. **Reservations:** suggested. **Address:** 9939 Universal Blvd 32819 **Location:** I-4 exit 72 (SR 528), 1.7 mi e to exit 2 (Orangewood Blvd), then 0.5 mi n; in Rosen Shingle Creek. **Parking:** on-site and valet. D CALL

ANTHONY'S COAL FIRED PIZZA 407/363-9466

Pizza. Casual Dining. **Address:** 8031 Turkey Lake Rd, Suite 300 32819

ANTOJITO'S AUTHENTIC MEXICAN CUISINE 407/363-8000 (10)

Mexican. Casual Dining. **Address:** 6000 Universal Blvd 32819

BAHAMA BREEZE ISLAND GRILLE 407/248-2499 (35)

Caribbean. Casual Dining. **Address:** 8849 International Dr 32817

BARTACO 407/801-8226 (17)

Specialty. Casual Dining. **Address:** 7600 Dr. Phillips Blvd 32819

BICE RISTORANTE 407/503-1415 (2)

Northern Italian. Fine Dining. **Address:** 5601 Universal Blvd 32819

BIG FIN SEAFOOD KITCHEN 407/615-8888 (49)

Seafood. Fine Dining. **Address:** 8046 Via Dellagio Way 32819

B-LINE DINER 407/352-4000 (45)

American. Casual Dining. **Address:** 9801 International Dr 32819

BOB MARLEY-A TRIBUTE TO FREEDOM 407/224-2264 (7)

Jamaican. Casual Dining. **Address:** 6000 Universal Blvd 32819

BONEFISH GRILL

Seafood. Fine Dining.

LOCATIONS:

Address: 7830 W Sand Lake Rd 32819
Phone: 407/355-7707 (30)

Address: 5463 Gateway Village Cir 32812
Phone: 407/816-6355 (2)

BORDER GRILL 407/352-0101 (1)

Mexican. Quick Serve. **Address:** 5695-A Vineland Rd 32819

BOSPHOROUS TURKISH CUISINE 407/352-6766 (21)

Turkish. Casual Dining. **Address:** 7600 Dr. Phillips Blvd, Suite 108 32819

CAFE TU TU TANGO 407/248-2222 (33)

Small Plates. Fine Dining. **Address:** 8625 International Dr 32819

CALA BELLA 407/996-9939 (42)

Regional Italian Fine Dining $23-$45

AAA Inspector Notes: Cala Bella translates to "beautiful creek," referring to the historic creek for which the resort is named. The elegant restaurant serves up Italian fare with Mediterranean and Tuscan influences. Menu selections include an antipasto sampler platter of imported cheeses and Italian-cured meats, chicken parmesan and veal Marsala. The pastry chef creates incredible desserts which offer a most delightful end to the meal. The refined staff offers excelled service. **Features:** full bar, patio dining. **Reservations:** suggested. **Address:** 9939 Universal Blvd 32819 **Location:** I-4 exit 72 (SR 528), 1.7 mi e to exit 2 (Orangewood Blvd), then 0.5 mi n; in Rosen Shingle Creek. **Parking:** on-site and valet. D CALL

CANVAS 407/313-7800 (8)

American. Casual Dining. **Address:** 13615 Sachs Ave 32827

CEDAR'S RESTAURANT 407/351-6000 (26)

Lebanese. Casual Dining. **Address:** 7732 W Sand Lake Rd 32819

CHARLEY'S STEAKHOUSE 407/363-0228 (31)

Steak. Fine Dining. **Address:** 8255 International Dr 32819

CHATHAM'S PLACE RESTAURANT 407/345-2992 (18)

Continental. Fine Dining. **Address:** 7575 Dr. Phillips Blvd 32819

CHRISTINI'S RISTORANTE ITALIANO 407/345-8770 (19)

Northern Italian Fine Dining $25-$68

AAA Inspector Notes: *Classic.* An area landmark since the early '80s, this esteemed restaurant upholds the fine-dining tradition of high-quality Italian cuisine crafted from only the freshest ingredients. Patrons enjoy the savory olives from Christini's own farm, satisfying house-made pasta dishes, and full-bodied and crisp wines from a well-varied wine list. A touch of elegance, a team of skilled servers and excellent cuisine make this an experience, not just a meal. Soft background music adds a romantic element. **Features:** full bar. **Reservations:** suggested. **Address:** 7600 Dr. Phillips Blvd 32819 **Location:** I-4 exit 74A (Sand Lake Rd), 0.7 mi w to Dr. Phillips Blvd, then just n; in Marketplace Shopping Center, near the clock tower. **Parking:** on-site and valet. D

CHROMA MODERN BAR + KITCHEN 407/955-4340 (9)

Small Plates. Casual Dining. **Address:** 6967 Lake Nona Blvd 32827

CIAO ITALIA RISTORANTE ITALIANO 408/354-0770 (48)

Italian. Fine Dining. **Address:** 6149 Westwood Blvd 32821

CITRON, AN AMERICAN BRASSERIE 407/206-2300 (7)

New American. Casual Dining. **Address:** 4040 Central Florida Pkwy 32837

COOPER'S HAWK WINERY & RESTAURANT 407/956-3400 (20)

American. Casual Dining. **Address:** 8005 International Dr 32819

COPPER CANYON GRILL 407/363-3933 (36)

American. Fine Dining. **Address:** 9101 International Dr, Suite 1220 32819

THE COWFISH SUSHI BURGER BAR 407/224-2275 (6)

Burgers Sushi. Casual Dining. **Address:** 6000 Universal Blvd #700 32819

CUBA LIBRE RESTAURANT & RUM BAR 407/226-1600 (39)

New Cuban. Casual Dining. **Address:** 9101 International Dr 32819

(See maps & indexes p. 197, 199, 202, 210.)

DIXIE BELLE'S CAFE 407/812-7012 (3)

Breakfast. Casual Dining. **Address:** 7125 S Orange Ave 32809

DRAGONFLY ROBATA GRILL-SUSHI LOUNGE 407/370-3359 (50)

Japanese Small Plates Sushi. Fine Dining. **Address:** 7972 Via Dellagio Way 32819

EDDIE V'S PRIME SEAFOOD 407/355-3011 (24)

Seafood. Fine Dining. **Address:** 7488 W Sand Lake Rd 32819

EVERGLADES RESTAURANT 407/996-9840 (46)

Regional Seafood Steak. Fine Dining. **Address:** 9840 International Dr 32819

FAMA'S RISTORANTE ITALIANO & PIZZERIA 407/239-1500 (49)

Italian Pizza. Casual Dining. **Address:** 5474 Central Florida Pkwy 32821

FIORENZO 407/352-4000 (44)

Italian. Fine Dining. **Address:** 9801 International Dr 32819

FISHBONES 407/352-0135 (16)

Seafood Steak. Fine Dining. **Address:** 6707 W Sand Lake Rd 32819

FLEMING'S PRIME STEAKHOUSE & WINE BAR 407/352-5706 (48)

Steak. Fine Dining. **Address:** 8030 Via Dellagio Way 32819

FRESCO MODERNE BRASSERIE 407/240-1000 (1)

American. Fine Dining. **Address:** 5445 Forbes Pl 32812

GARIBALDI MEXICAN CUISINE 407/888-2869 (1)

Mexican. Casual Dining. **Address:** 848 Sand Lake Rd 32809

HARD ROCK CAFE 407/351-7625 (5)

SAVE American. Casual Dining. **Address:** 6050 Universal Blvd 32819

THE H CUISINE 407/930-3020 (15)

Mediterranean. Fine Dining. **Address:** 7512 Dr. Phillips Blvd, Suite 80 32819

HEMISPHERE 407/825-1234 (4)

Steak Seafood. Casual Dining. **Address:** 9300 Jeff Fuqua Blvd (Airport Blvd) 32827

HIGHBALL & HARVEST 407/206-2400 (4)

New Southern. Casual Dining. **Address:** 4012 Central Florida Pkwy 32837

JACK'S PLACE 407/996-9700 (43)

Steak Seafood. Fine Dining. **Address:** 9700 International Dr 32819

JIMMY BUFFETT'S MARGARITAVILLE 407/224-2155 (9)

American. Casual Dining. **Address:** 6000 Universal Blvd, Suite 704 32819

THE KITCHEN 407/503-2430 (3)

New American. Casual Dining. **Address:** 5800 Universal Blvd 32819

KOSHER GRILL 407/392-2292 (13)

Kosher. Casual Dining. **Address:** 5615 International Dr 32819

MAGGIANO'S LITTLE ITALY 407/241-8650 (37)

Italian. Fine Dining. **Address:** 9101 International Dr, Suite 2400 32819

MEMORIES OF PERU 407/704-4014 (2)

Peruvian. Casual Dining. **Address:** 8204 Crystal Clear Ln, Suite 1600 32809

MOONFISH 407/363-7262 (23)

Seafood Steak. Fine Dining. **Address:** 7525 W Sand Lake Rd 32819

NAGOYA SUSHI 407/248-8558 (22)

Japanese Sushi. Casual Dining. **Address:** 7600 Dr. Phillips Blvd, Suite 66 32819

NEW PUNJAB INDIAN RESTAURANT 407/352-7887 (14)

Indian. Casual Dining. **Address:** 7451 International Dr 32819

NONA BLUE MODERN TAVERN 407/313-0027 (3)

American. Casual Dining. **Address:** 9685 Lake Nona Village Place 32827

THE OCEANAIRE SEAFOOD ROOM 407/363-4801 (40)

SAVE Seafood. Fine Dining. **Address:** 9101 International Dr, Suite 1002 32819

PADRINO'S CUBAN CUISINE 407/251-5107 (10)

Cuban. Casual Dining. **Address:** 13586 Village Park Dr, Suite 304 32837

THE PALM RESTAURANT 407/503-7256 (4)

American. Fine Dining. **Address:** 5800 Universal Blvd 32819

PAT O'BRIEN'S 407/224-2106 (8)

Cajun. Casual Dining. **Address:** 6000 Universal Blvd, S-723 32819

PHARMACY 407/985-2972 (51)

New American. Fine Dining. **Address:** 8060 Via Dellagio Way 32819

PRIMO 407/393-4444 (6)

New Italian Natural/Organic. Fine Dining. **Address:** 4040 Central Florida Pkwy 32837

ROY'S 407/352-4844 (29)

Pacific Rim Fusion. Fine Dining. **Address:** 7760 W Sand Lake Rd 32819

SAFFRON INDIAN CUISINE 407/674-8899 (27)

Indian. Casual Dining. **Address:** 7724 W Sand Lake Rd 32819

SEASONS 52 FRESH GRILL 407/354-5212 (25)

New American. Fine Dining. **Address:** 7700 Sand Lake Rd 32819

SEITO SUSHI 407/248-8888 (28)

New Japanese Sushi. Casual Dining. **Address:** 8031 Turkey Lake Rd, Suite 700 32819

SLATE 407/500-7528 (52)

New American. Casual Dining. **Address:** 8323 W Sand Lake Rd 32819

SONNY'S REAL PIT BAR-B-Q 407/859-7197

Barbecue. Casual Dining. **Address:** 7423 S Orange Blossom Tr 32809

SPENCER'S FOR STEAKS & CHOPS 407/313-8625 (47)

Steak. Fine Dining. **Address:** 6001 Destination Pkwy 32819

TAPA TORO 407/226-2929 (32)

Spanish. Casual Dining. **Address:** 8441 International Dr 32819

TAVERNA OPA 407/351-8660 (38)

Greek. Casual Dining. **Address:** 9101 International Dr, Suite 2240 32819

TEXAS DE BRAZIL 407/355-0355 (11)

Brazilian Steak. Casual Dining. **Address:** 5259 International Dr 32819

(See maps & indexes p. 197, 199, 202, 210.)

THAI SILK RESTAURANT 407/226-8997 (12)
Thai. Casual Dining. **Address:** 6803 S Kirkman Rd 32819

THAI THANI RESTAURANT 407/239-9733 (5)
Thai. Casual Dining. **Address:** 11025 S International Dr 32821

TOOJAY'S GOURMET DELI 407/355-0340
American. Casual Dining. **Address:** 7600 Dr. Phillips Blvd 32819

URBAIN 40 407/872-2640 (47)
American. Fine Dining. **Address:** 8000 Via Dellagio Way 32819

VITO'S CHOP HOUSE 407/354-2467 (34)
Steak Seafood. Fine Dining. **Address:** 8633 International Dr 32819

ORMOND BEACH (E-5) pop. 38,137, elev. 6'

• Hotels & Restaurants map & index p. 58

Pioneers of automobile racing, including R.E. Olds, founder of the Olds Motor Vehicle Company, sped their vehicles on the sands of Ormond Beach in the early and mid-1900s, giving the city its nickname "The Birthplace of Speed."

Ormond Beach Chamber of Commerce Welcome & Visitors Information Center: 165 W. Granada Blvd., Ormond Beach, FL 32174. **Phone:** (386) 677-3454.

BEST WESTERN CASTILLO DEL SOL
386/672-6711 (26)

AAA Benefit: Members save up to 15% and earn bonus points!

Address: 205 S Atlantic Ave 32176 **Location:** Oceanfront. I-95 exit 268 (SR 40/Granada Blvd), 5.4 mi e to SR A1A (Atlantic Ave), then 0.3 mi s. **Facility:** 147 units, some efficiencies. 7 stories, exterior corridors. **Pool:** outdoor. **Guest Services:** coin laundry. **Featured Amenity: breakfast buffet.**

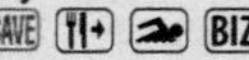

CLARION INN ORMOND BEACH 386/944-1500 (25)

Address: 1635 N US Hwy 1 32174 **Location:** I-95 exit 273 (US 1), just nw. **Facility:** 86 units. 2-3 stories, interior/exterior corridors. **Terms:** check-in 4 pm. **Amenities:** safes. **Pool:** outdoor. **Activities:** exercise room. **Featured Amenity: full hot breakfast.**

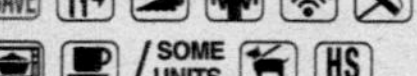

/ SOME UNITS

HAMPTON INN DAYTONA-ORMOND BEACH
386/677-9999 (27)

AAA Benefit: Members save 5% or more!

Address: 155 Interchange Blvd 32174 **Location:** I-95 exit 268 (SR 40/Granada Blvd), just w to Interchange Blvd, then just s. **Facility:** 84 units. 4 stories, interior corridors. **Terms:** check-in 4 pm. **Pool:** outdoor. **Activities:** exercise room. **Guest Services:** coin laundry. **Featured Amenity: full hot breakfast.**

CALL

/ SOME UNITS

SLEEP INN ORMOND BEACH 386/673-6030 (28)
Hotel. **Address:** 170 Williamson Blvd 32174

WHERE TO EAT

63 SOVEREIGN 386/238-9032 (20)
International. Casual Dining. **Address:** 63 W Granada Blvd 32174

BONEFISH GRILL 386/615-7889 (23)
Seafood. Fine Dining. **Address:** 814 S Atlantic Ave 32176

CHARLIE HORSE RESTAURANT 386/672-4347 (22)
American. Casual Dining. **Address:** 810 S Atlantic Ave 32176

COLT'S PIG STAND 386/898-0360 (14)
Barbecue. Quick Serve. **Address:** 1633 N US Hwy 1 32174

DUSTIN'S BAR-B-Q 386/677-5292
Barbecue. Quick Serve. **Address:** 1320 W Granada Blvd 32174

GENOVESE'S ITALIAN CAFE 386/677-3222 (16)
Italian Pizza. Casual Dining. **Address:** 183 E Granada Blvd 32176

GRIND GASTROPUB AND KONA TIKI BAR
386/672-7277 (19)
American. Gastropub. **Address:** 49 W Granada Blvd 32174

HULL'S SEAFOOD RESTAURANT & MARKET
386/673-8888 (21)
Seafood. Casual Dining. **Address:** 111 W Granada Blvd 32174

MARIO'S ITALIAN RESTAURANT & LOUNGE
386/677-2711 (24)
Italian. Casual Dining. **Address:** 521 S Yonge St 32174

PEACH VALLEY CAFE 386/615-0096 (15)
Breakfast Sandwiches. Casual Dining. **Address:** 185 E Granada Blvd 32176

STONEWOOD GRILL & TAVERN 386/671-1200 (17)
American. Fine Dining. **Address:** 100 S Atlantic Ave 32176

WILD RABBIT CAFE & BISTRO 386/256-7998 (18)
American. Casual Dining. **Address:** 48 E Granada Blvd 32176

OSCEOLA NATIONAL FOREST (A-8)

Elevations in the forest range from 120 ft. to 180 ft.

Near the Georgia border off US 90 approximately 12 miles east of US 441, Osceola National Forest encompasses 201,364 acres consisting of flat country dotted with ponds and swamps. Fishing is available in numerous streams and ponds. Hunting is permitted, but a special license is required in the Osceola Wildlife Management Area by the Florida Fish and Wildlife Conservation Commission *(see Good Facts To Know)*. Ocean Pond and Olustee Beach are major recreation areas within the forest. Phone (386) 752-2577. *See Recreation Areas Chart.*

PALATKA (D-3) pop. 10,558, elev. 28'

Judge Isaac Bronson, one of Palatka's foremost residents, was a member of the 25th U.S. Congress and was responsible for proposing the act by which Florida became a state. His restored home, Bronson-Mulholland House, 100 Madison St., was built in 1854 and is open to the public; phone (386) 329-0140. Adjacent to the home is the Putnam Historic Museum; phone (386) 385-3975 for hours. Rodman Reservoir, 10 miles southwest off SR 19, is a popular recreation destination, particularly for bass fishing. Several boat ramps are available in the area. *See Recreation Areas Chart.*

Putnam County Chamber of Commerce: 1100 Reid St., Palatka, FL 32177. **Phone:** (386) 328-1503.

HAMPTON INN BY HILTON RIVERFRONT 386/530-2420

SAVE Hotel. **Address:** 100 Memorial Pkwy 32177

AAA Benefit: Members save 5% or more!

HOLIDAY INN EXPRESS & SUITES-PALATKA NORTHWEST 386/325-2500

Hotel. **Address:** 3813 Reid St 32177

WHERE TO EAT

SONNY'S REAL PIT BAR-B-Q 386/328-4655

Barbecue. Casual Dining. **Address:** 425 Hwy 19 N 32177

PALM BAY pop. 103,190

• Hotels & Restaurants map & index p. 148

HOLIDAY INN EXPRESS HOTEL & SUITES PALM BAY 321/220-2003 27

Hotel. **Address:** 1206 SE Malabar Rd 32907

QUALITY INN PALM BAY 321/725-2952 26

Hotel. **Address:** 890 Palm Bay Rd NE 32905

WHERE TO EAT

SONNY'S REAL PIT BAR-B-Q 321/953-3997

Barbecue. Casual Dining. **Address:** 1020 Malabar Rd SE 32907

PALM COAST (C-10) pop. 75,180, elev. 10'

• Restaurants p. 250

GEM **WASHINGTON OAKS GARDENS STATE PARK,** 6400 N. Oceanshore Blvd., originally was part of Bella Vista Plantation owned by Gen. Joseph Hernandez, a militia general who commanded troops during the Second Seminole War. Extending from the Atlantic Ocean to the Matanzas River, the park covers more than 400 acres of Florida coastal scenery. Included are scenic tidal marshes, a scrub community, a beach and a hammock. Coquina rock outcroppings worn into unusual shapes by the sea give the beach area an unearthly appearance. Many species of shorebirds and marine and forest animals make their home in the park. *See Recreation Areas Chart.*

Formal gardens contain exotic plants from around the world; a history of the area is presented at the Young House Visitor Center. Guided walks are provided by request. **Time:** Allow 3 hours minimum. **Hours:** Daily 8-dusk. **Cost:** $5 (per private vehicle with two to eight people); $4 (motorcyclists or single-occupant private vehicle); $2 (per additional person or person arriving by bicycle or on foot). **Phone:** (386) 446-6780.

DAYS INN PALM COAST 386/627-7734

Hotel

Address: 120 Garden St N 32137 **Location:** I-95 exit 289 (Palm Coast Pkwy), just w to Boulder Rock Dr, just n to Plaza Dr, then just e. Located behind Home Depot. **Facility:** 119 units. 4 stories, interior corridors. **Amenities:** *Some:* safes. **Pool:** heated outdoor. **Activities:** exercise room. **Guest Services:** coin laundry. **Featured Amenity:** continental breakfast.

SAVE CALL BIZ

HS 

/ SOME UNITS

FAIRFIELD INN & SUITES BY MARRIOTT PALM COAST I-95 386/445-3450

SAVE Hotel. **Address:** 400 Old Kings Rd N 32137

AAA Benefit: Members save 5% or more!

HAMPTON INN & SUITES PALM COAST 386/439-8999

SAVE Hotel. **Address:** 150 Flagler Plaza Dr 32137

AAA Benefit: Members save 5% or more!

Save on travel, shopping, dining and more: AAA.com/discounts

HILTON GARDEN INN PALM COAST TOWN CENTER 386/586-2463

Hotel

AAA Benefit:
Members save 5% or more!

Address: 55 Town Center Blvd 32164 **Location:** I-95 exit 284 (SR 100), 0.5 mi w to Town Center Blvd, then just n. **Facility:** 121 units. 6 stories, interior corridors. **Pool:** heated outdoor. **Activities:** hot tub, exercise room. **Guest Services:** valet and coin laundry.

Hilton Garden Inn

New Beds & TVs. Great NE Florida stopover. 4 mi to Atlantic. Close to Daytona Beach, St. Augustine.

HOLIDAY INN EXPRESS HOTEL & SUITES PALM COAST-FLAGLER BEACH AREA 386/439-3939
Hotel. **Address:** 200 Flagler Plaza Dr 32137

RED ROOF PLUS+ PALM COAST 386/446-8180

Hotel

Address: 10 Kingswood Dr 32137 **Location:** I-95 exit 289 (Palm Coast Pkwy), just e to Kingswood Dr, then just sw; in Kingswood Center. **Facility:** 78 units. 3 stories, interior corridors. **Guest Services:** coin laundry. **Featured Amenity: full hot breakfast.**

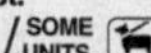

386, A FUSION OF FINE EATING 386/246-0070
New American. Casual Dining. **Address:** 5949 N Oceanshore Blvd 32137

CAPTAIN'S BBQ 386/597-2888
Barbecue. Quick Serve. **Address:** 5862 N Ocean Shore Blvd 32137

SONNY'S REAL PIT BAR-B-Q 386/446-5700
Barbecue. Casual Dining. **Address:** 25 Cypress Edge Dr 32137

PALMETTO pop. 12,606

- **Hotels & Restaurants map & index p. 300**

RIVERSIDE CAFE 941/729-4402 (30)
Seafood. Casual Dining. **Address:** 995 Riverside Dr 34221

PALM HARBOR pop. 57,439

- **Part of St. Petersburg-Clearwater and Beaches area — see map p. 275**

BUNGA RAYA RESTAURANT AND SUSHI BAR 727/754-7828
Cantonese Sushi. Casual Dining. **Address:** 4952 Ridgemoor Blvd 34685

EAST LAKE CAFE 727/772-0707
Breakfast Sandwiches. Casual Dining. **Address:** 3430 E Lake Rd 34685

THE LUCKY DILL DELI 727/789-5574
American. Casual Dining. **Address:** 33180 US Hwy 19 34684

MASSIMO'S ECLECTIC FINE DINING 727/784-1881
Italian. Casual Dining. **Address:** 31876 US 19 N 34684

MYSTIC FISH 727/771-1800
Continental. Fine Dining. **Address:** 3253 Tampa Rd W 34684

QUEEN'S PIZZA & RESTAURANT 727/474-3797
Italian Pizza. Casual Dining. **Address:** 3436 Tampa Rd E 34684

SONNY'S REAL PIT BAR-B-Q 727/785-5585
Barbecue. Casual Dining. **Address:** 30503 US Hwy 19 N 34684

THIRSTY MARLIN GRILL & BAR 727/784-3469
Seafood. Casual Dining. **Address:** 1023 Florida Ave 34683

PINELLAS PARK (H-1) pop. 49,079, elev. 13'

- **Hotels & Restaurants map & index p. 286**
- **Part of St. Petersburg-Clearwater and Beaches area — see map p. 275**

The Tackle Shack, 7801 66th St., offers instruction and rentals for kayaking, sailboating and scuba diving as well as scuba diving tours; phone (727) 546-5080.

TAMPA BAY AUTOMOBILE MUSEUM is at 3301 Gateway Centre Blvd. Vintage vehicles are displayed within a 16,000-square-foot gallery. Noteworthy exhibits include front-wheel-drive and rear-engine cars from the 1920s and '30s, which spearheaded engineering standards for the present-day automobile. Motorcars from Czechoslovakia, England, France, Germany, Ireland, Italy and United States of America are featured. A sole replica of the world's first self-propelled vehicle, the 1770 Fardier de Cugnot, also is showcased.

Time: Allow 1 hour minimum. **Hours:** Mon. and Wed.-Sat. 10-4, Sun. noon-4. Closed major holidays. **Cost:** $8; $6 (ages 55+); $5 (students with ID); free (ages 0-12). **Phone:** (727) 579-8226.

COUNTRY INN & SUITES BY RADISSON 727/545-5777 (55)
Hotel. **Address:** 8050 US Hwy 19 N 33781

WHERE TO EAT

CARMELITA'S MEXICAN RESTAURANT 727/545-8226
Mexican. Casual Dining. **Address:** 6218 66th St N 33781

JOTO'S PIZZA 727/544-5611 (82)
Pizza. Casual Dining. **Address:** 9119 Belcher Rd 33782

SONNY'S REAL PIT BAR-B-Q 727/546-8300
Barbecue. Casual Dining. **Address:** 4385 Park Blvd 33781

PLANT CITY (H-2) pop. 34,721, elev. 37'

• Part of Tampa area — see map p. 313

Plant City was named after Henry Bradley Plant, a wealthy railroad magnate, but the town is best known for its plant crop, the strawberry. The majority of all the winter strawberries in the United States is grown on farms surrounding Plant City. The annual Florida Strawberry Festival draws some 800,000 visitors in late February and early March; phone (813) 752-9194.

The town is home to the International Softball Federation, the world governing body for softball competition; phone (813) 864-0100.

A 700-acre reservoir created from a reclaimed phosphate mining area is the center of recreational activities in Edward Medard Park, 6140 Turkey Creek Rd.; phone (813) 757-3802. *See Recreation Areas Chart.*

The Pioneer/Heritage Museum, in the 1914 Plant City High School Community Center at 605 N. Collins St., has several exhibit rooms with period themes such as clothing, furnishings, medical equipment, farm implements and railroading; phone (813) 757-9226 for tour reservations.

Plant City Visitor Information Center: 1702 N. Park Rd., Plant City, FL 33563. **Phone:** (813) 754-7045.

DINOSAUR WORLD, 5145 Harvey Tew Rd., features more than 200 life-size dinosaur models in an outdoor setting. Uncover a life-size dinosaur replica in the boneyard, watch educational films in a cave and stroll through a garden filled with man-made dinosaur skeletons. In the Prehistoric Museum, inspect such authentic fossils as dinosaur bones and teeth found around the world, and gaze at five animatronic dinosaurs, including a pterodactyl, triceratops and a T-rex. A woolly mammoth exhibit, a geode excavation site and a cave show also are featured. Children may cavort on two playgrounds and play archeologist in a fossil dig; they can take home several real fossils, which may include shark teeth and dinosaur bone fragments.

Time: Allow 2 hours, 30 minutes minimum. **Hours:** Daily 9-5. **Cost:** $16.95; $14.95 (ages 60+); $11.95 (ages 3-12 includes fossil dig); free (ages 0-2 and active military with ID). Excavation Pass includes gem bag $22.75, $18.95 (ages 3-12). **Phone:** (813) 717-9865.

Where Diamonds make the difference:

AAA.com/travelguides/hotels

FAIRFIELD INN & SUITES BY MARRIOTT LAKELAND-PLANT CITY 813/757-6202

Hotel

AAA Benefit: Members save 5% or more!

Address: 4307 Sterling Commerce Dr 33566 **Location:** I-4 exit 25, just e on County Line Rd. **Facility:** 87 units. 3 stories, interior corridors. **Pool:** heated outdoor. **Activities:** exercise room. **Guest Services:** valet and coin laundry, area transportation. **Featured Amenity: continental breakfast.**

SAVE CALL BIZ HS

HAMPTON INN BY HILTON PLANT CITY 813/756-5600

SAVE Hotel. **Address:** 2702 Thonotosassa Rd 33563

AAA Benefit: Members save 5% or more!

WHERE TO EAT

19 NINETEEN SIXTEEN16 IRISH PUB 813/756-6504

Irish. Casual Dining. **Address:** 2309 W Thonotosassa Rd 33563

ABC PIZZA 813/752-5146

Italian. Casual Dining. **Address:** 114 N Alexander St 33566

BUDDY FREDDY'S COUNTRY BUFFET 813/754-5120

American. Casual Dining. **Address:** 1101 Goldfinch Dr 33566

DUKES BREWHOUSE 813/752-2700

American. Casual Dining. **Address:** 2212 James L Redman Pkwy 33566

EASTERN BUFFET 813/707-1199

Chinese. Quick Serve. **Address:** 1707 James L. Redman Pkwy 33563

FRED'S MARKET RESTAURANT 813/752-7763

Comfort Food. Buffet Style. **Address:** 1401 W Dr. Martin Luther King Jr Blvd 33565

JOHNSON'S BARBEQUE 813/759-0009

Barbecue. Casual Dining. **Address:** 1407 W Dr Martin Luther King Jr Blvd 33563

MI CASA MEXICAN RESTAURANT 813/752-0057

Mexican. Casual Dining. **Address:** 2613 Thonotosassa Rd 33563

NICK'S PIZZERIA & WINGS 813/757-5900

Pizza Sandwiches. Casual Dining. **Address:** 1707 James L Redman Pkwy 33563

O'BRIEN'S IRISH PUB & GRILL 813/764-8818

Irish. Casual Dining. **Address:** 1701 S Alexander St 33566

OLDE TOWN PIZZERIA & PASTA CO 813/752-5800

Italian. Casual Dining. **Address:** 3011 James L. Redman Pkwy 33566

PLANT CITY HOMETOWN BUFFET 813/754-4488

American. Quick Serve. **Address:** 1914 James L. Redman Pkwy 33566

SNELLGROVES RESTAURANT 813/752-3652

Comfort Food. Casual Dining. **Address:** 109 S Collins St 33566

SONNY'S REAL PIT BAR-B-Q 813/757-3118

Barbecue. Casual Dining. **Address:** 1102 Goldfinch Blvd 33565

STRAWBERRY HUT 813/752-3779

Sandwiches Desserts. Quick Serve. **Address:** 1505 N Wheeler St 33566

WASABI JAPANESE STEAK HOUSE & SUSHI BAR 813/754-8866

Japanese. Casual Dining. **Address:** 203 W Alexander St 33563

PONTE VEDRA BEACH

- **Hotels & Restaurants map & index p. 92**
- **Part of Jacksonville area — see map p. 84**

HILTON GARDEN INN JACKSONVILLE/PONTE VEDRA 904/280-1661 71

SAVE Hotel. **Address:** 45 PGA Tour Blvd 32082

AAA Benefit: Members save 5% or more!

THE LODGE & CLUB AT PONTE VEDRA BEACH

904/273-9500 70

Boutique Resort Hotel

Address: 607 Ponte Vedra Blvd 32082 **Location:** Oceanfront. SR A1A (3rd St), just e on 37th Ave to Ponte Vedra Blvd, 2.8 mi s. **Facility:** The oceanfront resort is in an area referred to as the "Palm Beach of North Florida." The inviting rooms are upscale and suites include living and kitchen areas. Recreational activities are abundant. 66 units. 2 stories, exterior corridors. **Parking:** on-site and valet. **Terms:** check-in 4 pm. **Amenities:** safes. **Dining:** 3 restaurants. **Pool:** heated outdoor. **Activities:** sauna, hot tub, steamroom, regulation golf, tennis, recreation programs, kids club, bicycles, lawn sports, health club, spa. **Guest Services:** valet laundry, area transportation.

SAVE ECO BIZ HS

/ SOME UNITS

PONTE VEDRA INN & CLUB

904/285-1111 69

Resort Hotel

Address: 200 Ponte Vedra Blvd 32082 **Location:** Oceanfront. SR A1A (3rd St), just e on 37th Ave to Ponte Vedra Blvd, then 1.3 mi s. **Facility:** Established in 1928, the sprawling property is on 300 acres of beautifully manicured grounds with a superb beach, world class spa and magnificent golf courses. Families will love the relaxed ambience. 249 units. 2 stories, interior/exterior corridors. **Parking:** on-site and valet. **Terms:** check-in 4 pm. **Amenities:** safes. **Dining:** 6 restaurants. **Pool:** heated outdoor. **Activities:** sauna, hot tub, steamroom, self-propelled boats, fishing, regulation golf, tennis, recreation programs, kids club, bicycles, playground, health club, spa. **Guest Services:** valet laundry, area transportation. *(See ad p. 253.)*

SAVE ECO BIZ HS

/ SOME UNITS

Discover North Florida's premier AAA Five-Diamond beach resort with endless family activities.

SAWGRASS MARRIOTT GOLF RESORT & SPA

904/285-7777 72

Resort Hotel

AAA Benefit: Members save 5% or more!

Address: 1000 PGA Tour Blvd 32082 **Location:** SR 202 (Butler Blvd), 4 mi s on SR A1A to PGA Tour Blvd, then just w. **Facility:** The PLAYERS Championship PGA tournament is played right next door to this resort which offers well-designed, modern rooms. Many offer great views of the ponds, waterfall or the resort grounds. 514 units, some two bedrooms. 2-7 stories, interior/exterior corridors. **Parking:** on-site (fee) and valet. **Terms:** check-in 4 pm. **Amenities:** safes. **Dining:** 6 restaurants. **Pool:** outdoor, heated outdoor. **Activities:** sauna, hot tub, steamroom, regulation golf, miniature golf, recreation programs in season, kids club, bicycles, health club, spa. **Guest Services:** valet and coin laundry, boarding pass kiosk, rental car service, area transportation.

SAVE ECO BIZ

/ SOME UNITS sHS

WHERE TO EAT

AL'S PIZZA 904/543-1494

Italian Pizza. Casual Dining. **Address:** 635 A1A N 32082

PUSSER'S BAR AND GRILLE 904/280-7766 91

Caribbean. Casual Dining. **Address:** 816 A1A Hwy N 32082

RESTAURANT MEDURE

904/543-3797 93

Fusion Fine Dining $21-$58

AAA Inspector Notes: Situated in an upscale shopping area, the restaurant offers a touch of sophistication and refinement. Décor elements include intriguing curves, angles and dim lighting that creates a romantic vibe. The menu features high-quality items from local and global markets. Two of the house favorites are the local fish Francaise and the Medure meatloaf. No meal is complete without the soufflé of the evening, a treat you won't want to miss. Live music is featured on Friday and Saturday evenings. **Features:** full bar, happy hour. **Reservations:** suggested. **Address:** 818 A1A N 32082 **Location:** 5.3 mi s of J Turner Butler Blvd. **Parking:** on-site and valet. D

RUTH'S CHRIS STEAK HOUSE 904/285-0014 92

Steak. Fine Dining. **Address:** 814 A1A N, Suite 103 32082

Mobile Battery Service

1-800-AAA-HELP
1-800-CAA-HELP

AAA.com/mobile
CAA.ca/mobile

▼ See AAA listing p. 252 ▼

North Florida's Premier Beach Resort

Set amidst lush landscapes and Atlantic beachfront shores,
Ponte Vedra Inn & Club features luxurious accommodations, 36 holes of golf, tennis courts, oceanfront pools and an award-winning spa.

For reservations, call **844.890.5026** or visit **PonteVedra.com**

STAY CONNECTED

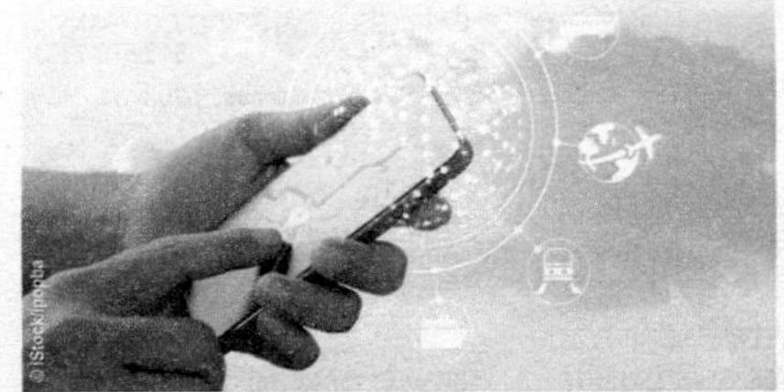

GET THE APP

AAA.com/mobile
CAA.ca/mobile

PORT ORANGE pop. 56,048, elev. 20'

• Hotels & Restaurants map & index p. 58

COUNTRY INN & SUITES BY RADISSON, PORT ORANGE-DAYTONA 386/760-0101 43

Hotel. **Address:** 5802 Journey's End Way 32127

WHERE TO EAT

AUNT CATFISH'S ON THE RIVER 386/767-4768 32

Southern Seafood. Casual Dining. **Address:** 4009 Halifax Dr 32127

DUSTIN'S BAR-B-Q 386/322-9177

Barbecue. Casual Dining. **Address:** 4908 Clyde Morris Blvd 32119

MALIBU BEACH GRILL 386/492-2968 35

New American. Fine Dining. **Address:** 5543 S Williamson Blvd 32128

MONTEREY GRILL 386/761-6868 34

American. Casual Dining. **Address:** 1665 Dunlawton Ave 32127

PORT ORANGE STEAKHOUSE 386/756-2660 33

Steak Seafood. Casual Dining. **Address:** 3851 S Nova Rd 32127

PORT RICHEY pop. 2,671

• Part of St. Petersburg-Clearwater and Beaches area — see map p. 275

HOMEWOOD SUITES BY HILTON TAMPA/PORT RICHEY 727/819-1000

SAVE Extended Stay Hotel. **Address:** 11115 US 19 N 34668

AAA Benefit: Members save 5% or more!

REDINGTON SHORES pop. 2,121

• Hotels & Restaurants map & index p. 286
• Part of St. Petersburg-Clearwater and Beaches area — see map p. 275

FRIENDLY TAVERN 727/393-4470 94

American. Casual Dining. **Address:** 18121 Gulf Blvd 33708

RIVERVIEW pop. 71,050

• Hotels & Restaurants map & index p. 338, 347
• Part of Tampa area — see map p. 313

HILTON GARDEN INN TAMPA/RIVERVIEW/BRANDON 813/626-6610 17

Hotel

Hilton Garden Inn **AAA Benefit:** Members save 5% or more!

Address: 4328 Garden Vista Dr 33578 **Location:** I-75 exit 254, 0.6 mi n on US 301, then just e on Crescent Park Dr. **Facility:** 119 units. 6 stories, interior corridors. **Terms:** check-in 4 pm. **Pool:** heated outdoor. **Activities:** hot tub, exercise room. **Guest Services:** valet and coin laundry, area transportation.

SAVE CALL

UPTOWN SUITES TAMPA RIVERVIEW 813/612-9550 16

Extended Stay Hotel. **Address:** 9321 Everhart Rd 33578

WHERE TO EAT

ACROPOLIS GREEK TAVERNA 813/654-2255 53

Greek. Casual Dining. **Address:** 6108 Winthrop Town Center Ave 33578

CHAI YO THAI CUISINE 813/671-6935 77

Thai. Casual Dining. **Address:** 11695 Boyette Rd 33569

CHINA 1 813/626-5577 51

Chinese. Quick Serve. **Address:** 3841 US 301 S 33578

CHINA PARK CHINESE FOOD 813/671-2333 75

Chinese. Quick Serve. **Address:** 11651 Boyette Rd 33569

CHINA STAR NEW YORK STYLE CHINESE RESTAURANT 813/671-0688 55

Chinese. Quick Serve. **Address:** 6925 US 301 S 33569

CHINA TASTE 813/671-6555

Chinese. Quick Serve. **Address:** 13172 US Hwy 301 S 33568

CRAZY CAFE 813/898-2839 52

Sushi. Casual Dining. **Address:** 3883 S US 301 33578

EAST COAST PIZZA 813/234-1700

Italian. Quick Serve. **Address:** 13340 Lincoln Rd 33578

EATS AMERICAN GRILL 813/655-3287 54

American. Casual Dining. **Address:** 6264 Winthrop Town Centre Ave 33578

FRED'S MARKET RESTAURANT 813/741-9101

Comfort Food. Casual Dining. **Address:** 6501 US 301 S 33578

THE HOT TOMATO OF RIVERVIEW 813/515-4179 78

Sandwiches Desserts. Quick Serve. **Address:** 10451 Gibsonton Dr 33578

ITALIAN KITCHEN CAFE 813/671-0953 56

Italian. Fine Dining. **Address:** 6915 US 301 S 33569

KAZBOR'S GRILLE 813/677-1673

American. Casual Dining. **Address:** 9992 US Hwy 301 S 33569

LITTLE HABANA CUBAN RESTAURANT 813/672-5111

Cuban. Casual Dining. **Address:** 13352 Lincoln Rd 33578

NEW CHINA NEW YORK STYLE CHINESE RESTAURANT 813/672-3888 76

Chinese. Quick Serve. **Address:** 9856 US 301 S 33569

PECK'S FLAME BROILED CHICKEN & CATERING COMPANY 813/570-7171

Chicken Barbecue. Quick Serve. **Address:** 8203 US Hwy 301 S 33569

SMOKIN' PIG BBQ 813/512-2500 50

Barbecue. Quick Serve. **Address:** 3834 US 301 S 33578

WESTSHORE PIZZA 813/672-2828

Pizza. Casual Dining. **Address:** 11643 Boyette Rd 33569

RUSKIN pop. 17,208

• Part of Tampa area — see map p. 313

HARBORSIDE SUITES AT LITTLE HARBOR 813/922-6000

Resort Condominium

Address: 536 Bahia Beach Blvd 33570 **Location:** Waterfront. 3.5 mi w of US 41 on Shell Point Rd. **Facility:** Set on many acres and Old Tampa Bay, the resort offers gorgeous sunset views and also a panoramic view of St. Petersburg. Units are spacious and offer that feeling of a home-away-from-home. 157 condominiums. 6 stories, interior/exterior corridors. **Dining:** 2 restaurants, also, Sunset Grill at Little Harbor, see separate listing, entertainment. **Pool:** heated outdoor. **Activities:** hot tub, beach access, fishing, tennis, playground, exercise room, massage. **Guest Services:** coin laundry.

WHERE TO EAT

CHINA WOK RUSKIN CHINESE FOOD 813/645-8088

Chinese. Quick Serve. **Address:** 3062 SR 674 33570

THE HOT TOMATO 813/938-1888

American. Quick Serve. **Address:** 2701 E College Ave 33570

SUNSET GRILL AT LITTLE HARBOR 813/607-2900

American. Casual Dining. **Address:** 602 Bahia Del Sol Dr 33570

SAFETY HARBOR (H-1) pop. 16,884, elev. 14'

• Hotels & Restaurants map & index p. 286
• Part of St. Petersburg-Clearwater and Beaches area — see map p. 275

Local Native Americans dipped into the area's five mineral springs long before the 1539 arrival of Hernando de Soto, who named the springs *Espiritu Santo*, meaning water of the Holy Spirit. Said to possess healing powers, the water first lured health-minded visitors to the area in the mid-1800s; by the early 1900s it was being bottled and shipped around the world. Today, Safety Harbor's calling card is its spa culture.

Safety Harbor Chamber of Commerce: 200 Main St., Safety Harbor, FL 34695. **Phone:** (727) 726-2890.

SAFETY HARBOR MUSEUM AND CULTURAL CENTER is at 329 Bayshore Blvd. S. The Pre-History exhibit displays tools, points, fossils and pottery tracing regional habitation dating back 12,000 years to the period of Spanish exploration. The Safety Harbor Heritage Gallery explains the importance of the mineral springs in area development through photographs and memorabilia. The City Gallery features temporary exhibits of local art. **Time:** Allow 1 hour minimum. **Hours:** Tues.-Fri. 11-4, Sat. 10-2. Closed major holidays. Phone ahead to confirm schedule. **Cost:** Donations. **Phone:** (727) 724-1562. GT

SAFETY HARBOR RESORT & SPA TRADEMARK COLLECTION BY WYNDHAM 727/726-1161 33

Historic Resort Hotel

Address: 105 N Bayshore Dr 34695 **Location:** Waterfront. Jct SR 590 (Main St) and Philippe Pkwy; downtown. **Facility:** World-renowned for its mineral springs and full-service spa facilities, the resort is located on Tampa Bay and the Espiritu Santo Springs. Rooms are spacious with many overlooking the bay and grounds. 172 units. 3-6 stories, interior corridors. **Parking:** on-site (fee) and street. **Terms:** check-in 4 pm. **Amenities:** safes. **Dining:** 2 restaurants. **Pool:** heated outdoor, heated indoor. **Activities:** sauna, hot tub, steamroom, fishing, tennis, recreation programs, bicycles, health club, spa. **Guest Services:** valet and coin laundry, area transportation. *(See ad p. 42.)*

SAVE BIZ SHS CALL /SOME UNITS

WHERE TO EAT

BURGER MONGER 727/726-4001

Burgers. Quick Serve. **Address:** 2454 N McMullen Booth Rd 34695

CRISPERS 727/210-6150

Sandwiches Soup. Quick Serve. **Address:** 100 Main St 34695

PARADISE RESTAURANT 727/725-1208 47

American. Casual Dining. **Address:** 443 Main St 34695

THE SANDWICH ON MAIN 727/773-6234 46

Sandwiches. Casual Dining. **Address:** 308 Main St 34695

SOUTHERN FRESH 727/216-6341 45

American Comfort Food. Casual Dining. **Address:** 122 3rd Ave N 34695

WHISTLE STOP GRILL & BAR 727/726-1956 48

American. Casual Dining. **Address:** 915 Main St 34695

ST. AUGUSTINE (B-10) pop. 12,975, elev. 7'

• Hotels p. 268 • Restaurants p. 269
• Hotels & Restaurants map & index p. 263, 266

As the oldest, continuously occupied European settlement in the United States, St. Augustine has played varied and prominent historic roles. Juan Ponce de León, in search of the legendary Fountain of Youth, landed in this area Apr. 3, 1513, and took possession of the region for Spain. In 1565 King Phillip II sent Pedro Menéndez de Avilés to colonize the new territory. Menéndez de Avilés arrived in Florida on the Feast Day of St. Augustine and named the landing site after the saint.

Its coastal location made the town both strategic and vulnerable. Pirates sacked St. Augustine in both the 16th and 17th centuries. Military importance soon came to the forefront as England extended its holdings southward down the coast. Spain responded by starting to build Castillo de San Marcos in 1672.

By the time St. Augustine was ceded to England in 1763, it had served as the seat of government for 30 missions as well as for all Spanish possessions in the regions of Florida and coastal Georgia. During the Revolutionary War, British loyalists from adjacent states sought refuge in St. Augustine.

(See maps & indexes p. 263, 266.)

In 1783 in recognition of Spain's assistance to the United States in its war against Britain, Florida was returned to Spain. Encouraged by Spanish land grants, many Americans moved onto property vacated by the English. Florida became a U.S. possession in 1821, and during the Second Seminole War in the 1830s, St. Augustine resumed a military role.

The quiet coastal town came to life in the 1880s when Henry Flagler began to develop the area as a winter resort and playground. With a railway link provided from New York, plush hotels were built and leisure activities such as golf and yachting awaited the city's guests.

Still preserving strong evidence of its Spanish origin, the Old City is being restored to a likeness of its colonial days; much of the historic area north of the Plaza de la Constitución is complete. Typical Spanish houses, with walled patios enclosing Old World gardens, line the many narrow streets.

Tolomato Cemetery, also known as the Old Spanish Cemetery, is at Cordova Street between Orange and Saragossa streets. Formerly the site of the Christian Native American village of Tolomato, the cemetery served as a Catholic burial ground 1784-1892 and is the burial site of Augustin Verot, the first bishop of St. Augustine. The cemetery is only open by request; information is available at the rectory entrance of the Cathedral of St. Augustine on Treasury Street.

South of the city on Anastasia Island, St. Augustine Beach provides a return to the present. Miles of wide, hard-packed sand beaches afford beach driving, swimming and surfing opportunities. Boating also is popular.

Tours of area attractions by horse-drawn carriage depart from the bayfront area next to Castillo de San Marcos. The city's historic sites can be seen in a different light during nightly ghost tours. Costumed guides tell eerie stories about the city and its historic buildings as part of walking tours conducted by Ghost Tours of St. Augustine; phone (904) 829-1122. The Trolley of the Doomed provides transportation to haunted sites such as the St. Augustine Lighthouse grounds and The Old Jail on tours offered by Ghosts & Gravestones; phone (866) 721-1844.

The Huguenot cemetery, between the City Gate and the Visitor Information Center, is open to the public anytime the gate is unlocked.

Note: Parking regulations are enforced strictly throughout the city. Yellow curbs are no-parking zones. A garage and paid parking spaces are available. *See St. Augustine Walking Tour map p. 257.*

St. Augustine & St. Johns County Visitors Information Center: 10 W. Castillo Dr., St. Augustine, FL 32084. **Phone:** (904) 825-1000.

Shopping: St. Augustine Outlets and St. Augustine Premium Outlets are both off I-95 exit 318 on SR 16.

The Old City

BLACK RAVEN ADVENTURES departs from the St. Augustine city marina at 111 Avenida Menendez. This 1.5-hour interactive journey aboard the *Black Raven,* a replica of a pirate ship that cruises Matanzas Bay, is a floating performance stage for pirate-themed entertainment. Adults and kids can participate in shipboard activities that range from singing, skits and sword-fighting to face painting, games and a rehearsed but unscripted show. Rum Runner is a 2-hour evening cruise for adults only; it features live entertainment and a full bar.

Hours: Departures daily at 2:15 and 6:15 (weather permitting). Rum Runner departs Fri.-Sat. at 8:15 p.m. Passengers must check in no later than 30 minutes before departure. Additional cruises are sometimes scheduled; phone ahead to verify times. **Cost:** $34.95; $24.95 (ages 3-12); $110.80 (family, two adults and two children ages 3-12, plus $24.95 for each additional child). Rum Runners $29.95. Reservations are recommended. **Phone:** (904) 826-0000, or (877) 578-5050 for reservations. GT

GEM **CASTILLO DE SAN MARCOS NATIONAL MONUMENT,** a Spanish fortress, is at Castillo Dr. and Avenida Menéndez. The oldest masonry fort in the continental United States, it was built 1672-95 of coquina, a soft local shellrock, as part of the defenses along the route of the treasure fleets. For many years the fort was the northernmost point of Spain's New World holdings.

The symmetrical fort has massive diamond-shaped bastions at each of its four corners, and 60 to 77 cannons once occupied the gun deck. Its 28-foot-high walls are skirted by a moat on three sides. A stairway leads to the gun deck overlooking the Old City Gate, quaint old streets and Matanzas Bay. Exhibits and a 25-minute video trace fort history, and costumed re-enactors give weapons demonstrations and presentations about Colonial life.

Until the mid-18th century this fortress defended St. Augustine. The English acquired the fort and Florida from Spain in 1763 at the end of the French and Indian War. Spain regained possession of Florida in 1784 as part of the Treaty of Paris.

Upon the acquisition of Florida in 1821, the fortress became part of the U.S. coastal defense system. It also was a military prison. Seminole leader Osceola was confined in the fort during the Second Seminole War. The fort's final military use was for imprisonment of some American soldiers during the Spanish-American War.

Metal detectors are not permitted. **Time:** Allow 1 hour minimum. **Hours:** Daily 8:45-5:15. Grounds are open daily 5:30 a.m.-midnight. Last ticket is sold 15 minutes before closing. Historic weapons demonstration Fri.-Sun. at 10:30, 11:30, 1:30, 2:30 and 3:30 (weather permitting); phone ahead to confirm schedule. Closed Thanksgiving and Christmas. **Cost:** $15; free (ages 0-15 when accompanied by a paying adult). Tickets are valid for 7 consecutive days. **Phone:** (904) 829-6506.

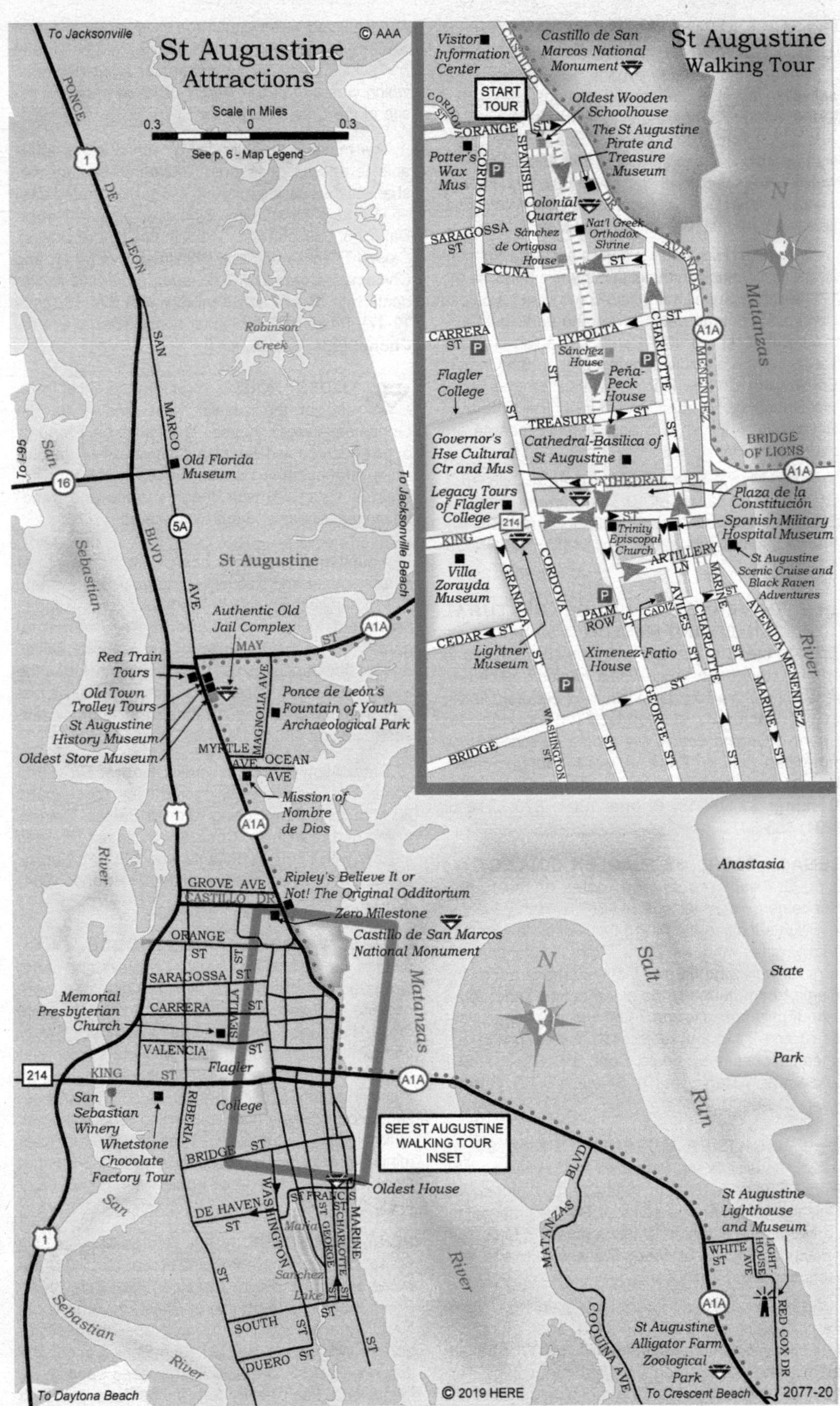
St Augustine Attractions
St Augustine Walking Tour
Scale in Miles
0.3 0 0.3
See p. 6 - Map Legend
© AAA
To Jacksonville
To Jacksonville Beach
To I-95
To Daytona Beach
To Crescent Beach
START TOUR
Visitor Information Center
Castillo de San Marcos National Monument
Oldest Wooden Schoolhouse
The St Augustine Pirate and Treasure Museum
Potter's Wax Mus
Colonial Quarter
Nat'l Greek Orthodox Shrine
Sánchez de Ortigosa House
Sánchez House
Peña-Peck House
Flagler College
Cathedral-Basilica of St Augustine
Governor's Hse Cultural Ctr and Mus
Legacy Tours of Flagler College
Plaza de la Constitución
Spanish Military Hospital Museum
Trinity Episcopal Church
St Augustine Scenic Cruise and Black Raven Adventures
Villa Zorayda Museum
Lightner Museum
Ximenez-Fatio House
Bridge of Lions
Matanzas River
Old Florida Museum
St Augustine
Authentic Old Jail Complex
Red Train Tours
Old Town Trolley Tours
St Augustine History Museum
Oldest Store Museum
Ponce de León's Fountain of Youth Archaeological Park
Mission of Nombre de Dios
Ripley's Believe It or Not! The Original Odditorium
Zero Milestone
Castillo de San Marcos National Monument
Memorial Presbyterian Church
San Sebastian Winery
Whetstone Chocolate Factory Tour
Flagler College
SEE ST AUGUSTINE WALKING TOUR INSET
Oldest House
Robinson Creek
San Sebastian River
Salt Run
Anastasia State Park
St Augustine Lighthouse and Museum
St Augustine Alligator Farm Zoological Park
© 2019 HERE
2077-20

(See maps & indexes p. 263, 266.)

GEM **COLONIAL QUARTER,** 33 St. George St., is a 2-acre historic park featuring hands-on activities, pictorial stories and demonstrations in a tour that explores three centuries of life in early St. Augustine. At the 16th Century Spanish First City, visitors can explore a replica archaeological dig, watch a 50-foot caravel ship being built by hand and meander down a boardwalk underneath flags that flew in St. Augustine over the centuries.

Costumed guides depict daily life through demonstrations of blacksmithing and gunsmithing at the 17th Century Spanish Fortified Town, where you can climb a 35-foot-tall watch tower and participate in a musket drill. At the 18th Century Spanish Garrison Town, explore a soldier's home; in the 18th Century British 14th Colony, learn how life changed under the British occupation and during the American Revolution. A British pub and Spanish taberna are on the premises.

Time: Allow 1 hour minimum. **Hours:** Daily 10-5. Guided tours depart at 10:30, noon, 1:30 and 3. Closed Christmas. **Cost:** $12.99; $6.99 (ages 5-15). **Phone:** (904) 342-2857 or (888) 991-0933. GT

GEM **GOVERNOR'S HOUSE CULTURAL CENTER AND MUSEUM** is at 48 King St. Exhibits blend technology with historic artifacts to tell the story of St. Augustine's founding based on research by the Florida Museum of Natural History at the University of Florida. First Colony: Our Spanish Origins details the area's role in shaping American history. **Time:** Allow 1 hour minimum. **Hours:** Daily 10-5. Closed Christmas. **Cost:** Free. **Parking:** $2.50-$15. **Phone:** (904) 823-2212 or (904) 825-5079.

LEGACY TOURS OF FLAGLER COLLEGE, 74 King St., explores several rooms of the former Ponce de León Hotel, built in 1887 by Henry Flagler. Highlights include the dining hall, which features 79 Tiffany glass windows. Eight Tiffany crystal chandeliers, artwork and Flagler family portraits adorn the Flagler room, formerly the grand parlor. **Time:** Allow 1 hour minimum. **Hours:** Tours typically depart daily at 10 and 2 but are subject to cancellation. Phone ahead to confirm schedule. **Cost:** $10; $8 (ages 65+ and active military with ID); $1 (ages 0-12). **Phone:** (904) 819-6400. GT

GEM **LIGHTNER MUSEUM,** 75 King St., is housed in the former Alcazar Hotel, built by Henry Flagler in 1888. In 1948 Otto C. Lightner, the Chicago publisher and editor of *Hobbies* magazine, converted the empty hotel into a museum to contain his vast collection of decorative and fine arts, artifacts and other antiques.

Four floors display furnishings, paintings, Victorian art glass, cut and blown glass, and natural history specimens. Other highlights include Oriental art, art nouveau works and the Victorian Village portraying 19th-century life. The museum's collections are displayed within the hotel's entertainment center where the spa level and ballroom were located and can still be seen. The former indoor swimming pool, which was one of the largest of its day, is now the site of the Cafe Alcazar.

The museum is self-guiding with docents available to answer questions. Nineteenth-century mechanical musical instruments are demonstrated daily at 11 and 2. **Time:** Allow 2 hours minimum. **Hours:** Daily 9-5. Last admission 30 minutes before closing. Closed Thanksgiving and Christmas Eve (at 2), and Christmas. **Cost:** $15; $12 (ages 65+, college students with ID and active military with ID); $8 (ages 12-17). Prices may be higher during special events. **Phone:** (904) 824-2874.

GEM **OLDEST HOUSE,** 14 St. Francis St. at the s. end of the seawall, also known as the González-Alvarez House, is said to be Florida's oldest documented Spanish Colonial dwelling. Built on a site occupied since the early 1600s, the present structure, with coquina walls and hand-hewn cedar beams, dates from the early 1700s.

A number of alterations brought the house into its current shape and size, reflecting both Spanish and British architectural styles. The house is furnished to represent its different periods. An ornamental garden typifies plants grown by the Spanish, British and American occupants. The complex includes the Page L. Edwards Gallery, highlighting the city's history through changing exhibits, and Manucy Museum, tracing 450 years of the state's history.

Time: Allow 1 hour minimum. **Hours:** Daily 9-5. Tours are given every half hour; the last tour departs 30 minutes before closing. Closed Easter, Thanksgiving and Christmas. **Cost:** $8; $7 (ages 55+ and military with ID); $4 (students with ID); $18 (family, two adults and up to five children). **Phone:** (904) 824-2872. GT

OLDEST WOODEN SCHOOLHOUSE, 14 St. George St., was built 1750-60 of cypress and cedar and is among the nation's oldest. Automated mannequins representing the professor and his students dressed in period clothing relate the school's history and explain the barter system, subjects studied and the use of the dunce cap. Schoolbooks, slates, old maps and other artifacts are displayed. The kitchen, separated from the main building to reduce the risk of fire, is open to the public. **Time:** Allow 30 minutes minimum. **Hours:** Daily 9-6 (also Fri.-Sat. 6-8 p.m.). **Cost:** $5; $4 (ages 6-12). **Phone:** (904) 824-0192 or (888) 653-7245.

PEÑA-PECK HOUSE, 143 St. George St., was built in the 1750s of native coquina stone. Originally the home of Spanish Royal Treasurer Juan Estevan de Peña, it became the home of British government in North America south of Canada after the Revolutionary War until 1785. Dr. Seth Peck bought the property in 1837. Displays include early Spanish artifacts and Peck family furnishings from the 18th

(See maps & indexes p. 263, 266.)

century. Much of the original artwork has been restored; the kitchen has been staged to appear as it did in 1840. **Time:** Allow 30 minutes minimum. **Hours:** Tours depart Sun.-Fri. 12:30-4, Sat. 10:30-4. Last tour begins 30 minutes before closing. Closed major holidays. **Cost:** Donations. **Phone:** (904) 829-5064. GT

ST. AUGUSTINE PIRATE & TREASURE MUSEUM is 1.5 mi. s. of SR 16 at 12 S. Castillo Dr. The museum houses more than 800 pirate artifacts, including such items as Captain Kidd's last voyage journal, an original Jolly Roger flag and an authentic pirate treasure chest. Original shipwreck treasures on display includes gold, silver, jewelry and weapons. Interactive displays enhance the experience. **Time:** Allow 45 minutes minimum. **Hours:** Daily 10-7. Closed Christmas. **Cost:** $12.99; $6.99 (ages 5-12). **Phone:** (904) 819-1444 or (877) 467-5863.

VILLA ZORAYDA MUSEUM, 83 King St., features Moorish architecture reminiscent of Spain's Alhambra Palace. The palatial residence was built of coquina and Portland cement in the 1880s by Franklin Smith and includes arches, columns, traceries and an interior courtyard as well as extensive collections of antiques, art and furnishings from the previous owners. Smith introduced the coquina construction method that was later used by Henry Flagler for his St. Augustine hotels. Audio tours are available in English, Spanish and French. Docent-led candlelight tours are available during the Christmas holidays.

Time: Allow 1 hour minimum. **Hours:** Mon.-Sat. 10-5, Sun. 11-4. Last tour departs 30 minutes before closing. Closed Easter, Thanksgiving, Christmas Eve and Christmas. **Cost:** Audio tours $10; $9 (ages 60+ and military with ID); $8 (ages 13-18 and students with ID); $5 (ages 8-12). Guided tours $17; $9 (ages 8-12). Reservations are required for guided tours. **Phone:** (904) 829-9887. GT

XIMENEZ-FATIO HOUSE, 20 Aviles St., is a well-preserved merchant's house and store dating to the Second Spanish Period 1783-1819. The house has been restored to the Territorial Period 1821-61, when it was operated as an inn. **Time:** Allow 30 minutes minimum. **Hours:** Tues.-Sat. 11-4. Tours are conducted on the half hour. Last tour begins 30 minutes before closing. **Cost:** $10; $8 (ages 65+ and students and military with ID); $20 (family). **Phone:** (904) 829-3575. GT

Other Points of Interest

GEM **AUTHENTIC OLD JAIL COMPLEX,** 167 San Marco Ave., centers on the history of the Old Jail, which was constructed by the same company that built Alcatraz; other things to do on-site include Florida Heritage Museum and Old Town Trolley Tours of St. Augustine. **Hours:** Daily 9-4:30. Closed Christmas. **Cost:** Old Jail $13.83; $7.44 (ages 6-12). Combinations and discounts available; phone ahead for schedule and admission. **Phone:** (904) 531-3248. GT

The Authentic Old Jail, 167 San Marco Ave., contains a large collection of weapons and displays that illustrate prison life in early St. Augustine. Costumed guides portray deputy sheriffs, their wives and jail prisoners. Visitors may tour the family's living quarters, which are in the same building as the prisoners' cells. Newspaper articles and photographs depict the history of the jail. **Time:** Allow 30 minutes minimum. **Hours:** Guided tours depart daily every 20 minutes 9-4:30. Closed Christmas. **Cost:** $12.45; $5.47 (ages 6-12). **Phone:** (904) 531-3248. GT

Old Town Trolley Tours, departing 167 San Marco Ave., offers a narrated 70-minute tour of the city with stops at 22 sites. Passengers may reboard the open-air trolleys at their own pace. **Hours:** Tours depart every 15-20 minutes daily 9-4:30. **Cost:** Fare (good for 3 days; includes admission to St. Augustine History Museum) $25.86; $10.35 (ages 6-12). Ticket is valid for 3 consecutive days. **Phone:** (904) 531-3248 or (888) 910-8687. GT

St. Augustine History Museum, 167 San Marco Ave., depicts Florida's growth from early Native American cultures through the Flagler era. Personal items and pictures of Henry Flagler are displayed along with a model railroad tracing the route he established between Jacksonville and Key West. Additional exhibits focus on the Florida Cracker, Fort Mose, Confederate items, 16th-century Spanish weapons, a life-size sunken ship and its treasures, and a replica of a Native American village. **Time:** Allow 1 hour minimum. **Hours:** Daily 8:30-5. Closed Christmas. **Cost:** $6.39; $5.33 (ages 6-12); free (with Old Town Trolley Tours ticket). **Phone:** (904) 531-3248.

MISSION OF NOMBRE DE DIOS is at 27 Ocean Ave., 5 blks. n. of the city gate on San Marco Ave. Pedro Menéndez de Avilés landed here Sept. 8, 1565, and established the first permanent community. A 208-foot stainless-steel cross marks the site of the founding of St. Augustine. The Shrine of Our Lady of La Leche and Mission Nombre de Dios Museum, which houses Menéndez's casket and exhibits, are on the grounds.

Time: Allow 1 hour minimum. **Hours:** Mon.-Sat. 9-5, Sun. noon-4. Museum Mon.-Sat. 9-4, Sun. noon-4. Closed Thanksgiving and Christmas. Phone ahead to confirm schedule. **Cost:** Donations. **Phone:** (904) 824-2809 or (800) 342-6529.

PONCE DE LEÓN'S FOUNTAIN OF YOUTH ARCHAEOLOGICAL PARK, e. of SR A1A (San Marco Ave.) on Williams St. to 11 Magnolia Ave., is on the site claimed to be Ponce de León's landing place Apr. 3, 1513 and the site of the 1565 Pedro Menendez settlement, the original location of St. Augustine.

(See maps & indexes p. 263, 266.)

The park contains the Timucuan Indian spring Ponce de León hoped was the Fountain of Youth. A cross of coquina stones excavated in 1909 is thought to be the claiming landmark. Remains of Christian Native American burials and archeological exhibits are on the grounds. Also located in the park is the reconstructed Mission Church of Nombre de Dios, built here in 1587 and a living-history blacksmith.

A planetarium offers a display about star navigation, and an observation deck provides views of marshland. Black powder and cannon firing demonstrations also are offered. **Time:** Allow 1 hour minimum. **Hours:** Daily 9-6. Last admission 1 hour before closing. Closed Christmas. **Cost:** $15; $14 (ages 60+ and active military with ID); $9 (ages 6-12); free (ages 0-5). **Phone:** (904) 829-3168 or (800) 356-8222.

GEM **ST. AUGUSTINE ALLIGATOR FARM ZOOLOGICAL PARK,** 1.75 mi. s.e. on SR A1A, on Anastasia Island, features a complete collection of the 23 crocodilian species, including rare white alligators. An elevated walkway winds through a rookery and over an alligator swamp. Florida wildlife shows are presented hourly. **Time:** Allow 2 hours minimum. **Hours:** Daily 9-6, Memorial Day-Labor Day; 9-5, rest of year. **Cost:** $26.99; $15.99 (ages 3-11). **Phone:** (904) 824-3337.

ST. AUGUSTINE LIGHTHOUSE AND MUSEUM is 1 mi. s.e. on SR A1A, then n. on Red Cox Dr. on Anastasia Island. St. Augustine's maritime past is reflected in this working lighthouse and restored keeper's house. Visitors may climb the 219 stairs to the top of the tower for a panoramic view of the city and its beaches. Highlights include exhibits illustrating the lives of lightkeepers and U.S. Coast Guard personnel who were stationed in St. Augustine during World War II. Shipwreck artifacts also are featured.

Themed guided tours are available; phone ahead to confirm schedule. **Hours:** Daily 9-7, Memorial Day-Labor Day; 9-6, rest of year. Last admission 15 minutes before closing. Guided behind-the-scenes tours depart on the hour 11-3. Closed Christmas. **Cost:** $12.95; $10.95 (ages 0-12 and 60+); free (active military with ID). Under 44 inches tall are not admitted to the lighthouse tower. **Phone:** (904) 829-0745. GT

GEM **WORLD GOLF HALL OF FAME & MUSEUM AT WORLD GOLF VILLAGE,** .5 mi. w. of I-95 exit 323, is a showcase for the game of golf. The World Golf Hall of Fame pays tribute to the history of the game and honors its members through exhibits of more than 3,000 pieces of memorabilia and artifacts, video presentations and interactive golfing activities. The village consists of the World Golf Hall of Fame & Museum, Hall of Fame Challenge Hole, a 3D IMAX theater, two championship golf courses, a golf academy, resort hotels, a convention center, restaurants and shopping.

Audio tours are available. **Hours:** Mon.-Sat. 10-6, Sun. noon-6. Last admission 45 minutes before closing. IMAX schedule varies; phone ahead. Closed Thanksgiving and Christmas. **Cost:** Museum (good for two consecutive days) and one shot at Challenge Hole $20.95; $19.95 (ages 55+ and military with ID); $10 (students with ID); $5 (ages 5-12). Audio tour $3 or two for $5. **Phone:** (904) 940-4133 for IMAX theater. GT

World Golf Hall of Fame IMAX Theater is .5 mi. w. of I-95 exit 323. The 300-seat 3D IMAX theater shows full-length feature films and documentaries on an 80-foot-wide, six-story-high screen. Film topics vary. **Hours:** Phone ahead to confirm schedule. **Cost:** Feature-length film $13; $12 (ages 55+ and students and military with ID); $10 (ages 3-12). Documentary $8.50; $7.50 (ages 55+ and students and military with ID); $6.50 (ages 3-12). **Phone:** (904) 940-4629 or (904) 940-4133.

AAA Walking Tours

The Old City

See St. Augustine Walking Tour map page p. 257.

The tour will take 1-2 hours, depending on your pace as well as the number of listed sites you visit and plaques you stop to read along the way. Those attractions appearing in bold type have detailed listings in The Old City section. Even if you decide not to visit a listed site, reading the listing when you reach that point should make the tour more interesting.

The best place to park is in the Historic Downtown Parking Facility adjacent to the Visitor Information Center, 10 W. Castillo Dr., across from the Castillo de San Marcos. Keep in mind that no automobiles are permitted on St. George Street north of the Plaza de la Constitución. (Most paid parking around there is enforced Mon.-Sat. 10-5 and federal holidays; phone ahead to confirm schedule.)

St. Augustine, compact and full of history, is a great place for a stroll. Influenced by the Timucuan Indians and placed under Spanish and English rule before becoming a U.S. territory, the city retains the flavors of its multicultured past. In the early 18th century, the walled city was entered through the City Gates, and this remains a logical place to begin a walk through Old St. Augustine. The Spanish built the wall surrounding the city in 1739 for defense; this gateway connected the wall, which was constructed of palm logs, dirt, cacti and coquina (soft limestone containing shell and coral fragments, quarried locally on Anastasia Island). The pillars, also made of coquina, were added in 1808. Closed at dusk, the gates protected the north end of the city. A replica of the log wall runs from the gates to the **Castillo de San Marcos,** which you can see by looking east toward the water. Looking west from the gates, you can see the Santo Domingo Redoubt, an important defensive position.

(See maps & indexes p. 263, 266.)

The Huguenot Cemetery, just north of the City Gates, serves as a final resting place for many non-Catholics, not solely French immigrants. An outbreak of yellow fever coupled with the fact that the Catholic cemetery inside the city walls would not accept Protestants brought about its founding in 1821.

Begin by heading south on narrow St. George Street, where second-story balconies add interest to simple buildings and whitewashed walls hide courtyards. More than 50 houses and craft shops have been restored or reconstructed on this pedestrians-only lane, where it seems there are always groups of school children on field trips.

The first spot the kids flock to is the **Oldest Wooden Schoolhouse,** on the right at 14 St. George St. The cedar building also served as a guardhouse during the Seminole Wars due to its proximity to the City Gates. If you can beat the crowd, check out its tabby floors (a mixture of crushed oyster shells and lime) and wooden peg construction.

The major part of the restoration area begins as you cross Fort Alley. The reconstructed **Colonial Quarter,** 33 St. George St., is a living-history museum demonstrating daily life in the 16th-, 17th- and 18th centuries. Noteworthy structures in the village include a Spanish soldier's dwelling, a leatherworker's shop and a blacksmith's forge.

Note the National Greek Orthodox Shrine, 41 St. George St., dedicated to the Greek colony of New Smyrna, where Greek immigrants were kept as servants. Its St. Photios Chapel is decorated with icons and frescoes depicting Greek Orthodox theology. Gold leaf highlights much of the chapel's artwork, and sounds of Byzantine music fill the halls.

On the west side of the block at the corner of Cuna Street is the Sánchez de Ortigosa House. Nearby are the reconstructed wooden buildings comprising the Peso de Burgo/Pellicer House, occupied by a Minorcan family 1763-83.

Proceed along St. George, enjoying the warm tones of ancient coquina stonework and the glimpses of courtyards between many of the buildings. At 105 St. George is the Sánchez House, a restored coquina and masonry building (now home to a crystal shop); house tours are offered.

As you cross Hypolita Street, look out for the sightseeing tram that shuffles by, accompanied by clanging bells.

Glance down Treasury Street, one of the narrowest streets in the Old City. On the left, the **Peña-Peck House** occupies the corner of Treasury and St. George; built in the 1690s for the Spanish treasurer, it was later occupied by a British doctor whose wife often used the house for high-society get-togethers. The art and furnishings reflect an extravagant lifestyle.

The tower on your left is part of the large **Cathedral-Basilica of St. Augustine,** which faces the Plaza de la Constitución. Founded in 1565, the parish holds what are said to be the country's oldest parish records, dating from 1594. The present cathedral was built in 1797 in the Spanish Mission style; following a fire in 1887 it was restored and its adjacent Spanish Renaissance-style bell tower was added. Inside the church, oil paintings are replicas of those found in the Vatican's Pauline Chapel. Victorian stained glass and sculpted marble also adorn the interior. (You might choose to visit the church later, as the route circles back this way.)

Cross Cathedral Place and continue south along St. George. To your left is the **Plaza de la Constitución,** which extends east toward the bay. Established in 1598 by an edict from King Phillip II, it was the hub of the original settlement. In the center is a monument dedicated to the Spanish Constitution of 1812.

The building to your right on the corner of St. George and King streets is the **Governor's House Cultural Center and Museum.** Dating to the 1700s, the site served as the headquarters for Spanish, English and territory governors 1595-1821. It is now home to the St. Augustine Preservation Board and contains interesting artifacts and Spanish treasure.

Turn right at King Street. At Cordova Street, the Casa Monica Hotel will be on your left. This Spanish/Moorish-style structure, one of three hotels owned by railroad magnate Henry Flagler, has a long history. Born as a grand hotel in 1887, it later served as the county courthouse for nearly 30 years before reopening in its present state.

Now look to the right. You can't miss the former Ponce de León Hotel—a huge Moorish-style palace with tall spires, turrets and a red-tiled roof. Built in 1888 by Henry Flagler as part of his grand plan to turn the city into an exclusive winter retreat, the hotel was the country's first major building to be crafted using poured concrete. The interior is posh: It features Tiffany stained glass, imported marble and carved oak. A beautiful courtyard, open to the public, leads to the foyer. Since 1968 the building has served as the main hall of Flagler College; it has what is arguably the fanciest student dining room. Guided tours are available.

Across the street from Flagler College is the third of Henry Flagler's hotels—the Spanish Renaissance Revival-style Alcazar Hotel, which also opened in 1888. Its design was based on the royal palace in Seville, Spain. Palm trees, fountains and a statue of Pedro Menéndez front the large building, which shelters City Hall and the **Lightner Museum.** Flagler would be proud—the museum's collection of decorative arts is quite affluent.

If you like, continue 1 block west on King Street to **Villa Zorayda Museum,** a smaller re-creation of the 13th-century Spanish Alhambra in Granada.

Retrace your steps along King to St. George. At the corner of St. George and King is Trinity Episcopal Church, established in 1830 and said to be the oldest Protestant church in Florida. Turn right onto St. George and make a left on narrow Artillery Lane to enter the city's oldest section.

(See maps & indexes p. 263, 266.)

At Aviles Street, turn right. At the corner of Cadiz Street is the two-story **Ximenez-Fatio House** (it's the one surrounded by the white picket fence). This late 18th-century coquina house has been restored and is furnished to reflect an 1850s boarding house.

Traipse back on Aviles, where galleries and boutiques reside. On the right, at 3 Aviles, is the **Spanish Military Hospital Museum** (once called the Hospital of our Lady Guadalupe), which has displays depicting day-to-day operations of the 18th century.

Head back to the Plaza de la Constitución by continuing north on Aviles. The market building to your right is a replica of the original. Turn right on Cathedral Street and walk for one block to Charlotte Street. From here you can see the life-size statue (on the east end of the plaza) of Juan Ponce de León, who landed in 1513. To the east the Bridge of Lions, a Mediterranean-style bridge built in 1927, crosses Matanzas Bay. Tile-roofed towers, arches and lion statues grace the structure, which is on the National Register of Historic Places.

Turn left on Charlotte and proceed north. A three-block walk past boutiques, antiques shops and bed and breakfast inns leads to Cuna Street. Look northeast from the corner of Charlotte and Cuna for a good view of the fort and bay. Turn left on Cuna, where more stores in restored buildings entice shoppers. At St. George, turn right. The City Gates, where you began your tour, is about a block north.

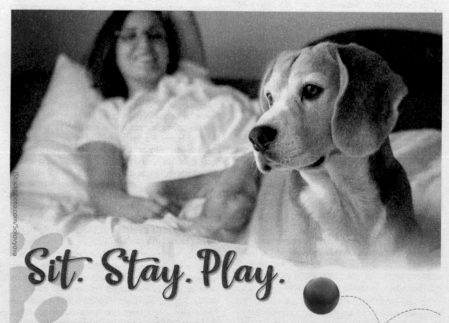

iStockphoto.com/Solovyova

Sit. Stay. Play.

Discover thousands of pet-friendly places to stay, play and dine. Get insight to guide your decisions. And enter your favorite photo in the next AAA Pet Travel Photo Contest*.

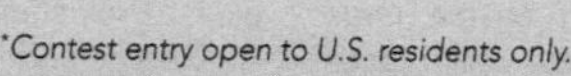

*Contest entry open to U.S. residents only.

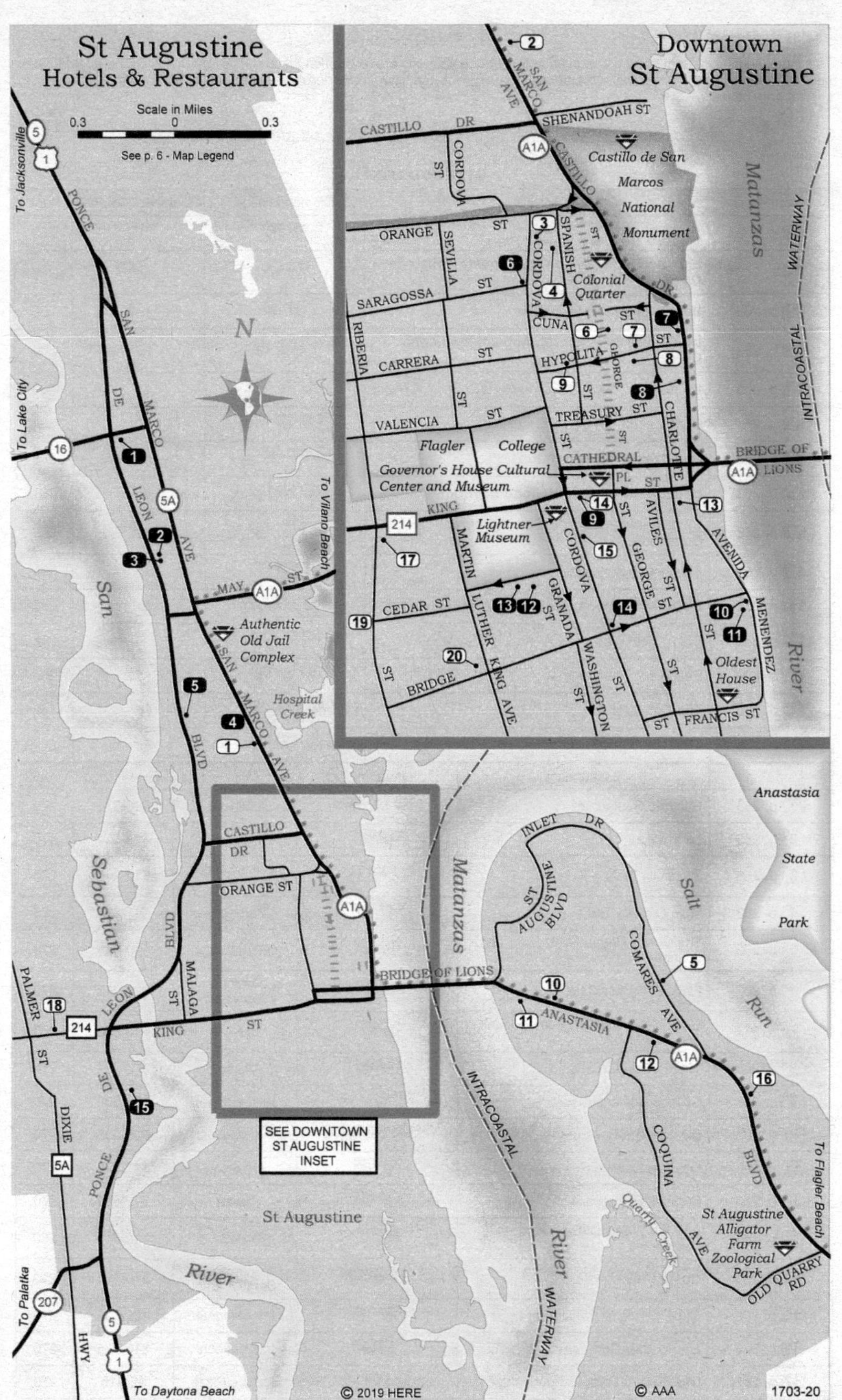

St Augustine
Hotels & Restaurants
Scale in Miles
0.3 0 0.3
See p. 6 - Map Legend
Downtown
St Augustine
Castillo de San Marcos National Monument
Colonial Quarter
Flagler College
Governor's House Cultural Center and Museum
Lightner Museum
Oldest House
Authentic Old Jail Complex
Anastasia State Park
St Augustine Alligator Farm Zoological Park
SEE DOWNTOWN ST AUGUSTINE INSET
To Jacksonville
To Lake City
To Vilano Beach
To Palatka
To Daytona Beach
To Flagler Beach
Matanzas River
San Sebastian River
St Augustine River
Salt Run
Hospital Creek
Quarry Creek
INTRACOASTAL WATERWAY
BRIDGE OF LIONS
© 2019 HERE
© AAA
1703-20

St. Augustine

This index helps you "spot" where approved hotels and restaurants are located on the corresponding detailed maps. Restaurant price range is a combination of lunch and/or dinner. Turn to the listing page for more information and consult display ads for special promotions.

For more details, rates and reservations: **AAA.com/travelguides/hotels**

ST. AUGUSTINE

Map Page	Hotels	Diamond Rated	Member Savings	Page
1 p. 263	Jaybird's Inn	2 diamonds		269
2 p. 263	**Hampton Inn by Hilton St. Augustine-Historic District**	2 diamonds	✔	269
3 p. 263	**Best Western Historical Inn**	2 diamonds	✔	268
4 p. 263	**Doubletree by Hilton St. Augustine Historic District**	3 diamonds	✔	269
5 p. 263	**Holiday Inn: St. Augustine-Historic**	3 diamonds	✔	269
6 p. 263	Casa de Suenos Bed & Breakfast	3 diamonds		268
7 p. 263	**Best Western Bayfront Inn**	2 diamonds	✔	268
8 p. 263	**Hilton St. Augustine Historic Bayfront**	3 diamonds	✔	269
9 p. 263	**Casa Monica Resort & Spa, Autograph Collection**	3 diamonds	✔	268
10 p. 263	Bayfront Marin House	3 diamonds		268
11 p. 263	**Bayfront Westcott House Bed & Breakfast Inn**	3 diamonds	✔	268
12 p. 263	Cedar House Inn	3 diamonds		268
13 p. 263	Peace and Plenty Inn	3 diamonds		269
14 p. 263	**The Collector Inn**	4 diamonds	✔	268
15 p. 263	**TRYP by Wyndham**	3 diamonds	✔	269

Map Page	Restaurants	Diamond Rated	Cuisine	Price Range	Page
1 p. 263	Raintree Restaurant	3 diamonds	Continental	$10-$34	270
2 p. 263	Le Pavillon	2 diamonds	Continental	$14-$34	270
3 p. 263	Michael's Tasting Room	3 diamonds	Spanish Small Plates	$12-$40	270
4 p. 263	Mojo Old City BBQ	2 diamonds	Barbecue	$11-$20	270
5 p. 263	The Conch House Restaurant and Lounge	2 diamonds	International	$10-$26	270
6 p. 263	Florida Cracker Cafe	2 diamonds	Regional American	$13-$17	270
7 p. 263	Casa Maya Mexican Seafood Grill and Tequila Bar	2 diamonds	Mexican	$10-$30	270
8 p. 263	Thai House and Sushi Bar	2 diamonds	Asian	$12-$24	270
9 p. 263	Collage Restaurant	3 diamonds	International	$29-$56	270
10 p. 263	Blackfly The Restaurant	3 diamonds	International	$19-$34	270
11 p. 263	Gas Full Service Restaurant	2 diamonds	American	$11-$30	270
12 p. 263	Fratelli's Restaurant	2 diamonds	Italian	$11-$24	270
13 p. 263	A1A Ale Works Brewery and Restaurant	2 diamonds	International	$10-$30	269
14 p. 263	**Costa Brava**	3 diamonds	Mediterranean Small Plates	$15-$64	270
15 p. 263	Old City House Restaurant	2 diamonds	International	$21-$36	270
16 p. 263	**Gypsy Cab Company**	2 diamonds	International	$10-$25	270
17 p. 263	One Twenty Three Burger House	1 diamond	Burgers Pizza	$9-$15	270

Map Page	Restaurants (cont'd)	Diamond Rated	Cuisine	Price Range	Page
18 p. 263	The Present Moment Cafe	◆◆	Vegan Natural/ Organic	$8-$16	270
19 p. 263	Ice Plant Bar	◆◆◆	New American	$10-$33	270
20 p. 263	Preserved Restaurant	◆◆◆	Southern	$15-$32	270

Make the Connection

AAA guidebooks are just the beginning. Open the door to a whole lot more on **AAA.com**. Get extra travel insight, more information and online booking.

Find this symbol for places to look, book and save on AAA.com.

iStockphoto.com_shapecharge

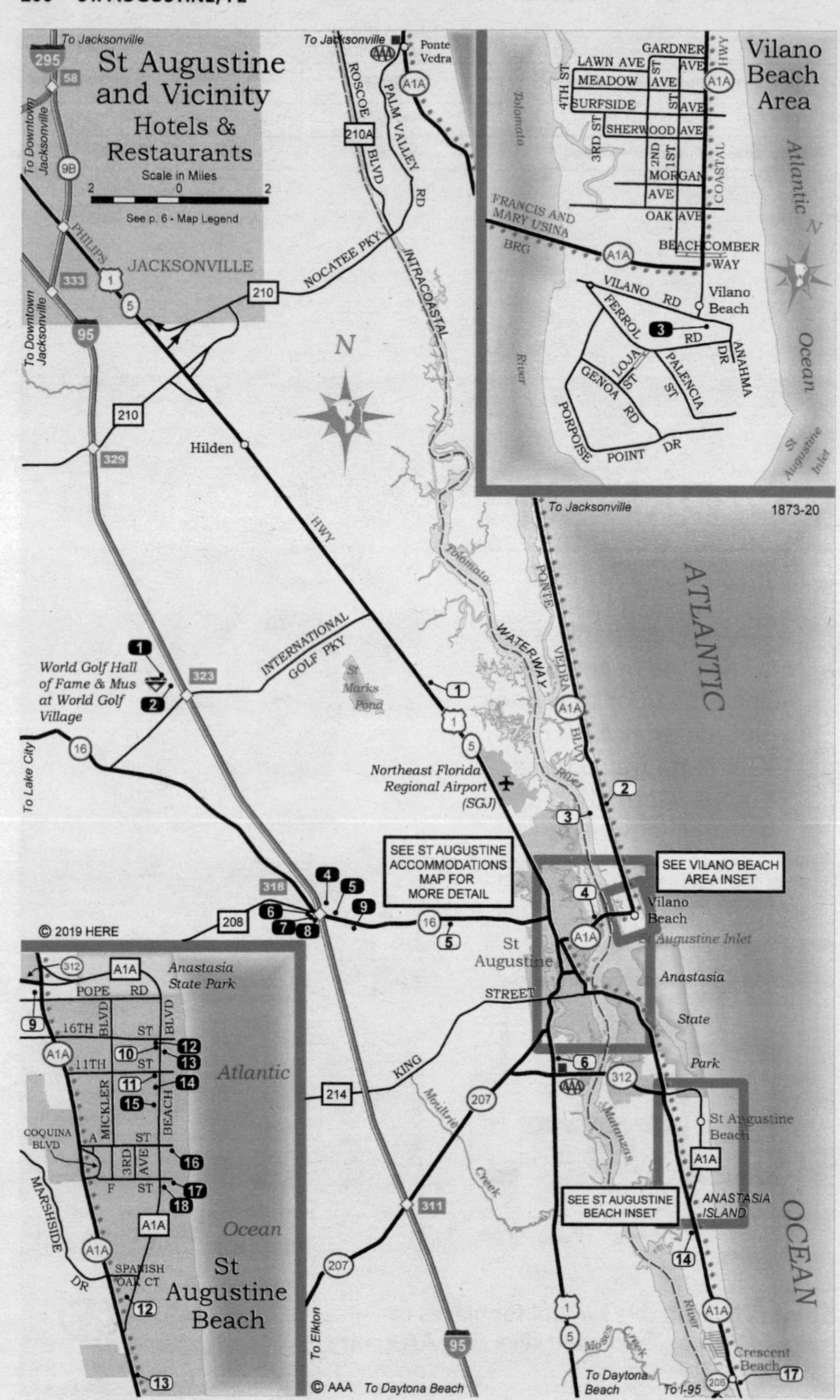
St Augustine and Vicinity
Hotels & Restaurants
Scale in Miles
See p. 6 - Map Legend
Vilano Beach Area
SEE ST AUGUSTINE ACCOMMODATIONS MAP FOR MORE DETAIL
SEE VILANO BEACH AREA INSET
SEE ST AUGUSTINE BEACH INSET
St Augustine Beach
To Jacksonville
To Downtown Jacksonville
JACKSONVILLE
Ponte Vedra
Hilden
World Golf Hall of Fame & Mus at World Golf Village
Northeast Florida Regional Airport (SGJ)
St Augustine
Vilano Beach
St Augustine Inlet
Anastasia State Park
ANASTASIA ISLAND
Crescent Beach
ATLANTIC OCEAN
To Lake City
To Elkton
To Daytona Beach
To I-95
1873-20
© 2019 HERE
© AAA

St. Augustine and Vicinity

This index helps you "spot" where approved hotels and restaurants are located on the corresponding detailed maps. Restaurant price range is a combination of lunch and/or dinner. Turn to the listing page for more information and consult display ads for special promotions.

For more details, rates and reservations: AAA.com/travelguides/hotels

ST. AUGUSTINE

Map Page	Hotels	Diamond Rated	Member Savings	Page
1 p. 266	Bluegreen Vacations Grande Villas at World Golf Village, an Ascend Resort Collection Member	◆◆◆		268
2 p. 266	Renaissance World Golf Village Resort	◆◆◆	✔	269
3 p. 266	Hampton Inn & Suites by Hilton St. Augustine-Vilano Beach	◆◆	✔	269
4 p. 266	**Fairfield Inn & Suites by Marriott St. Augustine I-95**	◆◆	✔	269
5 p. 266	Holiday Inn Express & Suites St Augustine North	◆◆◆		269
6 p. 266	Hampton Inn by Hilton St. Augustine I-95	◆◆	✔	269
7 p. 266	**Best Western Plus St. Augustine**	◆◆	✔	268
8 p. 266	Red Roof Inn St. Augustine	◆◆		269
9 p. 266	**Courtyard by Marriott St. Augustine I-95**	◆◆◆	✔	268

Map Page	Restaurants	Diamond Rated	Cuisine	Price Range	Page
1 p. 266	King's Head British Pub	◆◆	English	$10-$15	270
2 p. 266	The Reef	◆◆◆	Continental	$10-$39	270
3 p. 266	Aunt Kate's	◆◆	Seafood	$8-$26	269
4 p. 266	Kingfish Grill	◆◆	Seafood	$10-$30	270
5 p. 266	Wasabi Sushi King	◆◆	Japanese Sushi	$7-$43	270
6 p. 266	Creekside Dinery	◆◆	Seafood	$10-$24	270

ST. AUGUSTINE BEACH

Map Page	Hotels	Diamond Rated	Member Savings	Page
12 p. 266	**Hilton Garden Inn St. Augustine Beach**	◆◆◆	✔	271
13 p. 266	**Hampton Inn by Hilton St. Augustine Beach**	◆◆◆	✔	271
14 p. 266	**Best Western St. Augustine Beach Inn**	◆◆	✔	271
15 p. 266	**Courtyard by Marriott St. Augustine Beach**	◆◆◆	✔	271
16 p. 266	**House of Sea and Sun**	◆◆◆	✔	271
17 p. 266	Beachfront Bed & Breakfast	◆◆◆		270
18 p. 266	La Fiesta Ocean Inn & Suites	◆◆		271

Map Page	Restaurants	Diamond Rated	Cuisine	Price Range	Page
9 p. 266	Saigon Pho Bistro	◆◆	Vietnamese	$8-$12	271
10 p. 266	Sunset Grille	◆◆	American	$11-$40	271
11 p. 266	Cafe Eleven	◆	American	$8-$15	271
12 p. 266	Sea Oats Caffe	◆	Breakfast Sandwiches	$6-$11	271
13 p. 266	The World Famous Oasis Deck & Restaurant	◆◆	American	$9-$23	271
14 p. 266	Purple Olive	◆◆◆	International	$17-$35	271

CRESCENT BEACH

Map Page	Restaurant	Diamond Rated	Cuisine	Price Range	Page
17 p. 266	South Beach Grill	◆◆	International	$11-$26	53

(See maps & indexes p. 263, 266.)

BAYFRONT MARIN HOUSE 904/824-4301 10

Historic Bed & Breakfast. **Address:** 142 Avenida Menendez 32084

BAYFRONT WESTCOTT HOUSE BED & BREAKFAST INN
904/825-4602 11

Historic Bed & Breakfast

Address: 146 Avenida Menendez 32084 **Location:** 1 blk s of Bridge of Lions. **Facility:** Across the street from Matanzas Bay, this property with a Victorian-style setting dates as far back as 1880. The rooms are decorated with period antiques and modern touches of today. 16 units. 2 stories (no elevator), interior/exterior corridors. **Parking:** no self-parking. **Featured Amenity: full hot breakfast.**

BEST WESTERN BAYFRONT INN
904/824-4482 7

Motel

AAA Benefit: Members save up to 15% and earn bonus points!

Address: 16 Avenida Menendez 32084 **Location:** I-95 exit 318 (SR 16), 5.5 mi e to San Marco Ave, then 1.7 mi s; in historic district. **Facility:** 59 units. 2 stories (no elevator), exterior corridors. **Parking:** on-site (fee). **Pool:** outdoor.

SOME UNITS

BEST WESTERN HISTORICAL INN
904/829-9088 3

Motel

AAA Benefit: Members save up to 15% and earn bonus points!

Address: 2010 N Ponce de Leon Blvd 32084 **Location:** On US 1 (Ponce de Leon Blvd), 0.5 mi s of jct SR 16. **Facility:** 39 units, some two bedrooms and kitchens. 2 stories (no elevator), exterior corridors. **Pool:** outdoor. **Guest Services:** coin laundry. **Featured Amenity: breakfast buffet.**

CALL

BEST WESTERN PLUS ST. AUGUSTINE
904/824-9229 7

Hotel

AAA Benefit: Members save up to 15% and earn bonus points!

Address: 2465 SR 16 32092 **Location:** I-95 exit 318 (SR 16), just w. **Facility:** 68 units. 4 stories, interior corridors. **Pool:** outdoor. **Activities:** hot tub, exercise room. **Guest Services:** coin laundry.

CALL

BLUEGREEN VACATIONS GRANDE VILLAS AT WORLD GOLF VILLAGE, AN ASCEND RESORT COLLECTION MEMBER
904/940-2000 1

Vacation Rental Condominium. **Address:** 100 Front Nine Dr 32092

CASA DE SUENOS BED & BREAKFAST 904/824-0887 6

Historic Bed & Breakfast. **Address:** 20 Cordova St 32084

CASA MONICA RESORT & SPA, AUTOGRAPH COLLECTION
904/827-1888 9

Historic Hotel

AAA Benefit: Members save 5% or more!

Address: 95 Cordova St 32084 **Location:** Downtown; in historic district. Across from Lightner Museum and Flagler College. **Facility:** Since 1888 this historic property has served many functions, including as a courthouse. Rooms are tastefully appointed and include imported furnishings. Enjoy the amenities of the Serenata Beach Club. 138 units, some two and three bedrooms. 5 stories, interior corridors. **Parking:** valet only. **Terms:** check-in 4 pm. **Amenities:** safes. **Dining:** Costa Brava, see separate listing. **Pool:** heated outdoor. **Activities:** hot tub, exercise room, spa. **Guest Services:** valet laundry, area transportation.

SOME UNITS

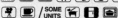

CEDAR HOUSE INN 904/829-0079 12

Historic Bed & Breakfast. **Address:** 79 Cedar St 32084

THE COLLECTOR INN
904/209-5800 14

Historic Boutique Hotel

Address: 149 Cordova St 32084 **Location:** Downtown; in historic district. Across from Lightner Museum. **Facility:** The buildings are set among beautiful, serene gardens. Antiques, hardwood floors and elegant furnishings keep the historic nature of the property. Each guest room has a living room and a kitchenette. 30 units, some two bedrooms. 2 stories (no elevator), interior/exterior corridors. **Parking:** valet only. **Amenities:** safes. **Pool:** heated outdoor. **Activities:** massage. **Guest Services:** valet laundry. **Featured Amenity: continental breakfast.**

CALL

SOME UNITS

COURTYARD BY MARRIOTT ST. AUGUSTINE I-95
904/826-4068 9

Hotel

AAA Benefit: Members save 5% or more!

Address: 2075 SR 16 32084 **Location:** I-95 exit 318 (SR 16), 0.3 mi e. **Facility:** 98 units. 3 stories, interior corridors. **Pool:** heated outdoor. **Activities:** hot tub, exercise room. **Guest Services:** valet and coin laundry, boarding pass kiosk.

COURTYARD

Near historic area, Dining & drinks at The Bistro, Free Wi-Fi, Outdoor pool & whirlpool, Fitness room.

(See maps & indexes p. 263, 266.)

DOUBLETREE BY HILTON ST. AUGUSTINE HISTORIC DISTRICT 904/825-1923 4

Hotel

AAA Benefit: Members save 5% or more!

Address: 116 San Marco Ave 32084 **Location:** Corner of Old Mission and San Marco aves; 0.5 mi n of downtown. **Facility:** 97 units. 5 stories, interior corridors. **Terms:** check-in 4 pm. **Amenities:** safes. **Pool:** heated outdoor. **Activities:** hot tub, exercise room. **Guest Services:** valet and coin laundry.

SAVE CALL / SOME UNITS HS

FAIRFIELD INN & SUITES BY MARRIOTT ST. AUGUSTINE I-95 904/810-9892 4

Hotel

Fairfield **AAA Benefit:** Members save 5% or more!

Address: 305 Outlet Mall Blvd 32084 **Location:** I-95 exit 318 (SR 16), just e, then just n. **Facility:** 86 units. 3 stories, interior corridors. **Amenities:** *Some:* safes. **Pool:** heated outdoor. **Activities:** hot tub, exercise room. **Guest Services:** valet and coin laundry. **Featured Amenity: continental breakfast.**

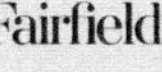

SAVE BIZ / SOME UNITS HS

HAMPTON INN & SUITES BY HILTON ST. AUGUSTINE-VILANO BEACH 904/827-9797 3

SAVE Hotel. **Address:** 95 Vilano Rd 32084

AAA Benefit: Members save 5% or more!

HAMPTON INN BY HILTON ST. AUGUSTINE-HISTORIC DISTRICT 904/829-1996 2

Hotel

AAA Benefit: Members save 5% or more!

Address: 2050 N Ponce de Leon Blvd 32084 **Location:** On US 1 (Ponce de Leon Blvd), 0.3 mi s of jct SR 16. **Facility:** 53 units. 3 stories, interior corridors. **Amenities:** safes. **Pool:** outdoor. **Activities:** hot tub, exercise room. **Guest Services:** valet and coin laundry. **Featured Amenity: breakfast buffet.**

SAVE ECO CALL

HAMPTON INN BY HILTON ST. AUGUSTINE I-95 904/824-4422 6

SAVE Hotel. **Address:** 2525 CR 208 32092

AAA Benefit: Members save 5% or more!

HILTON ST. AUGUSTINE HISTORIC BAYFRONT 904/829-2277 8

Hotel

AAA Benefit: Members save 5% or more!

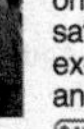

Address: 32 Avenida Menendez 32084 **Location:** I-95 exit 318 (SR 16), 5.5 mi e to San Marco Ave, then 1.8 mi s; in historic district. **Facility:** 72 units. 2 stories, interior corridors. **Parking:** valet only. **Terms:** check-in 4 pm. **Amenities:** safes. **Pool:** outdoor. **Activities:** hot tub, exercise room. **Guest Services:** valet and coin laundry.

SAVE ECO BIZ HS

HOLIDAY INN EXPRESS & SUITES ST AUGUSTINE NORTH 904/824-5151 5

Hotel. **Address:** 2300 SR 16 32084

HOLIDAY INN: ST. AUGUSTINE-HISTORIC 904/494-2100 5

Hotel

Address: 1302 N Ponce de Leon Blvd 32084 **Location:** 0.7 mi s of jct SR 16. **Facility:** 120 units. 4 stories, interior corridors. **Amenities:** *Some:* safes. **Pool:** outdoor. **Activities:** hot tub, exercise room. **Guest Services:** coin laundry.

SAVE ECO CALL BIZ HS

JAYBIRD'S INN 904/342-7938 1

Motel. **Address:** 2700 N Ponce de Leon Blvd 32084

PEACE AND PLENTY INN 904/829-8209 13

Historic Bed & Breakfast. **Address:** 87 Cedar St 32084

RED ROOF INN ST. AUGUSTINE 904/829-1999 8

Motel. **Address:** 2445 SR 16 32092

RENAISSANCE WORLD GOLF VILLAGE RESORT 904/940-8000 2

SAVE Resort Hotel. **Address:** 500 S Legacy Tr 32092

AAA Benefit: Members save 5% or more!

TRYP BY WYNDHAM 904/209-5580 15

Hotel

Address: 333 S Ponce de Leon Blvd 32084 **Location:** In historic district; 0.7 mi sw of center. **Facility:** 95 units. 5 stories, interior corridors. **Terms:** check-in 4 pm. **Amenities:** safes. **Pool:** heated outdoor. **Activities:** hot tub, exercise room. **Guest Services:** valet and coin laundry.

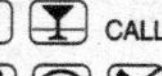

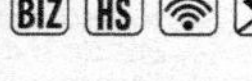

SAVE CALL BIZ HS

WHERE TO EAT

A1A ALE WORKS BREWERY AND RESTAURANT 904/829-2977 13

International. Gastropub. **Address:** 1 King St, Suite 101 32084

AUNT KATE'S 904/829-1105 3

Seafood. Casual Dining. **Address:** 612 Euclid Ave 32084

(See maps & indexes p. 263, 266.)

BLACKFLY THE RESTAURANT 904/201-6300 (10)

International. Casual Dining. **Address:** 108 Anastasia Blvd 32080

BONO'S PIT BAR-B-Q 904/794-9424

Barbecue. Casual Dining. **Address:** 2420 US 1 S 32086

CASA MAYA MEXICAN SEAFOOD GRILL AND TEQUILA BAR 904/823-0787 (7)

Mexican. Casual Dining. **Address:** 22 Hypolita St 32084

COLLAGE RESTAURANT 904/829-0055 (9)

International. Fine Dining. **Address:** 60 Hypolita St 32084

COLUMBIA RESTAURANT 904/824-3341

Spanish. Casual Dining. **Address:** 98 St. George St 32084

THE CONCH HOUSE RESTAURANT AND LOUNGE 904/829-8646 (5)

International. Casual Dining. **Address:** 57 Comares Ave 32080

COSTA BRAVA 904/810-6810 (14)

Mediterranean Small Plates Fine Dining $15-$64

AAA Inspector Notes: *Historic.* Enjoy a special experience in this upscale hotel, which dates to 1888. The dining rooms provide a mix of Southern Spain, Moroccan and contemporary décor elements with comfort and pleasing aesthetics in mind. There also is an appealing bar area between the lobby and restaurant. The menu highlights are divided into six sections including crudo, small plates, sharing plates, grill, entrées and desserts. The hunt platter, a charcuterie and cheese plate, is ideal for sharing. **Features:** full bar, Sunday brunch, happy hour. **Reservations:** suggested. **Address:** 95 Cordova St 32084 **Location:** Downtown; in historic district; in Casa Monica Resort & Spa, Autograph Collection. **Parking:** on-site (fee) and valet.

B L D CALL

CREEKSIDE DINERY 904/829-6113 (6)

Seafood. Casual Dining. **Address:** 160 Nix Boatyard Rd 32084

FLORIDA CRACKER CAFE 904/829-0397 (6)

Regional American. Casual Dining. **Address:** 81 St. George St 32084

FRATELLI'S RESTAURANT 904/819-1760 (12)

Italian. Casual Dining. **Address:** 415 Anastasia Blvd 32080

GAS FULL SERVICE RESTAURANT 904/217-0326 (11)

American. Casual Dining. **Address:** 9 Anastasia Blvd 32080

GYPSY CAB COMPANY 904/824-8244 (16)

International Casual Dining $10-$25

AAA Inspector Notes: Opened in 1983, this welcoming restaurant continues to draw a crowd. Purple, yellow and teal colors, as well as many eclectic, creative pieces of local art, create a vibrant aura. The "urban cuisine" menu, which features Southern, Cajun and Mediterranean influences, includes escargot, New York strip and braised lamb shank. The Key lime pie and chocolate mousse are sweet dessert temptations. **Features:** full bar, Sunday brunch. **Address:** 828 Anastasia Blvd 32080 **Location:** On SR A1A, 1 mi s of Bridge of Lions. **Parking:** on-site and street. L D

ICE PLANT BAR 904/829-6553 (19)

New American. Gastropub. **Address:** 110 Riberia St 32084

KINGFISH GRILL 904/824-2111 (4)

Seafood. Casual Dining. **Address:** 252 Yacht Club Dr 32084

KING'S HEAD BRITISH PUB 904/823-9787 (1)

English. Casual Dining. **Address:** 6460 US Hwy 1 N 32095

LE PAVILLON 904/824-6202 (2)

Continental. Casual Dining. **Address:** 45 San Marco Ave 32084

MICHAEL'S TASTING ROOM 904/810-2400 (3)

Spanish Small Plates. Casual Dining. **Address:** 25 Cuna St 32084

MOJO OLD CITY BBQ 904/342-5264 (4)

Barbecue. Casual Dining. **Address:** 5 Cordova St 32084

OLD CITY HOUSE RESTAURANT 904/826-0113 (15)

International. Casual Dining. **Address:** 115 Cordova St 32084

ONE TWENTY THREE BURGER HOUSE 904/687-2790 (17)

Burgers Pizza. Casual Dining. **Address:** 123 King St 32084

THE PRESENT MOMENT CAFE 904/827-4499 (18)

Vegan Natural/Organic. Casual Dining. **Address:** 224 W King St 32084

PRESERVED RESTAURANT 904/679-4940 (20)

Southern. Fine Dining. **Address:** 102 Bridge St 32084

RAINTREE RESTAURANT 904/824-7211 (1)

Continental. Casual Dining. **Address:** 102 San Marco Ave 32084

THE REEF 904/824-8008 (2)

Continental. Casual Dining. **Address:** 4100 Coastal Hwy 32084

SONNY'S REAL PIT BAR-B-Q 904/824-3315

Barbecue. Casual Dining. **Address:** 2720 SR 16 32092

THAI HOUSE AND SUSHI BAR 904/547-2095 (8)

Asian. Casual Dining. **Address:** 21 Hypolita St 32084

WASABI SUSHI KING 904/436-6688 (5)

Japanese Sushi. Casual Dining. **Address:** 965 SR 16, Suite 108/109 32084

ST. AUGUSTINE BEACH (D-4) pop. 6,176, elev. 10'

• Hotels & Restaurants map & index p. 266

Just 5 miles south of its notable neighbor St. Augustine, St. Augustine Beach is a quiet, relaxing vacation spot. Sea turtles nest here May through October, and furry creatures also enjoy the upscale beach community, as many of its businesses welcome dogs on a leash. On Wednesday mornings, bring your four-legged friend to the Wednesday Market at St. Johns County Pier Park (350 A1A Beach Blvd.), where 60-80 vendors purvey fresh produce, fine foods, and arts and crafts from 8-12:30. Pull up a lawn chair and attend a free summer concert at the same park on Wednesday evenings from mid-May to mid-October.

BEACHFRONT BED & BREAKFAST 904/461-8727 (17)

Bed & Breakfast. **Address:** 1 F St 32080

(See map & index p. 266.)

BEST WESTERN ST. AUGUSTINE BEACH INN
904/461-9990 **14**

Hotel

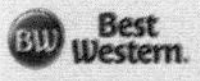
AAA Benefit: Members save up to 15% and earn bonus points!

Address: 541 A1A Beach Blvd 32080 **Location:** On Business Rt SR A1A, 1.3 mi s of jct SR 312 and A1A. **Facility:** 50 units, some two bedrooms and kitchens. 2 stories (no elevator), exterior corridors. **Pool:** outdoor. **Activities:** hot tub, beach access. **Guest Services:** coin laundry. **Featured Amenity: breakfast buffet.**

COURTYARD BY MARRIOTT ST. AUGUSTINE BEACH
904/940-3800 **15**

Hotel

COURTYARD **AAA Benefit:** Members save 5% or more!

Address: 605 A1A Beach Blvd 32080 **Location:** On Business Rt SR A1A; 1.3 mi s of jct SR 312 and A1A. **Facility:** 206 units. 4 stories, interior corridors. **Terms:** check-in 4 pm. **Pool:** outdoor. **Activities:** exercise room. **Guest Services:** coin laundry, boarding pass kiosk.

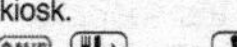  CALL 

HAMPTON INN BY HILTON ST. AUGUSTINE BEACH
904/471-4000 **13**

Hotel

AAA Benefit: Members save 5% or more!

Address: 430 A1A Beach Blvd 32080 **Location:** Oceanfront. On Business Rt SR A1A, 1.2 mi s of jct SR 312 and A1A. **Facility:** 100 units. 4 stories, interior corridors. **Terms:** check-in 4 pm. **Pool:** outdoor. **Activities:** hot tub, exercise room. **Featured Amenity: continental breakfast.**

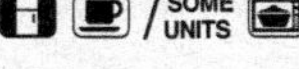 / SOME UNITS

HILTON GARDEN INN ST. AUGUSTINE BEACH
904/471-5559 **12**

Hotel

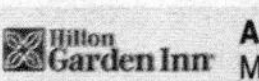
AAA Benefit: Members save 5% or more!

Address: 401 A1A Beach Blvd 32080 **Location:** Jct SR 312 and A1A, 1.1 mi e. **Facility:** 83 units. 3 stories, interior corridors. **Terms:** check-in 4 pm. **Pool:** outdoor. **Activities:** hot tub, exercise room. **Guest Services:** coin laundry.

 CALL

HOUSE OF SEA AND SUN
904/461-1716 **16**

Bed & Breakfast

Address: 2 B St 32080 **Location:** Oceanfront. Jct SR 312 and A1A, 1.9 mi s to B St, then just e. **Facility:** In a converted house built in the 1920s by the niece of Henry Flagler, the B&B overlooks the ocean and offers serenity. Some rooms have a private patio or balcony. Enjoy a gourmet breakfast daily. 7 units. 3 stories (no elevator), interior/exterior corridors. **Featured Amenity: full hot breakfast.**

/ SOME UNITS

LA FIESTA OCEAN INN & SUITES 904/471-2220 **18**
Motel. **Address:** 810 A1A Beach Blvd 32080

WHERE TO EAT

CAFE ELEVEN 904/460-9311 (11)
American. Casual Dining. **Address:** 501 A1A Beach Blvd 32080

PURPLE OLIVE 904/461-1250 (14)
International. Casual Dining. **Address:** 4255 A1A S, Suite 6 32080

SAIGON PHO BISTRO 904/461-9190 (9)
Vietnamese. Casual Dining. **Address:** 1935 A1A S 32080

SEA OATS CAFFE 904/471-7350 (12)
Breakfast Sandwiches. Casual Dining. **Address:** 1075 A1A Beach Blvd 32080

SUNSET GRILLE 904/471-5555 (10)
American. Casual Dining. **Address:** 421 A1A Beach Blvd 32080

THE WORLD FAMOUS OASIS DECK & RESTAURANT
904/471-3424 (13)
American. Casual Dining. **Address:** 4000 A1A S 32080

ST. CLOUD (G-4) pop. 35,183, elev. 63'

• **Hotels p. 272 • Restaurants p. 272**
• **Hotels & Restaurants map & index p. 197**
• **Part of Orlando area — see map p. 2**

The streets of downtown St. Cloud's historic business district, which features some 100 buildings and ranges from Florida to Massachusetts avenues and 8th through 13th streets, are lined with a variety of antique shops and retailers inviting treasure hunters with appliances, arts & crafts and furniture. The district plays host throughout the year to a number of special events, including a crawfish festival, car and motorcycle shows and live entertainment.

The town was founded in the early 1900s as a colony for elderly Civil War soldiers, eventually became an agricultural hub and now serves as an overflow tourist destination from its neighbors to the north, Walt Disney World® Resort and Orlando. The former Union fighters, many 70 years or older, were recruited for the area's purported climatic and health benefits. The 3 Cs of Florida farming—cane (sugar), cows and citrus—helped the area prosper until agriculture gave way to a tourist economy.

The St. Cloud Heritage Museum, located in the Veterans Memorial Library at 1012 Massachusetts Ave., offers a vast collection of pieces chronicling

(See map & index p. 197.)

city history as well as the stories of its founding individuals and organizations. Exhibits include area artifacts, articles, books and such items as historic records, photographs and postcards. The building was home to St. Cloud's first library and was built in 1922. For further information, phone (407) 957-7587 or (407) 414-2682, after hours.

Lakefront Park, 1104 Lakeshore Blvd., has a beach, fishing pier, marina and performing arts pavilion as well as bike and walking paths extending from Louisiana to Mississippi (avenues, that is). The 58-acre Peghorn Nature Park and Trail, 2101 Peghorn Way, offers nature programs; Hopkins Park, 620 E. 17th St., is home to a butterfly and vegetable garden. For program schedules and further information about these and other city parks, phone the St. Cloud Parks and Recreation Department at (407) 957-7243.

St. Cloud Greater Osceola Chamber of Commerce: 1200 New York Ave., St. Cloud, FL 34769. **Phone:** (407) 892-3671.

REPTILE WORLD SERPENTARIUM, 1 mi. e. on US 192 to 5705 E. Irlo Bronson Memorial Hwy., houses more than 50 species of snakes from around the world in glass display cases. Also featured are turtle, alligator and lizard exhibits. Venom programs are given daily at noon and 3. **Time:** Allow 1 hour, 30 minutes minimum. **Hours:** Tues.-Sun. 10-5. Venom shows are given at noon and 3. Closed Jan. 1, Easter, Thanksgiving, day after Thanksgiving, Christmas Eve, Christmas and Dec. 31. **Cost:** $11.50; $9.50 (ages 6-17); $8.50 (ages 3-5). **Phone:** (407) 892-6905.

Love the
Great Outdoors?

For getaways off the beaten path, visit AAA.com/campgrounds or AAA.com/maps for thousands of places to camp.

iStockphoto.com_pixelfit

BUDGET INN OF ST CLOUD 407/892-2858 17

Motel

Address: 602 13th St 34769 **Location:** On US 192/441, 0.5 mi e of the Water Tower, 2 mi w of jct CR 15. **Facility:** 17 units, some kitchens. 1 story, exterior corridors.

SAVE HS / SOME UNITS

WHERE TO EAT

CRABBY BILL'S 407/979-4001

Seafood. Casual Dining. **Address:** 1104 Lakeshore Dr 34769

SONNY'S REAL PIT BAR-B-Q 407/892-2285

Barbecue. Casual Dining. **Address:** 4475 13th St 34769

ST. PETE BEACH (H-1) pop. 9,346, elev. 5'

• **Restaurants p. 274**
• **Hotels & Restaurants map & index p. 286**
• **Part of St. Petersburg-Clearwater and Beaches area — see map p. 275**

A resort community on Long Key, St. Pete Beach is connected to the mainland by the St. Pete Beach Causeway and the Pinellas Bayway (toll). The town has good swimming beaches, several fishing piers and charter boat operations. Two trolleys, operated by PSTA, provide transportation in St. Pete Beach. The Central Avenue Trolley travels Central Avenue and Gulf Boulevard between St. Petersburg and Pass-A-Grille Beach. The Suncoast Beach Trolley travels Gulf Boulevard between Clearwater and St. Pete Beach; phone (727) 540-1900.

Tampa Bay Beaches Chamber of Commerce: 6990 Gulf Blvd., St. Pete Beach, FL 33706. **Phone:** (727) 360-6957 or (800) 944-1847.

Shopping: Dolphin Village Shopping Center, 4615 Gulf Blvd., has 30 specialty shops. The historic Corey Avenue area offers varied shops.

Nightlife: Lazy beach days call for lazy beach nights. At sundown, make your way to Crabby Bill's, 5100 Gulf Blvd., for the best crabs in town and take in fantastic views of the Gulf of Mexico and the Intracoastal Waterway from the tiki bar. After dinner, join the raucous crowd grooving to a one-man steel drum band at the Undertow Beach Bar, 3850 Gulf Blvd., where a bikini-clad waitstaff serves up frozen margaritas and sugary daiquiris. Keep track of the rubber duckies sailing around the bar's countertop moat, or head outside and put the Undertow's much-loved sand volleyball court to the test. Phone (727) 360-8858 for Crabby Bill's or (727) 368-9000 for the Undertow Beach Bar.

For an ultra-mellow, somewhat romantic and decidedly upscale experience head to The Don CeSar, a huge pink resort located on the beach where Gulf Boulevard connects to the SR 682 causeway. Order desserts from the outstanding in-house restaurant, then lounge on cushioned couches inside this historic hotel. Sit at a table in the elegant Lobby

(See map & index p. 286.)

Lounge, where an amazing pianist will play just about any song you call. Or, play Name That Tune to see who buys the next round; phone (727) 360-1881.

BAY PALMS WATERFRONT RESORT HOTEL AND MARINA 727/367-2791 **86**

Motel

Address: 4237 Gulf Blvd 33706 **Location:** Waterfront. On SR 699, 0.6 mi n of Pinellas Bayway. **Facility:** 15 units, some two bedrooms, efficiencies and kitchens. 2 stories (no elevator), exterior corridors. **Terms:** off-site registration. **Amenities:** safes. **Pool:** heated outdoor. **Activities:** boat dock, fishing. **Guest Services:** coin laundry.

/ SOME UNITS

BAYVIEW PLAZA WATERFRONT RESORT 727/367-2791 **85**

Motel

Address: 4321 Gulf Blvd 33706 **Location:** Waterfront. On SR 699, 0.6 mi n of Pinellas Bayway. **Facility:** 39 kitchen units. 2 stories (no elevator), interior/exterior corridors. **Terms:** off-site registration. **Amenities:** safes. **Pool:** heated outdoor. **Activities:** boat dock, fishing, exercise room. **Guest Services:** coin laundry.

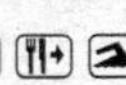

/ SOME UNITS

BEACH HOUSE SUITES BY THE DON CESAR 727/363-5050 **89**

Hotel

Address: 3860 Gulf Blvd 33706 **Location:** Oceanfront. On SR 699, 0.4 mi n of jct Pinellas Bayway. **Facility:** 70 kitchen units. 6 stories, exterior corridors. *Bath:* shower only. **Parking:** on-site (fee). **Terms:** check-in 4 pm. **Amenities:** safes. **Pool:** heated outdoor. **Activities:** hot tub, massage. **Guest Services:** complimentary laundry.

/ SOME UNITS

THE DON CESAR 727/360-1881 **90**

Classic Historic Resort Hotel

Address: 3400 Gulf Blvd 33706 **Location:** Oceanfront. On SR 699, jct Pinellas Bayway. **Facility:** Set on the Gulf of Mexico, the internationally recognized "pink palace" is a beacon to the beach. It boasts lavishly decorated public areas, specialty boutiques and a gorgeous pool and spa area. 277 units, some two bedrooms and kitchens. 10 stories, interior corridors. **Parking:** on-site (fee) and valet. **Terms:** check-in 4 pm. **Amenities:** video games, safes. **Dining:** 2 restaurants, also, Maritana Grille, Sea Porch Cafe, see separate listings, entertainment. **Pool:** heated outdoor. **Activities:** sauna, hot tub, steamroom, recreation programs, playground, game room, health club, spa. **Guest Services:** valet and coin laundry, area transportation.

CALL / SOME UNITS

For Any Occasion

AAA/CAA Members Save on Hotels

Great Rates, Great Brands, Great Guarantee

BW | Best Western Hotels & Resorts

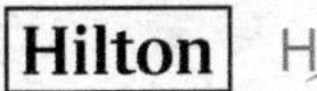

HYATT

VISIT over 1,100 AAA/CAA Offices | CLICK AAA.com/greatrates | CALL 1-866-222-7283

AAA Mobile
CAA Mobile

(See map & index p. 286.)

GRAND PLAZA BEACHFRONT RESORT & CONFERENCE CENTER 727/360-1811 84

Hotel. **Address:** 5250 Gulf Blvd 33706

HOTEL ZAMORA 727/456-8900 88

Hotel. **Address:** 3701 Gulf Blvd 33706

PALM CREST RESORT MOTEL 727/360-9327 87

Motel. **Address:** 3848 Gulf Blvd 33706

RUMFISH BEACH RESORT BY TRADEWINDS

727/360-5551 81

Resort Hotel

Address: 6000 Gulf Blvd 33706 **Location:** Oceanfront. On SR 699, 1.8 mi n of Pinellas Bayway. **Facility:** This beachside establishment offers a variety of room styles, sizes and features. The grounds are lovely with a waterfall and koi pond, hammocks, fire pits and a mechanical surfboard for the kids. 211 units, some two bedrooms and kitchens. 7 stories, interior/exterior corridors. **Parking:** on-site (fee). **Terms:** check-in 4 pm. **Amenities:** safes. **Dining:** 2 restaurants, nightclub, entertainment. **Pool:** heated outdoor. **Activities:** hot tub, cabanas, recreation programs, exercise room. **Guest Services:** valet and coin laundry.

SAVE ECO BIZ sHS

SIRATA BEACH RESORT

727/363-5100 83

Resort Hotel

Address: 5300 Gulf Blvd 33706 **Location:** Oceanfront. On SR 699, 1.2 mi n of Pinellas Bayway. **Facility:** Set on the Gulf of Mexico they offer a variety of activities such as personal water crafts, paddleboards, and parasailing. Rooms vary in size and configuration and many have great views of the beach. 382 units, some efficiencies and kitchens. 2-8 stories, interior/exterior corridors. **Parking:** on-site (fee). **Terms:** check-in 4 pm. **Amenities:** video games, safes. **Dining:** 3 restaurants, entertainment. **Pool:** heated outdoor. **Activities:** hot tub, cabanas, fishing, recreation programs, bicycles, playground, game room, exercise room. **Guest Services:** valet and coin laundry, boarding pass kiosk, rental car service.

SAVE ECO CALL BIZ sHS / SOME UNITS

TRADEWINDS ISLAND GRAND BEACH RESORT

727/367-6461 82

Resort Hotel

Address: 5500 Gulf Blvd 33706 **Location:** Oceanfront. On SR 699, 1 mi n of Pinellas Bayway. **Facility:** A winding stream—complete with paddleboats—meanders through the middle of this property, which is directly on the Gulf of Mexico. The resort offers several acres of tropically landscaped grounds. 585 units, some two bedrooms, kitchens and condominiums. 2-7 stories, interior/exterior corridors. **Parking:** on-site (fee) and valet. **Terms:** check-in 4 pm. **Amenities:** video games, safes. **Dining:** 3 restaurants, also, Palm Court Italian Grill, see separate listing, entertainment. **Pool:** heated outdoor. **Activities:** sauna, hot tub, cabanas, scuba diving, snorkeling, miniature golf, tennis, recreation programs, playground, lawn sports, health club, spa. **Guest Services:** valet and coin laundry.

SAVE ECO CALL BIZ sHS / SOME UNITS

WHERE TO EAT

BASIL LEAF THAI-SUSHI AND NOODLES 727/360-4000 125

Thai. Casual Dining. **Address:** 6395 Gulf Blvd 33706

BILLY'S STONE CRAB & LOBSTER 727/866-2115 135

Seafood. Casual Dining. **Address:** 1 Collany Rd 33715

CRABBY BILL'S 727/360-8858

Seafood. Casual Dining. **Address:** 5100 Gulf Blvd 33706

THE FROG POND RESTAURANT 727/363-7205 123

Breakfast Sandwiches. Casual Dining. **Address:** 7390 Gulf Blvd 33706

MARITANA GRILLE

727/360-1882 131

Continental Fine Dining
$30-$44

AAA Inspector Notes: Artistic presentations enhance creative entrées and add charm to any plate. For a light and tasty appetizer, try the foie gras or the tuna sashimi. The menu is seasonal and you may find on it items such as Anderson Ranch rack of lamb, diver scallops and Lake Meadows Cornish hen and Argentinian red shrimp. A private dining room and a chef's table are available for those wanting a more private meal. **Features:** full bar. **Reservations:** required. Semiformal attire. **Address:** 3400 Gulf Blvd 33706 **Location:** On SR 699, jct Pinellas Bayway; in The Don CeSar. **Parking:** on-site (fee) and valet. D CALL

PALM COURT ITALIAN GRILL 727/367-6461 128

Italian. Fine Dining. **Address:** 5500 Gulf Blvd 33706

SEA CRITTERS CAFE 727/360-3706 132

Seafood. Casual Dining. **Address:** 2007 Pass-A-Grille Way 33706

SEAHORSE TAVERN AND RESTAURANT 727/360-1734 134

Seafood. Casual Dining. **Address:** 800 Pass-A-Grille Way 33706

SEA PORCH CAFE 727/360-1884 130

Caribbean. Casual Dining. **Address:** 3400 Gulf Blvd 33706

SHELLS OF ST. PETE BEACH 727/826-0729 124

Seafood. Casual Dining. **Address:** 7081 Gulf Blvd 33706

SKIDDER'S RESTAURANT 727/360-1029 127

American. Casual Dining. **Address:** 5799 Gulf Blvd 33706

SNAPPER'S 727/367-3550 126

Seafood. Fine Dining. **Address:** 5895 Gulf Blvd 33706

SPINNERS ROOFTOP REVOLVING LOUNGE & BISTRO 727/360-1811 129

Steak Seafood. Fine Dining. **Address:** 5250 Gulf Blvd 33706

THE WHARF SEAFOOD RESTAURANT & WATERFRONT BAR

727/367-9469 133

Seafood Casual Dining
$5-$28

AAA Inspector Notes: A weathered exterior lends to the rustic appeal of this casual, nautically-themed restaurant which is located on the Intracoastal Waterway. Guests can enjoy great views of passing boats and wildlife while dining inside or on the waterside deck. House specials include grouper, tilapia, mahi mahi, fried seafood baskets, pasta dishes and sandwiches. **Features:** full bar, patio dining, happy hour. **Address:** 2001 Pass-A-Grille Way 33706 **Location:** On SR 699, 0.9 mi s of Pinellas Bayway; in Pass-A-Grille. L D

ST. PETERSBURG-CLEARWATER AND BEACHES

Such words as haven, refuge and sanctuary will likely spring to mind as you discover the St. Petersburg-Clearwater area's conglomeration of kitsch-crammed Florida highways and quaint main streets, Gulf Coast beach towns and strikingly untouched environs. Over the last few centuries, these idyllic surroundings have sheltered Tocobaga Indians, Spanish conquistadors and marauding pirates as well as, in more recent years, Greek sponge fishermen, condominium-loving snowbirds and culinary enthusiasts looking for the next best food places. Artistic enclaves from Dunedin to Gulfport safeguard creative expression in this perpetually inspiring milieu, while state parks, including Anclote Key Preserve and Honeymoon Island, protect delicate natural habitats and endangered fauna.

Whether you spend the day windsurfing on the Gulf or looking for where to eat in downtown St. Pete, you'll find yourself in good company. More than 13 million people vacation in this tranquil locale each year. Here, you can shop, dine and unwind in cities crisscrossing the Pinellas Peninsula, a 280-square-mile tract situated between Tampa Bay and the Gulf of Mexico, or explore the coastal communities of Pasco County, one of nine counties comprising a 980,000-acre expanse dubbed the "Nature Coast."

Since the late 1800s, tourism has been a key local industry. The completion of two bridges—the Gandy (1924) and the Courtney Campbell (1934), which linked Tampa with St. Petersburg and Clearwater respectively—helped firmly establish this expanse as a major travel destination. In fact, several elegant hotels and resorts built around the turn of the 19th century are still busy pampering discerning guests. Safety Harbor Resort and Spa, an elegant retreat built atop mineral springs, has welcomed travelers lured by the region's purported health benefits since the 1920s. St. Pete Beach's "pink palace," The Don CeSar, began operating in 1928 and remains a vacation hot spot.

This map shows cities in St. Petersburg-Clearwater and Beaches where you will find attractions, hotels and restaurants. Cities are listed alphabetically in this book on the following pages.

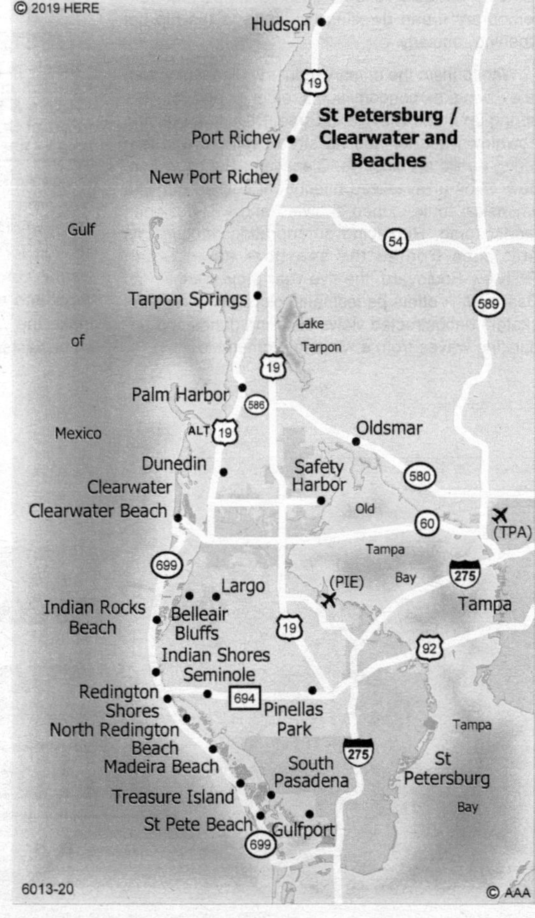

Home to Renaissance Vinoy, a Gatsby-era jewel overlooking Tampa Bay, St. Petersburg has long attracted wintering Northerners seeking a temperate climate and group travel enthusiasts. The city boasts an average 361 days of sunshine a year and holds the Guinness World Record for the most consecutive sunny days. Through the 1980s, St. Petersburg was widely known for its large population of sun-loving retirees; however, it has since emerged as a prominent cultural center. Today, you'll find nearly 30 art galleries and museums in town—from the expanded Morean Arts Center, featuring a permanent collection of Dale Chihuly's world-renowned glass art, to The Dalí Museum, an impressive waterfront abode for Salvador Dalí oil paintings, sculptures, photographs and other things to see.

Momentum also picked up on the sports scene with the addition of Major League Baseball's Tampa Bay Rays in 1998; 10 years later, the team won the American League Championship Series four games to three against the Boston Red Sox. Currently Florida's fourth largest city in terms of population, St. Petersburg continues to grow, with chic local restaurants, live music venues, upscale shops and contemporary urban dwellings catering to the hip set opening regularly.

With tourism the primary industry, Clearwater, too, is evolving, as condominiums, eateries and retailers spring up in the Cleveland Street District, a budding downtown quarter hosting street festivals and featuring public art displays. Clearwater Beach visitors now enjoy a revitalized beachfront decked out with whimsical turtle-topped showers and well-designed landscaping. Replacing deteriorating parking lots that once fronted the seashore along South Gulfview Boulevard, the five-year project known as Beach Walk offers pedestrians, bicyclists and in-line skaters unobstructed views of rolling dunes and undulating waves from a winding promenade.

Cultural heavyweight St. Petersburg draws erudite vacationers, and Clearwater's scenic vistas lure those seeking fun in the sun. But in this expansive destination area, these two captivating communities are just the crest of a foam-tipped wave. Many visitors choose to play on broad, graceful, white-sand beaches stretching for almost 35 miles from Crystal Beach south to Fort De Soto Park; others flock to Tarpon Springs to mingle with exuberant *Opa!*-shouting natives and eat at local restaurants during one of the city's food- and music-packed celebrations. Along with a wide variety of watery recreational pursuits and things to do, including saltwater fishing, scuba diving and canoeing, sightseeing opportunities abound in the vicinity—from Largo's arresting botanical gardens to Hubbard's Marina Cruises in Madeira Beach, where you can hop on a catamaran and scout the Gulf for dolphins. While a trip to the St. Petersburg-Clearwater area guarantees lots of R and R, you'll find your vacation also laced with a bit of adventure travel—no matter where your boogie board, kayak or beach cruiser takes you.

ST. PETERSBURG (E-8) pop. 244,769

• Hotels p. 293 • Restaurants p. 294
• Attractions map p. 282
• Hotels & Restaurants map & index p. 284, 286
• Part of St. Petersburg-Clearwater and Beaches area — see map p. 275

The American Medical Association was on to the bay area's bounty of recreational riches back in 1885, when it named St. Petersburg as an ideal destination for a "world health city." Near year-round warmth, broad beaches, a varied system of waterways and some 400 public parks and playgrounds make the region a true haven for adventure travel enthusiasts.

AAA
DISCOUNTS»REWARDS
DISCOUNTS
WITHOUT LIMITS
AAA.com/discounts

(See maps & indexes p. 284, 286.)

The Pinellas Trail, built along an abandoned railroad corridor, stretches 34 miles from Tarpon Springs to St. Petersburg. It provides opportunities for walking, jogging, bicycling and in-line skating. Many entry and exit points exist along the trail, with spurs going to Clearwater Beach and Honeymoon Island State Park. For information on things to do in St. Petersburg, contact the Pinellas County Parks and Conservation Resources, 12520 Ulmerton Rd. in Largo; phone (727) 582-2100.

Boasting an average 361 days of sunshine annually, St. Pete also allows for year-round golfing. The city's public and semiprivate courses include Baypointe, 9399 Commodore Dr., (850) 235-6950; Mainlands, 9445 Mainlands Blvd. W., (727) 577-4847; Mangrove Bay, 875 62nd Ave. N.E., (727) 893-7800; and Twin Brooks, 3800 22nd Ave. S., (727) 893-7445.

For racket pros, the St. Petersburg Tennis Center, 650 18th Ave. S., features 16 clay and four hard-surface courts; phone (727) 823-2225. For additional information phone the St. Petersburg Parks and Recreation Department at (727) 893-7441.

One of the world's largest shuffleboard clubs is at Mirror Lake Recreation Park in downtown St. Petersburg. Daily guest membership is available. The St. Petersburg Shuffleboard Club, next to Mirror Lake Recreation Park, open its shuffleboard lanes every Friday night and is among the fun things to do with friends in the area; phone (727) 822-2083.

If you'd rather exercise gray matter than muscles, try the St. Petersburg Chess Club on select days at 540 Fourth Ave. N. in Mirror Lake Recreation Park; phone (727) 822-1171. Or, contemplate at the First United Methodist Church, 212 Third. St. N., which houses a 10- by 18-foot stained-glass window of Da Vinci's masterpiece "The Last Supper"; phone (727) 894-4661.

A full season of symphonic presentations is brought to the area by the Florida Orchestra and by local dance companies. Performances take place at the Mahaffey Theater; (727) 893-7832 or (800) 874-9020 for ticket and schedule information.

Those seeking Broadway and off-Broadway plays should check out the American Stage Theater Company, the area's oldest professional theater at 163 Third St. N., for classical and contemporary plays in an intimate setting at the Raymond James Theatre that's ; phone (727) 823-7529. The St. Petersburg City Theatre, 4025 31st St. S., stages six major productions September through May; phone (727) 866-1973.

Get Downtown First Friday, a free street party offered in downtown on the first Friday of every month from 5:30-10 p.m, offers budget-friendly things for couples to do. The event features live jazz as well as arts and crafts.

Throughout the year, a number of other special events keep visitors busy. Williams Park; South Straub Park, next to the Museum of Fine Arts *(see attraction listing)* overlooking the inner harbor; and bayside Vinoy Park, near Straub Park, are settings for many St. Petersburg events and offer fun things to do with kids.

In late April or early May St. Petersburg hosts the St. Anthony's Triathlon. American Stage in the Park offers several weeks of professional theatrical productions under the stars mid-April to mid-May; phone (727) 823-7529. In late October or early November the city recognizes its ethnic groups during the International Folk Fair; offerings include folk dances and food places. To round out the year, the holiday Lighted Boat Parade takes place downtown at the waterfront in mid-December.

Sports fans flock to St. Pete to watch Major League Baseball's Tampa Bay Rays of the American League. The team plays April through September at Tropicana Field, 1 Tropicana Dr.; phone (727) 825-3137. The Rays' spring training games take place at Charlotte Sports Park, 2300 El Jobean Rd. in Port Charlotte; phone (941) 235-5010 for ticket information. The minor-league Charlotte Stone Crabs of Port Charlotte also play at the sports park; phone (941) 206-3511 or (941) 206-4487.

The St. Petersburg Kennel Club's Derby Lane track at 10490 Gandy Blvd. features greyhound racing most evenings and weekends; phone (727) 812-3339.

Note: Policies vary concerning admittance of children to pari-mutuel betting facilities. Phone for information.

The Downtown Looper trolley circles downtown St. Petersburg and affords visitors access to a variety of museums, shops and local restaurants. The trolleys operate Sun.-Thurs. 10-5, Fri.-Sat. 10-11:40; closed Martin Luther King Jr. Day, Thanksgiving and Christmas. Fare is 50c; 25c (ages 65+ and the physically impaired); free (ages 0-5), and exact change is required.

Shopping: Head to Beach Drive and peruse its upscale shopping establishments. Art showrooms, boutiques and long-established jewelers intermingle with cozy cafés and high-rise condos on this palm tree-lined thoroughfare, a lovely milieu prized by sightseeing pedestrians and gallivanting locals.

While you're prowling Beach Drive for things to see, stop in at Sundial, a collection of upscale shops and eateries at 153 Second Ave. N. between First and Second streets. Track down some new threads at its fashionable boutiques, including Chico's, Tommy Bahama and White House Black Market, take a load off in the courtyard beside a 30-foot-tall working solar sundial, or catch a flick at the 19-screen movie theater.

West of downtown St. Petersburg at Tyrone Boulevard and 22nd Avenue North, Tyrone Square Mall entices those stalking brand names. Fashion mavens can gather an impressive array of bulging bags from such tenants as Dillard's, JCPenney and Macy's at the shopping center, which also houses

Hit the Road with a Prepaid Card

Stay on budget during travel and use again to save for the next adventure.

Visit your local AAA office or **AAA.com/MemberPay** to learn more.

All products not available at all locations.

(See maps & indexes p. 284, 286.)

more than 170 specialty stores and is the focal point of a retail hub embracing several national chains.

With the sweet-and-salty scent of kettle corn hanging in the air, more than 100 vendors showcase their wares to the tune of funky jazz beats and energetic pop vocals at the Saturday Morning Market and offer fun things to do with kids. Drawn in by persuasive chalk signs ("World's Best Pineapple—2 for $5!"), sandaled browsers weave in and out of white tents sheltering delicate orchids, floppy sunhats, handmade jewelry and robust organic coffees. The downtown St. Petersburg event takes place in the Al Lang Stadium parking lot at First Avenue Southeast and First Street Southeast from 9 a.m. to 2 p.m., early October to late May; phone (727) 455-4921. The Saturday Morning Market also operates on a smaller scale at Williams Park, First Avenue North and Third Street North, from 9 a.m. to 1 p.m., June through August.

Drive along Central Avenue between the waterfront and 31st Street to discover pockets of retail space where merchants hawk everything from antique wardrobes to contemporary paintings to emo skateboarding accessories. Smell the roses at Green Bench Flowers, in business for more than 25 years, then satisfy your sweet tooth with a boxful of handmade truffles from the adjacent Schakolad Chocolate Factory, on the corner of Central Avenue and Fourth Street North. Though the decadent nibbles are likely to be gone by the time you reach Daddy Kool Records, 666 Central Ave., take care not to leave any chocolaty fingerprints on the indie store's selection of hard-to-find vinyl albums, CDs and music DVDs.

If you're searching for a vintage toy, mid-century modern chair or 19th-century chandelier, plant yourself inside Antique Galleries of St. Petersburg at 450 34th St. N. Nostalgic shoppers roam the marketplace, salivating over restored furniture, unusual knick-knacks, glitzy jewelry and other distinctive finds offered by more than 80 vendors.

Even if you're not a bookworm, you'll have a tough time overlooking Haslam's Book Store, said to be Florida's largest independent retailer of hardbacks and paperbacks. Eye-catching red and black letters on the side of the rambling showroom at 2025 Central Ave. invite passersby to "Come in and Browse Over 100,000 Titles From Art to Zoology and 'A' to 'Izzard.'" Established in 1933, the family-owned and operated business sits at the eastern border of the Grand Central District, a compact retail destination that garners attention mainly for its elegant and/or groovy secondhand commodities.

Nightlife: Things to do with kids include cheering on the Tampa Bay Rays alongside tenured patrons at family-operated Ferg's Sports Bar & Grill. You'll find the rambling patchwork structure sprouting out from a former gas station on Central Avenue, just north of Tropicana Field. Order the Ahi tuna nachos, or devour Ferg's scrumptious half-pound burger topped with honey barbecue sauce and allied cheeses (American and Swiss); phone (727) 822-4562.

For live riffs, catch a show at Jannus Live, 200 First Ave. N., said to be Florida's oldest outdoor concert venue. After jamming to the likes of such varied musical talents as Bleachers, Phantogram and Social Distortion, hit up a local restaurant or one of St. Petersburg's many dive bars for a few longnecks. About 3 blocks west of Jannus Live on Central Avenue, the Emerald Bar presents the requisite mishmash of bad bar décor (i.e., chintzy wood wall panels, linoleum and tired neon beer signs) complemented by loud jukebox music, occasional live music and cheap drinks. On Second Street North, the Ringside Café—an unusual St. Petersburg institution that once operated as a boarding house and boxing club—packs in down-to-earth blues aficionados with wailing performances by local bands, stiff libations and tasty bar grub. Phone (727) 565-0550 for Jannus Live box office, (727) 898-6054 for the Emerald Bar or (727) 894-8465 for the Ringside Café.

While daytime sightseers enjoy al fresco lunches, farmers markets, and arts and crafts tent sales along Central Avenue in downtown St. Petersburg, exuberant beer drinkers and wine connoisseurs swing by after dark. Survey incoming night owls from your perch on the wrought iron balcony of A Taste for Wine, a romantic establishment occupying the second floor of the bygone St. Charles Hotel, which offer plenty of things for couples to do. Nibble on artisan cheeses, bacon-wrapped scallops, and puff pastries filled with beef and mushrooms inside the comfy art-adorned lounge, where jazz, pop and folk artists often entertain laid-back weekenders; phone (727) 895-1623.

Of course, a trip to sun-kissed St. Petersburg isn't complete until you've slurped fruity beverages with bronzed, sandaled natives at Kahuna's Bar & Grill, 10515 N. Gandy Blvd. Though you can stop by this cozy tiki hut any day of the week for a casual game of pool or a few rounds of foosball, you'll often find aging Hawaiian shirt-wearing beach bums going up against college kids in fierce Hula-Hoop contests and fun-loving volleyball tournaments; phone (727) 576-7800.

St. Petersburg Chamber of Commerce: 100 Second Ave. N., Suite 150, St. Petersburg, FL 33701. **Phone:** (727) 821-4069.

CHIHULY COLLECTION, 720 Central Ave., is home to works by celebrated glass artist Dale Chihuly, whose brilliantly hued pieces are reminiscent of sea creatures and exotic flowers. Inside, the attention-grabbing "Ruby Red Icicle Chandelier" is suspended from the ceiling. Other holdings include such works as "Ikebana," "Macchia," "Niijima Floats" and "Persians." A video explores Chihuly's life and techniques.

Time: Allow 30 minutes minimum. **Hours:** Mon.-Sat. 10-5, Sun. noon-5. Closed Thanksgiving and Christmas. **Cost:** Combination ticket with Morean

(See maps & indexes p. 284, 286.)

Arts Center, Glass Studio (with live glassblowing demonstrations) and Morean Arts Center for Clay $19.95; $17.95 (ages 65+); $12.95 (students with ID); free (ages 0-5). **Phone:** (727) 822-7872.

THE DALÍ MUSEUM, jct. Bayshore Dr. S.E. and 5th Ave. S.E. at 1 Dalí Blvd., houses an unparalleled collection of Spanish artist Salvador Dalí's art; more than 2,000 works, comprising nearly 100 oil paintings, eight of which are Dalí masterworks. A geodesic glass sculpture (nicknamed The Enigma), made of 1,062 triangular-shaped glass pieces, sinuously wraps around a portion of the exterior. The museum's Avant-Garden is comprised of a subtropical grotto, a hedge labyrinth, a wish tree and a stone patio.

Inside, a helical spiral staircase climbs to the third floor where two exhibition galleries are located. The James Family Wing holds the permanent collection and the Hough Family Wing hosts all special exhibitions. The Dali Museum's preeminent collection represents every moment and medium of Dali's creative life. Paintings range from small impressionistic works to gigantic surrealistic montages. Sculptures, prints, photographs and other objects illustrate Dalí's artistic diversity. In addition to the extensive permanent collection, the museum showcases frequent special exhibitions curated from top worldwide collections. The museum also features a children's education classroom, a theater, family programs and special events.

Note: Free audio/visual guides are available in English, French, German, Portuguese, Russian and Spanish. **Time:** Allow 1 hour minimum. **Hours:** Daily 10-5:30 (also Thurs. 5:30-8). Last admission 15 minutes before closing. Free guided tours are generally given daily on the half-hour; phone ahead to confirm schedule. Closed Grand Prix weekend in March, Thanksgiving and Christmas. **Cost:** $24; $22 (ages 65+ and military, law enforcement, teachers and firefighters with ID); $17 (ages 13-17 and students ages 18+ with ID); $10 (ages 6-12 and to all Thurs. 5-8); free (ages 0-5). **Parking:** $10. **Phone:** (727) 823-3767 or (800) 442-3254. GT

EGMONT KEY STATE PARK is at the mouth of Tampa Bay, s.w. of Fort DeSoto Beach. The island, accessible only by boat, is a wildlife refuge and protects gopher tortoises, box turtles and a variety of nesting bird species. Bottlenose dolphins are a common sight for boaters and beachcombers. The island served as a camp for captured Seminoles and was occupied by the Union Navy during the Civil War. In 1898, due to the threat of the Spanish-American War, Fort Dade was built. An 1858 lighthouse also is on site. Recreational activities include seashell collecting, fishing, swimming, hiking, snorkeling and wildlife viewing. *See Recreation Areas Chart.*

Note: Private companies offer ferry services to the island at an additional cost. Visitors are advised to bring sufficient food and beverages as there are no shops on the island. **Time:** Allow 3 hours minimum. **Hours:** Daily 8-dusk. Phone ahead for ferry schedule and rates. **Cost:** Free. **Phone:** (727) 893-2627 for recorded park information, or (727) 398-6577 for ferry information.

THE FLORIDA HOLOCAUST MUSEUM, 55 Fifth St. S. at jct. First Ave. S., spreads a message of tolerance as it memorializes the millions of men, women and children lost during the Nazi regime's systematic killing of Jews and other civilian groups—including Poles, Jehovah's Witnesses, homosexuals and the disabled—during World War II. Holocaust survivors speak weekly and share their personal stories with visitors. An audio tour included with admission offers additional details about the permanent exhibit History, Heritage and Hope.

Somber visitors pause before interpretive panels, streaming film clips and timeworn documents relating the history of the state-sponsored genocide, while a variety of chilling artifacts—from armbands worn by Jews in the Warsaw Ghetto to bricks from a crematorium chimney—document the brutality of the period. Putting a human face on the tragedy is a photo wall spotlighting Holocaust-affected families before the war. Another photographic display showcases wartime heroes who helped Jews escape Nazi persecution. At the center of the museum sits a boxcar from Nazi-occupied Poland. One of the museum's most dramatic and disquieting pieces, it rests on railroad tracks from the Treblinka camp.

Temporary exhibitions presented on the second and third floors augment the stirring first-floor gallery space. Flash photography and video are prohibited. **Time:** Allow 2 hours minimum. **Hours:** Daily 10-5. Last admission 1 hour before closing. Docent-led tours depart Sat. at 1:30. Closed Jan. 1, Easter, Rosh Hashanah, Yom Kippur, Thanksgiving and Christmas. **Cost:** $16; $14 (ages 65+); $10 (college students and veterans with ID); $8 (ages 6-17); free (active military with ID). Under 16 must be with an adult. **Phone:** (727) 820-0100. GT

SAVE **GREAT EXPLORATIONS CHILDREN'S MUSEUM** is off I-275 exit 24, 1 mi. e. on 22nd Ave. N., then .5 mi. s. to 1925 Fourth St. N. This 24,000-square-foot children's museum offers hands-on and role playing exhibits, including Bella Brava Pizza Kitchen, My First Market, Fire Station 15, Bay News 9 on the Air, Pet Vet and Great Beginnings. **Time:** Allow 1 hour minimum. **Hours:** Mon.-Sat. 10-4:30, Sun. noon-4:30. **Cost:** $10; $9 (ages 55+); free (ages 0-1). **Phone:** (727) 821-8992.

MUSEUM OF FINE ARTS is at 255 Beach Dr. N.E. on the waterfront. Among the highlights of the comprehensive 18,000 piece art collection are works by de Kooning, Monet, Morisot, O'Keeffe, Rauschenberg and Whistler. Also on view are ancient Greek and Roman, pre-Columbian, Asian, African and Native American works and decorative arts. An extensive photography collection also is featured. Special exhibitions are presented in the Hazel Hough Wing,

(See maps & indexes p. 284, 286.)

a 39,000-square-foot exhibit space designed by noted architect Yann Weymouth.

Hours: Open Mon.-Sat. 10-5 (also Thurs. 5-8), Sun. noon-5. Guided tours depart Mon.-Sat. at 11 and 2, Sun. at 2. Last admission 45 minutes before closing. Closed Thanksgiving and Christmas. **Cost:** $20; $15 (ages 65+, college, Florida teachers and military with ID); $10 (ages 7-18 and students with ID). Prices may vary during special exhibits. **Phone:** (727) 896-2667. GT

THE PIER DISTRICT is at the foot of Second Ave. N.E. One of the most recognized landmarks on Florida's west coast, the building at the pier head was an inverted five-story pyramidal structure built in 1973. **Note:** Due to its age and related structural problems, the building was demolished in fall 2015. Plans are underway to rebuild The Pier structure and reopen in early 2019. The new pier will include shops, bicycle and walking trails, a fishing deck, restaurants, a beach, a coastal thicket, an observation deck, a splash pad, a playground and event space.

ST. PETERSBURG MUSEUM OF HISTORY is at 335 Second Ave. N.E. Permanent exhibits from a collection of 32,000 artifacts and 8,000 digitized photographs focus on the history of the Pinellas Peninsula, the 1914 origination of the first commercial airline flight in St. Petersburg, the 1920s tourist boom and the area's diverse heritage and neighborhoods. Permanent exhibits include Schrader's Little Cooperstown, highlighting the history of baseball and its importance to the area. Temporary exhibits, a student learning center and an archival library for history research also are available. **Time:** Allow 1 hour, 30 minutes minimum. **Hours:** Mon.-Sat. 10-5, Sun. noon-5. Closed Jan. 1, Easter, Thanksgiving and Christmas. **Cost:** $15; $12 (ages 65+); $9 (ages 6-17 and college students and military with ID). **Phone:** (727) 894-1052.

SUNKEN GARDENS is at 1825 Fourth St. N. In the 1920s avid gardener George Turner began charging visitors a nickel to stroll among his garden's lush foliage; he officially opened it to tourists in 1935. Today visitors can follow paths that meander among ponds, waterfalls and exotic plants. Butterflies, flamingos and macaws live in the garden. Horticultural programs are offered throughout the year. Pets are not permitted. Guided tours are available by appointment. **Time:** Allow 2 hours minimum. **Hours:** Mon.-Sat. 10-4:30, Sun. noon-4:30. Last admission 30 minutes before closing. **Cost:** $10; $8 (ages 55+); $4 (ages 2-11). **Phone:** (727) 551-3102. GT

WEEDON ISLAND PRESERVE is 1 mi. e. on 83rd Ave. (Patica Rd.) off Fourth St. N., then 1 mi. n.e. on San Martin Blvd., following signs to 1800 Weedon Dr. N.E. The 3,190-acre preserve is rich with a diversity of native flora and fauna and serves as a habitat for a variety of fish and wildlife. Recreational activities include hiking, fishing, canoeing and kayaking. Boardwalks and an observation tower overlook the mangroves and estuary. Free guided hikes through the mangroves are offered on Saturday mornings. A variety of nature and archaeology programs are available.

The Weedon Island Preserve Cultural and Natural History Center features the Connecting People and Place exhibit gallery depicting the estuary and the Native American and early 20th-century influences that helped shape the preserve. *See Recreation Areas Chart.*

Note: Visitors participating in guided and self-guiding tours are advised to take along plenty of water, a hat, sunscreen, sunglasses, insect repellent and snacks. **Time:** Allow 2 hours minimum. **Hours:** Preserve open daily dawn-dusk. Center open Thurs.-Sat. 9-4, Sun. 11-4. Guided tours are given Sat. 9-11. Preserve closed day after Thanksgiving and Christmas. Center closed major holidays. **Cost:** Free. **Phone:** (727) 453-6500. GT

Be Vacation Ready

Have your car checked out by a dependable AAA/CAA Approved Auto Repair facility.

AAA.com/autorepair

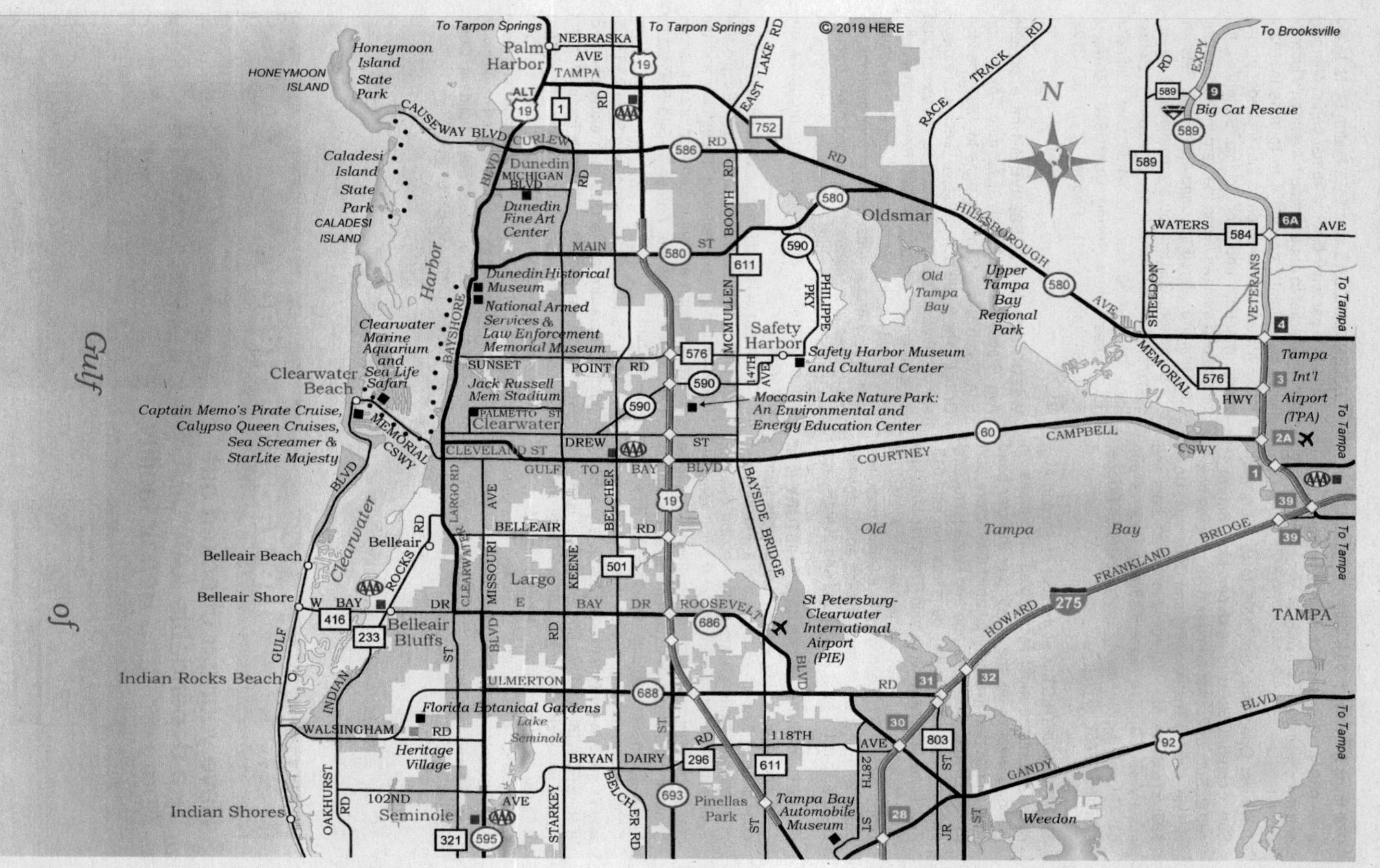

© 2019 HERE
To Brooksville
To Tampa
To Tarpon Springs
Big Cat Rescue
Tampa Int'l Airport (TPA)
TAMPA
Tampa Bay
Old Tampa Bay
Upper Tampa Bay Regional Park
Oldsmar
Safety Harbor
Safety Harbor Museum and Cultural Center
Moccasin Lake Nature Park: An Environmental and Energy Education Center
St Petersburg-Clearwater International Airport (PIE)
Tampa Bay Automobile Museum
Pinellas Park
Palm Harbor
Dunedin
Dunedin Fine Art Center
Dunedin Historical Museum
National Armed Services & Law Enforcement Memorial Museum
Jack Russell Mem Stadium
Clearwater
Largo
Florida Botanical Gardens
Lake Seminole
Heritage Village
Seminole
Belleair
Belleair Bluffs
Clearwater Harbor
Honeymoon Island State Park
HONEYMOON ISLAND
Caladesi Island State Park
CALADESI ISLAND
Clearwater Marine Aquarium and Sea Life Safari
Clearwater Beach
Captain Memo's Pirate Cruise, Calypso Queen Cruises, Sea Screamer & StarLite Majesty
Belleair Beach
Belleair Shore
Indian Rocks Beach
Indian Shores
Gulf of
Weedon
COURTNEY CAMPBELL CSWY
HOWARD FRANKLAND BRIDGE
BAYSIDE BRIDGE
GANDY BLVD
HILLSBOROUGH AVE
MEMORIAL HWY
VETERANS EXPY
WATERS AVE
SHELDON RD
RACE TRACK RD
EAST LAKE RD
PHILIPPE PKY
MCMULLEN BOOTH RD
GULF TO BAY BLVD
ROOSEVELT BLVD
ULMERTON RD
EAST BAY DR
WEST BAY DR
BELCHER RD
KEENE RD
MISSOURI AVE
BELLEAIR RD
CLEARWATER LARGO RD
ALT 19
CURLEW RD
MAIN ST
SUNSET POINT RD
DREW ST
CLEVELAND ST
NEBRASKA AVE
TAMPA RD
MICHIGAN BLVD
BAYSHORE BLVD
CAUSEWAY BLVD
MEMORIAL CSWY
GULF BLVD
INDIAN ROCKS RD
WALSINGHAM RD
102ND AVE
OAKHURST RD
STARKEY RD
BRYAN DAIRY RD
118TH AVE
28TH ST

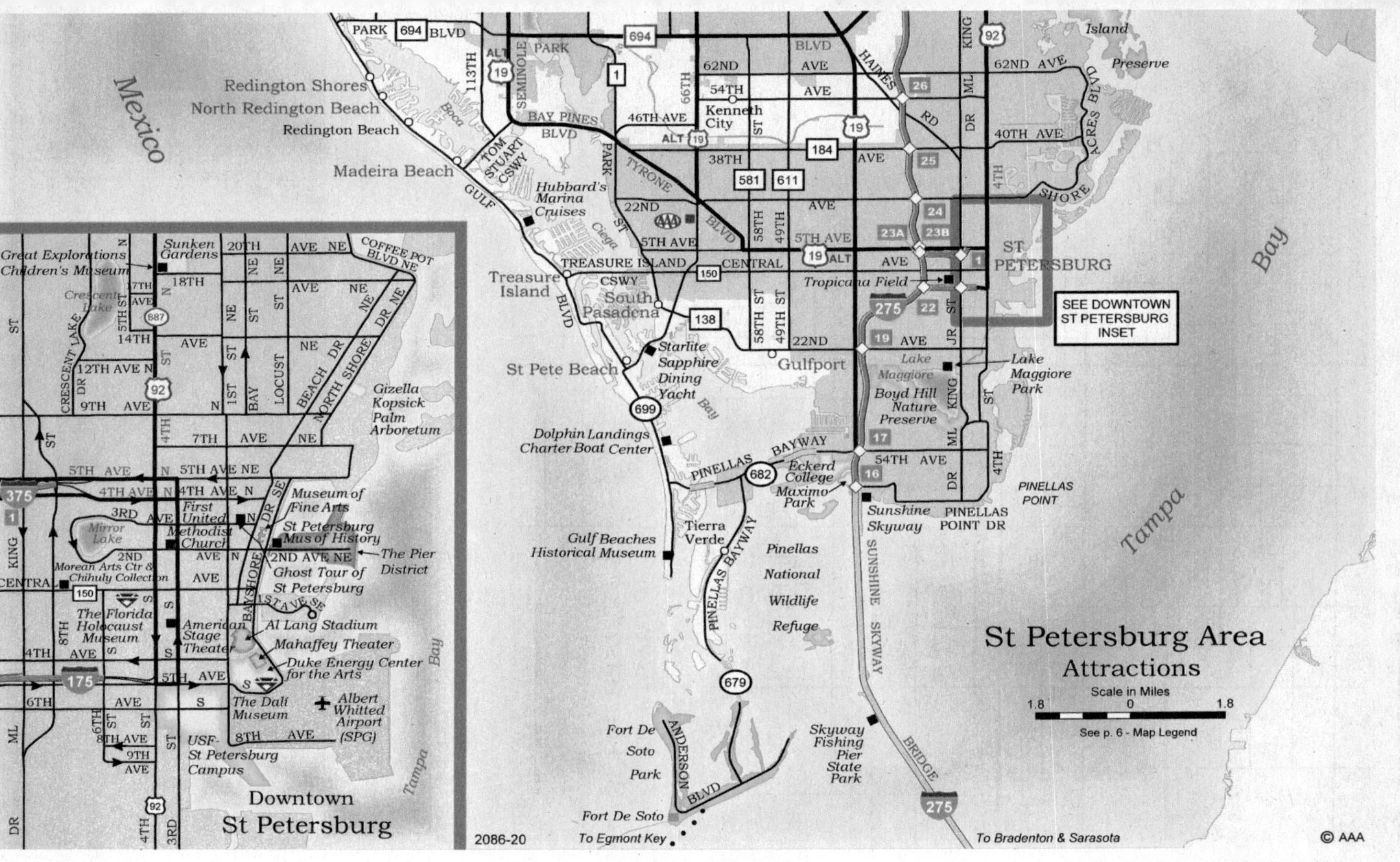
St Petersburg Area
Attractions
Scale in Miles
1.8
0
1.8
See p. 6 - Map Legend
© AAA
2086-20
SEE DOWNTOWN ST PETERSBURG INSET
Downtown St Petersburg
Tampa Bay
Mexico
Sunshine Skyway
Skyway Fishing Pier State Park
Fort De Soto Park
Fort De Soto
Pinellas National Wildlife Refuge
Gulf Beaches Historical Museum
Dolphin Landings Charter Boat Center
Starlite Sapphire Dining Yacht
Hubbard's Marina Cruises
Tropicana Field
Boyd Hill Nature Preserve
Lake Maggiore Park
Eckerd College
Maximo Park
Pinellas Point
Island Preserve
Redington Shores
North Redington Beach
Redington Beach
Madeira Beach
Treasure Island
St Pete Beach
South Pasadena
Gulfport
Kenneth City
Tierra Verde
St Petersburg
To Bradenton & Sarasota
To Egmont Key
Sunken Gardens
Great Explorations Children's Museum
Crescent Lake
Gizella Kopsick Palm Arboretum
Museum of Fine Arts
St Petersburg Mus of History
The Pier District
Ghost Tour of St Petersburg
Al Lang Stadium
Mahaffey Theater
Duke Energy Center for the Arts
Albert Whitted Airport (SPG)
The Dalí Museum
USF St Petersburg Campus
American Stage Theater
First United Methodist Church
Morean Arts Ctr & Chihuly Collection
The Florida Holocaust Museum
Mirror Lake

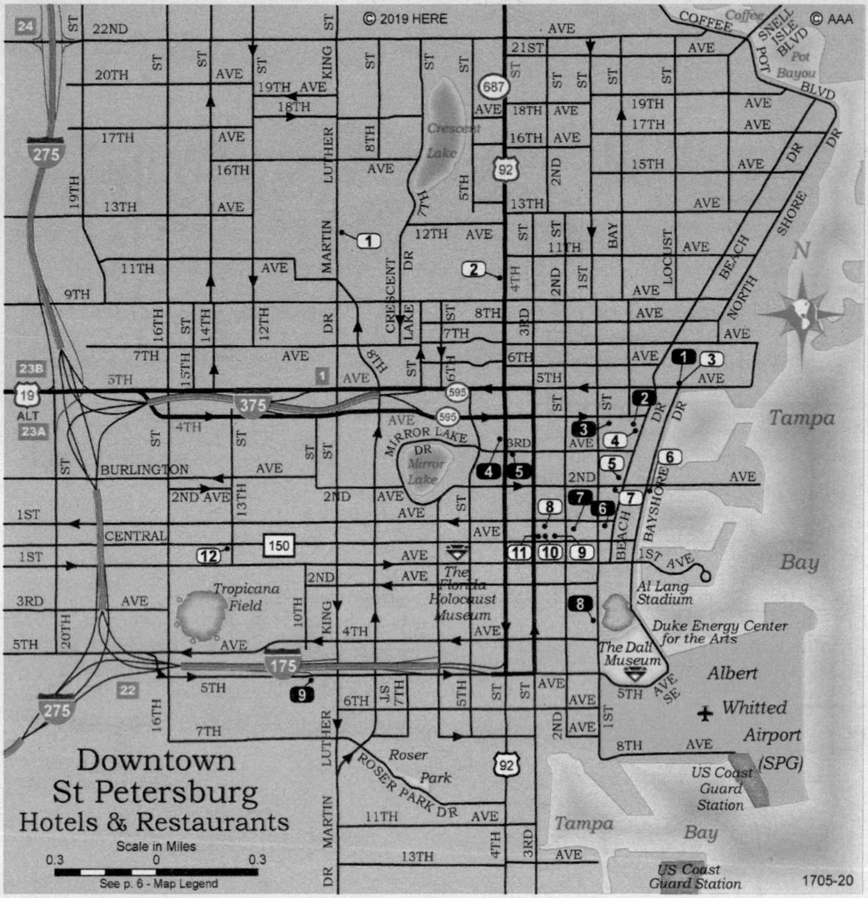

© 2019 HERE
© AAA
Downtown
St Petersburg
Hotels & Restaurants
Scale in Miles
0.3
0
0.3
See p. 6 - Map Legend
1705-20
Crescent Lake
Mirror Lake
Tropicana Field
The Florida Holocaust Museum
Al Lang Stadium
Duke Energy Center for the Arts
The Dali Museum
Albert Whitted Airport (SPG)
US Coast Guard Station
Roser Park
Tampa Bay
Coffee Pot Bayou

Hands-Free
IS NOT Risk-Free
Use hands-free systems cautiously and keep your focus on the road when driving.
AAA.com/Distraction

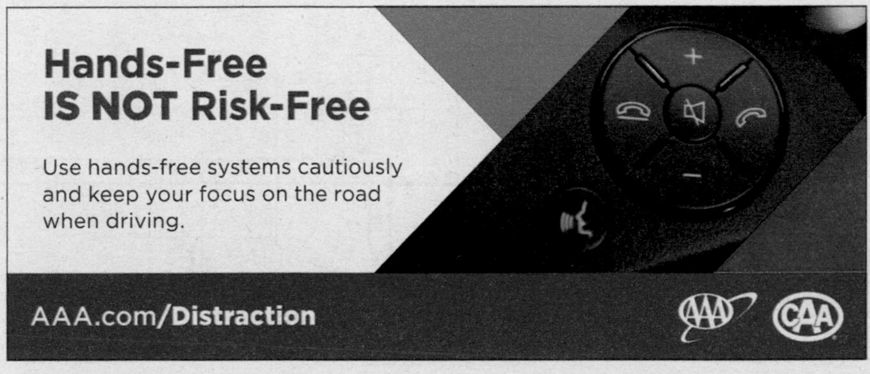

Downtown St. Petersburg

This index helps you "spot" where approved hotels and restaurants are located on the corresponding detailed maps. Restaurant price range is a combination of lunch and/or dinner. Turn to the listing page for more information and consult display ads for special promotions.

For more details, rates and reservations: AAA.com/travelguides/hotels

DOWNTOWN ST. PETERSBURG

Map Page	Hotels	Diamond Rated	Member Savings	Page
1 p. 284	**The Vinoy, Renaissance St. Petersburg Resort & Golf Club**	♦♦♦♦	✔	294
2 p. 284	The Birchwood At Lantern Lane	♦♦♦		293
3 p. 284	Watergarden Inn At The Bay	♦♦♦		294
4 p. 284	**Courtyard by Marriott St. Petersburg Downtown**	♦♦♦	✔	293
5 p. 284	The Inn On Third	♦♦		293
6 p. 284	**Hampton Inn & Suites St. Petersburg-Downtown**	♦♦♦	✔	293
7 p. 284	**Hyatt Place St. Petersburg/Downtown**	♦♦♦	✔	293
8 p. 284	Hilton St. Petersburg Bayfront	♦♦♦	✔	293
9 p. 284	**Staybridge Suites- St Petersburg Downtown**	♦♦♦	✔	293

Map Page	Restaurants	Diamond Rated	Cuisine	Price Range	Page
1 p. 284	Dairy Inn	♦	Sandwiches Desserts	$3-$8	294
2 p. 284	4th Street Shrimp Store Restaurant & Market	♦♦	Seafood	$8-$22	294
3 p. 284	Marchand's Bar & Grill	♦♦♦	Continental	$8-$40	294
4 p. 284	The Moon Under Water	♦♦	British	$10-$25	294
5 p. 284	Bella Brava	♦♦	Italian	$8-$27	294
6 p. 284	Fresco's Waterfront Bistro	♦♦	Italian	$11-$30	294
7 p. 284	Cassis American Brasserie	♦♦	European	$7-$37	294
8 p. 284	Yard of Ale St. Pete	♦♦	American	$7-$15	294
9 p. 284	Caddy's on Central	♦♦	American	$9-$19	294
10 p. 284	Central Avenue Oyster Bar	♦♦	Seafood	$8-$38	294
11 p. 284	Lucky Dill	♦	Sandwiches Deli	$7-$13	294
12 p. 284	Ferg's Sports Bar & Grill	♦	Burgers Sandwiches	$9-$16	294

Let Your Voice Be Heard

If your visit to a listed property doesn't meet your expectations, tell us about it.

AAA.com/MemberFeedback

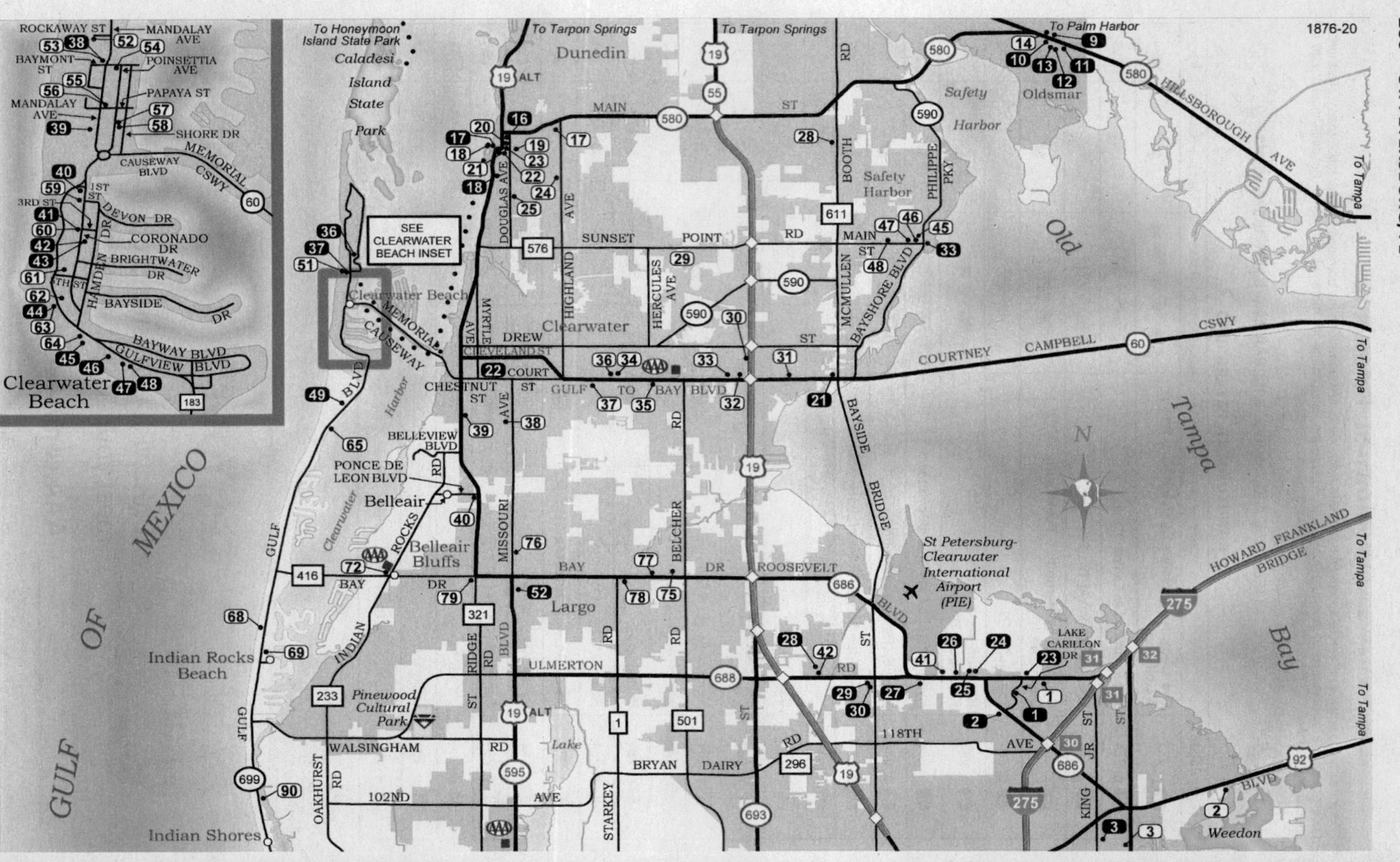

1876-20
To Tampa
To Palm Harbor
To Tarpon Springs
To Honeymoon Island State Park
Old Tampa Bay
Safety Harbor
Oldsmar
Dunedin
Clearwater
Largo
Belleair
Belleair Bluffs
Clearwater Beach
Caladesi Island State Park
St Petersburg-Clearwater International Airport (PIE)
Pinewood Cultural Park
Indian Rocks Beach
Indian Shores
Weedon
HOWARD FRANKLAND BRIDGE
COURTNEY CAMPBELL CSWY
BAYSIDE BRIDGE
HILLSBOROUGH AVE
MEMORIAL CAUSEWAY
SEE CLEARWATER BEACH INSET
GULF OF MEXICO

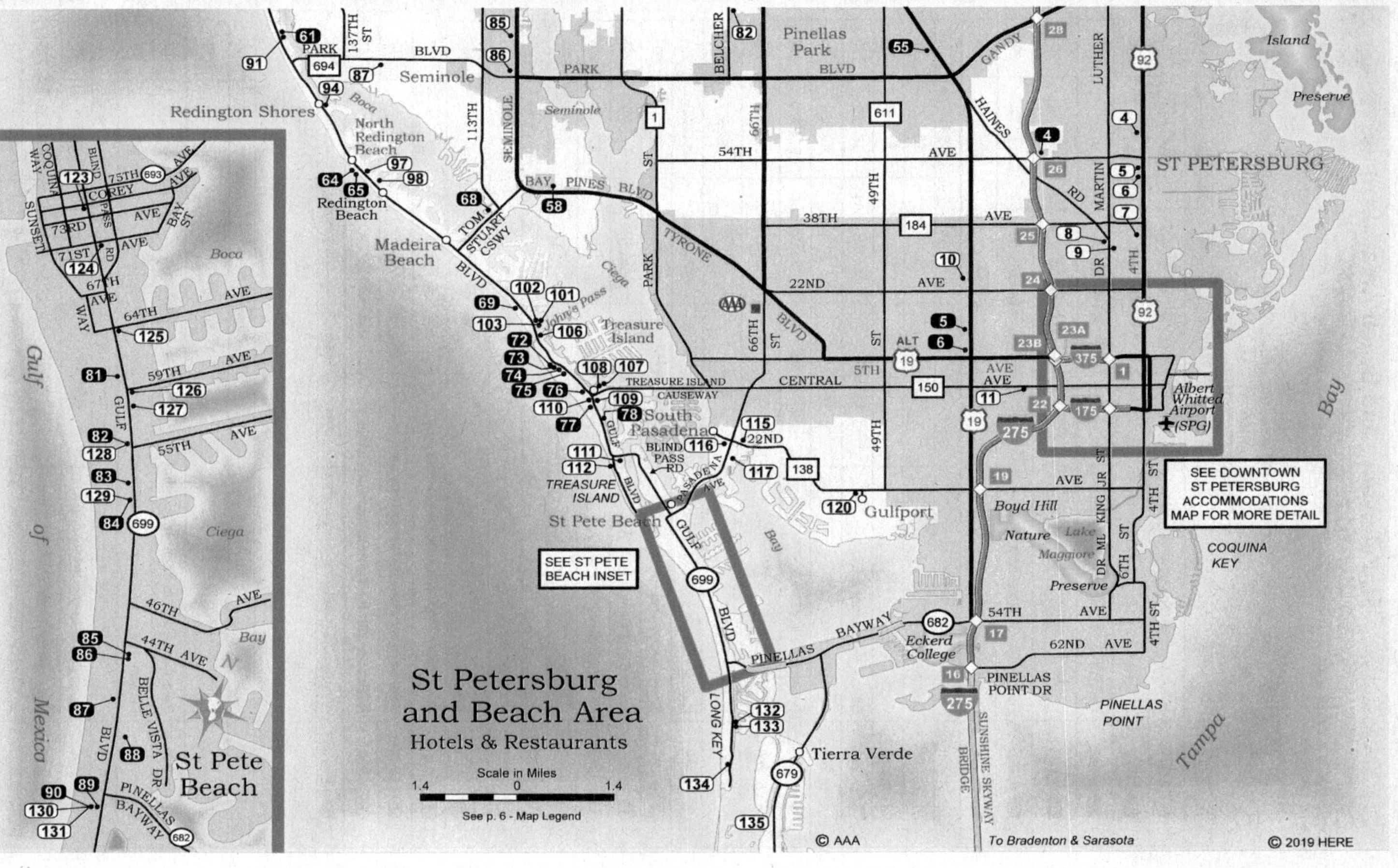
St Petersburg
and Beach Area
Hotels & Restaurants
Scale in Miles
1.4 0 1.4
See p. 6 - Map Legend
SEE DOWNTOWN ST PETERSBURG ACCOMMODATIONS MAP FOR MORE DETAIL
SEE ST PETE BEACH INSET
ST PETERSBURG
Pinellas Park
Seminole
Redington Shores
North Redington Beach
Redington Beach
Madeira Beach
Treasure Island
South Pasadena
St Pete Beach
Gulfport
Tierra Verde
Eckerd College
Boyd Hill Nature Preserve
Lake Maggiore
Albert Whitted Airport (SPG)
COQUINA KEY
PINELLAS POINT
LONG KEY
SUNSHINE SKYWAY BRIDGE
Tampa Bay
Boca Ciega Bay
Gulf of Mexico
To Bradenton & Sarasota
© 2019 HERE
© AAA

St. Petersburg and Beach Area

This index helps you "spot" where approved hotels and restaurants are located on the corresponding detailed maps. Restaurant price range is a combination of lunch and/or dinner. Turn to the listing page for more information and consult display ads for special promotions.

For more details, rates and reservations: AAA.com/travelguides/hotels

ST. PETERSBURG

Map Page	Hotels	Diamond Rated	Member Savings	Page
1 p. 286	Hilton St. Petersburg Carillon Park	♦♦♦	✔	294
2 p. 286	St. Petersburg Marriott Clearwater	♦♦♦	✔	294
3 p. 286	Comfort Inn & Suites Northeast Gateway	♦♦♦		294
4 p. 286	Holiday Inn Express Hotel & Suites St. Petersburg North	♦♦♦		294
5 p. 286	Holiday Inn St. Petersburg W	♦♦		294
6 p. 286	Days Inn Central	♦♦		294

Map Page	Restaurants	Diamond Rated	Cuisine	Price Range	Page
1 p. 286	Courtside Grille	♦♦	Continental	$9-$29	294
2 p. 286	Crab Shack	♦	Seafood	$7-$30	294
3 p. 286	Babalu Restaurant & Bar	♦♦	Comfort Food	$6-$29	294
4 p. 286	Paisano's Pizza 'n Pasta	♦♦	Italian	$9-$20	295
5 p. 286	Bonefish Grill	♦♦♦	Seafood	$14-$30	294
6 p. 286	Red Mesa Regional Mexican & Southwest Cuisine	♦♦	Mexican	$14-$29	295
7 p. 286	El Cap	♦	Burgers Sandwiches	$4-$7	294
8 p. 286	Casual Clam	♦♦	Seafood	$4-$32	294
9 p. 286	Siam Garden Thai Restaurant	♦♦	Thai	$7-$22	295
10 p. 286	Texas Cattle Company	♦♦	Steak Seafood	$15-$42	295
11 p. 286	Nitally's Thai-Mex Cuisine	♦♦	Thai	$5-$23	295

OLDSMAR

Map Page	Hotels	Diamond Rated	Member Savings	Page
9 p. 286	Hampton Inn & Suites Tampa-Northwest-Oldsmar	♦♦♦	✔	157
10 p. 286	Holiday Inn Express Hotel & Suites Tampa-Odsmar	♦♦♦		157
11 p. 286	Hilton Garden Inn Tampa Northwest/Oldsmar	♦♦♦	✔	157
12 p. 286	**Courtyard by Marriott Tampa-Oldsmar**	♦♦♦	✔	157
13 p. 286	**Residence Inn by Marriott Tampa/Oldsmar**	♦♦♦	✔	157

Map Page	Restaurant	Diamond Rated	Cuisine	Price Range	Page
14 p. 286	Flamestone American Grill	♦♦♦	American	$13-$37	157

DUNEDIN

Map Page	Hotels	Diamond Rated	Member Savings	Page
16 p. 286	Holiday Inn Express Hotel & Suites Clearwater North/Dunedin	♦♦♦		70
17 p. 286	**Best Western Plus Yacht Harbor Inn**	♦♦	✔	70
18 p. 286	**Fenway Hotel, Autograph Collection**	♦♦♦	✔	70

Map Page	Restaurants	Diamond Rated	Cuisine	Price Range	Page
17 p. 286	Julian's Little Italy	♦♦	Italian	$6-$17	70
18 p. 286	Bon Appetit Restaurant & Marina Cafe	♦♦♦	Continental	$11-$38	70
19 p. 286	Flanagan's Irish Pub & Restaurant	♦♦	Irish	$9-$15	70

Map Page	Restaurants (cont'd)	Diamond Rated	Cuisine	Price Range	Page
20 p. 286	Cafe Alfresco	◆◆	Italian	$9-$22	70
21 p. 286	Sea Sea Riders Restaurant	◆◆	Seafood	$9-$22	71
22 p. 286	Kelly's Chic-A-Boom-Room	◆◆	Continental	$7-$28	70
23 p. 286	Casa Tina	◆◆	Mexican	$8-$23	70
24 p. 286	The Restorative	◆◆	American	$20-$26	71
25 p. 286	Marguerite's Cafe and Catering	◆◆	Breakfast Sandwiches	$5-$10	71

CLEARWATER

Map Page	Hotels	Diamond Rated	Member Savings	Page
21 p. 286	Fairfield Inn & Suites by Marriott Clearwater Bayside	◆◆◆	✔	41
22 p. 286	Residence Inn by Marriott Clearwater Downtown	◆◆◆	✔	41
23 p. 286	**Homewood Suites by Hilton Clearwater**	◆◆◆	✔	41
24 p. 286	**Courtyard by Marriott St. Petersburg Clearwater**	◆◆◆	✔	41
25 p. 286	Fairfield Inn & Suites by Marriott St. Petersburg/Clearwater	◆◆	✔	41
26 p. 286	SpringHill Suites by Marriott St. Petersburg-Clearwater	◆◆◆	✔	42
27 p. 286	**Hampton Inn & Suites Clearwater/St. Petersburg**	◆◆◆	✔	41
28 p. 286	Holiday Inn Express Clearwater East-Icot Center	◆◆◆		41
29 p. 286	Residence Inn by Marriott St. Petersburg/Clearwater	◆◆◆	✔	41
30 p. 286	TownePlace Suites by Marriott St. Petersburg/Clearwater	◆◆	✔	42

Map Page	Restaurants	Diamond Rated	Cuisine	Price Range	Page
28 p. 286	Pickles Plus Deli	◆◆	Sandwiches Breakfast	$7-$11	43
29 p. 286	Queen's Pizza & Restaurant	◆◆	Italian	$6-$20	43
30 p. 286	Lenny's Restaurant	◆◆	Breakfast Sandwiches	$7-$14	43
31 p. 286	Pete & Shorty's Tavern	◆◆	American	$4-$16	43
32 p. 286	Green Market Cafe	◆	Natural/Organic Sandwiches	$8-$10	43
33 p. 286	**Oriental Super Buffet**	◆	Chinese	$9-$14	43
34 p. 286	Rumba Island Bar & Grill	◆◆	Caribbean	$8-$26	43
35 p. 286	Florida Subs & Gyros	◆	Sandwiches Burgers	$4-$9	43
36 p. 286	Papa's New York Diner	◆◆	Comfort Food	$2-$20	43
37 p. 286	Capogna's Dugout	◆	Sandwiches Pizza	$6-$20	43
38 p. 286	Thai Coconut Restaurant	◆◆	Thai	$8-$25	43
39 p. 286	O'Keefe's Tavern & Restaurant	◆◆	American	$8-$18	43
40 p. 286	Alfano's Restaurant	◆◆◆	Italian	$10-$40	43
41 p. 286	Bascom's Chop House Steaks & Fresh Seafood	◆◆◆	Steak Seafood	$10-$45	43
42 p. 286	Cafe Ponte	◆◆◆	Fusion	$9-$39	43

SAFETY HARBOR

Map Page	Hotel	Diamond Rated	Member Savings	Page
33 p. 286	**Safety Harbor Resort & Spa Trademark Collection by Wyndham** *(See ad p. 42.)*	◆◆◆	✔	255

Map Page	Restaurants	Diamond Rated	Cuisine	Price Range	Page
45 p. 286	Southern Fresh	◆◆	American Comfort Food	$3-$17	255

Map Page	Restaurants (cont'd)	Diamond Rated	Cuisine	Price Range	Page
46 p. 286	The Sandwich On Main	◆	Sandwiches	$6-$11	255
47 p. 286	Paradise Restaurant	◆◆	American	$5-$12	255
48 p. 286	Whistle Stop Grill & Bar	◆◆	American	$8-$19	255

CLEARWATER BEACH

Map Page	Hotels	Diamond Rated	Member Savings	Page
36 p. 286	Fairfield Inn & Suites by Marriott Clearwater Beach	◆◆◆	✔	44
37 p. 286	Palm Pavilion Inn	◆◆		45
38 p. 286	**Sandpearl Resort**	◆◆◆◆	✔	45
39 p. 286	**Hilton Clearwater Beach Resort & Spa**	◆◆◆	✔	44
40 p. 286	**Wyndham Grand Clearwater Beach** *(See ad p. 46.)*	◆◆◆◆	✔	47
41 p. 286	**Hyatt Regency Clearwater Beach Resort & Spa**	◆◆◆◆	✔	45
42 p. 286	**Residence Inn by Marriott Clearwater Beach**	◆◆◆	✔	45
43 p. 286	**SpringHill Suites by Marriott Clearwater Beach**	◆◆◆	✔	47
44 p. 286	**Opal Sands Resort**	◆◆◆◆	✔	45
45 p. 286	Holiday Inn & Suites	◆◆		44
46 p. 286	**Shephard's Beach Resort**	◆◆◆	✔	45
47 p. 286	Hampton Inn & Suites Clearwater Beach	◆◆◆	✔	44
48 p. 286	**Quality Beach Resort**	◆◆	✔	45
49 p. 286	**Sheraton Sand Key Resort**	◆◆◆	✔	47

Map Page	Restaurants	Diamond Rated	Cuisine	Price Range	Page
51 p. 286	Palm Pavilion Beachside Grill & Bar	◆◆	American	$7-$34	47
52 p. 286	Frenchy's Rockaway Grill	◆◆	Caribbean	$6-$23	47
53 p. 286	**Caretta On The Gulf**	◆◆◆◆	Continental	$12-$54	47
54 p. 286	Frenchy's Cafe	◆	Seafood	$7-$17	47
55 p. 286	Bobby's Bistro & Wine Bar	◆◆	Continental	$7-$29	47
56 p. 286	Bob Heilman's Beachcomber	◆◆◆	Steak Seafood	$9-$36	47
57 p. 286	Cooters Restaurant & Bar	◆◆	Seafood	$8-$27	47
58 p. 286	Frenchy's Saltwater Cafe	◆◆	Seafood	$8-$30	47
59 p. 286	**Ocean Hai** *(See ad p. 46.)*	◆◆◆◆	Asian Fusion	$14-$42	47
60 p. 286	**SHOR American Seafood Grill**	◆◆◆	Seafood Steak	$10-$46	48
61 p. 286	Frenchy's South Beach Cafe	◆◆	Seafood	$7-$19	47
62 p. 286	Post Corner Pizza	◆◆	American	$4-$21	47
63 p. 286	Sea-Guini	◆◆◆	Italian	$21-$44	47
64 p. 286	Taco Bus	◆	Mexican	$6-$13	48
65 p. 286	Backwater's On Sand Key	◆◆	Steak Seafood	$8-$29	47

LARGO

Map Page	Hotel	Diamond Rated	Member Savings	Page
52 p. 286	Holiday Inn Express & Suites Largo Central Park	◆◆◆		144

Map Page	Restaurants	Diamond Rated	Cuisine	Price Range	Page
75 p. 286	The Haus Coffee Shop	◆	Coffee/Tea Sandwiches	$4-$7	144
76 p. 286	Roosterfish Grill	◆◆	Seafood	$8-$21	144
77 p. 286	Café Classico Express	◆	Italian	$4-$25	144

Map Page	Restaurants (cont'd)	Diamond Rated	Cuisine	Price Range	Page
78 p. 286	Zio's Italian Market Deli & Bakery	◆	Italian	$6-$11	144
79 p. 286	Sages West Bay Bistro	◆◆	Italian	$8-$20	144

PINELLAS PARK

Map Page	Hotel	Diamond Rated	Member Savings	Page
55 p. 286	Country Inn & Suites by Radisson	◆◆◆		250

Map Page	Restaurant	Diamond Rated	Cuisine	Price Range	Page
82 p. 286	Joto's Pizza	◆◆	Pizza	$5-$23	250

SEMINOLE

Map Page	Hotel	Diamond Rated	Member Savings	Page
58 p. 286	Holiday Inn Express & Suites St. Petersburg-Madeira Beach	◆◆◆		309

Map Page	Restaurants	Diamond Rated	Cuisine	Price Range	Page
85 p. 286	Capo de Monte Italian Market	◆	Sandwiches Deli	$6-$15	309
86 p. 286	Brooklyn Pizza Company	◆◆	Pizza	$8-$24	309
87 p. 286	Joto's Pizza	◆◆	Pizza	$5-$23	309

INDIAN SHORES

Map Page	Hotel	Diamond Rated	Member Savings	Page
61 p. 286	Barefoot Beach Resort	◆◆◆		82

Map Page	Restaurants	Diamond Rated	Cuisine	Price Range	Page
90 p. 286	Caddy's Pub Waterfront Restaurant	◆◆	Seafood	$5-$28	82
91 p. 286	Salt Rock Grill	◆◆◆	Seafood	$15-$50	82

NORTH REDINGTON BEACH

Map Page	Hotels	Diamond Rated	Member Savings	Page
64 p. 286	DoubleTree Beach Resort by Hilton Hotel Tampa Bay-North Redington Beach	◆◆◆	✔	154
65 p. 286	Sails Resort Motel	◆◆		154

Map Page	Restaurants	Diamond Rated	Cuisine	Price Range	Page
97 p. 286	The Frog Pond Restaurant	◆◆	Breakfast Sandwiches	$6-$11	155
98 p. 286	The Conch Republic Grill & Raw Bar	◆◆	Seafood	$8-$30	155

MADEIRA BEACH

Map Page	Hotels	Diamond Rated	Member Savings	Page
68 p. 286	**Courtyard by Marriott St. Petersburg Clearwater/Madeira Beach**	◆◆◆	✔	146
69 p. 286	**Barefoot Beach Club**	◆◆	✔	146

Map Page	Restaurants	Diamond Rated	Cuisine	Price Range	Page
101 p. 286	The Hut Bar & Grill	◆◆	Sandwiches Burgers	$10-$17	146
102 p. 286	De Losa's Pizza & Italian Restaurant	◆	Italian	$6-$37	146
103 p. 286	Friendly Fisherman Waterfront Seafood Restaurant	◆◆	Seafood	$10-$35	146

TREASURE ISLAND

Map Page	Hotels	Diamond Rated	Member Savings	Page
72 p. 286	Sunset Vistas Beachfront Suites	◆◆◆		365
73 p. 286	**Residence Inn by Marriott St. Petersburg Treasure Island**	◆◆◆	✔	365
74 p. 286	**The Sea Chest**	◆◆	✔	365
75 p. 286	Jamaican on the Gulf	◆◆		364

TREASURE ISLAND (cont'd)

Map Page	Hotels (cont'd)	Diamond Rated	Member Savings	Page
76 p. 286	**Treasure Island Beach Resort**	◆◆◆	✔	365
77 p. 286	**Page Terrace Beachfront Hotel**	◆◆	✔	364
78 p. 286	Westwinds Waterfront Resort	◆◆◆		365

Map Page	Restaurants	Diamond Rated	Cuisine	Price Range	Page
106 p. 286	Gators Cafe & Saloon	◆	Seafood	$9-$22	365
107 p. 286	The Floridian	◆	Sandwiches	$4-$7	365
108 p. 286	Foxy's Cafe	◆◆	American	$5-$19	365
109 p. 286	VIP Lounge & Mexican Restaurant	◆	Mexican	$7-$23	365
110 p. 286	Sloppy Joe's On The Beach	◆◆	American	$9-$23	365
111 p. 286	Taco Bus	◆	Mexican	$6-$13	365
112 p. 286	Caddy's On The Beach	◆	Sandwiches Burgers	$6-$20	365

ST. PETE BEACH

Map Page	Hotels	Diamond Rated	Member Savings	Page
81 p. 286	**RumFish Beach Resort by TradeWinds**	◆◆	✔	274
82 p. 286	**TradeWinds Island Grand Beach Resort**	◆◆◆	✔	274
83 p. 286	**Sirata Beach Resort**	◆◆	✔	274
84 p. 286	Grand Plaza Beachfront Resort & Conference Center	◆◆		274
85 p. 286	**Bayview Plaza Waterfront Resort**	◆◆	✔	273
86 p. 286	**Bay Palms Waterfront Resort Hotel and Marina**	◆◆	✔	273
87 p. 286	Palm Crest Resort Motel	◆◆		274
88 p. 286	Hotel Zamora	◆◆◆		274
89 p. 286	**Beach House Suites by The Don CeSar**	◆◆◆	✔	273
90 p. 286	**The Don CeSar**	◆◆◆◆	✔	273

Map Page	Restaurants	Diamond Rated	Cuisine	Price Range	Page
123 p. 286	The Frog Pond Restaurant	◆◆	Breakfast Sandwiches	$7-$12	274
124 p. 286	Shells of St. Pete Beach	◆◆	Seafood	$11-$20	274
125 p. 286	Basil Leaf Thai-Sushi and Noodles	◆◆	Thai	$4-$24	274
126 p. 286	Snapper's	◆◆◆	Seafood	$18-$40	274
127 p. 286	Skidder's Restaurant	◆◆	American	$6-$25	274
128 p. 286	Palm Court Italian Grill	◆◆◆	Italian	$11-$34	274
129 p. 286	Spinners Rooftop Revolving Lounge & Bistro	◆◆◆	Steak Seafood	$11-$43	274
130 p. 286	Sea Porch Cafe	◆◆◆	Caribbean	$15-$42	274
131 p. 286	**Maritana Grille**	◆◆◆◆	Continental	$30-$44	274
132 p. 286	Sea Critters Cafe	◆◆	Seafood	$8-$13	274
133 p. 286	**The Wharf Seafood Restaurant & Waterfront Bar**	◆◆	Seafood	$5-$28	274
134 p. 286	Seahorse Tavern and Restaurant	◆◆	Seafood	$3-$8	274
135 p. 286	Billy's Stone Crab & Lobster	◆◆	Seafood	$8-$40	274

INDIAN ROCKS BEACH

Map Page	Restaurants	Diamond Rated	Cuisine	Price Range	Page
68 p. 286	Thai-Pan Alley & Bamboo Beach Bar	◆◆	Thai	$5-$16	82
69 p. 286	Guppy's on the Beach Seafood Grill & Bar	◆◆	Seafood	$9-$40	82

BELLEAIR BLUFFS

Map Page	Restaurant	Diamond Rated	Cuisine	Price Range	Page
(72) p. 286	E & E Stakeout Grill	◆◆◆	Continental	$16-$44	33

REDINGTON SHORES

Map Page	Restaurant	Diamond Rated	Cuisine	Price Range	Page
(94) p. 286	Friendly Tavern	◆	American	$8-$19	254

SOUTH PASADENA

Map Page	Restaurants	Diamond Rated	Cuisine	Price Range	Page
(115) p. 286	Spiros Pasadena Produce & Deli	◆	Greek	$4-$11	310
(116) p. 286	Horse & Jockey British Pub & Restaurant	◆◆	British	$8-$18	310
(117) p. 286	Ted Peters Famous Smoked Fish	◆	Seafood	$4-$23	310

GULFPORT

Map Page	Restaurant	Diamond Rated	Cuisine	Price Range	Page
(120) p. 286	Habana Cafe	◆◆	Cuban	$6-$22	79

DOWNTOWN ST. PETERSBURG

- **Restaurants p. 294**
- **Hotels & Restaurants map & index p. 284**
- **Part of St. Petersburg-Clearwater and Beaches area — see map p. 275**

THE BIRCHWOOD AT LANTERN LANE 727/896-1080 **2**

◆◆◆ Boutique Hotel. **Address:** 340 Beach Dr NE 33701

COURTYARD BY MARRIOTT ST. PETERSBURG DOWNTOWN 727/450-6200 **4**

◆◆◆ **Historic Hotel**

COURTYARD® **AAA Benefit:** Members save 5% or more!

Address: 300 4th St N 33701 **Location:** On US 92, jct 3rd Ave N. **Facility:** The location is fantastic as it is within walking distance of museums, the waterfront, and downtown dining and shopping venues. Spacious guest rooms are decorated in slick slate-gray tones. 128 units. 8 stories, interior corridors. **Parking:** valet only. **Pool:** heated indoor. **Activities:** hot tub, exercise room. **Guest Services:** valet and coin laundry, boarding pass kiosk.

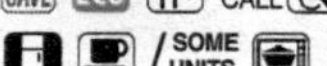

SAVE ECO CALL BIZ HS / SOME UNITS

HAMPTON INN & SUITES ST. PETERSBURG-DOWNTOWN 727/892-9900 **6**

Hotel

AAA Benefit: Members save 5% or more!

Address: 80 Beach Dr NE 33701 **Location:** Jct 1st Ave NE. **Facility:** 91 units. 4 stories, interior corridors. **Parking:** valet only. **Pool:** heated outdoor. **Activities:** exercise room. **Guest Services:** valet and coin laundry. **Featured Amenity: breakfast buffet.**

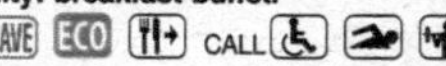

BIZ HS

HILTON ST. PETERSBURG BAYFRONT 727/894-5000 **8**

◆◆◆ SAVE Hotel. **Address:** 333 1st St S 33701

AAA Benefit: Members save 5% or more!

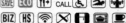

HYATT PLACE ST. PETERSBURG/DOWNTOWN 727/220-0950 **7**

◆◆◆ **Hotel**

HYATT PLACE® **AAA Benefit:** Members save up to 10%!

Address: 25 2nd St N 33701 **Location:** Jct Central Ave. **Facility:** 175 units. 13-15 stories, interior corridors. **Parking:** on-site (fee). **Pool:** heated outdoor. **Activities:** health club. **Guest Services:** valet and coin laundry. **Featured Amenity: breakfast buffet.**

SAVE CALL BIZ HS / SOME UNITS

THE INN ON THIRD 727/894-3248 **5**

◆◆ Historic Motel. **Address:** 342 3rd Ave N 33701

STAYBRIDGE SUITES- ST PETERSBURG DOWNTOWN 727/821-0777 **9**

◆◆◆ **Extended Stay Contemporary Hotel**

Address: 940 5th Ave S 33705 **Location:** I-275 exit 22, 0.4 mi se on US 175, jct Dr Martin Luther King Jr St. **Facility:** 119 kitchen units. 5 stories, interior corridors. **Pool:** heated outdoor. **Activities:** exercise room. **Guest Services:** complimentary and valet laundry, area transportation.

SAVE CALL BIZ HS / SOME UNITS

For complete hotel, dining and attraction listings: AAA.com/travelguides

(See map & index p. 284.)

THE VINOY, RENAISSANCE ST. PETERSBURG RESORT & GOLF CLUB 727/894-1000 1

Historic Resort Hotel

R RENAISSANCE® HOTELS **AAA Benefit:** Members save 5% or more!

Address: 501 5th Ave NE 33701 **Location:** Just n on Beach Dr; adjacent to Vinoy Park. **Facility:** Built in 1925 as a haven for the rich and famous, the hotel has been restored and modernized but retains its historical grandeur. Rooms range from cozy to spacious and are decorated in pleasing tones. 362 units. 7 stories, interior corridors. **Parking:** on-site (fee) and valet. **Terms:** check-in 4 pm. **Amenities:** safes. **Dining:** 4 restaurants, also, Marchand's Bar & Grill, see separate listing, entertainment. **Pool:** heated outdoor. **Activities:** sauna, hot tub, steamroom, marina, regulation golf, tennis, recreation programs, bicycles, health club, spa. **Guest Services:** valet and coin laundry, boarding pass kiosk, area transportation.

SAVE ECO CALL BIZ SHS / SOME UNITS

WATERGARDEN INN AT THE BAY 727/822-1700 3

Historic Boutique Bed & Breakfast. **Address:** 126 4th Ave NE 33701

WHERE TO EAT

4TH STREET SHRIMP STORE RESTAURANT & MARKET 727/822-0325 2

Seafood. Casual Dining. **Address:** 1006 4th St N 33701

BELLA BRAVA 727/895-5515 5

Italian. Casual Dining. **Address:** 204 Beach Dr NE 33701

CADDY'S ON CENTRAL 727/575-7939 9

American. Casual Dining. **Address:** 217 Central Ave 33701

CASSIS AMERICAN BRASSERIE 727/827-2927 7

European. Casual Dining. **Address:** 170 NE Beach Dr 33701

CENTRAL AVENUE OYSTER BAR 727/897-9728 10

Seafood. Casual Dining. **Address:** 249 Central Ave 33701

DAIRY INN 727/822-6971 1

Sandwiches Desserts. Quick Serve. **Address:** 1201 Dr. Martin Luther King Jr St N (9th St N) 33701

FERG'S SPORTS BAR & GRILL 727/822-4562 12

Burgers Sandwiches. Casual Dining. **Address:** 1320 Central Ave 33705

FRESCO'S WATERFRONT BISTRO 727/894-4429 6

Italian. Casual Dining. **Address:** 300 2nd Ave NE 33701

LONNI'S SANDWICHES, ETC. 727/894-1944

Sandwiches. Quick Serve. **Address:** 425 Central Ave 33701

LUCKY DILL 727/895-5859 11

Sandwiches Deli. Quick Serve. **Address:** 277 Central Ave 33701

MARCHAND'S BAR & GRILL 727/894-1000 3

Continental. Fine Dining. **Address:** 501 5th Ave NE 33701

THE MOON UNDER WATER 727/896-6160 4

British. Casual Dining. **Address:** 332 Beach Dr NE 33701

TIJUANA FLATS 727/823-5882

Tex-Mex. Quick Serve. **Address:** 944 4th St N, Suite 100 33701

YARD OF ALE ST. PETE 727/822-2027 8

American. Sports Bar. **Address:** 260 1st Ave N 33701

ST. PETERSBURG

• **Hotels & Restaurants map & index p. 286**
• **Part of St. Petersburg-Clearwater and Beaches area — see map p. 275**

COMFORT INN & SUITES NORTHEAST GATEWAY 727/563-9100 3

Hotel. **Address:** 875 94th Ave N 33702

DAYS INN CENTRAL 727/321-2958 6

Motel. **Address:** 650 34th St N 33713

HILTON ST. PETERSBURG CARILLON PARK 727/540-0050 1

SAVE Hotel. **Address:** 950 Lake Carillon Dr 33716

AAA Benefit: Members save 5% or more!

HOLIDAY INN EXPRESS HOTEL & SUITES ST. PETERSBURG NORTH 727/520-7800 4

Hotel. **Address:** 2171 54th Ave N 33714

HOLIDAY INN ST. PETERSBURG W 727/322-0770 5

Hotel. **Address:** 1200 34th St N 33713

ST. PETERSBURG MARRIOTT CLEARWATER 727/572-7800 2

SAVE Hotel. **Address:** 12600 Roosevelt Blvd 33716

AAA Benefit: Members save 5% or more!

WHERE TO EAT

BABALU RESTAURANT & BAR 727/576-7414 3

Comfort Food. Casual Dining. **Address:** 9246 4th St N 33702

BONEFISH GRILL 727/521-3434 5

Seafood. Fine Dining. **Address:** 5062 4th St N 33703

BURGER MONGER 727/592-4206

Burgers. Quick Serve. **Address:** 1325 4th St N 33701

CARMELITA'S MEXICAN RESTAURANT 727/545-2956

Mexican. Casual Dining. **Address:** 5211 Park St N 33709

CASUAL CLAM 727/895-2526 8

Seafood. Casual Dining. **Address:** 3336 Dr. Martin Luther King St N (9th St N) 33704

CODY'S ORIGINAL ROADHOUSE 727/345-1022

American. Casual Dining. **Address:** 4360 Park St N 33709

COURTSIDE GRILLE 727/561-7433 1

Continental. Casual Dining. **Address:** 110 Fountain Pkwy N 33716

CRAB SHACK 727/576-7813 2

Seafood. Casual Dining. **Address:** 11400 Gandy Blvd 33702

EL CAP 727/521-1314 7

Burgers Sandwiches. Casual Dining. **Address:** 3500 4th St N 33704

EVOS 727/571-3867

Natural/Organic. Quick Serve. **Address:** 2631 4th St N 33704

(See map & index p. 286.)

NITALLY'S THAI-MEX CUISINE 727/321-8424 (11)

Thai. Casual Dining. **Address:** 2462 Central Ave 33712

PAISANO'S PIZZA 'N PASTA 727/521-2656 (4)

Italian. Casual Dining. **Address:** 6000 4th St N 33703

RED MESA REGIONAL MEXICAN & SOUTHWEST CUISINE 727/527-8728 (6)

Mexican. Casual Dining. **Address:** 4912 4th St N 33703

SIAM GARDEN THAI RESTAURANT 727/822-0613 (9)

Thai. Casual Dining. **Address:** 3125 Dr. Martin Luther King Jr St N (9th St N) 33704

SONNY'S REAL PIT BAR-B-Q 727/341-2990

Barbecue. Casual Dining. **Address:** 3650 Tyrone Blvd 33710

TEXAS CATTLE COMPANY 727/527-3335 (10)

Steak Seafood. Casual Dining. **Address:** 2600 34th St N 33713

TIJUANA FLATS 727/209-0191

Tex-Mex. Quick Serve. **Address:** 2117 66th St N 33701

WESTSHORE PIZZA 727/895-5506

Pizza. Casual Dining. **Address:** 3187 4th St N 33704

SANFORD (F-4) pop. 53,570, elev. 20'

• **Hotels & Restaurants map & index p. 188**
• **Part of Orlando area — see map p. 2**

On Lake Monroe at the head of navigation on the St. Johns River, Sanford was established as a trading post in 1837. Gen. Henry R. Sanford bought 12,000 acres, including the townsite, in 1871 and established citrus groves.

The historic district, centered on First Street, contains structures dating back to 1883 and includes a former office building and hotel erected in 1887 for railroad entrepreneur Henry B. Plant. With the addition in recent years of cafés, pubs, art galleries and antique shops, downtown Sanford has become a hipster hangout. A refurbished 1922 silent movie and vaudeville house at 201 S. Magnolia Avenue is home to the Wayne Densch Performing Arts Center, a venue for the theater's repertory company and other performance troupes; phone (407) 321-8111.

RiverWalk, a 2-mile pedestrian way skirting the lake north of the historic district, provides waterfront picnicking and recreation space.

Amtrak's Auto Train transports passengers and their cars to and from Lorton, Va. To reach the station, take SR 46 (I-4 exit 101C) east to 600 Persimmon Ave. Phone (800) 872-7245 for arrival information or reservations.

Greater Sanford Regional Chamber of Commerce: 400 E. First St., Sanford, FL 32771. **Phone:** (407) 322-2212.

Shopping: First Street, in the downtown historic district, features a variety of shops with antiques, art, books and collectibles.

Self-guiding tours: Brochures for walking tours of the historic district are available from the chamber of commerce.

BEST WESTERN PLUS SANFORD AIRPORT/LAKE MARY
407/320-0845 (17)

Hotel

AAA Benefit: Members save up to 15% and earn bonus points!

Address: 3401 S Orlando Dr 32773 **Location:** I-4 exit 98, 4.5 mi e to US 17-92, then 0.7 mi n. **Facility:** 71 units. 4 stories, interior corridors. **Pool:** outdoor. **Activities:** picnic facilities, exercise room. **Guest Services:** valet and coin laundry. **Featured Amenity: breakfast buffet.**

SAVE CALL BIZ HS

/ SOME UNITS

COMFORT INN & SUITES NORTH ORLANDO/SANFORD
407/585-1580 (15)

Hotel

Address: 590 Ava Ct 32771 **Location:** I-4 exit 101C, 0.3 mi e to Hickman Dr, then just n; adjacent to Cracker Barrel. **Facility:** 107 units. 4 stories, interior corridors. **Pool:** outdoor. **Activities:** exercise room. **Guest Services:** valet and coin laundry, area transportation. **Featured Amenity: full hot breakfast.**

SAVE BIZ

SPRINGHILL SUITES BY MARRIOTT-ORLANDO NORTH/SANFORD
407/995-1000 (16)

Hotel

SPRINGHILL SUITES MARRIOTT

AAA Benefit: Members save 5% or more!

Address: 201 N Towne Rd 32771 **Location:** I-4 exit 101C, just se. **Facility:** 105 units. 5 stories, interior corridors. **Pool:** outdoor. **Activities:** exercise room. **Guest Services:** valet and coin laundry. **Featured Amenity: full hot breakfast.**

SAVE CALL BIZ HS

WHERE TO EAT

CAFFE POSITANO 407/531-1151 (49)

Italian Pizza. Casual Dining. **Address:** 1665 WP Ball Blvd 32771

CHIANTI'S PIZZA & PASTA 407/878-5900 (50)

Italian. Casual Dining. **Address:** 685 Towne Center Blvd 32771

COLONIAL ROOM RESTAURANT 407/323-2999 (44)

Comfort Food. Casual Dining. **Address:** 105 E 1st St 32771

THE CORNER CAFE HOME OF GOURMET2GO 407/322-3779 (43)

Deli. Quick Serve. **Address:** 101 W 1st St 32771

HOLLERBACH'S WILLOW TREE CAFE 407/321-2204 (41)

German. Casual Dining. **Address:** 205 E 1st St 32771

LASPADAS ORIGINAL PHILLY CHEESE STEAKS 407/322-1011 (46)

Sandwiches. Quick Serve. **Address:** 4301 W SR 46 32771

(See map & index p. 188.)

MARU SUSHI & GRILL 407/323-8108 (48)

Asian. Casual Dining. **Address:** 400 N Entrance Rd 32771

MEL'S FAMILY DINER 407/321-4294 (51)

Comfort Food. Casual Dining. **Address:** 3221 S Orlando Dr 32773

THE OLD JAILHOUSE KITCHEN & SPIRITS 407/548-6964 (42)

American. Casual Dining. **Address:** 113 S Palmetto Ave 32771

RIVERWALK PIZZERIA 407/915-5559 (47)

Italian Pizza. Casual Dining. **Address:** 5040 W SR 46 32771

SONNY'S REAL PIT BAR-B-Q 407/321-9295

Barbecue. Casual Dining. **Address:** 3506 Orlando Dr 32773

THE TENNESSEE TRUFFLE 407/942-3977 (45)

Southern. Casual Dining. **Address:** 125 W 1st St 32771

SARASOTA (F-8) pop. 51,917, elev. 18'

• Hotels p. 305 • Restaurants p. 307
• Hotels & Restaurants map & index p. 300

Although the origin of its name is not clear, the city has been a fixture on Sarasota Bay since the 1700s. The population was augmented by Scottish settlers in the 1880s, and the area became popular as a resort in the early part of the 20th century.

The circus is an integral part of Sarasota's past. In 1927 John Ringling selected the town for his Ringling Brothers and Barnum & Bailey Circus and made it his home. He exerted a major influence on the growth and development of the city because people from all over the world came to Sarasota to star in his show.

Sarasota, including the offshore islands of Casey Key, Lido Key, Longboat Key, St. Armand Key and Siesta Key, is a beach resort and art community. Hotels and residential and commercial areas ring Sarasota Bay, and the islands offer 35 miles of beaches that border the blue waters of the Gulf.

In the mainland section of the city is an array of performing arts groups, including Asolo Repertory Theatre, The Players Theatre, Sarasota Opera, Sarasota Orchestra, Sarasota Ballet, The Jazz Club of Sarasota and several vocal and chamber ensembles as well as an active theater district.

Performing arts facilities include The F.S.U. Center for the Performing Arts, 5555 N. Tamiami Tr., home to Asolo Repertory Theatre; Van Wezel Performing Arts Hall, 777 N. Tamiami Tr.; the Sarasota Opera House, 61 N. Pineapple Ave.; and Beatrice Friedman Symphony Center, 709 N. Tamiami Tr. The Florida Studio Theatre, 1241 N. Palm Ave., presents entertainment from drama to musicals; phone (941) 366-9000.

Since Sarasota is the city where golf was introduced to Florida from Scotland and where the first course was laid out in 1886, it is understandable that the sport remains popular; more than 30 courses are within minutes of downtown.

The Baltimore Orioles' spring training games take place in March at Ed Smith Stadium, 2700 12th St.; phone (941) 954-4101.

Sarasota Ski-A-Rees presents a free water ski show each Sunday at 2 p.m. from early February to early May and in October at Ken Thompson Park on City Island near the aquarium; phone (941) 388-1666.

Greyhound racing takes place year-round at Sarasota Kennel Club, 5400 Old Bradenton Rd.; phone (941) 355-7744.

Note: Policies vary concerning admittance of children to pari-mutuel betting facilities. Phone for information.

Visitor Sarasota County: 1945 Fruitville Rd., Sarasota, FL 34236. **Phone:** (941) 706-1253 or (800) 522-9799.

Shopping: Westfield Sarasota Square, 8201 S. Tamiami Tr., includes JCPenney, H&M and Old Navy among its 125 stores. St. Armands Circle and the vicinity contain more than 140 shops. Macy's is the anchor at Westfield Siesta Key, 3501 S. Tamiami Tr. The Mall at University Town Center, off I-75 exit 213 at the junction of Cattleman Road and University Parkway, is anchored by Dillard's, Macy's and Saks Fifth Avenue and has more than 100 stores and restaurants.

CROWLEY MUSEUM & NATURE CENTER is off I-75 exit 210, 10 mi. e. on Fruitville Rd. (SR 780), then 3 mi. s. to 16405 Myakka Rd. This 190-acre nature preserve includes trails through five habitats, a half-mile-long boardwalk over Maple Branch swamp and an observation tower overlooking the Myakka River. Also on site is a pioneer history area with a museum that includes a homesteader's cabin, sugar cane mill, two-story Cracker house circa 1889 and operating blacksmith shop. Chickens, horses and cracker cows are on the premises. A self-guiding tour, pioneer crafting workshops and demonstrations also are offered.

Time: Allow 3 hours minimum. **Hours:** Thurs.-Sun. 10-5, Oct.-May; Sat.-Sun. 10-5, rest of year. Closed Easter, Thanksgiving and Christmas. **Cost:** Self-guiding tour $5; $2 (ages 5-12). **Phone:** (941) 322-1000.

GEM **THE JOHN AND MABLE RINGLING MUSEUM OF ART** is 4 mi. n., just w. of US 41 at 5401 Bay Shore Rd. The fortune John Ringling derived from his circus, vast real estate, oil and railroad investments was well spent on his art museum and 1920s estate. The 66-acre complex, decorated with statues and dotted with banyan trees, offers a rose garden, a children's play area and a view of Sarasota Bay.

(See map & index p. 300.)

The museum was built in Italian Renaissance style, with an inner courtyard studded with many renowned sculptures from the Chiurazzi Foundry in Italy, including a bronze cast of Michelangelo's "David." The art collection includes significant holdings of American, European and non-Western art, with masterpieces from the 17th-century baroque period. Noteworthy is the Peter Paul Rubens collection and the James Turrell Skyspace. The Ulla R. and Arthur F. Searing Wing features a variety of changing exhibits year-round.

Ca' d'Zan, The Circus Museum and Tibbals Learning Center are on the museum's grounds *(see attraction listings)*.

Time: Allow 3 hours minimum. **Hours:** Grounds and gardens open daily 9:30-5:30. Museum open daily 10-5 (also Thurs. 5-8). Guided museum tours depart daily on the hour 11-4. Guided circus museum tours depart daily at noon and 1. Closed Jan. 1, Thanksgiving and Christmas. **Cost:** (also includes The Circus Museum and Tibbals Learning Center) $25; $23 (ages 65+); $15 (active military with ID and to all Thurs. 5-8); $5 (ages 6-17 and college students with ID). Museum of Art free to all Mon. Advance tickets are recommended. Prices may vary; phone ahead. A multiday pass also is available. **Phone:** (941) 359-5700, (941) 358-3180 for advance ticket information, or (941) 351-1660 for recorded information. GT 🍴

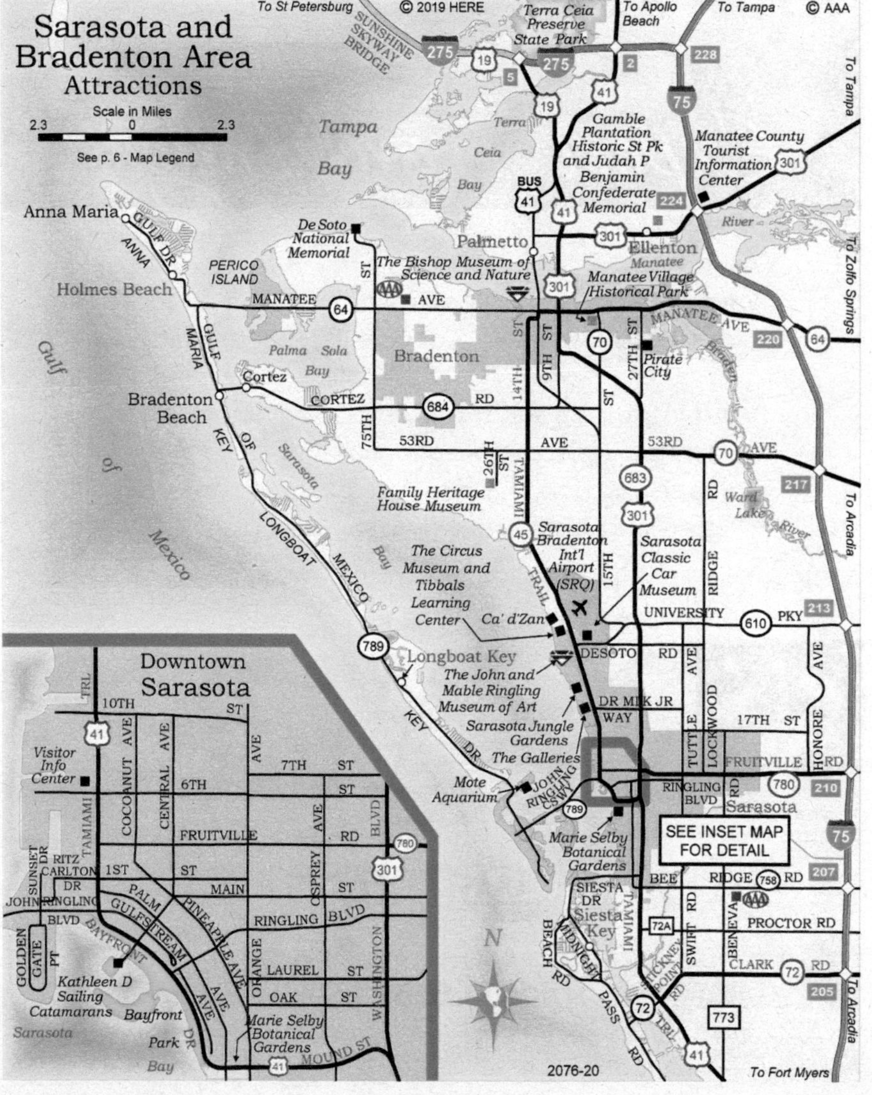

iStockphoto.com_LeoPatrizi

For travel and everyday activities, insight from those you trust can make a good experience great!

AAA inspectors and travel writers spend their days evaluating hotels, sampling menus and exploring new sights so you don't have to. Use their recommended picks and itineraries to find the best places to go, stay, dine and play.

Photo source iStockphoto.com

Get AAA travel information at club offices and on AAA.com for experiences you'll remember for a lifetime.

(See map & index p. 300.)

Ca' d'Zan (Ringling's Winter Residence) is at 5401 Bay Shore Rd. on the grounds of The John and Mable Ringling Museum of Art, and was completed in 1925 at a cost of $1.5 million. The 56-room, terra cotta mansion resembles a Venetian Gothic palace. Marble, tapestries and elaborately carved and gilded furniture dominate the interior. The mansion's first floor can be viewed on a self-guiding tour. The guided Mable's Tour includes the first and second floors; John's Tour includes floors two through five. Docent-led tours are limited; an admission time is provided with art museum ticketing. **Note:** Guided tours require climbing stairs and standing for long periods.

Hours: Daily 10-5. Guided tours depart on the hour 11-4. Grounds open daily 9:30-6. Closed Jan. 1, Thanksgiving and Christmas. **Cost:** Self-guiding tour $10. Mable's Tour $20. John's Tour $30. Combination ticket for Mable's and John's tours $40. Prices may vary; phone ahead. Admission includes The John and Mable Ringling Museum of Art and The Circus Museum. Advance tickets are recommended. **Phone:** (941) 359-5700, or (941) 358-3180 for advance ticketing. GT

The Circus Museum, 5401 Bay Shore Rd., on the grounds of The John and Mable Ringling Museum of Art, consists of displays of gilded parade wagons, calliopes, costumes, posters, photographs and a variety of circus memorabilia. Of special interest is an exhibit honoring famed circus performers.

Hours: Daily 10-5. Guided tours depart on the hour 11-3. Grounds open daily 9:30-6. Closed Jan. 1, Thanksgiving and Christmas. **Cost:** (also includes The John and Mable Ringling Museum of Art and Tibbals Learning Center) $25; $23 (ages 65+); $15 (active military with ID); $5 (ages 6-17 and college students with ID). Advance tickets are recommended. Prices may vary; phone ahead. **Phone:** (941) 359-5700, or (941) 358-3180 for advance ticket information. GT

Tibbals Learning Center is at 5401 Bay Shore Rd. on the grounds of The John and Mable Ringling Museum of Art. Handcrafted by Howard Tibbals, the miniature circus is said to be the world's largest and encompasses almost 4,000 square feet. Interactive galleries provide an up close experience. Restored circus posters also are on display. "The Greatest Show on Earth" mural depicts 45 circus performers.

Time: Allow 1 hour, 30 minutes minimum. **Hours:** Daily 10-5. Grounds open daily 9:30-6. Closed Jan. 1, Thanksgiving and Christmas. **Cost:** (also includes The John and Mable Ringling Museum of Art and The Circus Museum) $25; $23 (ages 65+); $15 (active military with ID); $5 (ages 6-17 and college students with ID). Advance tickets are recommended. Prices may vary; phone ahead. **Phone:** (941) 359-5700, or (941) 358-3180 for advance ticket information.

MYAKKA WILDLIFE TOURS, 9 mi. e. of I-75 exit 205 via SR 72, offers narrated tram tours through the wildlife habitats in Myakka River State Park *(see Recreation Areas Chart)*. Narrated airboat cruises on Upper Myakka Lake interpret the ecology of the lake and offer views of the animals. Binoculars are recommended.

Time: Allow 1 hour minimum. **Hours:** Tram tours daily at 1 and 2:30, Dec. 16-May 31. Airboat cruises daily at 10, 11:30 and 1 (also at 2:30, Dec. 16-May 31). **Cost:** Fare for each tour $14.98; $7.49 (ages 6-12). Apply for boarding pass upon arrival. Park entrance $6 (per private vehicle with two to eight people); $4 (motorcyclists or single-occupant private vehicle); $2 (per person arriving by bicycle or on foot). **Phone:** (941) 365-0100. GT

Traveling the world?

Before you go, purchase an International Driving Permit for a recognizable form of identification, even if you're not driving.

IDP
INTERNATIONAL DRIVING PERMIT
DRIVE THE WORLD!
U.S. residents apply at AAA offices.
Canadian residents apply at CAA offices.
Or visit us online:
AAA.com/IDP • CAA.ca/travelling/idp

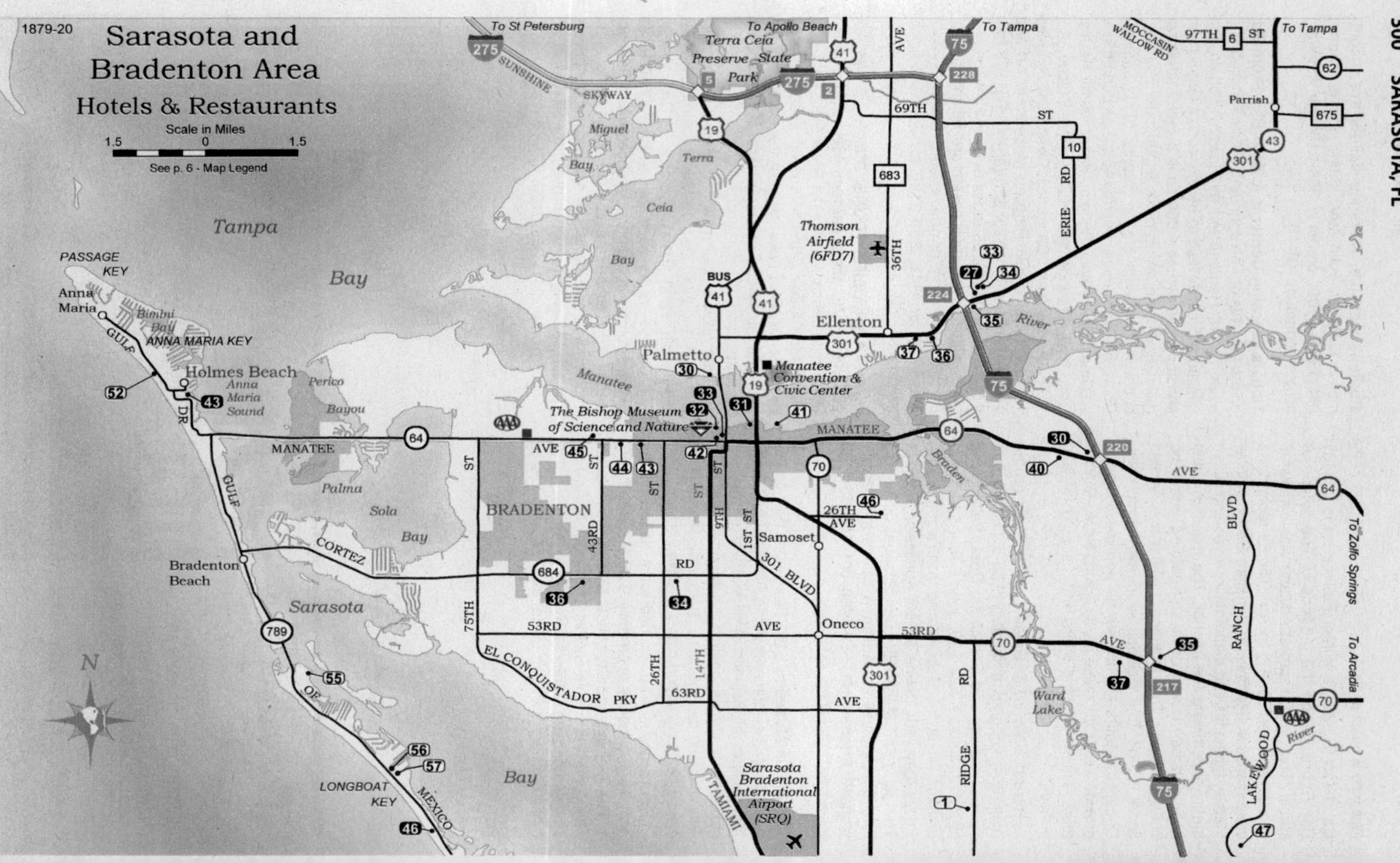

1879-20
Sarasota and
Bradenton Area
Hotels & Restaurants
Scale in Miles
1.5
0
1.5
See p. 6 - Map Legend
To St Petersburg
To Apollo Beach
To Tampa
To Tampa
To Zolfo Springs
To Arcadia
Terra Ceia Preserve State Park
SUNSHINE SKYWAY
Miguel Bay
Terra Ceia Bay
Tampa Bay
PASSAGE KEY
Anna Maria
Bimini Bay
ANNA MARIA KEY
Holmes Beach
Anna Maria Sound
Perico Bayou
Thomson Airfield (6FD7)
Ellenton
Palmetto
Manatee
Manatee Convention & Civic Center
The Bishop Museum of Science and Nature
River
Braden
MANATEE AVE
BRADENTON
Palma Sola Bay
CORTEZ
Bradenton Beach
Sarasota Bay
GULF DR
Samoset
Oneco
301 BLVD
26TH AVE
1ST ST
9TH ST
14TH ST
26TH ST
43RD ST
75TH ST
53RD AVE
63RD AVE
EL CONQUISTADOR PKY
TAMIAMI
Sarasota Bradenton International Airport (SRQ)
Ward Lake
RIDGE RD
RANCH BLVD
LAKEWOOD
River
ERIE RD
36TH AVE
69TH ST
97TH ST
MOCCASIN WALLOW RD
Parrish
LONGBOAT KEY
GULF OF MEXICO
N

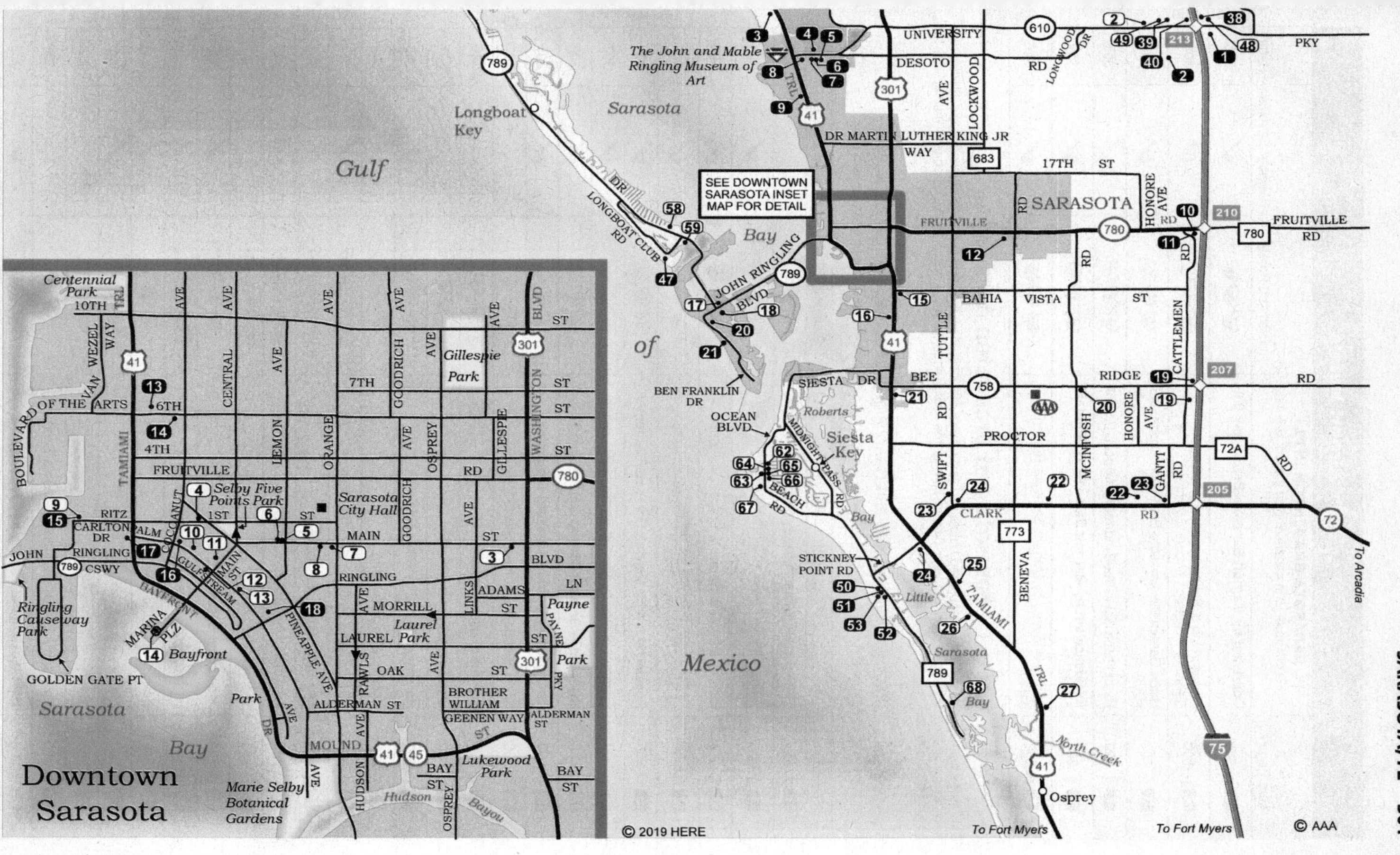

The John and Mable Ringling Museum of Art
Longboat Key
Sarasota Bay
Gulf of Mexico
SEE DOWNTOWN SARASOTA INSET MAP FOR DETAIL
SARASOTA
Siesta Key
Roberts Bay
Little Sarasota Bay
North Creek
Osprey
To Arcadia
To Fort Myers
To Fort Myers
© AAA
© 2019 HERE
Downtown Sarasota
Centennial Park
Gillespie Park
Selby Five Points Park
Sarasota City Hall
Ringling Causeway Park
Bayfront
Laurel Park
Payne Park
Lukewood Park
Marie Selby Botanical Gardens
Hudson Bayou

Airport Hotels

Map Page	SARASOTA-BRADENTON INT'L (Maximum driving distance from airport: 0.9 mi)	Diamond Rated	Member Savings	Page
8 p. 300	**Courtyard by Marriott Sarasota-Bradenton, 0.9 mi**	♦♦♦	✔	305
4 p. 300	Hampton Inn & Suites by Hilton Sarasota-Bradenton Airport, 0.7 mi	♦♦♦	✔	306
3 p. 300	Hilton Garden Inn Sarasota-Bradenton Airport, 0.8 mi	♦♦♦	✔	306
7 p. 300	**Hyatt Place Sarasota/Bradenton Airport, 0.5 mi**	♦♦♦	✔	306
5 p. 300	**Residence Inn by Marriott Sarasota-Bradenton, 0.7 mi**	♦♦♦	✔	306
6 p. 300	SpringHill Suites by Marriott Sarasota-Bradenton, 0.6 mi	♦♦♦	✔	307

Sarasota and Bradenton Area

This index helps you "spot" where approved hotels and restaurants are located on the corresponding detailed maps. Restaurant price range is a combination of lunch and/or dinner. Turn to the listing page for more information and consult display ads for special promotions.

For more details, rates and reservations: AAA.com/travelguides/hotels

SARASOTA

Map Page	Hotels	Diamond Rated	Member Savings	Page
1 p. 300	EVEN Hotels Sarasota-Lakewood Ranch	♦♦♦		305
2 p. 300	Homewood Suites by Hilton Sarasota University Park	♦♦♦	✔	306
3 p. 300	Hilton Garden Inn Sarasota-Bradenton Airport	♦♦♦	✔	306
4 p. 300	Hampton Inn & Suites by Hilton Sarasota-Bradenton Airport	♦♦♦	✔	306
5 p. 300	**Residence Inn by Marriott Sarasota-Bradenton**	♦♦♦	✔	306
6 p. 300	SpringHill Suites by Marriott Sarasota-Bradenton	♦♦♦	✔	307
7 p. 300	**Hyatt Place Sarasota/Bradenton Airport**	♦♦♦	✔	306
8 p. 300	**Courtyard by Marriott Sarasota-Bradenton**	♦♦♦	✔	305
9 p. 300	Super 8 of Sarasota Near Siesta Key	♦♦		307
10 p. 300	MainStay Suites Sarasota I-75	♦♦		306
11 p. 300	Sleep Inn Sarasota I-75	♦♦		307
12 p. 300	Homewood Suites by Hilton Sarasota	♦♦♦	✔	306
13 p. 300	**Hotel Indigo Sarasota**	♦♦♦	✔	306
14 p. 300	The Sarasota Modern, A Tribute Portfolio Hotel	♦♦♦♦	✔	307
15 p. 300	**The Ritz-Carlton, Sarasota**	♦♦♦♦	✔	307
16 p. 300	Art Ovation Hotel, Autograph Collection	♦♦♦♦	✔	305
17 p. 300	The Westin Sarasota	♦♦♦♦	✔	307
18 p. 300	**Aloft Hotel Sarasota**	♦♦♦	✔	305
19 p. 300	Hampton Inn Sarasota I-75 Bee Ridge	♦♦♦	✔	306
20 p. 300	**Holiday Inn Lido Beach**	♦♦♦	✔	306
21 p. 300	**Lido Beach Resort**	♦♦♦	✔	306
22 p. 300	Comfort Suites-Sarasota	♦♦♦		305
23 p. 300	Holiday Inn Express & Suites Sarasota East I-75	♦♦		306
24 p. 300	**Best Western Plus Siesta Key Gateway**	♦♦♦	✔	305

Map Page	Restaurants	Diamond Rated	Cuisine	Price Range	Page
1 p. 300	The Lazy Lobster	◆◆	Seafood	$13-$41	307
2 p. 300	Stonewood Grill & Tavern	◆◆◆	American	$11-$39	308
3 p. 300	Mediterraneo Ristorante Italiano	◆◆◆	Italian	$13-$32	307
4 p. 300	**The Bijou Cafe**	◆◆◆	Continental	$8-$45	307
5 p. 300	Mattison's City Grille	◆◆	Continental	$10-$36	307
6 p. 300	Patricks 1481	◆◆	American	$9-$28	308
7 p. 300	El Greco Mediterranean Cafe	◆◆	Greek	$7-$29	307
8 p. 300	Mélange	◆◆◆	New American	$10-$18	307
9 p. 300	Jack Dusty	◆◆◆	Seafood	$15-$36	307
10 p. 300	louies MODERN	◆◆◆	American	$12-$38	307
11 p. 300	Two Senoritas	◆◆	Mexican	$8-$17	308
12 p. 300	Cafe Epicure Restaurant Bakery	◆◆	Italian	$8-$32	307
13 p. 300	Caragiulos Italian-American Soul Food	◆◆	Italian	$10-$25	307
14 p. 300	Marina Jack	◆◆	Seafood	$10-$48	307
15 p. 300	**Michael's On East**	◆◆◆◆	Continental	$10-$41	308
16 p. 300	62 Bistrot	◆◆	French Breakfast Sandwiches	$8-$27	307
17 p. 300	Shore St. Armands	◆◆◆	New American	$10-$39	308
18 p. 300	Crab & Fin	◆◆◆	Seafood	$12-$130	307
19 p. 300	Madfish Grill	◆◆	Seafood	$9-$31	307
20 p. 300	Mi Pueblo El Restaurante Mexicano & Cantina	◆◆	Mexican	$9-$17	308
21 p. 300	Cafe Baci	◆◆◆	Northern Italian	$12-$32	307
22 p. 300	The Original Egg	◆◆	Breakfast Sandwiches	$8-$14	308
23 p. 300	4 & 20 Pasty Company	◆	British	$5-$8	307
24 p. 300	Sweet Berries Frozen Custard Sarasota	◆	Desserts Sandwiches	$5-$9	308
25 p. 300	Mattison's Forty-One	◆◆◆	Continental	$11-$36	307
26 p. 300	Waterfront Restaurant	◆◆	Steak Seafood	$9-$30	308
27 p. 300	Roessler's Restaurant	◆◆◆	Continental	$25-$35	308

ELLENTON

Map Page	Hotel	Diamond Rated	Member Savings	Page
27 p. 300	Hampton Inn Ellenton-Bradenton	◆◆◆	✓	71

Map Page	Restaurants	Diamond Rated	Cuisine	Price Range	Page
33 p. 300	Rippers Roadstand	◆	Burgers Hot Dogs	$3-$7	71
34 p. 300	Peach's Restaurant	◆◆	Breakfast Sandwiches	$4-$10	71
35 p. 300	Woody's River Roo Pub & Grill	◆	American	$7-$25	71
36 p. 300	Hickory Hollow Restaurant	◆	Comfort Food	$9-$26	71
37 p. 300	Shake Station	◆	Burgers Sandwiches	$4-$12	71

BRADENTON

Map Page	Hotels	Diamond Rated	Member Savings	Page
30 p. 300	**Best Western Plus Bradenton Hotel & Suites**	◆◆◆	✓	34

BRADENTON (cont'd)

Map Page	Hotels (cont'd)	Diamond Rated	Member Savings	Page
31 p. 300	**Courtyard by Marriott Bradenton/Sarasota Riverfront**	◆◆◆	✔	34
32 p. 300	SpringHill Suites by Marriott Bradenton Downtown/ Riverfront	◆◆◆	✔	34
33 p. 300	Hampton Inn & Suites Bradenton-Downtown Historic District	◆◆◆	✔	34
34 p. 300	**Best Western Plus Bradenton Gateway Hotel**	◆◆◆	✔	33
35 p. 300	Holiday Inn Express Inn & Suites Bradenton East-Lakewood Ranch	◆◆◆		34
36 p. 300	Holiday Inn Express Hotel & Suites Bradenton West	◆◆◆		34
37 p. 300	**Country Inn & Suites by Radisson-Bradenton**	◆◆◆	✔	34
38 p. 300	**Hyatt Place Sarasota/Lakewood Ranch**	◆◆◆	✔	34
39 p. 300	Courtyard by Marriott Sarasota University Park	◆◆◆	✔	34
40 p. 300	Hampton Inn & Suites Sarasota-University Park	◆◆◆	✔	34

Map Page	Restaurants	Diamond Rated	Cuisine	Price Range	Page
40 p. 300	D. Americo's Pizzeria	◆	Italian	$4-$20	34
41 p. 300	Caddy's at the Pointe	◆◆	Seafood	$9-$17	34
42 p. 300	the grill at O'Brick's	◆◆	American	$7-$34	34
43 p. 300	Peach's Restaurant	◆◆	Breakfast Sandwiches	$3-$9	34
44 p. 300	Shake Pit	◆	Sandwiches Desserts	$5-$7	35
45 p. 300	Sweet Berries Frozen Custard & Eatery	◆	Sandwiches Desserts	$5-$9	35
46 p. 300	Mixon's Groveside Cafe	◆	Sandwiches Pizza	$6-$8	34
47 p. 300	MacAllisters Grill & Tavern	◆◆	Irish	$9-$24	34
48 p. 300	Another Broken Egg Cafe	◆◆	Breakfast Sandwiches	$5-$15	34
49 p. 300	Anna's Deli	◆	Sandwiches	$4-$9	34

HOLMES BEACH

Map Page	Hotel	Diamond Rated	Member Savings	Page
43 p. 300	**Waterline Marina Resort & Beach Club, Autograph Collection**	◆◆◆	✔	81

Map Page	Restaurant	Diamond Rated	Cuisine	Price Range	Page
52 p. 300	Beach Bistro	◆◆◆	Continental	$27-$66	81

LONGBOAT KEY

Map Page	Hotels	Diamond Rated	Member Savings	Page
46 p. 300	**Zota Beach Resort**	◆◆◆	✔	145
47 p. 300	**The Resort At Longboat Key Club**	◆◆◆◆	✔	144

Map Page	Restaurants	Diamond Rated	Cuisine	Price Range	Page
55 p. 300	Mar Vista Dockside Restaurant & Pub	◆◆	Seafood	$9-$130	145
56 p. 300	Harry's Continental Kitchens	◆◆◆	Continental	$9-$41	145
57 p. 300	Euphemia Haye Restaurant	◆◆◆	Continental	$28-$55	145
58 p. 300	Dry Dock Waterfront Grill	◆◆	Seafood	$9-$36	145
59 p. 300	Chart House	◆◆◆	Seafood Steak	$22-$58 SAVE	145

SIESTA KEY

Map Page	Hotels	Diamond Rated	Member Savings	Page
50 p. 300	Tropical Beach Resorts	◆◆◆		310

SIESTA KEY (cont'd)

Map Page	Hotels (cont'd)	Diamond Rated	Member Savings	Page
51 p. 300	**The Capri at Siesta**	◆◆◆	✔	310
52 p. 300	**Siesta Palms By The Beach**	◆◆◆	✔	310
53 p. 300	**Siesta Key Inn**	◆◆◆	✔	310

Map Page	Restaurants	Diamond Rated	Cuisine	Price Range	Page
62 p. 300	The Old Salty Dog	◆◆	American	$8-$30	310
63 p. 300	Cafe Gabbiano Restaurant, Fine Wine And Bar	◆◆◆	Italian	$9-$42	310
64 p. 300	Village Cafe	◆◆	Breakfast Sandwiches	$8-$13	310
65 p. 300	Sun Garden Cafe	◆◆	American	$6-$15	310
66 p. 300	The Lobster Pot	◆◆	Seafood	$10-$38	310
67 p. 300	Daiquiri Deck Raw Bar	◆◆	Seafood	$10-$27	310
68 p. 300	**Turtles on Little Sarasota Bay**	◆◆	Seafood	$3-$34	310

PALMETTO

Map Page	Restaurant	Diamond Rated	Cuisine	Price Range	Page
30 p. 300	Riverside Cafe	◆◆	Seafood	$7-$17	250

ALOFT HOTEL SARASOTA 941/870-0900 18

◆◆◆ Hotel

AAA Benefit: Members save 5% or more!

Address: 1401 Ringling Blvd 34236 **Location:** Jct Palm Ave; downtown. **Facility:** 139 units. 10 stories, interior corridors. *Bath:* shower only. **Parking:** valet only. **Amenities:** safes. **Pool:** heated outdoor. **Activities:** hot tub, bicycles, health club. **Guest Services:** valet and coin laundry, area transportation.

  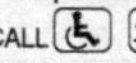 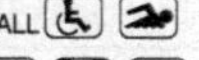   

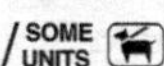

ART OVATION HOTEL, AUTOGRAPH COLLECTION 941/316-0808 16

◆◆◆◆ SAVE Boutique Contemporary Hotel. **Address:** 1255 N Palm Ave 34236

AAA Benefit: Members save 5% or more!

GET THE APP

Download today.
Connect every day.
AAA.com/mobile
CAA.ca/mobile

BEST WESTERN PLUS SIESTA KEY GATEWAY 941/924-4900 24

◆◆◆ Hotel

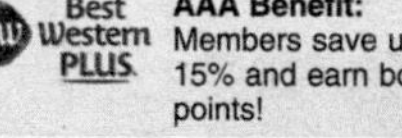

AAA Benefit: Members save up to 15% and earn bonus points!

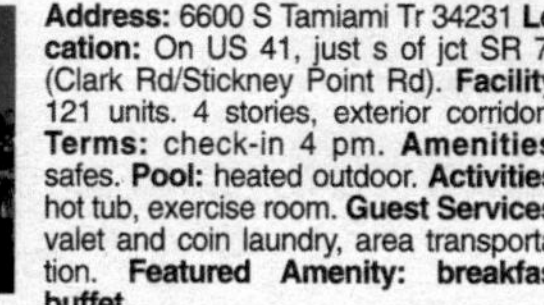

Address: 6600 S Tamiami Tr 34231 **Location:** On US 41, just s of jct SR 72 (Clark Rd/Stickney Point Rd). **Facility:** 121 units. 4 stories, exterior corridors. **Terms:** check-in 4 pm. **Amenities:** safes. **Pool:** heated outdoor. **Activities:** hot tub, exercise room. **Guest Services:** valet and coin laundry, area transportation. **Featured Amenity: breakfast buffet.**

COMFORT SUITES-SARASOTA 941/554-4475 22

◆◆◆ Hotel. **Address:** 5690 Honore Ave 34233

COURTYARD BY MARRIOTT SARASOTA-BRADENTON 941/355-3337 8

◆◆◆ Hotel

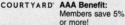

COURTYARD **AAA Benefit:** Members save 5% or more!

Address: 850 University Pkwy 34234 **Location:** Just e of jct US 41 (Tamiami Tr); jct Airport Cir; in Airport Business Park. **Facility:** 81 units. 3 stories, interior corridors. **Pool:** outdoor. **Activities:** exercise room. **Guest Services:** valet and coin laundry, boarding pass kiosk.

/ SOME UNITS

EVEN HOTELS SARASOTA-LAKEWOOD RANCH 941/782-4400 1

◆◆◆ Hotel. **Address:** 6231 Lake Osprey Dr 34240

(See map & index p. 300.)

HAMPTON INN & SUITES BY HILTON SARASOTA-BRADENTON AIRPORT 941/355-8140 **4**

SAVE Hotel. **Address:** 975 University Pkwy 34234

AAA Benefit: Members save 5% or more!

HAMPTON INN SARASOTA I-75 BEE RIDGE 941/371-1900 **19**

SAVE Hotel. **Address:** 5995 Cattleridge Blvd 34232

AAA Benefit: Members save 5% or more!

HILTON GARDEN INN SARASOTA-BRADENTON AIRPORT 941/552-1100 **3**

SAVE Hotel. **Address:** 8270 N Tamiami Tr 34243

AAA Benefit: Members save 5% or more!

HOLIDAY INN EXPRESS & SUITES SARASOTA EAST I-75 941/925-0631 **23**

Hotel. **Address:** 5730 Gantt Rd 34233

HOLIDAY INN LIDO BEACH 941/388-5555 **20**

Hotel

Address: 233 Ben Franklin Dr 34236 **Location:** On Lido Key at Lido Beach; 0.4 mi s of St. Armands Circle. **Facility:** 135 units. 7 stories, interior corridors. **Parking:** on-site (fee). **Amenities:** safes. **Dining:** 2 restaurants. **Pool:** heated outdoor. **Activities:** beach access, exercise room. **Guest Services:** complimentary and valet laundry, area transportation.

SAVE ECO CALL BIZ HS / SOME UNITS

HOMEWOOD SUITES BY HILTON SARASOTA 941/365-7300 **12**

SAVE Extended Stay Hotel. **Address:** 3470 Fruitville Rd 34237

AAA Benefit: Members save 5% or more!

HOMEWOOD SUITES BY HILTON SARASOTA UNIVERSITY PARK 941/309-3904 **2**

SAVE Extended Stay Hotel. **Address:** 305 N Cattlemen Rd 34243

AAA Benefit: Members save 5% or more!

HOTEL INDIGO SARASOTA 941/487-3800 **13**

Boutique Hotel

Address: 1223 Boulevard of the Arts 34236 **Location:** Jct US 41 (N Tamiami Tr). **Facility:** The hotel offers an inviting coastal theme with vibrant guest rooms and public areas that give one the feel of stepping into a beachside retreat, despite its location in the arts district. 95 units. 4 stories, interior corridors. *Bath:* shower only. **Parking:** on-site (fee). **Amenities:** safes. **Activities:** hot tub, bicycles, exercise room, massage. **Guest Services:** area transportation.

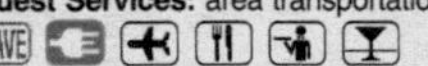

SAVE CALL BIZ HS / SOME UNITS

HYATT PLACE SARASOTA/BRADENTON AIRPORT 941/554-5800 **7**

Hotel

HYATT PLACE **AAA Benefit:** Members save up to 10%!

Address: 950 University Pkwy 34234 **Location:** Just e of US 41 (Tamiami Tr), jct Airport Cir. **Facility:** 114 units. 3 stories, interior corridors. **Pool:** heated outdoor. **Activities:** hot tub, picnic facilities, exercise room. **Guest Services:** valet and coin laundry, boarding pass kiosk, area transportation. **Featured Amenity:** **breakfast buffet.**

SAVE ECO CALL BIZ HS / SOME UNITS

LIDO BEACH RESORT 941/388-2161 **21**

Hotel

Address: 700 Ben Franklin Dr 34236 **Location:** Oceanfront. On Lido Key at Lido Beach; 0.8 mi s of St. Armands Circle. **Facility:** 222 units, some two bedrooms, efficiencies and kitchens. 4-14 stories, interior/exterior corridors. **Parking:** on-site (fee). **Terms:** check-in 4 pm. **Amenities:** safes. **Dining:** 3 restaurants, entertainment. **Pool:** heated outdoor. **Activities:** hot tub, fishing, recreation programs, bicycles, exercise room. **Guest Services:** valet and coin laundry, area transportation.

SAVE ECO CALL BIZ sHS / SOME UNITS

LIDO BEACH RESORT SARASOTA, FL

Beachfront resort with spacious rooms & condo-style suites. Close to world-class shopping & dining.

MAINSTAY SUITES SARASOTA I-75 941/500-4700 **10**

Extended Stay Hotel. **Address:** 5965A Brookhill Blvd 34232

RESIDENCE INN BY MARRIOTT SARASOTA-BRADENTON 941/358-1468 **5**

Extended Stay Hotel

Residence INN **AAA Benefit:** Members save 5% or more!

Address: 1040 University Pkwy 34234 **Location:** Just e of jct US 41 (Tamiami Tr). **Facility:** 78 kitchen units, some two bedrooms. 3 stories, interior corridors. **Pool:** heated outdoor. **Activities:** hot tub, exercise room. **Guest Services:** boarding pass kiosk.

SAVE ECO CALL BIZ HS / SOME UNITS

For exclusive AAA member savings and benefits: AAA.com/hertz

(See map & index p. 300.)

THE RITZ-CARLTON, SARASOTA 941/309-2000 **15**

Resort Hotel

THE RITZ-CARLTON **AAA Benefit:** Unequaled service at special member savings!

Address: 1111 Ritz-Carlton Dr 34236 **Location:** Waterfront. On US 41, jct John Ringling Blvd. **Facility:** A prime downtown location on the waterfront enhances this lovely hotel. Luxuries include a full-service spa and salon where you can pamper yourself and a separate first-class beach club facility. 266 units, some two bedrooms. 9 stories, interior corridors. **Parking:** on-site (fee) and valet. **Terms:** check-in 4 pm. **Amenities:** safes. **Dining:** 2 restaurants, also, Jack Dusty, see separate listing, entertainment. **Pool:** heated outdoor. **Activities:** sauna, hot tub, steamroom, fishing, tennis, recreation programs, kids club, bicycles, game room, lawn sports, health club, spa. **Guest Services:** valet laundry, boarding pass kiosk, rental car service, luggage security pick-up, area transportation.

SAVE ECO CALL BIZ HS  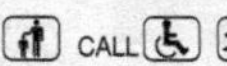  / SOME UNITS

THE SARASOTA MODERN, A TRIBUTE PORTFOLIO HOTEL 941/906-1290 **14**

SAVE Boutique Contemporary Retro Hotel. **Address:** 1290 Boulevard of the Arts 34236

AAA Benefit: Members save 5% or more!

SLEEP INN SARASOTA I-75 941/500-4700 **11**

Hotel. **Address:** 5965 Brookhill Blvd, Building A 34232

SPRINGHILL SUITES BY MARRIOTT SARASOTA-BRADENTON 941/358-3385 **6**

SAVE Hotel. **Address:** 1020 University Pkwy 34234

AAA Benefit: Members save 5% or more!

SUPER 8 OF SARASOTA NEAR SIESTA KEY 941/355-9326 **9**

Motel. **Address:** 4309 N Tamiami Tr 34234

THE WESTIN SARASOTA 941/217-4777 **17**

SAVE Hotel. **Address:** 1175 N Gulfstream Ave 34236

AAA Benefit: Members save 5% or more!

WHERE TO EAT

4 & 20 PASTY COMPANY 941/927-1421 (23)

British. Quick Serve. **Address:** 5638 Swift Rd 34231

62 BISTROT 941/954-1011 (16)

French Breakfast Sandwiches. Casual Dining. **Address:** 1962 Hillview St 34239

BARNACLE BILL'S SEAFOOD RESTAURANT & MARKET 941/365-6800

Seafood. Casual Dining. **Address:** 1526 Main St 34236

THE BIJOU CAFE 941/366-8111 (4)

Continental Fine Dining $8-$45

AAA Inspector Notes: In the heart of the theater and arts district, this stylish, upscale bistro draws diners in search of romance. Braised lamb shank, Australian rack of lamb, bijou roasted duck, organic chicken breast and steak au poivre are outstanding examples on a winning menu. The restaurant is owned and operated by Chef Jean Pierre Knaggs. **Features:** full bar, patio dining, happy hour. **Reservations:** suggested. **Address:** 1287 1st St 34236 **Location:** Between Cocoanut and Pineapple aves; downtown. **Parking:** on-site and valet. L D

CAFE BACI 941/921-4848 (21)

Northern Italian. Fine Dining. **Address:** 4001 S Tamiami Tr 34231

CAFE EPICURE RESTAURANT BAKERY 941/366-5648 (12)

Italian. Casual Dining. **Address:** 1298 N Palm Ave 34236

CARAGIULOS ITALIAN-AMERICAN SOUL FOOD 941/951-0866 (13)

Italian. Casual Dining. **Address:** 69 S Palm Ave 34236

COLUMBIA RESTAURANT 941/388-3987

Spanish. Casual Dining. **Address:** 411 St. Armands Cir 34236

CRAB & FIN 941/388-3964 (18)

Seafood. Fine Dining. **Address:** 420 St. Armands Cir 34236

EL GRECO MEDITERRANEAN CAFE 941/365-2234 (7)

Greek. Casual Dining. **Address:** 1592 Main St 34236

JACK DUSTY 941/309-2266 (9)

Seafood. Fine Dining. **Address:** 1111 Ritz-Carlton Dr 34236

THE LAZY LOBSTER 941/351-5515 (1)

Seafood. Casual Dining. **Address:** 7602 N Lockwood Ridge Rd 34243

LOUIES MODERN 941/552-9688 (10)

American. Casual Dining. **Address:** 1289 N Palm Ave 34236

MADFISH GRILL 941/377-3474 (19)

Seafood. Casual Dining. **Address:** 4059 Cattlemen Rd 34233

MARINA JACK 941/365-4232 (14)

Seafood. Casual Dining. **Address:** 2 Marina Plaza 34236

MATTISON'S CITY GRILLE 941/330-0440 (5)

Continental. Casual Dining. **Address:** 1 N Lemon Ave 34236

MATTISON'S FORTY-ONE 941/921-3400 (25)

Continental. Fine Dining. **Address:** 7275 S Tamiami Tr 34231

MEDITERRANEO RISTORANTE ITALIANO 941/365-4122 (3)

Italian. Casual Dining. **Address:** 1970 Main St 34236

MÉLANGE 941/953-7111 (8)

New American. Fine Dining. **Address:** 1568 Main St 34236

(See map & index p. 300.)

MICHAEL'S ON EAST 941/366-0007 (15)

Continental Fine Dining
$10-$41

AAA Inspector Notes: Creative dishes awaken your taste buds in this upscale restaurant. Such items as their spicy seafood gumbo whets the appetite and prepares you for their main course. Grilled salmon is just one of the popular choices and is attractively presented with a colorful vegetable medley. Staff members wear semi-formal attire and offer prompt, professional service throughout the course of your meal. **Features:** full bar, happy hour. **Reservations:** suggested. **Address:** 1212 East Ave S 34239 **Location:** On US 41, jct Bahia Vista Dr; in Midtown Plaza, east entrance. **Parking:** on-site and valet. L D CALL

MI PUEBLO EL RESTAURANTE MEXICANO & CANTINA 941/379-2880 (20)

Mexican. Casual Dining. **Address:** 4436 Bee Ridge Rd 34233

THE ORIGINAL EGG 941/922-2868 (22)

Breakfast Sandwiches. Casual Dining. **Address:** 4031 Clark Rd 34233

PATRICKS 1481 941/955-1481 (6)

American. Casual Dining. **Address:** 1481 Main St 34236

ROESSLER'S RESTAURANT 941/966-5688 (27)

Continental. Fine Dining. **Address:** 2033 Vamo Way 34238

SHORE ST. ARMANDS 941/296-0301 (17)

New American. Casual Dining. **Address:** 465 John Ringling Blvd 34236

SONNY'S REAL PIT BAR-B-Q 941/364-5833

Barbecue. Casual Dining. **Address:** 3926 S Tamiami Tr 34231

STONEWOOD GRILL & TAVERN 941/355-3315 (2)

American. Fine Dining. **Address:** 5415 University Pkwy 34201

SWEET BERRIES FROZEN CUSTARD SARASOTA 941/750-6771 (24)

Desserts Sandwiches. Quick Serve. **Address:** 2881 Clark Rd 34231

TIJUANA FLATS 941/330-0989

Tex-Mex. Quick Serve. **Address:** 1635 S Tamiami Tr 34243

TOMMY BAHAMA'S TROPICAL CAFE 941/388-2888

Caribbean. Casual Dining. **Address:** 300 John Ringling Blvd 34236

TOOJAY'S GOURMET DELI 941/362-3692

American. Casual Dining. **Address:** 3501 S Tamiami Tr 34239

TWO SENORITAS 941/366-1618 (11)

Mexican. Casual Dining. **Address:** 1355 Main St 34236

WATERFRONT RESTAURANT 941/921-1916 (26)

Steak Seafood. Casual Dining. **Address:** 7660 S Tamiami Tr 34231

SEBASTIAN (H-6) pop. 21,929, elev. 19'

In 1715 several ships of the Spanish fleet were lost in Sebastian Inlet during a hurricane. To this day, treasure hunters search the waters along Sebastian's coast for gold, jewelry and rare antiquities.

Skydiving and surfing are among the area's popular recreational activities. The Indian River Lagoon, the St. Sebastian River and Blue Cypress Lake are fishing hot spots and paradise for boaters. Pelican Island National Wildlife Refuge provides habitat for more than 30 species of birds; the refuge may be viewed only by boat.

Sebastian River Area Chamber of Commerce & Visitor's Center: 700 Main St., Sebastian, FL 32958. **Phone:** (772) 589-5969.

BEST WESTERN PLUS SEBASTIAN HOTEL & SUITES 772/388-9300

Hotel

AAA Benefit: Members save up to 15% and earn bonus points!

Address: 1655 US Hwy 1 32958 **Location:** I-95 exit 156 (Fellsmere Rd/CR 512), 6.5 mi e to US 1, then 1.2 mi n. **Facility:** 56 units, some two bedrooms and kitchens. 3 stories, interior corridors. **Amenities:** safes. **Pool:** heated outdoor. **Activities:** limited exercise equipment. **Guest Services:** coin laundry. **Featured Amenity: breakfast buffet.**

SAVE CALL BIZ / SOME UNITS

SEBRING (E-10) pop. 10,491, elev. 160'

Sebring (SEE-bring) was founded in 1911 by George E. Sebring, an ardent prohibitionist from Ohio; some early deeds contained bans against the use or sale of alcohol on the premises. The Atlantic Coast Railroad reached the town in 1912 and the land boom began. By 1920 there were nine resorts and the area was a popular winter resort for the affluent, and in 1926, the residents numbered 7,000. Following the land bust of 1924-26, the population dwindled to approximately 3,000. The establishment of the B-17 training facility Hendricks Field in World War II began the town's rebirth.

Today Sebring boasts some of the state's largest groves of citrus, lime and avocado trees. Sebring International Raceway plays host to automobile races, including March's grueling 12 Hours of Sebring, part of the American Le Mans Series; phone (800) 626-7223. Medal of Honor Park, on US 27 at the Agricultural Center, is an outside memorial dedicated to veterans.

Greater Sebring Chamber of Commerce: 227 US 27N, Sebring, FL 33870. **Phone:** (863) 385-8448.

CHILDREN'S MUSEUM OF THE HIGHLANDS, 901 US 27 N., has a child-size diner complete with a pizza oven, make-believe ethnic food and costumes. Other hands-on exhibits include a waterworks and a television station. Children can shop for groceries, paint their faces and make huge bubbles using materials provided by the museum. **Time:** Allow 1 hour, 30 minutes minimum. **Hours:** Tues.-Sat. 9-4. Closed major holidays. **Cost:** $5 (ages 1+). Children must be with an adult. **Phone:** (863) 451-5385.

GEM **HIGHLANDS HAMMOCK STATE PARK,** 4 mi. w. of US 27 on CR 634, is a 9,251-acre wilderness of lush, dense junglelike and subtropical vegetation and swamps, all accessible by an excellent system of paved drives, well-marked trails and elevated boardwalks. Trees range in age from more than 400 years to 1,000 years.

Highlands Hammock was Florida's first state park and opened to the public in 1931. The CCC was active in the park during the mid-1930s and '40s and developed additional facilities as well as planned for a botanical garden. The Florida State Civilian Conservation Corps Museum features displays about park history and short films about the park. Ranger-narrated tram tours of the park's remote areas are available year-round and park rangers conduct a variety of programs during the week, November through April. Inquire at the ranger station for schedules and locations. *See Recreation Areas Chart.*

Hours: Park open daily 8-dusk. Museum open daily 9-5. Tram tours depart Tues.-Fri. at 1 and 2:30, Sat.-Sun. at 1:30; tickets are available on a first-come, first-served basis at the Ranger Station beginning at 8. **Cost:** $6 (per private vehicle with two to eight people); $4 (motorcyclists or single-occupant private vehicle); $2 (per additional passenger or person arriving by bicycle or on foot). Tram tour $5; $3 (ages 6-12). **Phone:** (863) 386-6094, or (800) 326-3521 for camping reservations. GT

HOLIDAY INN EXPRESS & SUITES SEBRING 863/386-1115

Hotel. **Address:** 4400 US Hwy 27 N 33870

LA QUINTA INN & SUITES SEBRING 863/386-1000

Address: 4115 US Hwy 27 S 33870 **Location:** On US 27/98, just n of jct Sebring Pkwy. **Facility:** 77 units. 3 stories, interior corridors. **Amenities:** safes. **Pool:** heated outdoor. **Activities:** hot tub, exercise room. **Guest Services:** valet and coin laundry. **Featured Amenity: breakfast buffet.**

SAVE CALL BIZ HS

SOME UNITS

RESIDENCE INN BY MARRIOTT-SEBRING 863/314-9100

SAVE Extended Stay Contemporary Hotel. **Address:** 3221 Tubbs Rd 33870

AAA Benefit: Members save 5% or more!

SEVEN SEBRING RACEWAY HOTEL 863/655-7200

Address: 150 Midway Dr 33870 **Location:** Jct US 98, 1.4 mi n on Haywood Taylor Blvd; at entrance to Sebring International Raceway. **Facility:** 123 units, some efficiencies and kitchens. 4 stories, interior corridors. **Pool:** outdoor. **Activities:** exercise room, massage. **Guest Services:** valet and coin laundry, area transportation.

SOME UNITS

WHERE TO EAT

CODY'S ORIGINAL ROADHOUSE 863/402-0735

American. Casual Dining. **Address:** 521 US 27 N 33870

HIBACHI BUFFET 863/658-0977

Chinese Sushi. Quick Serve. **Address:** 2870 US 27 N 33870

SEBRING DINER 863/385-3434

Comfort Food Sandwiches. Casual Dining. **Address:** 4040 US Hwy 27 S 33872

SONNY'S REAL PIT BAR-B-Q 863/382-3820

Barbecue. Casual Dining. **Address:** 751 US 27 S 33870

SEFFNER pop. 7,579

- **Hotels & Restaurants map & index p. 338**
- **Part of Tampa area — see map p. 313**

COUNTRY INN & SUITES BY RADISSON TAMPA EAST/SEFFNER 813/675-8600 40

Address: 11551 Discovery Ln 33584 **Location:** I-4 exit 10, just n on CR 579. **Facility:** 83 units. 3 stories, interior corridors. **Pool:** outdoor. **Activities:** picnic facilities, exercise room. **Guest Services:** valet and coin laundry, area transportation. **Featured Amenity: full hot breakfast.**

SOME UNITS

HAMPTON INN & SUITES TAMPA EAST 813/630-4321 41

SAVE Hotel. **Address:** 11740 Tampa Gateway Blvd 33584

AAA Benefit: Members save 5% or more!

WHERE TO EAT

CHINA WOK CHINESE RESTAURANT 813/653-9998 71

Chinese. Quick Serve. **Address:** 11212 E Dr Martin Luther King Jr Blvd 33584

HUNGRY HARRY'S FAMOUS BAR-B-QUE 813/643-0063 72

Barbecue. Casual Dining. **Address:** 2006 S Parsons Ave 33584

YOUNG BIN CHINESE RESTAURANT 813/685-5458 70

Chinese. Casual Dining. **Address:** 720 Dr. Martin Luther King Jr Blvd W 33584

SEMINOLE pop. 17,233, elev. 36'

- **Hotels & Restaurants map & index p. 286**
- **Part of St. Petersburg-Clearwater and Beaches area — see map p. 275**

HOLIDAY INN EXPRESS & SUITES ST. PETERSBURG-MADEIRA BEACH 727/914-7107 58

Hotel. **Address:** 4816 100th Way N 33708

WHERE TO EAT

BROOKLYN PIZZA COMPANY 727/317-0044 86

Pizza. Casual Dining. **Address:** 10785 Park Blvd 33772

CAPO DE MONTE ITALIAN MARKET 727/394-7800 85

Sandwiches Deli. Quick Serve. **Address:** 8400 Seminole Blvd 33772

JOTO'S PIZZA 727/397-6661 87

Pizza. Casual Dining. **Address:** 13050 Park Blvd 33776

SIESTA KEY pop. 6,565

• Hotels & Restaurants map & index p. 300

THE CAPRI AT SIESTA 941/684-3244 (51)

Motel

Address: 6782 Sara Sea Cir 34242 **Location:** Just s of jct SR 72 (Stickney Point Rd) on Midnight Pass Rd, just w. **Facility:** 10 units, some efficiencies and kitchens. 1 story, exterior corridors. *Bath:* shower only. **Terms:** check-in 3:30 pm. **Amenities:** safes. **Activities:** beach access. **Guest Services:** complimentary laundry.

SIESTA KEY INN 941/349-4999 (53)

Extended Stay Motel

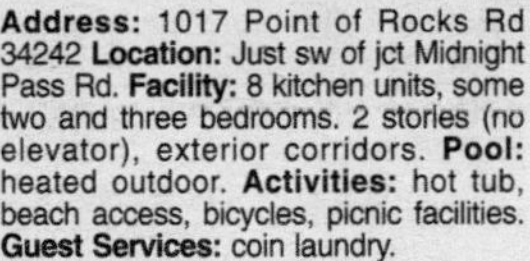

Address: 1017 Point of Rocks Rd 34242 **Location:** Just sw of jct Midnight Pass Rd. **Facility:** 8 kitchen units, some two and three bedrooms. 2 stories (no elevator), exterior corridors. **Pool:** heated outdoor. **Activities:** hot tub, beach access, bicycles, picnic facilities. **Guest Services:** coin laundry.

SIESTA PALMS BY THE BEACH 941/349-4999 (52)

Extended Stay Motel

Address: 1125-1127 Point of Rocks Rd 34242 **Location:** Jct Midnight Pass Rd. **Facility:** 8 kitchen units. 2 stories (no elevator), exterior corridors. **Terms:** off-site registration. **Pool:** heated outdoor. **Activities:** beach access, bicycles, picnic facilities.

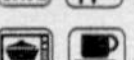
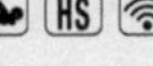

TROPICAL BEACH RESORTS 941/349-3330 (50)

Motel. **Address:** 6717 Sara Sea Cir 34242

WHERE TO EAT

CAFE GABBIANO RESTAURANT, FINE WINE AND BAR 941/349-1423 (63)

Italian. Casual Dining. **Address:** 5104 Ocean Blvd 34242

DAIQUIRI DECK RAW BAR 941/349-8697 (67)

Seafood. Casual Dining. **Address:** 5250 Ocean Blvd 34242

THE LOBSTER POT 941/349-2323 (66)

Seafood. Casual Dining. **Address:** 5157 Ocean Blvd 34242

THE OLD SALTY DOG 941/349-0158 (62)

American. Casual Dining. **Address:** 5023 Ocean Blvd 34242

SUN GARDEN CAFE 941/346-7170 (65)

American. Casual Dining. **Address:** 210 Avenida Madera 34242

TURTLES ON LITTLE SARASOTA BAY 941/346-2207 (68)

Seafood Casual Dining $3-$34

AAA Inspector Notes: Set on Little Sarasota Bay, this restaurant has been a popular dining spot since 1986. Enjoy potato-encrusted haddock, tilapia amandine, coconut-crusted mahi mahi or baked stuffed Gulf shrimp as you enjoy views of the bay and marina. You may spot a manatee or dolphin as you dine, depending on the time of the year. On Sunday they have a brunch that is served with a complimentary mimosa or Bloody Mary. **Features:** full bar, early bird specials, Sunday brunch. **Address:** 8875 Midnight Pass Rd 34242 **Location:** 2.7 mi s of jct SR 72; opposite Turtle Beach.

L D CALL

VILLAGE CAFE 941/349-2822 (64)

Breakfast Sandwiches. Casual Dining. **Address:** 5133 Ocean Blvd 34242

SOUTH PASADENA pop. 4,964

• Hotels & Restaurants map & index p. 286
• Part of St. Petersburg-Clearwater and Beaches area — see map p. 275

HORSE & JOCKEY BRITISH PUB & RESTAURANT 727/345-4995 (116)

British. Casual Dining. **Address:** 1155 Pasadena Ave S 33707

SPIROS PASADENA PRODUCE & DELI 727/384-0750 (115)

Greek. Quick Serve. **Address:** 6801 Gulfport Blvd 33707

TED PETERS FAMOUS SMOKED FISH 727/381-7931 (117)

Seafood. Quick Serve. **Address:** 1350 Pasadena Ave S 33707

SPRING HILL pop. 98,621

HAMPTON INN SPRING HILL 352/684-5000

SAVE Hotel. **Address:** 1344 Commercial Way 34606

AAA Benefit: Members save 5% or more!

MICROTEL INN & SUITES BY WYNDHAM, SPRING HILL 352/596-3444

Hotel. **Address:** 4881 Commercial Way 34606

Make the Connection

Find this symbol for places to look, book and save on AAA.com.

WHERE TO EAT

CODY'S ORIGINAL ROADHOUSE 352/683-8909

American. Casual Dining. **Address:** 3101 Commercial Way 34606

SONNY'S REAL PIT BAR-B-Q 352/597-3322

Barbecue. Casual Dining. **Address:** 4731 Commercial Way 34606

STARKE (C-2) pop. 5,449, elev. 150'

CAMP BLANDING MUSEUM AND MEMORIAL PARK is 11 mi. e. of jct. US 301 at 5629 SR 16W, at the main gate of Camp Blanding in building 3040. The museum, housed in a refurbished World War II barracks, contains photographs, weapons, artifacts and exhibits honoring the camp, which was a major training center during World War II. Outdoor exhibits include vehicles and artillery pieces as well as monuments and memorials to those who served in World War II and other 20th-century conflicts. **Time:** Allow 1 hour minimum. **Hours:** Park daily dawn-dusk. Museum daily noon-4. Closed Thanksgiving and Christmas. **Cost:** Free. **Phone:** (904) 682-3196. GT

BEST WESTERN STARKE 904/964-6744

Motel

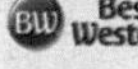
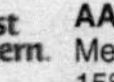

AAA Benefit: Members save up to 15% and earn bonus points!

Address: 1290 N Temple Ave 32091 **Location:** On US 301, 1 mi n from jct SR 100 (Reid St). **Facility:** 51 units. 2 stories (no elevator), exterior corridors. **Pool:** outdoor. **Featured Amenity: full hot breakfast.**

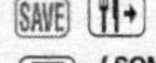
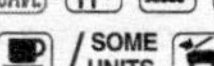

SOME UNITS

WHERE TO EAT

SONNY'S REAL PIT BAR-B-Q 904/964-8840

Barbecue. Casual Dining. **Address:** 230 S Temple Ave 32091

AAA Vacations® offers vacation options and experiences all over the world. In addition to our 24/7 Member Care and Best Price Guarantee*, we deliver value with every itinerary.

These exclusive values may include:

- Savings or spending credits
- Pre-night hotel stay
- Priority check-in
- ***And more!***
- Complimentary excursions
- Complimentary specialty dining
- Pre-paid gratuities

Call your AAA Travel Agent or visit AAA.com/AAAVacations

* If you book a qualifying *AAA Vacations®* cruise or tour package and find a valid better rate for the exact itinerary within 24 hours of your booking, AAA will match the lower rate and send you a $50 *AAA Vacations®* future travel credit certificate. Certain restrictions apply. Visit AAA.com/AAAVacations for full details.

Tampa

Then & Now

With the world's tourism mecca—Orlando—just 70 miles up the road, it might be easy to overlook the city by the bay as a major travel destination. But Tampa and its communities offer a number of fun things to do with friends and family. First, there's a theme park here: Busch Gardens Tampa preceded Walt Disney's dream by 12 years. With varied cultural offerings, world-class attractions, championship sports teams, water recreation opportunities and a vibrant Latin heritage, Tampa merits a closer look.

During the 18th century the bay belonged to pirates who left a decided influence on the area. The legendary Jose Gaspar may have pillaged his way to annual celebrity—Tampa's Gasparilla Pirate Festival takes place late January or early February. The NFL's Tampa Bay Buccaneers also take their name from this era.

In the late 1800s, railroads stimulated the tourist trade, attracting wealthy Northern vacationers. In 1891, royalty, financial bigwigs and luminaries attended the opening of Henry B. Plant's exclusive Tampa Bay Hotel, which is now part of the University of Tampa.

Cigars were once the city's mainstay, and brick and frame factories housing such companies as Hav-a-Tampa and Cuesta-Rey provided employment for Spanish, Italian and Cuban immigrants who labored at long tables hand-rolling tobacco leaves. Cigars are still produced, but the business community has diversified.

Tampa is now the foremost port of Florida's west coast and one of the nation's busiest, with petroleum, coal, steel and cement among its major inbound cargoes. A state-of-the-art cruise terminal welcomes passengers of several cruise lines bound for Caribbean and Latin American destinations.

Architecturally, Tampa admirably records the different periods of its growth. Older stucco homes with flat roofs, patios and wrought-iron balconies show a marked Spanish influence. The Tampa Convention Center, the Straz Center for the Performing Arts, and skyscrapers and luxury hotels added during the building boom of the 1980s and early 1990s heightened the city's once

(Continued on p. 314.)

AAA.com/travelguides—
more ways to look, book and save

Ybor City

Destination Tampa

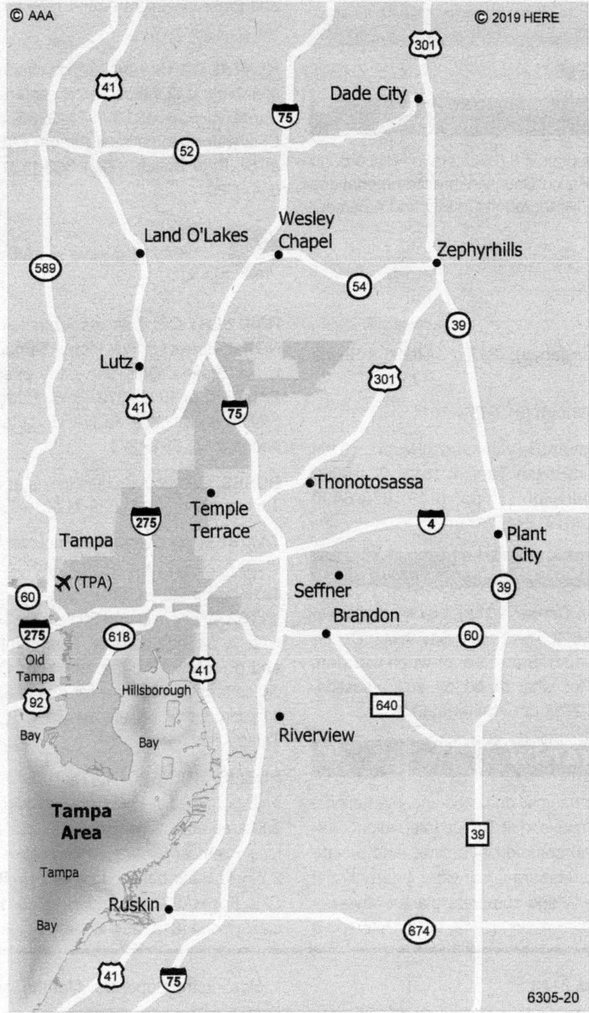

This map shows cities in the Tampa vicinity where you will find attractions, hotels and restaurants. Cities are listed alphabetically in this book on the following pages.

Fast Facts

ABOUT THE CITY

POP: 352,957 ▪ **ELEV:** 27 ft.

MONEY

SALES TAX: Sales tax is 8.5 percent in Hillsborough and 7 percent in Pasco County. An accommodations tax is 6 percent in Hillsborough County and 4 percent in Pasco County.

WHOM TO CALL

EMERGENCY: 911

POLICE (non-emergency): (813) 231-6130 ▪ Sheriff (813) 247-8200

FIRE (non-emergency): (813) 274-7011

HOSPITALS: AdventHealth Carrollwood, (813) 932-2222 ▪ AdventHealth Tampa, (813) 971-6000 ▪ Memorial Hospital of Tampa, (813) 873-6400 ▪ Tampa General, (813) 844-7000.

VISITOR INFORMATION

Tampa Bay Visitor Center: 201 N. Franklin St., Suite 102, Tampa, FL 33602. The Tampa Bay Visitor Center is open Mon.-Sat. 10-5, Sun. 11-5 for when you want additional advice for what to do on your vacation. **Phone:** (813) 226-2752 or (800) 448-2672.

TRANSPORTATION

AIR TRAVEL: Commercial domestic and international flights entering Tampa land at Tampa International Airport (TPA). Several commercial airlines and private planes use St. Petersburg-Clearwater International Airport (PIE). Private and corporate planes have access to Albert Whitted Airport (SPG) in St. Petersburg and Peter O. Knight Airport (TPF) in Tampa. *See Arriving, Air Travel.*

RENTAL CARS: Hertz, which offers discounts to AAA members, is at the car rental center at Tampa International Airport, (813) 874-3232; St. Petersburg-Clearwater International Airport, (727) 532-4801; and at St. Pete Beach, (727) 360-1631; or phone (800) 654-3080.

Book and save at AAA.com/hertz

RAIL SERVICE: Tampa's Amtrak station is at 601 N. Nebraska Ave. in downtown Tampa, behind historic Union Station. Daily service is offered; phone (813) 221-7600 or (800) 872-7245. Bus service to Union Station is available via HART routes 9, 12 and 400; phone (813) 254-4278.

BUSES: Greyhound Lines Inc. is at 610 E. Polk St. in Tampa; phone (813) 229-2174.

TAXIS: Major companies include United Cab Co., (813) 777-7777, and Yellow Cab Co., (813) 253-0121. Taxis are metered. Most cabs charge $2.50 to enter and $2.40 per mile and 30c per 60 seconds of waiting time. A taxi ride between Tampa International Airport and downtown Tampa, the Ybor City area and the cruise terminals costs a flat rate of $25 in either direction. Limousine service averages $65 per hour in the Tampa Bay area.

PUBLIC TRANSPORTATION: HART serves Tampa and its immediate suburbs, including shopping malls and area attractions. Service also includes the TECO Line Streetcar System, which makes 11 stops along a 2.7-mile track between downtown Tampa and Ybor City. For HART bus and streetcar fares and schedules, phone (813) 254-4278.

(Continued from p. 312.)
modest business district to a stature worthy of more established corporate centers.

On the waterfront, The Riverwalk, a 3-mile pedestrian promenade that parallels the Hillsborough River, has transformed the downtown landscape, opening up public access to Tampa's lovely waterfront and linking museums, parks, hotels, numerous places to eat and outdoor gathering places. Pedestrians can walk alongside the river beginning near The Florida Aquarium, passing Amalie Arena, Tampa Museum of Art and the Straz Center for the Performing Arts, and ending at Water Works Park.

Hosting the Super Bowl for the fourth time in 2009 served notice of the bay area's passion for sports, particularly football. The Tampa Bay Buccaneers took home the Super Bowl XXXVII trophy in 2003, the same year the Tampa Bay Storm arena football team won its fourth championship. In 2004, the Tampa Bay Lightning took the NHL's coveted Stanley Cup. Then there's Major League Baseball. From late February to early April, the Grapefruit League's spring training stint renders pro teams accessible to those who want to see how their favorites—including the 2008 American League Champion Tampa Bay Rays—are shaping up for the *real* season.

Must Do: AAA Editor's Picks

- Guide the family on a safari through **Busch Gardens Tampa** (3000 E. Busch Blvd.). You'll be transported to the countries and landscapes of Africa the moment you walk through the arches of this extraordinary 335-acre animal preserve and theme park.
- Immerse yourself in the Cuban culture of **Ybor City:** Learn about this district's historic cigar industry at **Ybor Chamber Visitor Information Center** (1600 E. 8th Ave.); take a walking tour offered by the **Ybor City Museum State Park** (1818 E. 9th Ave.); sample traditional *café con leche* and guava pastry for breakfast at La Tropicana Café (1822 E. 7th Ave.); and watch sensuous flamenco dancers while dining at the historic Columbia Restaurant (2117 E. 7th Ave). For things to do this weekend, live *la vida loca* (the crazy life) among thousands of club-hoppers along Seventh Avenue.
- Don your beach attire and take a trip to the **Gulf Coast beaches** on the Pinellas Peninsula. These are some of the best sandy shores in the nation when it comes to climate, water, sand and safety.
- Get acquainted with the man who turned Tampa into a winter resort at the **Henry B. Plant Museum** (401 W. Kennedy Blvd.) which occupies a wing of the railroad magnate's luxury 1891 hotel. The preserved Victorian-era building, with its sprawling veranda, ornate gingerbread trim and signature silver minarets, is part of the **University of Tampa.** During the annual Victorian Christmas Stroll, the halls are decked in 19th-century Christmas finery.
- Talk to the animals at **ZooTampa at Lowry Park** (1101 W. Sligh Ave.). Practice your bird calls in the zoo's free-flight aviaries, trumpet like the African elephants in the Ituri Forest and roar along with the white Bengal tigers in the Asian Gardens. See African creatures close up on the Safari Ride's train as it weaves around behind many of the zoo's animal enclosures. You can also feed giraffes, lorikeets and white rhinos, ride a camel or a llama, pet a stingray and gaze at Australian animals like kookaburras, koalas, wallabies and emus. At **Big Cat Rescue** (12802 Easy St.), spend the day on a 45-acre sanctuary among more than 140 rescued lions, tigers, bobcats and leopards.
- Take in the views at the **Tampa Museum of Art** (120 W. Gasparilla Plaza) on the waterfront of the Hillsborough River. The building itself is quite modern, wrapped in aluminum panels with LED lights peeking out of its perforations, while the view across the river features the University of Tampa's minarets. Inside, the view includes a wide range of styles such as Greek and Roman art dating as far back as 2300 B.C., contemporary photorealist oil paintings, photography from the 19th to 21st centuries and cutting-edge works by artists like Cindy Sherman.
- Indulge in some unique cuisine at **ū-lē-lē** (1810 N. Highland Ave.), one of Tampa's best local restaurants in its booming dining scene. Its blend of locally sourced foods and Native American dishes has the place packed every night, while its location on the Hillsborough River and The Riverwalk allows for marvelous views, especially at sunset. Adventurous diners will want to try Florida native chili, which includes alligator, wild boar and venison, or oysters on the half shell, harvested from local waters.
- Looking for fun things to do with friends this weekend? Attend a rock concert or an ice hockey game at **Amalie Arena** (401 Channelside Dr.). The arena is home base for the NHL's Tampa Bay Lightning and the AFL's Tampa Bay Storm and has recently hosted WWE wrestling events. Musical artists, including Ed Sheeran and Rush, also play at the arena. Simulated lightning bolts made by Tesla coils at the Lightning games make ice hockey even more exciting.
- Take a drive on the **Sunshine Skyway**, a 15-mile causeway spanning the mouth of Tampa Bay between the mainland north of Bradenton and the Pinellas Peninsula.

Sunshine Skyway

Tampa 1-day Itinerary

AAA editors suggest these activities for a great short vacation experience. Those staying in the area for a longer visit can access a 3-day itinerary at AAA.com/TravelGuides.

Morning

- Devote your day to Tampa's museums. Begin with an introduction to the early days at the **Tampa Bay History Center** (801 Old Water St.). Interactive exhibits cover periods of native habitation, Spanish exploration and events of the 20th century. A satellite of the Columbia Restaurant opens for lunch at 11.
- Complement your history lesson with a visit to the **Henry B. Plant Museum** in the restored Tampa Bay Hotel on the **University of Tampa** campus (401 W. Kennedy Blvd.). With its exotic minarets, domes and cupolas, Plant's Moorish-design hotel overlooking the Hillsborough River was a magnet for the Victorian-era's well-heeled. Peer into lavishly decorated rooms filled with antique furniture, period accessories and vintage clothing.
- Discover forces of nature, visit a lunar colony in 2070, encounter a real meteorite, climb a ropes course, learn all about STEAM careers, stargaze in the planetarium and experience future technologies, all at **MOSI (Museum of Science & Industry)** (4801 E. Fowler Ave.). Dozens of engaging exhibits appeal to all ages.
- If your inner Dr. Doolittle begs to come out, start out at **ZooTampa at Lowry Park** (1101 W. Sligh Ave.) where you can feed giraffes, ride a camel, pet a pony, interact with kangaroos, observe submerged manatees and giggle over monkeys in the primate exhibit.

Afternoon

- Get up close for a personal encounter with penguins at **The Florida Aquarium** (701 Channelside Dr.). Dive shows, animal feedings, touch tanks and a live coral reef place you within reach of the secrets of the sea.
- The Florida Aquarium is next to Sparkman Wharf, formerly Channelside Bay Plaza, where you can grab a bite at several casual eateries serving everything from Cedar Key oysters and Detroit-style pizza to Spanish tapas in trendy shipping containers.
- Burn off those lunch calories on Tampa's Riverwalk, a linear park that ambles beside the Hillsborough River. Begin at Fort Brooke Park (just south of Channelside at 601 Old Water St.), passing The Florida Aquarium, Amalie Arena, the Tampa Convention Center, Curtis Hixon Waterfront Park and the Tampa Museum of Art. On the way, break for a snack at The Sail (333 S. Franklin St.).

Evening

- Dinner options abound in Tampa. You may decide to start the evening with authentic Spanish-inspired cuisine and a flamenco show at one of Florida's oldest dining establishments. The **Columbia Restaurant** (2117 E. 7th Ave.) had its start as a lunch counter for cigar rollers in 1905 and is operated by descendants of founder Casimiro Hernandez. An informative menu tempts you with detailed descriptions of dishes prepared from original family recipes. (Flamenco performances—Monday through Saturday—are popular, so remember to make reservations in advance. There is a small cover charge for the show.)

Columbia Restaurant

- Shopping extends into the evening in Ybor. Between 15th and 17th streets you'll find vintage clothing, jewelry and artwork as well as cigar shops with wine and coffee bars (a few even offer cigar rolling demonstrations).
- For an American-style gourmet repast, the Tampa landmark **Bern's Steak House** (1208 S. Howard Ave.) in the Hyde Park neighborhood should suit you to a T (or a T-bone). This restaurant opened in 1956 and has built its reputation on the premise that preparing steak is an art form. Their menu features detailed descriptions of USDA Prime steak cuts including Châteaubriand and Delmonico.
- Spend your evening at the **Seminole Hard Rock Casino** (5223 N. Orient Rd.). Open 24 hours, you can hear the ringing bells of slot machines and the shuffling of cards until the wee hours of the morning.
- After dinner, return to Ybor City's Seventh Avenue and sample nightlife at a variety of clubs. See our Nightlife article for recommendations.

Top Picks for Kids

Under 13

- With more than interactive exhibits on topics including space, physics and robotics, **MOSI (Museum of Science & Industry)** (4801 E. Fowler Ave.) has fun things for kids and adults alike. They can immerse themselves in space at the planetarium and the simulated moon base, and then tackle the ropes course.
- At **ZooTampa at Lowry Park** (1101 W. Sligh Ave.), do more than simply look at the animals. Stand eye level with giraffes and feed them lettuce. Touch the smooth back of a stingray as it glides past in a shallow pool. Sit in on some of the daily shows and learn about birds of prey, elephants, penguins and other animals from the zoo keepers.
- **Adventure Island** (10001 N. McKinley Dr.) is a tropical-themed water park. Feel the excitement of the big slides, relax in the half-mile lazy river and play in children's areas complete with waterfalls, slides and bridges.
- Children will have fun learning at the 17 themed areas and during the daily programs at **Glazer Children's Museum** (110 W. Gasparilla Plaza). While here, kids can soar through the skies of New York, San Francisco and Tampa in a biplane, become a firefighter and drive a truck at the scaled-down fire station, and take the journey of a water droplet that evaporates into the sky and trickles back down into an aquifer.

Teens

- A visit to the **Tampa Museum of Art** (120 W. Gasparilla Plaza) will add a bit of culture to your trip. The permanent collections feature Greek and Roman antiquities as well as modern and contemporary art with a focus on photography. After dusk the building itself becomes a piece of art when the facade of LEDs, designed by Leo Villareal, lights up in a random sequence.
- Try one of the specialty pizzas at **Bavaro's Pizza Napoletana & Pastaria** (514 N. Franklin St.). The food is cooked in a wood-fired brick oven, and the ingredients are either imported from Italy or sourced locally.
- If shopping is what your teen is into, spend some time in **Hyde Park Village** (1602 W. Snow Ave.). This charming area has a delightful assortment of high-end and specialty shops as well as some great restaurants and cafés with outdoor seating. Enjoy the pleasant environment with a stroll through the butterfly garden, and check out the loading docks on Swann Avenue where local artists have painted murals.

All Ages

- Have a wild time at **Busch Gardens Tampa** (3000 E. Busch Blvd.), Tampa's premiere thrill-ride destination. Ride the big coasters for a thrill, and take a trip down Stanley Falls or through the Congo River Rapids to cool off. Encounter animals on the Serengeti Railway, or view these beautiful creatures from above on Skyway cable car. For the smaller ones in your group, Sesame Street Safari of Fun has rides and play areas that are perfectly sized. Check with a AAA Travel professional for available vacation packages.
- Get an up close view of Florida's marine life at **The Florida Aquarium** (701 Channelside Dr.). Visit the wetlands to see alligators, otters, great blue herons and roseate spoonbills. Travel farther south to the coral reef in Key West, and dive through the colorful ecosystems to a depth of 60 feet. Your journey's not over yet! Cross the Atlantic, and go to Africa where you'll spend time with black-footed penguins and ring-tailed lemurs.
- If you fancy a bit of baseball, catch a game during the **New York Yankees Spring Training** at George M. Steinbrenner Field (1 Steinbrenner Dr.). In the month of March the Yankees call Tampa home, and game day tickets are surprisingly affordable. Plan your trip well in advance though because tickets sell out quickly.
- Learn about Tampa and how the city developed at the **Tampa Bay History Center** (801 Old Water St.). The museum covers topics such as Spanish explorers, Seminole and Miccosukee tribes, and the cigar industry in Ybor City. The second floor has several interactive elements for kids. Plan to get a bite to eat while here. The famous **Columbia Restaurant,** one of the most popular restaurants in Tampa,has a satellite location, Columbia Café, in the lobby.

MOSI (Museum of Science & Industry)

Arriving

By Car

The major direct route to Tampa from the north is I-75, which traverses Florida's north-central lake district: The 62-mile stretch south of Wildwood is especially scenic. It is roughly paralleled by US 301 on the east and US 41 on the west. North of downtown I-75 changes to I-275, which merges with I-4 in mid-city. I-75 bypasses the city proper to the east, rejoining I-275 north of Bradenton.

Driving into Tampa from the south, US 41 parallels I-75, the main corridor from the southern Gulf Coast. From Daytona Beach in the east, I-4 angles across central Florida through Orlando, while older US 92 runs parallel from Lakeland. SR 60, a four-lane, divided highway, leads from Lake Wales. Running from the Gulf Coast west of Tampa, SR 60 connects to Clearwater, and I-275 travels to St. Petersburg.

Air Travel

Cheap airline flights can be found from numerous cities. Commercial flights entering Tampa land at Tampa International Airport (TPA). Several commercial airlines and private planes use St. Petersburg-Clearwater International Airport (PIE). Private and corporate planes have access to Albert Whitted Airport (SPG) in St. Petersburg and Peter O. Knight Airport (TPF) in Tampa.

Tampa International Airport is on the city's west side along Old Tampa Bay. The 1.4-mile-long SkyConnect train connects the airport, the economy garage and car rental center. To reach downtown Tampa, take I-275 north—though you'll actually be traveling east—and take the Ashley Street exit. Past this exit I-275 turns sharply northward, bisecting the city. Continue along I-275 to reach such destinations as the University of South Florida and Busch Gardens Tampa. Exit to I-4 east if you're heading for Ybor City, Plant City or Lakeland. Or take a cab: United and Yellow cabs provide service from the airport. Both have a minimum $15 fare from the airport; the flat rate to downtown (about 8 miles) or cruise terminal (about 9 miles) is about $25.

Pirate Water Taxi

To reach downtown St. Petersburg, take I-275 south, cross the bay on the 7-mile Howard Frankland Bridge, and proceed another 10 miles or so due south. From I-275, take I-375 into the northern half of downtown or I-175 into the southern half. Transportation from Tampa International to St. Petersburg is easily acquired. Supershuttle provides transfers from Tampa International to St. Petersburg and cities in Hernando, Pasco and Sarasota counties; phone (727) 572-1111 or (800) 282-6817.

St. Petersburg-Clearwater International Airport is about 10 miles across the bay from Tampa on SR 686 (Roosevelt Boulevard), near the west side of the W. Howard Frankland Bridge. Airport traffic exits northwest toward Clearwater or south, providing access to St. Petersburg and Tampa.

Hertz, which offers discounts to AAA members, is at the car rental center by Tampa International Airport, (813) 874-3232 or (800) 654-3080; St. Petersburg-Clearwater International Airport, (727) 532-4801; and at St. Pete Beach, (727) 360-1631; or phone (800) 654-3080.

Getting Around

Street System

Downtown Tampa is bracketed by water and has only a few major access routes. From I-275, take the Ashley Street exit. Also from the north, SR 45 (Nebraska Avenue) and one-way US 41 Bus. Rte. lead into downtown. Cass Street approaches from the west. From the east, use SR 60 (John F. Kennedy Boulevard).

Tampa also is laid out in a basic grid, with a few geographic variations. US 41 Bus. Rte. (Florida Avenue) divides east from west; John F. Kennedy Boulevard/Frank Adamo Drive (SR 60) separates north from south. Many streets in the downtown area are one way.

Five major east-west thoroughfares support cross-town traffic: SR 582 (Fowler Avenue), SR 580 (Busch Boulevard), US 92/US 41 (Hillsborough Avenue), SR 574 (Martin Luther King Jr. Boulevard), and the Crosstown Expressway (toll). Three others parallel I-275: on the west, SR 597/SR 580/US 92 (Dale Mabry Highway); through the central city, US 41/SR 45 (Nebraska Avenue); and on the east, SR 583 (56th Street).

Generally, downtown speed limits are 30 mph or as posted. Unless otherwise posted, a right turn is allowed on a red light after a complete stop. It is best to avoid taking an unfamiliar route during rush hours (about 7 to 9 a.m. and 4:30 to 6 p.m.).

If driving is not your thing, you can explore downtown Tampa by water. Pirate Water Taxi cruises along the Hillsborough River and has some 15 stops on its route. A fee is charged; phone (813) 390-3711 for rates and schedule.

Parking

Limited on-street parking is available in the downtown business sections and along major thoroughfares. Rates for municipal parking garages start at $1.20 per hour with a maximum of $9.50 per day. Metered lot parking and use of the Fort Brooke parking garage run $1.60 per hour (if using the garage for 6-24 hours, the rate is $9.50). For downtown parking information phone (813) 274-8179 or (813) 221-3686.

Shopping

Tampa's retail front offers an abundance of things to do, whether you prefer expansive malls with high-end merchandise or the diversity and uniqueness found in specialty shopping districts.

Malls

Dillard's, Neiman Marcus and Nordstrom anchor **International Plaza and Bay Street,** an upscale extreme shopping mall with an outdoor dining and entertainment center. In addition to nationally recognized department stores like Banana Republic and LOFT, women's fashions are well represented by designer boutiques Coach, Gucci, kate spade new york and Tory Burch; men's apparel by Abercrombie & Fitch, BOSS Hugo Boss and J.Crew; and children's togs by abercrombie kids, Janie and Jack, and Journeys Kidz. Teens won't feel left out with such stores as Forever 21, H&M and Urban Outfitters.

More than 200 retailers have all your shopping needs covered, from jewelry to home décor to electronics. A food court, two cappuccino bars and a children's play area provide R and R for weary shoppers, while 16 restaurants in the open-air Bay Street village adjoining the mall offer variety for lunch or post-shopping dinner. The complex is located at 2223 N. Westshore Blvd. at Boy Scout Boulevard, near Tampa International Airport, perfect for a last-minute trip at the end of your vacation; phone (813) 342-3790.

Westfield Citrus Park, 8021 Citrus Park Town Center off Veterans Expressway and Gunn Highway in west Tampa, is on one level lined end-to-end with 110 stores anchored by Dick's Sporting Goods, JCPenney and Macy's. Lampposts and an antique carousel add to the mall's Main Street ambience; phone (813) 926-4644 for mall information and (813) 926-9232 for the carousel. Dillard's, JCPenney, Macy's, Sears and 140 specialty shops and boutiques can be found at **Westfield Brandon,** 459 Brandon Town Center Dr. at the intersection of I-75 and SR 60 on Tampa's east side; phone (813) 661-6255.

University Mall, west of the University of South Florida at 2200 E. Fowler Ave., is one of the region's largest at 1.3 million square feet. The major stores

Hyde Park Village

operating here are Burlington Coat Factory and Dillard's Clearance Center, along with more than 100 specialty shops and places to eat; phone (813) 971-3466.

WestShore Plaza, off I-275 exit 40A at 250 WestShore Plaza, opened in 1967 and was the first of Tampa's enclosed malls. Dick's Sporting Goods, JCPenney and Macy's anchor the mall, which has more than 70 other stores and an international food court; phone (813) 286-0790.

Tampa Premium Outlets opened in October 2015 at 2300 Grand Cypress Dr. in Lutz, 20 miles north of Tampa at I-75 and SR 56. This newest addition to area shopping destinations has a Key West theme and houses Coach, Express, Fossil, Michael Kors, Nike, Polo Ralph Lauren, Saks Fifth Avenue OFF Fifth, Vera Bradley and about 80 other outlets; phone (813) 909-8716. In nearby Wesley Chapel, head to **The Shops at Wiregrass,** 28211 Paseo Dr., a pedestrian-friendly village with about 100 shops including Brighton, Champs Sports, The Children's Place and Pottery Barn, along with anchors Dillard's, JCPenney and Macy's; phone (813) 994-2242.

Last but not least, **Ellenton Premium Outlets,** 5641 Factory Shops Blvd., is about 40 miles south of Tampa, but well worth the drive for those who want to scout for bargains. There are more than 130 stores, including Aéropostale, BCBG MAX AZRIA, Bose, The Children's Place, Coach, Saks Fifth Avenue OFF 5th, Tommy Hilfiger, Vans and White House Black Market; phone (941) 729-8615.

Specialty Districts

Just off Bayshore Boulevard at Swann and South Dakota avenues in the historic Hyde Park neighborhood is **Hyde Park Village,** home to a delightful collection of more than 40 shops, restaurants and cafés. The residential area offers an Old World charm complemented by a cosmopolitan tempo. Shoppers can settle at a shady outdoor table or grab a bite at one of the eateries after perusing the upscale fashions at Anthropologie, Brooks Brothers and lululemon athletica, or before seeking out specialty items at more than two dozen shops, including Downtown Dogs, Pottery Barn, Sur La Table and west elm. Free garage parking encourages browsers or buyers to make a day of it; phone (813) 251-3500.

A short drive from Ybor City, and adjacent to the Florida Aquarium at the cruise ship docks, is **Sparkman Wharf**, 615 Channelside Dr., an entertainment and dining complex with several unique shops. Park in the garage across the street.

Defined by its location south of Kennedy Boulevard and north of Gandy Boulevard on the Interbay Peninsula, **South Tampa** yields some standouts in the shopping arena. **Seedlings,** 1530 S. Dale Mabry Hwy., offers everything you need for bringing up babies and toddlers, with a dash of style for modern mommies. You'll squeal with delight at the latest in car seats and strollers, fresh-frozen organic food, environmentally friendly bath products, books, clothes, toys and Sophie the giraffe teethers; phone (813) 251-5111. Right next door to Seedlings, you'll find **The Pink Palm,** 1532 S. Dale Mabry Hwy., the area's only Lilly Pulitzer signature store; phone (813) 259-9780.

Metropolitan Cigars

If you're familiar with ultrahip clothing lines by names like Dolce Vita, Sam & Lavi, Splendid and Velvet, you'll enjoy searching the racks at **Penelope T,** 3310 W. Bay to Bay Blvd., phone (813) 254-5740. Naming the boutique after 1960s model Penelope Tree, its native Floridian owners worked in the fashion industry in New York City before returning to Tampa and opening their shop in 2005.

The **Ybor City** shopping experience is as culturally rich and vibrant as its nightlife. Most of the activity centers on 10 blocks of Seventh and Eighth avenues bounded by 13th and 23rd streets, an area flush with local restaurants, cigar shops, nightclubs, cultural attractions, shops and other fun things to do. While you might find a national chain or two, most retailers are home-grown originals.

With vintage and reproduction apparel, hats, accessories and home décor items from the 1920s, '30s, '40s and '50s, **La France,** 1612 E. 7th Ave., offers a unique shopping experience along with a reputation for quality over its more than 40-year run in Ybor City; phone (813) 248-1381. At **Revolve Clothing Exchange,** 1620 E. 7th Ave., budget-conscious shoppers can trade in gently worn items for other used garments or cash. Don't be surprised to find brands like American Apparel, Diesel, Free People, Marc Jacobs and Nanette Lepore at greatly reduced prices; phone (813) 242-5970. Go to **Ybor Agora,** 1515 E. 7th Ave., for accoutrements for the home. This shop has an Asian vibe but will appeal to anyone who wants to dress up their abode with things like paper lanterns, pottery, fragrant candles and lamps; phone (813) 247-4141.

Cigar rolling is the very industry upon which the historic district was founded, and cigar shops, or *chinchales,* were once a mainstay. Although their numbers have dwindled over the years, there are still a few places where you can buy a hand-rolled stogie. Step inside one of the South's largest humidors during your trip to **Metropolitan Cigars,** 2014 E. 7th Ave.; phone (813) 248-3304. Sip an espresso and watch cigar rolling in the window at **La Faraona Cigars,** 1517 E. 7th Ave.; phone (813) 648-1422. Or enjoy Cuban coffee or wine with your smoke at **King Corona Cigars Café & Bar,** 1523 E. 7th Ave.; phone (813) 241-9109 or (888) 248-3812.

If buying or eyeballing local art is your thing, there are a couple of art galleries featuring works by local artists scattered throughout Ybor City. During the **Saturday Market,** Centennial Park, 1901 19th St., bursts into a riot of color and texture with artwork, crafts, produce, plants and gourmet foods; phone (813) 241-2442.

You can find souvenirs along with history books and locally made products at **Ybor City Museum State Park,** 1818 E. 9th Ave., and the **Ybor Chamber Visitor Information Center,** 1600 E. 8th Ave.; phone (813) 247-6323 and (813) 241-8838, respectively. After lunch at the oldest restaurant in Tampa, historic **Columbia Restaurant,** 2117 E. 7th Ave., visit the gift shop, which offers a full line of the restaurant's branded packaged foods, including salad dressing, sangria mix, seasonings and Cuban coffee; phone (813) 248-4961.

Specialty Shops

The atmosphere is as enticing as the offerings at the bay area's assorted specialty emporiums. Seek out these retailers for a one-of-a-kind shopping experience.

Fans of Swedish designs thronged to the grand opening of the **IKEA** store in 2009. With nearly 50 room displays and three complete model homes, this home design superstore has everything a DIY-er with modern decorating sensibilities could ask for: furniture with clean, contemporary lines; sofas with washable upholstery; ergonomic chairs; closet organizing systems; and lots of accessories including rugs, linens, lamps, artwork, cookware and cutlery. IKEA is at 1103 N. 22nd St. near the southeast corner of Ybor City; phone (813) 623-4532.

In nearby Lutz, Jewelry, contemporary crafts and fine art are the focus at **Dan Balk Jewelry Studios,** 1418 Julie Lagoon. What makes this shop unique is that it's a working silversmith studio, so you can take a 4-hour class for a fee and leave with a customized piece of your own design; phone (813) 728-4325.

Across the street from the University of Tampa is **Oxford Exchange,** 420 W. Kennedy Blvd. Its carefully curated collection of books combining new releases, classics, out-of-print and children's books is housed in a handsome 24,000-square-foot white brick building that began life as a hotel stable in 1891. You'll marvel at the shop's grand decor; modeled after shops and private clubs in London, it offers the feel of an English manor and features inlaid marble, pine and reclaimed white oak on its floors, leather-paneled walls and ceilings, leather club chairs and plush sofas, and a conservatory with a retractable glass roof covering the in-house restaurant. There's also a coffee bar, tea shop and a boutique that offers an eclectic selection of curiosities such as apothecary items, travel accessories, autographed books, statuettes and home fragrances. Phone (813) 253-0222.

If all this shopping has made you hungry, follow the fragrance of freshly baked Cuban bread to **Mauricio Faedo's Bakery,** across the street at 5150 N. Florida Ave.; phone (813) 237-2377. Open 24 hours a day (except on Saturday, when it closes at 1:30, and Sunday, when it closes at 5), this local favorite will satisfy cravings for pastries, doughnuts and breads just about anytime. Just a little further down the street in an adorable lime-green building is **Cleanse Apothecary,** 6500 N. Florida Ave., where you'll find handmade soaps, makeup bags, fragrances, body lotions and toiletries artfully arranged on mismatched antique furniture; phone (813) 374-0305.

Nightlife

Evening options in Tampa range from weekday happy-hour get-togethers at numerous local restaurants and bars to full-out weekend partying at velvet-rope dance clubs in Ybor City. Or maybe you'd

Oxford Exchange

prefer an evening of mellow jazz, twangy country sounds or high-energy pop music. Tampa's eclectic nightlife scene appeals to everyone.

Downtown

Downtown Tampa's business core is sprinkled with gentrified, after-five gathering places. **TAPS Restaurant, Bar & Lounge,** 777 N. Ashley Dr., pairs upscale decor with an extensive libations list, including more than 100 varieties of wine; phone (813) 463-1968. If you land in town on the first Thursday of the month, join locals at **Rock the Park** for music, food and drinks from 6:30-9:30 p.m. at **Curtis Hixon Waterfront Park,** 600 Ashley Dr.; phone (813) 274-8615. Any day of the week after 2 p.m. is a good time to mellow out at **The Sail Pavilion,** 333 S. Franklin St., an outdoor bar on The Riverwalk. You'll hear live music on the weekend and get a free shot at sunset. Leashed dogs get a free bowl of water; phone (813) 274-7778.

Tampa residents are passionate about their championship sports teams. Still, you don't have to be a sports nut to have a good time at **Hattrick's Sports Bar-Downtown Tampa,** 107 S. Franklin St. near Whiting Street; phone (813) 225-4288 for Hattrick's. **Four Green Fields,** 205 W. Platt St., should be on the radar of serious pub devotees; phone (813) 254-4444.

The place to go to see nationally known entertainers, especially rock and country artists, is **Amalie Arena,** 401 Channelside Dr.; phone (813) 301-6500. Musicians such as Paul McCartney, Roger Waters, Chance the Rapper, Enrique Iglesias and Pitbull have performed there.

Hyde Park

Hyde Park is one of Tampa's oldest established suburban neighborhoods and a hub of upscale living that's well worth the trip. Nightlife venues range from casual hangouts with spacious outdoor decks to wine bars to ultrachic intimate lounges. With luxurious décor, a velvet-roped preferred seating area, a dance floor and a dress code, **The Kennedy,** 2408 W. Kennedy Blvd., ranks among the classiest nightspots in the bay area; phone (813) 259-9669. **Hyde Park Café,** 1806 West Platt St., features a similar ambience plus elegant courtyard seating and resident DJs who keep the music going; phone (813) 254-2233.

If you're in the mood for dinner and a movie, kill two birds with one stone at **CinéBistro Hyde Park,** 1609 W. Swann Ave. Settle into a plush leather chair, sip a glass of merlot or a martini, and sup on an exquisite meal like fettuccine al forno while a current feature film plays on the screen; phone (813) 514-8300. Note that you must be age 21 or older to be admitted. When only an Irish pub will do, **Irish 31 Pub House & Eatery,** 1611 W. Swann Ave., is just the ticket with its cozy interior, an umbrella-covered outdoor deck, a sports bar vibe and Monday trivia nights; phone (813) 250-0031.

A concentration of watering holes frequented by residents and college students can be found along or adjacent to South Howard Avenue, commonly known as the **SoHo** district. Enjoy a spirit of camaraderie, sip a Guinness, play darts and listen to live music (on select nights) with loyal patrons on the deck of **MacDinton's Irish Pub & Restaurant,** 405 S. Howard Ave., or at **The Dubliner Irish Pub,** 2307 W. Azeele St., just off S. Howard Ave; phone (813) 251-8999 or (813) 258-2257, respectively. The SoHo lineup also includes **Tiny Tap Tavern,** 2105 W. Morrison Ave.; and **World of Beer,** 402 S. Howard Ave.

Ybor City

Timpano Chophouse, 1610 W. Swann Ave. in Hyde Park Village, is the perfect steal-away for a quiet evening of drinks and smooth music; phone (813) 254-5870. **Yard of Ale Soho,** 406 S. Howard Ave., provides sedate surroundings where aficionados can test their palate for vintages sans such distractions as brash bands and rowdy revelers; phone (813) 251-4433.

Ybor City

The historic cigar city is Tampa's smokin'-hot nightspot, especially on weekends when the overflow from a lively mix of dance clubs, hookah bars, lounges, microbreweries, martini bars and watering holes transforms the main strip of Seventh Avenue into an outdoor fiesta. Most bars and clubs here close at 3 a.m., so you can party into the wee hours.

Most bars offer DJ and/or live music ranging from acoustic to jazz to indie rock. Some of the most popular along Seventh and Eighth avenues are pirate-themed **Gaspar's Grotto,** 1805 E. 7th Ave., with two large outdoor bars and a covered patio; and **Coyote Ugly,** 1722 E. 7th Ave., where dancing on the bar is to be expected; phone (813) 248-5900 or (813) 241-8459. Get rowdy at **The Double Decker,** 1721 E. 7th Ave., a party saloon with karaoke, or at loud and gritty **Crowbar,** 1812 N. 17th St., specializing in high-energy bands appealing to twenty-somethings; phone (813) 248-2099 or (813) 241-8600, respectively. With different music and ambience on each of its five floors, **Club Prana,** 1619 E. 7th Ave., distinguishes itself as Ybor's chicest dance scene. Show your hip-hop moves in the plush first-floor lounge and later head to the rooftop bar for reggae music and an awesome view; phone (813) 241-4139.

If you prefer a more relaxed destination, slip into the **James Joyce Irish Pub,** 1724 E. 8th Ave., with two fireplaces and private nooks for reading the used books you'll find there (sip an Irish whiskey or one of 50 beers on tap); phone (813) 247-1896. A little off the beaten path is microbrewery **Coppertail Brewing Co.,** 2601 E. 2nd Ave. In an old brick warehouse across the street from IKEA, it makes for a good place to unwind after a shopping trip with a refreshing brew made on-site, and it also has a tasting room; phone (813) 247-1500.

Centro Ybor, 1600 E. 8th Ave., offers fun things to do in the historical entertainment complex, comedy club, eateries and a handful of shops; phone (813) 930-4660455 for movie information. **GameTime Tampa** is an alternative to the usual pub or nightclub; it features a sports bar with plenty of flat-screen TVs, but it also has pool tables, air hockey and a slew of arcade and video games, including Dance Dance Revolution, Guitar Hero, Pac-Man and a driving simulator. Players earn tickets that are redeemable for prizes, so this is a great option for families or date night; phone (813) 241-9675. For a side-splitting good time, slip into the **Improv Comedy Theater**; recent performers include Harland Williams and Amazing Johnathan. In its prime, the beautifully renovated 100-year-old building was a Spanish movie theater; phone (813) 864-4000. **Ybor City Wine Bar** appeals to a mellow crowd and has more than 200 boutique wines on its list; phone (813) 999-4966.

If your taste in nighttime entertainment veers toward something outside of "normal," step inside **The Castle,** 2004 N. 16th St., a two-story club that draws an unlikely combination of Ralph Lauren-clad college preps and black-garbed goth kids. On the first floor, both the music and crowd skew towards typical club fare, but in the second floor's dark, massive ballroom, you'll hear goth, industrial, techno, new wave, emo and other alternative beats. You'll also be visually stimulated by the club's habitués, who don leather, corsets, shredded tights and combat boots; phone (813) 247-7547.

For alternative music fans who love the energy of a live show, **The Orpheum,** 1915 E. 7th Ave., is the place to go. This venue has hosted shows by up-and-coming acts like Manchester Orchestra, Sleeping With Sirens and Dum Dum Girls; phone (813) 248-9500. You can check out live national bands at **The Ritz Ybor,** 1503 E. 7th Ave., which also has Saturday night dance parties with live deejays spinning EDM, pop and indie tunes; phone (813) 248-4050.

And when it's time to drag yourself home in the wee hours of morning, convenient and affordable flat-fee garage parking at two locations—Fifth Avenue at 16th Street and Eighth Avenue at 13th Street—takes the guesswork out of the closing-time conundrum "Where did I park the car?".

Channelside Bay Plaza

A major makeover is in the works for **Sparkman Wharf,** 615 Channelside Dr., an entertainment center with a large courtyard opening onto Garrison Channel, where cruise ships depart. When complete in 2020, the former Channelside Bay Plaza will include office lofts, retail, an open outdoor space with a lawn, outdoor dining and a beer garden.

In need of a frozen drink to cool down from a day in the hot Florida sun? Wet your whistle at **Wet Willie's** with a banana daiquiri, Bahama Mama or White Russian, or mix your own concoction from the self-serve bar; phone (813) 221-5650. At **LIT Premium Cigar Lounge,** choose a stogie from the walk-in humidor, sip a single malt scotch and settle into a comfortable chair just like your grandfather used to (there's also free Wi-Fi and flat-screen televisions); phone (813) 221-5548.

The Outer Limits

There are loads of fun places to go on the outskirts. Pull an all-nighter at SAVE **Hard Rock Cafe,** an upscale club worthy of celebrity patronage in the **Seminole Hard Rock Hotel & Casino.** Live music starts around 8 p.m. Wednesday through Sunday and goes into the wee hours of morning, long after most metro-area clubs have closed. The casino never closes, so there's plenty of opportunity before or after clubbing to try your luck at the tables. Located on Tampa's east side at 5223 N. Orient Rd., Seminole Hard Rock Hotel & Casino is an easy 30 minutes from Orlando; phone (813) 627-7757.

Coppertail Brewing Co.

Dallas Bull, a few miles from the casino at 3322 US 301 near the Florida State Fairgrounds, has been Tampa's stronghold of country music since 1979 and a favorite performance stage of top-name artists, including Dierks Bentley and Sam Hunt. With seven bars, two dance floors and a VIP lounge, this ain't no hole in the wall, pilgrim. Of course, there's the requisite mechanical bull; phone (813) 987-2855.

Skipper's Smokehouse Restaurant & Oyster Bar, off I-275 exit 52 at 910 Skipper Rd., is an unconventional music venue, perhaps not for everyone. Skipper's built its reputation on open jam nights featuring downhome blues and island rhythms, but now has a repertoire of Cajun, rock, funk, jazz and more. Performances typically take place Tues.-Sun. at 8 under the stars in an informal backyard arena (the "Skipperdome") with bench seating. A compound of weathered, fish-camp-style sheds covered with concert posters, autographed head shots of former performers, neon signs and music memorabilia resembles the junkyard digs of "Sanford and Son," but nobody seems to mind the look, especially when the music starts; phone (813) 971-0666.

Ciro's Speakeasy & Supper Club, 2109 Bayshore Blvd., is not a circa-1925 speakeasy in name only. Before you even step inside, you must know the secret password, which you'll get when you make a reservation; phone (813) 251-0022. Get in the mood by donning a fedora or flapper dress (not required, but it adds to the fun). Knock on the front door and give the password to the gent through the little window, and you're in. Take a seat at the bar and order a made-from-scratch Old-Fashioned or an absinthe cocktail, expertly prepared by a bartender in Prohibition-era garb (modern-day drinks also are available, but why not keep the theme going?). Jazz music plays in the background, and guests can sit in a private booth behind a curtain. The only thing this place is missing is a dance floor on which you can kick up your heels dancing the Charleston.

Jazzophiles will find that jazz clubs are few and far between in Tampa, but several local restaurants have risen to the occasion to fill the void. Tap your feet to the beats of jazz trios and quartets any night of the week at **The V Lounge** at **Eddie V's Prime Seafood,** 4400 W. Boy Scout Blvd. near Tampa International Airport; phone (813) 877-7290. At Italian restaurant **Donatello,** 232 N. Dale Mabry Hwy. about 4 miles southeast of the airport, sway to the swinging sounds of a pianist tickling the ivories on the lounge's baby grand, often accompanied by talented local musicians; phone (813) 875-6660. Then there's **Ybor City Jazz House,** 1611 E. 7th Ave., a three-level red-hot club where you can get cozy on the main floor's red velvet sofas while grooving to smokin' live jazz bands, strut your stuff on the second floor's dance floor or go up to the rooftop bar and get some air and a good view of Ybor City at night; phone (813) 642-6558.

Tampa Convention Center

Big Events

Tampa's calendar of events begins with the **Outback Bowl** at **Raymond James Stadium** on Dale Mabry Highway. This New Year's Day event matches college football's Southeastern Conference and Big 10 Conference champions. Mid-month brings the **Tampa Bay Black Heritage Festival,** a 10-day-long fete beginning in mid-January that honors African-American culture with such family-friendly events as a 2-day street festival, art exhibits, crafts, spoken word performances, music and ethnic food.

Around the turn of the 20th century, Tampa leaders introduced a citywide, pirate-themed festival based on the adventures of legendary buccaneer Jose Gaspar. **Gasparilla Pirate Fest** evolved into a full-blown mock pirate invasion followed by a downtown parade, an arts and crafts show and live entertainment on multiple stages. The tongue-in-cheek surrender of the city to swashbucklers kicks off in late January or early February with the arrival of the fully rigged *Jose Gasparilla*—a faithful replica of a Spanish galleon—at the **Tampa Convention Center.**

With so many events and fun things to do, February is a great time to vacation in Florida. First, catch daily parades, top-name entertainment, rodeo competitions, cook-offs, livestock shows, agriculture demonstrations, exhibits of everything from antique farm equipment to purebred canines and so much more at the **Florida State Fair,** which takes place over a 12-day period in early February. This all-American event has delighted Floridians for more than 100 years. Where else but a state fair would you make a meal of funnel cakes and corn dogs, stroll along a midway under the stars and step into the poultry barn to cast your vote for the best-looking chicken?

The promise of work in cigar factories lured Cuban, German, Italian and Spanish immigrants to Tampa's Ybor City in the late 19th century. **Fiesta Day**—once a day of rest for the workers—celebrates Ybor's rich ethnic heritage with lively music, multicultural entertainment, a colorful parade of flags, international food from nearby restaurants, cigar rolling demonstrations and contests for the best flan *and* the best flan eater. A high-spirited Latin tempo energizes the historic district during this celebration in late February.

Take advantage of March's cool spring temperatures and join the throng of art lovers wandering among more than 300 white-tented artists' booths filled with every genre imaginable during your trip to the **Gasparilla Festival of the Arts,** held on the first weekend of the month.

Early March is a good time to pick strawberries. If you can't make it to the farm, celebrate the harvest at the 11-day **Florida Strawberry Festival** in **Plant City,** 15 miles east of Tampa. Taste the freshest strawberry pies, cobblers, shortcakes and milkshakes, or buy a flat of berries and make your own. Although strawberries are the star of the show, this festival boasts a stellar lineup of country music performers. With exhibits, carnival rides, a midway and a parade, this event has all the flair of a state fair.

The **Apollo Beach Manatee Festival of the Arts,** held in Ruskin, has a dual mission: to preserve Florida's manatee population and to promote visual and performing arts. At this early March event you will find 100 booths of fine arts and crafts, live entertainment, food vendors and a beer garden as well as activities for children and lots of information about manatees and local wildlife.

In April, **Best of Tampa Bay,** sponsored by the David A. Straz, Jr. Center for the Performing Arts, features culinary creations from the area's top local restaurants. You also can eat, drink and be merry at the **Tampa Caribbean Festival** at the **Florida State Fairgrounds** in April. Celebrate the culture and history of the islands with Caribbean cuisine, parades, dance demonstrations, live deejays and soca, reggae and steel bands.

Whoever said "you have nothing to fear but fear itself" had obviously never been to **Howl-O-Scream** at **Busch Gardens Tampa.** Haunted houses, zombies, ghosts, vampires and a host of otherworldly creatures will scare you out of your wits on select nights from late September through late October.

The historic **Tampa Bay Hotel** is the perfect setting for a **Victorian Christmas Stroll.** Christmas trees, holiday greenery, lavish period decorations, vintage toys and elegantly wrapped packages adorn the hotel's Grand Hall and rooms of the **Henry B. Plant Museum** harking back to Christmas traditions of the past.

Sports & Rec

Tampa Bay area fans have the option to root for a home run; slap high-fives after a touchdown; count down the time during a power play; watch dogs chase a stuffed rabbit; or applaud as a favorite horse makes a photo finish. Plus, year-round warmth and a varied system of waterways and public parks make the region a true haven for outdoor and adventure travel enthusiasts.

Baseball Fans of professional baseball have more than their fair share of teams to cheer on in Tampa, including the city's own Major League Baseball team, the **Tampa Bay Rays** of the American League. They're at bat April through September at **Tropicana Field,** 1 Tropicana Dr., in St. Petersburg. Are you wondering why this Tampa team doesn't actually play in their home town? They've played at Tropicana Field since their inception in 1998, but their lease with the city doesn't expire until 2027; until then, phone (888) 326-7297 for tickets. You can also catch spring training for the Rays in March at **Charlotte Sports Park,** 2300 El Jobean Rd., in Port Charlotte; phone (941) 235-5010 for ticket information.

Gasparilla Pirate Fest

In spring, New York Yankees' fanatics can travel to catch the team's major and minor league games in Tampa. The MLB team plays at **George M. Steinbrenner Field,** 1 Steinbrenner Dr., from late February through late March. The facility's 10,000-seat stadium, fronted by a life-size bronze statue of the Yankees' former owner, is a replica of New York's old Yankee Stadium, which closed in 2008. Minor league's Class A **Tampa Yankees** (a New York Yankees affiliate) play April through August; for information phone (813) 875-7753 or (813) 879-2244.

Two other MLB Grapefruit League teams hold spring training on the Pinellas Peninsula: the **Philadelphia Phillies** and the **Toronto Blue Jays,** both of which have minor league affiliates that play ball locally. In summer the Phillies' **Clearwater Threshers** train at Clearwater's **Spectrum Field,** 601 Old Coachman Rd., and the **Dunedin Blue Jays** work out at **Florida Dunedin Stadium,** 373 Douglas Ave. in Dunedin. Both teams play a full minor league schedule; phone (727) 467-4457 for the Threshers or (727) 733-0429 for the Blue Jays.

Football The NFL's Tampa Bay Buccaneers, 2003 Super Bowl champs, play at Raymond James Stadium, 4201 N. Dale Mabry Hwy.; for ticket information phone (866) 582-2827. You can also take a stadium tour Monday through Thursday and some Fridays at 2:30 (a fee is charged); phone (813) 350-6500 for details. The Outback Bowl is played here on New Year's Day.

Hockey The NHL's **Tampa Bay Lightning,** winners of the 2004 Stanley Cup, hit the ice at **Amalie Arena,** 401 Channelside Dr., early October through mid-April. For information and tickets phone (813) 301-6600.

Horse Racing The only Thoroughbred track on Florida's west coast, **Tampa Bay Downs,** 11225 Race Track Rd., attracts horse racing devotees from near and far. The track has year-round simulcasting and holds live races Friday through Sunday, Wednesday and some Thursdays from early December to early May; post time is 12:25. For more information phone (813) 855-4401 or (866) 823-6967.

Note: Policies vary concerning admittance of children to pari-mutuel betting facilities. Phone for information.

Bicycling Tampa's busy roadways generally are not conducive to safe bicycling; however, scenic **Bayshore Boulevard** is a delightful exception. It offers a breezy ride along the western shore of Hillsborough Bay with pretty water views as a backdrop. **Suncoast Parkway Trail** parallels the toll road of the same name between the Veterans Expressway and State Road 50, and is generally separated from it by a buffer zone of plants and trees.

Cruise the periphery of **Downtown Tampa**; there are bike lanes on Tampa and Jackson streets and Nebraska Avenue, and more than 200 bike racks are scattered through the area. If you don't have a bike, rent one from downtown's **City Bike Tampa,** 212 E. Cass St.; phone (813) 225-1777. There's also **Coast Bike Share**, which has dozens of hubs throughout downtown Tampa where its bright blue bikes are stationed. Rental fees start at $8 per hour or $15 per month (for 60 minutes use per day); phone (813) 999-3300 for information.

You can also take a leisurely trip on foot or by bicycle along **The Riverwalk**, a wide paved path which runs along the banks of the Hillsborough River, beginning near The Florida Aquarium and passing the Tampa Bay History Center, Amalie Arena, the Tampa Convention Center and MacDill Park. It then goes past Curtis Hixon Waterfront Park, the Tampa Museum of Art, Glazer Children's Museum, the David A. Straz Jr. Center for the Performing Arts, and ends near Water Works Park and Spring. If you get a flat tire, take advantage of the walk's two bike repair stations. There's also plenty of signage along the walk to guide you.

The Riverwalk

Just south of downtown, peddle bayside on the **Davis Islands Trail,** beginning at Channel Drive and ending at Severn Boulevard near a seaplane basin next to Peter O. Knight Airport.

Fishing The waters of Hillsborough County yield bass, bream and perch. **Lake Thonotosassa,** northeast via SR 582, attracts freshwater fishing enthusiasts, and the docks off **Davis Islands** offer ample casting sites.

The central **Gulf Coast** offers some of the best saltwater fishing in the state. Boats can be chartered for inshore and offshore saltwater and freshwater fishing at **Clearwater Beach** and in other coastal communities.

In March and April, the Gulf of Mexico yields grouper, amberjack and king mackerel; in May and June, it's red snapper season. In November and December, head to the coast for gag grouper.

If you plan to fish on your vacation, freshwater and saltwater fishing licenses are sold at tackle shops, sporting goods and discount department stores and the county tax collector's office; phone (813) 635-5200 for information.

Golf With dozens of golf courses to choose from and weather that allows for year-round play, the Tampa Bay area is a true golfer's paradise and a great place to find things to do with friends. Some of the public and semi-private courses include **Babe Zaharias,** 11412 Forest Hills Dr., (813) 631-4374; **Bloomingdale Golfers Club,** 4113 Great Golfers Pl. in Valrico, (813) 685-4105; **The Claw at USF,** 13801 N. 46th St., (813) 632-6893; **Heritage Harbor,** 19502 Heritage Harbor Pkwy. in Lutz, (813) 949-4886; **Lake Jovita,** 12900 Lake Jovita Blvd. in Dade City, (352) 588-9200 or (877) 481-2652; **Northdale,** 4417 Northdale Blvd., (813) 962-0428; **Pebble Creek,** 10550 Regents Park Dr., (813) 973-3870; **Rocky Point,** 4151 Dana Shores Dr., (813) 673-4316; **Rogers Park,** 7910 N. 30th St., (813) 356-1670; **Saddlebrook,** 5700 Saddlebrook Way in Wesley Chapel, (813) 973-1111 or (800) 729-8383; **TPC Tampa Bay,** 5300 W. Lutz Lake Fern Rd. in Lutz, (813) 949-0090 or (866) 752-9872; and **Westchase,** 11602 Westchase Golf Dr., (813) 854-2331.

Hot Air Ballooning Tampa has its fair share of things for couples to do, as well. A champagne brunch accompanies hot air balloon flights that take off at sunrise and offer breathtaking views of the Tampa Bay area. For fares, flight schedules and departure locations phone **Big Red Balloon Sightseeing Adventures,** (813) 969-1518. You can also take to the skies with **American Balloons** in Land

O' Lakes or **Celebration Aviation**; phone (813) 243-9507 and (813) 884-5610 respectively.

Jogging and Walking Sunny weather encourages both visitors and locals to enjoy the outdoors. Four walking trails with a combined distance of 7.3 miles wind through scenic hardwood hammocks at **Hillsborough River State Park** *(see Recreation Areas Chart)* about 12 miles northeast to 15402 US 301 N.; phone (813) 987-6771.

For a sweeping view of Hillsborough Bay, nothing beats the 4.5-mile **Bayshore Boulevard Linear Park**, which begins at Columbus Statue Park and ends at Gandy Boulevard. The 10-foot-wide sidewalk is peppered with fitness stations along the way, and chances are you'll spot manatees and dolphins in the bay. On the opposite side of the street, you'll see Hyde Park's beautiful million-dollar homes.

In downtown Tampa, the **Riverwalk** runs alongside the Hillsborough River and passes numerous attractions, local restaurants, parks and hotels. The 2.5-mile walkway is open to pedestrians and runners.

Pound the asphalt on the 12-mile **Upper Tampa Bay Area Trail** in northwest Hillsborough County. The partially shaded trail begins at Memorial Highway and Montague Street with the northern terminus at Suncoast Parkway and W. Lutz Lake Fern Road; there are several water kiosks and benches on the trail. Phone (813) 801-6729 for a map and more information.

Commune with nature at **Sydney Dover Equestrian Trails**, 535 N. Dover Rd. in Apollo Beach, where you might be joined by hikers, runners, cyclists and horseback riders on 7.5 miles of smooth, wide grass and sand trails; phone (813) 757-3802.

Tennis The city-operated tennis facility at **Hillsborough Community College,** 4001 W. Tampa Bay Blvd., has 41 hard and clay courts; phone (813) 348-1173. There are eight lighted clay courts at the **Sandra W. Freedman Tennis Complex**, 59 Columbia Dr. on Davis Islands just south of downtown Tampa; phone (813) 259-1664. **Cal Dickson Tennis Center**, 4000 Watrous Ave. has eight courts open to the public; phone (813) 259-1893. For a complete list of playing courts, phone Tampa Parks and Recreation Department at (813) 274-8615.

Water Sports While there are two public beaches on the Tampa side of the bay—**Ben T. Davis Beach,** 7740 Courtney Campbell Causeway (SR 60) near the airport, and **Picnic Island Park,** 7409 Picnic Island Blvd. near Port Tampa—it's the Gulf beaches that draw lovers of water sports. Favorites are **Caladesi Island State Park** *(see Recreation Areas Chart)*, **Clearwater Beach** *(see place listing p. 43)*, **Fort De Soto Park** *(see Recreation Areas Chart)* and **St. Pete Beach** *(see place listing p. 272)*.

Hillsborough County parks also offer aquatic variety. Swimmers can dip into refreshing 72-degree spring water year-round at **Lithia Springs Regional Park,** 3932 Lithia Springs Rd. *(see Recreation Areas Chart)*; phone (813) 744-5572. The springs feed the **Alafia River**, the county's most popular canoeing destination; launches are available in Lithia

Bayshore Boulevard Linear Park

Springs Regional Park and in **Alderman's Ford Regional Park,** off CR 39 near Lithia at 9625 Canoe Launch Rd.; phone (813) 757-3801.

Picnic Island Park, 7409 Picnic Island Blvd., near the original encampment of Theodore Roosevelt's Rough Riders during the Spanish-American War, beckons boaters, swimmers, picnickers and anglers to its beach, pier and bay waters. The park is south of the Gandy Bridge (US 92) near MacDill Air Force Base and is accessible via Commerce Street; phone (813) 274-8615.

John Chesnut Sr. Park, 2200 E. Lake Rd. in Palm Harbor, accesses 5-mile-long Lake Tarpon; it allows motorized boats and is popular with waterskiers and users of personal watercraft. There's also a canoe trail (for non-motorized boats only), an elevated boardwalk that leads to a lookout tower, a dog park and playgrounds. Swimming is prohibited.

Paddle a rented canoe or kayak on Class II rapids at **Hillsborough River State Park**, 15402 N. US 301, or bask in the sun on the poolside lawn and cool off in the 1/2-acre swimming pool. Catch some bass, bream and catfish in the river, or just gaze at the bucolic view from a 1938 suspension bridge; phone (813) 987-6771 for information.

Other Diversions For enthusiasts of trapshooting (a type of clay pigeon shooting), the **Tampa Bay Sporting Clays**, 10514 Ehren Cutoff in Land O' Lakes, offers 260 acres of courses through palmetto and pine woods with one five-stand sporting clay and three wireless eight-station courses. There's also a 3D stationary archery course with 15 stations; phone (813) 929-6200.

Performing Arts

Tampa's spectrum of performing arts encompasses blockbuster Broadway musicals, symphony and chamber music concerts, children's shows and holiday spectaculars. Its keystone is the 335,000-square-foot **David A. Straz, Jr. Center for the Performing Arts,** the largest facility of its kind south of Washington, D.C.'s Kennedy Center. On the east bank of the Hillsborough River in downtown, the center plays host to a great variety of cultural things to do at its venues: the 2,610-seat **Carol Morsani Hall;** 1,042-seat **Ferguson Hall;** 268-seat **Jaeb Theater;** and 130-seat **Shimberg Playhouse.** Phone (813) 229-7827 or (800) 955-1045 for schedule, ticket information and group travel accomodations regarding each of these venues.

To learn about all the great things to do this weekend, grab a free copy of *Creative Loafing,* or the *Tampa Bay Times,* which are available throughout the city. The publications are filled with local news features; sections on where to eat, theater, film and music; and listings of upcoming events.

Film Downtown's 1,500-seat **Tampa Theatre,** a restored 1926 movie palace at 711 N. Franklin St., is a great spot to catch foreign films, cult movies, Hollywood classics and occasional concerts, especially if you're looking for unique things to do as a couple. Tours of the historic building also are offered; phone (813) 274-8981.

Music A full season of symphonic presentations is brought to the area by the **Florida Orchestra Inc.** and by local dance companies. Performances take place at David A. Straz, Jr. Center for the Performing Arts; phone (727) 892-3337 or (800) 662-7286 for ticket and schedule information.

Works for voice are presented by the **Master Chorale of Tampa Bay,** (813) 974-7726 and **Tampa Oratorio Singers,** (813) 666-5942. Performance locations vary.

Theater Broadway and off-Broadway theater plays are a big hit. **The Carrollwood Players,** 4333 Gunn Hwy. is a little-theater group presenting a variety of productions; phone (813) 265-4000. Comedies, musical revues and stage readings are offered at **The Gorilla Theatre,** 4419 N. Hubert Ave.; phone (813) 879-2914.

David A. Straz, Jr. Center for the Performing Arts' Shimberg Playhouse features local performing companies and improvisational groups, and the cozy Jaeb Theater presents plays and cabaret shows. The **Broadway** series brings the best of Broadway to Carol Morsani Hall. Phone the performing arts center at (813) 229-7827 before your trip.

ATTRACTIONS

For a complete list of attractions, visit AAA.com/travelguides/attractions

***AMERICAN VICTORY* MARINERS MEMORIAL & MUSEUM SHIP** is at 705 Channelside Dr. Berth #271. The memorial, an operational World War II-era military cargo ship named the SS *American*

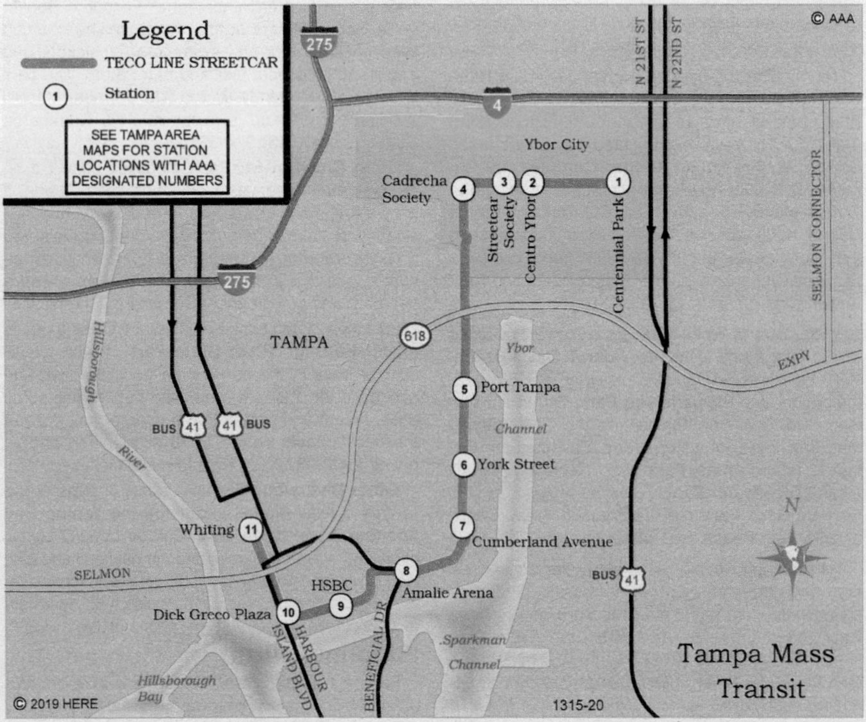

© AAA
© 2019 HERE
1315-20

Victory, is dedicated to those who built, served aboard and protected American merchant vessels. Completed in 1945, the ship served many roles in its history, such as delivering supplies to help rebuild Europe. Visitors can tour a variety of rooms and decks.

Time: Allow 1 hour minimum. **Hours:** Tues.-Sat. 10-5, Sun.-Mon. noon-5. Closed Easter, Thanksgiving and Christmas. **Cost:** $10; $8 (ages 65+); $5 (ages 5-12 and military with ID). **Phone:** (813) 228-8766. [bus] Cumberland Avenue, 7

GEM SAVE **BIG CAT RESCUE** is at 12802 Easy St. An accredited sanctuary for exotic cats that have been abused, abandoned or retired from performing acts, this 70-acre rehabilitation center offers guided walking tours of its grounds. Tigers, lions, bobcats, cougars, leopards, lynxes, ocelots and servals are among the approximately 50 cats living in the shaded sanctuary. Some of the cats had been kept as pets while others came from traveling acts and roadside zoos; most had been mistreated.

Enthusiastic tour guides divulge the back stories and educational facts about the cats featured on the 1.5-hour walking day tour. Visitors can also take a feeding tour, keeper tour and private tour, and there's a kids' tour for families with children ages 0-9. Guides talk about the dangers of keeping wild cats as pets. They also explain how big cats are inhumanely treated by breeders and exhibitors, provide information about laws that are in the works to prevent harm to captive exotic cats and teach the importance of respecting these noble beasts.

Big Cat Rescue had its beginnings in 1992 when the founder visited an animal auction and saved a young bobcat from becoming a stuffed den decoration. She later unknowingly visited a fur farm to purchase a bobcat kitten as a pet, only to learn that most of the remaining cats would be slaughtered and used in making fur coats. She rescued all 56 kittens and raised them, eventually building enclosures for them to live in.

Note: Visitors are advised to arrive 30 minutes before tours depart and wear comfortable, closed-toe shoes. Visitors are required to sign a release before taking the tour. Ages 0-9 are not permitted except on Kids' Tour. Photography is permitted. **Time:** Allow 2 hours minimum. **Hours:** Day tour Fri.-Wed. at 3. Other tour times vary; phone ahead for schedule. Closed Thanksgiving and Christmas. **Cost:** Day tour $39. Kids tour $29 (ages 0-9). Feeding tour $65. Keeper tour $125. Private tour $150. Rates may vary; phone ahead. Reservations are required. **Phone:** (813) 920-4130 for reservations. GT

GEM SAVE **BUSCH GARDENS TAMPA** is at 3000 E. Busch Blvd. (SR 580), 2 mi. e. of jct. I-275 exit 50 or 2 mi. w. of I-75 exit 265. The 335-acre adventure park features thrilling rides, live shows, shopping, dining and a major zoo with more than 300 species.

Cobra's Curse, a spin coaster for the whole family, features a vertical lift 70 feet high and a roller coaster that spins in different directions at 40 mph while a gigantic snake king stares you down.

Dive face down on a 335-foot drop tower, Falcon's Fury. At the thrill ride's highest point, riders pivot 90 degrees in midair to a face-down dive position. An instant later, they plunge straight down at 60 miles per hour.

Visitors watch in awe as cheetahs sprint across the plains of Cheetah Run. The hair-raising launch coaster Cheetah Hunt simulates a cheetah in pursuit of prey.

Jungala is a village nestled among towering trees where visitors can explore a three-story playland, soar on a zipline adventure, be launched into the sky from inside a 35-foot waterfall, connect up-close with orangutans and engage in a tug-of-war with a tiger.

SheiKra, one of seven heart-pounding roller coasters, is a floorless dive coaster that sends riders 200 feet up, then 90 degrees down. Among the kid-friendly attractions in the Sesame Street Safari of Fun area are Elmo's Treehouse Trek, Bert & Ernie's Watering Hole, the Air Grover coaster, the Zoe-patra & the Hippos of the Nile flume ride and The Count's Zambezi Rally car ride.

Edge of Africa offers a walking safari with hippos, lions, meerkats, vultures, Nile crocodiles and lemurs living in naturalistic habitats, remote encampments and African villages.

Myombe Reserve visitors can see lowland gorillas and chimpanzees in a naturalistic setting. The Serengeti Safari Tour takes riders through 65 acres and herds of free-roaming giraffes, zebras, rhinos, antelopes and ostriches. Kennels, strollers, wheelchairs and lockers can be rented. Allow a full day.

Hours: Generally opens daily between 9 and 10; closing times vary. Phone ahead to confirm schedule. **Cost:** $109.99; free (ages 0-2). Guided tours and encounters $29.99-$399.99. Keeper for a Day Tour $249.99. **Parking:** $25. **Phone:** (888) 800-5447. GT [restaurant]

GEM SAVE **THE FLORIDA AQUARIUM,** 701 Channelside Dr. on the downtown waterfront, is a 20,000-square-foot aquarium with themed areas featuring more than 30,000 aquatic creatures.

Wend your way through the Wetlands Trail, which realistically re-creates Florida swamplands with native trees, plants and gurgling freshwater streams (complete with their feathered, finned and furry inhabitants) under a nautilus-shaped glass dome. Ducks race each other in a long glass tank that's within arm's reach—you can even see their webbed feet paddling underwater. You also can watch cavorting otters do backflips, gaze at exotic marine birds such as white ibis and roseate spoonbills, and check out the turtles and native freshwater fish that dwell here.

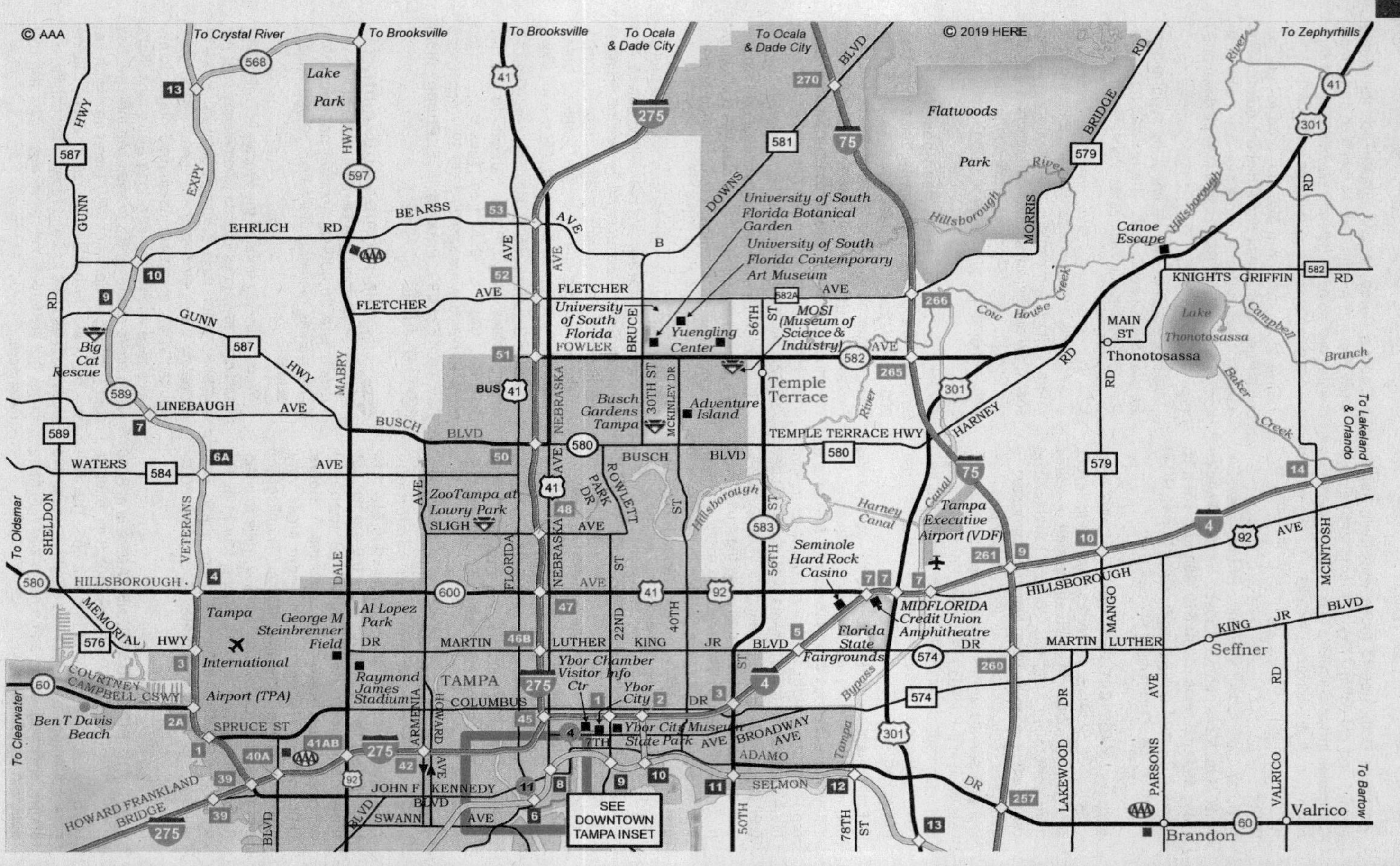

© AAA
To Crystal River
To Brooksville
To Brooksville
To Ocala & Dade City
To Ocala & Dade City
© 2019 HERE
To Zephyrhills
Lake Park
Flatwoods Park
Canoe Escape
Lake Thonotosassa
Thonotosassa
University of South Florida Botanical Garden
University of South Florida Contemporary Art Museum
University of South Florida
Yuengling Center
MOSI (Museum of Science & Industry)
Temple Terrace
Busch Gardens Tampa
Adventure Island
Big Cat Rescue
ZooTampa at Lowry Park
Tampa Executive Airport (VDF)
Seminole Hard Rock Casino
MIDFLORIDA Credit Union Amphitheatre
Florida State Fairgrounds
Seffner
To Lakeland & Orlando
To Oldsmar
Tampa International Airport (TPA)
George M Steinbrenner Field
Al Lopez Park
Raymond James Stadium
TAMPA
Ybor Chamber Visitor Info Ctr
Ybor City
Ybor City Museum State Park
Ben T Davis Beach
To Clearwater
HOWARD FRANKLAND BRIDGE
COURTNEY CAMPBELL CSWY
SEE DOWNTOWN TAMPA INSET
Brandon
Valrico
To Bartow

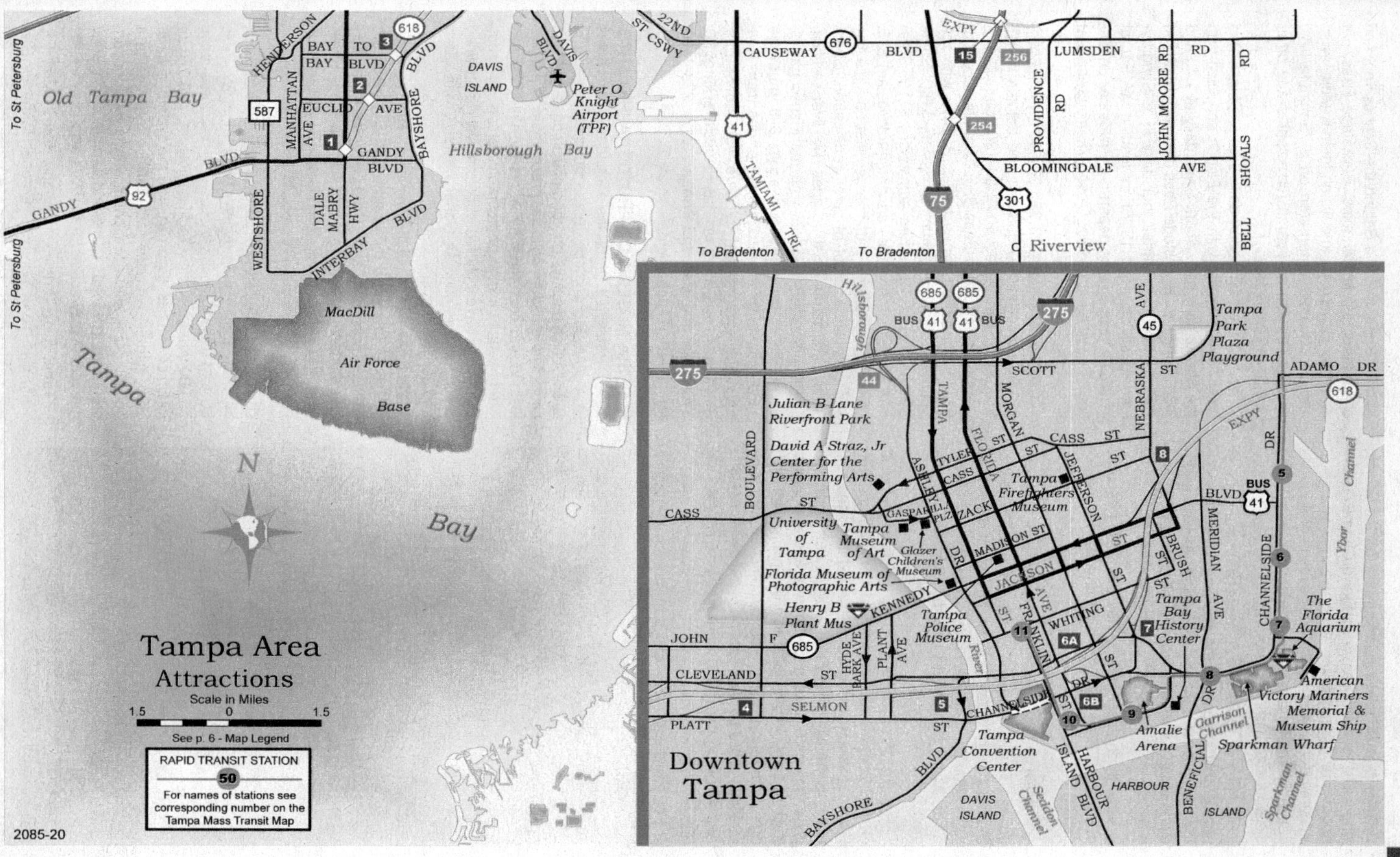
Tampa Area Attractions
Scale in Miles
1.5 0 1.5
See p. 6 - Map Legend
RAPID TRANSIT STATION
50
For names of stations see corresponding number on the Tampa Mass Transit Map
Downtown Tampa
Julian B Lane Riverfront Park
David A Straz, Jr Center for the Performing Arts
University of Tampa
Tampa Museum of Art
Glazer Children's Museum
Florida Museum of Photographic Arts
Henry B Plant Mus
Tampa Police Museum
Tampa Firefighters Museum
Tampa Park Plaza Playground
Tampa Bay History Center
Amalie Arena
Tampa Convention Center
The Florida Aquarium
American Victory Mariners Memorial & Museum Ship
Sparkman Wharf
Garrison Channel
Sparkman Channel
Seddon Channel
Ybor Channel
Hillsborough River
Davis Island
Harbour Island
MacDill Air Force Base
Peter O Knight Airport (TPF)
Old Tampa Bay
Hillsborough Bay
Tampa Bay
Riverview
To Bradenton
To St Petersburg
2085-20

Bays and Beaches concentrates on the wildlife who call the salty waters of Florida home. Learn about sea turtles, touch stingrays and sharks at Stingray Beach and visit a cross section of a Florida beach complete with several species of sun-loving birds grazing in the sand.

Journey to Madagascar focuses on the uniqueness of that region and the challenges that threaten the creatures that inhabit it. Features include an Indian Ocean exhibit, a hissing cockroach exhibit and a ring-tailed lemur.

Walk through a tunnel to see the living treasures of the Coral Reef exhibit, a replica of the underwater habitat of the Dry Tortugas islands near the Florida Keys. Residents of the 500,000-gallon tank include sand tiger sharks, sea turtles, angel fish, grouper, puffer fish, eels and snapper in an array of colors. Stop at Dragons Down Under, an exhibit devoted to Australian sea dragons, highly unusual marine creatures camouflaged by either leafy or weedy protrusions.

Have a close encounter of the watery kind at Ocean Commotion, where you can interact with talking animated versions of the exhibit's sea animals. In the No Bone Zone, visitors can touch sea stars, sea urchins, sea cucumbers and anemones. Kids can splash and play in the Splash Pad children's wet and dry playground, complete with a pirate ship, while parents cool off at the park's cantina. Animal programs include the Penguin Promenade and Otter Show.

For additional fees, take part in such interactive programs as Swim with the Fishes, Dive with the Sharks, Shark Swim, a Behind-the-Scenes Tour and shark feedings. At Penguins: Backstage Pass, pet these tuxedoed birds and watch them waddle, swim and eat. Board a catamaran on a 75-minute Wild Dolphin Cruise and search for dolphins and other wildlife in Tampa Bay.

The Florida Aquarium

Hours: Aquarium open daily 9:30-5. Splash Pad daily 10-4:45. Swim with the Fishes and Dive with the Sharks daily at 9. Shark Swim daily at 1:45 and 3:30. Penguins: Backstage Pass daily at 1:15, 2 and 2:45. Behind the Scenes tour daily at 1. Stingray-feeding talk daily at 1:15. Shark feeding talk Sat. at 11:30. Dolphin cruises depart daily (weather permitting); phone for schedule. Closed Thanksgiving and Christmas.

Cost: Aquarium $26.95; $24.95 (ages 60+); $21.95 (ages 3-11). Aquarium and dolphin cruise $55.90; $51.90 (ages 60+); $45.90 (ages 3-11). Penguins: Backstage Pass $30. Shark feeding tour $35. Behind-the-Scenes tour $12. Dive with the Sharks (includes aquarium admission) $160. Shark Swim (includes aquarium admission) $110. Swim with the Fishes (includes aquarium admission) $85. Dive with the Sharks participants must be ages 15+ and must show proof of diver certification. Shark Swim participants must be ages 9+; diver certification is not required. Swim with the Fishes participants must be ages 6+; ages 6-8 must be accompanied by a paying parent or guardian. Reservations are required for Dive with the Sharks, Shark Swim and Swim with the Fishes. **Parking:** $6; $10 (RVs and trailers). **Phone:** (813) 273-4000. GT Cumberland Avenue, 7

FLORIDA MUSEUM OF PHOTOGRAPHIC ARTS, 400 N. Ashley Dr., is on the second and third floors of a stunning six-story glass building called the Cube, which displays photographic images on its facade. The museum collects, preserves and exhibits historic and contemporary works by nationally and internationally known photographic artists. Previous exhibitions have included work from world-renowned photographers such as Gohar Dashti, Vivian Maier and Jerry Uelsmann.

Time: Allow 30 minutes minimum. **Hours:** Mon.-Fri. 11-6 (also Fri. 6-7 p.m.), Sat.-Sun. noon-5. Guided tours Sun. at 2. **Cost:** $10; $8 (ages 65+ and students and military with ID). **Parking:** Rivergate Plaza $5 per hour. Poe Garage $1.20 per hour. **Phone:** (813) 221-2222. GT Whiting, 11

GLAZER CHILDREN'S MUSEUM is off I-275 exit 44, then .5 mi. s.e. on Ashley Dr. N. at jct. W. Cass St. to 110 W. Gasparilla Plaza. In this three-story, 53,000-square-foot interactive museum, with 170 interactive exhibits, children follow the cycle of a water drop, captain a cruise ship, build a fort, design a house, dress like a firefighter, play a veterinarian, create art in various forms and explore engineering marvels. A play space for toddlers also is available.

Time: Allow 3 hours minimum. **Hours:** Mon.-Fri. 10-5, Sat. 10-6, Sun. 1-6. Closed Gasparilla Day (Jan. 26), Easter, Thanksgiving, Christmas Eve and

Christmas. Phone ahead to confirm schedule. **Cost:** $15; $12.50 (ages 65+ and active military, educators and first responders with ID); $10 (ages 1-12). Adults unaccompanied by children are not permitted. Children must be accompanied by an adult. **Phone:** (813) 443-3861. Whiting, 11

GEM **MOSI (MUSEUM OF SCIENCE & INDUSTRY),** 4801 E. Fowler Ave., contains more than 100 hands-on exhibits and demonstrations pertaining to science, technology, space, health and weather. Exhibits include Mission: Moonbase, featuring a simulated lunar colony; Idea Zone, a makerspace with robotics, 3D printing and prototyping; Connectus, which focuses on STEAM (Science, Technology, Engineering, Arts and Math) careers; and Core Science, which has interactive STEAM exhibits.

The multilevel Sky Trail Ropes Course dares you to defy gravity and your fears while testing your balance and dexterity. Make your way through the challenging ropes course that includes swinging steps, balance beams and trembling bridges 12 to 36 feet above ground level. The center also features Coleman Science Works Theater and Saunders Planetarium.

Note: Visitors are required to sign a release of liability before climbing the Sky Trail Ropes Course; clothing, height and weight restrictions apply. Open-toed shoes are not permitted on the Sky Trail; guests 42-47 inches tall must climb with an adult. Phone ahead for more details. **Hours:** Daily 10-5. Sky Trail Ropes Course Fri.-Sun. 10-5, weather permitting (last admission at 4:30). Closed Thanksgiving and Christmas. Phone ahead to confirm schedule. **Cost:** $12.95; $10.95 (ages 60+); $7.95 (ages 3-12). Sky Trail Ropes Course $7 with paid MOSI admission. Saunders Planetarium $5 with paid MOSI admission. An additional fee may be charged for special-engagement exhibits and films. **Phone:** (813) 987-6000, (813) 812-8774 or (800) 995-6674.

SAVE **TAMPA BAY HISTORY CENTER,** 801 Old Water St., interprets 12,000 years of Florida's history. Topics include Florida's first people, maritime activities, conquistadors, pirates, shipwrecks, and the cigar and cattle industries. Three floors of exhibits focus on the Gulf Coast, from prehistoric times to the present through artifacts, artwork, textiles, documents and furniture. Collections include more than 100 rare shipwreck artifacts recovered from Florida waters along with tools, clothing and ceremonial items from the Seminole Indians. **Time:** Allow 1 hour minimum. **Hours:** Daily 10-5 (10-3 on Dec. 24 and 31). Closed Thanksgiving and Christmas. **Cost:** $14.95; $12.95 (ages 65+ and military and students with ID); $10.95 (ages 7-17). Prices may vary; phone ahead. **Parking:** Parking is available for a fee at surrounding lots. **Phone:** (813) 228-0097. HSBC, 9

TAMPA MUSEUM OF ART, 120 W. Gasparilla Plaza in Curtis Hixon Waterfront Park, displays permanent and major traveling exhibitions with a focus on modern and contemporary art. The 66,000-square-foot building is encased in perforated aluminum panels accented by Leo Villareal's "Sky," an LED light display. Permanent collections include Greek and Roman antiquities as well as contemporary art in such mediums as oil paintings, lithographs, photography and sculpture. The museum faces the Hillsborough River with a view of the University of Tampa's minarets.

Florida Museum of Photographic Arts

Hours: Mon.-Thurs. 11-7 (also Fri. 7-8 p.m.); Sat.-Sun. 11-5. Closed Thanksgiving and Christmas. **Cost:** $15; $7.50 (ages 65+ and active military with ID and 1 guest); $5 (ages 6-18); free (ages 0-5 and college students with ID); by donation (Fri. 4-8). **Phone:** (813) 274-8130. Whiting, 11

TAMPA POLICE MUSEUM, 411 N. Franklin St., houses law enforcement equipment, vehicles, uniforms and memorabilia. One section documents the pursuit and capture of notorious criminals. **Time:** Allow 1 hour minimum. **Hours:** Mon.-Fri. 10-3 (based on staff availability). Phone ahead to confirm schedule. **Cost:** Free. **Phone:** (813) 276-3258. Whiting, 11

UNIVERSITY OF TAMPA, 401 W. Kennedy Blvd., was established in 1931 and serves approximately 9,000 undergraduate and graduate students. Encompassing 110 riverfront acres, the modern and historic downtown campus centers around Plant Hall, the former Tampa Bay Hotel. The Victorian-style building exemplifies Moorish revival architecture with minarets, domes and cupolas. The hotel was built in 1891 by transportation magnate Henry B. Plant, who was instrumental in the reconstruction of the South. The non-denominational Sykes Chapel and Center for Faith and Values, built in 2010, features a built-in Dobson pipe organ.

Time: Allow 30 minutes minimum. **Hours:** Campus tours are arranged through the Office of Admissions when school is in session. Closed Jan. 1, Thanksgiving, Christmas Eve, Christmas, day after Christmas, Dec. 30 and campus holidays. **Cost:** Free. **Phone:** (813) 253-6211 for campus tours. GT Whiting, 11

GEM **Henry B. Plant Museum** is housed in the south wing of Plant Hall at 401 W. Kennedy Blvd. Built in 1891 as the luxurious Tampa Bay Hotel by Henry Bradley Plant, a wealthy railroad magnate, the museum displays the Moorish Revival-style building's original collection of decorative arts and furnishings from the Gilded Age. The hotel, made of red brick and topped with stainless steel minarets and domes, cost $3,000,000 to build; the price includes much of the Victorian decor purchased by Plant and his wife during trips to Europe.

Hotel guests included Theodore Roosevelt, Babe Ruth, actress Sarah Bernhardt, author Stephen Crane and composer John Philip Sousa. Edison carbon filament light bulbs are the only lights used throughout the museum so that visitors may experience the hotel much like its original visitors. Exhibits are housed in 14 former guestrooms and re-create the first-class accommodations and activities of 1891.

A 14-minute video presentation highlights Tampa's Victorian-era lifestyle and tourism, and a live stage performance features character vignettes of the hotel's staff and guests. The 1-hour self-guiding audio tour features oral histories, commentary, music and sound effects. GEM A Victorian Christmas Stroll in December depicts a traditional 19th-century holiday.

Strollers, backpacks and large bags are not permitted. **Time:** Allow 1 hour minimum. **Hours:** Museum open Tues.-Sat. 10-5, Sun. noon-5, Jan.-Nov; daily 10-8, rest of year. Stage show Sun. at 2, Sept.-May. Victorian Christmas Stroll daily 10-8, Dec. 1-23. Closed Thanksgiving and Christmas. **Cost:** $10; $7 (ages 65+ and students with ID); $5 (ages 4-12). Audio tour and stage show free with admission. Victorian Christmas Stroll $15; $13 (ages 65+); $9 (ages 4-18). **Phone:** (813) 254-1891. Whiting, 11

YBOR CITY is bounded n. by 12th Ave., s. by Adamo Dr., e. by 26th St. and w. by Nebraska Ave. Ybor City was established by Don Vicente Martinez Ybor in 1886. Ybor moved his Key West cigar manufacturing business to the Tampa area to escape political and labor unrest resulting from the Cuban Freedom Movement. It soon became the Cigar Capital of the World, producing millions of cigars each year. By the 1960s, the cigar industry had waned, primarily due to the Cuban tobacco embargo.

The city is a busy entertainment district with strong Latin influences in music, food and culture. The historic district features cigar factories, shops and restaurants on brick streets lined with globe lampposts. Guided walking tours are available for a fee through Ybor City Museum State Park *(see attraction listing)*. **Time:** Allow 3 hours minimum. **Hours:** Ybor City Visitor Information Center Mon.-Sat. 10-5, Sun. noon-5. **Cost:** Free. **Phone:** (813) 241-8838 for Ybor City Visitor Information Center. GT Centro Ybor, 2

Ybor Chamber Visitor Information Center is at 1600 E. Eighth Ave., Suite B-104. Located within Tampa's historic cigar-manufacturing district, the center features cigar trade exhibits and a 7-minute video tracing the area's transformation from quiet swampland to bustling city. Maps for self-guiding walking tours are available. **Time:** Allow 15 minutes minimum. **Hours:** Mon.-Sat. 10-5, Sun. noon-5. **Cost:** Free. **Phone:** (813) 241-8838. Centro Ybor, 2

Ybor City Museum State Park, 3 blks. s. of I-4 exit 1 at 1818 E. Ninth Ave., is in a former bakery with huge brick ovens still intact. Displays depict Ybor City's founding by Don Vicente Martinez Ybor as well as the cigar industry, which brought many nationalities to Tampa. An 1895 cigar worker's cottage (La Casita) furnished in period is open by guided tour. Walking tours of Ybor City also are offered; reservations are required. A garden features statues, a fountain and picnic tables.

Time: Allow 30 minutes minimum. **Hours:** Wed.-Sun. 9-5. La Casita tours are given Wed.-Sun. on the hour 10-3. Closed Jan. 1, Thanksgiving and Christmas. **Cost:** Museum, garden and La Casita tour $4; free (ages 0-5). **Phone:** (813) 247-6323. GT Centennial Park, 1

GEM **ZOOTAMPA AT LOWRY PARK,** 1101 W. Sligh Ave., features iconic Florida species and wildlife from around the world. In Safari Africa and Ituri Forest, see animals such as okapi, pygmy hippos, meerkats and rhinos. An adorable colony of African penguins show off their expert swimming skills in a beach-themed habitat.

Enjoy behind-the-scenes views of dozens of animals including elephants and patas monkeys on a 15-minute narrated tram tour. Feel the rush on the new water adventure Roaring Springs. Trek to discover endangered Florida wildlife, then board a boat for a journey along a flowing stream and thrill to the roar of a three-story splashdown. The Florida Boardwalk harbors endangered Florida panthers, Florida black bears, river otters, Key deer and manatees. In the Asian Gardens, revel in the beauty of such rare or endangered species as Malayan tigers, clouded leopards, tapirs and Komodo dragons.

Wallaroo Station is an Australian-themed children's area where you can walk just a few footsteps away from wallabies and visit koalas. Kids can also enjoy the petting zoo and cool off in a water play area. Also enjoy the Tasmanian Tiger roller coaster, Boomers' Flyin' Bananas, Macaw Flyover, Bird of Prey Show, animal mingles and keeper chats.

Time: Allow 3 hours minimum. **Hours:** Daily 9:30-5 (weather permitting). Closed Thanksgiving and Christmas. **Cost:** $36.95; $27.95 (ages 3-11). Up-close signature encounters $25. Animal feedings $5. **Phone:** (813) 935-8552. GT

Sightseeing

Tampa Bay CityPASS saves you 54 percent on admission to the top five attractions in the Tampa Bay region. It includes discounted admission into Busch Gardens® Tampa Bay, The Florida Aquarium, ZooTampa at Lowry Park and Clearwater Marine Aquarium. Also included is an option ticket to either the Museum of Science & Industry (MOSI) OR Chihuly Collection presented by the Morean Arts Center.

The Tampa Bay CityPASS is available as a tech-friendly mobile ticket or a printed ticket booklet containing all the attraction admission tickets. Both options can be purchased online if you wish to purchase ahead of your trip. The CityPASS ticket booklet may also be purchased at any of the participating attractions. The Tampa Bay CityPASS is valid for 9 consecutive days once the first ticket is used. Credit cards accepted vary with the vendor attractions. Phone (888) 330-5008.

Driving Tours

With its scenic views of Hillsborough Bay, 4.5-mile-long Bayshore Boulevard is not only a popular walking and exercise area for residents but also a preferred driving destination. Among the beautiful residential neighborhoods to explore are Davis Islands, built on three man-made islands in the 1920s, and historic Hyde Park.

Walking Tours

Take in the sights, explore the local restaurants and delve into the city on foot. The Ybor Chamber Visitor Information Center, 1600 E. Eighth Ave., offers information about guided walking tours of historic Ybor City.

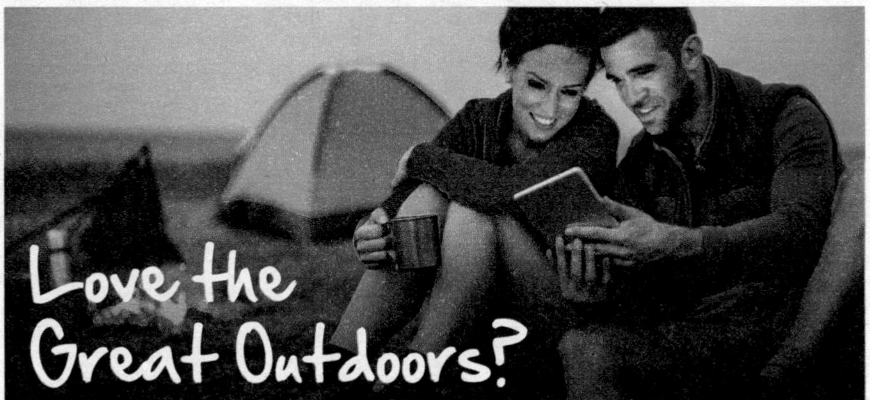

iStockphoto.com_pixelfit

When getting away means getting off the beaten path, visit AAA.com/campgrounds or AAA.com/maps for:

- Thousands of places to camp across the U.S. and Canada
- Complete mapping and travel information to plan your adventure

Look for locations with the trusted mark of approval.

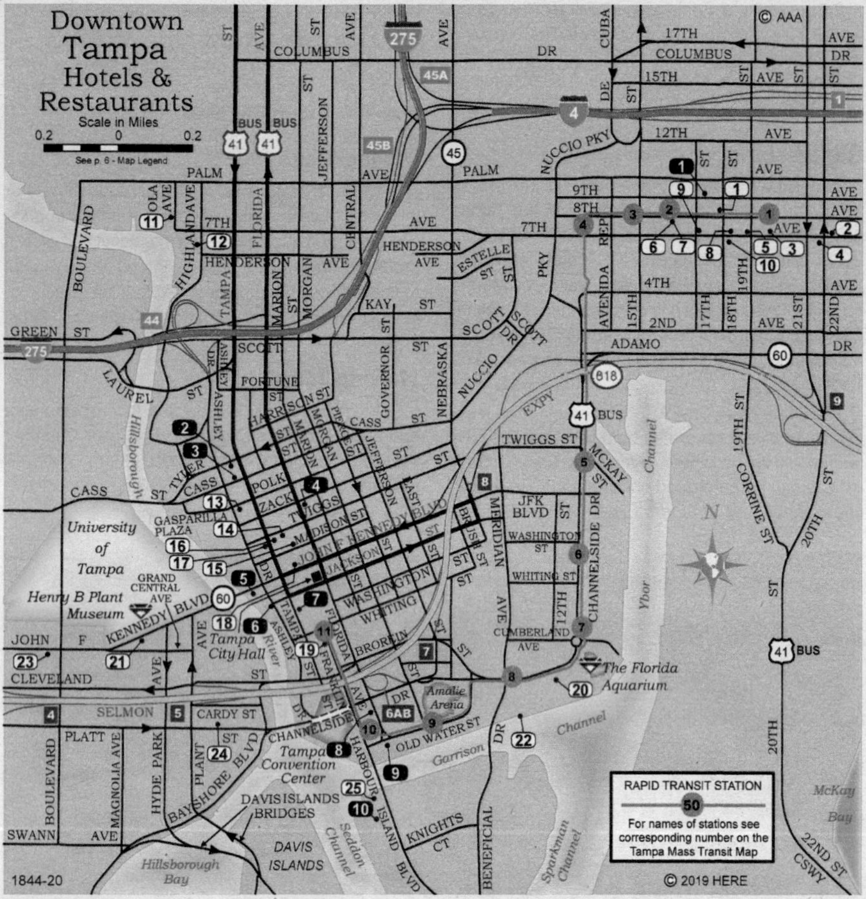

Downtown Tampa Hotels & Restaurants

Scale in Miles 0.2 0 0.2

See p. 6 - Map Legend

RAPID TRANSIT STATION 50 For names of stations see corresponding number on the Tampa Mass Transit Map

1844-20 © AAA © 2019 HERE

Downtown Tampa

This index helps you "spot" where approved hotels and restaurants are located on the corresponding detailed maps. Restaurant price range is a combination of lunch and/or dinner. Turn to the listing page for more information and consult display ads for special promotions.

For more details, rates and reservations: AAA.com/travelguides/hotels

DOWNTOWN TAMPA

Map Page	Hotels	Diamond Rated	Member Savings	Page
1 this page	Hilton Garden Inn/Tampa Ybor Historic District	◆◆◆	✔	350
2 this page	**Residence Inn by Marriott Tampa Downtown**	◆◆◆	✔	350
3 this page	**Courtyard by Marriott Tampa Downtown**	◆◆◆	✔	350
4 this page	**Le Meridien Tampa**	◆◆◆◆	✔	350
5 this page	**Aloft Tampa Downtown Hotel**	◆◆◆	✔	350
6 this page	Sheraton Tampa Riverwalk	◆◆◆	✔	350
7 this page	**Hilton Tampa Downtown**	◆◆◆	✔	350
8 this page	**Embassy Suites by Hilton Tampa Downtown Convention Center**	◆◆◆	✔	350
9 this page	**Tampa Marriott Water Street**	◆◆◆◆	✔	351

DOWNTOWN TAMPA (cont'd)

Map Page	Hotels (cont'd)	Diamond Rated	Member Savings	Page
10 p. 336	**The Westin Tampa Waterside**	♦♦♦	✔	351

Map Page	Restaurants	Diamond Rated	Cuisine	Price Range	Page
1 p. 336	James Joyce Irish Pub	♦♦	Irish	$7-$17	351
2 p. 336	Shrimp & Co Restaurant	♦♦	Seafood	$9-$20	351
3 p. 336	Sundays Delicatessen	♦	Breakfast Sandwiches	$4-$15	351
4 p. 336	Columbia Restaurant	♦♦♦	Spanish	$9-$39	351
5 p. 336	La Tropicana Cuban Cafe	♦	Cuban	$6-$9	351
6 p. 336	Samurai Blue Sushi & Sake Bar	♦♦	Japanese Sushi	$10-$25	351
7 p. 336	Jax Bar & Grill	♦♦	American	$7-$20	351
8 p. 336	Carmine's	♦♦	Spanish	$6-$33	351
9 p. 336	Bernini of Ybor	♦♦	Italian	$9-$34	351
10 p. 336	Gaspar's Grotto	♦♦	Sandwiches Pizza	$9-$20	351
11 p. 336	Steelbach	♦♦♦	Regional Southern	$10-$78	351
12 p. 336	u-le-le	♦♦♦	Natural/Organic	$8-$45	351
13 p. 336	Taps Restaurant Bar & Lounge	♦♦	American	$12-$22	351
14 p. 336	Bavaro's Pizza Napoletana & Pastaria	♦♦	Italian	$8-$19	351
15 p. 336	Taco Bus	♦	Mexican	$3-$9	351
16 p. 336	Eddie & Sams Pizza & Gelato Bar	♦	Italian	$3-$45	351
17 p. 336	Moxie's Cafe Coffeebar Caterer	♦	Breakfast Sandwiches	$6-$11	351
18 p. 336	Holy Hog Barbecue	♦	Barbecue	$7-$22	351
19 p. 336	Hattrick's Sports Bar-Downtown Tampa	♦♦	American	$8-$15	351
20 p. 336	Splitsville southern+ social	♦♦	American	$7-$19	351
21 p. 336	Mise en Place	♦♦♦	Mediterranean	$11-$41	351
22 p. 336	**Yacht Starship Dining Cruises**	♦♦♦	Continental	$60-$90	351
23 p. 336	Edison: Food+drink Lab	♦♦♦	Continental	$11-$39	351
24 p. 336	Four Green Fields	♦♦	Irish	$5-$15	351
25 p. 336	Jackson's Bistro-Bar & Sushi	♦♦♦	Steak Seafood	$11-$41	351

AAA/CAA Members Save on Hotels - For Any Occasion

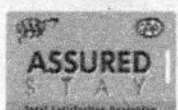

BW | Best Western. Hotels & Resorts

Hilton

HYATT

Marriott INTERNATIONAL

VISIT over 1,100 AAA/CAA Offices | CLICK AAA.com/greatrates | CALL 1-866-222-7283

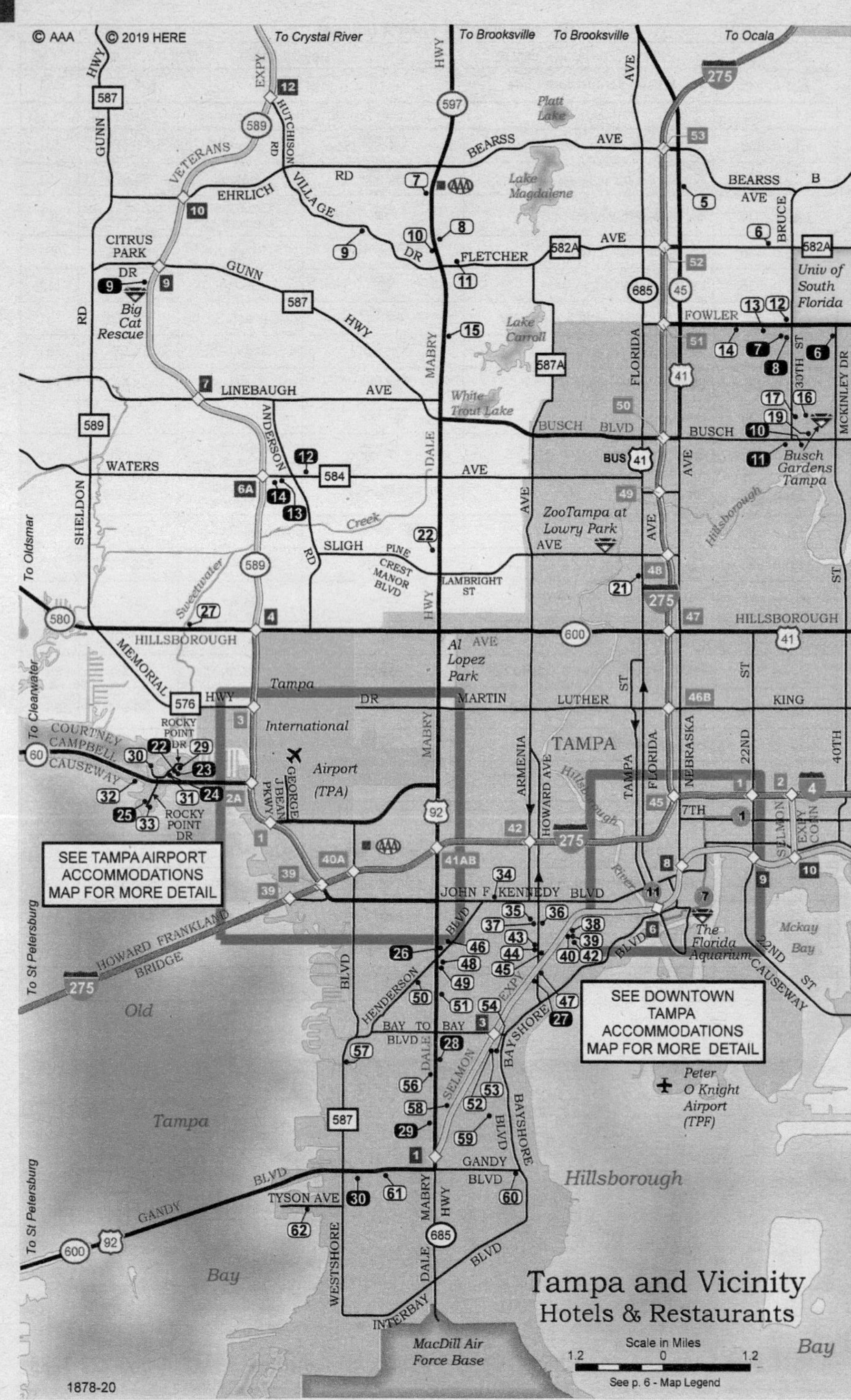

© AAA © 2019 HERE
To Crystal River
To Brooksville
To Brooksville
To Ocala
BEARSS AVE
EHRLICH RD
VILLAGE DR
FLETCHER AVE
GUNN HWY
CITRUS PARK
Big Cat Rescue
LINEBAUGH AVE
BUSCH BLVD
WATERS AVE
SLIGH AVE
PINE CREST MANOR BLVD
LAMBRIGHT ST
HILLSBOROUGH AVE
MEMORIAL HWY
FOWLER
Univ of South Florida
Busch Gardens Tampa
ZooTampa at Lowry Park
Platt Lake
Lake Magdalene
Lake Carroll
White Trout Lake
Al Lopez Park
Tampa International Airport (TPA)
MARTIN LUTHER KING
TAMPA
COURTNEY CAMPBELL CAUSEWAY
ROCKY POINT DR
SEE TAMPA AIRPORT ACCOMMODATIONS MAP FOR MORE DETAIL
HOWARD FRANKLAND BRIDGE
JOHN F. KENNEDY BLVD
HENDERSON BLVD
BAY TO BAY BLVD
BAYSHORE BLVD
SELMON EXPY
SEE DOWNTOWN TAMPA ACCOMMODATIONS MAP FOR MORE DETAIL
The Florida Aquarium
Mckay Bay
22ND ST CAUSEWAY
Peter O Knight Airport (TPF)
Old Tampa Bay
Hillsborough Bay
GANDY BLVD
TYSON AVE
WESTSHORE BLVD
DALE MABRY HWY
INTERBAY BLVD
MacDill Air Force Base
To Oldsmar
To Clearwater
To St Petersburg
To St Petersburg
Tampa and Vicinity
Hotels & Restaurants
Scale in Miles
1.2 0 1.2
See p. 6 - Map Legend
1878-20

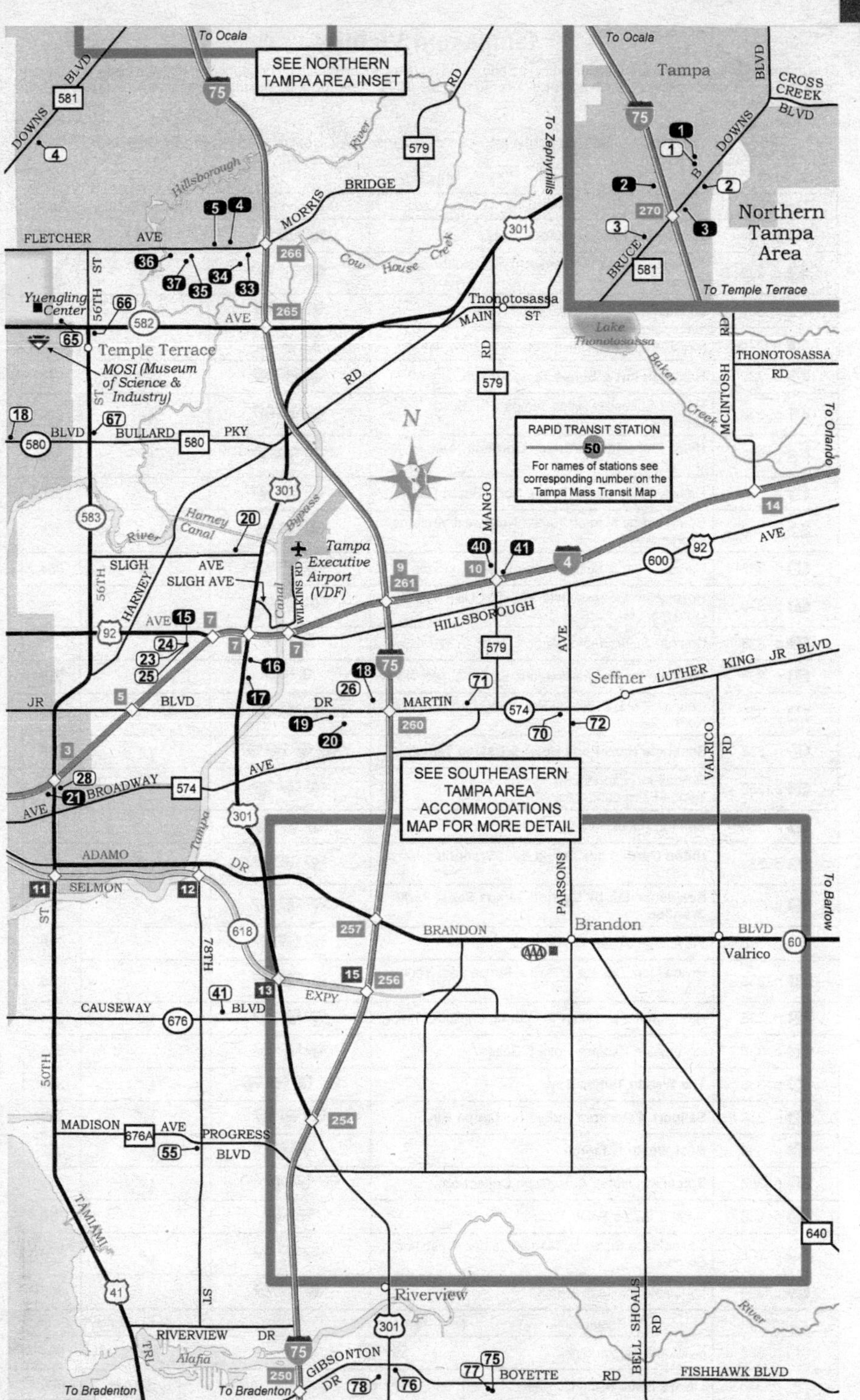

To Ocala
SEE NORTHERN TAMPA AREA INSET
Northern Tampa Area
Tampa
To Temple Terrace
Temple Terrace
Yuengling Center
MOSI (Museum of Science & Industry)
Thonotosassa
Lake Thonotosassa
To Zephyrhills
To Orlando
RAPID TRANSIT STATION
For names of stations see corresponding number on the Tampa Mass Transit Map
Tampa Executive Airport (VDF)
Seffner
SEE SOUTHEASTERN TAMPA AREA ACCOMMODATIONS MAP FOR MORE DETAIL
Brandon
Valrico
To Bartow
Riverview
To Bradenton
FLETCHER AVE
MORRIS BRIDGE RD
BULLARD PKY
SLIGH AVE
HILLSBOROUGH AVE
MARTIN LUTHER KING JR BLVD
BROADWAY AVE
ADAMO DR
SELMON EXPY
BRANDON BLVD
CAUSEWAY BLVD
MADISON AVE
PROGRESS BLVD
RIVERVIEW DR
GIBSONTON DR
BOYETTE RD
FISHHAWK BLVD
TAMIAMI TRL
MANGO RD
PARSONS AVE
VALRICO RD
BELL SHOALS RD
MCINTOSH RD
THONOTOSASSA RD
50TH ST
56TH ST
78TH ST

Tampa and Vicinity

This index helps you "spot" where approved hotels and restaurants are located on the corresponding detailed maps. Restaurant price range is a combination of lunch and/or dinner. Turn to the listing page for more information and consult display ads for special promotions.

For more details, rates and reservations: **AAA.com/travelguides/hotels**

TAMPA

Map Page	Hotels	Diamond Rated	Member Savings	Page
1 p. 338	Holiday Inn Express Hotel & Suites	♦♦♦		355
2 p. 338	SpringHill Suites by Marriott Tampa North/Tampa Palms	♦♦♦	✔	358
3 p. 338	La Quinta Inn & Suites Tampa North	♦♦♦		356
4 p. 338	Courtyard by Marriott Tampa North I-75 Fletcher	♦♦♦	✔	352
5 p. 338	**Hampton Inn & Suites Tampa North**	♦♦♦	✔	354
6 p. 338	Home2 Suites By Hilton Tampa USF/Busch Gardens	♦♦♦	✔	356
7 p. 338	**Hyatt Place Tampa/Busch Gardens** *(See ad p. 357.)*	♦♦♦	✔	356
8 p. 338	Holiday Inn & Suites Tampa North Busch Gardens	♦♦♦		355
9 p. 338	Courtyard by Marriott Tampa Northwest/Veterans Expressway	♦♦♦	✔	352
10 p. 338	Hampton Inn & Suites Tampa Busch Gardens	♦♦♦	✔	354
11 p. 338	Holiday Inn Express Hotel & Suites USF Busch Gardens	♦♦♦		356
12 p. 338	Comfort Suites Tampa Airport North	♦♦		352
13 p. 338	Hampton Inn Tampa-Veterans Expwy/Airport North	♦♦	✔	355
14 p. 338	Country Inn & Suites by Radisson, Tampa Airport North	♦♦♦		352
15 p. 338	**Seminole Hard Rock Hotel & Casino Tampa**	♦♦♦♦	✔	358
16 p. 338	Holiday Inn Express Suites Tampa-Fairground-Casino	♦♦♦		356
17 p. 338	Comfort Suites Tampa Fairgrounds-Casino	♦♦♦		352
18 p. 338	**Hilton Garden Inn Tampa East/Brandon** *(See ad p. 355.)*	♦♦♦	✔	355
19 p. 338	**Residence Inn by Marriott Tampa Sabal Park/ Brandon**	♦♦♦	✔	357
20 p. 338	Staybridge Suites-Tampa East	♦♦♦		358
21 p. 338	Holiday Inn Express & Suites Tampa East-Ybor City	♦♦♦		355
22 p. 338	Hampton Inn by Hilton Tampa-Airport/Rocky Point	♦♦♦	✔	354
23 p. 338	Holiday Inn Express Hotel & Suites	♦♦♦		355
24 p. 338	**The Westin Tampa Bay**	♦♦♦♦	✔	358
25 p. 338	**Sailport Waterfront Suites on Tampa Bay**	♦♦♦	✔	357
26 p. 338	**Best Western Tampa**	♦♦	✔	352
27 p. 338	**Epicurean Hotel, Autograph Collection**	♦♦♦♦	✔	353
28 p. 338	Hotel & Suites South Tampa	♦♦		356
29 p. 338	TownePlace Suites by Marriott Tampa Westshore South	♦♦♦	✔	358
30 p. 338	La Quinta Inn Tampa South	♦♦♦		356

Map Page	Restaurants	Diamond Rated	Cuisine	Price Range	Page
1 p. 338	Sukhothai Restaurant	♦♦	Thai	$9-$29	361
2 p. 338	Liang's Bistro Asian Cuisine	♦♦	Asian	$9-$19	360

Map Page	Restaurants (cont'd)	Diamond Rated	Cuisine	Price Range	Page
3 p. 338	Stonewood Grill & Tavern	◆◆◆	American	$11-$39	361
4 p. 338	Thai Ruby	◆◆	Thai	$8-$20	361
5 p. 338	**Skipper's Smokehouse Restaurant & Oyster Bar**	◆	Seafood	$5-$21	361
6 p. 338	Taco Bus	◆	Mexican	$3-$9	361
7 p. 338	Benjarong Thai	◆◆	Thai	$6-$20	359
8 p. 338	Vallarta's Restaurante Mexicano	◆◆	Mexican	$3-$19	361
9 p. 338	Slice Masters NY Pizzeria	◆	Italian	$5-$16	361
10 p. 338	Jasmine Thai Restaurant	◆◆	Thai	$11-$30	360
11 p. 338	Hibachi Buffet	◆	Chinese	$8-$14	360
12 p. 338	Chicken Salad Chick	◆	Chicken Sandwiches	$4-$9	359
13 p. 338	Saigon Bay Vietnamese Restaurant	◆◆	Vietnamese	$8-$16	360
14 p. 338	Pastries N Chaat Indian Street Food & Bakery	◆	Indian	$3-$15	360
15 p. 338	Holy Hog Barbecue	◆	Barbecue	$7-$22	360
16 p. 338	Dragonfire Grill	◆	American	$7-$11	359
17 p. 338	Zambia Smokehouse	◆	Barbecue	$7-$10	361
18 p. 338	Mel's Hot Dogs	◆	Hot Dogs Sandwiches	$4-$16	360
19 p. 338	Zagora Cafe	◆	Burgers Sandwiches	$7-$10	361
20 p. 338	Frontier Steakhouse	◆◆	Steak	$12-$41	359
21 p. 338	Rooster & The Till	◆◆◆	Continental	$13-$26	360
22 p. 338	Burger Culture	◆	Burgers Sandwiches	$7-$13	359
23 p. 338	RiSE Kitchen & Bakery	◆◆	American	$9-$29	360
24 p. 338	Hard Rock Cafe	◆◆	American	$12-$30 SAVE	360
25 p. 338	Council Oak Steaks & Seafood	◆◆◆	Steak	$23-$60	359
26 p. 338	Danny's All American Diner & Dairy Bar	◆	Burgers Sandwiches	$3-$10	359
27 p. 338	Pipo's & Son Cafeteria	◆	Spanish	$4-$13	360
28 p. 338	Brocato's Sandwich Shop	◆	Sandwiches Breakfast	$5-$15	359
29 p. 338	Bahama Breeze Island Grille	◆◆◆	Caribbean	$6-$24	359
30 p. 338	Galerie Restaurant	◆◆	Continental	$7-$25	359
31 p. 338	AQUA Bar & Grille	◆◆◆	Seafood	$9-$56	359
32 p. 338	Whiskey Joe's Bar & Grill	◆◆	Seafood	$10-$46	361
33 p. 338	The Rusty Pelican	◆◆◆	Seafood Steak	$10-$45	360
34 p. 338	Miguel's Mexican Seafood & Grill	◆◆	Mexican	$8-$33	360
35 p. 338	The Dubliner Irish Pub	◆◆	Irish	$8-$18	359
36 p. 338	Yard of Ale Soho	◆◆	Sandwiches Pizza	$6-$13	361
37 p. 338	MacDinton's Irish Pub & Restaurant	◆◆	Irish	$7-$14	360
38 p. 338	Goody Goody	◆◆	Comfort Food Breakfast	$4-$15	359
39 p. 338	CinéBistro Hyde Park	◆◆	Continental	$9-$30	359
40 p. 338	Irish 31 Pub House & Eatery	◆◆	Irish	$8-$26	360

Map Page	Restaurants (cont'd)	Diamond Rated	Cuisine	Price Range	Page
41 p. 338	Liborio's Latin Cafe & Catering	◆	Latin American	$3-$10	360
42 p. 338	Timpano Chophouse	◆◆◆	Continental	$11-$45	361
43 p. 338	717 South	◆◆◆	Italian	$9-$39	359
44 p. 338	Royal Palace Thai Restaurant	◆◆	Thai	$7-$20	360
45 p. 338	Haven	◆◆◆	Continental	$5-$22	360
46 p. 338	Bonefish Grill	◆◆◆	Seafood	$14-$30	359
47 p. 338	Bern's Steak House	◆◆◆	Steak Seafood	$24-$52	359
48 p. 338	Terra Gauha Brazilian Steakhouse	◆◆◆	Brazilian Steak	$16-$45	361
49 p. 338	Wright's Gourmet House	◆	Sandwiches Deli	$2-$12	361
50 p. 338	Holy Hog Barbecue	◆	Barbecue	$7-$22	360
51 p. 338	Indochinois Restaurant	◆◆	Vietnamese	$7-$19	360
52 p. 338	The Brunchery Restaurant & Catering	◆◆	Breakfast Sandwiches	$6-$10	359
53 p. 338	Pane' Rustica Bakery & Cafe	◆◆	Sandwiches Breads/Pastries	$6-$39	360
54 p. 338	Intelligent Gourmet	◆	Natural/Organic Sandwiches	$5-$13	360
55 p. 338	Pizza Pino	◆	Italian	$3-$17	360
56 p. 338	BJ's Alabama BBQ	◆	Barbecue	$6-$28	359
57 p. 338	Tate's Restaurant Pizzeria & Bar	◆◆	Italian	$8-$21	361
58 p. 338	Tampa Buffet	◆	Chinese	$7-$15	361
59 p. 338	Caffe Paradiso Ristorante Italiano	◆◆◆	Northern Italian	$11-$30	359
60 p. 338	Kojak's House of Ribs	◆◆	Barbecue	$7-$25	360
61 p. 338	Taco Bus	◆	Mexican	$3-$13	361
62 p. 338	Hula Bay Club Waterfront Restaurant & Bar	◆◆	Seafood	$9-$35	360

TEMPLE TERRACE

Map Page	Hotels	Diamond Rated	Member Savings	Page
33 p. 338	WoodSpring Suites	◆◆		363
34 p. 338	Hilton Garden Inn Tampa North	◆◆◆	✔	363
35 p. 338	**Residence Inn by Marriott Tampa North I-75 Fletcher**	◆◆◆	✔	363
36 p. 338	Holiday Inn Express Tampa N I-75 University Area	◆◆◆		363
37 p. 338	TownePlace Suites by Marriott Tampa North/I-75 Fletcher	◆◆	✔	363

Map Page	Restaurants	Diamond Rated	Cuisine	Price Range	Page
65 p. 338	CDB Pizza & Italian Restaurant	◆◆	Italian	$8-$24	363
66 p. 338	Tokyo Japanese Restaurant & Sushi Bar	◆◆	Japanese Sushi	$3-$29	363
67 p. 338	Vallartas Mexican Restaurant	◆◆	Mexican	$6-$18	363

SEFFNER

Map Page	Hotels	Diamond Rated	Member Savings	Page
40 p. 338	**Country Inn & Suites by Radisson Tampa East/Seffner**	◆◆◆	✔	309
41 p. 338	Hampton Inn & Suites Tampa East	◆◆◆	✔	309

Map Page	Restaurants	Diamond Rated	Cuisine	Price Range	Page
70 p. 338	Young Bin Chinese Restaurant	◆◆	Chinese	$5-$14	309

Map Page	Restaurants (cont'd)	Diamond Rated	Cuisine	Price Range	Page
71 p. 338	China Wok Chinese Restaurant	◆	Chinese	$5-$12	309
72 p. 338	Hungry Harry's Famous Bar-B-Que	◆	Barbecue	$4-$24	309

RIVERVIEW

Map Page	Restaurants	Diamond Rated	Cuisine	Price Range	Page
75 p. 338	China Park Chinese Food	◆	Chinese	$5-$13	254
76 p. 338	New China New York Style Chinese Restaurant	◆	Chinese	$7-$14	254
77 p. 338	Chai Yo Thai Cuisine	◆◆	Thai	$7-$20	254
78 p. 338	The Hot Tomato of Riverview	◆	Sandwiches Desserts	$3-$11	254

iStockphoto.com_LeoPatrizi

Make a good trip great with insight from AAA's travel experts. Use their recommended picks and itineraries to find best places to go, stay, dine and play.

Photo source iStockphoto.com

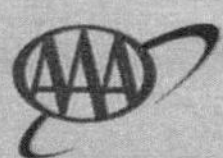

Get AAA travel information at club offices and on AAA.com for experiences you'll remember for a lifetime.

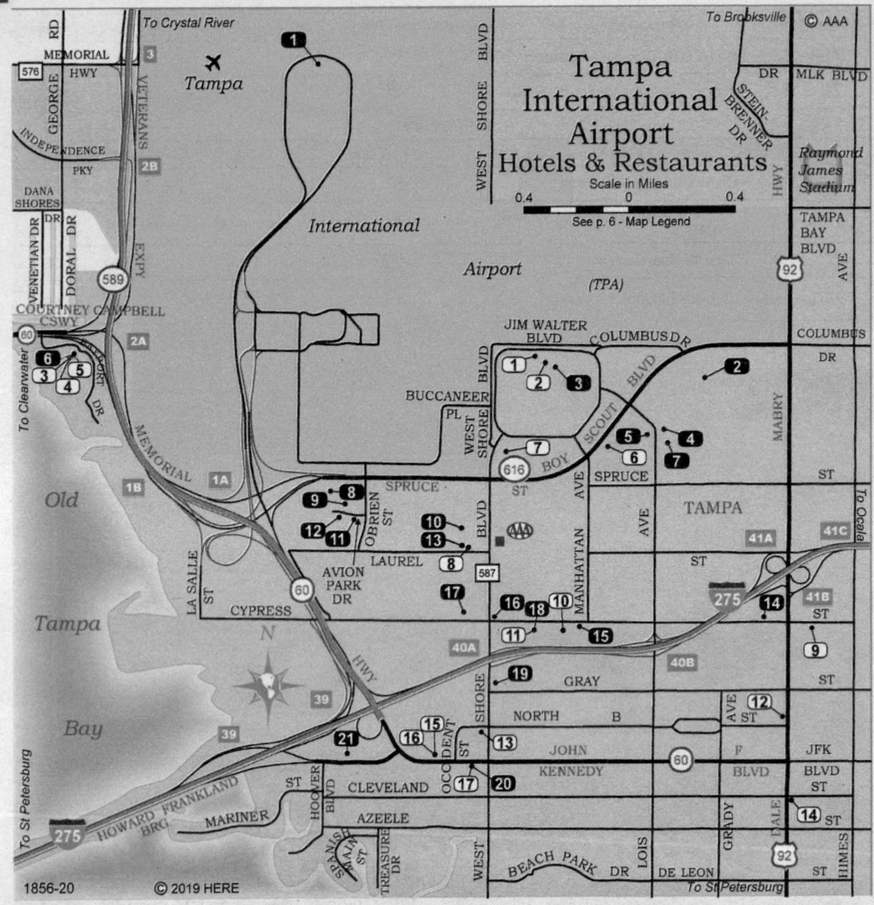

Airport Hotels

Map Page	TAMPA INTERNATIONAL (Maximum driving distance from airport: 4.4 mi)	Diamond Rated	Member Savings	Page
2 this page	**AC Hotels by Marriott Tampa Airport, 4.4 mi**	♦♦♦	✔	352
19 this page	**Embassy Suites by Hilton Tampa Airport Westshore, 3.8 mi**	♦♦♦	✔	353
7 this page	**Fairfield Inn & Suites by Marriott Tampa Westshore, 4.3 mi**	♦♦♦	✔	354
15 this page	**Four Points by Sheraton Tampa Airport Westshore, 3.7 mi**	♦♦♦	✔	354
6 this page	**Grand Hyatt Tampa Bay, 3.4 mi**	♦♦♦♦	✔	354
8 this page	**Hampton Inn & Suites Tampa Airport Avion Park Westshore, 3.0 mi**	♦♦♦	✔	354
13 this page	Hampton Inn Tampa-Airport/Westshore, 3.4 mi	♦♦	✔	355
12 this page	**Hilton Garden Inn Tampa Airport/Westshore, 2.9 mi**	♦♦♦	✔	355
4 this page	**Hilton Tampa Airport Westshore, 4.2 mi**	♦♦♦	✔	355
9 this page	**Homewood Suites by Hilton Tampa Westshore, 2.9 mi**	♦♦♦	✔	356

Map Page	**TAMPA INTERNATIONAL** (Maximum driving distance from airport: 4.4 mi) (cont'd)	Diamond Rated	Member Savings	Page
10 p. 344	**Hyatt Place Tampa Airport/Westshore, 3.4 mi**	◆◆◆	✔	356
16 p. 344	**Marriott Tampa Westshore, 3.4 mi**	◆◆◆	✔	356
3 p. 344	**Renaissance Tampa International Plaza Hotel, 4.2 mi**	◆◆◆◆	✔	357
5 p. 344	**Residence Inn by Marriott Tampa Westshore, 4.0 mi**	◆◆◆	✔	357
17 p. 344	**SpringHill Suites by Marriott Tampa/Westshore Airport, 3.8 mi**	◆◆◆	✔	358
1 p. 344	**Tampa Airport Marriott, on airport property**	◆◆◆	✔	358
11 p. 344	**TownePlace Suites by Marriott Tampa Westshore/Airport, 2.9 mi**	◆◆◆	✔	358

Tampa International Airport

This index helps you "spot" where approved hotels and restaurants are located on the corresponding detailed maps. Restaurant price range is a combination of lunch and/or dinner. Turn to the listing page for more information and consult display ads for special promotions.

For more details, rates and reservations: AAA.com/travelguides/hotels

TAMPA

Map Page	Hotels	Diamond Rated	Member Savings	Page
1 p. 344	**Tampa Airport Marriott**	◆◆◆	✔	358
2 p. 344	**AC Hotels by Marriott Tampa Airport**	◆◆◆	✔	352
3 p. 344	**Renaissance Tampa International Plaza Hotel**	◆◆◆◆	✔	357
4 p. 344	**Hilton Tampa Airport Westshore**	◆◆◆	✔	355
5 p. 344	**Residence Inn by Marriott Tampa Westshore**	◆◆◆	✔	357
6 p. 344	**Grand Hyatt Tampa Bay**	◆◆◆◆	✔	354
7 p. 344	**Fairfield Inn & Suites by Marriott Tampa Westshore**	◆◆◆	✔	354
8 p. 344	**Hampton Inn & Suites Tampa Airport Avion Park Westshore**	◆◆◆	✔	354
9 p. 344	**Homewood Suites by Hilton Tampa Westshore**	◆◆◆	✔	356
10 p. 344	**Hyatt Place Tampa Airport/Westshore**	◆◆◆	✔	356
11 p. 344	**TownePlace Suites by Marriott Tampa Westshore/Airport**	◆◆◆	✔	358
12 p. 344	**Hilton Garden Inn Tampa Airport/Westshore**	◆◆◆	✔	355
13 p. 344	Hampton Inn Tampa-Airport/Westshore	◆◆	✔	355
14 p. 344	**Courtyard by Marriott Tampa Westshore/Airport**	◆◆◆	✔	352
15 p. 344	**Four Points by Sheraton Tampa Airport Westshore**	◆◆◆	✔	354
16 p. 344	**Marriott Tampa Westshore**	◆◆◆	✔	356
17 p. 344	**SpringHill Suites by Marriott Tampa/Westshore Airport**	◆◆◆	✔	358
18 p. 344	**DoubleTree by Hilton Tampa Airport Westshore**	◆◆◆	✔	352
19 p. 344	**Embassy Suites by Hilton Tampa Airport Westshore**	◆◆◆	✔	353
20 p. 344	The Westshore Grand A Tribute Portfolio Hotel	◆◆◆		356
21 p. 344	Hotel Alba Tampa, Tapestry Collection by Hilton	◆◆◆	✔	356

Map Page	Restaurants	Diamond Rated	Cuisine	Price Range	Page
1 p. 344	The Cheesecake Factory	◆◆◆	International	$11-$32	359
2 p. 344	Rocco's Tacos & Tequila Bar	◆◆◆	Mexican	$4-$28	360

Map Page	Restaurants (cont'd)	Diamond Rated	Cuisine	Price Range	Page
3 p. 344	1823 Kitchen & Bar	◆◆◆	New American	$13-$32	359
4 p. 344	**Armani's**	◆◆◆◆	Northern Italian	$14-$58	359
5 p. 344	Oystercatchers Restaurant	◆◆◆	Seafood	$12-$58	360
6 p. 344	Roy's	◆◆◆	Pacific Rim Fusion	$26-$55	360
7 p. 344	Ocean Prime	◆◆◆	Seafood	$14-$60	360
8 p. 344	La Bamba Spanish American Restaurant	◆	Spanish	$5-$7	360
9 p. 344	J. Alexander's Redlands Grill	◆◆◆	American	$12-$34	360
10 p. 344	Charley's Steakhouse	◆◆◆	Steak	$16-$120	359
11 p. 344	Players Sports Pub	◆◆	Burgers Sandwiches	$10-$32	360
12 p. 344	Donatello	◆◆◆	Northern Italian	$16-$35	359
13 p. 344	Seasons 52 Fresh Grill	◆◆◆	New American	$8-$29	360
14 p. 344	Shells Casual Seafood	◆◆	Seafood	$8-$22	360
15 p. 344	P.F. Chang's China Bistro	◆◆◆	Chinese	$10-$27	360
16 p. 344	Maggiano's Little Italy	◆◆◆	Italian	$13-$46	360
17 p. 344	Shula's America's Steak House	◆◆◆	Steak	$12-$90	360

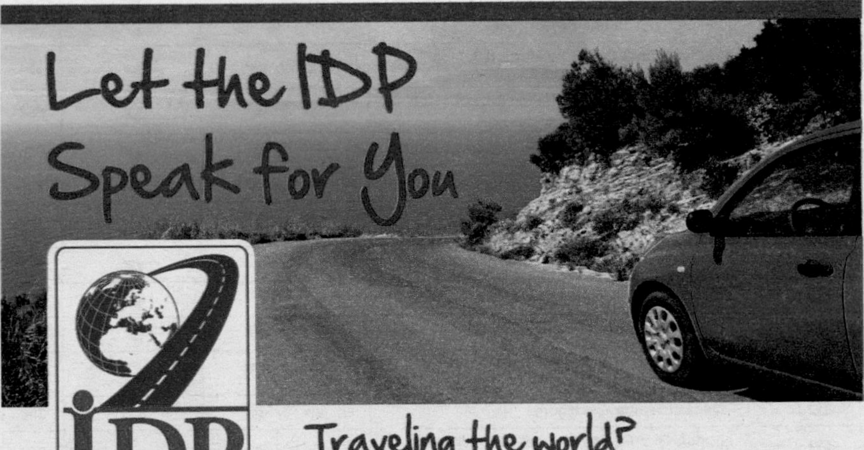

Traveling the world?

Before you go, purchase an International Driving Permit for a recognizable form of identification, even if you're not driving.

Translated into 10 languages, the IDP is valid in more than 150 countries — mandatory in some and highly recommended in others.

U.S. residents apply at AAA offices. Canadian residents apply at CAA offices. Or visit us online at: AAA.com/IDP or CAA.ca/travelling/idp

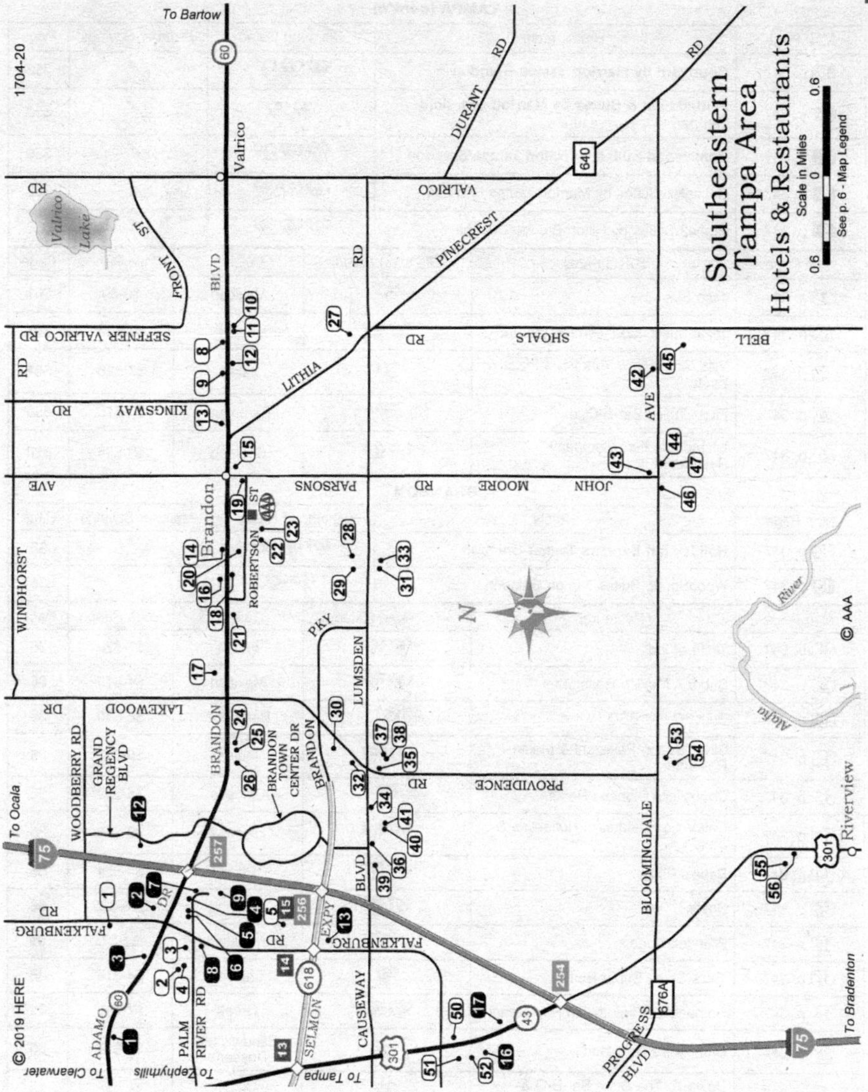

Southeastern Tampa Area

This index helps you "spot" where approved hotels and restaurants are located on the corresponding detailed maps. Restaurant price range is a combination of lunch and/or dinner. Turn to the listing page for more information and consult display ads for special promotions.

For more details, rates and reservations: AAA.com/travelguides/hotels

TAMPA

Map Page	Hotels	Diamond Rated	Member Savings	Page
1 this page	Clarion Inn Tampa Conference Center	◆◆		352
2 this page	Brandon Center Hotel	◆◆		352
3 this page	**Comfort Suites Tampa-Brandon**	◆◆	✔	352
4 this page	**Embassy Suites by Hilton Tampa-Brandon**	◆◆◆	✔	353

TAMPA (cont'd)

Map Page	Hotels (cont'd)	Diamond Rated	Member Savings	Page
5 p. 347	**Courtyard by Marriott Tampa Brandon**	◆◆◆	✔	352
6 p. 347	**Fairfield Inn & Suites by Marriott-Brandon/ Tampa**	◆◆	✔	353
7 p. 347	**Homewood Suites by Hilton Tampa/Brandon**	◆◆◆	✔	356
8 p. 347	SpringHill Suites by Marriott Tampa Brandon	◆◆◆	✔	358
9 p. 347	Home2 Suites by Hilton Brandon Tampa	◆◆◆	✔	356

Map Page	Restaurants	Diamond Rated	Cuisine	Price Range	Page
1 p. 347	Taco Bus	◆	Mexican	$3-$9	361
2 p. 347	Tokai Sushi Japanese Restaurant	◆◆	Japanese Sushi	$4-$27	361
3 p. 347	Villa Rina's New York Style Pizza & Pasta	◆	Italian	$7-$26	361
4 p. 347	First Choice Bar-B-Que	◆	Barbecue	$7-$15	359
5 p. 347	Islamorada Fish Company Restaurant	◆◆	Seafood	$9-$25	360

BRANDON

Map Page	Hotels	Diamond Rated	Member Savings	Page
12 p. 347	**Holiday Inn Express Tampa Brandon**	◆◆◆	✔	35
13 p. 347	WoodSpring Suites Tampa Brandon	◆◆		35

Map Page	Restaurants	Diamond Rated	Cuisine	Price Range	Page
8 p. 347	Taste of India	◆◆	Indian	$7-$20	36
9 p. 347	Sabor A Mexico Restaurant	◆◆	Mexican	$4-$19	36
10 p. 347	BubbaQue's BBQ	◆	Barbecue	$7-$30	35
11 p. 347	Silver Spoon Pakistani & Indian Restaurant	◆◆	Indian	$9-$17	36
12 p. 347	Chopsticks Chinese Restaurant	◆	Chinese	$5-$22	35
13 p. 347	Cali Viejo Restaurant Rotisserie & Bakery	◆◆	Colombian	$9-$20	35
14 p. 347	Babe's Pizza	◆◆	Pizza	$4-$24	35
15 p. 347	Shells	◆◆	Seafood	$10-$20	36
16 p. 347	Brandon Bagels	◆	Breakfast	$3-$7	35
17 p. 347	Top's China Super Buffet	◆	Chinese	$4-$16	36
18 p. 347	Romano's Greek Italian Restaurant	◆◆	Greek	$7-$18	36
19 p. 347	Campbell's Dairyland	◆	Sandwiches Desserts	$4-$37	35
20 p. 347	Down To The Bone Bar-B-Q & Catering	◆	Barbecue	$5-$30	35
21 p. 347	O'Toole's Irish Pub & Restaurant	◆◆	Irish	$8-$18	35
22 p. 347	Della's Delectables	◆	Sandwiches Deli	$3-$8	35
23 p. 347	Taste Of Berlin German Restaurant	◆◆	German	$8-$19	36
24 p. 347	Chicago's Best Burgers	◆	Burgers	$7-$10	35
25 p. 347	Ploy Thai Restaurant	◆◆◆	Thai Sushi	$9-$28	36
26 p. 347	Tres Amigos Cantina	◆◆	Mexican	$8-$16	36
27 p. 347	Jo-To Japanese Steak House & Sushi Bar	◆◆	Japanese	$6-$35	35
28 p. 347	La Septima Cafe	◆◆	Spanish	$5-$18	35
29 p. 347	Yokohama Japanese Restaurant and Sushi Bar	◆◆	Japanese Sushi	$5-$30	36

Map Page	Restaurants (cont'd)	Diamond Rated	Cuisine	Price Range	Page
30 p. 347	SQUARE 1 Burgers & Bar	2 diamonds	Burgers	$9-$18	36
31 p. 347	La Cubanita Cafe	1 diamond	Cuban	$3-$7	35
32 p. 347	Genghis Grill	2 diamonds	Chinese	$8-$14	35
33 p. 347	O'Brien's Irish Pub & Restaurant	2 diamonds	Irish	$9-$30	35
34 p. 347	First Watch	2 diamonds	Breakfast Sandwiches	$8-$11	35
35 p. 347	Bonefish Grill	3 diamonds	Seafood	$14-$30	35
36 p. 347	Fords Garage	2 diamonds	American	$7-$22	35
37 p. 347	Jasmine Thai Restaurant	3 diamonds	Thai	$7-$20	35
38 p. 347	Chick-N-Bones Cafe & Catering Company	1 diamond	Chicken Sandwiches	$5-$23	35
39 p. 347	Mellow Mushroom	2 diamonds	Pizza Sandwiches	$6-$25	35
40 p. 347	Lin's Garden Chinese Restaurant	1 diamond	Chinese	$5-$13	35
41 p. 347	KOIZI Endless Hibachi & Sushi Eatery	2 diamonds	Japanese Sushi	$11-$30	35
42 p. 347	Stonewood Grill & Tavern	3 diamonds	American	$11-$39	36
43 p. 347	Latin Grill	2 diamonds	Cuban	$5-$27	35
44 p. 347	China 1	1 diamond	Chinese	$5-$13	35
45 p. 347	Times Square Pizza	1 diamond	Pizza Sandwiches	$5-$25	36
46 p. 347	Olde Town Pizzeria Bloomingdale	2 diamonds	Pizza Sandwiches	$8-$27	35
47 p. 347	Recipe Box Diner	2 diamonds	Comfort Food Breakfast	$4-$9	36

RIVERVIEW

Map Page	Hotels	Diamond Rated	Member Savings	Page
16 p. 347	Uptown Suites Tampa Riverview	2 diamonds		254
17 p. 347	**Hilton Garden Inn Tampa/Riverview/Brandon**	3 diamonds	✔	254

Map Page	Restaurants	Diamond Rated	Cuisine	Price Range	Page
50 p. 347	Smokin' Pig BBQ	1 diamond	Barbecue	$7-$25	254
51 p. 347	China 1	1 diamond	Chinese	$5-$13	254
52 p. 347	Crazy Cafe	2 diamonds	Sushi	$8-$28	254
53 p. 347	Acropolis Greek Taverna	2 diamonds	Greek	$12-$27	254
54 p. 347	EATS American Grill	2 diamonds	American	$9-$19	254
55 p. 347	China Star New York Style Chinese Restaurant	1 diamond	Chinese	$2-$13	254
56 p. 347	Italian Kitchen Cafe	2 diamonds	Italian	$9-$20	254

Find AAA Inspected & Approved campgrounds at AAA.com/campgrounds

DOWNTOWN TAMPA

• Hotels & Restaurants map & index p. 336

ALOFT TAMPA DOWNTOWN HOTEL 813/898-8000 5

Hotel

AAA Benefit: Members save 5% or more!

Address: 100 W Kennedy Blvd 33602 **Location:** Waterfront. I-275 exit 44, 0.8 mi s. Whiting, 11. **Facility:** 130 units. 6 stories, interior corridors. *Bath:* shower only. **Parking:** valet only. **Amenities:** safes. **Pool:** heated outdoor. **Activities:** exercise room. **Guest Services:** valet and coin laundry.

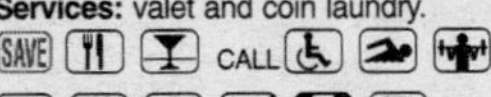

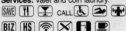

COURTYARD BY MARRIOTT TAMPA DOWNTOWN 813/229-1100 3

Hotel

COURTYARD **AAA Benefit:** Members save 5% or more!

Address: 102 E Cass St 33602 **Location:** I-275 exit 44, 0.6 mi sw on W Ashley Dr/Tampa St; exit 45A southbound, 1.5 mi sw on W Ashley Dr. Whiting, 11. **Facility:** 141 units. 6 stories, interior corridors. **Parking:** on-site (fee) and valet. **Terms:** check-in 4 pm. **Pool:** heated outdoor. **Activities:** exercise room. **Guest Services:** valet and coin laundry, boarding pass kiosk, area transportation.

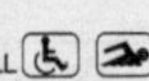

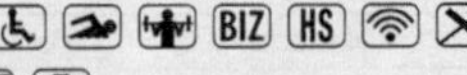

EMBASSY SUITES BY HILTON TAMPA DOWNTOWN CONVENTION CENTER 813/769-8300 8

Hotel

AAA Benefit: Members save 5% or more!

Address: 513 S Florida Ave 33602 **Location:** I-275 exit 44, 2.2 mi e on W Ashley Dr/Tampa St, then just se of jct SR 60 (Kennedy Blvd); exit 45A southbound, 3.7 mi e. Connected to Tampa Convention Center via skybridge. Dick Greco Plaza, 10. **Facility:** 360 units. 20 stories, interior corridors. **Parking:** on-site (fee) and valet. **Amenities:** safes. **Pool:** heated outdoor. **Activities:** exercise room. **Guest Services:** valet and coin laundry, rental car service, area transportation. **Featured Amenity:** **breakfast buffet.**

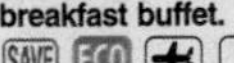

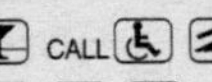

HILTON GARDEN INN/TAMPA YBOR HISTORIC DISTRICT 813/769-9267 1

Hotel. **Address:** 1700 E 9th Ave 33605

AAA Benefit: Members save 5% or more!

HILTON TAMPA DOWNTOWN 813/204-3000 7

Hotel

AAA Benefit: Members save 5% or more!

Address: 211 N Tampa St 33602 **Location:** I-275 exit 44, 0.8 mi s on Ashley Dr to Jackson St, then just e. Whiting, 11. **Facility:** 332 units. 17 stories, interior corridors. **Parking:** valet only. **Amenities:** safes. **Dining:** 2 restaurants. **Pool:** heated outdoor. **Activities:** hot tub, health club. **Guest Services:** valet laundry, area transportation.

LE MERIDIEN TAMPA 813/221-9555 4

Historic Boutique Hotel

Le MERIDIEN **AAA Benefit:** Members save 5% or more!

Address: 601 N Florida Ave 33602 **Location:** Just n of jct SR 60 (Kennedy Blvd), jct Twiggs St and Florida Ave. Whiting, 11. **Facility:** Located in the arts/entertainment district, the hotel was previously a federal courthouse. Upscale rooms vary in shape and size and were once judges' chambers, courtrooms and even holding cells. 130 units. 4 stories, interior corridors. **Parking:** valet only. **Amenities:** safes. **Pool:** outdoor. **Activities:** health club, massage. **Guest Services:** valet laundry, area transportation.

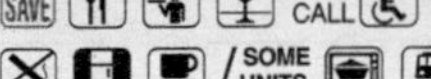

RESIDENCE INN BY MARRIOTT TAMPA DOWNTOWN 813/221-4224 2

Extended Stay Hotel

Residence INN. **AAA Benefit:** Members save 5% or more!

Address: 101 E Tyler St 33602 **Location:** I-275 exit 44, 0.5 mi se on W Ashley Dr/Tampa St; exit 45A southbound, 1.5 mi se on W Ashley Dr. Whiting, 11. **Facility:** 109 units, some two bedrooms, efficiencies and kitchens. 7 stories, interior corridors. **Parking:** on-site (fee). **Terms:** check-in 4 pm. **Pool:** heated outdoor. **Activities:** exercise room. **Guest Services:** valet and coin laundry, boarding pass kiosk, area transportation. **Featured Amenity:** **full hot breakfast.**

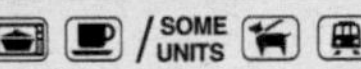

SHERATON TAMPA RIVERWALK 813/223-2222 6

Hotel. **Address:** 200 N Ashley Dr 33602

AAA Benefit: Members save 5% or more!

AAA.com/hertz—When your ideal road trip includes a comfortable ride

(See map & index p. 336.)

TAMPA MARRIOTT WATER STREET 813/221-4900 **9**

Hotel

AAA Benefit: Members save 5% or more!

Address: 700 S Florida Ave 33602 **Location:** Waterfront. I-275 exit 44, 2.2 mi e on W Ashley Dr/Tampa St, then just se of jct SR 60 (Kennedy Blvd); exit 45A southbound, 3.7 mi e. Opposite Tampa Convention Center. Dick Greco Plaza, 10. **Facility:** This hotel features striking public areas and impressive views of old Tampa Bay, Channelside and downtown Tampa. Rooms are decorated in pleasing tones; some floors are allergy friendly. 727 units. 27 stories, interior corridors. **Parking:** on-site (fee) and valet. **Terms:** check-in 4 pm. **Amenities:** video games, safes. **Pool:** heated outdoor. **Activities:** sauna, hot tub, marina, health club. **Guest Services:** valet and coin laundry, boarding pass kiosk, rental car service, area transportation.

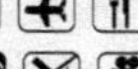

CALL

/ SOME UNITS

THE WESTIN TAMPA WATERSIDE 813/229-5000 **10**

Hotel

AAA Benefit: Members save 5% or more!

Address: 725 S Harbour Island Blvd 33602 **Location:** Waterfront. I-275 exit 44, 2.4 mi se on W Ashley Dr/Tampa St; exit 45A southbound, 3.9 mi se; on Harbour Island. Dick Greco Plaza, 10. **Facility:** 309 units. 12 stories, interior corridors. **Parking:** on-site (fee) and valet. **Amenities:** video games, safes. **Pool:** heated outdoor. **Activities:** exercise room, massage. **Guest Services:** valet laundry, boarding pass kiosk, area transportation.

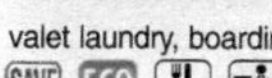
CALL

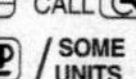

/ SOME UNITS

WHERE TO EAT

BAVARO'S PIZZA NAPOLETANA & PASTARIA 813/868-4440 (14)
Italian. Casual Dining. **Address:** 514 N Franklin St 33602

BERNINI OF YBOR 813/248-0099 (9)
Italian. Casual Dining. **Address:** 1702 E 7th Ave 33605

CARMINE'S 813/248-3834 (8)
Spanish. Casual Dining. **Address:** 1802 E 7th Ave 33605

COLUMBIA RESTAURANT 813/248-4961 (4)
Spanish. Casual Dining. **Address:** 2117 E 7th Ave 33605

EDDIE & SAMS PIZZA & GELATO BAR 813/229-8500 (16)
Italian. Quick Serve. **Address:** 203 E Twiggs St 33602

EDISON: FOOD+DRINK LAB 813/254-7111 (23)
Continental. Casual Dining. **Address:** 1934 W Kennedy Blvd 33606

FOUR GREEN FIELDS 813/254-4444 (24)
Irish. Casual Dining. **Address:** 205 W Platt St 33606

GASPAR'S GROTTO 813/248-5900 (10)
Sandwiches Pizza. Casual Dining. **Address:** 1805 E 7th Ave 33605

HATTRICK'S SPORTS BAR-DOWNTOWN TAMPA 813/225-4288 (19)
American. Casual Dining. **Address:** 107 S Franklin St 33602

HOLY HOG BARBECUE 813/223-4464 (18)
Barbecue. Quick Serve. **Address:** 302 E Kennedy Blvd 33602

JACKSON'S BISTRO-BAR & SUSHI 813/277-0339 (25)
Steak Seafood. Fine Dining. **Address:** 601 S Harbour Island Blvd, Suite 100 33602

JAMES JOYCE IRISH PUB 813/247-1896 (1)
Irish. Casual Dining. **Address:** 1724 E 8th Ave 33605

JAX BAR & GRILL 813/241-9675 (7)
American. Casual Dining. **Address:** 1600 8th Ave E 33605

LA TROPICANA CUBAN CAFE 813/247-4040 (5)
Cuban. Casual Dining. **Address:** 1822 E 7th Ave 33605

MISE EN PLACE 813/254-5373 (21)
Mediterranean. Fine Dining. **Address:** 442 W Kennedy Blvd 33606

MOXIE'S CAFE COFFEEBAR CATERER 813/221-4510 (17)
Breakfast Sandwiches. Quick Serve. **Address:** 514 N Tampa St 33602

SAMURAI BLUE SUSHI & SAKE BAR 813/242-6688 (6)
Japanese Sushi. Casual Dining. **Address:** 1600 E 8th Ave, Suite C208 33605

SHRIMP & CO RESTAURANT 813/374-0192 (2)
Seafood. Casual Dining. **Address:** 2202 E 7th Ave 33606

SPLITSVILLE SOUTHERN+ SOCIAL 813/514-2695 (20)
American. Casual Dining. **Address:** 615 Channelside Dr 33602

STEELBACH 813/693-5478 (11)
Regional Southern. Casual Dining. **Address:** 1902 N Ola Ave 33602

SUNDAYS DELICATESSEN 813/304-2041 (3)
Breakfast Sandwiches. Quick Serve. **Address:** 1930 E 7th Ave 33605

TACO BUS 813/397-2800 (15)
Mexican. Quick Serve. **Address:** 505 Franklin St 33602

TAPS RESTAURANT BAR & LOUNGE 813/463-1968 (13)
American. Casual Dining. **Address:** 777 N Ashley Dr 33602

U-LE-LE 813/999-4952 (12)
Natural/Organic. Casual Dining. **Address:** 1810 N Highland Ave 33602

YACHT STARSHIP DINING CRUISES 813/223-7999 (22)

Continental Fine Dining $60-$90

AAA Inspector Notes: This yacht offers an attraction and dining all in one. Guests cruise Old Tampa Bay and enjoy panoramic views of downtown Tampa while they dine and then dance to live music. A hospitable staff makes for a memorable evening. Brunches are also offered. It is recommended to look at their website for lunch and brunch dates as these are sporadic. **Features:** full bar. **Reservations:** required. **Address:** 603 Channelside Dr 33602 **Location:** Just s of jct SR 60 (Kennedy Blvd); in Channelside. Amalie Arena, 8. **Parking:** on-site (fee).

L D CALL

TAMPA

• Restaurants p. 359
• Hotels & Restaurants map & index p. 338, 344, 347

AC HOTELS BY MARRIOTT TAMPA AIRPORT

813/350-4020 **2**

Contemporary Hotel

AAA Benefit: Members save 5% or more!

Address: 4020 W Boy Scout Blvd 33607 **Location:** Jct Jim Walter Blvd. **Facility:** 175 units. 6 stories, interior corridors. **Terms:** check-in 4 pm. **Amenities:** safes. **Pool:** heated outdoor. **Activities:** exercise room. **Guest Services:** valet and coin laundry.

BEST WESTERN TAMPA

813/490-2378 **26**

Hotel

AAA Benefit: Members save up to 15% and earn bonus points!

Address: 734 S Dale Mabry Hwy 33609 **Location:** I-275 exit 41A, 1.4 mi sw on US 92. **Facility:** 54 units, some two bedrooms. 3 stories, interior corridors. **Terms:** check-in 4 pm. **Pool:** outdoor. **Activities:** exercise room. **Guest Services:** coin laundry. **Featured Amenity: breakfast buffet.**

 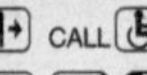  

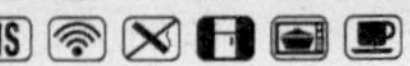

BRANDON CENTER HOTEL 813/661-8888 **2**

Hotel. **Address:** 10110 Horace Ave 33619

CLARION INN TAMPA CONFERENCE CENTER 813/621-5555 **1**

Motel. **Address:** 9331 Adamo Dr 33619

COMFORT SUITES TAMPA AIRPORT NORTH 813/880-8938 **12**

Hotel. **Address:** 5421 W Waters Ave 33634

COMFORT SUITES TAMPA-BRANDON

813/630-4444 **3**

Hotel

Address: 9932 E Adamo Dr 33619 **Location:** I-75 exit 257, 0.5 mi w on SR 60. **Facility:** 69 units, some kitchens. 4 stories, interior corridors. **Pool:** heated outdoor. **Activities:** exercise room. **Guest Services:** valet and coin laundry. **Featured Amenity: full hot breakfast.**

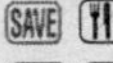  

COMFORT SUITES TAMPA FAIRGROUNDS-CASINO 813/868-7770 **17**

Hotel. **Address:** 4506 Oak Fair Blvd 33610

COUNTRY INN & SUITES BY RADISSON, TAMPA AIRPORT NORTH 813/881-1800 **14**

Hotel. **Address:** 8109 Benjamin Rd 33634

COURTYARD BY MARRIOTT TAMPA BRANDON

813/661-9559 **5**

Hotel

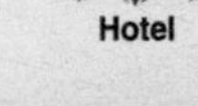

COURTYARD **AAA Benefit:** Members save 5% or more!

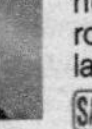

Address: 10152 Palm River Rd 33619 **Location:** I-75 exit 257, 0.4 mi w on SR 60, just s on Falkenburg Rd, then just e. **Facility:** 90 units. 3 stories, interior corridors. **Amenities:** video games. **Pool:** heated indoor. **Activities:** exercise room. **Guest Services:** valet and coin laundry, boarding pass kiosk.

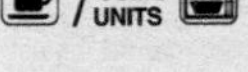

COURTYARD BY MARRIOTT TAMPA NORTH I-75 FLETCHER 813/978-9898 **4**

Hotel. **Address:** 13575 Cypress Glen Ln 33637

AAA Benefit: Members save 5% or more!

COURTYARD BY MARRIOTT TAMPA NORTHWEST/VETERANS EXPRESSWAY 813/920-2011 **9**

Hotel. **Address:** 12730 Citrus Park Ln 33625

AAA Benefit: Members save 5% or more!

COURTYARD BY MARRIOTT TAMPA WESTSHORE/ AIRPORT

813/874-0555 **14**

Hotel

COURTYARD **AAA Benefit:** Members save 5% or more!

Address: 3805 W Cypress St 33607 **Location:** I-275 exit 41A, just s on US 92 (Dale Mabry Hwy), then just w. **Facility:** 145 units. 4 stories, interior corridors. **Pool:** heated outdoor. **Activities:** exercise room. **Guest Services:** valet and coin laundry, boarding pass kiosk, area transportation.

DOUBLETREE BY HILTON TAMPA AIRPORT WESTSHORE

813/879-4800 **18**

Hotel

AAA Benefit: Members save 5% or more!

Address: 4500 W Cypress St 33607 **Location:** I-275 exit 40A, exit 39A northbound, just nw on Westshore Blvd, then just e. **Facility:** 489 units. 5-10 stories, interior corridors. **Amenities:** safes. **Dining:** 2 restaurants. **Pool:** heated outdoor. **Activities:** hot tub, exercise room. **Guest Services:** valet and coin laundry, area transportation.

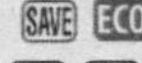 

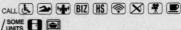

(See maps & indexes p. 338, 344, 347.)

EMBASSY SUITES BY HILTON TAMPA AIRPORT WESTSHORE 813/875-1555 19

Hotel

AAA Benefit: Members save 5% or more!

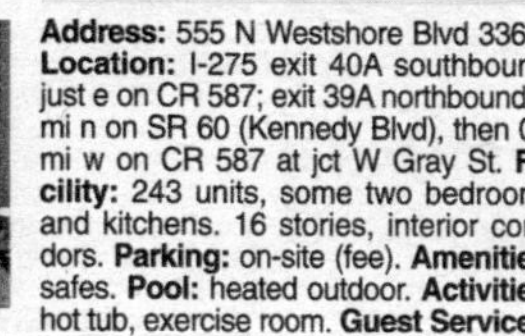

Address: 555 N Westshore Blvd 33609 **Location:** I-275 exit 40A southbound, just e on CR 587; exit 39A northbound, 1 mi n on SR 60 (Kennedy Blvd), then 0.5 mi w on CR 587 at jct W Gray St. **Facility:** 243 units, some two bedrooms and kitchens. 16 stories, interior corridors. **Parking:** on-site (fee). **Amenities:** safes. **Pool:** heated outdoor. **Activities:** hot tub, exercise room. **Guest Services:** valet and coin laundry, area transportation. **Featured Amenity:** **breakfast buffet.**

   CALL  

EMBASSY SUITES BY HILTON TAMPA-BRANDON 813/653-1905 4

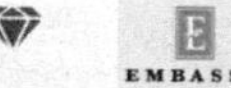

Hotel

AAA Benefit: Members save 5% or more!

Address: 10220 Palm River Rd 33619 **Location:** I-75 exit 257, just w on SR 60, just s on Falkenburg Rd, then just e. **Facility:** 147 units. 5 stories, interior corridors. **Terms:** check-in 4 pm. **Amenities:** safes. **Pool:** heated outdoor. **Activities:** exercise room. **Guest Services:** valet and coin laundry, boarding pass kiosk, rental car service. **Featured Amenity:** **full hot breakfast.**

  CALL 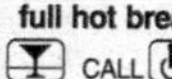 

EPICUREAN HOTEL, AUTOGRAPH COLLECTION 813/999-8700 27

Boutique Hotel

AUTOGRAPH COLLECTION HOTELS **AAA Benefit:** Members save 5% or more!

Address: 1207 S Howard Ave 33606 **Location:** I-275 exit 42, 1 mi s on Armenia Ave, just e on Azeele St, then 0.8 mi s. **Facility:** Located in the old Hyde Park area, the hotel boasts an urban chic décor with a flair for epicurean tastes, as the name suggests. Room décor is a mix of repurposed industrial with a culinary influence. 137 units, some kitchens. 4 stories, interior corridors. **Parking:** on-site (fee) and valet. **Terms:** check-in 4 pm. **Amenities:** safes. **Dining:** 2 restaurants. **Pool:** heated outdoor. **Activities:** bicycles, exercise room, spa. **Guest Services:** valet laundry, boarding pass kiosk.

SAVE CALL BIZ HS / SOME UNITS

FAIRFIELD INN & SUITES BY MARRIOTT-BRANDON/TAMPA 813/661-9719 6

Hotel

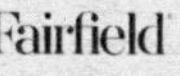

Fairfield **AAA Benefit:** Members save 5% or more!

Address: 10150 Palm River Rd 33619 **Location:** I-75 exit 257, 0.4 mi w on SR 60, just s on Falkenburg Rd, then just e. **Facility:** 107 units. 3 stories, interior corridors. **Amenities:** video games. **Pool:** heated outdoor. **Activities:** limited exercise equipment. **Guest Services:** valet and coin laundry. **Featured Amenity:** **continental breakfast.**

 CALL  BIZ

 / SOME UNITS 

Get INVOLVED and Keep Teens Safe

Exploring the countryside or visiting nearby cities can be perfect opportunities to teach your teens good habits and rules of the road — before and after they learn to drive.

TeenDriving.AAA.com | DriveRight.CAA.ca

(See maps & indexes p. 338, 344, 347.)

FAIRFIELD INN & SUITES BY MARRIOTT TAMPA WESTSHORE
813/872-0044 **7**

Hotel

Fairfield **AAA Benefit:** Members save 5% or more!

Address: 2215 N Lois Ave 33607 **Location:** Just s of jct Boy Scout Rd. **Facility:** 129 units. 5 stories, interior corridors. **Pool:** heated outdoor. **Activities:** exercise room. **Guest Services:** valet and coin laundry, boarding pass kiosk, area transportation.

SAVE CALL BIZ HS 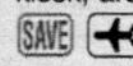  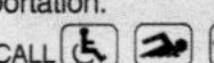  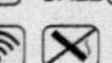 

FOUR POINTS BY SHERATON TAMPA AIRPORT WESTSHORE
813/873-8675 **15**

Hotel

AAA Benefit: Members save 5% or more!

Address: 4400 W Cypress St 33607 **Location:** I-275 exit 40A southbound, just nw on CR 587 (Westshore Blvd); exit 39A northbound, 1 mi n on SR 60 (Kennedy Blvd), 0.9 mi nw on CR 587, then just e. **Facility:** 261 units. 8 stories, interior corridors. **Amenities:** safes. **Pool:** heated indoor. **Activities:** exercise room. **Guest Services:** valet and coin laundry.

SAVE ECO BIZ HS  

GRAND HYATT TAMPA BAY
813/874-1234 **6**

Hotel

GRAND | HYATT **AAA Benefit:** Members save up to 10%!

Address: 2900 Bayport Dr 33607 **Location:** Waterfront. On SR 60, at east end of Courtney Campbell Cswy. **Facility:** This property sits on 35 acres of lushly landscaped grounds overlooking Old Tampa Bay and next to an ecologically protected salt marsh. Rooms offer city and bay views and are beautifully decorated. 442 units. 13 stories, interior/exterior corridors. **Parking:** on-site (fee) and valet. **Amenities:** safes. **Dining:** 1823 Kitchen & Bar, Armani's, Oystercatchers Restaurant, see separate listings. **Pool:** heated outdoor. **Activities:** sauna, hot tub, self-propelled boats, tennis, bicycles, lawn sports, trails, health club. **Guest Services:** valet laundry, boarding pass kiosk, area transportation.

SAVE ECO CALL BIZ sHS / SOME UNITS 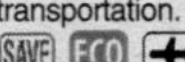     

HAMPTON INN & SUITES TAMPA AIRPORT AVION PARK WESTSHORE
813/287-8500 **8**

Hotel

AAA Benefit: Members save 5% or more!

Address: 5329 Avion Park Dr 33607 **Location:** I-275 exit 40A southbound, 0.7 mi n on Westshore Blvd; exit 39A northbound, 1 mi e on SR 60 (Kennedy Blvd), 1.2 mi n on Westshore Blvd, just w on Spruce St, then just s on O'Brien St; in Avion Park Westshore. **Facility:** 178 units. 8 stories, interior corridors. **Pool:** heated outdoor. **Activities:** exercise room. **Guest Services:** valet and coin laundry, area transportation.

SAVE CALL BIZ HS / SOME UNITS 

HAMPTON INN & SUITES TAMPA BUSCH GARDENS
813/605-5233 **10**

SAVE Hotel. **Address:** 3333 E Busch Blvd 33612

AAA Benefit: Members save 5% or more!

HAMPTON INN & SUITES TAMPA NORTH
813/903-6000 **5**

Hotel

AAA Benefit: Members save 5% or more!

Address: 8210 Hidden River Pkwy 33637 **Location:** I-75 exit 266, 0.8 mi w on CR 582 (Fletcher Ave); at Hidden River Corporate Park. **Facility:** 126 units, some kitchens. 4 stories, interior corridors. **Amenities:** video games. **Pool:** outdoor. **Activities:** exercise room. **Guest Services:** valet and coin laundry, area transportation. **Featured Amenity: full hot breakfast.**

SAVE CALL BIZ HS / SOME UNITS     

HAMPTON INN BY HILTON TAMPA-AIRPORT/ROCKY POINT
813/289-6262 **22**

SAVE Hotel. **Address:** 3035 N Rocky Point Dr 33607

AAA Benefit: Members save 5% or more!

Love the great outdoors? Find places to camp at AAA.com/campgrounds

(See maps & indexes p. 338, 344, 347.)

HAMPTON INN TAMPA-AIRPORT/WESTSHORE
813/287-0778 13

SAVE Hotel. **Address:** 4817 W Laurel St 33607

AAA Benefit: Members save 5% or more!

HAMPTON INN TAMPA-VETERANS EXPWY/AIRPORT NORTH
813/901-5900 13

SAVE Hotel. **Address:** 5628 W Waters Ave 33634

AAA Benefit: Members save 5% or more!

HILTON GARDEN INN TAMPA AIRPORT/WESTSHORE
813/289-2700 12

Hotel

Hilton Garden Inn **AAA Benefit:** Members save 5% or more!

Address: 5312 Avion Park Dr 33607 **Location:** I-275 exit 40A southbound, 0.7 mi n on Westshore Blvd; exit 39A northbound, 1 mi e on SR 60 (Kennedy Blvd), 1.2 mi n on Westshore Blvd, just w on Spruce St, then just s on O'Brien St; in Avion Park Westshore. **Facility:** 171 units. 6 stories, interior corridors. **Pool:** heated outdoor. **Activities:** hot tub, exercise room. **Guest Services:** valet and coin laundry, boarding pass kiosk, area transportation.

    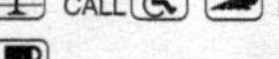

SAVE ECO CALL BIZ HS

For exclusive AAA member savings and benefits:

AAA.com/hertz

HILTON GARDEN INN TAMPA EAST/BRANDON
813/626-6700 18

Hotel

Hilton Garden Inn **AAA Benefit:** Members save 5% or more!

Address: 10309 Highland Manor Dr 33610 **Location:** I-75 exit 260 southbound; exit 260B northbound, just w on SR 574 (Dr. Martin Luther King Jr Blvd), just n on Park Oaks Blvd, then just e; in Highland Oaks. **Facility:** 152 units. 6 stories, interior corridors. **Amenities:** video games. **Pool:** heated outdoor. **Activities:** hot tub, exercise room. **Guest Services:** valet and coin laundry, area transportation. *(See ad this page.)*

SAVE CALL BIZ HS

HILTON TAMPA AIRPORT WESTSHORE
813/877-6688 4

Hotel

Hilton HOTELS & RESORTS **AAA Benefit:** Members save 5% or more!

Address: 2225 N Lois Ave 33607 **Location:** I-275 exit 40B, 0.8 mi n. **Facility:** 238 units. 12 stories, interior corridors. **Amenities:** safes. **Pool:** heated outdoor. **Activities:** tennis, exercise room. **Guest Services:** valet laundry, area transportation.

SAVE ECO CALL BIZ HS / SOME UNITS

HOLIDAY INN & SUITES TAMPA NORTH BUSCH GARDENS
813/971-7690 8

Hotel. **Address:** 11310 N 30th St 33612

HOLIDAY INN EXPRESS & SUITES TAMPA EAST-YBOR CITY
813/533-0400 21

Hotel. **Address:** 2520 N 50th St 33619

HOLIDAY INN EXPRESS HOTEL & SUITES
813/287-8585 23

Hotel. **Address:** 3025 N Rocky Point Dr 33607

HOLIDAY INN EXPRESS HOTEL & SUITES
813/910-7171 1

Hotel. **Address:** 8310 Galbraith Rd 33647

▼ *See AAA listing this page* ▼

Hilton Garden Inn®

Hilton Garden Inn
Tampa East/Brandon

10309 Highland Manor Drive
Tampa, FL 33610

813-626-6700

(See maps & indexes p. 338, 344, 347.)

HOLIDAY INN EXPRESS HOTEL & SUITES USF BUSCH GARDENS 813/936-8200 11

Hotel. **Address:** 2807 E Busch Blvd 33612

HOLIDAY INN EXPRESS SUITES TAMPA-FAIRGROUND-CASINO 813/490-1000 16

Hotel. **Address:** 8610 Elm Fair Blvd 33610

HOME2 SUITES BY HILTON BRANDON TAMPA 813/612-5950 9

SAVE Extended Stay Contemporary Hotel. **Address:** 10323 Palm River Rd 33619

AAA Benefit: Members save 5% or more!

HOME2 SUITES BY HILTON TAMPA USF/BUSCH GARDENS 813/750-8844 6

SAVE Extended Stay Hotel. **Address:** 11606 N McKinley Dr 33612

AAA Benefit: Members save 5% or more!

HOMEWOOD SUITES BY HILTON TAMPA/BRANDON 813/685-7099 7

Extended Stay Hotel

AAA Benefit: Members save 5% or more!

Address: 10240 Palm River Rd 33619 **Location:** I-75 exit 257, 0.4 mi w on SR 60, just s on S Falkenburg Rd, then 0.3 mi e. **Facility:** 126 kitchen units, some two bedrooms. 7 stories, interior corridors. **Pool:** heated outdoor. **Activities:** hot tub, exercise room. **Guest Services:** valet and coin laundry. **Featured Amenity: full hot breakfast.**

SAVE ECO CALL BIZ HS / SOME UNITS

HOMEWOOD SUITES BY HILTON TAMPA WESTSHORE 813/282-1950 9

Extended Stay Hotel

AAA Benefit: Members save 5% or more!

Address: 5325 Avion Park Dr 33607 **Location:** I-275 exit 40A southbound, 0.7 mi n on Westshore Blvd; exit 39A northbound, 1 mi e on Kennedy Blvd (SR 60), 1.2 mi n on Westshore Blvd, just w on Spruce St, then just s on O'Brien St; in Avion Park Westshore. **Facility:** 144 kitchen units, some two bedrooms. 7 stories, interior corridors. **Pool:** heated outdoor. **Activities:** exercise room. **Guest Services:** valet and coin laundry.

SAVE ECO CALL BIZ HS / SOME UNITS

HOTEL ALBA TAMPA, TAPESTRY COLLECTION BY HILTON 813/289-1950 21

SAVE Hotel. **Address:** 5303 W Kennedy Blvd 33609

AAA Benefit: Members save 5% or more!

HOTEL & SUITES SOUTH TAMPA 813/832-4656 28

Motel. **Address:** 3314 S Dale Mabry Hwy 33629

HYATT PLACE TAMPA AIRPORT/WESTSHORE 813/282-1037 10

Hotel

AAA Benefit: Members save up to 10%!

Address: 4811 W Main St 33607 **Location:** I-275 exit 40A southbound, 0.5 mi n on Westshore Blvd; exit 39A northbound, 1 mi e on SR 60 (John F Kennedy Blvd), 1 mi n on Westshore Blvd, then just w. **Facility:** 124 units. 6 stories, interior corridors. **Pool:** heated outdoor. **Activities:** exercise room. **Guest Services:** valet laundry, boarding pass kiosk, area transportation. **Featured Amenity: breakfast buffet.**

SAVE CALL BIZ HS

HYATT PLACE

Free shuttle within 2 miles including the airport, stadium, two malls and hundreds of restaurants

HYATT PLACE TAMPA/BUSCH GARDENS 813/979-1922 7

Hotel

HYATT PLACE **AAA Benefit:** Members save up to 10%!

Address: 11408 N 30th St 33612 **Location:** I-275 exit 51, 1.8 mi e on SR 582 (Fowler Ave), then just s. **Facility:** 126 units. 6 stories, interior corridors. **Parking:** on-site (fee). **Amenities:** safes. **Pool:** heated outdoor. **Activities:** exercise room. **Guest Services:** valet laundry. **Featured Amenity: breakfast buffet.** *(See ad p. 357.)*

SAVE CALL BIZ HS

THE WESTSHORE GRAND A TRIBUTE PORTFOLIO HOTEL 813/286-4030 20

Hotel. **Address:** 4860 W Kennedy Blvd 33609

LA QUINTA INN & SUITES TAMPA NORTH 813/971-7676 3

Hotel. **Address:** 17301 Dona Michelle Dr 33647

LA QUINTA INN TAMPA SOUTH 813/835-6262 30

Hotel. **Address:** 4620 W Gandy Blvd 33611

MARRIOTT TAMPA WESTSHORE 813/287-2555 16

Hotel

AAA Benefit: Members save 5% or more!

Address: 1001 N Westshore Blvd 33607 **Location:** I-275 exit 40A southbound, just nw on CR 587; exit 39A northbound, 1 mi n on SR 60 (Kennedy Blvd), then 0.9 mi nw on CR 587. **Facility:** 310 units. 13 stories, interior corridors. **Terms:** check-in 4 pm. **Pool:** heated outdoor, heated indoor. **Activities:** exercise room. **Guest Services:** valet and coin laundry, area transportation.

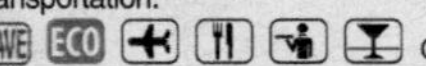

(See maps & indexes p. 338, 344, 347.)

RENAISSANCE TAMPA INTERNATIONAL PLAZA HOTEL

813/877-9200 3

Boutique Hotel

R RENAISSANCE HOTELS **AAA Benefit:** Members save 5% or more!

Address: 4200 Jim Walter Blvd 33607 **Location:** I-275 exit 40A southbound, 0.7 mi n on Westshore Blvd; exit 39A northbound, 1 mi e on Kennedy Blvd (SR 60), then 1.2 mi n on Westshore Blvd; at International Plaza and Bay St. **Facility:** Located next to the International Plaza, this upscale hotel is a world away from the norm. Guest rooms vary in size and are elegantly decorated in slate gray and tan tones. 293 cottages. 8 stories, interior corridors. **Parking:** on-site and valet. **Terms:** check-in 4 pm. **Amenities:** safes. **Pool:** heated outdoor. **Activities:** hot tub, health club. **Guest Services:** valet laundry, area transportation.

  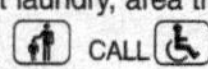 CALL  BIZ

 sHS

RESIDENCE INN BY MARRIOTT TAMPA SABAL PARK/ BRANDON

813/627-8855 19

Extended Stay Hotel

Residence INN **AAA Benefit:** Members save 5% or more!

Address: 9719 Princess Palm Ave 33619 **Location:** I-75 exit 260 southbound; exit 260B northbound, just w on SR 574 (Dr. Martin Luther King Jr Blvd), just s on Falkenburg Rd, then 0.4 mi w; in Sabal Corporate Park. **Facility:** 102 units, some two bedrooms and kitchens. 3 stories, interior corridors. **Pool:** heated outdoor. **Activities:** exercise room. **Guest Services:** valet and coin laundry.

  CALL  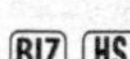 BIZ HS  

 / SOME UNITS

RESIDENCE INN BY MARRIOTT TAMPA WESTSHORE

813/877-7988 5

Extended Stay Hotel

Residence INN **AAA Benefit:** Members save 5% or more!

Address: 4312 W Boy Scout Blvd 33607 **Location:** I-275 exit 40B, 0.8 mi n on Lois Ave. **Facility:** 160 kitchen units, some two bedrooms. 8 stories, interior corridors. **Pool:** heated outdoor. **Activities:** hot tub, exercise room. **Guest Services:** valet and coin laundry, boarding pass kiosk.

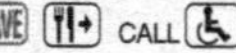 CALL 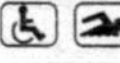 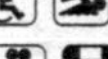  BIZ

HS  

/ SOME UNITS 

SAILPORT WATERFRONT SUITES ON TAMPA BAY

813/281-9599 25

Vacation Rental Condominium

Address: 2506 Rocky Point Dr 33607 **Location:** Waterfront. I-275 exit 39 southbound; exit 39B northbound, 3 mi w on SR 60, then just s. **Facility:** Set on Old Tampa Bay, this property offers one- and two-bedroom fully equipped condos with a living room and spectacular views of the bay from a private balcony. 194 condominiums. 3 stories, interior/exterior corridors. **Pool:** heated outdoor. **Activities:** fishing, lawn sports, picnic facilities, exercise room. **Guest Services:** valet and coin laundry, boarding pass kiosk, rental car service, area transportation.

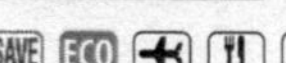   HS  

For complete hotel, dining and attraction listings: AAA.com/travelguides

▼ See AAA listing p. 356 ▼

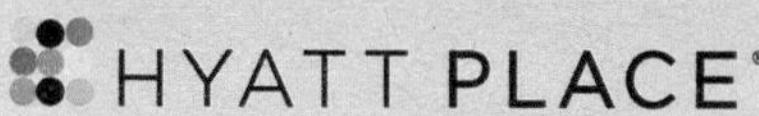

tampa/busch gardens

Welcome to a different place

- Oversized guest rooms
- Plush Hyatt Grand Bed®
- 24 hr Stay Fit® Center
- 24-hour food options, Lobby bar, Starbucks
- Complimentary hotel wide Wi-Fi
- Outdoor heated pool
- Complimentary breakfast for members when booked on Hyatt.com

11408 N. 30th Street • Tampa, FL 33612
813-979-1922 • tampabuschgardens.place.hyatt.com

(See maps & indexes p. 338, 344, 347.)

SEMINOLE HARD ROCK HOTEL & CASINO TAMPA 813/627-7625 15

Contemporary Resort Hotel

Address: 5223 N Orient Rd 33610 **Location:** I-4 exit 6, just w. **Facility:** This large facility offers outstanding amenities and spacious guest rooms. Bathrooms are decorated with very trendy art deco-inspired touches. The casino is the sixth largest in the world. 239 units. 12 stories, interior corridors. **Parking:** on-site and valet. **Terms:** check-in 4 pm. **Amenities:** safes. **Dining:** 7 restaurants, also, Council Oak Steaks & Seafood, Hard Rock Cafe, RiSE Kitchen & Bakery, see separate listings, entertainment. **Activities:** spa. **Guest Services:** valet laundry.

SAVE CALL BIZ HS / SOME UNITS

SPRINGHILL SUITES BY MARRIOTT TAMPA BRANDON 813/623-9990 8

SAVE Hotel. **Address:** 1051 S Falkenburg Rd 33619

AAA Benefit: Members save 5% or more!

SPRINGHILL SUITES BY MARRIOTT TAMPA NORTH/TAMPA PALMS 813/558-0300 2

SAVE Hotel. **Address:** 5396 Primrose Lake Cir 33647

AAA Benefit: Members save 5% or more!

SPRINGHILL SUITES BY MARRIOTT TAMPA/WESTSHORE AIRPORT 813/639-9600 17

Hotel

SPRINGHILL SUITES MARRIOTT **AAA Benefit:** Members save 5% or more!

Address: 4835 W Cypress St 33607 **Location:** I-275 exit 40A southbound, just n on Westshore Blvd, then just w; exit 39A northbound, 1 mi e on John F Kennedy Blvd, 0.9 mi n on Westshore Blvd, then just w. **Facility:** 149 units. 6 stories, interior corridors. **Amenities:** video games. **Pool:** heated outdoor. **Activities:** hot tub, exercise room. **Guest Services:** valet and coin laundry, boarding pass kiosk. **Featured Amenity: breakfast buffet.**

SAVE ECO CALL BIZ HS

Love the Great Outdoors?

For getaways off the beaten path, visit AAA.com/campgrounds

iStockphoto.com_pixelfit

STAYBRIDGE SUITES-TAMPA EAST 813/227-4000 20

Extended Stay Hotel. **Address:** 3624 N Falkenburg Rd 33619

TAMPA AIRPORT MARRIOTT 813/879-5151 1

Hotel

MARRIOTT **AAA Benefit:** Members save 5% or more!

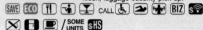

Address: 4200 George J Bean Pkwy 33607 **Location:** I-275 exit 39, exit 39B northbound, 2 mi w on SR 60; at Tampa International Airport. **Facility:** 298 units. 8 stories, interior corridors. **Parking:** on-site (fee) and valet. **Dining:** 2 restaurants. **Pool:** heated outdoor. **Activities:** health club, massage. **Guest Services:** valet and coin laundry, boarding pass kiosk, luggage security pick-up.

SAVE ECO CALL BIZ / SOME UNITS sHS

TOWNEPLACE SUITES BY MARRIOTT TAMPA WESTSHORE/AIRPORT 813/282-1081 11

Extended Stay Hotel

TOWNEPLACE SUITES MARRIOTT **AAA Benefit:** Members save 5% or more!

Address: 5302 Avion Park Dr 33607 **Location:** I-275 exit 40A southbound, 0.7 mi n on Westshore Blvd; exit 39A northbound, 1 mi e on SR 60 (Kennedy Blvd), 1.2 mi n on Westshore Blvd, just w on Spruce St, then just s on O'Brien St; in Avion Park Westshore. **Facility:** 122 kitchen units, some two bedrooms. 4 stories, interior corridors. **Pool:** heated outdoor. **Activities:** exercise room. **Guest Services:** valet and coin laundry, area transportation.

SAVE ECO CALL BIZ HS / SOME UNITS

TOWNEPLACE SUITES BY MARRIOTT TAMPA WESTSHORE SOUTH 813/542-4500 29

SAVE Extended Stay Hotel. **Address:** 4505 S Dale Mabry Hwy 33611

AAA Benefit: Members save 5% or more!

THE WESTIN TAMPA BAY 813/281-0000 24

Contemporary Hotel

WESTIN HOTELS & RESORTS **AAA Benefit:** Members save 5% or more!

Address: 7627 Courtney Campbell Cswy 33607 **Location:** Waterfront. On SR 60, at east end of causeway. **Facility:** Located on the waterfront, a short drive to downtown Tampa, sports and concert venues and museums, this modern hotel features guest rooms with fabulous views of Tampa Bay. 244 units, some efficiencies. 16 stories, interior corridors. **Parking:** on-site (fee) and valet. **Amenities:** safes. **Dining:** AQUA Bar & Grille, see separate listing. **Pool:** heated indoor. **Activities:** hot tub, beach access, motor boats, health club, massage. **Guest Services:** valet laundry, boarding pass kiosk, luggage security pick-up, area transportation.

SAVE CALL BIZ HS / SOME UNITS

(See maps & indexes p. 338, 344, 347.)

WHERE TO EAT

1823 KITCHEN & BAR 813/874-1234 (3)

New American. Fine Dining. **Address:** 2900 Bayport Dr 33607

717 SOUTH 813/250-1661 (43)

Italian. Fine Dining. **Address:** 717 S Howard Ave 33606

ABC PIZZA

Italian. Casual Dining.

LOCATIONS:

Address: 7512 W Hillsborough Ave 33615 **Phone:** 813/884-3495

Address: 1242 W Hillsborough Ave 33603 **Phone:** 813/237-3324

ANTHONY'S COAL FIRED PIZZA

Pizza. Casual Dining.

LOCATIONS:

Address: 13020 N Dale Mabry Hwy 33618 **Phone:** 813/265-2625

Address: 1901 S Dale Mabry Hwy 33629 **Phone:** 813/258-2625

AQUA BAR & GRILLE 813/675-8700 (31)

Seafood. Fine Dining. **Address:** 7627 Courtney Campbell Cswy 33607

ARMANI'S 813/207-6800 (4)

Northern Italian Fine Dining $14-$58

AAA Inspector Notes: Overlooking Old Tampa Bay, this romantic, upscale Italian restaurant is on the top floor of the hotel. Specializing in Northern Tuscan cuisine, veal is the house specialty. Popular dishes include braised veal shank, frutti de mare, Hudson Valley duck, and lobster ravioli. Diners can order antipasto directly from the chef or let the waiter help with some 30 selections. **Features:** full bar. **Reservations:** required. Semiformal attire. **Address:** 2900 Bayport Dr 33607 **Location:** On SR 60, at east end of Courtney Campbell Cswy; in Grand Hyatt Tampa Bay. **Parking:** on-site and valet. D CALL

BAHAMA BREEZE ISLAND GRILLE 813/289-7922 (29)

Caribbean. Casual Dining. **Address:** 3045 N Rocky Point Dr E 33607

BENJARONG THAI 813/265-2667 (7)

Thai. Casual Dining. **Address:** 14402 N Dale Mabry Hwy 33618

BERN'S STEAK HOUSE 813/251-2421 (47)

Steak Seafood. Fine Dining. **Address:** 1208 S Howard Ave 33606

BJ'S ALABAMA BBQ 813/374-0219 (56)

Barbecue. Quick Serve. **Address:** 3423 S Dale Mabry Hwy 33629

BONEFISH GRILL 813/876-3535 (46)

Seafood. Fine Dining. **Address:** 3665 Henderson Blvd 33609

BROCATO'S SANDWICH SHOP 813/248-9977 (28)

Sandwiches Breakfast. Quick Serve. **Address:** 5021 E Old Columbus Dr 33619

THE BRUNCHERY RESTAURANT & CATERING 813/831-4694 (52)

Breakfast Sandwiches. Casual Dining. **Address:** 3225 S MacDill Ave 33629

BURGER CULTURE 813/992-7444 (22)

Burgers Sandwiches. Quick Serve. **Address:** 6920 N Dale Mabry Hwy 33602

BURGER MONGER

Burgers. Quick Serve.

LOCATIONS:

Address: 3838 W Neptune St 33609 **Phone:** 813/254-0290

Address: 10412 N Dale Mabry Hwy 33618 **Phone:** 813/968-6860

CAFFE PARADISO RISTORANTE ITALIANO 813/835-6622 (59)

Northern Italian. Fine Dining. **Address:** 4205 S MacDill 33611

CHARLEY'S STEAKHOUSE 813/353-9706 (10)

Steak. Fine Dining. **Address:** 4444 W Cypress St 33607

THE CHEESECAKE FACTORY 813/353-4200 (1)

International. Casual Dining. **Address:** 2223 N Westshore Blvd, Suite B201 33607

CHERRY'S 813/685-3465

American. Casual Dining. **Address:** 10033 E Adamo Dr 33619

CHICKEN SALAD CHICK 813/910-4300 (12)

Chicken Sandwiches. Quick Serve. **Address:** 2790 E Fowler Ave 33617

CINÉBISTRO HYDE PARK 813/514-8300 (39)

Continental. Casual Dining. **Address:** 1609 W Swann Ave 33606

CODY'S ORIGINAL ROADHOUSE 813/855-2787

American. Casual Dining. **Address:** 11202 W Hillsborough Ave 33635

COUNCIL OAK STEAKS & SEAFOOD 813/627-7600 (25)

Steak. Fine Dining. **Address:** 5223 N Orient Rd 33610

CRISPERS 813/969-2445

Sandwiches Soup. Quick Serve. **Address:** 15726 N Dale Mabry Hwy 33618

DANNY'S ALL AMERICAN DINER & DAIRY BAR 813/740-0606 (26)

Burgers Sandwiches. Quick Serve. **Address:** 4406 N Falkenburg Rd 33610

DONATELLO 813/875-6660 (12)

Northern Italian. Fine Dining. **Address:** 232 N Dale Mabry Hwy 33609

DRAGONFIRE GRILL 813/884-4386 (16)

American. Quick Serve. **Address:** 3000 E Busch Blvd 33612

THE DUBLINER IRISH PUB 813/258-2257 (35)

Irish. Casual Dining. **Address:** 2307 Azeele St 33606

EVOS 813/258-3867

Natural/Organic. Quick Serve. **Address:** 609 S Howard Ave 33606

FIRST CHOICE BAR-B-QUE 813/621-7434 (4)

Barbecue. Quick Serve. **Address:** 10113 Adamo Dr 33619

FRONTIER STEAKHOUSE 813/621-3050 (20)

Steak. Casual Dining. **Address:** 8602 E Sligh Ave 33610

GALERIE RESTAURANT 813/739-8821 (30)

Continental. Casual Dining. **Address:** 3050 N Rocky Point Dr W 33607

GOODY GOODY 813/308-1925 (38)

Comfort Food Breakfast. Casual Dining. **Address:** 1601 W Swann Ave 33606

GREEN IGUANA BAR & GRILL 813/837-1234

American. Casual Dining. **Address:** 4029 S Westshore Blvd 33611

(See maps & indexes p. 338, 344, 347.)

HARD ROCK CAFE 813/627-7757 (24)
SAVE American. Casual Dining. **Address:** 5223 N Orient Rd 33601

HAVEN 813/258-2233 (45)
Continental. Casual Dining. **Address:** 2208 W Morrison Ave 33606

HIBACHI BUFFET 813/960-8668 (11)
Chinese. Quick Serve. **Address:** 13151 N Dale Mabry Hwy 33618

HOLY HOG BARBECUE 813/282-4647 (50)
Barbecue. Quick Serve. **Address:** 4004 Henderson Blvd 33629

HOLY HOG BARBECUE 813/961-4464 (15)
Barbecue. Quick Serve. **Address:** 11417 N Dale Mabry Hwy 33618

HULA BAY CLUB WATERFRONT RESTAURANT & BAR 813/837-4852 (62)
Seafood. Casual Dining. **Address:** 5210 W Tyson Ave 33611

INDOCHINOIS RESTAURANT 813/254-3757 (51)
Vietnamese. Casual Dining. **Address:** 1912 S Dale Mabry Hwy 33629

INTELLIGENT GOURMET 813/287-2253 (54)
Natural/Organic Sandwiches. Quick Serve. **Address:** 3225 S MacDill Ave 33629

IRISH 31 PUB HOUSE & EATERY 813/250-0031 (40)
Irish. Casual Dining. **Address:** 1611 W Swann Ave 33606

ISLAMORADA FISH COMPANY RESTAURANT 813/655-2000 (5)
Seafood. Casual Dining. **Address:** 10501 Palm River Rd 33619

J. ALEXANDER'S REDLANDS GRILL 813/354-9006 (9)
American. Casual Dining. **Address:** 913 Dale Mabry Hwy 33609

JASMINE THAI RESTAURANT 813/968-1501 (10)
Thai. Casual Dining. **Address:** 13248 N Dale Mabry Hwy 33618

KOJAK'S HOUSE OF RIBS 813/837-3774 (60)
Barbecue. Casual Dining. **Address:** 2808 W Gandy Blvd 33611

LA BAMBA SPANISH AMERICAN RESTAURANT 813/287-2575 (8)
Spanish. Quick Serve. **Address:** 4815 W Laurel St 33607

LIANG'S BISTRO ASIAN CUISINE 813/978-1225 (2)
Asian. Casual Dining. **Address:** 17515 Bruce B Downs Blvd 33647

LIBORIO'S LATIN CAFE & CATERING 813/623-1318 (41)
Latin American. Quick Serve. **Address:** 8210 E Causeway Blvd 33619

MACDINTON'S IRISH PUB & RESTAURANT 813/251-8999 (37)
Irish. Casual Dining. **Address:** 405 S Howard Ave 33606

MAGGIANO'S LITTLE ITALY 813/288-9000 (16)
Italian. Fine Dining. **Address:** 203 Westshore Plaza 33609

MEL'S HOT DOGS 813/985-8000 (18)
Hot Dogs Sandwiches. Quick Serve. **Address:** 4136 E Busch Blvd 33617

MIGUEL'S MEXICAN SEAFOOD & GRILL 813/876-2587 (34)
Mexican. Casual Dining. **Address:** 3035 W Kennedy Blvd 33609

MR. EMPANADA
Cuban. Quick Serve.
LOCATIONS:
Address: 7543 W Hillsborough Ave 33615 **Phone:** 813/249-6233
Address: 3953 W Kennedy Blvd 33609 **Phone:** 813/872-6233
Address: 10023 N Dale Mabry Hwy 33618 **Phone:** 813/908-6202
Address: 4836 N Armenia Ave 33603 **Phone:** 813/879-6232

OCEAN PRIME 813/490-5288 (7)
Seafood. Fine Dining. **Address:** 2205 N Westshore Blvd 33607

OYSTERCATCHERS RESTAURANT 813/207-6815 (5)
Seafood. Fine Dining. **Address:** 2900 Bayport Dr 33607

PANE' RUSTICA BAKERY & CAFE 813/902-8828 (53)
Sandwiches Breads/Pastries. Casual Dining. **Address:** 3225 S MacDill Ave 33629

PASTRIES N CHAAT INDIAN STREET FOOD & BAKERY 813/512-2632 (14)
Indian. Quick Serve. **Address:** 1811 E Fowler Ave 33612

P.F. CHANG'S CHINA BISTRO 813/289-8400 (15)
Chinese. Fine Dining. **Address:** 219 Westshore Plaza 33609

PIPO'S & SON CAFETERIA 813/882-0184 (27)
Spanish. Quick Serve. **Address:** 7233 W Hillsborough Ave 33634

PIZZA PINO 813/671-4200 (55)
Italian. Quick Serve. **Address:** 5529 S 78th St 33619

PLAYERS SPORTS PUB 813/998-2255 (11)
Burgers Sandwiches. Casual Dining. **Address:** 4500 W Cypress St 33607

RISE KITCHEN & BAKERY 813/627-7625 (23)
American. Casual Dining. **Address:** 223 N Orient Rd 33610

ROCCO'S TACOS & TEQUILA BAR 813/800-8226 (2)
Mexican. Casual Dining. **Address:** 2223 N Westshore Blvd 33607

ROOSTER & THE TILL 813/374-8940 (21)
Continental. Casual Dining. **Address:** 6500 N Florida Ave 33604

ROYAL PALACE THAI RESTAURANT 813/258-5893 (44)
Thai. Casual Dining. **Address:** 811 S Howard Ave 33606

ROY'S 813/873-7697 (6)
Pacific Rim Fusion. Fine Dining. **Address:** 4342 W Boy Scout Blvd 33607

THE RUSTY PELICAN 813/281-1943 (33)
Seafood Steak. Fine Dining. **Address:** 2425 N Rocky Point Dr 33607

SAIGON BAY VIETNAMESE RESTAURANT 813/971-0854 (13)
Vietnamese. Casual Dining. **Address:** 2373 E Fowler Ave 33612

SEASONS 52 FRESH GRILL 813/286-1152 (13)
New American. Fine Dining. **Address:** 204 N Westshore Blvd 33609

SHELLS CASUAL SEAFOOD 813/875-3467 (14)
Seafood. Casual Dining. **Address:** 202 S Dale Mabry Hwy 33609

SHULA'S AMERICA'S STEAK HOUSE 813/286-4366 (17)
Steak. Fine Dining. **Address:** 4860 W Kennedy Blvd 33609

(See maps & indexes p. 338, 344, 347.)

SKIPPER'S SMOKEHOUSE RESTAURANT & OYSTER BAR 813/971-0666 (5)

Seafood
Casual Dining
$5-$21

AAA Inspector Notes: This extremely casual restaurant has been around since 1980 and is eclectically decorated in a Bohemian style. It's popular for their outdoor stage area, which offers local bands a venue to perform. The restaurant and oyster bar serves Florida fare with Caribbean and Louisiana accents. Menu selections include clam, mullet, basa, catfish, scallops, grouper, mahi mahi, oysters, alligator, crab, shrimp, wings, ribs and conch chowder. **Features:** full bar, patio dining. **Address:** 910 Skipper Rd 33613 **Location:** I-275 exit 51, just e on Fletcher Ave, 0.8 mi n on Nebraska Ave, then just e. L D LATE

SLICE MASTERS NY PIZZERIA 813/341-1414 (9)
Italian. Casual Dining. **Address:** 4538 W Village Dr 33624

SONNY'S REAL PIT BAR-B-Q
Barbecue. Casual Dining.
LOCATIONS:
Address: 10010 E Adamo Dr 33619 **Phone:** 813/621-8784
Address: 15412 N Dale Mabry Hwy 33618
Phone: 813/960-3595

STONEWOOD GRILL & TAVERN 813/978-0388 (3)
American. Fine Dining. **Address:** 17050 Palm Pointe Dr 33647

SUKHOTHAI RESTAURANT 813/615-2345 (1)
Thai. Casual Dining. **Address:** 18101 Highwoods Preserve Pkwy 33647

TACO BUS 813/643-0027 (1)
Mexican. Quick Serve. **Address:** 301 S Falkenburg Rd 33619

TACO BUS 813/977-6808 (6)
Mexican. Quick Serve. **Address:** 2320 E Fletcher Ave 33612

TACO BUS 813/831-0550 (61)
Mexican. Quick Serve. **Address:** 4308 W Gandy Blvd 33611

TAMPA BUFFET 813/805-2929 (58)
Chinese. Quick Serve. **Address:** 3904 S Dale Mabry Hwy 33611

TATE'S RESTAURANT PIZZERIA & BAR 813/832-5675 (57)
Italian. Casual Dining. **Address:** 3342 S Westshore Blvd 33629

TERRA GAUHA BRAZILIAN STEAKHOUSE 813/999-4332 (48)
Brazilian Steak. Fine Dining. **Address:** 1808 S Dale Mabry Hwy 33629

THAI RUBY 813/558-0570 (4)
Thai. Casual Dining. **Address:** 15319 Amberly Dr 33647

TIJUANA FLATS
Tex-Mex. Quick Serve.
LOCATIONS:
Address: 2782 E Fowler Ave 33612 **Phone:** 813/975-0800
Address: 10019 N Dale Mabry Hwy 33618
Phone: 813/849-6900

TIMPANO CHOPHOUSE 813/254-5870 (42)
Continental. Casual Dining. **Address:** 1610 W Swann Ave 33606

TOKAI SUSHI JAPANESE RESTAURANT 813/621-3332 (2)
Japanese Sushi. Casual Dining. **Address:** 10115 E Adamo Dr 33619

VALLARTA'S RESTAURANTE MEXICANO 813/264-7691 (8)
Mexican. Casual Dining. **Address:** 13731-37 N Dale Mabry Hwy 33618

VILLA RINA'S NEW YORK STYLE PIZZA & PASTA 813/654-6449 (3)
Italian. Quick Serve. **Address:** 10073 Adamo Dr 33619

WESTSHORE PIZZA 813/832-5331
Pizza. Casual Dining. **Address:** 4802 W Bay Court Ave 33611

WHISKEY JOE'S BAR & GRILL 813/281-0770 (32)
Seafood. Casual Dining. **Address:** 7720 W Courtney Campbell Cswy 33607

WRIGHT'S GOURMET HOUSE 813/253-3838 (49)
Sandwiches Deli. Quick Serve. **Address:** 1200 S Dale Mabry Hwy 33629

YARD OF ALE SOHO 813/251-4433 (36)
Sandwiches Pizza. Casual Dining. **Address:** 406 S Howard Ave 33606

ZAGORA CAFE 813/884-4386 (19)
Burgers Sandwiches. Quick Serve. **Address:** 3000 E Busch Blvd 33612

ZAMBIA SMOKEHOUSE 813/884-4386 (17)
Barbecue. Quick Serve. **Address:** 3000 E Busch Blvd 33612

TARPON SPRINGS (G-1) pop. 23,484, elev. 18'

• Hotels p. 362 • Restaurants p. 362
• Part of St. Petersburg-Clearwater and Beaches area — see map p. 275

Tarpon Springs became an important center for sponge diving when Greek divers came to the area in the early 1900s. Although the industry has diminished, the Greek influence still is evident in the remaining historic Sponge Dock area, where natural sponges, shops and a variety of ethnic restaurants and bakeries are plentiful. Sponge-diving exhibitions, scenic cruises and deep-sea fishing charters are available from the dock area.

Spring Bayou, one block west of downtown, is home to manatees and dolphins in winter and the site where men dive for the cross during the Epiphany Celebration in January. Nearby Crescent Circle features lovely Victorian homes. The Tarpon Springs Heritage Museum, 100 Beekman Ln. in Craig Park, features a variety of items pertaining to the Victorian era as well as a video presentation about the history of the sponge-diving industry; phone (727) 937-0686.

A replica of St. Sophia's in Constantinople, the 1943 St. Nicholas Greek Orthodox Cathedral, at the corner of Pinellas Avenue (US 19A) and Orange Street, is the center of colorful pageantry during Greek festivals; phone (727) 937-3540. St. Michael Shrine at 113 Hope St. reflects the Greek culture through its artwork and murals.

The Safford House, at 23 Parkin Ct., was home to Anson Safford and his family. Safford was one of the city's founders. His sister, Mary Jane, was the first practicing female physician in Florida; phone (727) 937-1130.

Tarpon Springs also offers two sandy beaches on the Gulf of Mexico: Fred Howard Park, 1700 Sunset Dr.; and Sunset Beach, 1800 Gulf Rd.

Tarpon Springs Chamber of Commerce: 1 N. Pinellas Ave., Tarpon Springs, FL 34689. **Phone:** (727) 937-6109.

Shopping: More than 100 gift shops and homespun Greek eateries dot the historic Sponge Docks area; you'll find most establishments on Dodecanese Boulevard and along Athens Street. Munch on sticky baklava chunks as you putter past tour boat operators bellowing the latest cruise times and neat sale racks displaying sandals of every color and dimension. Along with a myriad of sea-harvested products, including loofahs and natural sponges, local businesses proffer a variety of keepsakes—from shell jewelry and safari hats to tropical wind chimes and hand-rolled cigars. Break up your afternoon of Florida kitsch by visiting Tarpon Springs' historic downtown, home to a handful of antiques dealers operating on Tarpon Avenue.

BROOKER CREEK PRESERVE ENVIRONMENTAL EDUCATION CENTER is at 3940 Keystone Rd. The 25,000-square-foot center features permanent exhibits focusing on natural Florida and local history, while temporary displays include art. Guided hikes, programs and workshops are available year-round. Boardwalks and a network of nature trails provide bird-watching opportunities. Sightings include deer, turkey and gopher tortoises. **Time:** Allow 2 hours minimum. **Hours:** Preserve open daily 7-dusk; closed Christmas. Center Thurs.-Sat. 9-4; closed major holidays. **Cost:** Donations. **Phone:** (727) 453-6800. GT

LEEPA-RATTNER MUSEUM OF ART is at 600 Klosterman Rd. Located on the Tarpon Springs campus of St. Petersburg College, the museum features modern works of art by Allen Leepa, Abraham Rattner, Esther Gentle and their contemporaries, including Pablo Picasso, Marc Chagall, Georges Rouault and Max Ernst. Contemporary pieces by Florida and southeastern artists also are featured. The Challenge of Art Interactive Gallery includes hands-on activities. Changing exhibitions also are offered.

Time: Allow 2 hours minimum. **Hours:** Tues.-Wed. and Sat. 10-5, Thurs. 10-8, Fri. 10-4, Sun. 1-5. Docent-led tours are offered Sun. at 2; otherwise by appointment. Closed major holidays. **Cost:** $7; $6 (ages 62+); by donation (to all Thurs. 5-8); free (ages 0-18 and students and active military with ID). **Phone:** (727) 712-5762. GT

SUN LINE CRUISES departs from the sponge docks at 18 and 510 Dodecanese Blvd. Narrated by a trained naturalist, this 2-hour cruise traverses the Anclote River and Gulf of Mexico. Visitors learn about the area's history, local sponging and fishing industries, and wildlife. Sightings may include dolphins, eagles, osprey, herons and a variety of birds in a protected nesting area. The tour includes a 30-minute stop at Anclote Key, where swimming, shelling and wildlife viewing are possible. Binoculars are available on loan throughout the tour. Weekend sunset tours and visits to the Anclote Lighthouse also are offered seasonally.

Time: Allow 1 hour, 30 minutes minimum. **Hours:** 2-hour cruise departs daily. Reservations with 24 hours advance notice are requested. Phone ahead to confirm schedule. **Cost:** SeaFari Island Adventure $18.95; $17.95 (ages 62+); $9.95 (ages 2-10). Prices are subject to change. Phone ahead for current prices. Reservations are recommended. **Phone:** (727) 944-4468 or (727) 943-2164. GT

HAMPTON INN & SUITES TARPON SPRINGS 727/945-7755
Three Diamond SAVE Hotel. **Address:** 39284 US 19 N 34689

AAA Benefit: Members save 5% or more!

WHERE TO EAT

CODY'S ORIGINAL ROADHOUSE 727/937-1022
Two Diamond American. Casual Dining. **Address:** 39870 US 19 N 34689

COSTA'S RESTAURANT 727/938-6890
Two Diamond Greek. Casual Dining. **Address:** 521 Athens St 34689

HELLAS BAKERY & RESTAURANT 727/943-2400
Two Diamond Greek. Casual Dining. **Address:** 785 Dodecanese Blvd 34689

QUEEN'S PIZZA AND RESTAURANT 727/939-1791
Two Diamond Italian. Casual Dining. **Address:** 40949 US 19 N 34689

RUSTY BELLIES WATERFRONT GRILL 727/934-4047
Two Diamond Seafood. Casual Dining. **Address:** 937 Dodecanese Blvd 34689

TAVARES (F-3) pop. 13,951, elev. 66'

• Part of Orlando area — see map p. 2

With a number of small planes buzzing around Lake Dora, this small community exemplifies "America's Seaplane City," but there's also a hint of the past with a walkable downtown and quaint Tavares Union Station (305 E. Ruby St.).

Alexander St. Clair-Abrams, a New Orleans businessman with ties to newspapers and the railroad, founded and named this small community after a Portuguesee ancestor in 1880. His goal of it becoming the state capital was not realized, but Tavares did become the county seat of Lake County in 1887.

Hurricane Irma blew through the town Sept. 10, 2017, and destroyed the marina and seaplane base; seaplanes are lining up along temporary docks on Lake Dora. **Note:** A new marina and seaplane base (150 E. Ruby St.) is scheduled to open late 2020; phone (352) 742-6267 for more information.

Wooton Park, 100 E. Ruby St., is along the shores of Lake Dora and the site of many community events. Open daily dawn-dusk, it features docks, a fishing pier, playground and seaplane-themed splash pad (April through September); phone (352) 742-6267.

COMFORT INN & SUITES 352/253-2378
Hotel. **Address:** 1380 E Burleigh Blvd 32778

WHERE TO EAT

ANGELO'S ITALIAN RESTAURANT 352/343-2757
Italian. Casual Dining. **Address:** 2270 Vindale Rd 32778

HURRICANE DOCKSIDE GRILL 352/508-5137
American. Casual Dining. **Address:** 3351 W Burleigh Blvd 32778

TEMPLE TERRACE pop. 24,541

• **Hotels & Restaurants map & index p. 338**
• **Part of Tampa area — see map p. 313**

HILTON GARDEN INN TAMPA NORTH 813/342-5000 34
SAVE Hotel. **Address:** 13305 Tampa Oaks Blvd 33637

AAA Benefit: Members save 5% or more!

HOLIDAY INN EXPRESS TAMPA N I-75 UNIVERSITY AREA 813/972-9800 36
Hotel. **Address:** 13294 Telecom Dr 33637

RESIDENCE INN BY MARRIOTT TAMPA NORTH I-75 FLETCHER 813/972-4400 35

Extended Stay Hotel

Residence INN **AAA Benefit:** Members save 5% or more!

Address: 13420 N Telecom Pkwy 33637 **Location:** I-75 exit 266, 1.1 mi w on Fletcher Ave (CR 582A), then just s; in Telecom Tampa Park. **Facility:** 78 kitchen units, some two bedrooms. 3 stories, interior corridors. **Terms:** check-in 4 pm. **Pool:** heated outdoor. **Activities:** picnic facilities, exercise room. **Guest Services:** valet and coin laundry.

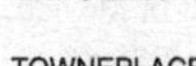
SAVE CALL BIZ HS / SOME UNITS

TOWNEPLACE SUITES BY MARRIOTT TAMPA NORTH/I-75 FLETCHER 813/975-9777 37
SAVE Extended Stay Hotel. **Address:** 6800 Woodstork Rd 33637

AAA Benefit: Members save 5% or more!

WOODSPRING SUITES 813/513-0050 33
Extended Stay Hotel. **Address:** 12162 Morris Bridge Rd 33637

WHERE TO EAT

CDB PIZZA & ITALIAN RESTAURANT 813/985-1336 65
Italian. Casual Dining. **Address:** 5104 E Fowler Ave 33617

GATOR'S DOCKSIDE 813/341-4445
American. Casual Dining. **Address:** 5840 Fowler Ave 33617

TOKYO JAPANESE RESTAURANT & SUSHI BAR 813/983-1822 66
Japanese Sushi. Casual Dining. **Address:** 5711 E Fowler Ave 33617

VALLARTAS MEXICAN RESTAURANT 813/987-2720 67
Mexican. Casual Dining. **Address:** 9255 N 56th St 33617

THE VILLAGES pop. 51,442

HAMPTON INN & SUITES-THE VILLAGES 352/259-8246
SAVE Hotel. **Address:** 11727 NE 63rd Dr 32162

AAA Benefit: Members save 5% or more!

THE WATERFRONT INN 352/753-7535

Hotel

Address: 1105 Lakeshore Dr 32162 **Location:** Waterfront. 2.9 mi w of jct US 27/441 on CR 466, then just s on Morse Blvd. **Facility:** 118 units. 4 stories, interior corridors. **Amenities:** safes. **Dining:** Amelia's Restaurant and The Lakeside Lounge, see separate listing, entertainment. **Pool:** heated outdoor. **Activities:** hot tub, exercise room. **Guest Services:** coin laundry.

SAVE BIZ HS

WHERE TO EAT

AMELIA'S RESTAURANT AND THE LAKESIDE LOUNGE 352/753-7535
Seafood Steak. Casual Dining. **Address:** 1105 Lakeshore Dr 32162

CODY'S ORIGINAL ROADHOUSE 352/259-8500
American. Casual Dining. **Address:** 1041 Lakeshore Dr 32162

REDSAUCE 352/750-2930
Italian. Casual Dining. **Address:** 1000 Canal St 32162

TAKIS GREEK & ITALIAN RESTAURANT 352/430-3630
Greek Pizza. Casual Dining. **Address:** 13761 US Hwy 441 32159

THONOTOSASSA (H-2) pop. 13,014, elev. 49'

• **Part of Tampa area — see map p. 313**

Fort Foster, on the Hillsborough River in nearby Hillsborough River State Park *(see Recreation Areas Chart)*, was used as a battle post and supply depot during the Second Seminole War. Abandoned in 1838 because of disease and the miserable, damp conditions, the fort and the bridge it guarded have been reconstructed on the original site. A tram transports visitors to the fort for a fee. Seasonal guided tours are available (weather permitting); phone (813) 987-6771.

RECREATIONAL ACTIVITIES

Canoeing

- **Canoe Escape** is in John B. Sargeant Park, 12702 US 301. **Hours:** Daily 9-5. Guided 3-hour interpretive canoe trips are available Wed. at 11 or by appointment with 48 hours notice. Self-guiding and guided tours are available. **Cost:** Reservations are recommended. **Phone:** (813) 986-2067. GT

TITUSVILLE (D-10) pop. 43,761, elev. 18'

• **Hotels p. 364 • Restaurants p. 364**
• **Hotels & Restaurants map & index p. 50**

Named for founder Col. Henry T. Titus in 1874, Titusville once was a citrus shipping point and commercial fishing port. The establishment of Kennedy Space Center *(see place listing p. 105)* brought the

(See map & index p. 50.)

Space Age—and increased tourism—to this small mainland city.

SAVE **AMERICAN POLICE HALL OF FAME & MUSEUM,** 6350 Horizon Dr., displays more than 10,000 items relating to law enforcement. Exhibits include a mock crime scene, a forensic area and specialty cars. An indoor memorial lists the names of U.S. police officers killed in the line of duty since 1960. A 24-lane shooting range is available. **Time:** Allow 1 hour minimum. **Hours:** Daily 10-6. Closed Thanksgiving and Christmas. **Cost:** $13; $10 (ages 65+ and active military with ID); $8 (ages 4-12); $2 (active and retired law enforcement officers and family survivors); free (ages 0-3). **Phone:** (321) 264-0911.

VALIANT AIR COMMAND WARBIRD AIR MUSEUM, 6600 Tico Rd. at the Space Coast Regional Airport, following signs, features aviation memorabilia dating from World War I to the present. Exhibits include model planes, uniforms, artifacts and up to 50 vintage warbird aircraft in three restoration and exhibition hangars. **Time:** Allow 2 hours minimum. **Hours:** Daily 9-5. Closed Jan. 1, Thanksgiving and Christmas. **Cost:** $20; $18 (ages 60+ and active and retired military with ID); $10 (students with ID); $5 (ages 5-12). **Phone:** (321) 268-1941.

BEST WESTERN SPACE SHUTTLE INN
321/269-9100 14

Hotel

Best Western **AAA Benefit:** Members save up to 15% and earn bonus points!

Address: 3455 Cheney Hwy 32780 **Location:** I-95 exit 215 (SR 50), just e. **Facility:** 129 units. 2 stories (no elevator), exterior corridors. **Dining:** Durango Steakhouse, see separate listing. **Pool:** outdoor. **Activities:** exercise room. **Featured Amenity: full hot breakfast.**

SAVE CALL

/ SOME UNITS

DAYS INN TITUSVILLE KENNEDY SPACE CENTER
321/269-4480 18

Motel. **Address:** 3755 Cheney Hwy 32780

FAIRFIELD INN & SUITES BY MARRIOTT-TITUSVILLE/ KENNEDY SPACE CENTER 321/385-1818 15

Fairfield **AAA Benefit:** Members save 5% or more!

Address: 4735 Helen Hauser Blvd 32780 **Location:** I-95 exit 215 (SR 50), just w. **Facility:** 96 units. 4 stories, interior corridors. **Pool:** heated outdoor. **Activities:** exercise room. **Guest Services:** valet and coin laundry. **Featured Amenity: full hot breakfast.**

SAVE CALL BIZ

HAMPTON INN TITUSVILLE/I-95 KENNEDY SPACE CENTER
321/383-9191 16

SAVE Hotel. **Address:** 4760 Helen Hauser Blvd 32780

AAA Benefit: Members save 5% or more!

HOLIDAY INN TITUSVILLE-KENNEDY SPACE CENTER
321/383-0200 17

Hotel. **Address:** 4715 Helen Hauser Blvd 32780

TOWNEPLACE SUITES BY MARRIOTT KENNEDY SPACE CENTER
321/603-0811 19

SAVE Extended Stay Hotel. **Address:** 4815 Helen Hauser Blvd 32780

AAA Benefit: Members save 5% or more!

WHERE TO EAT

DIXIE CROSSROADS SEAFOOD RESTAURANT
321/268-5000 9

American. Casual Dining. **Address:** 1475 Garden St 32796

DURANGO STEAKHOUSE 321/264-2499

Steak Seafood. Casual Dining. **Address:** 3455 Cheney Hwy 32780

EL LEONCITO MEXICAN & CUBAN RESTAURANT
321/267-1159 11

Mexican. Casual Dining. **Address:** 4280 S Washington Ave 32780

KELSEY'S PIZZERIA EATERY 321/268-5555 10

Italian Pizza. Casual Dining. **Address:** 2845 Garden St 32796

SONNY'S REAL PIT BAR-B-Q 321/385-2665

Barbecue. Casual Dining. **Address:** 2900 Cheney Hwy 32780

TREASURE ISLAND (H-1) pop. 6,705, elev. 3'

- **Hotels & Restaurants map & index p. 286**
- **Part of St. Petersburg-Clearwater and Beaches area — see map p. 275**

Located on a barrier island in the Gulf of Mexico, about 8 miles west of St. Petersburg, Treasure Island offers 4 miles of tranquil beaches for sun worshippers. Landlubbers also can pick up a club or racquet at Treasure Bay Golf and Tennis (10315 Paradise Blvd.). If you want to hit the water, fishing charters are plentiful, and there's paddle boarding and parasailing for thrill seekers. On Gulf Boulevard, 1950s-era motels will delight fans of midcentury architecture.

JAMAICAN ON THE GULF 727/360-6981 75

Vacation Rental Condominium. **Address:** 11660 Gulf Blvd 33706

PAGE TERRACE BEACHFRONT HOTEL
727/367-1997 77

Address: 10500 Gulf Blvd 33706 **Location:** Oceanfront. On SR 699, just s of jct Treasure Island Cswy. **Facility:** 36 units, some efficiencies and kitchens. 3 stories (no elevator), interior/exterior corridors. **Amenities:** safes. **Pool:** heated outdoor. **Guest Services:** coin laundry.

SAVE BIZ HS

(See map & index p. 286.)

RESIDENCE INN BY MARRIOTT ST. PETERSBURG TREASURE ISLAND 727/367-2761 **73**

Extended Stay Hotel

Residence INN. **AAA Benefit:** Members save 5% or more!

Address: 11908 Gulf Blvd 33706 **Location:** Oceanfront. On SR 699, 0.7 mi n of jct Treasure Island Cswy. **Facility:** 105 units, some two bedrooms, three bedrooms and kitchens. 6-9 stories, interior/exterior corridors. **Terms:** check-in 4 pm. **Amenities:** safes. **Pool:** heated outdoor. **Activities:** hot tub, exercise room. **Guest Services:** valet and coin laundry. **Featured Amenity: breakfast buffet.**

SAVE CALL SOME UNITS

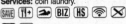

THE SEA CHEST 727/360-5501 **74**

Motel

Address: 11780 Gulf Blvd 33706 **Location:** Oceanfront. On SR 699, 0.5 mi n of jct Treasure Island Cswy. **Facility:** 21 units, some efficiencies and kitchens. 2 stories (no elevator), interior/exterior corridors. **Pool:** heated outdoor. **Guest Services:** coin laundry.

SUNSET VISTAS BEACHFRONT SUITES 727/360-1600 **72**

Vacation Rental Condominium. **Address:** 12000 Gulf Blvd 33706

TREASURE ISLAND BEACH RESORT 727/322-7022 **76**

Resort Hotel

Address: 10800 Gulf Blvd 33706 **Location:** Oceanfront. On SR 699, just n of Treasure Island Cswy. **Facility:** Located on the Gulf of Mexico, each guest room offers fantastic views of the water and beach as well as gorgeous sunsets. Rooms vary in size and are smartly decorated in soothing blue tones. 77 kitchen units, some two bedrooms. 6 stories, exterior corridors. *Bath:* shower only. **Terms:** check-in 4 pm. **Amenities:** safes. **Pool:** heated outdoor. **Activities:** hot tub, exercise room. **Guest Services:** valet and coin laundry.

SOME UNITS

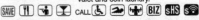

WESTWINDS WATERFRONT RESORT 727/363-4807 **78**

Vacation Rental Condominium. **Address:** 10265 Gulf Blvd 33706

WHERE TO EAT

CADDY'S ON THE BEACH 727/360-4993 **112**

Sandwiches Burgers. Casual Dining. **Address:** 9000 W Gulf Blvd 33706

THE FLORIDIAN 727/367-6662 **107**

Sandwiches. Quick Serve. **Address:** 230 107th Ave 33706

FOXY'S CAFE 727/363-3699 **108**

American. Casual Dining. **Address:** 160 107th Ave 33706

GATORS CAFE & SALOON 727/367-8951 **106**

Seafood. Casual Dining. **Address:** 12754 Kingfish Dr 33706

SLOPPY JOE'S ON THE BEACH 727/367-1600 **110**

American. Casual Dining. **Address:** 10650 Gulf Blvd 33706

TACO BUS 727/360-8226 **111**

Mexican. Quick Serve. **Address:** 9641 Gulf Blvd 33706

VIP LOUNGE & MEXICAN RESTAURANT 727/360-5062 **109**

Mexican. Casual Dining. **Address:** 10625 Gulf Blvd 33706

VENICE (F-8) pop. 20,748, elev. 13'

• Restaurants p. 366

As its name implies, Venice has a distinct Mediterranean ambience with Northern Italian influences. The city's location on the Gulf makes it a popular destination for boating, fishing and golfing. Visitors can comb the beaches for fossilized shark teeth, which range in size from one-eighth-inch to 3 inches.

Venice Area Chamber of Commerce: 597 Tamiami Trail S., Venice, FL 34285-2424. **Phone:** (941) 488-2236.

BEST WESTERN PLUS AMBASSADOR SUITES VENICE 941/480-9898

Hotel

AAA Benefit: Members save up to 15% and earn bonus points!

Address: 400 Commercial Ct 34292 **Location:** I-75 exit 193, just w on CR 765 (Jacaranda Blvd), then just n. **Facility:** 83 units. 3 stories, interior corridors. **Pool:** heated outdoor. **Activities:** exercise room. **Guest Services:** valet and coin laundry.

SAVE ECO CALL BIZ HS

FAIRFIELD INN & SUITES BY MARRIOTT VENICE 941/488-4343

Hotel

Fairfield **AAA Benefit:** Members save 5% or more!

Address: 2935 Executive Dr 34292 **Location:** I-75 exit 193, just w on CR 765 (Jacaranda Blvd), then just s; in Sarasota Interstate Business Center. **Facility:** 103 units. 4 stories, interior corridors. **Pool:** heated outdoor. **Activities:** hot tub, exercise room. **Guest Services:** valet and coin laundry. **Featured Amenity: breakfast buffet.**

SAVE CALL BIZ HS

HAMPTON INN & SUITES VENICE BAYSIDE/SOUTH SARASOTA 941/488-5900

SAVE Hotel. **Address:** 881 Venetia Bay Blvd 34292

AAA Benefit: Members save 5% or more!

HOTEL VENEZIA A RAMADA HOTEL 941/308-7700

Boutique Motel

Address: 425 US 41 Bypass N 34285 **Location:** 0.4 mi n of jct Venice Ave (CR 772). **Facility:** Just a short drive from the beach and downtown shopping and dining, this very modern property has stark white with tan tones in the public spaces. Room styles vary; all are decorated in earth tones. 146 units. 2 stories, exterior corridors. **Terms:** check-in 4 pm. **Amenities:** safes. **Pool:** heated outdoor. **Activities:** hot tub, picnic facilities, exercise room. **Guest Services:** valet and coin laundry.

SAVE BIZ HS / SOME UNITS

INN AT THE BEACH 941/484-8471

Motel. **Address:** 725 W Venice Ave 34285

VENICE BEACH VILLAS 941/488-1580

Extended Stay Motel. **Address:** 501 W Venice Ave 34285

WHERE TO EAT

BRITISH OPEN PUB & RESTAURANT 941/492-9227

British. Casual Dining. **Address:** 367 Jacaranda Blvd 34285

CAFE VENICE 941/484-1855

Continental. Casual Dining. **Address:** 116 Venice Ave 34285

CHINA TASTE 941/485-8887

Chinese. Quick Serve. **Address:** 329 Jacaranda Blvd 34292

THE CROW'S NEST MARINA RESTAURANT & TAVERN 941/484-9551

Seafood. Casual Dining. **Address:** 1968 Tarpon Center Dr 34285

MI PUEBLO EL RESTAURANTE MEXICANO & CANTINA 941/486-0005

Mexican. Casual Dining. **Address:** 530 US 41 Bypass S 34285

MYAKKA RIVER OYSTER BAR 941/423-9616

Seafood. Casual Dining. **Address:** 121 Playmore Dr 34293

NTINOS FAMILY RESTAURANT & PIZZERIA 941/485-4474

Italian. Casual Dining. **Address:** 660 S Tamiami Tr 34285

SHARKY'S ON THE PIER 941/488-1456

Seafood Casual Dining $10-$29

AAA Inspector Notes: Fish mounted on the walls and maritime decorations convey a fitting theme in this busy, gulf-front restaurant. Market-fresh fish can be broiled, blackened, grilled or fried. The menu features Gulf shrimp, macadamia grouper, baby back ribs, filet mignon and New York strip. Outside dining on their deck features a separate menu and a tiki bar. The beach is known for shark tooth gathering, sun bathing and fishing from the pier which is located on-site. **Features:** full bar, patio dining. **Address:** 1600 S Harbor Dr 34285 **Location:** On US 41 business route, 0.5 mi w via Venice Ave, 2 mi s; at Venice Fishing Pier. L D

SONNY'S REAL PIT BAR-B-Q 941/484-1327

Barbecue. Casual Dining. **Address:** 406 Venice Bypass 34292

TOMATILLO'S FRESH MEX 941/412-4832

Mexican. Quick Serve. **Address:** 339 Commercial Ct 34292

VERO BEACH (H-6) pop. 15,220, elev. 17'

McKee Botanical Garden, 350 US 1, features orchids, water lilies, palm trees and dense tropical vegetation on the remaining 18 acres of an 80-acre jungle garden created in the 1930s by William Lyman Phillips for northern industrialist Arthur McKee. It was one of Florida's first public gardens; phone (772) 794-0601.

The Vero Beach Museum of Art, 3001 Riverside Park Dr., is home to several galleries focusing on American and International artists; phone (772) 231-0707.

Sebastian Inlet State Park *(see Recreation Areas Chart)*, 15 miles north on SR A1A, preserves more than 900 acres of barrier island for recreation and wildlife protection. In addition to 3 miles of beach for swimming, surfing and snorkeling, the park has nature trails and a Volksport walking trail. Interpretive programs and two museums also are available; phone (321) 984-4852.

Indian River County Chamber of Commerce: 1216 21st St., Vero Beach, FL 32960. **Phone:** (772) 567-3491.

MCLARTY TREASURE MUSEUM, 13 mi. n. on SR A1A, is at the s. end of Sebastian Inlet State Park at 13180 SR A1A. The museum's historical displays include artifacts and a diorama of the 1715 *Spanish Plate Fleet* and the shipwreck salvors' camp, including salvage materials. "The Queens Jewels and the 1715 Fleet," an A&E Channel production, tells the story of the ill-fated journey that was ended by a hurricane off the Florida coast, and the ongoing salvaging operations to recover the treasure. **Time:** Allow 1 hour minimum. **Hours:** Daily 10-4. Last show begins 45 minutes before closing. Closed major holidays. **Cost:** $2; free (ages 0-5). **Phone:** (772) 589-2147.

THE CARIBBEAN COURT BOUTIQUE HOTEL 772/231-7211

Boutique Hotel. **Address:** 1601 S Ocean Dr 32963

COSTA D' ESTE BEACH RESORT & SPA 772/562-9919

Boutique Resort Hotel

Address: 3244 Ocean Dr 32963 **Location:** Oceanfront. I-95 exit 147 (SR 60), 8.7 mi e to Indian River Blvd, 1 mi n to Merril P Barber Bridge/SR 60, 1.7 mi e to Ocean Dr, then just s. **Facility:** This hotel is serenely situated on the Atlantic Ocean. The driveway features interesting architectural elements and an attractive fountain. 94 units. 5 stories, interior corridors. **Parking:** on-site (fee) and valet. **Terms:** check-in 4 pm. **Amenities:** safes. **Dining:** The Wave Kitchen & Bar, see separate listing. **Pool:** heated outdoor. **Activities:** hot tub, steamroom, cabanas, self-propelled boats, snorkeling, bicycles, exercise room, spa. **Guest Services:** valet laundry. **Featured Amenity: full hot breakfast.**

SAVE CALL BIZ SHS / SOME UNITS

COUNTRY INN & SUITES BY RADISSON, VERO BEACH I-95 772/257-0252

Hotel. **Address:** 9330 19th Ln 32966

DISNEY'S VERO BEACH RESORT 407/939-7540

Resort Hotel. **Address:** 9250 Island Grove Terrace 32963

HAMPTON INN VERO BEACH 772/770-4299

Hotel. **Address:** 9350 19th Ln 32966

AAA Benefit: Members save 5% or more!

KIMPTON VERO BEACH HOTEL & SPA 772/231-5666

Boutique Hotel

Address: 3500 Ocean Dr 32963 **Location:** Oceanfront. On Ocean Dr, just n of SR 60. **Facility:** The oceanfront property has set the bar very high for luxury in the area! The Atlantic Ocean serves as the backdrop to paradise during your relaxing stay. Watch a beautiful sunrise and enjoy the surf. 111 units, some two bedrooms and kitchens. 5 stories, interior/exterior corridors. **Parking:** valet only. **Terms:** check-in 4 pm. **Amenities:** safes. **Dining:** 2 restaurants. **Pool:** heated outdoor. **Activities:** sauna, hot tub, self-propelled boats, snorkeling, recreation programs, bicycles, exercise room, spa. **Guest Services:** valet laundry.

   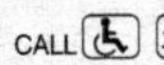 CALL  

 / SOME UNITS

WHERE TO EAT

AMERICAN ICON BREWERY 772/934-4266

American. Casual Dining. **Address:** 1133 19th Pl 32960

BIG APPLE PIZZA & PASTA 772/569-8900

Italian Pizza. Casual Dining. **Address:** 5970 20th St 32966

DAGWOOD'S DELI & SUB SHOP 772/778-1900

Deli Sandwiches. Quick Serve. **Address:** 835 17th St 32960

FISHACK 772/770-0977

Seafood. Casual Dining. **Address:** 1931 Old Dixie Hwy 32960

THE LEMON TREE RESTAURANT 772/231-0858

American. Casual Dining. **Address:** 3125 Ocean Dr 32963

MAISON MARTINIQUE RESTAURANT 772/231-7299

New American. Fine Dining. **Address:** 1603 S Ocean Dr 32963

MR. MANATEE'S 772/569-9151

Seafood. Casual Dining. **Address:** 30 Royal Palm Pointe 32960

MULLIGAN'S BEACH HOUSE BAR & GRILL 772/492-6744

American. Casual Dining. **Address:** 1025 Beachland Blvd 32963

OCEAN GRILL 772/231-5409

Steak Seafood Fine Dining $10-$39

AAA Inspector Notes: *Historic.* Built by entrepreneur Waldo Sexton, this restaurant has been a staple in the community since 1941. Nestled on a sandy beach of the Atlantic Ocean, a rustic appeal can be found in the all-wood facade and interior where windows afford scenic views of the rolling waves of the ocean. The menu features a variety of seafood, steak and chicken dishes. The seafood is as fresh as it comes and the steaks are all dry-aged for optimal tenderness. **Features:** full bar. **Address:** 1050 Sexton Plaza 32963 **Location:** E of SR A1A, at end of SR 60. L D CALL 

RIVERSIDE CAFE 772/234-5550

Seafood Sandwiches. Casual Dining. **Address:** 3341 Bridge Plaza Dr 32963

SONNY'S REAL PIT BAR-B-Q 772/770-4190

Barbecue. Casual Dining. **Address:** 5001 20th St 32960

TOOJAY'S GOURMET DELI 772/569-6070

American. Casual Dining. **Address:** 555 21st St 32960

THE WAVE KITCHEN & BAR 772/410-0100

New American. Fine Dining. **Address:** 3244 Ocean Dr 32963

WALDO

BEST WESTERN WALDO INN & SUITES 352/468-2500

Hotel

 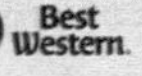

AAA Benefit: Members save up to 15% and earn bonus points!

Address: 17230 NE US 301 32694 **Location:** Jct NE SR 24 and US 301; 2.8 mi n. **Facility:** 51 units. 2 stories, interior corridors. **Terms:** check-in 4 pm. **Amenities:** safes. **Pool:** outdoor. **Activities:** exercise room. **Guest Services:** coin laundry. **Featured Amenity: breakfast buffet.**

 CALL  

/ SOME UNITS

WEIRSDALE (C-9) elev. 98'

THE GRAND OAKS MUSEUM, 3000 Marion County Rd., is located on a 400-acre equestrian-themed resort tucked into the rolling hills of Florida's horse breeding and training country. The museum displays a painstakingly curated collection of more than 160 restored antique carriages, including an 1850 dress chariot owned by Emperor Franz Josef of Austria; guests can also learn about equine history. The grounds include trails, arenas, an RV park and cottages. Grand Oaks hosts more than 40 events and horse shows featuring hunters, jumpers and dressage each year. Carriage and horseback rides and carriage driving lessons are available.

Note: The museum is temporarily closed. Renovations are scheduled to be completed by 2019; phone ahead for updates. **Phone:** (352) 750-5500 or (866) 500-2237.

WESLEY CHAPEL pop. 44,092

- **Restaurants p. 368**
- **Part of Tampa area — see map p. 313**

BEST WESTERN WESLEY CHAPEL 813/345-2000

Hotel

 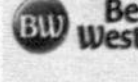

AAA Benefit: Members save up to 15% and earn bonus points!

Address: 5639 Oakley Blvd 33544 **Location:** I-75 exit 279, just w on SR 54, then just n. **Facility:** 73 units. 3 stories, interior corridors. **Amenities:** safes. **Pool:** outdoor. **Activities:** exercise room. **Guest Services:** valet and coin laundry. **Featured Amenity: breakfast buffet.**

 CALL  

HAMPTON INN & SUITES TAMPA/WESLEY CHAPEL
813/973-2288

SAVE Hotel. **Address:** 2740 Cypress Ridge Blvd 33544

AAA Benefit: Members save 5% or more!

HILTON GARDEN INN TAMPA-WESLEY CHAPEL
813/591-6907

Hotel. **Address:** 26640 Silver Maple Pkwy 33544

HOLIDAY INN EXPRESS TAMPA NORTH WESLEY CHAPEL
813/803-7899

Hotel. **Address:** 2775 Cypress Ridge Blvd 33544

WHERE TO EAT

BURGER MONGER 813/991-4242

Burgers. Quick Serve. **Address:** 1656 Bruce B Downs Blvd 33544

CANTINA LAREDO 813/907-3068

Mexican. Casual Dining. **Address:** 2000 Piazza Ave 33543

SONNY'S REAL PIT BAR-B-Q 813/994-8989

Barbecue. Casual Dining. **Address:** 5324 Bruce B Downs Blvd (CR 581) 33543

VALLARTA'S RESTAURANTE MEXICANO 813/907-5161

Mexican. Casual Dining. **Address:** 5335 Village Market 33543

WEST MELBOURNE pop. 18,355

• Hotels & Restaurants map & index p. 148

COURTYARD BY MARRIOTT MELBOURNE WEST
321/724-6400 19

COURTYARD **AAA Benefit:** Members save 5% or more!

Address: 2101 W New Haven Ave 32904 **Location:** I-95 exit 180, 3.1 mi e on US 192. **Facility:** 146 units. 3 stories, interior corridors. **Pool:** heated outdoor. **Activities:** exercise room. **Guest Services:** valet and coin laundry, boarding pass kiosk. **Featured Amenity:** full hot breakfast.

/ SOME UNITS

FAIRFIELD INN & SUITES BY MARRIOTT MELBOURNE PALM BAY/VIERA
321/722-2220 21

Fairfield **AAA Benefit:** Members save 5% or more!

Address: 4355 W New Haven Ave 32904 **Location:** I-95 exit 180, just e on US 192. **Facility:** 83 units. 4 stories, interior corridors. **Pool:** heated outdoor. **Activities:** exercise room. **Guest Services:** valet and coin laundry. **Featured Amenity:** full hot breakfast.

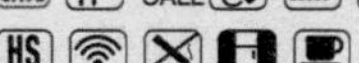

/ SOME UNITS

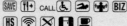

HAMPTON INN & SUITES BY HILTON WEST MELBOURNE-PALM BAY ROAD
321/372-7445 23

SAVE Hotel. **Address:** 4520 Durham Dr 32904

AAA Benefit: Members save 5% or more!

HAMPTON INN MELBOURNE 321/956-6200 20

SAVE Hotel. **Address:** 194 Coastal Ln 32904

AAA Benefit: Members save 5% or more!

HOLIDAY INN EXPRESS & SUITES 321/345-4186 22

Hotel. **Address:** 2255 Coastal Ln 32904

WILDWOOD pop. 6,709

COMFORT INN & SUITES WILDWOOD–THE VILLAGES
352/748-0507

Hotel

Address: 1224 S Main St 34785 **Location:** Florida Tpke exit 304, just n on US 301. **Facility:** 62 units. 3 stories, interior corridors. **Amenities:** safes. **Pool:** heated outdoor. **Activities:** exercise room. **Guest Services:** coin laundry. **Featured Amenity: full hot breakfast.**

SAVE ECO CALL BIZ HS / SOME UNITS

DAYS INN WILDWOOD 352/748-7766

Motel. **Address:** 551 E SR 44 34785

WINTER GARDEN pop. 34,568

• Hotels & Restaurants map & index p. 188, 197, 202

• Part of Orlando area — see map p. 2

THE GROVE RESORT ORLANDO 407/545-7500 82

Hotel

Address: 14501 Grove Resort Ave 34787 **Location:** Waterfront. Jct SR 429 and US 192; 3.3 mi w, then just n on Avalon Rd. **Facility:** 565 kitchen units, some two and three bedrooms. 7 stories, interior corridors. **Parking:** on-site (fee). **Terms:** check-in 4 pm. **Amenities:** safes. **Dining:** 2 restaurants, also, Valencia Restaurant, see separate listing. **Pool:** heated outdoor. **Activities:** sauna, hot tub, cabanas, self-propelled boats, boat dock, fishing, recreation programs, exercise room, spa. **Guest Services:** complimentary laundry.

SAVE CALL BIZ

SPRINGHILL SUITES BY MARRIOTT ORLANDO AT FLAMINGO CROSSINGS
407/507-1200 12

Hotel

SPRINGHILL SUITES MARRIOTT **AAA Benefit:** Members save 5% or more!

Address: 13279 Flamingo Crossings Blvd 34787 **Location:** SR 429 exit 8, just n. **Facility:** 248 units. 6 stories, interior corridors. **Terms:** check-in 4 pm. **Pool:** heated outdoor. **Activities:** hot tub, picnic facilities, exercise room. **Guest Services:** valet and coin laundry, area transportation. **Featured Amenity:** breakfast buffet.

SAVE CALL

(See maps & indexes p. 188, 197, 202.)

TOWNEPLACE SUITES BY MARRIOTT ORLANDO AT FLAMINGO CROSSINGS® TOWN CENTER/WESTERN ENTRANCE (407)507-1300 13

Extended Stay Hotel

AAA Benefit: Members save 5% or more!

Address: 13295 Flamingo Crossings Blvd 34787 **Location:** SR 429 exit 8, just n. **Facility:** 250 efficiency kitchen units, some two bedrooms. 6 stories, interior corridors. **Terms:** check-in 4 pm, cancellation fee imposed. **Pool:** heated outdoor. **Activities:** hot tub, picnic facilities, exercise room. **Guest Services:** valet and coin laundry, area transportation. **Featured Amenity: breakfast buffet.**

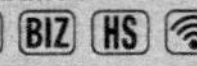

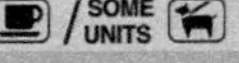

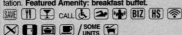

TOWNEPLACE SUITES BY MARRIOTT

Extended stay property, located less than a mile from the western entrance to Walt Disney World®.

WHERE TO EAT

4 LOCOS TACOS 407/554-2312 (140)

Mexican. Casual Dining. **Address:** 360 W Plant St 34787

4 RIVERS SMOKEHOUSE 407/474-8377

Barbecue. Quick Serve. **Address:** 1047 S Dillard St 34787

BONEFISH GRILL 407/654-6093

Seafood. Fine Dining. **Address:** 3279 Daniels Rd, Suite 108 34787

THE CHEF'S TABLE AT THE EDGEWATER AND TASTING ROOM 407/230-4837 (139)

American. Casual Dining. **Address:** 99 W Plant St 34777

THAI BLOSSOM RESTAURANT 407/905-9917 (138)

Thai. Casual Dining. **Address:** 99 W Plant St 34787

TIJUANA FLATS 407/656-4855

Tex-Mex. Quick Serve. **Address:** 13770 W Colonial Dr 34787

VALENCIA RESTAURANT 407/545-7500 (44)

Continental. Casual Dining. **Address:** 14501 Grove Resort Ave 34787

WINTER HAVEN (E-9) pop. 33,874, elev. 164'

• **Restaurants p. 370**

Winter Haven is surrounded by more than 40 freshwater lakes, many of which are joined by canals to form a navigable chain of lakes ideal for family recreation and water sports such as boating, fishing and skiing.

Greater Winter Haven Chamber of Commerce: 401 Ave. B N.W., Winter Haven, FL 33881. **Phone:** (863) 293-2138.

LEGOLAND FLORIDA RESORT, 4 mi. w. on SR 540 at jct. US 27 and SR 540 at 1 LEGOLAND Way, offers themed zones on 150 acres with more than 50 family-oriented interactive attractions, shows and rides, including four rollercoasters and a botanical garden. Some 65 million LEGO bricks were used in the construction of the zones, including Miniland USA, which features such miniaturized cities and places as Las Vegas; Washington, D.C.; New York City; Florida, featuring Daytona International Speedway and Kennedy Space Center.

Other zones include the toddler-oriented DUPLO Valley; Fun Town, featuring a 4D theater and carousel; Star Wars: The Force Awakens MINILAND Model Display; medieval-themed LEGO Kingdoms; LEGO Technic, featuring the Great LEGO Race VR coaster and AQUAZONE Wave Racers; Imagination Zone, where guests can build cars and robots from LEGO bricks; Pirates' Cove, a water stunt show; Land of Adventure, where riders take adventurous journeys through a prehistoric jungle and ancient Egypt; LEGO City, a child-sized "town" where kids can drive a LEGO car and receive a LEGOLAND Florida driver's license; Heartlake City, an area based on LEGO Friends. LEGO NINJAGO. THE LEGO® MOVIE™ WORLD is the newest expansion featuring three new rides and numerous attractions, all inspired by the characters and themes of the worldwide blockbuster THE LEGO® MOVIE™ and the exciting big-screen animated adventure sequel THE LEGO® MOVIE™ 2: The Second Part.

Hours: Opens daily at 10. Closing times vary; check website to confirm schedule. **Cost:** 1 day $99.99; 2 days $119.99; Free (ages 0-2). Combination ticket with LEGOLAND Florida Water Park 1 day $124.99; 2 days $144.99; Free (ages 0-2). **Parking:** Standard $23. **Phone:** (877) 350-5346.

LEGOLAND Florida Water Park is 4 mi. w. on SR 540 at jct. US 27 and SR 540 at 1 LEGOLAND Way. Designed to appeal to younger children, the water park's LEGO-themed offerings include a gentle wave pool and several slides. Build-A-Raft River is a lazy river with soft LEGO bricks that kids can grab from the water and attach to their inner-tube rafts as they float along. DUPLO Splash Safari and Joker Soaker are interactive water playgrounds. Water slides include Splash Out, which has three slides, including one with a 60-foot drop, and Twin Chasers, a 375-foot-long enclosed waterslide.

Hours: Opens daily at 10:30, Mar.-Oct. Closing times vary; check website to confirm schedule. **Cost:** (includes LEGOLAND Florida Resort) $124.99 (1 day); $144.99 (2 days); Free (ages 0-2). **Phone:** (877) 350-5346.

COURTYARD BY MARRIOTT WINTER HAVEN 863/292-3000

SAVE Hotel. **Address:** 6225 Cypress Gardens Blvd SE 33884

AAA Benefit: Members save 5% or more!

HAMPTON INN WINTER HAVEN 863/299-9251

SAVE Hotel. **Address:** 202 Cypress Gardens Blvd 33880

AAA Benefit: Members save 5% or more!

HOLIDAY INN OF WINTER HAVEN 863/292-2100

Hotel. **Address:** 200 Cypress Gardens Blvd 33880

LEGOLAND FLORIDA RESORT 863/551-3600

Contemporary Resort Hotel

Address: One LEGOLAND Way 33884 **Location:** Waterfront. 2.7 mi e of jct US 17 on SR 540 (Cypress Gardens Blvd). **Facility:** Geared toward children, this resort is LEGO themed. Kids have their own bunk bed area while adults can relax in their own space. The pirate-, adventure, and kingdom-themed rooms are popular. 152 two-bedroom units. 5 stories, interior corridors. **Parking:** on-site and valet. **Terms:** check-in 4 pm. **Amenities:** safes. **Dining:** 2 restaurants, entertainment. **Pool:** heated outdoor. **Activities:** recreation programs, kids club, picnic facilities, trails. **Featured Amenity: full hot breakfast.**

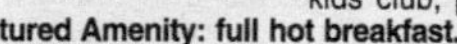
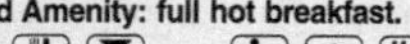

SAVE CALL HS / SOME UNITS

WHERE TO EAT

BUFFET CITY 863/292-9898

Japanese Sushi. Quick Serve. **Address:** 810 Cypress Gardens Blvd 33880

CRISPERS 863/401-8899

Sandwiches Soup. Quick Serve. **Address:** 416 Citi Centre St 33880

SCHACK'S BAR-B-QUE 863/324-1537

Barbecue. Casual Dining. **Address:** 3000 Cypress Gardens Rd 33884

SONNY'S REAL PIT BAR-B-Q 863/293-4744

Barbecue. Casual Dining. **Address:** 4600 Recker Hwy 33880

WINTER PARK (D-10) pop. 27,852, elev. 96'

• **Hotels & Restaurants map & index p. 188, 195**
• **Part of Orlando area — see map p. 2**

Moss-draped oaks line the residential streets of Winter Park, a community of beautiful homes and picturesque lakes. The campus of Rollins College features brick streets and Mediterranean-style buildings on the shores of Lake Virginia; maps for self-guiding tours are available. The small, private college is at the foot of Park Avenue, a popular shopping district with a varied selection of upscale boutiques, galleries and restaurants.

Hannibal Square Heritage Center, 642 W. New England Ave., recounts the settlement of Winter Park's African-American community with oral histories, photographs, art displays and artifacts; phone (407) 539-2680.

Winter Park Chamber of Commerce: 151 W. Lyman Ave., Winter Park, FL 32789. **Phone:** (407) 644-8281 or (877) 972-4282.

Shopping: On Saturday mornings, make a beeline to the Winter Park Farmers Market, 200 W. New England Ave., for fresh local produce, pastries, plants and cheeses. Head one block east to Park Avenue for an assortment of shops, galleries and restaurants with a European feel.

Winter Park Village is just a short drive from Park Avenue and features shops such as LOFT, Pier I Imports and White House Black Market, along with several restaurants and a 20-screen movie theater.

ALBIN POLASEK MUSEUM AND SCULPTURE GARDENS is 1.3 mi. e. of US 17/92 at 633 Osceola Ave. (SR 426). Three galleries and lush gardens on the shores of Lake Osceola display the sculptures and paintings of the Czech-American artist. Noteworthy is a wooden nativity Polasek created at age 15. Tours provide insight into how the sculptor lived and worked. **Hours:** Tues.-Sat. 10-4, Sun. 1-4. Guided tours depart Tues.-Sat. at 10:30, 11:45, 1:30 and 3; Sun. at 1:30 and 3. Closed major holidays. **Cost:** $5; $4 (ages 60+); $3 (students with ID); free (ages 0-12). **Phone:** (407) 647-6294.

GT Winter Park, 10

GEM **THE CHARLES HOSMER MORSE MUSEUM OF AMERICAN ART,** 445 N. Park Ave., contains a comprehensive collection of works by Louis Comfort Tiffany, a celebrated and influential designer of the late 19th and early 20th century. In addition to the brilliant jewel-toned leaded-glass lamps and windows the talented artist is best known for, visitors will find *objets d'art* such as Tiffany jewelry exquisitely handcrafted of enamel and semiprecious gems circa 1905-20, and detailed drawings and oil paintings created by Tiffany. The collection also features blown-glass pieces including vases in the forms of pansies, lilies and carnations as well as wine and liqueur glasses, all in resplendent shades of violet, gold, ruby, aqua and rose.

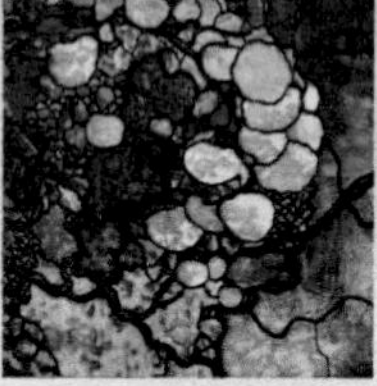

A highlight is the Byzantine-Romanesque chapel Tiffany designed for the 1893 World's Columbian Exposition in Chicago, a masterpiece that includes a baptistery, a 1,000-pound cross-shaped chandelier, 16 mosaic columns, a mosaic altar and stained-glass windows.

Many of the stained-glass windows on exhibit were installed at Laurelton Hall, Tiffany's country estate built on Long Island 1902-05. The estate burned down in 1957, but many pieces were rescued from the ruins by Hugh and Jeannette McKean, the Winter Park couple who assembled the Morse collection. Painstakingly restored to their original splendor, these treasures are on display in the museum's Laurelton Hall wing.

(See maps & indexes p. 188, 195.)

The exhibit features pieces that provide insight into the lifestyle of the wealthy in the early 20th century, including partially re-created rooms from Laurelton Hall that include many original pieces. The re-created dining room holds an original rug patterned with dark blue medallions as well as two replicas that visitors may walk on. The room also includes original leaded-glass windows in a wisteria design that features stunning shades of purple and green.

In another large room, the striking Daffodil Terrace contains eight 11-foot-tall columns topped with yellow and green glass daffodils that support a coffered ceiling under which Tiffany and his guests may have enjoyed a cool spring breeze. A cell phone audio tour of Laurelton Hall is available.

The museum's permanent collection also includes late 19th- and 20th-century Arts and Crafts and Art Nouveau furnishings, American art pottery, American paintings and decorative art.

Flash photography, selfie sticks, backpacks, large bags and large strollers are not permitted in the building. **Time:** Allow 1 hour minimum. **Hours:** Tues.-Sat. 9:30-4 (also Fri. 4-8, Nov.-Apr., Easter weekend, July 4 and Christmas Eve), Sun. 1-4. Guided tours depart Tues.-Thurs. at 11 and 2:30. **Cost:** $6; $5 (ages 60+); $1 (students with ID); free (ages 0-11 and to all Fri. 4-8, Nov.-Apr., Easter, July 4 and Christmas Eve). **Phone:** (407) 645-5311. GT Winter Park, 10

CORNELL FINE ARTS MUSEUM, 1000 Holt Ave. at Lake Virginia on the Rollins College campus, displays permanent and changing exhibits of American and European works of art ranging from the Renaissance to contemporary. **Time:** Allow 1 hour minimum. **Hours:** Tues.-Fri. 10-4 (also Tues. 4-7), Sat.-Sun. noon-5. Guided tours depart Sat. at 1. Closed major holidays and between exhibitions. **Cost:** Free. **Phone:** (407) 646-2526. GT Winter Park, 10

SCENIC BOAT TOURS, leaving from the foot of E. Morse Blvd., provide narrated 1-hour cruises aboard an 18-passenger pontoon boat past many of Winter Park's opulent lakeside estates and landmarks. **Time:** Allow 1 hour, 30 minutes minimum. **Hours:** Departures daily on the hour 10-4. Closed Christmas. **Cost:** Fare $14; $7 (ages 2-11). Cash or check only. **Phone:** (407) 644-4056. GT Winter Park, 10

Save on travel, shopping and more: AAA.com/discounts

THE ALFOND INN AT ROLLINS 407/998-8090 1

Boutique Hotel

Address: 300 E New England Ave 32789 **Location:** I-4 exit 87 (Fairbanks Ave), 2 mi e to Park Ave, just n to New England Ave, then just e. Winter Park, 10. **Facility:** Public areas are striking and feature hand-picked artwork showcasing various artists. Elegant rooms with vibrant colors, custom furnishings and cozy bedding make it easy to rest at the end of the day. 112 units. 5 stories, interior corridors. **Parking:** valet only. **Terms:** check-in 4 pm. **Amenities:** safes. **Pool:** heated outdoor. **Activities:** lawn sports, exercise room, massage. **Guest Services:** valet laundry.

SAVE CALL BIZ / SOME UNITS

WHERE TO EAT

310 PARK SOUTH 407/647-7277 18
New American. Casual Dining. **Address:** 310 S Park Ave 32789

4 RIVERS SMOKEHOUSE 407/474-8377
Barbecue. Casual Dining. **Address:** 2103 W Fairbanks Ave 32789

ARMANDO'S CUCINA ITALIANA & PIZZERIA 407/951-8930 20
Italian. Casual Dining. **Address:** 463 W New England Ave 32789

BOARDWALK PIZZA 407/671-6880 135
Italian. Casual Dining. **Address:** 5419 Lake Howell Rd 32792

BOSPHOROUS TURKISH CUISINE 407/644-8609 13
Turkish. Casual Dining. **Address:** 108 S Park Ave 32789

THE BRIARPATCH 407/628-8651 10
American. Casual Dining. **Address:** 252 N Park Ave 32789

BRIO TUSCAN GRILLE 407/622-5611 6
Italian. Fine Dining. **Address:** 480 N Orlando Ave 32789

BUBBALOU'S BODACIOUS BAR-B-QUE 407/628-1212
Barbecue. Casual Dining. **Address:** 1471 Lee Rd 32789

BULLA GASTROBAR 321/214-6120 19
Spanish Small Plates. Gastropub. **Address:** 110 S Orlando Ave 32789

CAFE DE FRANCE 407/647-1869 25
French. Fine Dining. **Address:** 526 S Park Ave 32789

THE CHEESECAKE FACTORY 407/644-4220 4
International. Casual Dining. **Address:** 520 N Orlando Ave, Suite 110 32789

COCINA 214 407/790-7997 14
Tex-Mex. Fine Dining. **Address:** 151 E Welbourne Ave 32789

THE COOP 407/843-2667 15
Southern Comfort Food. Quick Serve. **Address:** 610 W Morse Blvd 32789

CRISPERS 407/622-4403
Sandwiches Soup. Quick Serve. **Address:** 480 N Orlando Ave 32789

(See maps & indexes p. 188, 195.)

CROISSANT GOURMET 407/622-7753 12

Breads/Pastries Breakfast. Quick Serve. **Address:** 120 E Morse Blvd 32789

ETHOS VEGAN KITCHEN INC 407/228-3898 29

Vegan. Casual Dining. **Address:** 601-B S New York Ave 32789

FLEMING'S PRIME STEAKHOUSE & WINE BAR 407/699-9463 2

Steak. Fine Dining. **Address:** 933 N Orlando Ave 32789

THE GLASS KNIFE 407/500-2253 24

Desserts. Casual Dining. **Address:** 276 S Orlando Ave 32789

HILLSTONE 407/740-4005 22

American. Fine Dining. **Address:** 215 S Orlando Ave 32789

LUMA ON PARK 407/599-4111 17

New American. Fine Dining. **Address:** 290 S Park Ave 32789

ORCHID THAI CUISINE 407/331-1400 9

Thai. Fine Dining. **Address:** 305 N Park Ave 32789

PANNULLO'S ITALIAN RESTAURANT 407/629-7270 16

Italian. Casual Dining. **Address:** 216 S Park Ave 32789

PARK AVENUE PIZZA 407/599-9199 21

Italian Pizza. Quick Serve. **Address:** 119 E Lyman Ave 32789

P.F. CHANG'S CHINA BISTRO 407/622-0188 8

Chinese. Fine Dining. **Address:** 436 N Orlando Ave 32789

PIZZERIA VALDIANO 407/628-5333 7

Pizza. Quick Serve. **Address:** 510 N Orlando Ave, Suite 103 32789

POWER HOUSE CAFE 407/645-3616 23

Sandwiches. Quick Serve. **Address:** 111 E Lyman Ave 32789

PRATO 407/262-0050 11

Italian. Casual Dining. **Address:** 124 N Park Ave 32789

THE RAVENOUS PIG 407/628-2333 30

American. Fine Dining. **Address:** 565 W Fairbanks Ave 32789

RUTH'S CHRIS STEAK HOUSE 407/622-2444 3

Steak. Fine Dining. **Address:** 610 N Orlando Ave 32789

SCRATCH 407/325-5165 27

Small Plates. Fine Dining. **Address:** 223 W Fairbanks Ave 32789

SONNY'S REAL PIT BAR-B-Q 407/671-2002

Barbecue. Casual Dining. **Address:** 3390 University Blvd 32792

THAI PLACE 407/644-8449 5

Thai. Casual Dining. **Address:** 501 N Orlando Ave, Suite 319 32789

TIBBY'S NEW ORLEANS KITCHEN 407/672-5753 1

Cajun. Casual Dining. **Address:** 2203 Aloma Ave 32792

TIJUANA FLATS

Tex-Mex. Quick Serve.

LOCATIONS:

Address: 1955 Aloma Ave 32789 **Phone:** 407/679-2132

Address: 7608 University Blvd 32792 **Phone:** 407/673-2456

UMI 407/960-3993 26

Japanese Fusion. Casual Dining. **Address:** 525 S Park Ave 32789

YULEE pop. 11,491

• Part of Jacksonville area — see map p. 84

BEST WESTERN PLUS FIRST COAST INN & SUITES 904/225-0182

Hotel

AAA Benefit: Members save up to 15% and earn bonus points!

Address: 462577 SR 200 32097 **Location:** I-95 exit 373 (SR 200/A1A), just e. **Facility:** 62 units. 3 stories, interior corridors. **Pool:** outdoor. **Activities:** hot tub, exercise room. **Guest Services:** coin laundry. **Featured Amenity: breakfast buffet.**

CALL

/ SOME UNITS

COMFORT INN 904/225-2600

Hotel. **Address:** 76043 Sidney Pl 32097

HOLIDAY INN EXPRESS & SUITES JACKSONVILLE NORTH - FERNANDINA 904/849-0200

Hotel. **Address:** 76071 Sidney Pl 32097

WHERE TO EAT

OLIVE COVE ITALIAN KITCHEN 904/849-1688

Italian Pizza. Casual Dining. **Address:** 463646 SR 200 32097

WILLIE JEWELL'S OLD SCHOOL BAR-B-Q 904/849-1298

Barbecue. Quick Serve. **Address:** 463155 SR 200 32097

ZEPHYRHILLS pop. 13,288

• Part of Tampa area — see map p. 313

MICROTEL INN & SUITES BY WYNDHAM ZEPHYRHILLS 813/783-2211

Hotel. **Address:** 7839 Gall Blvd 33541

WHERE TO EAT

CONEY ISLAND DRIVE-INN 813/602-8396

American. Quick Serve. **Address:** 5327 Gall Blvd 33542

SONNY'S REAL PIT BAR-B-Q 813/782-4272

Barbecue. Casual Dining. **Address:** 6606 Gall Blvd 33542

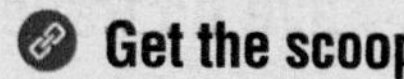

from AAA inspectors:

AAA.com/travelguides/restaurants

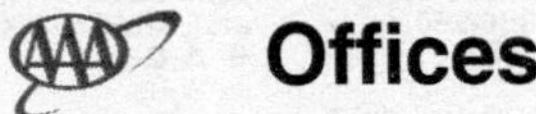

Offices

Main office listings are shown in **BOLD TYPE** and toll-free member service numbers appear in *ITALIC TYPE*.
All are closed Saturdays, Sundays and holidays unless otherwise indicated.
The addresses, phone numbers and hours for any AAA/CAA office are subject to change.
The type of service provided is designated below the name of the city where the office is located:

- ✚ Auto travel services, including books and maps, and on-demand TripTik® routings.
- ● Auto travel services, including selected books and maps, and on-demand TripTik® routings.
- ■ Books/maps only, no marked maps or on-demand TripTik® routings.
- ▲ Travel Agency Services, cruise, tour, air, car and rail reservations; domestic and international hotel reservations; passport photo services; international and domestic travel guides and maps; travel money products; and International Driving Permits. In addition, assistance with travel related insurance products including trip cancellation, travel accident, lost luggage, trip delay and assistance products.
- ✪ Insurance services provided. If only this icon appears, only insurance services are provided at that office.
- ☾ Car Care Plus Facility provides car care services.
- ▣ Electric vehicle charging station on premises.

AAA NATIONAL OFFICE: 1000 AAA DRIVE, HEATHROW, FLORIDA 32746-5063, (407) 444-7000

CENTRAL FLORIDA

BELLEAIR BLUFFS—AUTO CLUB GROUP - SOUTHERN REGION, 100 N INDIAN ROCKS RD, 33770. WEEKDAYS (M-F) 8:30-5:30. (727) 584-7678 ✚ ▲ ✪

BRADENTON—AUTO CLUB GROUP - SOUTHERN REGION, 6210 MANATEE AVE W, 34209. WEEKDAYS (M-F) 8:30-5:30. (941) 798-2221 ✚ ▲ ✪

BRANDON—AUTO CLUB GROUP - SOUTHERN REGION, 415 W ROBERTSON ST, 33511. WEEKDAYS (M-F) 8:30-5:30. (813) 681-5761 ✚ ▲ ✪

CLEARWATER—AUTO CLUB GROUP - SOUTHERN REGION, 2170 RAINBOW DR, 33765. WEEKDAYS (M-F) 8:30-5:30. (727) 448-2600 ✚ ▲ ✪

CLERMONT—AUTO CLUB GROUP - SOUTHERN REGION, 12340 ROPER BLVD, 34711. WEEKDAYS (M-F) 8:30-5:30. (352) 394-5503 ✪

DAYTONA BEACH—AUTO CLUB GROUP - SOUTHERN REGION, 2525 INT'L SPEEDWAY BLVD, 32114. WEEKDAYS (M-F) 8:30-5:30. (386) 252-0531 ✚ ▲ ✪

GAINESVILLE—AUTO CLUB GROUP - SOUTHERN REGION, 1201 NW 13TH ST, 32601. WEEKDAYS (M-F) 8:30-5:30. (352) 373-7801 ✚ ▲ ✪

HEATHROW—AUTO CLUB GROUP - SOUTHERN REGION, 1000 AAA DR #28, 32746. WEEKDAYS (M-F) 8:30-5:30. (407) 444-4240 ✚ ▲ ✪ ▣

JACKSONVILLE—AUTO CLUB GROUP - SOUTHERN REGION, 4320 DEERWOOD LK PKY #109, 32216. WEEKDAYS (M-F) 8:30-5:30. (904) 565-7722 ✚ ▲ ✪

LAKELAND—AUTO CLUB GROUP - SOUTHERN REGION, 1457 E MEMORIAL BLVD, 33801. WEEKDAYS (M-F) 8:30-5:30. (863) 688-7921 ✚ ▲ ✪

LAKEWOOD RANCH—AUTO CLUB GROUP - SOUTHERN REGION, 11531 PALMBRUSH TRL, 34202. WEEKDAYS (M-F) 8:30-5:30. (941) 756-0606 ✚ ▲ ✪

LEESBURG—AUTO CLUB GROUP - SOUTHERN REGION, 1708 CITRUS BLVD, 34748. WEEKDAYS (M-F) 8:30-5:30. (352) 787-8800 ✚ ▲ ✪

MELBOURNE—AUTO CLUB GROUP - SOUTHERN REGION, 4100 N WICKHAM RD #101, 32935. WEEKDAYS (M-F) 8:30-5:30. (321) 253-9100 ✚ ▲ ✪

OCALA—AUTO CLUB GROUP - SOUTHERN REGION, 3033 SW COLLEGE RD #101, 34474. WEEKDAYS (M-F) 8:30-5:30. (352) 237-6251 ✚ ▲ ✪

ORANGE PARK—AUTO CLUB GROUP - SOUTHERN REGION, 555 BLANDING BLVD STE 1, 32073. WEEKDAYS (M-F) 8:30-5:30. (904) 272-2010 ✚ ▲ ✪

ORLANDO—AUTO CLUB GROUP - SOUTHERN REGION, 626 N ALAFAYA TRL #106, 32828. WEEKDAYS (M-F) 8:30-5:30. (407) 380-3920 ✪

ORLANDO—AUTO CLUB GROUP - SOUTHERN REGION, 7339 W SAND LAKE RD # 424, 32819. WEEKDAYS (M-F) 8:30-5:30. (407) 351-5610 ✚ ▲ ✪

PALM HARBOR—AUTO CLUB GROUP - SOUTHERN REGION, 32050 US HWY 19 N, 34684. WEEKDAYS (M-F) 8:30-5:30. (727) 789-7850 ✚ ▲ ✪ ▣

PONTE VEDRA—AUTO CLUB GROUP - SOUTHERN REGION, 840 A1A N #180, 32082. WEEKDAYS (M-F) 8:30-5:30. (904) 280-8181 ✚ ▲ ✪

PORT RICHEY—AUTO CLUB GROUP - SOUTHERN REGION, 10532 DEVCO DR, 34668. WEEKDAYS (M-F) 8:30-5:30. (727) 868-9523 ✚ ▲ ✪

SARASOTA—AUTO CLUB GROUP - SOUTHERN REGION, 3844 BEE RIDGE RD, 34233. WEEKDAYS (M-F) 8:30-5:30. (941) 929-2299 ✚ ▲ ✪

SEMINOLE—AUTO CLUB GROUP - SOUTHERN REGION, 9200 SEMINOLE BLVD, 33772. WEEKDAYS (M-F) 8:30-5:30. (727) 398-3120 ✚ ▲ ✪

SPRING HILL—AUTO CLUB GROUP - SOUTHERN REGION, 1410 PINEHURST DR, 34606. WEEKDAYS (M-F) 8:30-5:30. (352) 683-3446 ✚ ▲ ✪

ST. AUGUSTINE—AUTO CLUB GROUP - SOUTHERN REGION, 172 STATE RD 312, 32086. WEEKDAYS (M-F) 8:30-5:30. (904) 825-0298 ■ ▲ ✪

ST. PETERSBURG—AUTO CLUB GROUP - SOUTHERN REGION, 1518 66TH ST N, 33710. WEEKDAYS (M-F) 8:30-5:30. (727) 344-6850 ✚ ▲ ✪

SUN CITY CENTER—AUTO CLUB GROUP - SOUTHERN REGION, 4868 SUN CITY CENTER BLV, 33573. WEEKDAYS (M-F) 8:30-5:30. (813) 633-4880 ✚ ▲ ✪

TAMPA—AUTO CLUB GROUP - SOUTHERN REGION, 14755 N DALE MABRY, 33618. WEEKDAYS (M-F) 8:30-5:30. (813) 963-2121 ✚ ▲ ✪

TAMPA—AUTO CLUB GROUP - SOUTHERN REGION, 1701 N WESTSHORE BLVD, 33607. WEEKDAYS (M-F) 7:30-6:00, SAT 8:00-4:00. (813) 289-5800 ✚ ▲ ✪ ☾ ▣

TAMPA—AUTO CLUB GROUP - SOUTHERN REGION, 20315 BRUCE B DOWNS BLVD, 33647. WEEKDAYS (M-F) 8:30-5:30. (813) 929-3430 ✚ ▲ ✪

THE VILLAGES—AUTO CLUB GROUP - SOUTHERN REGION, 1068 LAKE SUMTER LANDING, 32162. WEEKDAYS (M-F) 8:30-5:30. (352) 751-1888 ✚ ▲

THE VILLAGES—AUTO CLUB GROUP - SOUTHERN REGION, 955 BICHARA BLVD, 32159. WEEKDAYS (M-F) 8:30-5:30. (352) 753-2500 + ▲ ✪

TRINITY—AUTO CLUB GROUP - SOUTHERN REGION, 10700 ST RD 54 #102 & 103, 34655. WEEKDAYS (M-F) 8:30-5:30. (727) 375-2404 + ▲ ✪

VENICE—AUTO CLUB GROUP - SOUTHERN REGION, 2100 S TAMIAMI TRL, 34293. WEEKDAYS (M-F) 8:30-5:30. (941) 493-2100 + ▲ ✪

VERO BEACH—AUTO CLUB GROUP - SOUTHERN REGION, 495 21ST, 32960. WEEKDAYS (M-F) 8:30-5:30. (772) 770-3400 + ▲ ✪

WINTER PARK—AUTO CLUB GROUP - SOUTHERN REGION, 783 S ORLANDO AVE, 32789. WEEKDAYS (M-F) 8:30-5:30. (407) 647-1033 + ▲ ✪

Make the Connection

AAA guidebooks are just the beginning. Open the door to a whole lot more on **AAA.com**. Get extra travel insight, more information and online booking.

Find this symbol for places to look, book and save on AAA.com.

iStockphoto.com_shapecharge

Photo Credits

Page numbers are in bold type. Picture credit abbreviations are as follows:
■ (i) numeric sequence from top to bottom, left to right ■ (AAA) AAA Travel library.

- (Cover) Kennedy Space Center, Cape Canaveral / © Kennedy Space Center
- **2** (i) © iStockphoto.com / surfbabe
- **2** (ii) © AAA / Thuyvi Gates
- **2** (iii) © AAA / Inspector 511
- **2** (iv) Courtesy of Visit Tampa Bay
- **8** (i) © AAA / Thuyvi Gates
- **8** (ii) © iStockphoto.com / Sean Pavone
- **9** © iStockphoto.com / S. Greg Panosian
- **10** (i) Chronicle / Alamy Stock Photo
- **10** (ii) © Disney
- **13** (i) © AAA / Thuyvi Gates
- **13** (ii) Courtesy of Epicurean Hotel, Autograph Collection
- **13** (iii) © AAA / Inspector 39
- **13** (iv) © iStockphoto.com / dosecreative
- **13** (v) Courtesy of Kennedy Space Center Visitor Center Complex
- **14** (i) © AAA / Thuyvi Gates
- **14** (ii) © iStockphoto.com / Wirepec
- **14** (iii) © iStockphoto.com / BristolDen
- **14** (iv) Courtesy of Kennedy Space Center Visitor Complex
- **83** © iStockphoto.com / peeterv
- **86** © iStockphoto.com / surfbabe
- **87** © iStockphoto.com / normawilson
- **88** © iStockphoto.com / benedek
- **89** © iStockphoto.com / Ken Badgley
- **159** © AAA / Inspector 511
- **162** Courtesy of Kennedy Space Center Visitor Complex
- **163** Courtesy of The Charles Hosmer Morse Museum of American Art
- **164** Courtesy of Gatorland
- **165** © iStockphoto.com / Michael Warren
- **166** © iStockphoto.com / JPForte
- **167** © AAA / Thuyvi Gates
- **168** © AAA / Sherry Mims
- **169** © AAA / Sherry Mims
- **170** © AAA / Diana Beyer
- **171** © AAA / Thuyvi Gates
- **172** © AAA / Thuyvi Gates
- **173** © AAA / Thuyvi Gates
- **174** Courtesy of Florida Department of Environmental Protection, Division of Recreation and Parks
- **176** Courtesy of Enzian Theater
- **180** © AAA / Janet Brindle Reddick
- **181** Courtesy of SeaWorld Parks & Resorts Orlando
- **183** © AAA / Inspector 87
- **312** © iStockphoto.com / benedek
- **315** © iStockphoto.com / Boogich
- **316** Courtesy of Columbia Restaurant
- **317** Courtesy of the MOSI (Museum of Science & Industry)
- **318** Matt May / Alamy Stock Photo
- **319** © AAA / Patricia Miller
- **320** © iStockphoto.com / cookelma
- **321** © AAA / Patricia Miller
- **322** © Keir Magoulas / Visit Tampa Bay
- **323** Courtesy of Visit Tampa Bay
- **324** Courtesy of Visit Tampa Bay
- **325** Courtesy of Visit Tampa Bay
- **326** © Keir Magoulas / Visit Tampa Bay
- **327** Courtesy of Visit Tampa Bay
- **332** Courtesy of Visit Tampa Bay
- **333** Courtesy of Visit Tampa Bay

Get INVOLVED and Keep Teens Safe

Exploring the countryside or visiting nearby cities can be perfect opportunities to teach your teens good habits and rules of the road — before and after they learn to drive.

TeenDriving.AAA.com
DriveRight.CAA.ca

Hit the Road with Foreign Currency

A treasure trove of artisan masterpieces awaits.

Visit your local AAA office or **AAA.com/ForeignCurrency** to learn more.

All products not available at all locations.

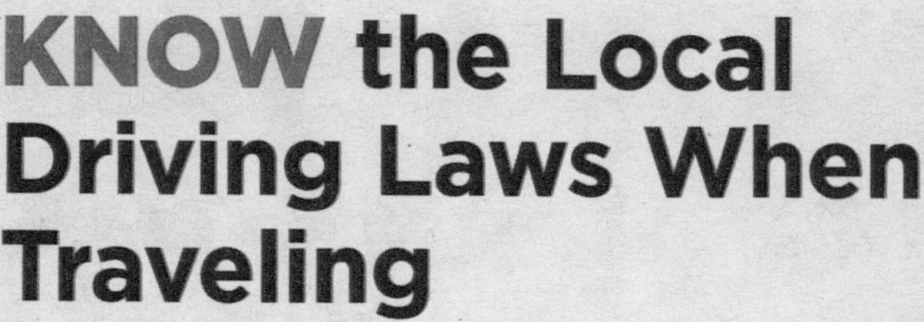

Wherever you travel, know the local laws that govern motor vehicle operation and registration.

DrivingLaws.AAA.com

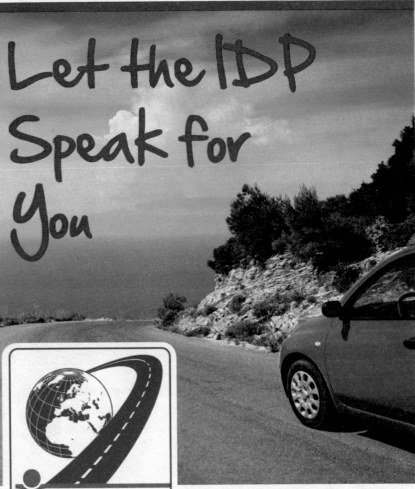

Let the IDP Speak for You

IDP
INTERNATIONAL DRIVING PERMIT
DRIVE THE WORLD!

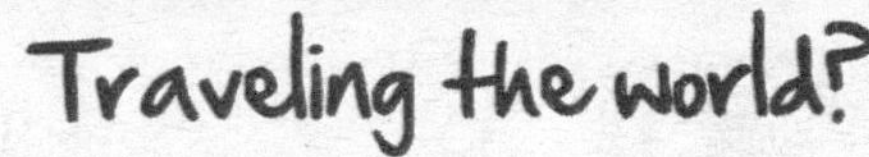

Before you go, purchase an International Driving Permit for a recognizable form of identification, even if you're not driving.

Translated into 10 languages, the IDP is valid in more than 150 countries — mandatory in some and highly recommended in others.

U.S. residents apply at AAA offices. Canadian residents apply at CAA offices.
Or visit us online at: AAA.com/IDP or CAA.ca/travelling/idp

iStockphoto.com_LeoPatrizi

For travel and everyday activities, insight from those you trust can make a good experience great!

AAA inspectors and travel writers spend their days evaluating hotels, sampling menus and exploring new sights so you don't have to. Use their recommended picks and itineraries to find the best places to go, stay, dine and play.

Photo source iStockphoto.com

Get AAA travel information at club offices and on AAA.com for experiences you'll remember for a lifetime.

Hit the Road with a Prepaid Card

Stay on budget during travel and use again to save for the next adventure.

Visit your local AAA office or **AAA.com/MemberPay** to learn more.

All products not available at all locations.

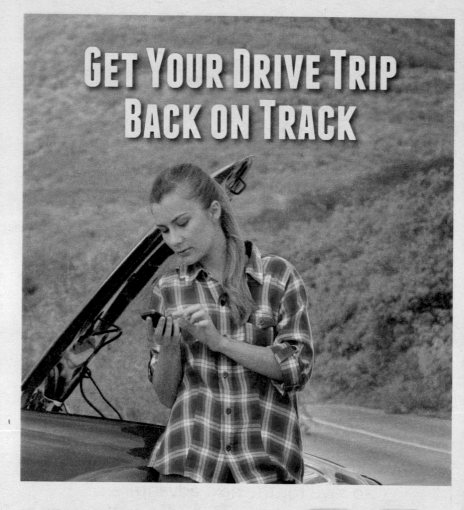

GET YOUR DRIVE TRIP BACK ON TRACK

When a drive trip takes an unexpected turn, use the **MOBILE APP** or go **ONLINE** to quickly request roadside service.

- New, more intuitive user interface
- Easier service request submissions
- Frequent status updates
- Service Tracker feature to follow service vehicle en route to your location

AAA.com/mobile
CAA.ca/mobile